Humaniti

Dallas Public Li

500 Common C
Proverbs and Colloquial
Expressions

500 Common Chinese Proverbs and Colloquial Expressions is a dictionary of key Chinese proverbs or *suyu*. *Suyu* are vivid and colorful expressions widely used in the Chinese language. The smooth use of *chengyu* in Chinese writing and of *suyu* in spoken Chinese not only makes communication more effective, it is also an indicator of mastery of the language.

This dictionary will provide an ideal resource for all intermediate to advanced learners of Chinese. Concise and practical, it draws upon a large corpus of authentic language data to present 500 of the most commonly used Chinese *suyu*. The *suyu* are listed and organized according to their frequency, enabling easy and convenient access for the reader.

Each proverb listing:

- is given in both simplified and traditional characters
- offers an English translation, followed by English equivalents
- is followed by two examples, written in Chinese, Pinyin and English, plus explanations and usage notes.

Examples are given in the form of dialogues reflecting typical situations, and helpful cultural annotations are provided throughout. A Pinyin index, a stroke index and a Chinese word index are presented at the back of the book and accompanying audio is also available for free download at **www.routledge.com/9780415501491**. Recorded by native speakers and covering the whole range of proverbs, expressions and example sentences featured in the book, this invaluable resource will help students to build up strong comprehension and communication skills.

This dictionary is suitable both for classroom use and independent study and will be of keen interest to students and teachers of Chinese alike.

Liwei Jiao is Lecturer in Chinese at the University of Pennsylvania, USA. His publications include *500 Common Chinese Idioms: An Annotated Frequency Dictionary* (co-authored with Cornelius C. Kubler and Weiguo Zhang, Routledge 2011) and *The Routledge Advanced Chinese Multimedia Course: Crossing Cultural Boundaries* (co-authored with Kunshan Carolyn Lee, Hsin-hsin Liang and Julian K. Wheatley, Routledge 2009).

Benjamin M. Stone is a graduate student at the University of Pennsylvania, USA. He possesses extensive experience in translating and interpreting Mandarin Chinese in a wide variety of professional contexts.

"The 500 proverbs and colloquial expressions collected in this book provide a precious window on Chinese culture, as well as an invaluable aid to learning the language. The book is an immensely useful reference toward understanding the Chinese mind, for both the learner and the teacher."

W.S.-Y. Wang, *Professor Emeritus, University of California at Berkeley; Academician of Academia Sinica; Editor of the* Journal of Chinese Linguistics

"This is an extraordinary dictionary with a creative and effective glossary that includes stylistic-register usages and historical resources. It is composed, for the first time, by first rate experts in the field. This dictionary will serve not only for Chinese learners and teachers, but also professionals who are interested in Chinese proverbs."

Professor Shengli Feng, *The Chinese University of Hong Kong*

"This book is a valuable resource I would recommend to any serious learners of Mandarin Chinese at intermediate level or above. It is essentially two books in one: with a Pinyin index, a stroke index, and a word index, this is an easy-to-use reference dictionary, while with two typical authentic examples for each of the 500 *suyu* items in the dictionary arranged according to their frequency of use, including their Pinyin glosses, literal translations, functional translations as well as usage guides and cultural notes, the book provides an excellent reader suitable for independent study."

Dr Richard Xiao, *Director of Lancaster University Confucius Institute*

"With copious examples and annotations, this collection of colourful expressions is bound to be an enriching addition to any learner's library."

Professor Zheng-sheng Zhang, *Editor of the* Journal of the Chinese Language Teachers Association (JCLTA)

500 Common Chinese Proverbs and Colloquial Expressions

An annotated frequency dictionary

Liwei Jiao and Benjamin M. Stone

Routledge
Taylor & Francis Group

LONDON AND NEW YORK

First published 2014
by Routledge
2 Park Square, Milton Park, Abingdon, Oxon OX14 4RN

and by Routledge
711 Third Avenue, New York, NY 10017

Routledge is an imprint of the Taylor & Francis Group, an informa business

© 2014 Liwei Jiao and Benjamin M. Stone

British Library Cataloguing in Publication Data
A catalogue record for this book is available from the British Library

Library of Congress Cataloging in Publication Data
Jiao, Liwei.
    500 common Chinese proverbs and colloquial expressions : an annotated
frequency dictionary / Liwei Jiao, Benjamin M. Stone.
        pages cm
    Includes index.
    1. Proverbs, Chinese.   2. Chinese language–Terms and phrases.   3. Chinese
language–Dictionaries–English.   I. Stone, Benjamin M., author.   II. Title.
III. Title: Five hundred common Chinese proverbs and colloquial expressions.
    PN6519.C5J54 2014
    398.9'951–dc23

                                                    2013015161

ISBN: 978-0-415-50148-4 (hbk)
ISBN: 978-0-415-50149-1 (pbk)
ISBN: 978-1-315-88458-5 (ebk)

Typeset in GraphSwift Light
by Graphicraft Limited, Hong Kong

Printed and bound in Great Britain by
TJ International Ltd, Padstow, Cornwall

To my students in Section 8, Class of 1998 at International College
of Chinese Language and Culture, Renmin University of China.

—Liwei Jiao

To my family.

—Benjamin Stone

Contents

Introduction viii
    Characteristics of Chinese suyu viii
    Why suyu *are important to learners of Chinese* ix
    Special characteristics of this dictionary x
    How the entries of this dictionary were determined xi
    Background of the compilation of this dictionary and acknowledgments xii

List of abbreviations and grammatical terms in character-by-character
translation xiv

List of entries xv

Structure of entries xxi

500 common Chinese proverbs and colloquial expressions 1

Appendix one: Pinyin index of 500 common Chinese proverbs and
colloquial expressions 387

Appendix two: stroke index of 500 common Chinese proverbs and
colloquial expressions 395

Appendix three: Chinese word index of 500 common Chinese
proverbs and colloquial expressions 401

Introduction

500 Common Chinese Proverbs and Colloquial Expressions: An Annotated Frequency Dictionary is a dictionary of common Chinese proverbs and colloquial expressions known as *suyu*. *Suyu* are an important constituent part of the Chinese language, which Chinese language learners must not neglect. This dictionary, which lists and organizes *suyu* according to their frequency – as determined by a sociolinguistic survey of more than 900 Chinese university students – is designed primarily for Chinese learners at the intermediate level or above whose first language is English, as well as teachers of Chinese as a second/foreign language. Besides being used as a reference work, this dictionary is also suitable for classroom use and independent study.

Characteristics of Chinese *suyu*

The definition of *suyu* in Chinese is relatively broad and does not completely coincide with the definition of the English word 'proverb.' What this book catalogues are Chinese proverbs and colloquial expressions, to be referred to hereafter as *suyu*. This book's definition of *suyu* is as follows: they are phrases or sentences that are widely employed by the general population in colloquial discourse, whose actual meanings are more than the sum of their parts, are mainly employed in expressing ridicule or criticism, and whose structure is relatively fixed. Some examples of *suyu* would be 吃豆腐, whose literal meaning 'to eat tofu' comes to mean 'to take advantage of a woman;' 皇上不急太监急 which, while literally meaning 'the emperor is rested and at ease while the eunuch is excessively concerned,' is used to describe a situation in which the person involved is calm and collected, but observers are very anxious. Specifically speaking, *suyu* should have the following characteristics:

1) *Suyu* are evocative and ingenious. In most circumstances, they are the best, most articulate form of expression for a given situation. For example, if one wishes to articulate how someone has overstepped their bounds, both 得寸进尺 (given-inch-advance-foot) and 得陇望蜀 (get-a tip of Southwestern China-hope-the whole Southwestern China) are acceptable, although the latter is possibly too literal. However, neither expression has a humorous connotation. In contrast, the *suyu* 蹬鼻子上脸 (climb-nose-mount-face) is both humorous in meaning and widely used in informal conversations. Similarly, 天上掉馅饼 (sky-upon-fall-stuffed-pancake) is the most apt translation of 'to have something fall into one's lap,' while 躲得过初一，躲不过十五 vividly invokes the idea that 'you cannot avoid something forever,' by making the analogy that you can avoid 初一, the first day of a lunar month with a new moon, but you cannot avoid its counterpart, 十五, the fifteenth day of a lunar month.

2) *Suyu* are used by the general population. However, this characteristic does not preclude the use of *suyu* by political leaders or public figures in some situations. It is general knowledge that Mao Zedong and Deng Xiaoping liked using *suyu*, with some of their most famous *suyu* including, among others: 纸老虎 (paper tigers), 墙头草 (fence-sitters), 东方不亮西方亮 (while something is not workable in one place, it might be workable somewhere else), 摸着石头过河 (to cross the river by touching stones), and 不管白猫黑猫，能捉老鼠就是好猫 (it does not matter whether a cat is black or white so long as it catches mice).

3) *Suyu* are mainly colloquial. However, this does not preclude one from using *suyu* on formal occasions or in writing in order to elicit a special reaction from the audience. Also, based on our observations, the rapid proliferation of the internet has led internet users to begin using more *suyu* in their pursuit of fresh, pithy expressions, therein indirectly influencing the vernacular of the media.

4) The actual meanings of *suyu* come not from a literal, character-by-character translation, but rather from the proverb's analogical or synecdochic meaning. For example, consider the sentence 他不是省油的灯. The portion of the proverb, 不是省油的灯 does not actually mean 'a non kerosene-saving lamp,' but rather, 'a real piece of work.'

5) *Suyu* mainly express derogatory or critical sentiments. Take, for example, 占着茅坑不拉屎 (to be a dog in the manger), or 临时抱佛脚 (fair weather atheists turn to god in a pinch). About half of the entries in this dictionary carry either a strongly or slightly derogatory connotation, and the most common word in the 500 entries is 不, which appears 119 times in total. However, there are also many neutral *suyu*, such as 一个萝卜一个坑 (each has his own task and there is nobody to spare).

6) The structures of *suyu* are relatively fixed. For example, while one can say 一个萝卜一个坑, meaning, literally, 'one radish, one hole,' the proverb does not maintain its implied meaning of 'each has his own task and there is nobody to spare' if the structure is changed. We cannot say 'two radishes, two holes.' Neither can we say 'one sweet potato, one hole.' However, the structures of a number of *suyu*, mainly those embodied in short phrases, can be slightly adjusted. In some instances, it is fine to insert a few components. For example, 吃豆腐, meaning, literally, 'to eat tofu,' actually means 'to come on to,' or 'to take advantage of.' However, one can say 吃**她**的豆腐, or 吃**小姑娘**的豆腐, to yield the phrases, 'take advantage of **her**,' or 'come on to **a young woman**.'

7) The constituent parts of *suyu* are mostly objects or activities which are closely associated with the daily life of the general population. The most common words in the entries included in this dictionary include 人 (people), 吃 (to eat), 打 (to hit, to beat and many other meanings), 水 (water), 马 (horse), 眼 (eye), 狗 (dog), 虎 (tiger), 鸡 (chicken), 风 (wind), 山 (mountain), 脚 (foot), and 刀 (knife).

Why *suyu* are important to learners of Chinese

Suyu are vivid and colorful expressions that are widely and liberally used by Chinese people. Those people who use *suyu* often and well in everyday life project a cultural sophistication, expressive ability, sense of humor, and bonhomie, which facilitates their acceptance by others and makes them the center of attention. Using *suyu* in certain special situations can work wonders. For decades, countless politicians and economists argued over a still-socialist China's adoption of a capitalist path and were unable to resolve certain resulting theoretical questions. However, with one *suyu*, 不管黑猫白猫，能捉老鼠就是好猫 (it does not matter whether a cat is black or white so long as it catches mice), Deng Xiaoping promptly settled the dispute. Examples like this cause people to admire the importance of *suyu*. They are a shortcut to establishing a rapport with Chinese people.

It is generally difficult for non-immersion learners of Chinese to come into contact with genuine *suyu*. Even if these learners should happen to encounter a Chinese person, the language environment outside of China, and considerations of practicality, discourage the Chinese from using *suyu* in communicating with Chinese language learners. Moreover, due to the duality of *suyu*, it is not easy for learners of Chinese to quickly guess their implied meaning. They sometimes even develop mistaken – and potentially embarrassing – understandings of *suyu*. Recall, for example, the *suyu* 吃豆腐. The component words, 吃 (eat) and 豆腐 (tofu) are both quite simple, however, when put together, their meaning changes significantly, as shown earlier.

Special characteristics of this dictionary

We hope this dictionary will come to be an indispensable aid to many Chinese language learners and teachers. As such, we have included a number of distinguishing features, which are as follows:

1) This dictionary has identified, and lists the 500 most common Chinese *suyu* according to their frequency of use. In this manner, learners of Chinese can be sure about which *suyu* are important and should be learned first. Knowledge of these 500 *suyu* will be sufficient for use in daily life or work situations, when conducting business, or even when writing.

2) This dictionary contains accurate English translations and annotations. For example, the *suyu* 会哭的孩子有奶吃, when translated literally, means 'if a baby is good at pretending to cry, it will be rewarded with its mother's milk.' However, given the context of its usage and the functional meaning of the phrase (the squeaky wheel gets the grease), this dictionary has more logically and correctly translated 奶 (milk) as 母乳 (breast milk). Additionally, English translations of Chinese example dialogues were structured, where possible, to adhere closely to the syntactical organization of the Chinese, in order to make it easy for students to learn the characters for words and phrases they are unfamiliar with.

3) This dictionary is concise, practical, and convenient for educational purposes. The entry for each *suyu* includes: the *suyu* itself (in simplified and traditional Chinese characters), Pinyin romanization, a character-by-character translation in English, implied meaning in English, functional translation in English (for most entries), two suitable examples (in Chinese, Pinyin, and English), usage, variants (if any), and notes. Most examples take the form of dialogues reflecting commonly encountered situations.

4)   Because it is very difficult for non-native learners of Chinese to grasp the degree of sarcasm or abrasiveness associated with a given *suyu*, this dictionary separates the tone of *suyu* into four categories in the annotations: humorous, neutral, slightly derogatory, and derogatory. As such, when employing *suyu*, users of this dictionary will not make egregious and potentially embarrassing errors in usage. For example, when recommending that some leader retire, one would not use a strongly derogatory *suyu* such as 占着茅坑不拉屎 (to be like a dog in the manger). The chart depicted below is included for all entries except the 21 which have complimentary connotations.

humorous	neutral	slightly derogatory	derogatory

5)   This dictionary contains necessary cultural annotations. For each entry, we have made a judgment as to whether or not there is a serious gap in relevant cultural understanding between native English and Chinese speakers. In cases where we deemed it necessary, cultural gaps are addressed and further explained. For example, while the practice of foot binding may be one that native English speakers are familiar with, the deeper social and cultural connotations of this custom provide the meaning of the *suyu* 露马脚 and, as such, the tradition is explained in that entry's cultural note.

6)   This dictionary also includes a large number of relevant Chinese idioms (*chengyu*) to contrast or complement the *suyu* and make the language even more vivid. For example, the Chinese idiom 视而不见 (to turn a blind eye to) appears in the example sentence for 睁着眼睛说瞎话 (to tell bald-faced lies).

As should be clear from the analysis above, *500 Common Chinese Proverbs and Colloquial Expressions* should satisfy the educational needs of Chinese language learners at the intermediate level or higher, enabling them to gain a grasp of the most common *suyu* in the Chinese language one by one. Alternatively, we hope this dictionary will provide significant assistance to Chinese language instructors who, when preparing for class or explaining *suyu* to their students, may select those *suyu* which are most likely to be encountered, and refer to the usage notes and example sentences in this dictionary.

How the entries of this dictionary were determined

As there was no existing corpus of *suyu* organized by frequency prior to the inception of this volume, the writing of this dictionary necessitated the compilation of a frequency ordered corpus of *suyu* using sociolinguistic methods. In order to compile this list, 902 Chinese university students from different regions of China were surveyed to gauge their familiarity with hundreds of different Chinese *suyu*. For each *suyu*, participants were asked to choose among the following options:

A)   I have never heard this *suyu* before.
B)   I occasionally hear others (not counting my family, relatives, friends, classmates, colleagues, or instructors) use this *suyu* colloquially.

C) I have heard this *suyu* used colloquially by someone close to me (including my family, relatives, friends, classmates, colleagues or instructors).

D) I believe I can use this *suyu* appropriately.

E) I have used this *suyu* either in written or spoken form.

At the end of the survey, each participant was asked to list the ten *suyu* that he or she used most often, even if they were not featured on the survey list.

While, on the face of it, it may seem that we have surveyed only a small number of individual university students, our survey methodology is workable because what we were really surveying were the groups to which these students belong. As each survey participant is a member of a larger social or cultural group – be it a family, an affinity group, or a cultural movement – each participant's responses indirectly reflect the influence and general linguistic tendencies of the groups to which they belong as well as the groups to which their acquaintances belong. This trickle-down diversity makes up for what would otherwise be an excessively homogeneous survey group.

This survey was conducted primarily in June of 2012, whereas compilation and selection of possible entries started as early as 2007. One of the authors, Liwei Jiao, was present when most of the surveys were being conducted. The authors wish to sincerely thank all of the following Chinese faculty and their students for their participation in this survey:

Professor Bo Zhang and his students at Nankai University,

Professor Lei Liang, Professor Qibin Ran, Professor Jia Guo and Ms. Minyuan Wang and their students and classmates at Nankai University,

Professor Xiujuan Shi and her students at Tianjin Normal University,

Dr. Shitie Yang, Dr. Yujian Xiang, and Ms. Yanli Liu and their students at Huaibei Normal University,

Professor Lijian Liu and his students at Zhejiang Normal University,

Ms. Yuhui Shi and her students at Xuzhou Normal University,

Dr. Qiaoling Cao and her students at China Criminal Police University,

Mr. Xiaoning Han and his students at Qingdao University,

Professor Yingzhi Na and his students at Qingdao Technical College,

Professor Lintao Zhao and his students at Hebei University,

Dr. Xiaohua Xu and her students at Capital University of Economics and Business.

Background of the compilation of this dictionary and acknowledgments

This dictionary is the sister volume to *500 Common Chinese Idioms*, and both books were jointly conceived in 2007. The research for this volume proceeded gradually from 2007 until the completion of *500 Common Chinese Idioms* in 2010. In the fall of 2010, Benjamin Stone joined this project, and we have worked together towards the completion of this book since then.

The authors wish to express here their appreciation to the following people for their assistance in the compilation of this dictionary: Professor Shuiguang Deng of Zhejiang University, Professor Zepeng Wang of Nankai University, Professor

Hsin-hsin Liang of University of Virginia, Ms. Xuefei Hao of Washington University in St. Louis, Mr. William Xuefeng Wang, Mr. Jinsong Fan, and Mr. Lizhong Jiao. Special thanks go to Professor William Labov of University of Pennsylvania for his advice on how to conduct the survey of entries. The authors also would like to thank their editors at Routledge, Ms. Andrea Hartill, Ms. Samantha Vale Noya, Ms. Isabelle Cheng, Ms. Sarah May and Ms. Jill Campbell for their support of this project. Finally, the authors would be remiss not to also thank our families for their crucial support, without which this dictionary would surely never have seen the light of day.

Liwei Jiao
Benjamin Stone

List of abbreviations and grammatical terms in character-by-character translation

's: possessive
ed: past tense
ing: present progressive tense
MW: measure word

List of entries

1	好马不吃回头草	40	三个臭皮匠，顶个诸葛亮
2	小菜一碟	41	脚踩两只船
3	太阳从西边出来	42	此地无银三百两
4	说曹操，曹操到	43	吃不到葡萄就说葡萄酸
5	乌鸦嘴	44	心急吃不了热豆腐
6	二百五	45	家常便饭
7	吃一堑，长一智	46	癞蛤蟆想吃天鹅肉
8	睁着眼睛说瞎话	47	天无绝人之路
9	近朱者赤，近墨者黑	48	走后门
10	物以稀为贵	49	瞎猫碰上死耗子
11	王婆卖瓜，自卖自夸	50	好汉不吃眼前亏
12	站着说话不腰疼	51	解铃还须系铃人
13	天下没有不散的筵席	52	肥水不流外人田
14	天上掉馅饼	53	心有余而力不足
15	己所不欲，勿施于人	54	不分青红皂白
16	睁眼瞎	55	睁一只眼，闭一只眼
17	跳进黄河洗不清	56	破罐子破摔
18	拍马屁	57	种瓜得瓜，种豆得豆
19	情人眼里出西施	58	萝卜白菜，各有所爱
20	打酱油	59	狗嘴里吐不出象牙
21	不怕一万，就怕万一	60	三天打鱼，两天晒网
22	走着瞧	61	一朝被蛇咬，十年怕井绳
23	不管三七二十一	62	英雄难过美人关
24	吃着碗里的，看着锅里的	63	刀子嘴，豆腐心
25	钻牛角尖	64	一失足成千古恨
26	人不可貌相，海水不可斗量	65	哪壶不开提哪壶
27	林子大了，什么鸟都有	66	炒鱿鱼
28	鸡毛蒜皮	67	人往高处走，水往低处流
29	鲜花插在牛粪上	68	说得比唱得好听
30	醉翁之意不在酒	69	强扭的瓜不甜
31	猴年马月	70	老掉牙
32	眼不见为净	71	搬起石头砸自己的脚
33	姜是老的辣	72	卖关子
34	留得青山在，不怕没柴烧	73	一分钱一分货
35	拿得起，放得下	74	九牛二虎之力
36	以其人之道还治其人之身	75	敬酒不吃吃罚酒
37	走桃花运	76	躲得过初一，躲不过十五
38	成事不足，败事有余	77	吃香的，喝辣的
39	皇上不急太监急	78	小儿科

79 一个巴掌拍不响
80 牛头不对马嘴
81 以小人之心，度君子之腹
82 车到山前必有路
83 鸡蛋里挑骨头
84 吃不了兜着走
85 打肿脸充胖子
86 三十六计走为上
87 当耳旁风
88 恨铁不成钢
89 你走你的阳关道，我过我的独木桥
90 过了这个村，就没这个店
91 抱佛脚
92 有钱能使鬼推磨
93 有其父必有其子
94 不见棺材不落泪
95 三长两短
96 纸包不住火
97 好戏在后头
98 吹牛皮
99 欲速则不达
100 家家有本难念的经
101 墙头草
102 替罪羊
103 近水楼台先得月
104 小巫见大巫
105 过河拆桥
106 一不做，二不休
107 以牙还牙，以眼还眼
108 跑了和尚跑不了庙
109 绿帽子
110 识时务者为俊杰
111 井水不犯河水
112 一棵树上吊死
113 放鸽子
114 一步一个脚印
115 上梁不正下梁歪
116 不入虎穴，焉得虎子
117 赔了夫人又折兵
118 有心栽花花不长，无心插柳柳成荫
119 八字还没一撇
120 有眼不识泰山
121 出气筒
122 八九不离十
123 无风不起浪
124 得便宜卖乖
125 不是省油的灯
126 家丑不可外扬
127 背黑锅
128 兔子不吃窝边草
129 铁饭碗
130 冰冻三尺，非一日之寒
131 远亲不如近邻
132 下马威
133 天下乌鸦一般黑
134 不到黄河心不死
135 狗急了跳墙
136 狗眼看人低
137 只许州官放火，不许百姓点灯
138 偷鸡摸狗
139 死马当活马医
140 新官上任三把火
141 对号入座
142 十万八千里
143 露马脚
144 公说公有理，婆说婆有理
145 上刀山，下火海
146 打退堂鼓
147 磨刀不误砍柴工
148 风马牛不相及
149 一山不容二虎
150 眼里揉不得沙子
151 三下五除二
152 泼冷水
153 杀鸡给猴看
154 生米做成熟饭
155 初生牛犊不怕虎
156 铁公鸡
157 无事不登三宝殿
158 马后炮
159 掉链子
160 纸老虎
161 狐狸精
162 丑话说在前头
163 半路杀出个程咬金
164 麻雀虽小，五脏俱全
165 虎毒不食子
166 小不忍则乱大谋
167 打狗还得看主人
168 万事俱备，只欠东风
169 不管黑猫白猫，会捉老鼠就是好猫
170 真金不怕火炼
171 狗改不了吃屎
172 杀手锏

173 饥不择食
174 对事不对人
175 皮笑肉不笑
176 双刃剑
177 热脸贴冷屁股
178 好了伤疤忘了疼
179 醋坛子
180 君子之交淡如水
181 三个和尚没水吃
182 赶鸭子上架
183 小白脸
184 放长线，钓大鱼
185 依葫芦画瓢
186 隔墙有耳
187 巧妇难为无米之炊
188 不是吃素的
189 嫁鸡随鸡，嫁狗随狗
190 打开天窗说亮话
191 人算不如天算
192 小动作
193 远水解不了近渴
194 占着茅坑不拉屎
195 碰一鼻子灰
196 死猪不怕开水烫
197 换汤不换药
198 救命稻草
199 明枪易躲，暗箭难防
200 谋事在人，成事在天
201 三个女人一台戏
202 有鼻子有眼
203 枪打出头鸟
204 碰钉子
205 蹬鼻子上脸
206 吃豆腐
207 眉毛胡子一把抓
208 偷鸡不成反蚀把米
209 众人拾柴火焰高
210 快刀斩乱麻
211 吃软饭
212 一着不慎，满盘皆输
213 听风就是雨
214 鸿门宴
215 吃哑巴亏
216 眼中钉、肉中刺
217 舍不得孩子套不住狼
218 挂羊头、卖狗肉
219 煮熟的鸭子飞了

220 常在河边走，哪有不湿鞋
221 三脚猫
222 吃闭门羹
223 三十年河东，三十年河西
224 土包子
225 树大招风
226 酒逢知己千杯少
227 当一天和尚撞一天钟
228 是骡子是马拉出来遛遛
229 一个鼻孔出气
230 身在曹营心在汉
231 瘦死的骆驼比马大
232 树欲静而风不止
233 丑媳妇早晚也得见公婆
234 胜者王侯败者贼
235 下三烂
236 上了贼船
237 病急乱投医
238 打如意算盘
239 龙生龙，凤生凤
240 不看僧面看佛面
241 雷声大、雨点小
242 脸红脖子粗
243 一棍子打死
244 拿鸡蛋碰石头
245 没有不透风的墙
246 人怕出名猪怕壮
247 山中无老虎，猴子称大王
248 杀鸡焉用宰牛刀
249 大树底下好乘凉
250 跑龙套
251 七大姑，八大姨
252 一是一，二是二
253 多个朋友多条路
254 下台阶
255 打小算盘
256 坐山观虎斗
257 羊毛出在羊身上
258 一口吃成个胖子
259 屋漏偏逢连阴雨
260 老油条
261 捅马蜂窝
262 小意思
263 倒打一耙
264 陈芝麻、烂谷子
265 一条龙
266 四两拨千斤

267   前怕狼，后怕虎
268   吃水不忘挖井人
269   有仇不报非君子
270   不倒翁
271   干打雷，不下雨
272   鸡飞狗跳
273   事后诸葛亮
274   落水狗
275   板上钉钉
276   一碗水端平
277   烫手的山芋
278   笑掉大牙
279   一回生，二回熟
280   鱼与熊掌不可得兼
281   咸鱼翻身
282   一根绳上的蚂蚱
283   趟浑水
284   狗腿子
285   用在刀刃上
286   鸡飞蛋打
287   胳膊扭不过大腿
288   饱汉不知饿汉饥
289   笑面虎
290   二
291   给力
292   母老虎
293   五十步笑百步
294   门外汉
295   前人栽树，后人乘凉
296   烂泥扶不上墙
297   关公面前耍大刀
298   高不成，低不就
299   胳膊肘往外扭
300   长痛不如短痛
301   酒香不怕巷子深
302   一条路走到黑
303   不是鱼死，就是网破
304   冰山一角
305   身体是革命的本钱
306   说风凉话
307   紧箍咒
308   唱双簧
309   开空白支票
310   保护伞
311   一个萝卜一个坑
312   狗咬狗
313   唱高调

314   打水漂
315   开小差
316   两面派
317   一盘散沙
318   和稀泥
319   敲竹杠
320   扯后腿
321   穿小鞋
322   给他一点颜色看看
323   天高皇帝远
324   拣软柿子捏
325   打马虎眼
326   千里马
327   打擦边球
328   摸着石头过河
329   半路出家
330   老狐狸
331   一窝蜂
332   开夜车
333   手心手背都是肉
334   缩头乌龟
335   走过场
336   做文章
337   吃大锅饭
338   戴高帽
339   秋后算账
340   僧多粥少
341   坐冷板凳
342   不当家不知柴米贵
343   红眼病
344   葫芦里卖的是什么药
345   三句话不离本行
346   糖衣炮弹
347   树倒猢狲散
348   硬骨头
349   二虎相争，必有一伤
350   拆东墙，补西墙
351   大鱼吃小鱼
352   狐狸尾巴露出来了
353   开绿灯
354   歪瓜裂枣
355   小辫子
356   一头雾水
357   隔行如隔山
358   一亩三分地
359   成也萧何，败也萧何
360   大水冲了龙王庙

361	乱弹琴	408	出来混的，总要还的
362	挤牙膏	409	画虎不成反类犬
363	墙倒众人推	410	大意失荆州
364	莫须有	411	卸磨杀驴
365	拿鸡毛当令箭	412	躺着都中枪
366	捅破窗户纸	413	脚正不怕鞋歪
367	三字经	414	有奶就是娘
368	苍蝇不叮无缝的蛋	415	肉烂在锅里
369	大跌眼镜	416	说你胖你就喘
370	说一千，道一万	417	擦屁股
371	绊脚石	418	皇帝女儿不愁嫁
372	过五关、斩六将	419	一朝天子一朝臣
373	求爷爷、告奶奶	420	活人让尿憋死
374	羡慕嫉妒恨	421	走马灯
375	打掉门牙往肚里咽	422	花无百日红
376	唱对台戏	423	东风压倒西风
377	分一杯羹	424	岁月是把杀猪刀
378	变色龙	425	丁是丁，卯是卯
379	独木不成林	426	多年的媳妇熬成婆
380	既生瑜，何生亮？	427	强将手下无弱兵
381	撂挑子	428	头痛医头，脚痛医脚
382	敲门砖	429	拉不出屎来怨茅房
383	试金石	430	东方不亮西方亮
384	火烧眉毛	431	老牛拉破车
385	空手套白狼	432	放卫星
386	一瓶子不满，半瓶子晃荡	433	鸡同鸭讲
387	脱了裤子放屁	434	一锅端
388	借东风	435	老皇历
389	白开水	436	家花没有野花香
390	鲤鱼跳龙门	437	又想当婊子又想立牌坊
391	强龙压不住地头蛇	438	遮羞布
392	这山望着那山高	439	耍花枪
393	光脚的不怕穿鞋的	440	又要马儿跑，又要马儿不吃草
394	不成功，便成仁	441	牛不喝水强按头
395	滚刀肉	442	摆乌龙
396	久病成良医	443	各打五十大板
397	枕边风	444	一个将军一个令
398	一锤子买卖	445	抱大腿
399	横挑鼻子竖挑眼	446	砸了锅
400	唱空城计	447	会哭的孩子有奶吃
401	一刀切	448	二一添作五
402	旧瓶装新酒	449	风一阵，雨一阵
403	两面三刀	450	剃头挑子一头热
404	一把钥匙开一把锁	451	远来的和尚会念经
405	打一巴掌，给个甜枣	452	揪辫子
406	先君子后小人	453	小姐的身子丫鬟的命
407	尺有所短，寸有所长	454	只见树木，不见森林

455   屁股决定脑袋
456   兔子尾巴长不了
457   骑马找马
458   敲锣边儿
459   扣帽子
460   拔出萝卜带出泥
461   满嘴跑火车
462   温水煮青蛙
463   万金油
464   树挪死，人挪活
465   按下葫芦起了瓢
466   到什么山唱什么歌
467   拔根汗毛比腰粗
468   阎王好见，小鬼难搪
469   不见兔子不撒鹰
470   当面锣，对面鼓
471   眼大肚子小
472   浅水养不了大鱼
473   吃别人嚼过的馍不香
474   起大早，赶晚集
475   打不着狐狸惹身骚
476   多面手
477   鸟枪换炮

478   矬子里拔将军
479   给个棒槌就当针
480   捧臭脚
481   咬人的狗不露齿
482   炒冷饭
483   一只羊是赶，一群羊也是放
484   虱子多了不咬，账多了不愁
485   攒鸡毛，凑掸子
486   骑脖子拉屎
487   指着和尚骂秃子
488   蚂蚱也是肉
489   背着抱着一般沉
490   一言堂
491   乱拳打死老师傅
492   端起碗来吃肉，放下筷子骂娘
493   出头的椽子先烂
494   一马勺坏一锅
495   终日打雁，让雁啄了眼
496   老鸹嫌猪黑
497   别人牵驴你拔橛
498   仔卖爷田不心疼
499   萝卜快了不洗泥
500   接地气

Structure of entries

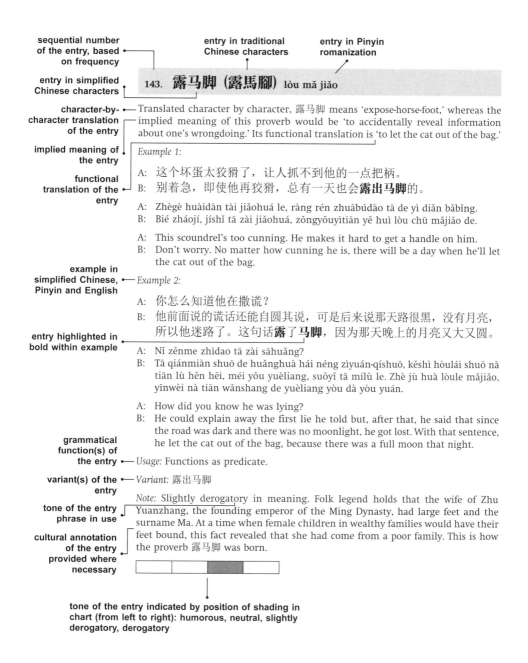

sequential number of the entry, based on frequency

entry in traditional Chinese characters

entry in Pinyin romanization

entry in simplified Chinese characters

143. 露马脚 (露馬腳) lòu mǎ jiǎo

character-by-character translation of the entry

Translated character by character, 露马脚 means 'expose-horse-foot,' whereas the implied meaning of this proverb would be 'to accidentally reveal information about one's wrongdoing.' Its functional translation is 'to let the cat out of the bag.'

implied meaning of the entry

functional translation of the entry

Example 1:

A: 这个坏蛋太狡猾了，让人抓不到他的一点把柄。

B: 别着急，即使他再狡猾，总有一天也会**露出马脚**的。

A: Zhège huàidàn tài jiǎohuá le, ràng rén zhuābúdào tā de yì diǎn bǎbǐng.

B: Bié zháojí, jíshǐ tā zài jiǎohuá, zǒngyǒuyìtiān yě huì lòu chū mǎjiǎo de.

A: This scoundrel's too cunning. He makes it hard to get a handle on him.

B: Don't worry. No matter how cunning he is, there will be a day when he'll let the cat out of the bag.

example in simplified Chinese, Pinyin and English

Example 2:

A: 你怎么知道他在撒谎？

B: 他前面说的谎话还能自圆其说，可是后来说那天路很黑，没有月亮，所以他迷路了。这句话**露了马脚**，因为那天晚上的月亮又大又圆。

entry highlighted in bold within example

A: Nǐ zěnme zhīdao tā zài sāhuǎng?

B: Tā qiánmiàn shuō de huǎnghuà hái néng zìyuán-qíshuō, kěshì hòulái shuō nà tiān lù hěn hēi, méi yǒu yuèliang, suǒyǐ tā mílù le. Zhè jù huà lòule mǎjiǎo, yīnwèi nà tiān wǎnshang de yuèliang yòu dà yòu yuán.

A: How did you know he was lying?

B: He could explain away the first lie he told but, after that, he said that since the road was dark and there was no moonlight, he got lost. With that sentence, he let the cat out of the bag, because there was a full moon that night.

grammatical function(s) of the entry

Usage: Functions as predicate.

variant(s) of the entry

Variant: 露出马脚

tone of the entry phrase in use

Note: Slightly derogatory in meaning. Folk legend holds that the wife of Zhu Yuanzhang, the founding emperor of the Ming Dynasty, had large feet and the surname Ma. At a time when female children in wealthy families would have their feet bound, this fact revealed that she had come from a poor family. This is how the proverb 露马脚 was born.

cultural annotation of the entry provided where necessary

tone of the entry indicated by position of shading in chart (from left to right): humorous, neutral, slightly derogatory, derogatory

500 common Chinese proverbs and colloquial expressions

1. 好马不吃回头草 (好馬不吃回頭草)
hǎo mǎ bù chī huí tóu cǎo

Translated character by character, 好马不吃回头草 means 'good-horse-not-eat-turn-around-grass,' whereas the implied meaning of this proverb would be 'a good man doesn't backtrack.'

Example 1:

A: 我已经决定要离开现在的公司了，可是公司又提出给我加薪。你看我应该走还是留？

B: **好马不吃回头草**。你还是走吧。

A: Wǒ yǐjīng juédìng yào líkāi xiànzài de gōngsī le, kěshì gōngsī yòu tíchū gěi wǒ jiāxīn. Nǐ kàn wǒ yīnggāi zǒu háishì liú?

B: Hǎo mǎ bù chī huítóu cǎo. Nǐ háishì zǒu ba.

A: I already decided that I was going to leave the company I'm at now, but they're discussing giving me a raise. What do you think, should I leave or should I stay?

B: A good man doesn't backtrack. You should still leave.

Example 2:

A: 听说他们想复婚呢。

B: **好马不吃回头草**，那已经是过去的一页了。

A: Tīngshuō tāmen xiǎng fùhūn ne.

B: Hǎo mǎ bù chī huítóu cǎo, nà yǐjīng shì guòqù de yí yè le.

A: I've heard they want to remarry.

B: A good man doesn't backtrack. They've already turned over a new leaf.

Usage: Used singly.

Note: Neutral or humorous in meaning.

2. 小菜一碟 (小菜一碟) xiǎo cài yì dié

Translated character by character, 小菜一碟 means 'small-dish-one-plate,' whereas the implied meaning of this proverb would be 'something that can be done very easily.' Its functional equivalent is 'a piece of cake.'

Example 1:

A: 这个国家的篮球队对于美国队来说简直是**小菜一碟**。美国队的替补阵容都能把他们打得稀里哗啦的。

A: Zhège guójiā de lánqiú duì duìyú Měiguó duì láishuō jiǎnzhí shì xiǎo
    cài yì dié. Měiguó duì de tìbǔ zhènróng dōu néng bǎ tāmen dǎ de xīlǐhuālā
    de.

A: This country's basketball team really is a piece of cake for the American team.
    Even the American substitutes could clean their clocks.

Example 2:

A: 我外甥女今年要毕业了，你能不能把她安排进交通局工作？

B: 不就是交通局嘛，**小菜一碟**。

A: Wǒ wàishēngnǚ jīnnián yào bìyè le, nǐ néngbùnéng bǎ tā ānpái jìn jiāotōngjú
    gōngzuò?

B: Bú jiùshì jiāotōngjú ma, xiǎo cài yì dié.

A: My sister's daughter is graduating this year. Would you be able to arrange a
    job for her at the Traffic Department?

B: We're talking about the Traffic Department, right? It'll be a piece of cake.

Usage: Functions as predicative.

Note: Neutral or humorous in meaning.

3. 太阳从西边出来 (太陽從西邊出來)
tàiyáng cóng xī biān chūlai

Translated character by character, 太阳从西边出来 means 'sun-from-west-side-come-
out,' whereas the implied meaning of this proverb would be 'something is very
unlikely to happen.' Its functional translation is 'hell freezes over.'

Example 1:

A: 他工作三年了，今天第一次加班。

B: **太阳从西边出来**了吧？要不肯定是他的电脑、手机、手表上的时间
    同时晚了。

A: Tā gōngzuò sān nián le, jīntiān dì-yī cì jiābān.

B: Tàiyáng cóng xībiān chūláile ba? Yàobù kěndìng shì tā de diànnǎo, shǒujī,
    shǒubiǎo shàng de shíjiān tóngshí wǎn le.

A: He's been working for three years now. Today's the first time he's worked late.

B: Has hell frozen over? Otherwise his computer, phone, and watch are all running
    slow at the same time.

Example 2:

A: 你们的关系恢复了吗？

B: 我已经跟他一刀两断，如果想恢复关系，除非**太阳从西边出来**。

A: Nǐmen de guānxi huīfù le ma?

B: Wǒ yǐjīng gēn tā yìdāo-liǎngduàn, rúguǒ xiǎng huīfù guānxi, chúfēi tàiyáng cóng xībiān chūlái.

A: Have you reconciled with him?

B: I already broke things off with him. If he wants to reconcile our relationship, it won't happen unless hell freezes over.

Usage: Functions as predicate or used singly.

Note: Slightly derogatory and humorous in meaning.

4. 说曹操，曹操到 (说曹操，曹操到)
shuō Cáo Cāo, Cáo Cāo dào

Translated character by character, 说曹操，曹操到 means 'speak-Cao Cao, Cao Cao-arrive,' whereas the implied meaning of this proverb would be 'someone appears right after you have said their name.' Its functional translation is 'Speak of the devil (and he shall appear).'

Example 1:

A: 今天晚上的饭局谁做东呢？

B: 老刘啊！他刚抱上孙子。
    （老刘进来。）

A: 这不，**说曹操，曹操就到**。

A: Jīntiān wǎnshang de fànjú shéi zuòdōng ne?

B: Lǎo Liú a! Tā gāng bàoshàng sūnzi.
    (Lǎo Liú jìnlái.)

A: Zhè bú, shuō Cáo Cāo, Cáo Cāo jiù dào.

A: Who is hosting tonight's dinner party?

B: Old Liu! He's just become a grandfather.
    (Old Liu enters)

A: Speak of the devil.

Example 2:

A: 我得给王局长打个电话。
    （王局长从远处出现。）

B: 不用打了，**说曹操，曹操到**。

A: Wǒ děi gěi Wáng júzhǎng dǎ gè diànhuà.
     (Wáng júzhǎng cóng yuǎnchù chūxiàn.)
B: Búyòng dǎ le, shuō Cáo Cāo, Cáo Cāo dào.

A: I should give Director Wang a call.
     (Director Wang appears from a distance)
B: There's no need. Speak of the devil and he shall appear.

Usage: Used singly.

Variant: 说曹操，曹操就到

Note: Neutral or humorous in meaning.

5.   乌鸦嘴 (烏鴉嘴) wūyā zuǐ

Translated character by character, 乌鸦嘴 means 'crow-mouth,' whereas the implied meaning of this proverb would be 'a person who is believed to bring bad luck.' Its functional translation is 'jinx.'

Example 1:

A: 他又预测巴西队会夺冠。
B: 他是个有名的**乌鸦嘴**，看好哪个队哪个队倒霉。

A: Tā yòu yùcè Bāxī duì huì duóguàn.
B: Tā shì gè yǒumíng de wūyāzuǐ, kàn hǎo nǎ ge duì nǎ ge duì dǎoméi.

A: He once again predicted that Brazil would win the championship.
B: He's a well-known jinx. Whichever team he favors gets unlucky.

Example 2:

A: 有我保佑，你一定成功。
B: 闭上你那只**乌鸦嘴**！

A: Yǒu wǒ bǎoyòu, nǐ yídìng chénggōng.
B: Bì shàng nǐ nà zhī wūyāzuǐ!

A: With my blessing, you will definitely succeed.
B: Shut your jinx mouth!

Usage: Functions as object or predicative.

Note: Slightly derogatory in meaning.

6. 二百五 (二百五) èr bǎi wǔ

Translated character by character, 二百五 means 'two-hundred-fifty,' whereas the implied meaning of this proverb would be 'an idiot.' Its functional translation is 'halfwit,' or 'pea-brain.'

Example 1:

A: 你能告诉我怎么用电子表格求和吗？

B: **二百五**，连电子表格都不会，以后怎么做秘书？

A: Nǐ néng gàosù wǒ zěnme yòng diànzǐbiǎogé qiúhé ma?
B: Èrbǎiwǔ, lián diànzǐbiǎogé dōu búhuì, yǐhòu zěnme zuò mìshū?

A: Can you show me how to do a summation on Excel?
B: You pea-brain! If you can't even use Excel, how can you become a secretary?

Example 2:

A: 别人跟他说了要再研究研究，可是他非得逼着人家当面作决定，人家只能拒绝了。

B: 他真是个**二百五**，听不出来别人话里有话。

A: Biérén gēn tā shuōle yào yánjiu yánjiu, kěshì tā fēiděi bīzhe rénjia dāngmiàn zuò juédìng, rénjia zhǐnéng jùjué le.
B: Tā zhēn shì gè èrbǎiwǔ, tīng bù chūlai biérén huàlǐyǒuhuà.

A: They told him they needed to think more about it, but he forced them to make a decision on the spot. They had no choice but to reject him.
B: He really is a halfwit. He can't read between the lines.

Usage: Functions as noun.

Note: Derogatory in meaning.

7. 吃一堑，长一智 (吃一堑，長一智) chī yí qiàn, zhǎng yí zhì

Translated character by character, 吃一堑，长一智 means 'fall-once-pit-increase-bit-wisdom,' whereas the implied meaning of this proverb would be 'to derive wisdom from one's mistakes.' Its functional translation is 'a fall in the pit, a gain in your wit.'

Example 1:

A: 你没事吧？

B: 我没事，就是汽车废了。下次我再也不喝酒了。

A: **吃一堑，长一智**。

B: 是，就算花钱买个教训吧。

A: Nǐ méishì ba?
B: Wǒ méishì, jiùshì qìchē fèi le. Xiàcì wǒ zài yě bù hējiǔ le.
A: Chī yí qiàn, zhǎng yí zhì.
B: Shì, jiù suàn huāqián mǎi gè jiàoxùn ba.

A: Are you OK?
B: I'm alright, just my car's wrecked. Next time I'm not drinking.
A: A fall in the pit, a gain in your wit.
B: Yeah, it's like paying to learn a lesson.

Example 2:

A: 中国的企业在与外国的企业打官司时，因为对国际惯例不熟悉而败
     诉。不过，**吃一堑，长一智**，以后再打类似的官司时就有经验了。

A: Zhōngguó de qǐyè zài yǔ wàiguó de qǐyè dǎ guānsī shí, yīnwèi duì guójì guànlì
     bù shúxi ér bàisù. Búguò, chī yí qiàn, zhǎng yí zhì, yǐhòu zài dǎ lèishì de
     guānsī shí jiù yǒu jīngyàn le.

A: When Chinese corporations participate in lawsuits with foreign corporations,
     they lose because they aren't familiar with international practices. However,
     a fall in the pit is a gain in your wit. When faced with similar lawsuits in the
     future, they will have experience.

Usage: Functions as predicate or used singly.

Note: Neutral in meaning.

8. 睁着眼睛说瞎话 (睜著眼睛説瞎話)
zhēng zhe yǎnjing shuō xiā huà

Translated character by character, 睁着眼睛说瞎话 means 'open-ed-eyes-tell-lies,'
whereas the implied meaning of this proverb would be 'to say what one knows to
be untrue.' Its functional translation is 'to flout reality,' 'to tell bald-faced lies,' or
'to lie through one's teeth.'

Example 1:

A: 他太不诚实了，常常**睁着眼睛说瞎话**，连他父母都骗。

A: Tā tài bù chéngshí le, chángcháng zhēngzhe yǎnjing shuō xiā huà, lián tā
     fùmǔ dōu piàn.

A: He's so dishonest. He often tells bald-faced lies, even to his parents.

Example 2:

A: 那家电视台**睁着眼睛说瞎话**，赤裸裸地攻击别的国家，而对自己国
     家的问题却视而不见。

A: Nà jiā diànshìtái zhēngzhe yǎnjing shuō xiā huà, chìluǒluǒ de gōngjī biéde
    guójiā, ér duì zìjǐ guójiā de wèntí què shì'érbújiàn.

A: That TV station is flouting reality. It plainly slanders other countries, but turns
    a blind eye towards its own country's problems.

Usage: Functions as predicate.

Note: Slightly derogatory in meaning.

---

9. 近朱者赤，近墨者黑 (近朱者赤，近墨者黑)
jìn zhū zhě chì, jìn mò zhě hēi

Translated character by character, 近朱者赤，近墨者黑 means 'close-red-person-red,
close-black-person-black,' whereas the implied meaning of this proverb would be
'one is marked by the company one keeps.'

Example 1:

A: 最近你交往的人里面有一些不三不四的人，你得小心。
B: 爸，我知道。我跟他们只是认识而已，算不上朋友。
A: 那也不行，**近朱者赤，近墨者黑**，时间久了也会染上恶习。

A: Zuìjìn nǐ jiāowǎng de rén lǐmiàn yǒu yìxiē bùsān-búsì de rén, nǐ děi xiǎoxīn.
B: Bà, wǒ zhīdào. Wǒ gēn tāmen zhǐshì rènshí éryǐ, suànbúshàng péngyǒu.
A: Nà yě bú xíng, jìn zhū zhě chì, jìn mò zhě hēi, shíjiān jiǔle yě huì rǎnshàng èxí.

A: You've been interacting with a few shady characters recently. You should be careful.
B: Dad, I know. They're just acquaintances, I wouldn't call them friends.
A: That's also an issue. One is marked by the company one keeps. After a while,
    their vices will rub off on you.

Example 2:

A: 这位政治家年轻时曾是白宫的实习生，与总统接触较多。现在这位
   政治家的做事风格与那位总统一模一样，所谓**近朱者赤，近墨者黑**。

A: Zhè wèi zhèngzhìjiā niánqīng shí céng shì Báigōng de shíxíshēng, yǔ zǒngtǒng
    jiēchù jiào duō. Xiànzài zhè wèi zhèngzhìjiā de zuòshì fēnggé yǔ nà wèi
    zǒngtǒng yìmú-yíyàng, suǒwèi jìn zhū zhě chì, jìn mò zhě hēi.

A: This politician was a White House intern in his youth. He had a good amount
    of contact with the president. Now, he does things in exactly the same manner
    as that president. It's as they say: one is marked by the company one keeps.

Usage: Used singly.

Note: Neutral in meaning.

10. 物以稀为贵 (物以稀為貴) wù yǐ xī wéi guì

Translated character by character, 物以稀为贵 means 'goods-by-rare-be-expensive,' whereas the implied meaning of this proverb would be 'scarcity makes something valuable.' Its functional translation would be 'that which is rare is dear.'

Example 1:

A: 收藏市场的普遍原则是**物以稀为贵**。

A: Shōucáng shìchǎng de pǔbiàn yuánzé shì wù yǐ xī wéi guì.

A: The rule in the collectors' market is that which is rare is dear.

Example 2:

A: 据说真正的龙井茶树不多，**物以稀为贵**，因此清明节前的龙井茶被炒成了天价。

A: Jùshuō zhēnzhèng de Lóngjǐng chá shù bù duō, wù yǐ xī wéi guì, yīncǐ qīngmíngjié qián de Lóngjǐng chá bèi chǎo chéng le tiānjià.

A: I've heard there aren't many true Longjing tea trees. That which is rare is dear, so the price of Longjing tea picked before Tomb Sweeping Day was speculated to high heaven.

Usage: Functions as predicate or used singly.

Note: Neutral in meaning.

11. 王婆卖瓜，自卖自夸 (王婆賣瓜，自賣自誇)
wáng pó mài guā, zì mài zì kuā

Translated character by character, 王婆卖瓜，自卖自夸 means 'nanny-Wang-sell-melon, self-sell-self-brag,' whereas the implied meaning of this proverb would be 'to praise one's own work.' Its functional translation is 'every potter praises his own pot.'

Example 1:

A: 他又在吹嘘他儿子怎么怎么棒呢。

B: **老王卖瓜，自卖自夸**。他那个儿子，学习成绩在班上倒数第一，他还真好意思夸奖。

A: Tā yòu zài chuīxū tā érzǐ zěnme zěnme bàng ne.

B: Lǎo Wáng mài guā, zì mài zì kuā. Tā nàgè érzǐ, xuéxí chéngjì zài bān shàng dàoshǔ dì-yī, tā hái zhēn hǎoyìsi kuājiǎng.

A: He's boasting about how his son's so great again.

B: Every potter praises his own pot. That son of his has the worst grades in his class and yet he somehow still praises him.

Example 2:

A: 他的评论有"**王婆卖瓜**"的嫌疑，对自己的产品表扬多，对其他家的产品批评多。

A: Tā de pínglùn yǒu "Wáng pó mài guā" de xiányí, duì zìjǐ de chǎnpǐn biǎoyáng duō, duì qítā jiā de chǎnpǐn pīpíng duō.

A: His comment smacked of a potter praising his own pot. He praised his own products a lot and criticized other people's products a lot.

Usage: Used singly.

Variant: 老王卖瓜，自卖自夸

Note: Slightly derogatory in meaning.

12. 站着说话不腰疼 (站著说話不腰疼)
zhàn zhe shuōhuà bù yāo téng

Translated character by character, 站着说话不腰疼 means 'stand-ing-speak-not-waist-ache,' whereas the implied meaning of this proverb would be 'easier said than done.' Its functional translation would be 'to be an armchair quarterback' or 'talk is cheap.'

Example 1:

A: 这事儿还不容易，要是我早就办完了。
B: 你是**站着说话不腰疼**，真的让你干，未必比我快呢。

A: Zhè shìr hái bù róngyi, yàoshi wǒ zǎo jiù bàn wán le.
B: Nǐ shì zhànzhe shuōhuà bù yāo téng, zhēnde ràng nǐ gàn, wèibì bǐ wǒ kuài ne.

A: This should be easy. If it were me, it would have been finished a long time ago.
B: You're an armchair quarterback. If you really were to do it, you wouldn't necessarily be faster than me.

Example 2:

A: 政府应该再追加三百亿人民币在这个项目上。
B: **站着说话不腰疼**，三百亿哪儿那么容易来啊？

A: Zhèngfǔ yīnggāi zài zhuījiā sānbǎi yì rénmínbì zài zhège xiàngmù shang.
B: Zhànzhe shuōhuà bù yāo téng, sānbǎi yì nǎr nàme róngyi lái a?

A: The government should supplement this program with another 30 billion RMB.
B: Talk is cheap. Since when has it been easy to find 30 billion?

Usage: Functions as predicate.

Note: Slightly derogatory and humorous in meaning.

13. 天下没有不散的筵席 (天下没有不散的筵席)
tiānxià méiyǒu bú sàn de yánxí

Translated character by character, 天下没有不散的筵席 means 'heaven-under-not-have-not-dispersed-banquet,' whereas the implied meaning of this proverb would be 'nothing good lasts forever.' Its functional translation is 'all good things must come to an end.'

Example 1:

A: 留步吧，**天下没有不散的筵席**，多保重！

A: Liúbù ba, tiānxià méiyǒu bú sàn de yánxí, duō bǎozhòng!

A: Don't bother to see me out. All good things must come to an end. Take care of yourself!

Example 2:

A: 时间过得真快，转眼一个月过去了，真舍不得离开你们。
B: **天下没有不散的筵席**，以后保持联系。

A: Shíjiān guò de zhēn kuài, zhuǎnyǎn yígè yuè guòqù le, zhēn shěbudé líkāi nǐmen.
B: Tiānxià méiyǒu bú sàn de yánxí, yǐhòu bǎochí liánxì.

A: Time really flew. A month went by in the blink of an eye. I really hate to part with you guys.
B: All good things must come to an end. Keep in touch.

Usage: Used singly.

Note: Neutral in meaning.

14. 天上掉馅饼 (天上掉餡餅) tiānshang diào xiànbǐng

Translated character by character, 天上掉馅饼 means 'sky-upon-fall-stuffed-pancake,' whereas the implied meaning of this proverb would be 'to receive a windfall without working.' Its functional translation is 'to have something fall into your lap.'

Example 1:

A: 你怎么不努力工作呢？
B: 我运气好，下午就去买彩票，说不定中两百万呢。
A: 你就等着**天上掉馅儿饼**吧，有饿死你的一天。

A: Nǐ zěnme bù nǔlì gōngzuò ne?
B: Wǒ yùnqì hǎo, xiàwǔ jiù qù mǎi cǎipiào, shuōbúdìng zhòng liǎng bǎi wàn ne.
A: Nǐ jiù děngzhe tiānshang diào xiànrbǐng ba, yǒu è sǐ nǐ de yì tiān.

A: Why aren't you working hard?

B: I have good luck. I'm going to buy lotto tickets this afternoon, who says I won't win two million dollars?

A: You just wait for money to fall into your lap. One day you'll starve.

Example 2:

A: 有人幻想国家富裕了，人民的生活水平自然会提高，不工作也能过上好日子，于是他们天天盼望**天上掉馅儿饼**。

A: Yǒu rén huànxiǎng guójiā fùyù le, rénmín de shēnghuó shuǐpíng zìrán huì tígāo, bù gōngzuò yě néng guò shang hǎo rìzi, yúshì tāmen tiāntiān pànwàng tiānshang diào xiànrbǐng.

A: Some people fantasize that when the country becomes prosperous, the citizens' quality of life will naturally rise, and even if they don't work they can still live well. So, they're always waiting for something to just fall into their laps.

Usage: Functions as object.

Note: Slightly derogatory and humorous in meaning.

15. 己所不欲，勿施于人 (己所不欲，勿施於人)
jǐ suǒ bú yù, wù shī yú rén

Translated character by character, 己所不欲，勿施于人 means 'oneself-what-not-desire, not-impose-on-others,' whereas the implied meaning of this proverb would be 'don't treat others differently than you would like to be treated.' Its functional translation is 'do unto others as you would have them do unto you.'

Example 1:

A: 他这样要求别人也太过分了。

B: 是啊，连他自己都做不到，**己所不欲，勿施于人**嘛。

A: Tā zhèyàng yāoqiú biérén yě tài guòfèn le.

B: Shì a, lián tā zìjǐ dōu zuò bú dào, jǐ suǒ bú yù, wù shī yú rén ma.

A: He's going too far by asking that of others.

B: Yeah, even he wouldn't do that. Do unto others as you would have them do unto you.

Example 2:

A: 你这样做恐怕不合适吧？

B: 怎么不合适？

A: 你再想想，如果别人这样对待你，你会高兴吗？**己所不欲，勿施于人**。

A: Nǐ zhèyàng zuò kǒngpà bù héshì ba?

B: Zěnme bù héshì?

A: Nǐ zài xiǎngxiǎng, rúguǒ biérén zhèyàng duìdài nǐ, nǐ huì gāoxìng ma? Jǐ suǒ
bú yù, wù shī yú rén.

A: I'm afraid it would be inappropriate for you to do that.

B: How is it inappropriate?

A: Think about it. If other people treated you like that, would you be happy? Do
unto others as you would have them do unto you.

Usage: Used singly.

Note: Neutral in meaning.

16. 睁眼瞎 (睜眼瞎) zhēng yǎn xiā

Translated character by character, 睁眼瞎 means 'open-eyes-blind,' whereas the
implied meaning of this proverb would be 'a bad judge of character.'

Example 1:

A: 我真是个**睁眼瞎**，怎么没看出他是个披着人皮的狼！

A: Wǒ zhēn shì gè zhēngyǎnxiā, zěnme méi kànchū tā shì gè pīzhe rén pí de
láng!

A: I'm such a bad judge of character. How could I not see that he was a wolf in
sheep's clothing?

Example 2:

A: 他是个**睁眼瞎**。他老婆在外面跟别人搞，他好像一点儿都不知道。

B: 谁知道呢？没准儿他是睁一只眼、闭一只眼。

A: Tā shì gè zhēngyǎnxiā. Tā lǎopo zài wàimiàn gēn biérén gǎo tā hǎoxiàng yìdiǎnr
dōu bù zhīdào.

B: Shéi zhīdào ne? Méizhǔnr tā shì zhēng yì zhī yǎn, bì yì zhī yǎn.

A: He's a bad judge of character. His wife is having an affair and he seems not
to have a clue.

B: Who knows? Who's to say he's not just turning a blind eye?

Usage: Functions as predicative.

Note: Slightly derogatory in meaning.

17. 跳进黄河洗不清 (跳進黃河洗不清)
tiào jìn Huáng Hé xǐ bù qīng

Translated character by character, 跳进黄河洗不清 means 'jump-in-Yellow River-wash-unable-clean.' Its functional translation is 'to be unable to clear one's name.'

Example 1:

A: 那位有前途的政治家与一个名声很不好的女人泡夜店的照片被曝光了。

B: 完了，这下他**跳进黄河也洗不清**了，以后肯定会被政治对手攻击的。

A: Nà wèi yǒu qiántú de zhèngzhìjiā yǔ yígè míngshēng hěn bù hǎo de nǚrén pào yèdiàn de zhàopiàn bèi bàoguāng le.

B: Wán le, zhèxià tā tiào jìn Huáng Hé yě xǐ bù qīng le, yǐhòu kěndìng huì bèi zhèngzhì duìshǒu gōngjī de.

A: That picture of the politician with the bright future and a girl with a bad reputation at a nightclub has surfaced.

B: That's it, this time there's no way he can clear his name. He will definitely be attacked by his political adversaries for this in the future.

Example 2:

A: 昨晚公司失窃了，丢了很多现金。监控录像只发现老李一个人进去过。

B: 以老李的人品不会偷东西啊。不过，他**跳到黄河里都洗不清**了。

A: Zuó wǎn gōngsī shīqiè le, diūle hěnduō xiànjīn. Jiānkòng lùxiàng zhǐ fāxiàn Lǎo Lǐ yígè rén jìnqù guò.

B: Yǐ Lǎo Lǐ de rénpǐn búhuì tōu dōngxi a. Búguò, tā tiào dào Huáng Hé lǐ dōu xǐ bù qīng le.

A: The company was robbed last night. A lot of cash was taken. The surveillance tapes show that only Lao Li had gone in.

B: It's not in Lao Li's nature to steal, but now there's no way for him to clear his name.

Usage: Functions as predicate or predicative.

Variants: 跳到黄河(也)洗不清

Note: Neutral or humorous in meaning. The Yellow River has a lot of silt in it and is very murky. The more one washes, the dirtier one gets.

18.   拍马屁 (拍馬屁) pāi mǎ pì

Translated character by character, 拍屁股 means 'hit-butt,' whereas the implied meaning of this proverb would be 'to fawn over.' Its functional translation is 'to suck up to.'

Example 1:

A: 她既有工作能力，又善于**拍**上司的**马屁**，所以提升很快。

A: Tā jì yǒu gōngzuò nénglì, yòu shànyú pāi shàngsī de mǎ pì, suǒyǐ tíshēng hěn kuài.

A: She's a good worker and she's good at sucking up to her superiors, so she was promoted quickly.

Example 2:

A: 老板，您的领带真漂亮，跟您的西装最配了。
B: 你少**拍马屁**，这条领带我都戴了八回了，你怎么第一次说好？

A: Lǎobǎn, nín de lǐngdài zhēn piàoliang, gēn nín de xīzhuāng zuì pèi le.
B: Nǐ shǎo pāimǎpì, zhè tiáo lǐngdài wǒ dōu dàile bā huí le, nǐ zěnme dì-yī cì shuō hǎo?

A: Boss, your tie is really nice. It goes great with your suit.
B: Stop sucking up to me. I've already worn this tie eight times. Why is this the first time you've commented on it?

Usage: Functions as predicate.

Note: Derogatory in meaning.

19.   情人眼里出西施 (情人眼裏出西施)
qíngrén yǎn lǐ chū Xīshī

Translated character by character, 情人眼里出西施 means 'lover-eyes-in-come out of-Xishi,' whereas the implied meaning of this proverb would be 'one's lover always appears beautiful to oneself.' However, it should be noted that this expression is exclusively used to refer to girls or women. Its functional translation is 'love is blind,' or 'beauty is in the eye of the beholder.'

Example 1:

A: 他老婆也太丑了。
B: **情人眼里出西施**，他认为漂亮就行。

A: Tā lǎopo yě tài chǒu le.
B: Qíngrén yǎn lǐ chū Xīshī, tā rènwéi piàoliang jiù xíng.

A: His wife is hideous.
B: Beauty is in the eye of the beholder; as long as he thinks she's pretty, it's OK.

Example 2:

A: 听说他们两个人在谈恋爱呢。你觉得他们合适吗？男的高富帅，女的可是相貌平平啊！

B: **情人眼里出西施，**那个男的应该更重视女朋友的内在美吧。

A: Tīngshuō tāmen liǎng gè rén zài tán liàn'ài ne. Nǐ juéde tāmen héshì ma? Nánde gāofùshuài, nǔde kě shì xiàngmào píngpíng a!

B: Qíngrén yǎn lǐ chū Xīshī, nàgè nánde yīnggāi gèng zhòngshì nǔpéngyǒu de nèizàiměi ba.

A: I heard they are dating. Do you think they are a good match? The boy is tall, rich and handsome, but the girl is too plain looking!

B: Beauty is in the eye of the beholder. That boy obviously cares more about the inner beauty of his girlfriend.

Usage: Used singly.

Note: Neutral or humorous in meaning. Xishi (c. 506 BC) was one of the renowned Four Beauties of ancient China.

20. 打酱油 (打酱油) dǎ jiàngyóu

Translated character by character, 打酱油 means 'get-soy-sauce,' whereas the implied meaning of this proverb would be 'it's none of my business.' Its functional translation would be 'I couldn't care less,' or 'that's above my pay grade.'

Example 1:

A: 请问您对中东局势有什么看法？

B: 抱歉，我要去**打酱油**。

A: Qǐngwèn nín duì Zhōngdōng júshì yǒu shénme kànfǎ?

B: Bàoqiàn, wǒ yào qù dǎ jiàngyóu.

A: Excuse me, what's your view on the situation in the Middle East?

B: I'm sorry, that's above my pay grade.

Example 2:

A: 您是来欢迎总统的吗？

B: 不是，我是来**打酱油**的。

A: Nín shì lái huānyíng zǒngtǒng de ma?

B: Búshì, wǒ shì lái dǎ jiàngyóu de.

A: Are you here to welcome the president?

B: No, I couldn't care less.

Usage: Functions as predicate.

Note: Humorous or neutral in meaning. This *suyu* is Chinese Internet slang dating from 2008. When responding to a TV reporter's commentary on some issue (an elementary school student refusing to look at pornographic and violent content on the internet), someone said, "What does this have to do with me? I'm here to '打酱油' (get some soy sauce)," meaning that he was indifferent to current events and government. '他不是打酱油的' is a very popular usage, meaning that the person in question is not a bystander, but someone wielding great influence on a certain topic or issue.

21. 不怕一万，就怕万一 (不怕一萬，就怕萬一)
bú pà yí wàn, jiù pà wànyī

Translated character by character, 不怕一万，就怕万一 means 'not-fear-one-ten thousand, just-fear-one-ten thousandth,' whereas the implied meaning of this proverb would be 'to be prepared for all eventualities.' Its functional translation is 'one can never be too careful.'

Example 1:

A: 孩子，晚上太晚了千万别出门。
B: 妈，没事儿的，我们学校安全得很。
A: 那也不行，**不怕一万，就怕万一**。尤其是周末晚上，有些人喝醉了酒，很危险。

A: Háizi, wǎnshang tài wǎn le qiānwàn bié chūmén.
B: Mā, méishìr de, wǒmen xuéxiào ānquán de hěn.
A: Nà yě bùxíng, bú pà yí wàn, jiù pà wànyī. Yóuqí shì zhōumò wǎnshàng, yǒuxiē rén hēzuì le jiǔ, hěn wēixiǎn.

A: Child, when it's too late at night, don't, under any circumstances, go out.
B: Mom, it's not an issue. Our school is incredibly safe.
A: That's not good enough. You can never be too careful. Especially on weekend nights, some people get drunk; it's very dangerous.

Example 2:

A: 老板，明天的谈判我们万无一失了。
B: **不怕一万，就怕万一**。你们还是要准备一套应急方案。

A: Lǎobǎn, míngtiān de tánpàn wǒmen wànwú-yìshī le.
B: Bú pà yí wàn, jiù pà wànyī. Nǐmen háishì yào zhǔnbèi yí tào yìngjí fāng'àn.

A: Boss, we're guaranteed success in tomorrow's negotiation.
B: One can never be too careful. You guys still need to prepare an emergency plan.

Usage: Used singly.

Variant: 不怕一万，只怕万一

Note: Neutral in meaning.

---

22. 走着瞧 (走著瞧) zǒu zhe qiáo

Translated character by character, 走着瞧 means 'walk-ing-look.' Its functional translation is 'wait and see.'

Example 1:

A: 这次你输定了。
B: 不要高兴太早，**走着瞧**吧。

A: Zhècì nǐ shū dìng le.
B: Búyào gāoxìng tài zǎo, zǒuzheqiáo ba.

A: This time you're definitely going to lose.
B: Don't celebrate too soon. Just wait and see.

Example 2:

A: 你再赔偿我名誉损失费20万。
B: 我已经给你精神损失费20万了，现在又要名誉损失费。你不要把我逼急了，逼急了我什么样的事都能干出来，不信咱们**走着瞧**。

A: Nǐ zài péicháng wǒ míngyù sǔnshīfèi 20 wàn.
B: Wǒ yǐjīng gěi nǐ jīngshen sǔnshīfèi 20 wàn le, xiànzài yòu yào míngyù sǔnshīfèi. Nǐ búyào bǎ wǒ bī jí le, bī jí le wǒ shénmeyàng de shì dōu néng gàn chūlái, bú xìn zánmen zǒuzheqiáo.

A: Pay me another 200,000 RMB for libel damages.
B: I already gave you 200,000 RMB for emotional distress; now you also want libel damages? Don't push me too hard. When I'm pushed, I'm capable of anything. If you don't believe me, just wait and see.

Usage: Functions as predicate.

Note: Slightly derogatory or neutral in meaning.

23. 不管三七二十一 (不管三七二十一)
bùguǎn sān qī èrshíyī

Translated character by character, 不管三七二十一 means 'not-care-three-(times)-seven-twenty-one,' whereas the implied meaning of this proverb would be 'to act recklessly.' Its functional translation is 'to throw caution to the wind.'

Example 1:

A: 这款电子产品你根本不懂有什么用处，怎么一下子买了两个？

B: 那不是圣诞节大减价嘛，**不管**三七二十一，先买回家再说，以后再慢慢看怎么用。

A: Zhè kuǎn diànzǐ chǎnpǐn nǐ gēnběn bù dǒng yǒu shénme yòngchu, zěnme yíxiàzi mǎile liǎng gè?

B: Nà búshì Shèngdànjié dàjiǎnjià ma, bùguǎn sān qī èrshíyī, xiān mǎi huí jiā zàishuō, yǐhòu zài mànmānr kàn zěnme yòng.

A: You actually don't know what this gadget does; why did you impulsively buy two?

B: Wasn't it a big Christmas sale? I threw caution to the wind and bought two; I'll figure out how to use them later.

Example 2:

A: 你今天说话可伤了不少人。

B: 只要我站在正义的立场上，我才**不管**三七二十一。

A: Nǐ jīntiān shuōhuà kě shānle bùshǎo rén.

B: Zhǐyào wǒ zhàn zài zhèngyì de lìchǎng shang, wǒ cái bùguǎn sān qī èrshíyī ne.

A: You hurt a lot of people with what you said today.

B: As long as I am on the side of justice, I throw caution to the wind.

Usage: Functions as predicate or used singly.

Note: Slightly derogatory in meaning.

24. 吃着碗里的，看着锅里的 (吃著碗裏的，看著鍋裏的) chī zhe wǎn lǐ de, kàn zhe guō lǐ de

Translated character by character, 吃着碗里的，看着锅里的 means 'eat-ing-bowl-inside, watch-ing-pot-inside,' whereas the implied meaning of this proverb would be 'to eat what's in one's bowl while eyeing the pot.' Its functional translation is 'to be unsatisfied with what one has.'

Example 1:

A:　好像他在勾引他小姨子。

B:　这家伙太花心了，**吃着碗里的，看着锅里的**。

A:　Hǎoxiàng tā zài gōuyǐn tā xiǎoyízi.

B:　Zhè jiāhuo tài huāxīn le, chīzhe wǎn lǐ de, kànzhe guō lǐ de.

A:　It seems he's after his wife's sister.

B:　This guy is so unfaithful. He's eating what's in his bowl while eyeing the pot.

Example 2:

A:　他们公司已经得到政府的很大的订单了，现在又要起诉竞争对手，说对方不公平竞争。

B:　他们的胃口也太大了，**吃着碗里的，看着锅里的**。

A:　Tāmen gōngsī yǐjīng dédào zhèngfǔ de hěn dà de dìngdān le, xiànzài yòu yào qǐsù jìngzhēng duìshǒu, shuō duìfāng bù gōngpíng jìngzhēng.

B:　Tāmen de wèikǒu yě tài dà le, chīzhe wǎn lǐ de, kànzhe guō lǐ de.

A:　Their company already got a very big order from the government and now he's also going to sue his competitors, saying they didn't play fair.

B:　They're too greedy, eating what's in their bowls while eyeing the pot.

Usage: Used singly.

Variants: 吃着碗里的，想着锅里的；吃着碗里的，望着锅里的

Note: Slightly derogatory and humorous in meaning.

25. 钻牛角尖 (鑽牛角尖) zuān niú jiǎo jiān

Translated character by character, 钻牛角尖 means 'squeeze-bull-horn-tip,' whereas the implied meaning of this proverb would be 'to go down a dead end,' or 'to split hairs.'

Example 1:

A:　欧洲人学语言有优势，一般人都会两三种语言。

B:　不对，很多英国人只会英语。

A:　你这个人怎么**钻牛角尖**啊？我是总的来说。

A:　Ōuzhōu rén xué yǔyán yǒu yōushì, yìbān rén dōu huì liǎng-sān zhǒng yǔyán.

B:　Búduì, hěnduō Yīngguó rén zhǐ huì Yīngyǔ.

A:　Nǐ zhègè rén zěnme zuān niú jiǎo jiān a? Wǒ shì zǒngdeláishuō.

A:　Europeans have an advantage in learning languages. An average European can speak two or three languages.

B:　No, a lot of English people can only speak English.

A:　Why are you splitting hairs? I was speaking in generalities.

Example 2:

A: 他怎么样？

B: 勤奋有余，灵活不足，看问题太**钻牛角尖**。

A: Tā zěnmeyàng?

B: Qínfèn yǒuyú, línghuó bùzú, kàn wèntí tài **zuān niú jiǎo jiān**.

A: How is he?

B: He's excessively diligent, but not flexible enough. He's too closed-minded in dealing with problems.

Usage: Functions as predicate.

Note: Slightly derogatory in meaning.

26. 人不可貌相，海水不可斗量 (人不可貌相，海水不可斗量) rén bù kě mào xiàng, hǎi shuǐ bù kě dǒu liáng

Translated character by character, 人不可貌相，海水不可斗量 means 'person-not-by-appearance-judged, ocean-water-not-by-*volume unit*-measure,' whereas the implied meaning of this proverb would be 'you cannot judge something by appearance only.' Its functional translation is 'you can't judge a book by its cover.'

Example 1:

A: 他平常看起来很不起眼，可是在昨天的大场面上表现得恰到好处，一看就是见过世面的。看来真是**人不可貌相，海水不可斗量**。

A: Tā píngcháng kàn qǐlái hěn bùqǐyǎn, kěshì zài zuótiān de dàchǎngmiàn shàng biǎoxiàn de qiàdàohǎochù, yí kàn jiùshì jiànguò shìmiàn de. Kànlái zhēnshì **rén bùkě mào xiàng, hǎishuǐ bùkě dǒu liáng**.

A: He usually looks very undistinguished, but he conducted himself perfectly at yesterday's occasion. He seemed, at a glance, cultured. It looks like you really can't judge a book by its cover.

Example 2:

A: 你看他这身打扮，能有什么本事？

B: 别这么说，**人不可貌相，海水不可斗量**。史蒂夫·乔布斯还只穿黑色高领衫和牛仔裤呢，谁敢小看他？

A: Nǐ kàn tā zhè shēn dǎbàn, néng yǒu shénme běnshì?

B: Bié zhème shuō, **rén bùkě mào xiàng, hǎishuǐ bùkě dǒu liáng**. Shǐdìfū Qiáobùsī hái zhǐ chuān hēisè gāolǐngshān hé niúzǎikù ne, shuí gǎn xiǎokàn tā?

A: Look at the way he dresses! What could he be good at?

B: Don't say that. You can't judge a book by its cover. Steve Jobs just wears a black turtleneck and jeans, and who would dare to look down on him?

Usage: Used singly.

Variant: 人不可貌相

Note: Neutral in meaning.

27. 林子大了，什么鸟都有 (林子大了，什麼鳥都有)
línzi dà le, shénme niǎo dōu yǒu

Translated character by character, 林子大了，什么鸟都有 means 'woods-be-big, any-bird-all-exist,' whereas the implied meaning of this proverb would be 'some people really are weird.' Its functional translation is 'there are all kinds of fish in the sea.'

Example 1:

A: 有的政府官员去嫖妓，完了以后还让妓女开发票，他们回去以后可以报销。什么人啊！

B: **真是林子大了，什么鸟都有**。

A: Yǒude zhèngfǔ guānyuán qù piáojì, wánle yǐhòu hái ràng jìnǔ kāi fāpiào, tāmen huíqù yǐhòu kěyǐ bàoxiāo. Shénme rén a!

B: Zhēnshì línzi dà le, shénme niǎo dōu yǒu.

A: When some government officials frequent brothels, they make the prostitutes give them a receipt so that they can claim reimbursement (from the government) when they get back. What characters!

B: There really are all kinds of fish in the sea!

Example 2:

A: 我听说有个人倒着拿着报纸看。

B: **林子大了，什么鸟都有**。

A: Wǒ tīngshuō yǒu gè rén dàozhe názhe bàozhǐ kàn.

B: Línzi dà le, shénme niǎo dōu yǒu.

A: I heard there's a person who reads the newspaper upside down.

B: There are all kinds of fish in the sea.

Usage: Used singly.

Note: Slightly derogatory in meaning.

28. 鸡毛蒜皮 (雞毛蒜皮) jī máo suàn pí

Translated character by character, 鸡毛蒜皮 means 'chicken-feathers-garlic-skins.' Its functional translation is 'trivial,' or 'trivialities.'

Example 1:

A: 王哥，你能不能帮我看一下我的电脑，死机了。
B: 这点儿**鸡毛蒜皮**的小事也找我，我的时间那么不值钱啊？去，买个新的去。

A: Wáng gē, nǐ néngbunéng bāng wǒ kàn yíxià wǒde diànnǎo, sǐjī le.
B: Zhè diǎnr jī máo suàn pí de xiǎoshì yě zhǎo wǒ, wǒde shíjiān nàme bù zhíqián a? Qù, mǎi gè xīn de qù.

A: Brother Wang, could you take a quick look at my computer? It crashed.
B: Is my time really worth that little, bothering me with such trivial matters? Go buy a new one.

Example 2:

A: 咱们头儿大事干不了，整天讲一些**鸡毛蒜皮**的事情，都烦死我了。

A: Zánmen tóur dà shì gàn bùliǎo, zhěngtiān jiǎng yìxiē jī máo suàn pí de shìqing, dōu fán sǐ wǒ le.

A: Our leader can't handle big issues, and talks about trivial matters all the time. I'm sick of it.

Usage: Functions as attributive.

Note: Slightly derogatory in meaning.

29. 鲜花插在牛粪上 (鮮花插在牛糞上)
xiān huā chā zài niú fèn shàng

Translated character by character, 鲜花插在牛粪上 means 'fresh-flower-stick-in-cow-dung,' whereas the implied meaning of this proverb would be 'a beautiful woman is married to an old or ugly man.'

Example 1:

A: 那个大美女怎么嫁给了一个老头子？**鲜花插在牛粪上**，太可惜了！
B: 别这么说。是各取所需，老头子是亿万富翁。

A: Nàgè dà měinǚ zěnme jiàgěi le yígè lǎotóuzi? Xiānhuā chā zài niú fèn shàng, tài kěxī le!
B: Bié zhème shuō. Shì gè qǔ suǒ xū, lǎotóuzi shì yìwànfùwēng.

A: How did that gorgeous woman marry an old fart? It's a May-December marriage. What a pity!

B: Don't say that. They each get what they want. That old fart is a multi-billionaire.

Example 2:

A: 她又高又漂亮，她老公又矮又丑。两个人怎么结婚了呢？

B: **一朵鲜花插在牛粪上**了。

A: Tā yòu gāo yòu piàoliang, tā lǎogōng yòu ǎi yòu chǒu. Liǎng gè rén zěnme jiéhūn le ne?

B: Yì duǒ xiānhuā chā zài niú fèn shàng le.

A: She's tall and beautiful, her husband is short and ugly, how did those two get married?

B: It's a May-December marriage.

Usage: Functions mainly as predicative or predicate.

Note: Derogatory in meaning.

---

30. 醉翁之意不在酒 (醉翁之意不在酒)
zuì wēng zhī yì bú zài jiǔ

Translated character by character, 醉翁之意不在酒 means 'drunk-man-'s-intention-not-at-wine,' whereas the implied meaning of this proverb would be 'to have an ulterior motive.'

Example 1:

A: 我们的谈判僵持住了。对方说请我们去看戏，说是放松一下。

B: 他们没有那么简单，肯定是**醉翁之意不在酒**啊。

A: Wǒmen de tánpàn jiāngchí zhù le. Duìfāng shuō qǐng wǒmen qù kànxì, shuō shì fàngsōng yíxià.

B: Tāmen méiyǒu nàme jiǎndān, kěndìng shì zuì wēng zhī yì bú zài jiǔ a.

A: Our negotiations have ground to a halt. Our counterparts say they want to invite us to see a play. They say they want to relax for a while.

B: That's not the whole story. They definitely have ulterior motives.

Example 2:

A: 李小姐喜欢艺术。他三番五次请李小姐去参观名人画展。

B: **醉翁之意不在酒**。他大概对李小姐本人更感兴趣。

A: Lǐ xiǎojiě xǐhuan yìshù. Tā sānfān-wǔcì qǐng Lǐ xiǎojiě qù cānguān míngrén huàzhǎn.

B: Zuì wēng zhī yì bú zài jiǔ. Tā dàgài duì Lǐ xiǎojiě běnrén gèng gǎn xìngqù.

A: Ms. Li likes art. He's invited Ms. Li to visit celebrity art exhibitions over and over.

B: He has ulterior motives. He's probably more interested in Ms. Li.

Usage: Functions as predicate or used singly.

Note: Humorous or neutral in meaning.

31. 猴年马月 (猴年馬月) hóu nián mǎ yuè

Translated character by character, 猴年马月 means 'monkey-year-horse-month,' whereas the implied meaning of this proverb would be 'in the remote future.' Its functional translation is 'it'll be a cold day in hell when,' or 'god knows when.'

Example 1:

A: 政府说要在市中心建一座公园，都说了二十年了，还没有动静，不知道**猴年马月**才能建成。

A: Zhèngfǔ shuō yào zài shì zhōngxīn jiàn yí zuò gōngyuán, dōu shuōle èrshí nián le, hái méiyǒu dòngjing, bù zhīdao hóu nián mǎ yuè cáinéng jiànchéng.

A: The government says they want to build a park in the city center. They've been saying that for twenty years now and they still haven't started. God only knows when they'll finish.

Example 2:

A: 你打算什么时候买房子？

B: 房价那么高，只靠工资，**猴年马月**也买不起一套房子啊！

A: Nǐ dǎsuàn shénme shíhòu mǎi fángzi?

B: Fángjià nàme gāo, zhǐ kào gōngzī, hóu nián mǎ yuè yě mǎibuqǐ yí tào fángzi a!

A: When are you planning on buying a house?

B: With real estate prices as high as they are and relying only on my salary, it'll be a cold day in hell when I can buy a house.

Usage: Functions as adverbial.

Variants: 牛年马月; 驴年马月

Note: Neutral or humorous in meaning.

32. 眼不见为净 (眼不見為淨) yǎn bú jiàn wéi jìng

Translated character by character, 眼不见为净 means 'eyes-not-see-is-clean,' whereas the implied meaning of this proverb would be 'to not worry about things that do not happen in front of one's eyes.' Its functional translation is 'What somebody doesn't know/see can't hurt them.'

Example 1:

A: 这家小饭馆看起来黑乎乎的，卫生吗？

B: 别管卫生不卫生的，先填饱肚子再说。**眼不见为净**，大饭店也未必很干净。

A: Zhè jiā xiǎo fànguǎn kàn qǐlái hēihūhu de, wèishēng ma?

B: Bié guǎn wèishēng bú wèishēng de, xiān tiánbǎo dùzǐ zàishuō. Yǎn bú jiàn wéi jìng, dà fàndiàn yě wèibì hěn gànjìng.

A: This little restaurant looks filthy. Is it hygienic?

B: Don't worry about the hygiene, just eat up. What you don't know can't hurt you. Even big restaurants aren't necessarily very clean.

Example 2:

A: 你儿子最近给你添了不少麻烦。

B: 咳，好在他在外国，我就**眼不见为净**了，否则早该给气死了。

A: Nǐ érzǐ zuìjìn gěi nǐ tiānle bùshǎo máfan.

B: Hài, hǎozài tā zài wàiguó, wǒ jiù yǎn bú jiàn wéi jìng le, fǒuzé zǎo gāi gěi qìsǐ le.

A: Your son has been a real handful for you lately.

B: Oh, it's a good thing he's abroad. What I don't see can't hurt me. Otherwise I'd have gone ballistic a long time ago.

Usage: Functions mainly as predicate.

Note: Neutral in meaning.

33. 姜是老的辣 (薑是老的辣) jiāng shì lǎo de là

Translated character by character, 姜是老的辣 means 'ginger-is-older-spicy,' whereas the implied meaning of this proverb would be 'people become more capable as they get older.' Its functional translation is 'with experience comes wisdom.'

Example 1:

A: 你的电脑的问题我五分钟就解决了。

B: 哇！**姜还是老的辣**，您真厉害。

A: Nǐde diànnǎo de wèntí wǒ wǔ fēnzhōng jiù jiějué le.
B: Wà! Jiāng háishì lǎo de là, nín zhēn lìhai.

A: I fixed the problem with your computer in just five minutes.
B: Wow! With experience comes wisdom. You're amazing.

Example 2:

A: 里根用"星球大战"计划拖垮了前苏联的经济，用和平演变瓦解了前苏联和东欧国家的意识形态。前苏联及东欧社会主义国家就这么轻易地被里根解体了。
B: 里根当总统的时候都七十多岁了，不过，**姜是老的辣**，他太老谋深算了。

A: Lǐgēn yòng Xīngqiú Dàzhàn jìhuà tuōkuǎle qián Sūlián de jīngjì, yòng hépíng yǎnbiàn wǎjiěle qián Sūlián hé Dōng Ōu guójiā de yìshi xíngtài. Qián Sūlián jí Dōng Ōu shèhuìzhǔyì guójiā jiù zhème qīngyì de bèi Lǐgēn wǎjiě le.
B: Lǐgēn dāng zǒngtǒng de shíhou dōu qīshí duō suì le, búguò, jiāng shì lǎo de là, tā tài lǎomóu-shēnsuàn le.

A: President Reagan used the 'Star Wars program' to wear down the former Soviet Union's economy and broke down the Soviet Union and Eastern Europe's ideology through peaceful evolution. The Soviet Union and socialist Eastern European countries were so easily broken up by Reagan.
B: When Reagan was president, he was already in his seventies. But with experience comes wisdom. He's a wily old fox.

Usage: Used singly.

Note: Neutral or humorous in meaning.

---

34. 留得青山在，不怕没柴烧 (留得青山在，不怕没柴燒) liú dé qīng shān zài, bú pà méi chái shāo

Translated character by character, 留得青山在，不怕没柴烧 means 'leave-green-mountain-remain, not-fear-no-firewood-burn,' whereas the implied meaning of this proverb would be 'where there's life, there's hope.'

Example 1:

A: 你怎么又喝起酒来了？
B: 喝不喝有什么区别？反正是没前途了。
A: 没出息！不就是被解职了吗？你才三十五岁，以后有的是机会。**留得青山在，不怕没柴烧**。把酒瓶扔掉！

A:　Nǐ zěnme yòu hē qǐ jiǔ lái le?

B:　Hē bù hē yǒu shénme qūbié? Fǎnzhèng shì méi qiántú le.

A:　Méi chūxi! Bú jiùshì bèi jiězhí le ma? Nǐ cái sānshíwǔ suì, yǐhòu yǒudeshì jīhuì. Liú dé qīngshān zài, bú pà méi chái shāo. Bǎ jiǔpíng rēngdiào!

A:　Why have you started drinking alcohol again?

B:　What difference does it make if I drink or not? I have no future anyway.

A:　You have no drive! Weren't you only laid off? You're just 35, there will be plenty of opportunity in the future. Where there's life, there's hope. Throw that bottle away!

Example 2:

A:　（病人）我吃不下了。

B:　再吃两口吧，身体要紧，别的事都可以往后放放。**留得青山在，不怕没柴烧**。

A:　(bìng rén) Wǒ chī bú xià le.

B:　Zài chī liǎng kǒu ba, shēntǐ yàojǐn, biéde shì dōu kěyǐ wǎnghòu fàngfàng. Liú dé qīngshān zài, bú pà méi chái shāo.

A:　(sick person) I can't eat anymore.

B:　Eat two more bites. Your body is the most important thing; everything else can be dealt with after. Where there's life, there's hope.

Usage: Used singly.

Note: Neutral in meaning.

35. 拿得起，放得下 (拿得起，放得下) ná de qǐ, fàng de xià

Translated character by character, 拿得起，放得下 means 'able-to-pick up, able-to-put down,' whereas the implied meaning of this proverb would be 'to be able to accept whatever happens to oneself.' Its functional translation is 'to be able to go with the flow.'

Example 1:

A:　我不应该当众跟他吵架。

B:　吵就吵了，这种事得**拿得起，放得下**，没什么大不了的。

A:　Wǒ bù yīnggāi dāngzhòng gēn tā chǎojià.

B:　Chǎo jiù chǎo le, zhè zhǒng shì děi ná de qǐ, fàng de xià, méi shénme dàbùliǎo de.

A:　I shouldn't argue with him in public.

B:　It was just an argument. With these sorts of things, you have to be able to go with the flow. It's nothing major.

Example 2:

A: 她老公可是个好男人。

B: 怎么讲？

A: 工作社交、家里家外，什么事都**拿得起，放得下**。

A: Tā lǎogōng kě shì gè hǎo nánrén.

B: Zěnme jiǎng?

A: Gōngzuò shèjiāo, jiālǐ jiāwài, shénme shì dōu ná de qǐ, fàng de xià.

A: Her husband really is a good man.

B: What do you mean?

A: At work or in social situations, at home or away from home, no matter what, he's able to go with the flow.

Usage: Functions as predicate.

Note: Neutral or complimentary in meaning.

36. 以其人之道还治其人之身 (以其人之道還治其人之身) yǐ qí rén zhī dào huán zhì qí rén zhī shēn

Translated character by character, 以其人之道还治其人之身 means 'using-that-person-'s-way-return-treat-that-person-'s-body,' whereas the implied meaning of this proverb would be 'to take revenge on someone by treating them as they treat others.' Its functional translation is 'to give someone a taste of their own medicine,' or 'to pay back in one's own coin.'

Example 1:

A: 既然他拿我的私生活炒作，那么我们**以其人之道还治其人之身**，把他上大学时吸大麻的事透露给媒体。

A: Jìrán tā ná wǒde sīshēnghuó chǎozuò, nàme wǒmen yǐ qí rén zhī dào huán zhì qí rén zhī shēn, bǎ tā shàng dàxué shí xī dàmá de shì tòulù gěi méitǐ.

A: Since he was publicizing my private life, we gave him a taste of his own medicine, and disclosed to the media that he smoked marijuana in college.

Example 2:

A: 两个国家关系看起来挺好的，怎么这次在联合国安理会投票时A国没有支持B国呢？

B: 那是因为B国在A国申办奥运会时没有投A国的票，现在A国只是**以其人之道还治其人之身**。

A: Liǎng gè guójiā guānxi kàn qǐlái tǐng hǎo de, zěnme zhècì zài Liánhéguó Ānlǐhuì tóupiào shí A guó méi yǒu zhīchí B guó ne?

B: Nà shì yīnwèi B guó zài A guó shēnbàn Àoyùnhuì shí méiyǒu tóu A guó de piào, xiànzài A guó zhǐshì yǐ qí rén zhī dào huán zhì qí rén zhī shēn.

A: The two countries' relations appear to be quite good. Why did country A not support country B in this UN Security Council vote?

B: That's because country B didn't vote for country A when they were in the running for hosting the Olympics. Now country A is just paying country B back in its own coin.

Usage: Functions as predicate.

Note: Neutral in meaning.

---

37. 走桃花运 (走桃花運) *zǒu táo huā yùn*

Translated character by character, 走桃花运 means 'get-peach-blossom-luck,' whereas the implied meaning of this proverb would be 'lucky, specifically with regards to women.' Its functional translation is 'lucky in love.'

Example 1:

A: 李小姐答应今天晚上跟我一起去看电影。

B: 你小子**走桃花运**了，多少人想请李小姐去都没成啊！

A: Lǐ xiǎojiě dāying jīntiān wǎnshang gēn wǒ yìqǐ qù kàn diànyǐng.

B: Nǐ xiǎozi zǒu táohuāyùn le, duōshǎo rén xiǎng qǐng Lǐ xiǎojiě qù dōu méi chéng a!

A: Ms. Li said she would go see a movie with me tonight.

B: You, kid, are lucky in love. So many people want to ask Ms. Li to a movie, but to no avail!

Example 2:

A: 那个算命先生告诉他今年下半年他一定会**走桃花运**，明年就能结婚生子。

A: Nàgè suànmìng xiānshēng gàosù tā jīnnián xià bàn nián tā yídìng huì zǒu táohuāyùn, míngnián jiù néng jiéhūn shēngzǐ.

A: That fortune teller told him that he will definitely be lucky in love in the second half of this year and that he's going to get married and have a baby next year.

Usage: Functions as predicate.

Note: Neutral in meaning.

38. 成事不足，败事有余 (成事不足，败事有餘)
chéng shì bù zú, bài shì yǒu yú

Translated character by character, 成事不足，败事有余 means 'accomplish-thing-not-enough, failed-thing-have-excess,' whereas the implied meaning of this proverb would be 'to be unable to successfully complete anything, but have a tendency to ruin everything.' Its functional translation is 'everything one touches turns to dust.'

Example 1:

A: 他平常吹得厉害，可是什么事都做不好。这件事又搞砸了。

B: **成事不足，败事有余**。他的工作合同明年就不要续签了。

A: Tā píngcháng chuī de lìhai, kěshì shénme shì dōu zuò bù hǎo. Zhè jiàn shì yòu gǎo zá le.

B: Chéng shì bù zú, bài shì yǒu yú. Tā de gōngzuò hétóng míngnián jiù búyào xùqiān le.

A: He usually blows a lot of smoke, but he can't do anything well. He screwed this up too.

B: Everything he touches turns to dust. You shouldn't renew his employment contract next year.

Example 2:

A: 老马，小朱这个人怎么样啊？

B: 老胡，小朱是个**成事不足，败事有余**的家伙。用他的时候得小心。

A: Lǎo Mǎ, Xiǎo Zhū zhègè rén zěnmeyàng a?

B: Lǎo Hú, Xiǎo Zhū shì gè chéng shì bù zú, bài shì yǒu yú de jiāhuo. Yòng tā de shíhòu děi xiǎoxīn.

A: Old Ma, what's Little Zhu like?

B: Old Hu, Little Zhu is the sort of guy where everything he touches turns to dust. You have to be careful when you use him.

Usage: Functions as predicate or attributive.

Note: Slightly derogatory or neutral in meaning.

39. 皇上不急太监急 (皇上不急太監急)
huángshang bù jí tàijian jí

Translated character by character, 皇上不急太监急 means 'His Majesty-not-worry-eunuch-worry,' whereas the implied meaning of this proverb would be, 'the emperor is rested and at ease while the eunuch is excessively concerned.' Its functional translation is, 'the person involved is calm and collected, but observers are very worried.'

Example 1:

A:　快点走吧！会议就要开始了。

B:　急什么啊？**皇上不急太监急**，领导还在那儿喝茶呢。

A:　Kuài diǎn zǒu ba! Huìyì jiùyào kāishǐ le.

B:　Jí shénme a? Huángshang bù jí tàijian jí, lǐngdǎo hái zài nàr hēchá ne.

A:　Move faster! The meeting is about to start.

B:　Where's the fire? You're fretting over nothing; our boss is still over there drinking tea.

Example 2:

A:　恐怕小赵这次要被裁掉了。

B:　**皇上不急太监急**。你没看见小赵整天笑呵呵的嘛。你急什么啊？

A:　Kǒngpà Xiǎo Zhào zhècì yào bèi cáidiào le.

B:　Huángshang bù jí tàijian jí. Nǐ méi kànjian Xiǎo Zhào zhěngtiān xiàohēhē de ma. Nǐ jí shénme a?

A:　I'm afraid Little Zhao is going to be let go this time.

B:　If he's not concerned, you shouldn't be concerned. Haven't you seen Little Zhao smiling all day? What are you worried about?

Usage: Used singly or as predicate.

Variants: 皇帝不急太监急; 皇上不急急太监

Note: Slightly derogatory or neutral in meaning. Because a 太监 (eunuch) is unable to reproduce, one must be extremely careful when using this proverb in conversation with Chinese men – especially those who are already married but do not have children.

40. 三个臭皮匠，顶个诸葛亮（三個臭皮匠，頂個諸葛亮）sān gè chòu pí jiàng, dǐng gè Zhūgé Liàng

Translated character by character, 三个臭皮匠，顶个诸葛亮 means 'three-MW-common-cobblers, surpass-a-Zhuge Liang,' whereas the implied meaning of this proverb would be 'three inferior minds are better than one great one.' Its functional translation is 'two heads are better than one.'

Example 1:

A:　老王，这事我们能行吗？

B:　能，一定能。**三个臭皮匠，顶个诸葛亮**。我们一共十多个人，怎么也能想出一个好办法来。

A: Lǎo Wáng, zhè shì wǒmen néng xíng ma?

B: Néng, yídìng néng. Sān gè chòu píjiàng, dǐng gè Zhūgé Liàng. Wǒmen yígòng shí duō gè rén, zěnme yě néng xiǎngchū yígè hǎo bànfǎ lái.

A: Lao Wang, can we get this thing done?

B: Yes, absolutely. Two heads are better than one. Together, we're more than ten people; we will come up with a good solution one way or another.

Example 2:

A: 我们的对手是哈佛的高材生啊？

B: 我们好歹也是常春藤联盟的，再说我们人多，**三个臭皮匠，顶个诸葛亮**，肯定能竞争过他。

A: Wǒmen de duìshǒu shì Hāfó de gāocáishēng a?

B: Wǒmen hǎodǎi yě shì Chángchūnténg liánméng de, zàishuō wǒmen rén duō, sān gè chòu píjiàng, dǐng gè Zhūgé Liàng, kěndìng néng jìngzhēng guò tā.

A: Our opponent is a distinguished Harvard student?

B: At any rate, we're also Ivy Leaguers, and there are a lot of us. Two heads are better than one. We can definitely beat him.

Usage: Used singly.

Variant: 三个臭皮匠，赛过诸葛亮

Note: Humorous in meaning. Zhuge Liang (诸葛亮 181–234) was a chancellor of Kingdom Shu during the Three Kingdoms period. He is popularly recognized as the smartest person in the history of China.

41.　脚踩两只船 (腳踩兩隻船) jiǎo cǎi liǎng zhī chuán

Translated character by character, 脚踩两只船 means 'foot-step-two-MW-boat.' Its implied meaning is 'to have a foot in both camps.'

Example 1:

A: 他**脚踩两只船**，同时跟两个女孩子谈恋爱。

B: 这就不道德了，对爱情不够尊重。

A: Tā jiǎo cǎi liǎng zhī chuán, tóngshí gēn liǎng gè nǚháizi tán liàn'ài.

B: Zhè jiù bú dàodé le, duì àiqíng búgòu zūnzhòng.

A: He's got a foot in both camps, carrying on relationships with two women at the same time.

B: That's just not right. He doesn't have the proper respect for love.

Example 2:

A:　她够圆滑的，既跟保守派打得火热，又被激进派看成他们的人。

B:　她能**脚踩两只船**，而且踩得很稳，水平够高的。

A:　Tā gòu yuánhuá de, jì gēn bǎoshǒupài dǎ de huǒrè, yòu bèi jījìnpài kàn chéng tāmen de rén.

B:　Tā néng jiǎo cǎi liǎng zhī chuán, érqiě cǎi de hěn wěn, shuǐpíng gòu gāo de.

A:　She's very sly. She gets on well with the conservatives and the progressives see her as one of them.

B:　She can have a foot in both camps and stay firmly planted. She's good.

Usage: Functions as predicate.

Variants: 脚踩(or 踏)两只(or 条)船

Note: Slightly derogatory in meaning.

42.　此地无银三百两 (此地無銀三百兩)
cǐ dì wú yín sānbǎi liǎng

Translated character by character, 此地无银三百两 means 'this-place-not-have-silver-three-hundred-tael,' whereas the implied meaning of this proverb would be 'to expose oneself due to unconvincing denial.' Its functional translation is 'methinks the lady doth protest too much,' or 'telltale sign/action.'

Example 1:

A:　在昨天的匿名投票中，因为有一个人反对，这项计划流产了。

B:　谁干的？太缺德了。不过，这样也好，我们可以节省一笔不小的开支。

A:　不用再解释了，你这是**此地无银三百两**，大家心里都清楚是谁投的反对票。

A:　Zài zuótiān de nìmíng tóupiào zhōng, yīnwèi yǒu yígè rén fǎnduì, zhè xiàng jìhuà liúchǎn le.

B:　Shéi gàn de? Tài quēdé le. Búguò, zhèyàng yě hǎo, wǒmen kěyǐ jiéshěng yì bǐ bùxiǎo de kāizhī.

A:　Búyòng zài jiěshì le, nǐ zhè shì cǐ dì wú yín sānbǎi liǎng, dàjiā xīnli dōu qīngchu shì shéi tóu de fǎnduìpiào.

A:　In last night's anonymous voting, because one person opposed, the plan was aborted.

B:　Who was it? That's so evil. But the silver lining is that we can save a great deal of expenditures.

A:　You don't need to explain any further, methinks the lady doth protest too much. Everyone knows perfectly well who voted against it.

Example 2:

A: 警察把一群与一起强奸案有关联的人叫到一起，说受害人在罪犯的右手腕上留下了一道不深的牙痕。所有的人都没动，只有一个人下意识地看了一下他的右手腕。这一举动无疑是**此地无银三百两**，警察据此把这个人列为重点怀疑对象。

A: Jǐngchá bǎ yì qún yǔ yì qǐ qiángjiān'àn yǒu guānlián de rén jiào dào yìqǐ, shuō shòuhàirén zài zuìfàn de yòu shǒuwàn shàng liúxiàle yí dào bù shēn de yá hén. Suǒyǒu de rén dōu méi dòng, zhǐyǒu yígè rén xiàyìshi de kànle yíxià tā de yòu shǒuwàn. Zhè yī jǔdòng wúyí shì cǐ dì wú yín sānbǎi liǎng, jǐngchá jù cǐ bǎ zhègè rén liè wéi zhòngdiǎn huáiyí duìxiàng.

A: The police called a group of people who were implicated in a rape case together, saying the victim left a set of shallow toothmarks on the right wrist of the criminal. No one moved, but one person unconsciously looked quickly at his right wrist. This action was undoubtedly a telltale sign and, on this evidence, the police made this person their primary suspect.

Usage: Functions as predicate.

Note: Slightly derogatory and humorous in meaning.

---

43. 吃不到葡萄就说葡萄酸 (吃不到葡萄就说葡萄酸)
chī bú dào pútao jiù shuō pútao suān

Translated character by character, 吃不到葡萄就说葡萄酸 means 'eat-not-able-grape-then-say-grape-sour,' whereas the implied meaning of this proverb would be 'to downplay the value of something one wanted but couldn't get.' Its functional translation, is 'sour grapes.'

Example 1:

A: 就那份工作，请我去我都不去。
B: 真的吗？你当初可是申请来着，不要**吃不到葡萄就说葡萄酸**。

A: Jiù nà fèn gōngzuò, qǐng wǒ qù wǒ dōu bú qù.
B: Zhēnde ma? Nǐ dāngchū kěshì shēnqǐng láizhe, búyào chī bú dào pútao jiù shuō pútao suān.

A: I wouldn't take that job even if they offered it to me.
B: Really? You applied for it in the first place. No need for sour grapes.

Example 2:

A: 王小姐明天就嫁人喽！
B: 嫁就嫁呗，嫁了个花花公子，等着哭去吧。
A: 这话我听起来怎么酸溜溜的，你不要**吃不到葡萄就说葡萄酸**啊。

A: Wáng xiǎojiě míngtiān jiù jiàrén lou!
B: Jià jiù jià bei, jiàle gè huāhuāgōngzǐ, děngzhe kū qù ba.
A: Zhè huà wǒ tīng qǐlái zěnme suānliūliu de, nǐ búyào chī bú dào pútao jiù shuō
    pútao suān a.

A: Miss Wang is getting married tomorrow!
B: Let her get married. When she marries that playboy, she'll end up in tears.
A: Why do I feel like you're jealous? There's no need for sour grapes.

Usage: Functions as predicate.

Note: Slightly derogatory in meaning.

44. 心急吃不了热豆腐 (心急吃不了熱豆腐)
xīn jí chī bù liǎo rè dòufu

Translated character by character, 心急吃不了热豆腐 means 'heart-anxious-eat-not-able-hot-tofu,' whereas the implied meaning of this proverb would be 'being overly hasty will actually slow one down in the long run.' Its functional translation is 'more haste, less speed.'

Example 1:

A: 机会这么好，我们赶快动手吧！
B: 再观望两天，**心急吃不了热豆腐**，现在先准备好。

A: Jīhuì zhème hǎo, wǒmen gǎnkuài dòngshǒu ba!
B: Zài guānwàng liǎng tiān, xīn jí chī bùliǎo rè dòufu, xiànzài xiān zhǔnbèi
    hǎo.

A: With such a good opportunity, we should move on it quickly!
B: Let's wait and see for another two days. More haste, less speed. We need to
    prepare everything first.

Example 2:

A: 这么好的女孩儿，快去追吧！
B: 不急，**心急吃不了热豆腐**。

A: Zhème hǎo de nǚháir, kuài qù zhuī ba!
B: Bù jí, xīn jí chī bùliǎo rè dòufu.

A: What a good girl, go get her quickly!
B: Don't rush. More haste, less speed.

Usage: Used singly.

Note: Neutral in meaning.

45. 家常便饭 (家常便飯) jiā cháng biàn fàn

Translated character by character, 家常便饭 means 'home-style-convenient-food,' whereas the implied meaning of this proverb would be 'ordinary,' or 'to be expected.' Its functional translation is 'run of the mill' or 'par for the course.'

Example 1:

A: 那对夫妻对孩子过于严厉，逼孩子学弹钢琴，只要孩子练不好，少睡觉或不让吃饭是**家常便饭**。

A: Nà duì fūqī duì háizi guòyú yánlì, bī háizi xué tán gāngqín, zhǐyào háizi liàn bùhǎo, shǎo shuìjiào huò bú ràng chīfàn shì jiācháng biànfàn.

A: That couple is overly strict with their children. They force their kids to learn to play the piano and if they play badly, sleep deprivation or withholding of food is run of the mill.

Example 2:

A: 他是工作狂，夜里工作到两、三点是**家常便饭**。

A: Tā shì gōngzuòkuáng, yèlǐ gōngzuò dào liǎng-sān diǎn shì jiācháng biànfàn.

A: He's a workaholic. For him to work until two or three in the morning is par for the course.

Usage: Functions as predicative.

Note: Neutral in meaning.

46. 癩蛤蟆想吃天鹅肉 (癩蛤蟆想吃天鵝肉)
làiháma xiǎng chī tiān'é ròu

Translated character by character, 癩蛤蟆想吃天鹅肉 means 'ugly-toad-want-eat-swan's-meat,' whereas the implied meaning of this proverb would be 'to seek to secure something requiring a higher social position or greater abilities.' Its functional translation is 'to be out of one's league' or 'to (want/try to) punch above one's weight.'

Example 1:

A: 他的梦中情人就是现代版的玛丽莲·梦露。
B: 他也不拿镜子照照自己，简直是**癩蛤蟆想吃天鹅肉**。

A: Tā de mèngzhōng qíngrén jiùshì xiàndàibǎn de Mǎlìlián Mènglù.
B: Tā yě bù ná jìngzi zhàozhào zìjǐ, jiǎnzhí shì làiháma xiǎng chī tiān'é ròu.

A: His dream girl is a modern-day Marilyn Monroe.
B: Has he taken a look at himself? He's out of his league.

Example 2:

A: 听说一千人申请了这个职位，连他也申请了。

B: **癞蛤蟆也想吃天鹅肉**，怪不得这么多人申请。

A: Tīngshuō yì qiān rén shēnqǐng le zhège zhíwèi, lián tā yě shēnqǐng le.

B: Làiháma yě xiǎng chī tiān'é ròu, guàibude zhème duō rén shēnqǐng.

A: I heard a thousand people applied for this position. Even he applied.

B: Everyone wants/tries to punch above his weight. No wonder so many people applied.

Usage: Functions as predicative or used singly.

Note: Derogatory in meaning. Normally used with regard to an unattractive man pursuing a pretty woman.

---

47. 天无绝人之路 (天無絕人之路) tiān wú jué rén zhī lù

Translated character by character, 天无绝人之路 means 'heaven-no-repel-person-road,' whereas the implied meaning of this proverb would be 'no obstacle is insurmountable.' Its functional translation is 'there's always a way (to get) around things' or 'there is always a way out.'

Example 1:

A: 董事长，我们有救了！银行同意贷款了！

B: 真是**天无绝人之路**啊！去，马上准备办手续！

A: Dǒngshìzhǎng, wǒmen yǒu jiù le! Yínháng tóngyì dàikuǎn le!

B: Zhēn shì tiān wú jué rén zhī lù a! Qù, mǎshàng zhǔnbèi bàn shǒuxù!

A: Chairman, we've been saved! The bank has agreed to a loan!

A: There really is always a way out! Go, we'll prepare to process it immediately!

Example 2:

A: 现在大的就业环境不景气，她投了上百份工作申请都没有回音。然而，**天无绝人之路**，就在她完全丧失信心的时候，离她家极近的一家公司招聘了她。

A: Xiànzài dà de jiùyè huánjìng bù jǐngqì, tā tóule shàng bǎi fèn gōngzuò shēnqǐng dōu méiyǒu huíyīn. Rán'ér, tiān wú jué rén zhī lù, jiù zài tā wánquán sàngshī xìnxīn de shíhòu, lí tā jiā jí jìn de yì jiā gōngsī zhāopìn le tā.

A: Currently, the broader employment situation is weak; she applied for hundreds of jobs and hasn't heard back from any. But, there's always a way out. Just when she lost hope, a company right near her home hired her.

Usage: Functions as adverbial or used singly.

Note: Neutral in meaning.

48. 走后门 (走後門) zǒu hòu mén

Translated character by character, 走后门 means 'walk-back-door,' whereas the implied meaning of this proverb would be 'to use connections or influence to one's advantage.' Its functional translation is 'to get in through the back door.'

Example 1:

A: 听说小李马上要提副局长了。
B: 又是**走后门**呗，谁都知道他老爸是市长。

A: Tīngshuō Xiǎo Lǐ mǎshàng yào tí fù júzhǎng le.
B: Yòu shì zǒuhòumén bei. Shéi dōu zhīdao tā lǎobà shì shìzhǎng.

A: I hear that Little Li will soon be promoted to vice-director (of a bureau).
B: More back-door dealings. Everyone knows his old man is the mayor.

Example 2:

A: 她工作上没什么本事，但是拉关系、**走后门**很有一套。
B: 别眼红，你有这资本也可以走啊？

A: Tā gōngzuò shàng méi shénme běnshì, dànshì lā guānxi, zǒuhòumén hěn yǒu yí tào.
B: Bié yǎnhóng, nǐ yǒu zhè zīběn yě kěyǐ zǒu a?

A: She is not particularly capable at her job, but she is quite good at establishing connections and using them to her advantage.
B: Don't be jealous. If you had her social capital, wouldn't you do the same?

Usage: Functions mainly as predicate. In Mandarin, 门 is usually retroflexed as 'ménr.'

Note: Derogatory in meaning.

49. 瞎猫碰上死耗子 (瞎貓碰上死耗子)
xiā māo pèng shàng sǐ hàozi

Translated character by character, 瞎猫碰上死耗子 means 'blind-cat-run-into-dead-mouse,' whereas the implied meaning of this proverb would be 'a total fluke.' Its functional translation is 'even a broken clock is right twice a day', or 'even a blind squirrel finds a nut once in a while.'

Example 1:

A: 他对股票一窍不通，就买了一只股票，半个月后那只股票翻了番，
他赚了一大笔钱。

B: **瞎猫碰上死耗子**呗。我们怎么没有这么好的运气。

A: Tā duì mǎi gǔpiào yíqiào-bùtōng, jiù mǎile yì zhī gǔpiào, bàn gè yuè hòu nà
zhī gǔpiào fānle fān, tā zhuànle yí dà bǐ qián.

B: Xiā māo pèng shàng le sǐ hàozi bei. Wǒmen zěnme méiyǒu zhème hǎo de
yùnqi?

A: He bought stock without knowing a thing about them. After a half a month,
that stock had doubled in price, and he made a pretty penny.

B: Even a blind squirrel finds a nut once in a while. Why don't we have such
good luck?

Example 2:

A: 现在工作这么难找，这家伙怎么一下子就找到了？

B: **瞎猫碰上了死耗子**。我听说他给那家公司打电话，误打误撞打进了
董事长办公室，偏巧那天董事长不知道怎么心血来潮，没让秘书
接，而是自己接了电话。董事长一听，说打错了；不过，他那天心
情特别好，竟然让秘书把他的电话转给人事部。人事部及有关部门
以为董事长亲自推荐来的，他跟董事长肯定有很硬的关系，于是面
试手续一路绿灯。这个傻小子稀里糊涂地就找到了工作。真是瞎猫
碰上死耗子了！要不然哪家公司会看上这个傻小子。

A: Xiànzài gōngzuò zhème nán zhǎo, zhè jiāhuo zěnme yíxiàzi jiù zhǎo dào le?

B: Xiā māo pèng shàng le sǐ hàozi. Wǒ tīngshuō tā gěi nà jiā gōngsī dǎ diànhuà,
wùdǎ-wùzhuàng dǎ jìnle dǒngshìzhǎng bàngōngshì, piānqiǎo nà tiān
dǒngshìzhǎng bù zhīdao zěnme xīnxuè-láicháo, méi ràng mìshu jiē, érshì zìjǐ
jiēle diànhuà. Dǒngshìzhǎng yì tīng, shuō dǎ cuò le; búguò, tā nà tiān xīnqíng
tèbié hǎo, jìngrán ràng mìshū bǎ tā de diànhuà zhuǎn gěi rénshìbù. Rénshìbù
jí yǒuguān bùmén yǐwéi dǒngshìzhǎng qīnzì tuījiàn lái de, tā gēn dǒngshìzhǎng
kěndìng yǒu hěn yìng de guānxi, yúshì miànshì shǒuxù yílù lǜdēng. Zhège
shǎxiǎozi xīlihútu de jiù zhǎo dàole gōngzuò. Zhēnshi xiā māo pèng shàng le
sǐ hàozi le! Yàobùrán nǎ jiā gōngsī huì kàn shàng zhège shǎxiǎozi.

A: With employment so hard to find, how did this guy instantly find a job?

B: Even a blind squirrel finds a nut once in a while. I heard that when he called
that company, he accidentally called the chairman's office and, as luck would
have it, that day, the chairman, by some impulse, wouldn't let his secretary
answer, but rather answered the phone himself. As soon as the chairman
picked up, he said he'd misdialed, however, the chairman was in a good mood
that day and, surprisingly, had his secretary put this guy through to HR. HR
and the other relevant departments thought that the chairman had personally
recommended this guy, and that he definitely was close with the chairman,

so they 'green lighted' the interview process. This silly man muddled through and found a job. It really is sheer dumb luck! Otherwise, what company would look kindly on this idiot's application?

Usage: Used singly.

Note: Slightly derogatory and humorous in meaning. Usually the speaker's words have a sense of envy when he comments on others.

50. 好汉不吃眼前亏 (好漢不吃眼前虧)
hǎo hàn bù chī yǎn qián kuī

Translated character by character, 好汉不吃眼前亏 means 'good-man-not-eat-eyes-front-loss,' whereas the implied meaning of this proverb would be 'a wise man knows when to retreat.' Its functional translation is 'you have to know when to hold 'em and when to fold 'em,' or 'discretion is the better part of valor.'

Example 1:

A: 我就是不服他们。

B: 算了，**好汉不吃眼前亏**。想找他们算账以后有的是机会。

A: Wǒ jiùshì bù fú tāmen.

B: Suànle, hǎohàn bù chī yǎnqián kuī. Xiǎng zhǎo tāmen suànzhàng yǐhòu yǒudeshì jīhuì.

A: I refuse to obey them.

B: Forget about it, you have to know when to hold 'em and when to fold 'em. If you want to settle the score with them, there will be plenty of opportunities in the future.

Example 2:

A: 对方人越来越多，他看情况不妙，**好汉不吃眼前亏**，说话的语气马上软了下来。

A: Duìfāng rén yuèláiyuè duō, tā kàn qíngkuàng búmiào, hǎohàn bù chī yǎnqián kuī, shuōhuà de yǔqì mǎshàng ruǎnle xiàlái.

A: As the opposing side grew in number, he realized the situation was dire. As discretion is the better part of valor, his manner of speaking immediately softened.

Usage: Used singly.

Note: Humorous in meaning.

51. 解铃还须系铃人 (解鈴還須繫鈴人)
jiě líng hái xū jì líng rén

Translated character by character, 解铃还须系铃人 means 'untie-bell-still-need-tie-bell-person,' whereas the implied meaning of this proverb would be 'the person who created a problem can solve it.' Its functional translation is 'he that hides can find.'

Example 1:

A: 她那么不开心，你去劝劝她吧？

B: 为什么让我去？

A: 你别装傻，她不开心还不是因为你？**解铃还须系铃人**，只有你才能让她高兴起来。

A: Tā nàme bù kāixīn, nǐ qù quànquàn tā ba?

B: Wèishénme ràng wǒ qù?

A: Nǐ bié zhuāngshǎ, tā bù kāixīn hái búshì yīnwèi nǐ? Jiě líng hái xū jì líng rén, zhǐyǒu nǐ cáinéng ràng tā gāoxìng qǐlái.

A: She's so unhappy. Can you go talk to her?

B: Why me?

A: Don't play dumb. Isn't she unhappy because of you? He that hides can find. You're the only one that can cheer her up.

Example 2:

A: 中美之间的矛盾是美国挑起的，**解铃还须系铃人**，只要美方道歉，中方是不会计较的。

A: Zhōng-měi zhījiān de máodùn shì Měiguó tiǎoqǐ de, jiě líng hái xū jì líng rén, zhǐyào Měi fāng dàoqiàn, Zhōng fāng shì búhuì jìjiào de.

A: The conflict between China and the US was stirred up by the US. He that hides can find. If the US apologizes, China won't dwell on it.

Usage: Used singly.

Variant: 解铃还需系铃人

Note: Neutral in meaning.

52. 肥水不流外人田 (肥水不流外人田)
féi shuǐ bù liú wài rén tián

Translated character by character, 肥水不流外人田 means 'rich-water-not-flow-others'-field,' whereas the implied meaning of this proverb would be 'one does not allow benefits created by one's own work to accrue to others.'

Example 1:

A: 为什么有的公司合同上规定离开那个公司后两年内不能进入同一行业的其他公司工作？

B: 是为了**肥水不流外人田**，同行是冤家。

A: Wèishénme yǒude gōngsī hétong shàng guīdìng líkāi nàgè gōngsī hòu liǎng nián nèi bùnéng jìnrù tóngyī hángyè de qítā gōngsī gōngzuò?

B: Shì wèile féishuǐ bù liú wàirén tián, tóngháng shì yuānjia.

A: Why do some companies' employment contracts stipulate that an employee cannot join another company in the same field within two years of having left?

B: It's in order not to allow others to benefit from their investment in the employee. Companies in the same field are competitors.

Example 2:

A: 博彩业是地方政府税收的重要来源。有的州赌博不合法，于是人们到附近的州去赌。因此不少州为了增加税收，防止**肥水流入外人田**，正在努力使赌博合法化。

A: Bócǎiyè shì dìfāng zhèngfǔ shuìshōu de zhòngyào láiyuán. Yǒude zhōu dǔbó bù héfǎ, yúshì rénmen dào fùjìn de zhōu qù dǔ. Yīncǐ bùshǎo zhōu wèile zēngjiā shuìshōu, fángzhǐ féishuǐ liúrù wàirén tián, zhèngzài nǔlì shǐ dǔbó héfǎhuà.

A: The gaming industry is an important source of tax revenue for local governments. Gambling is illegal in some states and, as a result, people travel to nearby states to gamble. Because of this, in order to increase tax revenues and not allow others to benefit from their own residents, many states are currently working hard to legalize gambling.

Usage: Used singly.

Note: Humorous or neutral in meaning.

---

53. 心有余而力不足 (心有餘而力不足)
xīn yǒu yú ér lì bù zú

Translated character by character, 心有余而力不足 means 'heart-have-excess-but-strength-not-enough,' whereas the implied meaning of this proverb would be 'to want to do something but lack the strength.' Its functional translation is 'to run out of steam.'

Example 1:

A: 总统刚上台的时候高调宣称要进行医疗制度改革，但是这绝非易事。一年之后总统就显得**心有余而力不足**了。

A: Zǒngtǒng gāng shàngtái de shíhòu gāodiào xuānchēng yào jìnxíng yīliáo zhìdù gǎigé, dànshì zhè juéfēi yìshì. Yī nián zhīhòu zǒngtǒng jiù xiǎnde xīn yǒuyú ér lì bùzú le.

A: When the president first took office, he grandly proclaimed that he would carry out a reform of the healthcare system, but this was no easy task. One year later, the president appears to be running out of steam.

Example 2:

A: 他年青的时候每天只睡五个小时，其它时间都工作。但是四十岁以后他感到**心有余而力不足**了。

A: Tā niánqīng de shíhòu měitiān zhǐ shuì wǔ gè xiǎoshí, qítā shíjiān dōu gōngzuò. Dànshì sìshí suì yǐhòu tā gǎndào xīn yǒuyú ér lì bùzú le.

A: When he was young, he would sleep only five hours a night, working the rest of the time. But, after he turned forty years old, he feels he's running out of stream.

Usage: Functions as predicative or predicate. It is usually used after '感到' or '显得.'

Note: Neutral in meaning.

---

54. 不分青红皂白 (不分青红皂白) bù fēn qīng hóng zào bái

Translated character by character, 不分青红皂白 means 'not-distinguish-cyan-red-black-white,' whereas the implied meaning of this proverb would be 'indiscriminate.'

Example 1:

A: 只要他看到不满意的地方，**不分青红皂白**，就把相关人批评一顿。

A: Zhǐyào tā kàn dào bù mǎnyì de dìfang, bù fēn qīng hóng zào bái, jiù bǎ xiāngguān rén pīpíng yí dùn.

A: If he sees something that doesn't please him, he indiscriminately chastises the relevant people.

Example 2:

A: 闯进来一群蒙面人，**不问青红皂白**，见人就打，见东西就砸。

A: Chuǎng jìnlái yì qún méngmiàn rén, bú wèn qīng hóng zào bái, jiàn rén jiù dǎ, jiàn dōngxi jiù zá.

A: A group of masked men rushed in, indiscriminately hitting anyone they saw and breaking anything they saw.

Usage: Functions as adverbial or predicate.

Variant: 不问青红皂白

Note: Derogatory in meaning.

55. 睁一只眼，闭一只眼 (睜一隻眼，閉一隻眼)
zhēng yì zhī yǎn, bì yì zhī yǎn

Translated character by character, 睁一只眼，闭一只眼 means 'open-one-MW-eye, shut-one-MW-eye,' whereas the implied meaning of this proverb would be 'with one eye closed.' Its functional translation is 'to turn a blind eye.'

Example 1:

A: 因为路上的车不多，所以警察对于超速现象**睁一只眼，闭一只眼**。

A: Yīnwèi lùshang de chē bù duō, suǒyǐ jǐngchá duìyú chāosù xiànxiàng zhēng yì zhī yǎn, bì yì zhī yǎn.

A: Because there weren't many cars on the road, the police turned a blind eye to speeding.

Example 2:

A: 他嘴上总是说要严厉反腐败。
B: 是啊，可是对他自己的家属和下属的违法行为却**睁一只眼，闭一只眼**。

A: Tā zuǐshang zǒngshì shuō yào yánlì fǎn fǔbài.
B: Shì a, kěshì duì tā zìjǐ de jiāshǔ hé xiàshǔ de wéifǎ xíngwéi què zhēng yì zhī yǎn, bì yì zhī yǎn.

A: He's always saying we need to stringently fight corruption.
B: Yes, but he actually turns a blind eye to the illegal actions of his own family and inferiors.

Usage: Functions as predicate.

Note: Slightly derogatory in meaning.

56. 破罐子破摔 (破罐子破摔) pò guànzi pò shuāi

Translated character by character, 破罐子破摔 means 'broken-jar-neglected-smash,' whereas the implied meaning of this proverb would be 'to write oneself off as hopeless and act recklessly.' Its functional translation is 'go into a tailspin.' It can also mean 'a vicious cycle.'

Example 1:

A: 他出狱以后好好儿干了几个月，现在又游手好闲了。
B: 得注意了，防止他**破罐子破摔**，应该尽力帮助他。

A: Tā chūyù yǐhòu hǎohāor gànle jǐgè yuè, xiànzài yòu yóushǒu-hàoxián le.
B: Děi zhùyì le, fángzhǐ tā pò guànzi pò shuāi, yīnggāi jìnlì bāngzhù tā.

A: For a few months after he got out of jail, he kept busy. Now he's just lolling around.

B: You need to be careful. You should do your best to help him in order to prevent his going into a tailspin.

Example 2:

A: 两个月内被两个男朋友抛弃了，现在她好像无所谓了。

B: 她那是**破罐子破摔**，咳，都是那两个男人害的。

A: Liǎng gè yuè nèi bèi liǎng gè nánpéngyǒu pāoqì le, xiànzài tā hǎoxiàng wúsuǒwèi le.

B: Tā nà shì pò guànzi pò shuāi, hài, dōushi nà liǎng gè nánrén hài de.

A: Two boyfriends have left her within the last two months. She seems desensitized now.

B: It's a vicious cycle. It's all those two men's fault.

Usage: Functions as predicate.

Note: Slightly derogatory in meaning.

57. 种瓜得瓜，种豆得豆 (種瓜得瓜，種豆得豆)
zhòng guā dé guā, zhòng dòu dé dòu

Translated character by character, 种瓜得瓜，种豆得豆 means 'plant-melon-get-melon, sow-bean-get-bean,' whereas the implied meaning of this proverb would be 'one's fortunes are determined by one's actions.' Its functional translation is 'you reap what you sow.'

Example 1:

A: 他怎么懂这么多稀奇古怪的东西？

B: 人家工作之余，总是坚持读书、看报、上网，所以懂。你整天抽烟、喝酒、打麻将，怎么能懂这些高深的知识？**种瓜得瓜，种豆得豆**嘛。

A: Tā zěnme dǒng zhème duō xīqí-gǔguài de dōngxi?

B: Rénjia gōngzuò zhīyú, zǒngshì jiānchí dúshū, kàn bào, shàngwǎng, suǒyǐ dǒng. Nǐ zhěngtiān chōuyān, hējiǔ, dǎ májiàng, zěnme néng dǒng zhèxiē gāoshēn de zhīshi? Zhòng guā dé guā, zhòng dòu dé dòu ma.

A: How does he understand so many whimsical things?

B: Because he's always reading books, reading newspapers, and surfing the Internet in his spare time. You spend all of your time smoking, drinking, and playing Mahjong. How would you understand these profound things? You reap what you sow.

Example 2:

A: 教师的责任重大，因为他们的一举一动都对学生产生巨大的影响，所谓**种瓜得瓜，种豆得豆**。

A: Jiàoshī de zérèn zhòngdà, yīnwèi tāmen de yìjǔ-yídòng dōu duì xuéshēng chǎnshēng jùdà de yǐngxiǎng, suǒwèi zhòng guā dé guā, zhòng dòu dé dòu.

A: A teacher's responsibility is enormous, because their every move has a huge influence on their students. As they say, you reap what you sow.

Usage: Used singly.

Note: Neutral in meaning.

58. 萝卜白菜，各有所爱 (蘿蔔白菜，各有所愛)
luóbo báicài, gè yǒu suǒ ài

Translated character by character, 萝卜白菜，各有所爱 means 'turnip-cabbage, each-have-what-loves,' whereas the implied meaning of this proverb would be 'different people like different things.' Its functional translation is 'there's no accounting for taste,' or 'different strokes for different folks.'

Example 1:

A: 她这身打扮，跟斑马似的。
B: **萝卜白菜，各有所爱**。只要她自己喜欢就好。

A: Tā zhè shēn dǎbàn, gēn bānmǎ shìde.
B: Luóbo báicài, gè yǒu suǒ ài. Zhǐyào tā zìjǐ xǐhuan jiù hǎo.

A: Made up like that, she looks like a zebra.
B: Different strokes for different folks. As long as she likes it, it's fine.

Example 2:

A: 西方人喜欢吃半生不熟的牛肉，北京人喜欢吃臭豆腐，**萝卜白菜，各有所爱**。

A: Xīfāngrén xǐhuan chī bànshēng-bùshú de niúròu, Běijīngrén xǐhuan chī chòudòufu, luóbo báicài, gè yǒu suǒ ài.

A: Westerners like to eat half-raw, rare beef. Beijingers like to eat smelly tofu. There's no accounting for taste.

Usage: Used singly.

Variant: 萝卜青菜，各有所爱

Note: Neutral or humorous in meaning.

59. 狗嘴里吐不出象牙 (狗嘴裏吐不出象牙)
gǒu zuǐ lǐ tǔ bù chū xiàng yá

Translated character by character, 狗嘴里吐不出象牙 means 'dog-mouth-inside-spit-not-out-elephant-tusk,' whereas the implied meaning of this proverb would be 'you won't get anything clean out of a filthy mouth.' Its functional translation is 'what can you expect from a hog but a grunt?'

Example 1:

A: 他说你因为喝酒被警察抓走了。

B: **狗嘴里吐不出象牙**，我那是帮助警察说明情况，我根本没喝酒。

A: Tā shuō nǐ yīnwèi hējiǔ bèi jǐngchá zhuā zǒu le.

B: Gǒu zuǐ li tǔ bù chū xiàngyá. Wǒ nà shì bāngzhù jǐngchá shuōmíng qíngkuàng, wǒ gēnběn méi hējiǔ.

A: He said that you were picked up by the police because you were drinking.

B: What can you expect from a hog but a grunt? What I was doing was helping explain the situation to the police. I actually wasn't drinking.

Example 2:

A: 他在背后常常说别人的坏话。

B: 他就是那种人，**狗嘴里吐不出象牙**，不说别人坏话就活不了。

A: Tā zài bèihòu chángcháng shuō biérén de huàihuà.

B: Tā jiùshì nà zhǒng rén, gǒu zuǐ li tǔ bù chū xiàngyá, bù shuō biérén huàihuà jiù huó bùliǎo.

A: He often speaks ill of others behind their backs.

B: That's the kind of person he is; what can you expect from a hog but a grunt? He would die if he couldn't speak ill of others.

Usage: Used singly.

Variant: 狗嘴吐不出象牙

Note: Derogatory and humorous in meaning.

60. 三天打鱼，两天晒网 (三天打魚，兩天曬網)
sān tiān dǎ yú, liǎng tiān shài wǎng

Translated character by character, 三天打鱼，两天晒网 means 'three-days-catch-fish, two-days-dry-net,' whereas the implied meaning of this proverb would be 'to lack perseverance and continuity.' Its functional translation is 'to blow hot and cold.'

Example 1:

A: 他做事情没有毅力，**三天打鱼，两天晒网**。

A: Tā zuò shìqing méiyǒu yìlì, **sān tiān dǎ yú, liǎng tiān shài wǎng**.

A: He doesn't have any perseverance. He blows hot and cold.

Example 2:

A: 练钢琴需要耐心，要天天练，不能三**天打鱼，两天晒网**。

A: Liàn gāngqín xūyào nàixīn, yào tiāntiān liàn, bùnéng sān tiān dǎ yú, liǎng tiān shài wǎng.

A: Learning to play the piano requires endurance. You must practice every day; you can't blow hot and cold.

Usage: Functions as predicate.

Note: Slightly derogatory in meaning.

---

61. 一朝被蛇咬，十年怕井绳 (一朝被蛇咬，十年怕井繩) yì zhāo bèi shé yǎo, shí nián pà jǐng shéng

Translated character by character, 一朝被蛇咬，十年怕井绳 means 'once-by-snake-bitten, ten-years-fear-well-rope,' whereas the implied meaning of this proverb would be 'to avoid or be scared of something after a bad experience or setback.' Its functional translation is 'once bitten, twice shy.'

Example 1:

A: 几年前他几乎把所有的钱都投进股票市场，结果几乎赔光了。现在他再也不敢进入股市了，**一朝被蛇咬，十年怕井绳**。

A: Jǐ nián qián tā jīhū bǎ suǒyǒu de qián dōu tóujìn gǔpiào shìchǎng, jiéguǒ jīhū péi guāng le. Xiànzài tā zài yě bùgǎn jìnrù gǔshì le, yì zhāo bèi shé yǎo, shí nián pà jǐngshéng.

A: A few years ago, he almost put all of his money into the stock market and he almost lost his shirt. Now he doesn't dare invest in stocks; once bitten, twice shy.

Example 2:

A: 你怎么看见大狗就躲着走啊？
B: 我小时候挨过狗咬，现在看见狗就哆嗦，**一朝被蛇咬，十年怕井绳**。

A: Nǐ zěnme kànjiàn dà gǒu jiù duǒzhe zǒu a?
B: Wǒ xiǎoshíhòu áiguò gǒu yǎo, xiànzài kànjiàn gǒu jiù duōsuo, yì zhāo bèi shé yǎo, shí nián pà jǐngshéng.

A: Why did you avoid the big dog when you saw it?
B: When I was little, I was bitten by a dog. Now when I see a dog I tremble; once bitten, twice shy.

Usage: Used singly.

Note: Neutral in meaning.

62. 英雄难过美人关 (英雄難過美人關)
yīngxióng nán guò měirén guān

Translated character by character, 英雄难过美人关 means 'hero-difficult-go through-beautiful-person-pass.' Its functional translation is 'no man can resist the charms of a beautiful woman.'

Example 1:

A: 前总统在经济上的贡献非常伟大，可是婚外恋毁了他的名声。
B: **英雄难过美人关**，总统也不例外。

A: Qián zǒngtǒng zài jīngjì shàng de gòngxiàn fēicháng wěidà, kěshì hūnwàiliàn huǐle tā de míngshēng.
B: Yīngxióng nán guò měirén guān, zǒngtǒng yě bú lìwài.

A: The former president had great success with the economy, but his extramarital affairs sullied his reputation.
B: No man can resist the charms of a beautiful woman, not even the president.

Example 2:

A: 老板，我们的谈判对手非常强硬啊！寸步不让。
B: 那好吧，明天换一批人去谈，派年轻漂亮的去，**英雄难过美人关**，或许对方会让一些步。

A: Lǎobǎn, wǒmen de tánpàn duìshǒu fēicháng qiángyìng a! Cùn bù bú ràng.
B: Nà hǎo ba, míngtiān huàn yì pī rén qù tán, pài niánqīng piàoliang de qù, yīngxióng nán guò měirén guān, huòxǔ duìfāng huì ràng yìxiē bù.

A: Boss, our negotiation counterpart is extraordinarily tough! He won't give an inch!
B: Alright. Tomorrow we'll sub a new group of people in to negotiate. We will send a pretty, young woman. No man can resist the charms of a beautiful woman; maybe our counterpart will give a little.

Usage: Used singly.

Note: Neutral or slightly derogatory in meaning.

63. 刀子嘴，豆腐心（刀子嘴，豆腐心）dāozi zuǐ, dòufu xīn

Translated character by character, 刀子嘴，豆腐心 means 'knife-mouth, tofu-heart,' whereas the implied meaning of this proverb would be 'to seem hard and intimidating, but be kind at heart.' Its functional translation is 'to be a softie at heart,' or 'someone's bark is worse than their bite.'

Example 1:

A: 她说话也太严厉了，真让人难以接受。

B: 不要太在意，她一向**刀子嘴，豆腐心**。人挺好的，就是说话不太讲究方式。

A: Tā shuōhuà yě tài yánlì le, zhēn ràng rén nányǐ jiēshòu.

B: Búyào tài zàiyì, tā yíxiàng dāozi zuǐ, dòufu xīn. Rén tǐng hǎo de, jiùshì shuōhuà bú tài jiǎngjiu fāngshì.

A: She speaks too severely; it makes people reluctant to comply.

B: Don't let it bother you, her bark is always worse than her bite. She's a good person, she just isn't too discerning in her manner of speech.

Example 2:

A: 他爸爸是典型的**刀子嘴，豆腐心**，不会真正伤人。

A: Tā bàba shì diǎnxíng de dāozi zuǐ, dòufu xīn, búhuì zhēnzhèng shāng rén.

A: His father is a typical softie. He couldn't really hurt a person.

Usage: Functions as predicate or predicative.

Note: Humorous in meaning.

64. 一失足成千古恨（一失足成千古恨）
yì shī zú chéng qiān gǔ hèn

Translated character by character, 一失足成千古恨 means 'one-lost-step-become-all-time-regret,' whereas the implied meaning of this proverb would be 'the results of some mistakes cannot be undone.' Its functional translation is 'one false step brings everlasting grief.'

Example 1:

A: 我的同学中有人抽大麻。

B: 儿子，你可千万别学他们。这东西沾上就上瘾，**一失足成千古恨**啊！

A: Wǒde tóngxué zhōng yǒu rén chōu dàmá.
B: érzi, nǐ kě qiānwàn bié xué tāmen. Zhè dōngxi zhān shàng jiù shàngyǐn, yì shīzú chéng qiāngǔ hèn a!

A: Some of my classmates smoke marijuana.
B: Son, whatever you do, don't follow their example. If you try it you'll get addicted. One false step brings everlasting grief.

Example 2:

A: 我就要这样做下去！
B: 我警告你，你现在是站在悬崖边上，再不回头就一**失足成千古恨**了。

A: Wǒ jiùyào zhèyàng zuò xiàqù!
B: Wǒ jǐnggào nǐ, nǐ xiànzài shì zhàn zài xuányá biān shàng, zài bù huítóu jiù yì shīzú chéng qiāngǔ hèn le.

A: I'm just going to do it this way.
B: I'm warning you, you're standing on the brink now and if you don't step back, you'll make a fatal mistake.

Usage: Used singly.

Note: Neutral in meaning.

65. 哪壶不开提哪壶 (哪壶不開提哪壺)
nǎ hú bù kāi tí nǎ hú

Translated character by character, 哪壶不开提哪壶 means 'which-pot-not-boiling-pick up-which-pot,' whereas the implied meaning of this proverb would be 'to intentionally draw attention to someone's faults.' Its functional translation is 'rub someone's nose in it.'

Example 1:

A: 你路考过了没有？
B: 你怎么**哪壶不开提哪壶**？没看见我是坐着公交车回来的吗？

A: Nǐ lùkǎo guòle méiyǒu?
B: Nǐ zěnme nǎ hú bù kāi tí nǎ hú? Méi kànjiàn wǒ shì zuòzhe gōnggòngqìchē huílái de ma?

A: Have you taken your driving test?
B: Why do you have to rub my nose in it? Didn't you see I took the bus back?

Example 2:

A: 你为什么**哪壶不开提哪壶**？

B: 我怎么了？

A: 刚才你跟那两个人聊天，他们俩明明是大胖子，你却一个劲儿地说肥胖的坏处。你这不是存心让他们难堪吗？

A: Nǐ wèishénme nǎ hú bù kāi tí nǎ hú?

B: Wǒ zěnme le?

A: Gāngcái nǐ gēn nà liǎng gè rén liáotiān, tāmen míngmíng shì dà pàngzi, nǐ què yígèjìnr de shuō féipàng de huàichu. Nǐ zhè búshì cúnxīn ràng tāmen nánkān ma?

A: Why did you rub their noses in it?

B: What did I do?

A: Just now, when you were talking to those two people; they were clearly obese, and you were constantly talking about the disadvantages of being fat. Were you deliberately trying to embarrass them?

Usage: Functions as predicate.

Note: Slightly derogatory and humorous in meaning.

66. 炒鱿鱼 (炒鱿魚) chǎo yóu yú

Translated character by character, 炒鱿鱼 means 'fry-squid' whereas the implied meaning of this proverb would be 'to fire someone.' Its functional translation is 'to give someone a pink slip,' or 'to can someone.'

Example 1:

A: 怎么这么不开心？

B: 被**炒鱿鱼**了，这是半年以来的第二次。

A: Zěnme zhème bù kāixīn?

B: Bèi chǎo yóuyú le, zhè shì bànnián yǐlái de dì-èr cì.

A: Why are you so unhappy?

B: I got canned. This is the second time in the last half year.

Example 2:

A: 球队成绩不好，老板的第一个反应就是**炒**主教练的**鱿鱼**。

A: Qiúduì chéngjì bùhǎo, lǎobǎn de dì-yī gè fǎnyìng jiùshì chǎo zhǔjiàoliàn de yóuyú.

A: The boss's first reaction to the team's poor record was to give the head coach a pink slip.

Usage: Functions as predicate.

Note: Neutral or humorous in meaning.

67. 人往高处走，水往低处流（人往高處走，水往低處流） rén wǎng gāo chù zǒu, shuǐ wǎng dī chù liú

Translated character by character, 人往高处走，水往低处流 means 'people-towards-high-place-move, water-towards-low-place-flow,' whereas the implied meaning of this proverb would be 'it is in man's nature to strive for better.'

Example 1:

A: 贵公司开出的条件的确非常诱人，只是我与现在的公司还有两年的合同，而且现在的公司对我也很不错。

B: 这个我知道，不过，**人往高处走，水往低处流**。我相信，你现在的公司对你的行为一定会理解的。

A: Guì gōngsī kāichū de tiáojiàn díquè fēicháng yòurén, zhǐshì wǒ yǔ xiànzài de gōngsī hái yǒu liǎng nián de hétóng, érqiě xiànzài de gōngsī duì wǒ yě hěn búcuò.

B: Zhègè wǒ zhīdao, búguò, rén wǎng gāochù zǒu, shuǐ wǎng dīchù liú. Wǒ xiāngxìn, nǐ xiànzài de gōngsī duì nǐde xíngwéi yídìng huì lǐjiě de.

A: Your company's terms of employment are really extremely attractive. It's only that I still have two years on my contract with the company I'm with now. Also, this company I am with now is pretty good to me too.

B: I know that, but it's in man's nature to strive for better. I believe the company you are with would definitely understand your actions.

Example 2:

A: **人往高处走，水往低处流**。清华、北大的毕业生不是出了国，就是留在北京或到上海这样的大城市工作，几乎没有人去小城市，更不用说农村了。

A: Rén wǎng gāochù zǒu, shuǐ wǎng dīchù liú. Qīnghuá, Běidà de bìyèshēng búshì chūle guó, jiùshì liú zài Běijīng huò dào Shànghǎi zhèyàng de dà chéngshì gōngzuò, jīhū méiyǒu rén qù xiǎo chéngshì, gèngbúyòngshuō nóngcūn le.

A: It is in man's nature to strive for better. If graduates of Tsinghua and Beida don't leave the country, they stay in large cities like Beijing and Shanghai. Almost none of them go to small cities, to say nothing of the countryside.

Usage: Used singly.

Note: Complimentary in meaning.

68. 说得比唱得好听 (説的比唱的好聽)
shuō de bǐ chàng de hǎo tīng

Translated character by character, 说得比唱得好听 means 'speak-relative to-sing-sound-pleasant,' whereas the implied meaning of this proverb would be 'to speak eloquently but untruthfully.'

Example 1:

A: 你听我说，是这么一回事。

B: 我再也不信你的话了。你这个大骗子，**说得比唱得都好听**。

A: Nǐ tīng wǒ shuō, shì zhème yìhuíshì.

B: Wǒ zài yě bú xìn nǐde huà le. Nǐ zhègè dà piànzi, shuō de bǐ chàng de dōu hǎotīng.

A: Listen to me. This is how it is.

B: I'm not believing you anymore. You're such a liar. It sounds good, but it's all empty words.

Example 2:

A: 他是个夸夸其谈的家伙，**说得比唱得好听**，就是不干实事。

A: Tā shì gè kuākuā-qítán de jiāhuo, shuō de bǐ chàng de hǎotīng, jiùshì bú gàn shíshì.

A: He's the kind of guy who talks big. He speaks eloquently, but it's all empty words, and he doesn't do anything.

Usage: Functions as predicate.

Variant: 说得比唱得还好听

Note: Slightly derogatory in meaning.

69. 强扭的瓜不甜 (強扭的瓜不甜) qiáng niǔ de guā bù tián

Translated character by character, 强扭的瓜不甜 means 'forcibly-pick-ed-melon-not-sweet,' whereas the implied meaning of this proverb would be 'forcing an issue when the time is not right will yield undesirable results.' Its functional translation is 'you can lead a horse to water but you can't make him drink.'

Example 1:

A: 我一定要把他们俩的婚事给撮合成。

B: 算了吧，**强扭的瓜不甜**。孩子们都不同意，你就省省心吧。

A: Wǒ yídìng yào bǎ tāmen liǎ de hūnshì gěi cuōhé chéng.

B: Suànle ba, qiáng niǔ de guā bù tián. Háizǐmen dōu bù tóngyì, nǐ jiù shěngshěng xīn ba.

A:　I definitely want to set those two up to marry each other.

B:　Forget about it. You can lead a horse to water, but you can't make him drink. They aren't willing to get married. Just save your breath.

Example 2:

A:　看在您的面子上，这笔生意我做了。

B:　别这样，**强扭的瓜不甜**，如果你心里不痛快，那就算了。

A:　Kàn zài nín de miànzi shàng, zhè bǐ shēngyì wǒ zuò le.

B:　Bié zhèyàng, qiáng niǔ de guā bù tián, rúguǒ nǐ xīnlǐ bú tòngkuài, nà jiù suàn le.

A:　For the sake of your reputation, I'll do this business deal.

B:　Don't do that. You can lead a horse to water, but you can't make him drink. If you're not happy about it, just forget it.

Usage: Used singly.

Variant: 强拗的瓜不甜 (less common)

Note: Neutral or humorous in meaning.

70.　老掉牙 (老掉牙) lǎo diào yá

Translated character by character, 老掉牙 means 'old-fall-out-teeth' whereas the implied meaning of this proverb would be 'out-of-date.' Its functional translation is 'tired old.'

Example 1:

A:　我给你们讲一个故事。从前有一个美丽但是恶毒的王后，她有一面镜子……

B:　别讲了，这个**老掉牙**的故事我都能倒着讲了，不就是《白雪公主》的故事吗？

A:　Wǒ gěi nǐmen jiǎng yígè gùshi. Cóngqián yǒu yígè měilì dànshì èdú de wánghòu, tā yǒu yí miàn jìngzi ......

B:　Bié jiǎng le, zhègè lǎodiàoyá de gùshi wǒ dōu néng dàozhe jiǎng le, bú jiù shì "Báixuě gōngzhǔ" de gùshi ma?

A:　I'll tell you a story. There once was a beautiful but evil queen. She had a mirror . . .

B:　Stop. I know that tired old story forwards and backwards. It's Snow White, right?

Example 2:

A:　他至今还开着一辆二十世纪九十年代的**老掉牙**的福特车。

A:　Tā zhìjīn hái kāizhe yí liàng èrshí shìjì jiǔshí niándài de lǎodiàoyá de Fútè chē.

A:　To this day, he still drives a tired old Ford from the 90s.

Usage: Functions as attributive.

Note: Slightly derogatory and humorous in meaning.

71. 搬起石头砸自己的脚 (搬起石頭砸自己的腳)
bān qǐ shítou zá zìjǐ de jiǎo

Translated character by character, 搬起石头砸自己的脚 means 'lift-up-stone-smash-own-foot,' whereas the implied meaning of this proverb would be 'to fall into a pit of one's own digging.' Its functional translation is 'to shoot oneself in the foot.'

Example 1:

A: 很多年前她伙同很多人制定了一项规定，57岁可以留任高管，而58岁必须离任。当时她就是为了把一名58岁的高管赶下台。

B: 现在好了，她自己也58岁了，别人又把这条规定拿出来对付她了，她没想到**搬起的石头砸了自己的脚**。

A: Hěnduō nián qián tā huǒtóng hěnduō rén zhìdìngle yí xiàng guīdìng, 57 suì kěyǐ liúrèn gāoguǎn, ér 58 suì bìxū lírèn. Dāngshí tā jiùshì wèile bǎ yì míng 58 suì de gāoguǎn gǎn xià tái.

B: Xiànzài hǎo le, tā zìjǐ yě 58 suì le, biérén yòu bǎ zhè tiáo guīdìng ná chūlai duìfù tā le, tā méi xiǎngdao bān qǐ de shítou zále zìjǐ de jiǎo.

A: Many years ago, she colluded with many others in drawing up a rule that a 57-year-old could retain their spot in the top brass, but at 58, one had to leave one's post. At the time, she did this to force a 58-year-old supervisor to step down.

B: It's funny to see that, now that she's 58 years old herself, others have used this rule to deal with her. She didn't realize that she was shooting herself in the foot.

Example 2:

A: 美国一味地促使美元贬值，结果**搬起石头砸自己的脚**，国内物价飞涨，通货膨胀出现了。

A: Měiguó yíwèi de cùshǐ Měiyuán biǎnzhí, jiéguǒ bān qǐ shítou zá zìjǐ de jiǎo, guónèi wùjià fēizhǎng, tōnghuòpéngzhàng chūxiàn le.

A: America blindly pushed for the devaluation of the dollar. In the end, they shot themselves in the foot, as prices in domestic markets soared and inflation occurred.

Usage: Functions as predicate.

Note: Slightly derogatory and humorous in meaning.

72. 卖关子 (賣關子) mài guānzi

Translated character by character, 卖关子 means 'sell-cliff-hanger,' whereas the implied meaning of this proverb would be 'to stop telling a story at its climax.' Its functional translation is 'to leave someone hanging.'

Example 1:

A: 那个人是谁？你快点儿告诉我！
B: 她啊，你肯定认识。你再猜猜？
A: 哎呀，你就别**卖关子**了！快点儿说吧。

A: Nàgè rén shì shéi? Nǐ kuàidiǎnr gàosù wǒ!
B: Tā a, nǐ kěndìng rènshí. Nǐ zài cāicāi?
A: Āiya, nǐ jiù bié màiguānzi le! Kuàidiǎnr shuō ba.

A: Who is that? Tell me now!
B: Her? You definitely know her. Take another guess.
A: Ugh, don't leave me hanging! Tell me quickly.

Example 2:

A: 大家都听得津津有味的时候，他**卖**了一个**关子**，忽然停了下来。

A: Dàjiā dōu tīng de jīnjīn-yǒuwèi de shíhòu, tā màile yígè guānzi, hūrán tíngle xiàlái.

A: When everyone was listening intently, he stopped abruptly, leaving them hanging.

Usage: Functions as predicate.

Note: Neutral in meaning.

73. 一分钱一分货 (一分錢一分貨) yī fēn qián yī fēn huò

Translated character by character, 一分钱一分货 means 'one-cent-money-one-cent-goods,' whereas the implied meaning of this proverb would be 'one penny buys a penny's worth of something.' Its functional translation is 'you get what you pay for.'

Example 1:

A: 你这家店的东西比别的家的贵很多啊？
B: 小姐，您是识货的人，**一分钱一分货**。我这家店的保证是正品，别人家的我就不好意思说了。

A: Nǐ zhè jiā diàn de dōngxi bǐ biéde jiā de guì hěn duō a?
B: Xiǎojiě, nín shì shí huò de rén, yī fēn qián yī fēn huò. Wǒ zhè jiā diàn de bǎozhèng shì zhèngpǐn, biérén jiā de wǒ jiù bùhǎoyìsī shuō le.

A: Your store's wares are much more expensive than those of other stores, aren't they?

B: Miss, you're a discerning woman. You get what you pay for. At this store, you're guaranteed authentic goods; I can't say that about other people's stores.

Example 2:

A: 这个破包，没用几次，肩带就断了。

B: 在哪儿买的？在小摊儿上买的吧？**一分钱一分货**，以后还得买名牌。

A: Zhègè pò bāo, méi yòng jǐ cì, jiāndài jiù duàn le.

B: Zài nǎr mǎi de? Zài xiǎotānr shàng mǎi de ba? Yī fēn qián yī fēn huò, yǐhòu hái děi mǎi míngpái.

A: I haven't used this bag more than a few times and the shoulder strap just broke.

B: Where'd you buy it? You bought it at the little cart, right? You get what you pay for. In the future, you need to buy name brands.

Usage: Used singly.

Note: Neutral in meaning.

74. 九牛二虎之力 (九牛二虎之力) jiǔ niú èr hǔ zhī lì

Translated character by character, 九牛二虎之力 means 'nine-cows-two-tigers-'s-strength,' whereas the implied meaning of this proverb would be 'an enormous effort.' Its functional translation is 'a Herculean effort.'

Example 1:

A: 她费尽**九牛二虎之力**才请到这么多名人来捧场。

A: Tā fèi jìn jiǔ niú èr hǔ zhī lì cái qǐng dào zhème duō míngrén lái pěngchǎng.

A: Through Herculean effort, she got this many famous people to come for support.

Example 2:

A: 他费了**九牛二虎之力**，终于把汽车修好了。

A: Tā fèile jiǔ niú èr hǔ zhī lì, zhōngyú bǎ qìchē xiū hǎo le.

A: He put in a Herculean effort and finally fixed his car.

Usage: Functions as object and usually used after '费了.'

Note: Neutral in meaning.

75. 敬酒不吃吃罚酒 (敬酒不吃吃罰酒)
jìng jiǔ bù chī chī fá jiǔ

Translated character by character, 敬酒不吃吃罚酒 means 'toast-wine-not-drink-drink-forfeit-wine,' whereas the implied meaning of this proverb would be 'to acquiesce to something after having refused someone's first overture.'

Example 1:

A: 你同意不同意。
B: 不同意，就是不同意！
A: 你不要**敬酒不吃吃罚酒**！

A: Nǐ tóngyì bù tóngyì.
B: Bù tóngyì, jiùshì bù tóngyì!
A: Nǐ búyào jìng jiǔ bù chī chī fá jiǔ!

A: Do you agree?
B: No means no!
A: Don't make me make you.

Example 2:

A: 老板，他还是不来。
B: 我们这么给他面子他都不来，看来他是**敬酒不吃吃罚酒**。

A: Lǎobǎn, tā háishì bú lái.
B: Wǒmen zhème gěi tā miànzi tā dōu bù lái, kànlái tā shì jìng jiǔ bù chī chī fá jiǔ.

A: Boss, he's still not coming.
B: We give him face and he doesn't come? It seems he wants to do this the hard way.

Usage: Functions as predicate.

Note: Derogatory in meaning. Carries a threatening connotation in dialogue with others. Be discerning with its use.

76. 躲得过初一，躲不过十五 (躲得過初一，躲不過十五) duǒ de guò chū-yī, duǒ bù guò shíwǔ

Translated character by character, 躲得过初一，躲不过十五 means 'avoid-able-first of the month-avoid-not-able-the fifteenth,' whereas the implied meaning of this proverb would be 'one may get off today, but not necessarily tomorrow.' Its functional translation is 'you can't avoid something forever,' or 'you can't keep something up forever.'

Example 1:

A: 这次会议上，我不想提那件事了。

B: 老赵，**躲得过初一，躲不过十五**，早晚得说啊。

A: Zhècì huìyì shàng, wǒ bù xiǎng tí nà jiàn shì le.

B: Lǎo Zhào, **duǒ de guò chū-yī, duǒ bú guò shíwǔ**, zǎowǎn děi shuō a.

A: I don't want to bring that issue up in this meeting.

B: Old Zhao, you can't avoid it forever. Sooner or later you'll have to bring it up.

Example 2:

A: 政府用增加支出的方式躲过了这次经济危机。

B: **躲得过初一，躲不过十五**，生产上不去，以后的问题只能是越来越麻烦。

A: Zhèngfǔ yòng zēngjiā zhīchū de fāngshì duǒguòle zhècì jīngjì wēijī.

B: **Duǒ de guò chū-yī, duǒ bú guò shíwǔ**, shēngchǎn shàng bú qù, yǐhòu de wèntí zhǐnéng shì yuèláiyuè máfan.

A: The government weathered this economic crisis by increasing expenditures.

B: They can't keep this up forever. If production doesn't increase, the problem will only get worse.

Usage: Used singly.

Note: Neutral in meaning. 初一 is the first day of the Chinese lunar month, which also means a new moon, whereas 十五 is the fifteenth day and a full moon. 初一 and 十五 here stand for the two extremes of one thing, implying that it encompasses all possibilities.

77. 吃香的，喝辣的 (吃香的，喝辣的)
chī xiāng de, hē là de

Translated character by character, 吃香的，喝辣的 means 'eat-delicious-(food)-drink-spicy-(drinks),' whereas the implied meaning of this proverb would be 'to eat and drink well.' Its functional translation is 'to live in the lap of luxury.'

Example 1:

A: 你看她多有福气？

B: 怎么有福气？

A: 嫁个又有钱又体贴的好老公，不用工作，**吃香的，喝辣的**，要什么有什么。多好！

A: Nǐ kàn tā duō yǒu fúqì?

B: Zěnme yǒu fúqì?

A: Jià gè yòu yǒu qián yòu tǐtiē de hǎo lǎogōng, búyòng gōngzuò, chī xiāng de,
    hē là de, yào shénme yǒu shénme. Duō hǎo!

A: Look how fortunate she is.
B: How is she fortunate?
A: She married a rich and considerate husband. She doesn't need to work, she
    lives in the lap of luxury, and she has everything she wants. How wonderful!

Example 2:

A: 好好跟着我干，保管你**吃香的喝辣的**。

A: Hǎohāo gēnzhe wǒ gàn, bǎoguǎn nǐ chī xiāng de hē là de.

A: Stick with me and I'll keep you in the lap of luxury.

Usage: Functions as predicate.

Note: Neutral in meaning.

78. 小儿科 (小兒科) xiǎo ér kē

Translated character by character, 小儿科 means 'small-child-department (of a
hospital),' whereas the implied meaning of this proverb would be 'pediatrics
department.' Its functional translation is 'child's play' or 'easy.'

Example 1:

A: 今天我学会了怎么群发电子邮件。
B: 就这个啊？太**小儿科**了。

A: Jīntiān wǒ xué huì le zěnme qúnfā diànzǐ yóujiàn.
B: Jiù zhègè a? Tài xiǎo'érkē le.

A: I learned how to send group emails today.
B: That's it? That's child's play.

Example 2:

A: 经理准备让小白去前台工作。
B: 天啊？让一个堂堂的北大毕业生去干这种**小儿科**的工作？经理怎么
    了？

A: Jīnglǐ zhǔnbèi ràng Xiǎo Bái qù qiántái gōngzuò.
B: Tiān a? Ràng yígè tángtáng de Běidà bìyèshēng qù gàn zhèzhǒng xiǎo'érkē de
    gōngzuò? Jīnglǐ zěnme le?

A: The manager is preparing to send Xiao Bai to work at the front desk.
B: My god! Sending a dignified Peking University graduate student to do such a
    simple job? What is the matter with the manager?

Usage: Functions mainly as predicate or attributive.

Note: Humorous and slightly derogatory in meaning.

79. 一个巴掌拍不响 (一個巴掌拍不響)
yí gè bāzhang pāi bù xiǎng

Translated character by character, 一个巴掌拍不响 means 'one-MW-hand-clap-no-sound,' whereas the implied meaning of this proverb would be 'one hand alone cannot clap.' Its functional translation is 'it takes two to tango.'

Example 1:

A: 你们怎么还不结婚啊？

B: **一个巴掌拍不响**，我着急她不着急啊！

A: Nǐmen zěnme hái bù jiéhūn a?
B: yígè bāzhang pāi bù xiǎng, wǒ zháojí tā bù zháojí a!

A: How are you guys still not married?
B: It takes two to tango. I'm anxious to get married but she's not!

Example 2:

A: 咱们怎么才能吸引外资呢？

B: 是啊，**一个巴掌拍不响**，我们的条件够好的了，可是老外不了解我们，他们怎么来啊？

A: Zánmen zěnme cái néng xīyǐn wàizī ne?
B: Shì a, yígè bāzhang pāi bù xiǎng, wǒmen de tiáojiàn gòu hǎo de le, kěshì lǎowài bù liǎojiě wǒmen, tāmen zěnme lái a?

A: What do we need to do to attract foreign investment?
B: Yes, it takes two to tango. Our terms are sufficiently attractive but, since the foreigners don't understand us, why would they come to us?

Usage: Used singly.

Note: Neutral in meaning.

80. 牛头不对马嘴 (牛頭不對馬嘴) niú tóu bú duì mǎ zuǐ

Translated character by character, 牛头不对马嘴 means 'cow-head-not-match-horse-mouth,' whereas the implied meaning of this proverb would be 'incongruous or inconsistent.' Its functional translation is 'incongruous,' or 'neither here nor there.'

Example 1:

A: 他后半夜才回家，老婆问他干什么去了。他一会儿说陪客户吃饭去了，一会儿又说在办公室加班，回答得**牛头不对马嘴**。老婆知道他肯定有外遇了。

A: Tā hòu bànyè cái huíjiā, tā lǎopo wèn tā gàn shénme qù le. Tā yíhuìr shuō péi kèhù chīfàn qù le, yíhuìr yòu shuō zài bàngōngshì jiābān, niútóu bú duì mǎzuǐ. Tā lǎopo zhīdao tā kěndìng yǒu wàiyù le.

A: He got home after midnight and his wife asked him what he had been out doing. He said for a while that he had been eating with clients, he also said for a while that he had been working overtime at the office. He answered incongruously; his wife knew that he definitely was having an affair.

Example 2:

A: 什么是儒家思想？
B: 嗯…，就是不喝酒、不吃肉、不结婚。
A: 你说的这是什么啊！**牛头不对马嘴**。

A: Shénme shì Rújiā sīxiǎng?
B: En, jiùshì bù hējiǔ, bù chīròu, bù jiéhūn.
A: Nǐ shuō de zhè shì shénme a! Niútóu bú duì mǎzuǐ.

A: What is Confucianism?
B: Um . . . It's not drinking alcohol, not eating meat, and not getting married.
A: What are you saying? That's neither here nor there.

Usage: Functions as complement of verbs like '回答' or '说', or used singly.

Variant: 驴头不对马嘴; 驴唇不对马嘴 (驴 lǘ, donkey. 唇 chún, lip)

Note: Slightly derogatory and humorous in meaning.

81. 以小人之心，度君子之腹 (以小人之心度君子之腹)
yǐ xiǎorén zhī xīn, dúo jūnzǐ zhī fù

Translated character by character, 以小人之心, 度君子之腹 means 'using-mean-person-'s-mind, judge-gentleman-'s-belly,' whereas the implied meaning of this proverb would be 'to seek to size up a virtuous person using an immoral person's heuristics.' Its functional translation is 'to project one's shortcomings on someone.'

Example 1:

A: 副局长写匿名信检举局长贪污。

B: 地球上的人都知道副局长贪污而局长清廉，副局长纯粹是**以小人之心度君子之腹**。

A: Fù júzhăng xiě nìmíngxìn jiǎnjǔ júzhǎng tānwū.

B: Dìqiú shàng de rén dōu zhīdao fù jú hǎng tānwū ér júzhǎng qīnglián, fù
    júzhǎng chúncuì shì yǐ xiǎorén zhī xīn dúo jūnzǐ zhī fù.

A: The deputy director wrote an anonymous letter accusing the director of
    embezzlement.

B: Everyone in the world knows that the deputy director is dirty and the director
    is clean. The deputy director is purely projecting his shortcomings on the
    director.

Example 2:

A: 你跟你的女秘书是不是关系太亲密了？

B: 我们只是工作上的关系。

A: 真的吗？没有别的吗？

B: 你不要**以小人之心度君子之腹**，谁都跟你一样是个大色狼吗？

A: Nǐ gēn nǐde nǚ mìshū shìbúshì guānxì tài qīnmì le?

B: Wǒmen zhǐ shì gōngzuò shàng de guānxì.

A: Zhēn de ma? Méiyǒu biéde ma?

B: Nǐ búyào yǐ xiǎorén zhī xīn dúo jūnzǐ zhī fù, shuí dōu gēn nǐ yíyàng shì gè dà
    sèláng ma?

A: Isn't your relationship with your secretary too intimate?

B: We just have a working relationship.

A: Really? Nothing else?

B: Don't project your shortcomings on others. Not everyone is a lecher like you.

Usage: Functions as predicative or predicate.

Note: Slightly derogatory or neutral in meaning.

82. 车到山前必有路 (車到山前必有路)
chē dào shān qián bì yǒu lù

Translated character by character, 车到山前必有路 means 'cart-arrive-mountain-
front-must-have-road,' whereas the implied meaning of this proverb would be 'what
problems exist will be dealt with.' Its functional translation is 'we'll cross that
bridge when we come to it.'

Example 1:

A: 我们得想个好办法，这样下去不妙。

B: 你着什么急嘛！**车到山前必有路**，到时候就有办法了。

A: Wǒmen děi xiǎng gè hǎo bànfǎ, zhèyàng xiàqù búmiào.

B: Nǐ zháo shénme jí ma! Chē dào shān qián bì yǒu lù, dào shíhou jiù yǒu
    bànfǎ le.

A: We have to think of a good solution. Continuing like this doesn't look promising.

B: What're you nervous about? We'll cross that bridge when we come to it. When the time comes, there will be a way.

Example 2:

A: 下一步怎么做？

B: 下一步啊？我还没想好，不过，**车到山前必有路**，过两天再说。

A: Xiàyíbù zěnme zuò?

B: Xiàyíbù a? Wǒ hái méi xiǎnghǎo, búguò, chē dào shān qián bì yǒu lù, guò liǎngtian zàishuō.

A: What do we do next?

B: The next step? I haven't really thought about it, but we'll cross that bridge when we come to it. Let's come back to it in two days.

Usage: Used singly.

Note: Neutral in meaning.

83.   鸡蛋里挑骨头 (雞蛋裏挑骨頭) jīdàn lǐ tiāo gútou

Translated character by character, 鸡蛋里挑骨头 means 'chicken-egg-inside-pick out-bone,' whereas the implied meaning of this proverb would be 'to find fault.' Its functional translation is 'to nitpick' or 'to find quarrel in a straw.'

Example 1:

A: 你看，左侧车门上有一道划痕。

B: 朋友，我卖的是二手车，不是新车，你这不是**鸡蛋里挑骨头**吗？

A: Nǐ kàn, zuǒcè chēmén shàng yǒu yí dào huáhén.

B: Péngyou, wǒ mài de shì èrshǒuchē, búshì xīnchē, nì zhè búshì jīdàn lǐ tiāo gútou ma?

A: Look, there's a scratch on the car's left-hand door.

B: Buddy, what I'm selling are second-hand cars, not new cars. Aren't you just finding quarrel in a straw?

Example 2:

A: 我们的报告一共一百页，里面只有两个标点符号错误，可是上司却说我们工作态度不认真。

B: 分明**鸡蛋里挑骨头**，存心找我们的麻烦。

A: Wǒmen de bàogào yígòng yìbài yè, lǐmiàn zhǐyǒu liǎng gè biāodiǎn fúhào cuòwù, kěshì shàngsi què shuō wǒmen gōngzuò tàidù bú rènzhēn.

B: Fēnmíng jīdàn lǐ tiāo gútou, cúnxīn zhǎo wǒmen de máfan.

A: Our report was one hundred pages in total, containing only two punctuation errors, but our superiors said our work ethic was poor.

B: They're clearly nitpicking, deliberately trying to cause us trouble.

Usage: Functions as predicate.

Note: Slightly derogatory in meaning.

84.   吃不了兜着走 (吃不了兜著走) chī bù liǎo dōu zhe zǒu

Translated character by character, 吃不了兜着走 means 'eat-not-able-wrap-ed-leave,' whereas the implied meaning of this proverb would be 'to be unable to bear the consequences of failure.'

Example 1:

A: 就凭你们几个也想来闹事！告诉你们，赶快滚，不滚的话让你们**吃不了兜着走**。

A: Jiù píng nǐmen jǐ gè yě xiǎng lái nàoshì! Gàosu nǐmen, gǎnkuài gǔn, bù gǔn dehuà ràng nǐmen chī bùliǎo dōuzhe zǒu.

A: You can't make trouble here! I'm warning you, you better scram now. If you don't, I'll make you bear the consequences.

Example 2:

A: 我们这次只是想试探一下对手，没想到他们跟咱们玩儿真的，要打价格战。我们还是收手吧。

B: 不行，再坚持三天。

A: 那我们的风险太大了，弄不好**吃不了**可得**兜着走**啊！

A: Wǒmen zhècì zhǐshì xiǎng shìtàn yíxià duìshǒu, méixiàngdào tāmen gēn zánmen wánr zhēnde, yào dǎ jiàgézhàn. Wǒmen háishi shōushǒu ba.

B: Bùxíng, zài jiānchí sān tiān.

A: Nà wǒmen de fēngxiǎn tài dà le, nòngbùhǎo chī bùliǎo kě děi dōuzhe zǒu a!

A: This time, we just wanted to test our opponent. We didn't expect they would really engage with us, wanting to start a price war. We should pull back.

B: No. Let's keep it up for three days.

A: Then our exposure to risk will be too great. If we mess this up, we won't be able to bear the consequences.

Usage: Functions as predicate.

Note: Derogatory in meaning.

85. 打肿脸充胖子 (打腫臉充胖子)
dǎ zhǒng liǎn chōng pàngzi

Translated character by character, 打肿脸充胖子 means 'slam-swollen-face-pretend-fat-man,' whereas the implied meaning of this proverb would be 'to keep up appearances (often by spending beyond one's means).' Its functional translation is 'to puff oneself up at one's own cost.'

Example 1:

A: 她买了一个两千多美元的包。

B: 别**打肿脸充胖子**，她的收入就那么点儿，谁不知道。

A: Tā mǎile yígè liǎngqiān duō Měiyuán de bāo.
B: Bié dǎ zhǒng liǎn chōng pàngzi, tāde shōurù jiù nàme diǎnr, shéi bù zhīdào.

A: She bought a bag that cost more than $2,000.
B: She shouldn't puff herself up. She has very little income, everybody knows that.

Example 2:

A: 政府又捐了一千万美元给那个国家。

B: 又**打肿脸充胖子**呢。有钱给自己国家失业的人花不好吗？

A: Zhèngfǔ yòu juānle yìqiān wàn Měiyuán gěi nàge guójiā.
B: Yòu dǎ zhǒng liǎn chōng pàngzi ne. Yǒu qián gěi zìjǐ guójiā shīyè de rén huā bùhǎo ma?

A: The government donated another ten million dollars to that country.
B: They're spending money they don't have again. Is it not worth it to give your money to your own country's jobless?

Usage: Functions as predicate.

Note: Slightly derogatory in meaning.

86. 三十六计走为上 (三十六計走為上)
sānshíliù jì zǒu wéi shàng

Translated character by character, 三十六计走为上 means 'the-thirty-sixth-stratagem-flee-is-best,' whereas the implied meaning of this proverb would be 'running away is the best option.' Its functional translation is 'to get out while the going's good' or 'to get while the getting's good.'

Example 1:

A: 这里是是非之地，非常危险，我该怎么办？

B: 你还是**三十六计走为上**吧。

A: Zhè lǐ shì shìfēizhīdì, fēicháng wēixiǎn, wǒ gāi zěnme bàn?
B: Nǐ hái shì sānshíliù jì zǒu wéi shàng ba.

A: This is a sketchy area, it's very dangerous. What should I do?
B: You should get while the getting's good.

Example 2:

A: 眼看企业一年不如一年，已经没有复兴的希望了，他就**三十六计走为上**，主动辞职了。

A: Yǎnkàn qǐyè yì nián bùrú yì nián, yǐjīng méiyǒu fùxīng de xīwàng le, tā jiù sānshíliù jì zǒu wéi shàng, zhǔdòng cízhí le.

A: He saw that the company was getting worse and worse with each passing year and it was already beyond saving. So, he got while the getting was good and resigned voluntarily.

Usage: Functions as predicate or used singly.

Note: Neutral in meaning.

87. 当耳旁风 (當耳旁風) dāng ěr páng fēng

Translated character by character, 当耳旁风 means 'take as-ear-side-wind,' whereas the implied meaning of this proverb would be 'to be completely disregarded.' Its functional translation is 'to roll off like water off a duck's back.'

Example 1:

A: 她总是把我的警告**当耳旁风**。

A: Tā zǒngshì bǎ wǒde jǐnggào dāng ěrpángfēng.

A: She always lets my warnings roll off like water off a duck's back.

Example 2:

A: 我是认真的，你别把我的话**当耳旁风**。

A: Wǒ shì rènzhēn de, nǐ bié bǎ wǒde huà dāng ěrpángfēng.

A: I'm serious, don't let what I say roll off like water off a duck's back.

Usage: Functions as predicate.

Variant: 当耳边风

Note: Slightly derogatory in meaning.

88. 恨铁不成钢 (恨鐵不成鋼) hèn tiě bù chéng gāng

Translated character by character, 恨铁不成钢 means 'regret-iron-not-become-steel,' whereas the implied meaning of this proverb would be 'to hold someone to a higher standard with the hope that they will improve.' Its functional translation is 'to expect better from someone.'

Example 1:

A: 我理解你，**恨铁不成钢**，但是你打你儿子也不对啊？

A: Wǒ lǐjiě nǐ, hèn tiě bù chéng gāng, dànshì nǐ dǎ nǐ érzi yě búduì a?

A: I get it, you expect better from him, but isn't it also wrong to hit your son?

Example 2:

A: 他用一种**恨铁不成钢**的眼神望着这个他全力培养了二十年的接班人。

A: Tā yòng yìzhǒng hèn tiě bù chéng gāng de yǎnshén wàngzhe zhègè tā quánlì péiyǎngle èrshí nián de jiēbānrén.

A: He watched the protégé he had poured himself into training for twenty years with an expression in his eyes of expecting better from him.

Usage: Functions as predicate or attributive.

Note: Neutral in meaning.

89. 你走你的阳关道，我过我的独木桥
(你走你的陽關道，我過我的獨木橋)
nǐ zǒu nǐ de yáng guān dào, wǒ guò wǒ de dú mù qiáo

Translated character by character, 你走你的阳关道，我过我的独木桥 means 'you-walk-your-broad-way, I-cross-my-single-plank-foot-bridge,' whereas the implied meaning of this proverb would be 'we should part ways.' Its functional translation is 'let's go our separate ways.'

Example 1:

A: 我们能不能再谈谈？

B: 不必了。以后**你走你的阳关道，我过我的独木桥**，就当两个人从来不认识。

A: Wǒmen néngbùnéng zài tántan?

B: Búbì le. Yǐhòu nǐ zǒu nǐde yángguāndào, wǒ guò wǒde dúmùqiáo, jiù dāng liǎng gè rén cónglái bú rènshi.

A: Can we talk again?

B: There's no need. We should go our separate ways. It'll be as though we never met.

Example 2:

A: 话不要说得那么绝情！

B: 就是这么绝情！从今以后，**你走你的阳关道，我过我的独木桥**，各不相干。

A: Huà búyào shuō de nàme juéqíng!

B: Jiùshì zhème juéqíng! Cóngjīn yǐhòu, nǐ zǒu nǐde yángguāndào, wǒ guò wǒde dúmùqiáo, gè bù xiānggān.

A: Don't be so heartless when you speak!

B: I'm just that heartless! From now on, we'll go our own separate ways. Our paths won't cross.

Usage: Used singly.

Note: Slightly derogatory and humorous in meaning.

90. 过了这个村，就没这个店 (過了這個村，就沒這個店) guò le zhè ge cūn, jiù méi zhè ge diàn

Translated character by character, 过了这个村，就没这个店 means 'pass-ed-this-MW-village, then-no-this-MW-inn,' whereas the implied meaning of this proverb would be, 'there is no other inn once you pass this village.' Its functional translation is, 'opportunity seldom knocks twice,' or 'it's now or never.'

Example 1:

A: 我们再等等吧，没准儿下周还降价呢。

B: 别，我看不会降了，没准儿还升呢。快点买吧，**过了这个村，就没这个店**了。

A: Wǒmen zài děngděng ba, méizhǔnr xià zhōu hái jiàngjià ne.

B: Bié, wǒ kàn búhuì jiàng le, méizhǔnr hái shēng ne. Kuàidiǎn mǎi ba, guòle zhègè cūn, jiù méi zhègè diàn le.

A: Let's wait a little longer. The price might drop again next week.

B: No, I don't think the price will go lower, it might rise. Buy it quickly, opportunity seldom knocks twice.

Example 2:

A: 我们的关系进展不快。

B: 赶快去追吧，**过了这个村，可就没这个店**了。等她出了国，你上哪儿去追啊？

A: Wǒmen de guānxi jìnzhǎn bú kuài.

B: Gǎnkuài qù zhuī ba, guòle zhègè cūn, kě jiù méi zhègè diàn le. Děng tā chūle guó, nǐ shàng nǎr qù zhuī a?

A: Our relationship isn't progressing very fast.

B: Hurry up and get her; it's now or never. Once she leaves the country, how will you win her over?

Usage: Used singly. You can insert a '可' in front of the '就' in order to express emphasis.

Note: Neutral or humorous in meaning.

91. 抱佛脚 (抱佛腳) bào fó jiǎo

Translated character by character, 抱佛脚 means 'embrace-Buddha-foot,' whereas the implied meaning of this proverb would be 'to cram,' or 'to normally not see someone, but grovel at their feet when their help is needed.' Its functional translation is 'to cram,' or 'fair weather atheists turn to god in a pinch.'

Example 1:

A: 我们还是请大学同学小刘帮忙吧？

B: 咳，大学毕业二十年都没有联系过，现在我们**临时抱佛脚**，求到人家头上，人家会怎么想？

A: Wǒmen háishì qǐng dàxué tóngxué Xiǎo Liú bāngmáng ba?

B: Hài, dàxué bìyè èrshí nián dōu méiyǒu liánxì guò, xiànzài wǒmen línshí bào fó jiǎo, qiú dào rénjiā tóu shàng, rénjiā huì zěnme xiǎng?

A: Should we ask our college classmate Little Liu to help us out?

B: Huh? We graduated 20 years ago and haven't been in contact with him. If we ask a favor of him now like fair weather atheists turning to god in a pinch, what would he think?

Example 2:

A: 他是语言学家，可是被邀请去做一个关于中国农村民主政治的报告，推脱不掉，所以他只好**临时抱佛脚**，找了一本权威入门书，匆匆看了看，就去做报告了。

A: Tā shì yǔyánxuéjiā, kěshì bèi yāoqǐng qù zuò yígè guānyú Zhōngguó nóngcūn mínzhǔ zhèngzhì de bàogào, tuītuō bú diào, suǒyǐ tā zhǐhǎo línshí bào fó jiǎo, zhǎole yì běn quánwēi rùmén shū, cōngcōng kànlekàn, jiù qù zuò bàogào le.

A: He's a linguist, but he was invited to do a report about democratic governance in rural China, and he couldn't get out of it, so he's just cramming. He found an authoritative introductory book, skimmed it, and went to do his report.

Usage: Functions as predicate.

Variant: 临时抱佛脚

Note: Slightly derogatory in meaning.

92. 有钱能使鬼推磨 (有錢能使鬼推磨)
yǒu qián néng shǐ guǐ tuī mò

Translated character by character, 有钱能使鬼推磨 means 'have-money-can-make-ghost-push-millstone,' whereas the implied meaning of this proverb would be 'money makes many things possible.' Its functional translation is 'money talks.'

Example 1:

A: 你的新公司要开业了，准备请谁来剪彩？
B: 功夫巨星张三。
A: 请得来吗？
B: 已经定了。**有钱能使鬼推磨**。当然我们下了本钱。

A: Nǐde xīn gōngsī yào kāiyè le, zhǔnbèi qǐng shéi lái jiǎncǎi?
B: Gōngfu jùxīng Zhāng Sān.
A: Qǐng de lái ma?
B: Yǐjīng dìng le. Yǒu qián néng shǐ guǐ tuī mò. Dāngrán wǒmen xiàle běnqian.

A: Your new company is about to open for business. Who are you going to invite to cut the ribbon?
B: Kung Fu superstar, Mr. X.
A: Can you get him?
B: It's already set. Money talks. Of course, we paid for it.

Example 2:

A: 他的人生哲学就是**有钱能使鬼推磨**，所以他做任何事都用钱来开路。

A: Tā de rénshēng zhéxué jiùshì yǒu qián néng shǐ guǐ tuī mò, suǒyǐ tā zuò rènhé shì dōu yòng qián lái kāilù.

A: His life philosophy is that money talks. So, whatever he's doing, he always uses money to clear the way.

Usage: Used singly.

Note: Neutral or humorous in meaning.

93. 有其父必有其子 (有其父必有其子) yǒu qí fù bì yǒu qí zǐ

Translated character by character, 有其父必有其子 means 'have-that-father-must-have-that-son,' whereas the implied meaning of this proverb would be 'the son is like the father.' Its functional translation is 'like father, like son,' or 'the apple doesn't fall far from the tree.'

Example 1:

A: 他绯闻不断。

B: 不难理解。他爸爸就是个有名的花花公子，**有其父必有其子**。

A: Tā fēiwén búduàn.

B: Bú nán lǐjiě. Tā bàba jiùshì gè yǒumíng de huāhuāgōngzǐ, yǒu qí fù bì yǒu qí zǐ.

A: He's always involved in sex scandals.

B: It's not hard to understand why. His father is a well-known playboy. The apple doesn't fall far from the tree.

Example 2:

A: 我儿子将来还要靠你提携呢。

B: 哪里，你贵为省长，**有其父必有其子**，将来令郎还能更上一层楼呢。

A: Wǒ érzi jiānglái háiyào kào nǐ tíxié ne.

B: Nǎlǐ, nǐ guì wéi shěngzhǎng, yǒu qí fù bì yǒu qí zǐ, jiānglái lìngláng hái néng gèng shàng yì céng lóu ne.

A: My son will still need to rely on your guidance in the future.

B: I don't think so. You're the provincial governor and the apple doesn't fall far from the tree. Your son will rise to the next level.

Usage: Used singly.

Note: Neutral in meaning.

94. 不见棺材不落泪 (不見棺材不落淚)
bú jiàn guāncai bú luò lèi

Translated character by character, 不见棺材不落泪 means 'not-see-coffin-not-shed-tear,' whereas the implied meaning of this proverb would be 'to hold out hope until faced with the grim reality.'

Example 1:

A: 好，咱们比做俯卧撑，看谁做得多。

B: 我看你是**不见棺材不落泪**，谁先来？

A: Hǎo, zánmen bǐ zuò fǔwòchēng, kàn shéi zuò de duō.

B: Wǒ kàn nǐ shì bú jiàn guāncai bú luòlèi, shéi xiān lái?

A: OK, let's have a push-up contest and see who can do the most.

B: I think you're holding out hope until faced with the grim reality. Who's going first?

Example 2:

A: 我没有借过你的东西。

B: 你真是**不见棺材不落泪**，等会儿我把你亲笔写的借条拿来给你看。

A: Wǒ méiyǒu jièguo nǐde dōngxi.

B: Nǐ zhēnshì bú jiàn guāncai bú luòlèi, děnghuìr wǒ bǎ nǐ qīnbǐ xiě de jiètiáo nálái gěi nǐ kàn.

A: I didn't borrow your stuff.

B: You really are holding out hope until faced with the grim reality. In a moment, I'll bring you the loan slip that was written by your own hand.

Usage: Functions mainly as predicative or predicate.

Note: Derogatory and humorous in meaning.

95. 三长两短 (三長兩短) sān cháng liǎng duǎn

Translated character by character, 三长两短 means 'three-long-two-short,' whereas the implied meaning of this proverb would be 'unexpected misfortune befalls someone.' Its functional translation is 'god forbid anything should happen to someone.'

Example 1:

A: 他都九十多岁了，还想坐飞机来咱们这里。

B: 我看就算了。这么大年纪了，还要坐十个钟头的飞机，万一有个三**长两短**，我们负不起责任啊。

A: Tā dōu jiǔshí duō suì le, hái xiǎng zuò fēijī lái zánmen zhèlǐ.

B: Wǒ kàn jiù suàn le. Zhème dà niánjì le, hái yào zuò shí gè zhōngtóu de fēijī, wànyī yǒu gè sāncháng-liǎngduǎn, wǒmen fù bù qǐ zérèn a.

A: He's more than 90 years old, and he still wants to fly here.

B: I think we should forget about it. At this age, making him take a ten-hour flight; god forbid something should happen to him; we couldn't bear the guilt.

Example 2:

A: 孩子跟我吵架后就走了，两天没回家了，万一……

B: 别太担心。她大了，又是懂事的孩子，很快就会回来的。

A: 如果她有个三**长两短**，我也不活了。

A: Háizi gēn wǒ chǎojià hòu jiù zǒu le, liǎng tiān méi huíjiā le, wànyī ......
B: Bié tài dānxīn. Tā dà le, yòu shì dǒngshì de háizi, hěn kuài jiù huì huílái de.
A: Rúguǒ tā yǒu gè sāncháng-liǎngduǎn, wǒ yě bù huó le.

A: My child left after we fought and hasn't come home in two days. What if . . . ?
B: Don't worry too much. She's a grown and worldly child, she'll come back soon.
A: God forbid something should happen to her; I would die.

Usage: Functions as object.

Note: Neutral in meaning.

96. 纸包不住火 (紙包不住火) zhǐ bāo bú zhù huǒ

Translated character by character, 纸包不住火 means 'paper-contain-not-able-fire,' whereas the implied meaning of this proverb would be 'the truth cannot be supressed.' Its functional translation is 'the truth always comes out,' 'truth will out,' or 'there is no concealing the truth.'

Example 1:

A: 咱俩把这笔钱私分了，只要咱俩不说，谁也不知道。
B: 大哥，**纸包不住火**啊！如果被发现了，咱俩可都要进监狱的。

A: Zán liǎ bǎ zhè bǐ qián sīfēn le, zhǐyào zán liǎ bù shuō, shéi yě bù zhīdao.
B: Dàgē, zhǐ bāo bú zhù huǒ a! Rúguǒ bèi fāxiàn le, zán liǎ kě dōu yào jìn jiānyù de.

A: Let's split the cash between the two of us. So long as neither of us snitches, no one will know.
B: Brother, there's no concealing the truth. If we are found out, both of us will definitely end up in jail.

Example 2:

A: 煤矿井下出了事故，死了十个人。矿主想隐瞒，但是**纸包不住火**，三天以后有人把这件事告诉了记者。

A: Méikuàng jǐng xià chūle shìgù, sǐle shí gè rén. Kuàngzhǔ xiǎng yǐnmán, dànshì zhǐ bāo bú zhù huǒ, sān tiān yǐhòu yǒu rén bǎ zhè jiàn shì gàosù le jìzhě.

A: An accident happened in a coal mine and ten people died. The mine manager wanted to cover it up, but the truth always comes out. Three days later, someone tipped a reporter off to the incident.

Usage: Used singly.

Note: Neutral in meaning.

97. 好戏在后头 (好戲在後頭) hǎo xì zài hòutou

Translated character by character, 好戏在后头 means 'good-drama-is-behind,' whereas the implied meaning of this proverb would be 'the best or most surprising events have not yet come to pass.' Its functional translation is 'the best is yet to come,' or 'you ain't seen nothing yet.'

Example 1:

A: 这两位名人在媒体上的争吵终于完了。

B: 完了？还早着呢。我保证**好戏还在后头**呢。

A: Zhè liǎng wèi míngrén zài méitǐ shàng de zhēngchǎo zhōngyú wán le.

B: Wán le? Hái zǎo zhe'ne. Wǒ bǎozhèng hǎo xì hái zài hòutou ne.

A: These two celebrities' media fight has finally ended.

B: Ended? It's still early. I guarantee the best is yet to come.

Example 2:

A: 那家公司最近出了一点儿麻烦，高层不和的消息已经公开化了。

B: 等着瞧吧，**好戏在后头**。听说他们的竞争对手准备跟他们打价格战了。

A: Nà jiā gōngsī zuìjìn chūle yìdiǎnr máfan, gāocéng bùhé de xiāoxī yǐjīng gōngkāihuà le.

B: Děngzheqiáo ba, hǎo xì zài hòutou. Tīngshuō tāmen de jìngzhēng duìshǒu zhǔnbèi gēn tāmen dǎ jiàgézhàn le.

A: That company recently ran into a little trouble. It has already become common knowledge that there is dissension in the ranks of the management.

B: Just wait and see, you ain't seen nothing yet. I hear their competitor is preparing to engage in a price war with them.

Usage: Used singly.

Variant: 好戏还在后头

Note: Neutral or humorous in meaning.

98. 吹牛皮 (吹牛皮) chuī niú pí

Translated character by character, 吹牛皮 means 'blow-ox-skin,' whereas the implied meaning of this proverb would be 'to talk oneself up.' Its functional translation is 'to blow smoke.'

Example 1:

A: 我能喝十五瓶啤酒，而且不醉。

B: **吹牛皮**呢吧？十五天喝十五瓶还差不多。

A: Wǒ néng hē shíwǔ píng píjiǔ, érqiě bú zuì.

B: Chuīniúpí ne ba? Shíwǔ tiān hē shíwǔ píng hái chàbuduō.

A: I can drink fifteen bottles of beer and not get drunk.

B: You're blowing smoke, right? Fifteen bottles in fifteen days is more like it.

Example 2:

A: 不是我跟你们**吹牛皮**，就这点儿小事儿，如果是我，早就办完了。

A: Búshì wǒ gēn nǐmen chuīniúpí, jiù zhè diǎnr xiǎoshìr, rúguǒ shì wǒ, zǎo jiù bànwán le.

A: I'm not blowing smoke, but if I was dealing with this minor issue, I'd have been done a long time ago.

Usage: Functions as predicate.

Note: Slightly derogatory in meaning.

99.　欲速则不达 (欲速則不達) yù sù zé bù dá

Translated character by character, 欲速则不达 means 'want-fast-instead-not-arrive' whereas the implied meaning of this proverb would be 'rushing to complete something will often result in errors causing the project to be finished late.' Its functional translation is 'more haste, less speed.'

Example 1:

A: 教练，我都练了两个小时的发球了，怎么还练啊？

B: 发球是打网球的基本功。如果连发球都发不好，就更谈不上接球和回球了。今天一天都练发球，别着急，**欲速则不达**。

A: Jiàoliàn, wǒ dōu liànle liǎng gè xiǎoshí de fāqiú le, zěnme hái liàn a?

B: Fāqiú shì dǎ wǎngqiú de jīběngōng. Rúguǒ lián fāqiú dōu fā bù hǎo, jiù gèng tánbúshàng jiēqiú hé huíqiú le. Jīntiān yì tiān dōu liàn fāqiú, bié zháojí, yù sù zé bù dá.

A: Coach, I've practiced serving for two hours already; how are we still practicing?

B: Serving is a basic skill of tennis. If you can't serve well, don't even think about returning. We're practicing serving all day today. Don't worry about it. More haste, less speed.

Example 2:

A: 你追上那个女孩儿没有？

B: 还没有呢。不过这种事不能太着急，着急的结果是**欲速则不达**。

A: Nǐ zhuī shàng nàgè nǚháir méiyǒu?

B: Hái méiyǒu ne. Búguò zhè zhǒng shì bùnéng tài zháojí, zháojí de jiéguǒ shì yù sù zé bù dá.

A: Did you get that girl?
B: Not yet. But you can't rush this sort of thing. More haste, less speed.

Usage: Functions as predicate.

Note: Neutral in meaning.

100. 家家有本难念的经 (家家有本難念的經)
jiā jiā yǒu běn nán niàn de jīng

Translated character by character, 家家有本难念的经 means 'family-family-have-a-hard-chant-scripture,' whereas the implied meaning of this proverb would be 'every family has its hardships.' Its functional translation is 'we all have our burdens to bear.'

Example 1:

A: 我那个儿子啊，有多动症。我老公又常常出差，家庭重担都落到我头上了。我快坚持不住了。

B: 真够辛苦你的了。**家家有本难念的经**，我的公公、婆婆都不用提了……

A: Wǒ nàgè érzi a, yǒu duōdòngzhèng. Wǒ lǎogōng yòu chángcháng chūchāi, jiātíng zhòngdàn dōu luò dào wǒ tóushang le. Wǒ kuài jiānchí bú zhù le.
B: Zhēn gòu xīnkǔ nǐ de le. Jiā jiā yǒu běn nán niàn de jīng, wǒde gōnggong, pópo dōu búyòng tí le.

A: My son has ADHD and my husband often goes abroad for work. All of our family's burdens fall on my shoulders. I can't take it much longer.
B: You deal with so much! But we all have our own burdens to bear. Let's not even talk about my father-in-law and mother-in-law . . .

Example 2:

A: 总统的工作多轻松，什么事都有人给干了。
B: 未必，**每个人都有一本难念的经**。我听说有一次总统喝完酒以后在雨里大哭，说上届政府给他留下的财政赤字太多。

A: Zǒngtǒng de gōngzuò duō qīngsōng, shénme shì dōu yǒu rén gěi gàn le.
B: Wèibì, měi gè rén dōu yǒu yì běn nán niàn de jīng. Wǒ tīngshuō yǒu yí cì zǒngtǒng hē wán jiǔ yǐhòu zài yǔ lǐ dàkū, shuō shàng jiè zhèngfǔ gěi tā liúxià de cáizhèng chìzì tài duō.

A: The president's job is so relaxed, everything is done for him by someone.
B: Not necessarily. Everyone has their own burdens to bear. I hear that, one time, after the president had been drinking, he was sobbing in the rain, saying that the budget deficit left to him by the previous administration was too big.

Usage: Used singly.

Variants: 家家都有（一）本难念的经; 人人都有难念的经

Note: Neutral in meaning.

101. 墙头草 (墻頭草) qiáng tóu cǎo

Translated character by character, 墙头草 means 'wall-top-grass.' Its functional translation, as popularized with Mao's usage, is 'fence sitter.'

Example 1:

A: 我们得争取他的支持。

B: 不必，他是棵**墙头草**，典型的投机分子，很不可靠。

A: Wǒmen děi zhēngqǔ tāde zhīchí.

B: Búbì, tā shì kē qiángtóu cǎo, diǎnxíng de tóujīfènzi, hěn bù kěkào.

A: We have to earn his support.

B: There's no need, he's a fence sitter. He's a typical speculator – very unreliable.

Example 2:

A: 政治评论员又开始说另一个总统候选人的好话了。

B: 这不奇怪，因为那个候选人在民调中又领先了。政治评论员都是**墙头草**，哪边儿风硬哪边儿倒。

A: Zhèngzhì pínglùnyuán yòu kāishǐ shuō lìngyígè zǒngtǒng hòuxuǎnrén de hǎohuà le.

B: Zhè bù qíguài, yīnwèi nàgè hòuxuǎnrén zài míndiào zhōng yòu lǐngxiān le. Zhèngzhì pínglùnyuán dōu shì qiángtóu cǎo, nǎbiānr fēng yìng nǎbiānr dǎo.

A: The political pundits have begun talking up yet another presidential candidate.

B: That's not surprising, because that candidate is the front-runner in polls. Political pundits are all fence sitters; they lean whichever way the wind blows.

Usage: Functions as object.

Note: Slightly derogatory in meaning.

102. 替罪羊 (替罪羊) tì zuì yáng

Translated character by character, 替罪羊 means 'substitute-crime-goat,' whereas the implied meaning of this proverb would be 'one who is made to take the blame for something.' Its functional translation is 'a scapegoat,' or 'a sacrificial lamb.'

Example 1:

A: 那件事是两个人一起做的，结果一个人没事，另一个人成了**替罪羊**。

A: Nà jiàn shì shì liǎng gè rén yìqǐ zuò de, jiéguǒ yígè rén méishì, lìngyígè rén chéngle tìzuìyáng.

A: Two people did that together. In the end, one of them got off and the other became the sacrificial lamb.

Example 2:

A: 听说王市长的秘书被抓了起来。

B: 当**替罪羊**了。谁都知道，如果市长不同意，秘书敢那样做吗？

A: Tīngshuō Wáng shìzhǎng de mìshū bèi zhuāle qǐlái.

B: Dāng tìzuìyáng le. Shéi dōu zhīdào, rúguǒ shìzhǎng bù tóngyì, mìshū gǎn nàyàng zuò ma?

A: I hear Mayor Wang's secretary has been arrested.

B: He's a scapegoat. Everyone knows that if the mayor didn't approve it, the secretary wouldn't have dared do that.

Usage: Functions as object.

Note: Neutral in meaning.

---

103. 近水楼台先得月 (近水樓臺先得月)
jìn shuǐ lóu tái xiān dé yuè

Translated character by character, 近水楼台先得月 means 'near-water-pavilion-first-get-moonlight,' whereas the implied meaning of this proverb would be 'to enjoy the benefits of a favorable position.'

Example 1:

A: 费城有世界顶尖的沃顿商学院，按说**近水楼台先得月**，周围地区应该很富裕。可是为什么不远处就破破烂烂呢？

B: 你会开车吗？汽车的观后镜都有盲点。沃顿商学院周围的地区就是盲点。

A: Fèichéng yǒu shìjiè dǐngjiān de Wòdùn Shāngxuéyuàn, ànshuō jìn shuǐ lóu tái xiān dé yuè, zhōuwéi dìqū yīnggāi hěn fùyù. Kěshì wèishénme bùyuǎnchù jiù pòpòlànlàn ne?

B: Nǐ huì kāichē ma? Qìchē de guānhòujìng dōu yǒu mángdiǎn. Wòdùn Shāngxuéyuàn zhōuwéi de dìqū jiùshì mángdiǎn.

A: Wharton, the world's best business school, is in Philadelphia. The city should benefit from Wharton's proximity, and the surrounding area should be very affluent. So, why are there dilapidated areas not far from Wharton?

B: Can you drive? A car's rear view mirrors have blind spots. The area surrounding Wharton is a blind spot.

Example 2:

A: 广东顺德等城市，因为邻近香港的关系，**近水楼台先得月**，很快就发展起来了。

A: Guǎngdōng Shùndé děng chéngshì, yīnwèi línjìn Xiānggǎng de guānxi, jìn shuǐ lóu tái xiān dé yuè, hěn kuài jiù fāzhǎn qǐlái le.

A: Because of their proximity to Hong Kong, cities like Shunde in Guangdong Province benefit from their favorable location, becoming developed very quickly.

Usage: Used singly.

Note: Neutral in meaning.

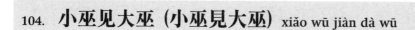

104. 小巫见大巫 (小巫見大巫) xiǎo wū jiàn dà wū

Translated character by character, 小巫见大巫 means 'small-witch-meet-sorceress,' whereas the implied meaning of this proverb would be 'to be nothing in comparison to.' Its functional translation is 'to pale in comparison with,' or 'doesn't hold a candle to.'

Example 1:

A: 我家乡的桥非常长。
B: 我见过，不过跟我家乡的金门大桥比起来真是**小巫见大巫**。

A: Wǒ jiāxiāng de qiáo fēicháng cháng.
B: Wǒ jiànguò, búguò gēn wǒ jiāxiāng de Jīnmén Dàqiáo bǐ qǐlái zhēn shì xiǎo wū jiàn dà wū.

A: The bridge in my hometown is extremely long.
B: I've seen it, but it really doesn't hold a candle to my hometown's Golden Gate Bridge.

Example 2:

A: 他的胃大极了，可以吃十个热狗。
B: 十个热狗？那跟世界大胃王比简直就是**小巫见大巫**。大胃王可以吃60多个。

A: Tā de wèi dà jí le, kěyǐ chī shí gè règǒu.
B: Shí gè règǒu? Nà gēn shìjiè dàwèiwáng bǐ jiǎnzhí jiùshì xiǎo wū jiàn dà wū. Dàwèiwáng kěyǐ chī liùshí duō gè.

A: He's got a huge appetite. He can eat ten hot dogs.

B: Ten hot dogs? That really pales in comparison to the world eating champion. The eating champion can eat more than 60.

Usage: Functions as predicative.

Note: Humorous in meaning.

105. 过河拆桥 (過河拆橋) guò hé chāi qiáo

Translated character by character, 过河拆桥 means 'cross-river-dismantle-bridge,' whereas the implied meaning of this proverb would be 'to get rid of someone as soon as they've done their job.' Its functional translation is 'to kick someone to the curb when they've outlived their usefulness.'

Example 1:

A: 别再找我了，你烦不烦？

B: 你也太没人性了，**过**了**河**就**拆桥**，想当初你是怎么求我帮助你来着？

A: Bié zài zhǎo wǒ le, nǐ fán bù fán?

B: Nǐ yě tài méi rénxìng le, guòle hé jiù chāi qiáo, xiǎngdāngchū nǐ shì zěnme qiú wǒ bāngzhù nǐ láizhe?

A: Stop bothering me! Aren't you an annoying one?

B: You're heartless, kicking me to the curb once I've outlived my usefulness. Have you forgotten how you begged for my help before?

Example 2:

A: 你得小心，他是个**过河拆桥**的人。

A: Nǐ děi xiǎoxīn, tā shì gè guò hé chāi qiáo de rén.

A: You need to be careful. He's the sort of person who'll kick you to the curb once you outlive your usefulness to him.

Usage: Functions as predicate or attributive.

Note: Derogatory in meaning.

106. 一不做，二不休 (一不做，二不休) yī bú zuò, èr bù xiū

Translated character by character, 一不做，二不休 means 'first-not-do, second-not-stop,' whereas the implied meaning of this proverb would be 'as one has already started something, one might as well play the situation out.' Its functional translation is 'go (the) whole hog,' or 'in for a penny, in for a pound.'

Example 1:

A:　既然我们要告这个主治医生，索性一**不做，二不休**，连这家医院及
　　卫生部一起告。

A:　Jìrán wǒmen yào gào zhègè zhǔzhì yīshēng, suǒxìng yī bú zuò, èr bù xiū, lián
　　zhè jiā yīyuàn jí wèishēngbù yìqǐ gào.

A:　Since we're going to sue the physician-in-charge, we might as well go the whole
　　hog, and even sue the hospital and Ministry of Health at the same time.

Example 2:

A:　你父母死活不同意我们的婚事，怎么办？
B:　你已经跟我父母闹翻了，你就一**不做，二不休**，干脆带我走吧。

A:　Nǐ fùmǔ sǐhuó bù tóngyì wǒmen de hūnshì, zěnme bàn?
B:　Nǐ yǐjīng gēn wǒ fùmǔ nào fān le, nǐ jiù yī bú zuò, èr bù xiū, gàncuì dài wǒ zǒu ba.

A:　Your parents will never approve of our marriage. What can we do?
B:　You've already fallen out with my parents. In for a penny, in for a pound. Just
　　take me away.

Usage: Functions as predicate.

Note: Neutral in meaning.

---

107. 以牙还牙，以眼还眼 (以牙還牙，以眼還眼)
yǐ yá huán yá, yǐ yǎn huán yǎn

Translated character by character, 以牙还牙，以眼还眼 means 'use-tooth-repay-
tooth, use-eye-repay-eye' whereas the implied meaning of this proverb would be
'to repay an insult with retribution of a similar magnitude.' Its functional translation
is 'an eye for an eye and a tooth for a tooth.'

Example 1:

A:　美国对中国出口的纺织品征收附加关税，中国**以牙还牙，以眼还
　　眼**，停止进口美国的农产品。

A:　Měiguó duì Zhōngguó chūkǒu de fǎngzhīpǐn zhēngshōu fùjiā guānshuì,
　　Zhōngguó yǐ yá huán yá, yǐ yǎn huán yǎn, tíngzhǐ jìnkǒu Měiguó de nóngchǎnpǐn.

A:　China responded with an eye for an eye to America's levying additional tariffs
　　on China's exported textile products, stopping the import of American
　　agricultural products.

Example 2:

A:　她把我害得这么惨，我要**以牙还牙，以眼还眼**，也让她没有好日子过。

A: Tā bǎ wǒ zhěng de zhème cǎn, wǒ yào yǐ yá huán yá, yǐ yǎn huán yǎn, yě ràng tā méiyǒu hǎo rìzǐ guò.

A: She hurt me so badly. I want an eye for an eye. I want to make her miserable.

Usage: Functions as predicate.

Variant: 以牙还牙

Note: Neutral in meaning.

108.   跑了和尚跑不了庙 (跑了和尚跑不了廟)
pǎo le héshang pǎo bù liǎo miào

Translated character by character, 跑了和尚跑不了庙 means 'run-ed-monk-run-not-able-temple,' whereas the implied meaning of this proverb would be 'a monk may run away but the temple cannot.' Its functional translation is 'you can run, but you can't hide.'

Example 1:

A: 肇事司机逃逸了。
B: **跑了和尚跑不了庙**，有目击者记下了车牌号。

A: Zhàoshì sījī táoyì le.
B: Pǎole héshang pǎo bùliǎo miào, yǒu mùjīzhě jìxiale chēpáihào.

A: The driver who caused the accident left the scene.
B: He can run, but he can't hide. A witness took down his license plate number.

Example 2:

A: 外资老板卷钱跑了。
B: 不怕，**跑了和尚跑不了庙**，一方面冻结他公司的所有帐号，另一方面在他的国家起诉他。

A: Wàizī lǎobǎn juǎnqián pǎo le.
B: Bú pà, pǎole héshang pǎo bùliǎo miào, yìfāngmiàn dòngjié tā gōngsī de suǒyǒu zhànghào, lìngyìfāngmiàn zài tāde guójiā qǐsù tā.

A: The boss took the foreign investment and disappeared.
B: Don't worry. He can run, but he can't hide. We've frozen his company's account and we're suing him in his country.

Usage: Used singly.

Variant: 跑得了和尚跑不了庙

Note: Neutral in meaning.

109. 绿帽子 (綠帽子) lǜ màozi

Translated character by character, 绿帽子 means 'green-hat.' Its functional translation is 'cuckold.'

Example 1:

A: 他老婆跟她老板有不正当男女关系。

B: 给他戴了顶大**绿帽子**。

A: Tā lǎopo gēn tā lǎobǎn yǒu bú zhèngdàng nánnǚ guānxi.

B: Gěi tā dài le dǐng dà lǜ màozi.

A: His wife had an affair with his boss.

B: She made him a cuckold.

Example 2:

A: 他们刚结婚，妻子就给丈夫送了一顶**绿帽子**。

A: Tāmen gāng jiéhun, qīzi jiù gěi zhàngfu sòngle yì dǐng lǜ màozi.

A: They had just gotten married and his wife made him a cuckold.

Usage: Functions as object. There is usually a verb '戴' and a measure word '顶' in front of this *suyu*.

Note: Derogatory in meaning.

110. 识时务者为俊杰 (識時務者為俊傑)
shí shí wù zhě wéi jùn jié

Translated character by character, 识时务者为俊杰 means 'understand-current-situation-person-is-smart-person.' Its functional translation is 'he who understands the times is a wise man.'

Example 1:

A: 你看现在的形势，如果你不主动辞职，也会被董事会免职。**识时务者为俊杰**，你还是主动辞了吧。

A: Nǐ kàn xiànzài de xíngshì, rúguǒ nǐ bù zhǔdòng cízhí, yě huì bèi dǒngshìhuì miǎnzhí. Shí shíwù zhě wéi jùnjié, nǐ háishì zhǔdòng cíle ba.

A: Take a look at the situation. If you don't voluntarily resign, you will be relieved by the board of directors. He who understands the times is a wise man. You should resign voluntarily.

Example 2:

A: 我们的专业就业前景很糟糕，而且十年二十年也改善不了。很多人都换专业了，包括我。你也换一个就业前景好的吧，**识时务者为俊杰**嘛。

A: Wǒmen de zhuānyè jiùyè qiánjǐng hěn zāogāo, érqiě shí nián èrshí nián yě gǎishàn bùliǎo. Hěnduō rén dōu huàn zhuānyè le, bāokuò wǒ. Nǐ yě huàn yígè jiùyè qiánjǐng hǎo de ba, shí shíwù zhě wéi jùnjié ma.

A: The prospects for employment in our profession are awful, and they won't improve in the next ten or twenty years. A lot of people have changed professions, including myself. You should also change to a profession with good prospects. He who understands the times is a wise man.

Usage: Used singly.

Note: Neutral in meaning.

111. 井水不犯河水 (井水不犯河水) jǐng shuǐ bú fàn hé shuǐ

Translated character by character, 井水不犯河水 means 'well-water-not-encroach-river-water,' whereas the implied meaning of this proverb would be 'to mind one's own business.' Its functional translation is 'to stay in one's own lane.'

Example 1:

A: 小刘，你这样做太过分了。
B: 老马，这件事跟你没有一点关系，咱们**井水不犯河水**。你的事我不搀和，我的事也用不着你管。

A: Xiǎo Liú, nǐ zhèyàng zuò tài guòfèn le.
B: Lǎo Mǎ, zhè jiàn shì gēn nǐ méiyǒu yìdiǎn guānxi, zánmen jǐngshuǐ bú fàn héshuǐ. Nǐde shì wǒ bù chānhuo, wǒde shì yě yòngbùzháo nǐ guǎn.

A: Little Liu, that's going too far.
B: Old Ma, this has nothing to do with you. Let's stay in our own lanes. I don't meddle in your business, so my affairs don't need your oversight.

Example 2:

A: 两家服装店紧挨着，一家主营高档服装，一家主营中低档服装。过去几十年来两家店**井水不犯河水**，各赚各的钱，关系倒挺愉快的。

A: Liǎng jiā fúzhuāngdiàn jǐn āizhe, yì jiā zhǔyíng gāodàng fúzhuāng, yì jiā zhǔyíng zhōng-dīdàng fúzhuāng. Guòqù jǐshí nián lái liǎng jiā diàn jǐngshuǐ bú fàn héshuǐ, gè zhuàn gè de qián, guānxi dào tǐng yúkuài de.

A: There were two adjacent clothing stores, one mainly dealt in high-grade clothing, one mainly dealt in low- to middle-grade clothing. Over the past decades, these two stores have kept to themselves, each making its own money and staying in its own lane.

Usage: Functions as predicate.

Variant: 河水不犯井水 (less common)

Note: Slightly derogatory or neutral in meaning.

112. 一棵树上吊死 (一棵樹上吊死) yī kē shù shàng diào sǐ

Translated character by character, 一棵树上吊死 means 'a-MW-tree-on-hang-dead,' whereas the implied meaning of this proverb would be 'to be inflexible and stubborn.'

Example 1:

A: 我老公又赌博，在外面还有女人。我下半辈子该怎么过啊？

B: 你非得**在一棵树上吊死**啊？不能离婚吗？

A: Wǒ lǎogōng yòu dǔbó, zài wàimiàn háiyǒu nǚrén. Wǒ xià bàn bèizǐ gāi zěnme guò a?

B: Nǐ fēiděi zài yī kē shù shàng diào sǐ a? Bùnéng líhūn ma?

A: My husband gambles and he has a mistress. Is this how I'll spend the rest of my life?

B: Why do you insist on being so stubborn? Can't you divorce him?

Example 2:

A: 企业发展得多元化，什么赚钱做什么，不能**在一棵树上吊死**。

A: Qǐyè fāzhǎn děi duōyuánhuà, shénme zuànqián zuò shénme, bùnéng zài yī kē shù shàng diào sǐ.

A: A company needs to develop in a diversified manner, doing whatever makes money. It can't put all of its eggs in one basket.

Usage: Functions as predicate.

Variant: 在一棵树上吊死

Note: Slightly derogatory and humorous in meaning.

113. 放鸽子 (放鴿子) fàng gēzi

Translated character by character, 放鸽子 means 'release-pigeon,' whereas the implied meaning of this proverb would be 'to let someone wait in vain.' Its functional translation is 'to stand someone up,' or 'to leave someone in the lurch.'

Example 1:

A: 怎么这么早就回来了？

B: 被她**放鸽子**了。等了一个钟头也没来。

A: Zěnme zhème zǎo jiù huílái le?

B: Bèi tā fànggēzi le. Děngle yígè zhōngtóu yě méi lái.

A: Why are you back so early?

B: She stood me up. I waited for an hour and she didn't come.

Example 2:

A: 这件事咱们得重新考虑。

B: 什么？你不是答应好了吗？现在反悔，这不是**放**我**鸽子**吗？

A: Zhè jiàn shì zánmen děi chóngxīn kǎolǜ.

B: Shénme? Nǐ búshì dāyìng hǎole ma? Xiànzài fǎnhuǐ, zhè búshì fàng wǒ gēzi ma?

A: We need to reconsider this issue.

B: What? Didn't you already agree? If you go back on your word now, wouldn't you be leaving me in the lurch?

Usage: Functions as predicate or predicative.

Note: Neutral in meaning.

114. 一步一个脚印 (一步一個腳印) yí bù yí gè jiǎoyìn

Translated character by character, 一步一个脚印 means 'one-step-one-MW-foot-print,' whereas the implied meaning of this proverb would be 'to do something at an even pace.' Its functional translation is 'to take something one step at a time.'

Example 1:

A: 他虽然起步晚，但是**一步一个脚印**，最终取得了比同龄人大得多的成就。

A: Tā suīrán qǐbù wǎn, dànshì yí bù yígè jiǎoyìn, zuìzhōng qǔdé le bǐ tónglíngrén dà de duō de chéngjiù.

A: While he got started late, he took it one step at a time and, in the end, he achieved much greater success than others his age.

Example 2:

A: 你怎么这么马虎？出了这么多错！

B: 我太着急了。

A: 着急没有用，做事得**一步一个脚印**。

A: Nǐ zěnme zhème mǎhu? Chūle zhème duō cuò!

B: Wǒ tài zháojí le.

A: Zháojí méiyǒu yòng, zuòshì děi yí bù yígè jiǎoyìn.

A: How were you so careless? You made so many errors!

B: I'm too impatient.

A: There's no use being impatient. You need to take things one step at a time.

Usage: Functions as adverbial or attributive.

Note: Complimentary in meaning.

115.　上梁不正下梁歪 (上樑不正下樑歪)
shàng liáng bú zhèng xià liáng wāi

Translated character by character, 上梁不正下梁歪 means 'upper-beam-not-straight-lower-beam-deviate,' whereas the implied meaning of this proverb would be 'when those in authority stray from righteousness, those below them will follow suit.' Its functional translation is 'a crooked stick will have a crooked shadow.'

Example 1:

A: 这个单位的人怎么都不认真工作？

B: 看看他们的领导就行了，一年也上不了两、三天班。**上梁不正下梁歪**，底下的人肯定好不了。

A: Zhègè dānwèi de rén zěnme dōu bú rènzhēn gōngzuò?

B: Kànkàn tāmen de lǐngdǎo jiù xíng le, yì nián yě shàng bùliǎo liǎng, sān tiān bān. Shàng liáng bú zhèng xià liáng wāi, dǐxià de rén kěndìng hǎo bùliǎo.

A: Why are all of the people in this work unit not working hard?

B: If you take a look at their leader, you'll understand. He hardly works two or three days a year. A crooked stick will have a crooked shadow, so his underlings definitely can't be good.

Example 2:

A: 某市公安局长因为庇护黑社会最终入狱，因为**上梁不正下梁歪**，他手下的警察也大多因为跟黑社会有勾结而入狱或辞职。

A: Mǒu shì gōng'ānjúzhǎng yīnwèi bìhù hēishèhuì zuìzhōng rùyù, yīnwèi shàng liáng bú zhèng xià liáng wāi, tā shǒuxià de jǐngchá yě dàduō yīnwèi gēn hēishèhuì yǒu gōujié ér rùyù huò cízhí.

A: Some city's chief of police was finally thrown in jail for protecting the mafia. Because a crooked stick will cast a crooked shadow, the majority of the policemen under his command were also jailed or resigned for colluding with the mob.

Usage: Used singly.

Note: Slightly derogatory or neutral in meaning.

116. 不入虎穴，焉得虎子 (不入虎穴，焉得虎子)
bú rù hǔ xuè, yān dé hǔ zǐ

Translated character by character, 不入虎穴，焉得虎子 means 'not-enter-tiger-den, how-get-tiger-cub,' whereas the implied meaning of this proverb would be 'one must take risks in order to get something good.' Its functional translation is 'nothing good comes without risk.'

Example 1:

A: 你一个人去太危险了。我派两个人保护你吧。

B: 不行，人多目标大。再说，**不入虎穴，焉得虎子**？

A: Nǐ yígè rén qù tài wēixiǎn le. Wǒ pài liǎng gè rén bǎohù nǐ ba.

B: Bùxíng, rén duō mùbiāo dà. Zàishuō, bú rù hǔ xuè, yān dé hǔ zǐ?

A: Going by yourself is too dangerous. I'll assign two people to protect you.

B: No, more people make a bigger target. Moreover, nothing good comes without risk!

Example 2:

A: 你不用任何防护设施就去海里拍摄大白鲨袭击别的鲨鱼的场景，这也太危险了！

B: **不入虎穴，焉得虎子**！放心吧，我命大，不会出事的。

A: Nǐ búyòng rènhé fánghù shèshī jiù qù hǎi lǐ pāishè dàbáishā xíjī biéde shāyú de chǎngjǐng, zhè yě tài wēixiǎn le!

B: Bú rù hǔ xuè, yān dé hǔ zǐ! Fàngxīn ba, wǒ mìngdà, búhuì chūshì de.

A: You just jump in the ocean to film great white sharks attacking other sharks without any protective apparatus? That's too dangerous!

B: Nothing good comes without risk! Relax, I'm invincible; nothing's going to happen to me.

Usage: Used singly.

Note: Complimentary in meaning.

117. 赔了夫人又折兵 (賠了夫人又折兵)

péi le fūren yòu zhé bīng

Translated character by character, 赔了夫人又折兵 means 'lose-ed-wife-also-lose-soldier,' whereas the implied meaning of this proverb would be 'to suffer serious losses concurrently.' Its functional translation is 'to suffer a double loss.'

Example 1:

A: 他这次惨了。

B: 怎么了？

A: 为了选总统，把参议员的工作辞了。结果不但没有选上总统，还因为涉嫌非法使用捐款而被司法机关调查了，最后老婆也跟他离婚了。

B: 真是**赔了夫人又折兵**。

A: Tā zhèxià cǎn le.

B: Zěnme le?

A: Wèile xuǎn zǒngtǒng, bǎ cānyìyuán de gōngzuò cí le. Jiéguǒ búdàn méiyǒu xuǎn shang zǒngtǒng, hái yīnwèi shèxián fēifǎ shǐyòng juānkuǎn ér bèi sīfǎ jīguān diàochá le, zuìhòu lǎopo yě gēn tā líhūn le.

B: Zhēn shì péile fūren yòu zhé bīng.

A: He's in bad shape.

B: What's wrong?

A: In order to run for president, he gave up his seat in the Senate. In the end, he not only wasn't elected president but, as he was suspected of illegal use of campaign funds, was investigated by the authorities. In the end, his wife divorced him too.

Example 2:

A: 甲公司收购了乙公司，本想强强联手，结果事与愿违，不但前乙公司经营越来越差，甲公司也受到很大的负面影响。对甲公司来说，**赔了夫人又折兵**。

A: Jiǎ gōngsī shōugòule yǐ gōngsī, běn xiǎng qiángqiáng liánshǒu, jiéguǒ shìyǔyuànwéi, búdàn qián yǐ gōngsī jīngyíng yuèláiyuè chà, jiǎ gōngsī yě shòudàole hěn dà de fùmiàn yǐngxiǎng. Duì jiǎ gōngsī láishuō, péile fūren yòu zhé bīng.

A: Company A acquired company B. They originally wanted to merge two leaders in the field but, in the end, they got the opposite. Not only did the former company B's business get worse and worse, company A was also subject to serious negative influences. To company A, it was a double loss.

Usage: Functions as predicate.

Note: Slightly derogatory and humorous in meaning.

118. 有心栽花花不长，无心插柳柳成荫 (有心栽花花不長，無心插柳柳成蔭)

yǒu xīn zāi huā huā bù zhǎng, wú xīn chā liǔ liǔ chéng yīn

Translated character by character, 有心栽花花不长，无心插柳柳成荫 means 'have-intention-plant-flower-flower-not-grow,   no-intention-plant-willow-willow-become-shade,' whereas the implied meaning of this proverb would be 'to fail to accomplish what one diligently tries to do, but succeed in that which one ignores.' Its functional translation is 'to unknowingly benefit from an unexpected course of events.'

Example 1:

A: 她本来是大学教授，搞法律的，没想到**无心插柳**，写了一本关于孩子教育的书，一下子成了媒体上的红人。

A: Tā běnlái shì dàxué jiàoshòu, gǎo fǎlǜ de, méi xiǎng dào wú xīn chā liǔ, xiěle yì běn guānyú háizǐ jiàoyù de shū, yíxiàzǐ chéng le méitǐ shàng de hóngrén.

A: She used to be a university law professor. She never imagined that, after writing a book about child education, she would unknowingly become a media darling overnight.

Example 2:

A: 那个面包师不小心在给顾客的面包上抹上了一层芥末，结果出现了**无心插柳**的效果。这种面包大卖，最后成了这家面包房的招牌。

A: Nàgè miànbāoshī bù xiǎoxīn zài gěi gùkè de miànbāo shàng mǒ shàng le yì céng jièmo, jiéguǒ chūxiàn le wú xīn chā liǔ de xiàoguǒ. Zhè zhǒng miànbāo dà mài, zuìhòu chéngle zhè jiā miànbāofáng de zhāopái.

A: That pastry chef accidentally applied a coat of mustard on the bread that he gave to his clients, resulting in an unexpected effect. That kind of bread sold well and, in the end, became the pastry shop's calling card.

Usage: Functions as predicate.

Variant: 无心插柳(柳成荫)

Note: Neutral in meaning.

119. 八字还没一撇 (八字還沒一撇) bā zì hái méi yì piě

Translated character by character, 八字还没一撇 means '"eight"-still-not-have-a-*pie* (the first stroke in the character "eight"),' whereas the implied meaning of this proverb would be 'it hasn't even begun.'

Example 1:

A: 你那个画展准备得怎么样了？

B: 别提了，**八字还没一撇**呢，场地、时间都还没定好呢。

A: Nǐ nàge huàzhǎn zhǔnbèi de zěnmeyàng le?

B: Bié tí le, bā zì hái méi yì piě ne, chǎngdì, shíjiān dōu hái méi dìng hǎo ne.

A: How is preparation for your art exhibit going?

B: Don't even talk about it. It hasn't even begun. I still haven't confirmed the time or location yet.

Example 2:

A: 你跟女朋友什么时候结婚？

B: 早着呢，**八字还没一撇**。

A: Nǐ gēn nǚpéngyou shénme shíhou jiéhūn?

B: Zǎo zhe ne, bā zì hái méi yì piě.

A: When are you and your girlfriend going to get married?

B: It's still early. It's still far from done.

Usage: Used singly.

Variant: 八字没一撇

Note: Neutral or humorous in meaning.

120. 有眼不识泰山 (有眼不識泰山) yǒu yǎn bù shí Tài Shān

Translated character by character, 有眼不识泰山 means 'have-eyes-not-recognize-Tai-Mountain,' whereas the implied meaning of this proverb would be 'to fail to recognize a famous person.' Its functional translation is 'to entertain angels unawares,' or 'wouldn't recognize someone if they came up and introduced themselves.'

Example 1:

A: 这个门卫连市长的身份证都查，真是**有眼不识泰山**。

A: Zhège ménwèi lián shìzhǎng de shēnfènzhèng dōu chá, zhēnshì yǒu yǎn bù shí Tài Shān.

A: This security guard even checks the mayor's ID. He wouldn't recognize President Obama if he came up and introduced himself.

Example 2:

A: 你没听说过我的名字吗？XYZ。

B: 对不起，X部长，我**有眼不识泰山**，请您原谅。

A: Nǐ méi tīngshuō guò wǒde míngzì ma? XYZ.

B: Duìbùqǐ, X bùzhǎng, wǒ yǒu yǎn bù shí Tài Shān, qǐng nín yuánliàng.

A: Haven't you heard of me? I'm XYZ.

B: I'm sorry, Minister X. I am entertaining angels unawares. Please forgive me.

Usage: Functions as predicate or predicative.

Note: Slightly derogatory in meaning.

---

121. 出气筒 (出氣筒) chū qì tǒng

Translated character by character, 出气筒 means 'release-anger-pump,' whereas the implied meaning of this proverb would be 'someone whom another person takes their anger out on.' Its functional translation is 'punching bag.'

Example 1:

A: 他酒后常常打老婆。

B: 他老婆真可怜，就是他的一个**出气筒**。

A: Tā jiǔ hòu chángcháng dǎ lǎopo.

B: Tā lǎopo zhēn kělián, jiù shì tā de yígè chūqìtǒng.

A: He often beats his wife when he's drunk.

B: His wife's really pitiful. She's just a punching bag to him.

Example 2:

A: 他在外面受辱，回来拿我当**出气筒**，见到我就大喊大叫。

A: Tā zài wàimiàn shòu rǔ, huílái ná wǒ dāng chūqìtǒng, jiàn dào wǒ jiù dàhǎn-dàjiào.

A: When he gets humiliated when he's away, he comes back and makes me his punching bag. When he sees me, he starts screaming.

Usage: Functions as predicative or object.

Note: Neutral in meaning.

---

122. 八九不离十 (八九不離十) bā jiǔ bù lí shí

Translated character by character, 八九不离十 means 'eight-nine-not-far from-ten,' whereas the implied meaning of this proverb would be 'not far off.' Its functional translation is 'close to the mark.'

Example 1:

A: 这件事办得怎么样了？

B: **八九不离十**，您就放心吧。

A: Zhè jiàn shì bàn de zěnmeyàng le?

B: Bā jiǔ bù lí shí, nín jiù fàngxīn ba.

A: How well was the issue taken care of?

B: It was close to the mark. Don't worry about it.

Example 2:

A: 我看这个小姑娘将来一定不得了。

B: 你怎么知道？

A: 我都八十岁了，经历过多少事啊！虽然不敢说百分之百，但是**八九不离十**。

Λ: Wǒ kàn zhègè xiǎogūniang jiānglái yídìng bùdéliǎo.

B: Nǐ zěnme zhīdao?

A: Wǒ dōu bāshí duō suì le, jīnglì guo duōshao shì a! Suīrán bùgǎn shuō bǎi fēn zhī bǎi, dànshi bā jiǔ bù lí shí.

A: I can tell this lady is going to be unbearable.

B: How can you tell?

A: I'm 80 years old, I've experienced so much! While I don't dare say for sure, I can't be far off.

Usage: Used singly or functions as predicate.

Note: Neutral in meaning.

123. 无风不起浪 (無風不起浪) wú fēng bù qǐ làng

Translated character by character, 无风不起浪 means 'no-wind-not-raise-wave,' whereas the implied meaning of this proverb would be 'there is often fact underlying pervasive rumors.' Its functional translation is 'there's no smoke without fire.'

Example 1:

A: 小报上都在炒作州长的婚外情呢。我看不像真的。州长看起来人不错。

B: 那倒不一定。**无风不起浪**，肯定有点儿问题；否则凭空捏造的新闻大家谁看啊？

A: Xiǎobào shàng dōu zài chǎozuò zhōuzhǎng de hūnwàiqíng ne. Wǒ kàn bú xiàng zhēnde. Zhōuzhǎng kàn qǐlái rén búcuò.

B: Nà dào bùyídìng. Wú fēng bù qǐ làng, kěndìng yǒudiǎnr wèntí; fǒuzé píngkōng niēzào de xīnwén dàjiā shéi kàn a?

A: The tabloids are all hyping the governor's extramarital affairs. I don't think it's true. The governor seems like a decent person.

B: That might not be the case. There's no smoke without fire. There's definitely some issue, otherwise who would read baseless, fabricated news?

Example 2:

A: 邮票刚涨完价，有人说再过几个月还要涨呢。不会吧？

B: **无风不起浪**。邮政局一直亏损，国家都不愿意补贴了，那只好涨邮费了。

A: Yóupiào gāng zhǎng wán jià, yǒurén shuō zài guò jǐ gè yuè hái yào zhǎng ne. Búhuì ba?

B: Wú fēng bù qǐ làng. Yóuzhèngjú yìzhí kuīsǔn, guójiā dōu bú yuànyì bǔtiē le, nà zhǐhǎo zhǎng yóufèi le.

A: The price of stamps just went up; people are saying that in a few months it'll rise again. That can't be, right?

B: There's no smoke without fire. The postal service is constantly losing money, and the government isn't willing to subsidize them anymore, so they have no choice but to raise postage.

Usage: Functions mainly as predicate.

Note: Neutral in meaning.

124.　得便宜卖乖 (得便宜賣乖) dé piányi mài guāi

Translated character by character, 得便宜卖乖 means 'receive-benefit-brag,' whereas the implied meaning of this proverb would be 'to not admit that one has received a benefit.'

Example 1:

A: 他还找领导诉苦呢，就他得到的好处最多，**得了便宜还卖乖**，好像他受到了不公正的待遇似的。

A: Tā hái zhǎo lǐngdǎo sùkǔ ne, jiù tā dédào de hǎochù zuìduō, déle piányi hái mài guāi, hǎoxiàng tā shòudào le bù gōngzhèng de dàiyu shìde.

A: He even goes to the boss to complain and he gets the most out of it. He refuses to admit that he has been benefitting, but it seems like he has gotten unfair treatment.

Example 2:

A: 你别**得了便宜卖乖**，我不跟你计较就是了，你还有完没完？

A: Nǐ bié déle piányi mài guāi, wǒ bù gēn nǐ jìjiào jiù shì le, nǐ hái yǒu wán méi wán?

A: Don't deny that you benefitted. I'm not going to argue about this with you. Are you done talking?

Usage: Functions as predicate.

Variants: 捡便宜卖乖; 占便宜卖乖; 讨便宜卖乖

Note: Slightly derogatory in meaning.

---

125. 不是省油的灯 (不是省油的燈) bú shì shěng yóu de dēng

Translated character by character, 不是省油的灯 means 'not-is-save-oil-lamp,' whereas the implied meaning of this proverb would be 'is not a kerosene-saving lamp.' Its functional translation is 'a real son of a bitch' or 'a real piece of work.'

Example 1:

A: 上次跟同事吵架之后，现在他安静多了。
B: 他可**不是省油的灯**。你看着吧，后面肯定有好戏看。

A: Shàng cì gēn tóngshì chǎojià zhīhòu, xiànzài tā ānjìng duō le.
B: Tā kě búshì shěng yóu de dēng. Nǐ kànzhe ba, hòumiàn kěndìng yǒu hǎo xì kàn.

A: After fighting with his colleague last time, he is now much calmer
B: He really is a piece of work. Watch, there'll be some interesting drama later.

Example 2:

A: 千万别惹她的麻烦。
B: 怎么了？她又没长三头六臂。
A: 她呀，麻烦着呢，绝对**不是省油的灯**，你尽量躲远点儿。

A: Qiānwàn bié rě tā de máfan.
B: Zěnme le? Tā yòu méi zhǎng sāntóu-liùbì.
A: Tā ya, máfan zhe ne, juéduì búshì shěng yóu de dēng, nǐ jìnliàng duǒ yuǎn diǎnr.

A: Whatever you do, don't provoke her.
B: What's wrong? She's not superwoman.
A: Her? She's a real handful, a real son of a bitch. Do your best to stay away from her.

Usage: Functions as predicative.

Note: Slightly derogatory in meaning. '一盏' (盏 is measure word for 灯) can be added in front of 省油, but generally is not necessary.

126. 家丑不可外扬 (家醜不可外揚) jiā chǒu bù kě wài yáng

Translated character by character, 家丑不可外场 means 'family-shame-not-suitable-for-outside-publicize,' whereas the implied meaning of this proverb would be 'don't discuss embarrassing family issues in public.' Its functional translation is 'don't wash your dirty laundry/linen in public.'

Example 1:

A: 这件事就咱们几个知道，**家丑不可外扬**，谁也不许说出去。

A: Zhè jiàn shì jiù zánmen jǐ gè zhīdào, jiā chǒu bùkě wài yáng, shéi yě bùxǔ shuō chūqù.

A: Only the few of us know about this issue. One doesn't wash dirty linen in public; no one is allowed to discuss this with outsiders.

Example 2:

A: 妈，您看您的宝贝女儿把我给挠的，胳膊全破了。

B: 这件事以后再说。但是，**家丑不可外扬**。明天上班别人要是问了，就说是走路不小心自己摔的。

A: Mā, nín kàn nín de bǎobèi nǚ'ér bǎ wǒ gěi náo de, gēbo quán pò le.

B: Zhè jiàn shì yǐhòu zài shuō. Dànshì, jiā chǒu bùkě wài yáng. Míngtiān shàngbān biérén yàoshì wèn le, jiù shuō shì zǒulù bù xiǎoxīn zìjǐ shuāi de.

A: Mom, look how your baby daughter scratched me. My whole arm is scratched up.

B: We'll talk about this later, but don't wash your dirty linen in public. If people at the office ask you tomorrow, just say you accidentally fell while walking.

Usage: Used singly.

Note: Neutral in meaning.

127. 背黑锅 (背黑鍋) bēi hēi guō

Translated character by character, 背黑锅 means 'carry on back-black-pot,' whereas the implied meaning of this proverb would be 'to take the blame for someone else.' Its functional translation is 'to take the rap,' or 'be left holding the bag.'

Example 1:

A: 小李，明天你跟媒体解释一下为什么我们反对现在就改革医疗保险制度。

B: 局长，又让我**背黑锅**，媒体还不得把我骂死啊。

A:　Xiǎo Lǐ, míngtiān nǐ gēn méitǐ jiěshì yíxià wèishénme wǒmen fǎnduì xiànzài jiù gǎigé yīliáo bǎoxiǎn zhìdù.

B:　Júzhǎng, yòu ràng wǒ bēi hēi guō, méitǐ hái bùděi bǎ wǒ mà sǐ a.

A:　Little Li, explain to the media tomorrow why we oppose reforming the healthcare system at this point.

B:　Director, you're making me take the rap again. The media will definitely ream me out.

Example 2:

A:　外交部长主动辞职了。

B:　这是在为总统**背黑锅**，谁都知道是总统做的错误决策。

A:　Wàijiāo bùzhǎng zhǔdòng cízhí le.

B:　Zhè shì zài wèi zǒngtǒng bēi hēi guō, shéi dōu zhīdao shì zǒngtǒng zuò de cuòwù juédìng.

A:　The foreign minister resigned.

B:　He is taking the rap for the president. Everyone knows it was the president's misguided policy.

Usage: Functions as predicate. '为/替 + sb' is often said before '背黑锅.'

Note: Neutral in meaning.

128.　兔子不吃窝边草 (兔子不吃窩邊草)
tùzi bù chī wō biān cǎo

Translated character by character, 兔子不吃窝边草 means 'hare-not-eat-hole-around-grass,' whereas the implied meaning of this proverb would be 'even a villain doesn't harm the next door neighbors.'

Example 1:

A:　咱们商店周围的居民把购物车推到他们房子附近，还不给送回来。我们得警告他们一下。

B:　算了，**兔子不吃窝边草**，我们还得跟这些邻居搞好关系，吃点儿亏就吃点儿亏吧。

A:　Zánmen shāngdiàn zhōuwéi de jūmín bǎ gòuwùchē tuī dào tāmen fángzi fùjìn, hái bú sòng huílái. Wǒmen děi jǐnggào tāmen yíxià.

B:　Suàn le, tùzi bù chī wō biān cǎo, wǒmen hái děi gēn zhèxiē línju gǎo hǎo guānxi, chī diǎnr kuī jiù chī diǎnr kuī ba.

A:　The people living around our store push shopping carts to their homes and don't bring them back. We should warn them.

B:　Forget about it. Even a villain doesn't harm the next door neighbors. We need to have good relations with our neighbors. If it means eating a loss, we'll eat a loss.

Example 2:

A: 你好像喜欢上了你们办公室的小李。

B: 是这样。

A: 我劝你赶快打住。**兔子不吃窝边草**，再说，小李可是有妇之夫啊。这事儿传出去好说不好听啊。

A: Nǐ hǎoxiàng xǐhuan shàng le nǐmen bàngōngshì de Xiǎo Lǐ.

B: Shì zhèyàng.

A: Wǒ quàn nǐ gǎnkuài dǎzhù. Tùzi bù chī wō biān cǎo, zàishuō, Xiǎo Lǐ kě shì yǒufùzhīfū a. Zhè shìr chuán chūqù hǎo shuō bù hǎo tīng a.

A: You seem to have taken a liking to Little Li from your office.

B: I have.

A: I'd recommend you snap out of it quickly; even a villain doesn't harm the next door neighbors. Besides, Little Li is a married man. If this got out, it would make juicy gossip.

Usage: Used singly.

Note: Humorous or neutral in meaning.

---

129. 铁饭碗 (鐵飯碗) tiě fàn wǎn

Translated character by character, 铁饭碗 means 'iron-rice-bowl,' whereas the implied meaning of this proverb would be 'a very secure job.' Its functional translation is 'a cradle-to-grave job,' 'cradle-to-grave job security.'

Example 1:

A: 当个中学老师有什么意思？

B: 那是**铁饭碗**，很多人抢着当呢。

A: Dāng gè zhōngxué lǎoshī yǒu shénme yìsī?

B: Nà shì tiěfànwǎn, hěnduō rén qiǎngzhe dāng ne.

A: What's interesting about being a high school teacher?

B: It's a cradle-to-grave job. A lot of people are competing to be one.

Example 2:

A: 听说公交系统要私有化了。

B: 早该打破他们的**铁饭碗**了。

A: Tīngshuō gōngjiāo xìtǒng yào sīyǒuhuà le.

B: Zǎo gāi dǎ pò tāmen de tiěfànwǎn le.

A: I've heard they're going to privatize the public transit system.

B: They should've done away with their cradle-to-grave job security long ago.

Usage: Functions mainly as object, often after verbs like '打破', '丢掉', '破除', '端着', '捧着' etc.

Note: Neutral in meaning.

130. 冰冻三尺，非一日之寒 (冰凍三尺，非一日之寒)
bīng dòng sān chǐ, fēi yí rì zhī hán

Translated character by character, 冰冻三尺，非一日之寒 means 'ice-frozen-three-feet, not-one-day-'s-cold,' whereas the implied meaning of this proverb would be 'great happenings do not occur spontaneously, but, rather, are the result of an underlying condition that has accumulated over time.' Its functional translation is 'Rome wasn't built in a day.'

Example 1:

A: 这家公司怎么有这么多矛盾？

B: **冰冻三尺，非一日之寒**，矛盾越积越深，几乎解决不了了。

A: Zhè jiā gōngsī zěnme yǒu zhème duō máodùn?

B: Bīng dòng sān chǐ, fēi yí rì zhī hán, máodùn yuè jī yuè shēn, jīhū jiějué bùliǎo le.

A: How does this company have this many problems?

B: Rome wasn't built in a day. As the problems accumulated, they got worse. The situation is almost unsalvageable now.

Example 2:

A: 中东问题怎么这么复杂？

B: **冰冻三尺，非一日之寒**。从二十世纪四十年代起就有冲突，一直到现在。

A: Zhōngdōng wèntí zěnme zhème fùzá?

B: Bīng dòng sān chǐ, fēi yí rì zhī hán. Cóng èrshí shìjì sìshí niándài qǐ jiù yǒu chōngtū, yìzhí dào xiànzài.

A: How is the Middle East issue so complicated?

B: Rome wasn't built in a day. There have been conflicts ever since the 1940s.

Usage: Used singly.

Note: Neutral in meaning.

131. 远亲不如近邻 (遠親不如近鄰) yuǎn qīn bù rú jìn lín

Translated character by character, 远亲不如近邻 means 'distant-relative-not-better-near-neighbor' whereas the implied meaning of this proverb would be 'neighbors may be more helpful than distant friends.' Its functional translation is 'better a close neighbor than a distant brother.'

Example 1:

A: 你跟你的邻居的关系怎么那么好？

B: 邻里关系非常重要，**远亲不如近邻**。如果有事的话，邻居往往能帮不小的忙。

A: Nǐ gēn nǐde línjū de guānxì zěnme nàme hǎo?

B: Línlǐ guānxì fēicháng zhòngyào, yuǎn qīn bùrú jìn lín. Rúguǒ yǒushì de huà, línjū wǎngwǎng néng bāng bù xiǎo de máng.

A: How do you have such a good relationship with your neighbor?

B: Neighborly relations are very important. Better a close neighbor than a distant brother. If you have a problem, your neighbor can usually help a great deal.

Example 2:

A: 中国与哈萨克斯坦虽然在历史上往来不多，但两国相邻，**远亲不如近邻**，因此加强中哈关系格外重要。

A: Zhōngguó yǔ Hāsākèsītǎn suīrán zài lìshǐ shàng wǎnglái bù duō, dàn liǎng guó xiānglín, yuǎn qīn bù rú jìn lín, yīncǐ jiāqiáng Zhōng-Hā guānxì géwài zhòngyào.

A: While China and Kazakhstan haven't had much contact in history, the two countries border each other. Better a close neighbor than a distant brother; so strengthening Sino-Kazakh relations is especially important.

Usage: Used singly.

Note: Neutral in meaning.

132. 下马威 (下馬威) xià mǎ wēi

Translated character by character, 下马威 means 'dismount-horse-imposing manner,' whereas the implied meaning of this proverb would be 'an action taken to establish an imposing air or advantageous position for oneself.' Its functional translation is 'opening gambit.'

Example 1:

A: 他那么大年纪了还能整篇背诵林肯的《葛底斯堡演说》，真了不起。

B: 是了不起，同时也是给我们年青人一个**下马威**，老同志对西方的了
    解并不比年青人少。

A: Tā nàme dà niánjì le hái néng zhěng piān bèisòng Línkěn de "Gědǐsībǎo
    Yǎnshuō", zhēn liǎobùqǐ.
B: Shì liǎobùqǐ, tóngshí yě shì gěi wǒmen niánqīngrén yígè xiàmǎwēi, lǎotóngzhì
    duì xīfāng de liǎojiě bìng bù bǐ niánqīngrén shǎo.

A: That he can still recite Lincoln's whole Gettysburg Address at such an old age
    is really amazing.
B: It is amazing. At the same time, it's his opening gambit for us young folk. This
    old guy's understanding of the West is no less than that of young people.

Example 2:

A: 他刚上任怎么这么凶！
B: 要给大家一个**下马威**，现在他说了算。

A: Tā gāng shàngrèn zěnme zhème xiōng!
B: Yào gěi dàjiā yígè xiàmǎwēi, xiànzài tā shuōle suàn.

A: He's only just started; how is he so intimidating?
B: It's his opening gambit for everyone. Now, what he says goes.

Usage: Functions as object.

Note: Neutral in meaning.

133. 天下乌鸦一般黑 (天下烏鴉一般黑)
tiānxià wūyā yìbān hēi

Translated character by character, 天下乌鸦一般黑 means 'heaven-under-crow-same-
black,' whereas the implied meaning of this proverb would be 'there is no difference
between bad people the world over.' Its functional translation is 'they're all the
same.'

Example 1:

A: 这家工厂对我们剥削得太厉害了，要不我们换家工厂吧？
B: 我看算了吧。**天下乌鸦一般黑**，说不定下家比这家还黑呢。

A: Zhè jiā gōngchǎng duì wǒmen bōxuē de tài lìhai le, yàobù wǒmen huàn jiā
    gōngchǎng ba?
B: Wǒ kàn suànle ba. Tiānxià wūyā yìbān hēi, shuōbúdìng xià jiā bǐ zhè jiā hái
    hēi ne.

A: This factory seriously exploits us, why don't we switch factories?
B: Forget about it; they're all the same. Who's to say that the next factory won't
    be worse than this one?

Example 2:

A: 你的新男朋友怎么样？

B: **天下乌鸦一般黑**，跟上一个一样，也很花心。男人没一个好东西。

A: Nǐde xīn nánpéngyou zěnmeyàng?

B: Tiānxià wūyā yìbān hēi, gēn shàng yígè yíyàng, yě hěn huāxīn. Nánrén méi yígè hǎodōngxi.

A: How is your new boyfriend?

B: They're all the same; this one's the same as the last, unfaithful. Men have no redeeming qualities.

Usage: Used singly.

Note: Slightly derogatory in meaning.

134. 不到黄河心不死 (不到黄河心不死)
bú dào Huáng Hé xīn bù sǐ

Translated character by character, 不到黄河心不死 means 'not-arrive-Yellow-River-heart-not-die,' whereas the implied meaning of this proverb would be 'to not give up until one is unable to continue.' Its functional translation is 'it's not over 'til it's over.'

Example 1:

A: 我向你保证那个城市一点儿也不好玩儿。

B: 我听别人说过还不错，所以我想去看看。

A: 你呀，**不到黄河心不死**。后悔以后别跟我说。

A: Wǒ xiàng nǐ bǎozhèng nàgè chéngshì yìdiǎnr yě bù hǎowánr.

B: Wǒ tīng biérén shuōguò hái búcuò, suǒyǐ wǒ xiǎng qù kànkàn.

A: Nǐ ya, bú dào Huáng Hé xīn bù sǐ. Hòuhuǐ yǐhòu bié gēn wǒ shuō.

A: I guarantee you that city isn't any fun at all.

B: I've heard from other people that it's pretty nice, so I want to go see it.

A: With you, it's never over 'til it's over. Don't come whining to me when you regret it.

Example 2:

A: 他虽然笨点儿，但是有股**不到黄河心不死**的劲儿，以后应该会有些出息的。

A: Tā suīrán bèn diǎnr, dànshì yǒu gǔ bú dào Huáng Hé xīn bù sǐ de jìnr, yǐhòu yīnggāi huì yǒuxiē chūxi de.

A: He might be a little dumb, but he has that 'it's not over 'til it's over' spirit. He should have some success.

Usage: Functions mainly as attributive or predicate.

Variant: 不到黄河不死心

Note: Neutral in meaning.

135. 狗急了跳墙 (狗急了跳墙) *gǒu jí le tiào qiáng*

Translated character by character, 狗急了跳墙 means 'dog-desperate-ed-jump-wall,' whereas the implied meaning of this proverb would be 'a desperate person is capable of anything.' Its functional translation is 'despair gives courage even to a coward.'

Example 1:

A: 我们不能逼得太急了。
B: 小心他**狗急了跳墙**。

A: Wǒmen bùnéng bī de tài jí le.
B: Xiǎoxīn tā gǒu jíle tiào qiáng.

A: We can't push too hard.
A: Be careful; despair gives courage even to a coward.

Example 2:

A: 他已经黔驴技穷了，我们可以好好收拾收拾他了。
B: 得防止他**狗急跳墙**，这个家伙什么事都做得出来。

A: Tā yǐjīng Qiánlú-jìqióng le, wǒmen kěyǐ hǎohāo shōushi shōushi tā le.
B: Děi fángzhǐ tā gǒu jí tiào qiáng, zhègè jiāhuo shénme shì dōu zuò de chūlai.

A: They're already on their last legs; now we can take care of them.
B: You need to keep him from deriving courage from despair. This guy is capable of anything.

Usage: Functions as predicate.

Variant: 狗急跳墙

Note: Slightly derogatory and humorous in meaning.

136. 狗眼看人低 (狗眼看人低) *gǒu yǎn kàn rén dī*

Translated character by character, 狗眼看人低 means 'dog-eye-look-people-down,' whereas the implied meaning of this proverb would be 'to be snobbish.' Its functional translation is 'to have one's nose in the air,' or 'to be stuck-up.'

Example 1:

A: 他对办公室的秘书、清洁工、门卫等从来都是高高在上的样子。

B: **狗眼看人低**，希望他别忘了他自己以前不过是个货车司机。

A: Tā duì bàngōngshì de mìshū, qīngjiégōng, ménwèi děng cónglái dōu shì gāogāo-zàishàng de yàngzi.

B: Gǒu yǎn kàn rén dī, xīwàng tā bié wàngle tā zìjǐ yǐqián búguò shì gè huòchē sījī.

A: He seems to always act aloof towards the secretary, janitor, security guard, etc. in the office.

B: He's stuck-up. I hope he doesn't forget that he was once merely a truck driver.

Example 2:

A: 你刚退休，他跟你说话怎么就这个味儿了？

B: 这家伙**狗眼看人低**。我没退休以前他在我面前跟狗似的。

A: Nǐ gāng tuìxiū, tā gēn nǐ shuōhuà zěnme jiù zhège wèir le?

B: Zhè jiāhuo gǒu yǎn kàn rén dī. Wǒ méi tuìxiū yǐqián tā zài wǒ miànqián gēn gǒu shìde.

A: You just retired. How could he talk to you like that?

B: That guy's got his nose in the air. But, before I retired, he was sycophantic towards me.

Usage: Used singly.

Note: Derogatory in meaning.

---

137. 只许州官放火，不许百姓点灯
（只許州官放火，不許百姓點燈）
zhǐ xǔ zhōu guān fàng huǒ, bù xǔ bǎixìng diǎn dēng

Translated character by character, 只许州官放火，不许百姓点灯 means 'only-allow-prefecture-official-set-fire, not-allow-common-people-light-lamp,' whereas the implied meaning of this proverb would be 'those in power may do as they desire while common people are restricted.' Its functional translation is 'one man may steal a horse while another may not look over a hedge.'

Example 1:

A: 我听说你停车又挨罚了。

B: 我就在商店门口停了两分钟，进去买了一瓶矿泉水，警察就给了二百块钱的罚单。他们的警车不执行公务的时候也是随便停车，怎么不给他们自己罚单。这是什么世道？**只许州官放火，不许百姓点灯**，让小老百姓怎么活啊？

A: Wǒ tīngshuō nǐ tíngchē yòu āi fá le.

B: Wǒ jiù zài shāngdiàn ménkǒu tíngle liǎng fēnzhōng, jìnqù mǎile yì píng kuàngquánshuǐ, jǐngchá jiù gěile èrbǎi kuài qián de fádān. Tāmen de jǐngchē bù zhíxíng gōngwù de shíhòu yě shì suíbiàn tíngchē, zěnme bù gěi tāmen zìjǐ fádān. Zhè shì shénme shìdao? Zhǐ xǔ zhōuguān fàng huǒ, bùxǔ bǎixìng diǎn dēng, ràng xiǎolǎobǎixìng zěnme huó a?

A: I heard you got another parking fine.

B: I parked in front of the store for two minutes and went in to buy a bottle of water, and the policeman gave me a $200 ticket. When they aren't on duty they park their cop cars wherever they please; why don't they give themselves tickets? What a society we live in! One man may steal a horse while another may not look over a hedge. How can common people get by?

Example 2:

A: 美国总是指责别的国家侵犯人权，而对自己国内的问题视而不见，也不允许其他的国家批评她，只许她自己放火，不许别的国家点灯。

A: Měiguó zǒngshì zhǐzé biéde guójiā qīnfàn rénquán, ér duì zìjǐ guónèi de wèntí shì'érbújiàn, yě bù yǔnxǔ qítā de guójiā pīpíng tā, zhǐ xǔ tā zìjǐ fàng huǒ, bù xǔ biéde guójiā diǎn dēng.

A: America always points out when other countries violate human rights, but turns a blind eye to domestic issues and doesn't allow other countries to criticize it. One man may steal a horse while another may not look over a hedge.

Usage: Used singly.

Note: Slightly derogatory and humorous in meaning.

---

138. 偷鸡摸狗 (偷雞摸狗) tōu jī mō gǒu

Translated character by character, 偷鸡摸狗 means 'steal-chicken-pilfer-dog,' whereas the implied meaning of this proverb would be 'to philander,' or 'to pilfer.'

Example 1:

A: 他初中没毕业就不上学了，也没有工作，人品又不好，常干些**偷鸡摸狗**的事。

A: Tā chūzhōng méi bìyè jiù bú shàngxué le, yě méiyǒu gōngzuò, rénpǐn yòu bùhǎo, cháng gàn xiē tōujī-mōgǒu de shì.

A: When he didn't graduate from junior high, he stopped going to school, and he doesn't have a job either. He's not a good person. He often philanders around.

Example 2:

A: 他都一大把岁数了，还干**偷鸡摸狗**的勾当，专门骗没有社会经验的小姑娘。

A: Tā dōu yí dà bǎ suìshù le, hái gàn **tōujī-mōgǒu** de gòudang, zhuānmén piàn méiyǒu shèhuì jīngyàn de xiǎo gūniang.

A: He's good and old already, but he's still involved in con jobs. He specifically cons young women with no street smarts.

Usage: Functions as attributive or predicate.

Note: Derogatory in meaning.

---

139. 死马当活马医 (死馬當活馬醫) *sǐ mǎ dāng huó mǎ yī*

Translated character by character, 死马当活马医 means 'dead-horse-as-alive-horse-cure,' whereas the implied meaning of this proverb would be 'to make a last attempt to save a hopeless situation.' Its functional translation is 'to make a Hail Mary effort.'

Example 1:

A: 现在咱们单位问题这么大，他来当一把手能行吗？

B: 我看也够呛，不过**死马当活马医**，说实话神仙也救不了我们。

A: Xiànzài zánmen dānwèi wèntí zhème dà, tā lái dāng yìbǎshǒu néng xíng ma?

B: Wǒ kàn yě gòuqiàng, búguò **sǐ mǎ dāng huó mǎ yī**, shuō shíhuà shénxiān yě jiù búliǎo wǒmen.

A: Our work unit's problems are so huge. Is he capable of being the boss?

B: I looked long and hard, but it's a Hail Mary pass. To be honest, not even an immortal could save us.

Example 2:

A: 股市这么低迷，这项宏观经济政策能起作用吗？

B: **死马当活马医**吧，有好办法的话绝不会用现在的办法。

A: Gǔshì zhème dīmí, zhè xiàng hóngguān jīngjì zhèngcè néng qǐ zuòyòng ma?

B: **Sǐ mǎ dāng huó mǎ yī** ba, yǒu hǎo bànfǎ de huà jué búhuì yòng xiànzài de bànfǎ.

A: With the stock market so depressed, can this macroeconomic policy be effective?

B: It's a Hail Mary effort. If there were a good solution, we absolutely wouldn't be pursuing this policy.

Usage: Used singly or functions as predicate.

Note: Neutral in meaning.

140. 新官上任三把火 (新官上任三把火)
xīn guān shàng rèn sān bǎ huǒ

Translated character by character, 新官上任三把火 means 'new-official-take-office-three-MW-fire,' whereas the implied meaning of this proverb would be 'to make drastic changes to an organization upon taking charge.'

Example 1:

A: 王市长**新官上任三把火**，第一把火就把市政府工作人员裁员百分之二十。

A: Wáng shìzhǎng xīn guān shàngrèn sān bǎ huǒ, dì-yī bǎ huǒ jiù bǎ shìzhèngfǔ gōngzuò rényuán cáiyuán bǎi fēn zhī èrshí.

A: Mayor Wang made drastic changes when he took office. The first thing he did was lay off 20 percent of municipal government employees.

Example 2:

A: 报纸主编**新官上任三把火**，增加了地方版块的内容，增加了社论，也增加了广告。结果在很短时间内把一份死气沉沉的报纸办得有声有色。

A: Bàozhǐ zhǔbiān xīn guān shàngrèn sān bǎ huǒ, zēngjiā le dìfang bǎnkuài de nèiróng, zēngjiā le shèlùn, yě zēngjiā le guǎnggào. Jiéguǒ zài hěn duǎn shíjiān nèi bǎ yí fèn sǐqìchénchén de bàozhǐ bàn de yǒushēng-yǒusè.

A: The new editor in chief made drastic changes when he took charge. He added to the local news section, increased editorials, and increased ads. As a result, in a very short time, he revived a lifeless paper.

Usage: Functions as predicate or used singly.

Note: Neutral or humorous in meaning.

141. 对号入座 (對號入座) duì hào rù zuò

Translated character by character, 对号入座 means 'according-number-enter-seat,' whereas the implied meaning of this proverb would be 'to make a connection.'

Example 1:

A: 你什么意思？

B: 唉，我是讲笑话，你别**对号入座**啊？

A: Nǐ shénme yìsī?

B: Èi, wǒ shì jiǎng xiàohuà, nǐ bié duìhào rùzuò a?

A: What do you mean?
B: Huh? I'm joking. Don't read into it.

Example 2:

A: 你怎么看出来这部话剧讽刺的是哪些人？
B: 你听话剧里的主人公的姓名是不是有些奇怪？你只要根据谐音，就**可以对号入座**了。

A: Nǐ zěnme kàn chūlái zhè bù huàjù fěngcì de shì nǎxiē rén?
B: Nǐ tīng huàjù lǐ de zhǔréngōng de xìngmíng shì búshì yǒuxiē qíguài? Nǐ zhǐyào gēnjù xiéyīn, jiù kěyǐ duìhào rùzuò le.

A: How can you tell that this play is satirizing them?
B: Doesn't the protagonist's name sound a little odd? If you change the pronunciation, everything will fall into place.

Usage: Functions as predicate.

Note: Neutral in meaning. In order to prevent lawsuits, the opening credits of movies and TV shows often say: This story is purely fictional, please don't 对号入座.

142. 十万八千里 (十萬八千里) shí wàn bā qiān lǐ

Translated character by character, 十万八千里 means 'ten-ten thousand-eight-thousand-miles,' whereas the implied meaning of this proverb would be 'to have a long way to go.' Its functional translation is 'worlds apart.'

Example 1:

A: 他就是当代的孔圣人！
B: 你别忽悠了，他跟孔夫子相差何止**十万八千里**！

A: Tā jiù shì dāngdài de Kǒng shèngrén!
B: Nǐ bié hūyōu le, tā gēn Kǒngfūzǐ xiāngchà hézhǐ shí wàn bā qiān lǐ!

A: He is a modern Confucius!
B: Don't jerk me around. He and Confucius are worlds apart!

Example 2:

A: 她理想的世界与现实简直相差**十万八千里**。这让她难以接受。

A: Tā lǐxiǎng de shìjiè yǔ xiànshí jiǎnzhí xiāngchà shí wàn bā qiān lǐ. Zhè ràng tā nányǐ jiēshòu.

A: Her ideal world is truly worlds apart from the reality. It's hard for her to accept.

Usage: Functions as object.

Note: Neutral in meaning.

143. 露马脚 (露馬腳) lòu mǎ jiǎo

Translated character by character, 露马脚 means 'expose-horse-foot,' whereas the implied meaning of this proverb would be 'to accidentally reveal information about one's wrongdoing.' Its functional translation is 'to let the cat out of the bag.'

Example 1:

A: 这个坏蛋太狡猾了，让人抓不到他的一点把柄。

B: 别着急，即使他再狡猾，总有一天也会**露出马脚**的。

A: Zhège huàidàn tài jiǎohuá le, ràng rén zhuābúdào tā de yì diǎn bǎbǐng.

B: Bié zháojí, jíshǐ tā zài jiǎohuá, zǒngyǒuyìtiān yě huì lòu chū mǎjiǎo de.

A: This scoundrel's too cunning. He makes it hard to get a handle on him.

B: Don't worry. No matter how cunning he is, there will be a day when he'll let the cat out of the bag.

Example 2:

A: 你怎么知道他在撒谎？

B: 他前面说的谎话还能自圆其说，可是后来说那天路很黑，没有月亮，所以他迷路了。这句话**露**了**马脚**，因为那天晚上的月亮又大又圆。

A: Nǐ zěnme zhīdao tā zài sāhuǎng?

B: Tā qiánmiàn shuō de huǎnghuà hái néng zìyuán-qíshuō, kěshì hòulái shuō nà tiān lù hěn hēi, méi yǒu yuèliang, suǒyǐ tā mílù le. Zhè jù huà lòule mǎjiǎo, yīnwèi nà tiān wǎnshang de yuèliang yòu dà yòu yuán.

A: How did you know he was lying?

B: He could explain away the first lie he told but, after that, he said that since the road was dark and there was no moonlight, he got lost. With that sentence, he let the cat out of the bag, because there was a full moon that night.

Usage: Functions as predicate.

Variant: 露出马脚

Note: Slightly derogatory in meaning. Folk legend holds that the wife of Zhu Yuanzhang, the founding emperor of the Ming Dynasty, had large feet and the surname Ma. At a time when female children in wealthy families would have their feet bound, this fact revealed that she had come from a poor family. This is how the proverb 露马脚 was born.

144. 公说公有理，婆说婆有理 (公說公有理，婆說婆有理) gōng shuō gōng yǒu lǐ, pó shuō pó yǒu lǐ

Translated character by character, 公说公有理，婆说婆有理 means 'grandpa-say-grandpa-reasonable, grandma-say-grandma-reasonable,' whereas the implied meaning of this proverb would be 'each side believes it is correct,' or 'both sides have their merits.'

Example 1:

A: 有人说加税能促进经济发展，而也有人说减税能促进经济发展，双方都有例证，对这个问题，真是**公说公有理，婆说婆有理**。

A: Yǒurén shuō jiāshuì néng cùjìn jīngjì fāzhǎn, ér yě yǒurén shuō jiǎnshuì néng cùjìn jīngjì fāzhǎn, shuāngfāng dōu yǒu lìzhèng, duì zhège wèntí, zhēn shì gōng shuō gōng yǒulǐ, pó shuō pó yǒulǐ.

A: Some people say increasing taxes can promote economic development, but other people say cutting taxes can promote economic development. Both sides have evidence, but, on this issue, both sides have their merits.

Example 2:

A: 两口子吵架，**公说公有理，婆说婆有理**，外人根本判断不出到底谁有理。

A: Liǎngkǒuzi chǎojià, gōng shuō gōng yǒulǐ, pó shuō pó yǒulǐ, wàirén gēnběn pànduàn bù chū dàodǐ shéi yǒulǐ.

A: When the couple was fighting, each believed they were right. The onlookers really couldn't decide who was, in fact, correct.

Usage: Functions mainly as predicate.

Note: Neutral in meaning.

145. 上刀山，下火海 (上刀山，下火海) shàng dāo shān, xià huǒ hǎi

Translated character by character, 上刀山，下火海 means 'climb-knife-mountain, go into-fire-sea,' whereas the implied meaning of this proverb would be 'no matter the inconvenience or danger.' Its functional translation is 'come hell or high water.'

Example 1:

A: 这件事就拜托你了。

B: 哪儿的话！别说这点儿事，就是**上刀山，下火海**我也去办。

A: 好，真是好哥们儿。

A: Zhè jiàn shì jiù bàituō nǐ le.
B: Nǎr de huà! Bié shuō zhè diǎnr shì, jiùshì shàng dāo shān, xià huǒ hǎi wǒ yě qù bàn.
A: Hǎo, zhēn shì hǎo gēmenr.

A: I beg you this one thing.
B: Don't say that! Even for something bigger, I'd take care of it for you, come hell or high water.
A: Good. You're really a good guy.

Example 2:

A: 他有一种不怕死的劲头儿，所以**上刀山，下火海**，什么事都敢干。

A: Tā yǒu yìzhǒng bú pà sǐ de jìntóur, suǒyǐ shàng dāo shān, xià huǒ hǎi, shénme shì dōu gǎn gàn.

A: He's fearless so, come hell or high water, he'll do anything.

Usage: Functions as predicate.

Note: Neutral in meaning.

146. 打退堂鼓 (打退堂鼓) dǎ tuì táng gǔ

Translated character by character, 打退堂鼓 means 'beat-retreat-hall-drum,' whereas the implied meaning of this proverb would be 'to withdraw from an endeavor.' Its functional translation is 'to beat a retreat.'

Example 1:

A: 我看，这事咱们往后放一放吧？
B: 怎么，你想**打退堂鼓**了？

A: Wǒ kàn, zhè shì zánmen wǎnghòu fàng yí fàng ba?
B: Zěnme, nǐ xiǎng dǎ tuìtánggǔ le?

A: I think we should push this issue back.
B: What? You want to beat a retreat?

Example 2:

A: 在她最艰难的时刻曾经想过**打退堂鼓**；不过，后来咬牙坚持了下来。

A: Zài tā zuì jiānnán de shíkè céngjīng xiǎngguò dǎ tuìtánggǔ; búguò, hòulái yǎoyá jiānchí le xiàlái.

A: In her darkest moment, she once considered beating a retreat, but then, she gritted her teeth and trudged on.

Usage: Functions as predicate.

Note: Neutral in meaning.

147. 磨刀不误砍柴工 (磨刀不誤砍柴工)
mó dāo bú wù kǎn chái gōng

Translated character by character, 磨刀不误砍柴工 means 'sharpen-knife-not-delay-cut-firewood-work,' whereas the implied meaning of this proverb would be 'preparing fully and properly will speed the task at hand.' Its functional translation is 'a beard well lathered is half shaved.'

Example 1:

A: 我的羽毛球水平怎么提高得这么慢？

B: 我观察你的步法有问题。你还是先把步法练习好吧。**磨刀不误砍柴工**。如果步法有问题，很难提高水平。

A: Wǒde yǔmáoqiú shuǐpíng zěnme tígāo de zhème màn?

B: Wǒ guānchá nǐde bùfǎ yǒu wèntí. Nǐ háishì xiān bǎ bùfǎ liànxí hǎo ba. Mó dāo bú wù kǎn chái gōng. Rúguǒ bùfǎ yǒu wèntí, hěn nán tígāo shuǐpíng.

A: How is my badminton game improving so slowly?

B: I see your footwork is bad. You should practice your footwork first. A beard well lathered is half shaved. If your footwork is bad, it's difficult to improve your game.

Example 2:

A: 公司对新员工的培训是绝对必要的，因为**磨刀不误砍柴工**。培训能使员工在以后减少错误。

A: Gōngsī duì xīn yuángōng de péixùn shì juéduì bìyào de, yīnwèi mó dāo bú wù kǎn chái gōng. Péixùn néng shǐ yuángōng zài yǐhòu jiǎnshǎo cuòwù.

A: The company's training of new employees is absolutely necessary, because a beard well lathered is half shaved. Training can reduce the number of mistakes employees make in the future.

Usage: Used mainly singly.

Note: Complimentary in meaning.

148. 风马牛不相及 (風馬牛不相及) fēng mǎ niú bù xiāng jí

Translated character by character, 风马牛不相及 means 'wind-horse-ox-not-mutual-relate,' whereas the implied meaning of this proverb would be 'to be utterly unrelated.' Its functional translation is 'to be as different as chalk and cheese' or 'as different as night and day.'

Example 1:

A: 今天讲座的题目是 "孔子弹琴与梵高画画"，你要去听吗？

B: 我不去，这两件事之间有什么联系？简直**风马牛不相及**。

A: Jīntiān jiǎngzuò de tímù shì "Kǒng zǐ tánqín yǔ Fàngāo huà huà", nǐ yào qù tīng ma?

B: Wǒ bú qù, zhè liǎng jiàn shì zhījiān yǒu shénme liánxì? Jiǎn zhí fēng mǎ niú bù xiāng jí.

A: The topic of today's lecture is "Confucius playing the zither and Van Gogh painting." Do you want to go?

B: No. What do those things have in common? They're really as different as chalk and cheese.

Example 2:

A: 他想象力很丰富。

B: 怎么丰富？

A: 把**风马牛不相及**的博弈论引入了经济学，开创了一门新学科。

A: Tā xiǎngxiànglì hěn fēngfù.

B: Zěnme fēngfù?

A: Bǎ fēng mǎ niú bù xiāng jí de bóyìlùn yǐnrù le jīngjìxué, kāichuàng le yì mén xīn xuékē.

A: His imagination is very active.

B: How so?

A: He incorporated the completely unrelated discipline of game theory into economics, creating a new field.

Usage: Functions as predicate or attributive.

Note: Slightly derogatory and humorous in meaning.

149. 一山不容二虎 (一山不容二虎) yī shān bù róng èr hǔ

Translated character by character, 一山不容二虎 means 'one-mountain-not-accommodate-two-tigers,' whereas the implied meaning of this proverb would be 'two tigers cannot share one mountain.'

Example 1:

A: 科比和奥尼尔怎么只赢了三个总冠军？
B: 两个人都是顶尖球星，但是**一山不容二虎**，在湖人队，两个人都想当独一无二的老大，所以最后几年两个人不和。

A: Kēbǐ hé Àoní'ěr zěnme zhǐ yíngle sān gè zǒngguànjūn?
B: Liǎng gè rén dōu shì dǐngjiān qiúxīng, dànshì yī shān bù róng èr hǔ, zài Húrén duì, liǎng gè rén dōu xiǎng dāng dúyī-wú'èr de lǎodà, suǒyǐ zuìhòu jǐ nián liǎng gè rén bùhé.

A: How have Kobe and Shaq only won three championships?
B: Both are top-notch players, but two tigers cannot share one mountain. On the Lakers, they both want to be top dog, so in the last few years, they haven't gelled.

Example 2:

A: 这个公司以后麻烦大了。
B: 怎么讲？
A: 首席执行官与董事长对企业的发展战略观点不同，**一山不容二虎**，以后肯定会出乱子。

A: Zhège gōngsī yǐhòu máfan dà le.
B: Zěnme jiǎng?
A: Shǒuxí zhíxíngguān yǔ dǒngshìzhǎng duì qǐyè de fāzhǎn zhànluè guāndiǎn bùtóng, yī shān bù róng èr hǔ, yǐhòu kěndìng huì chū luànzi.

A: This company is going to have a lot of trouble later on.
B: What do you mean?
A: The CEO and the chairman of the board have different views regarding the company's development strategy. Two tigers cannot share one mountain; in the future, it'll definitely come to a head.

Usage: Used singly.

Variant: 一山容不下二虎

Note: Neutral in meaning.

150. 眼里揉不得沙子 (眼裏揉不得沙子)
yǎn lǐ róu bù de shāzi

Translated character by character, 眼里揉不得沙子 means 'eye-in-rob-not-bearable-sand,' whereas the implied meaning of this proverb would be 'one doesn't want to allow small mistakes or slights to pass.' Its functional translation is 'to not let things slide.'

Example 1:

A: 新老板来了，怎么大家都这么努力？

B: 你没看出来吗？新老板是个**眼里揉不得沙子**的人，老实点儿吧。

A: Xīn lǎobǎn lái le, zěnme dàjiā dōu zhème nǔlì?

B: Nǐ méi kàn chūlái ma? Xīn lǎobǎn shì gè yǎn lǐ róu bù de shāzi de rén, lǎoshí diǎnr ba.

A: Why is everyone so diligent since the new boss got here?

B: Can't you see? The new boss isn't one to let things slide. You should be a little better behaved.

Example 2:

A: 她喜欢争强好胜，**眼里揉不进一粒沙子**，不想吃一点儿亏，因此常跟别人吵架。

A: Tā xǐhuan zhēngqiáng-hǎoshèng, yǎn lǐ róu bú jìn yí lì shāzi, bù xiǎng chī yìdiǎnr kuī, yīncǐ cháng gēn biérén chǎojià.

A: She likes to excel over others, she can't let things slide, and doesn't like to lose, so she often fights with others.

Usage: Functions as predicate or attributive.

Variant: 眼里容不得沙子

Note: Neutral in meaning.

---

151. 三下五除二 (三下五除二) sān xià wǔ chú èr

Translated character by character, 三下五除二 means '(add) three-get-five-(but) take off-two,' whereas the implied meaning of this proverb would be 'in no time (flat),' or 'deftly.'

Example 1:

A: 他三**下五**除二就把一个大西瓜切成了32块。

A: Tā sān xià wǔ chú èr jiù bǎ yígè dà xīgua qiē chéng le 32 kuài.

A: He cut a watermelon into 32 pieces in no time flat.

Example 2:

A: 我的汽车不能启动了，我以为出了大问题，没想到我的朋友三**下五除**二就把汽车修好了，前后不超过十五分钟。

A: Wǒde qìchē bùnéng qǐdòng le, wǒ yǐwéi chūle dà wèntí, méi xiǎng dào wǒde péngyou sān xià wǔ chú èr jiù bǎ qìchē xiūhǎo le, qiánhòu bú chāoguò shíwǔ fēnzhōng.

A: My car wouldn't start, so I thought there was a big problem. I wouldn't have thought that my friend could repair it in no time, taking less than fifteen minutes.

Usage: Functions as adverbial.

Note: Neutral in meaning.

152.   泼冷水 (潑冷水) pō lěng shuǐ

Translated character by character, 泼冷水 means 'pour-cold-water,' whereas the implied meaning of this proverb would be 'to be discouraging or negative about someone's ideas or hopes.' Its functional translation is 'to pour cold water on.'

Example 1:

A: 这个年青人太不实际了。
B: 不过我们也要从另一个角度看，那就是有热情，所以我们不能总 **泼冷水**，还要适当鼓励。

A: Zhège niánqīngrén tài bù shíjì le.
B: Búguò wǒmen yě yào cóng lìngyígè jiǎodù kàn, nà jiù shì yǒu rèqíng, suǒyǐ wǒmen bùnéng zǒng pōlěngshuǐ, hái yào shìdāng gǔlì.

A: This young person is so unrealistic.
B: But we also have to look at it from another vantage point. That's just enthusiasm, so we can't always pour cold water on his ideas; we have to encourage him appropriately.

Example 2:

A: 在年终大会上，公司领导层给员工**泼了一盆冷水**，说明年不再涨工资，并且裁员百分之三十。

A: Zài niánzhōng dàhuì shàng, gōngsī lǐngdǎo céng gěi yuángōng pōle yì pén lěngshuǐ, shuō míngnián búzài zhǎng gōngzī, bìngqiě cáiyuán bǎi fēn zhī sānshí.

A: At the annual meeting, the company's management poured cold water on the employees' hopes, saying salaries wouldn't be increased next year and 30 percent of the employees would be laid off.

Usage: Functions as predicate.

Note: Derogatory in meaning.

153. 杀鸡给猴看 (殺雞給猴看) shā jī gěi hóu kàn

Translated character by character, 杀鸡给猴看 means 'kill-chicken-for-monkey-see,' whereas the implied meaning of this proverb would be 'to punish someone in order to ensure the obedience of others.' Its functional translation is 'to throw the book at someone to set an example.'

Example 1:

A: 学校为什么这么严厉地处罚了那个作弊的学生？

B: 学校**杀鸡给猴看**，现在学生的学习风气太差了，尤其是考试风气。

A: Xuéxiào wèishénme zhème yánlì de chǔfále nàge zuòbì de xuésheng?

B: Xuéxiào shā jī gěi hóu kàn, xiànzài xuésheng de xuéxí fēngqì tài chà le, yóuqí shì kǎoshì fēngqì.

A: Why did the school punish the student who cheated so severely?

B: The school was throwing the book at him to set an example. Students' study habits are so bad, particularly with regards to test-taking.

Example 2:

A: 新市长上任以后不久，就找个借口把公安局长撤职了。公安局长的资历可老了。

B: 这是**杀鸡给猴看**，是在树立威信，别人不听话就得落相同的下场。

A: Xīn shìzhǎng shàngrèn yǐhòu bùjiǔ, jiù zhǎo gè jièkǒu bǎ gōng'ān júzhǎng chèzhí le. Gōng'ān júzhǎng de zīlì kě lǎo le.

B: Zhè shì shā jī gěi hóu kàn, shì zài shùlì wēixìn, biéren bù tīnghuà jiù děi luò xiāngtóng de xiàchǎng.

A: Soon after the new mayor took office, he sought out an excuse to dismiss the police chief. The chief's record of service was quite long.

B: That's throwing the book at him to make an example. He's establishing a reputation for himself that those who don't obey him will suffer a similar fate.

Usage: Functions as predicate. '猴' is usually rendered '猴儿' in colloquial expression.

Note: Humorous or neutral in meaning.

154. 生米做成熟饭 (生米做成熟飯)
shēng mǐ zuò chéng shú fàn

Translated character by character, 生米做成熟饭 means 'raw-rice-made-into-cooked-rice,' whereas the implied meaning of this proverb would be 'something has already been done and cannot be undone.' Its functional translation is 'the die is cast,' or 'what's done is done.'

Example 1:

A: 这对年青人的父母本来反对他们的婚事，可是两个人已经怀孕，**生米做成了熟饭**，父母没有办法，只好答应让他们结婚。

A: Zhè duì niánqīngrén de fùmǔ běnlái fǎnduì tāmen de hūnshì, kěshì liǎng gè rén yǐjīng huáiyùn, shēng mǐ zuò chéng le shú fàn, fùmǔ méiyǒu bànfǎ, zhǐhǎo dāyìng ràng tāmen jiéhūn.

A: This young couple's parents initially opposed their marriage, but they've already conceived a child. The die is cast. Their parents don't have any choice. They should say that they'll allow them to get married.

Example 2:

A: 要是上头反对怎么办？
B: 我们把事情先做了，**生米做成熟饭**，上头虽然不高兴，最多不过批评几句罢了。

A: Yàoshì shàngtou fǎnduì zěnme bàn?
B: Wǒmen bǎ shìqíng xiān zuò le, shēng mǐ zuò chéng shú fàn, shàngtou suīrán bù gāoxìng, zuìduō búguò pīpíng jǐ jù bà le.

A: And what if the higher-ups are opposed?
B: Let's get it done first. The die is cast. While the boss will be angry, at the most he'll criticize us a little and that's it.

Usage: Functions as predicate.

Variant: 生米煮成（了）熟饭

Note: Neutral or humorous in meaning. Often said in reference to two people consummating a relationship.

---

155. 初生牛犊不怕虎 (初生牛犢不怕虎)
chū shēng niú dú bú pà hǔ

Translated character by character, 初生牛犊不怕虎 means 'newly-born-calf-not-fear-tiger,' whereas the implied meaning of this proverb would be 'the young are not fearful.' Its functional translation is 'youth knows no fear.'

Example 1:

A: 我担心做不好。
B: 担心什么！你这么年青，得有一种**初生牛犊不怕虎**的精神。年青人犯错误是可以原谅的，但是不能原谅的是胆小怕事，缩手缩脚。

A: Wǒ dānxīn zuò bù hǎo.

B: Dānxīn shénme! Nǐ zhème niánqīng, děi yǒu yìzhǒng chū shēng niúdú bú pà hǔ de jīngshen. Niánqīngrén fàn cuòwù shì kěyǐ yuánliàng de, dànshì bùnéng yuánliàng de shì dǎnxiǎo pàshì, suōshǒu-suōjiǎo.

A: I'm afraid I won't be able to do well.

B: What're you afraid of! At this young age, you should have a 'youth knows no fear' mindset. If young people make mistakes, they can be forgiven; but what can't be forgiven is being timid and afraid to take on responsibilities, and shrinking from challenges.

Example 2:

A: 这个年轻选手**初生牛犊不怕虎**，面对世界排名第一的选手，打得很勇敢，很有自信。

A: Zhègè niánqīng xuǎnshǒu chū shēng niúdú bú pà hǔ, miànduì shìjiè páimíng dì-yī de xuǎnshǒu, dǎ de hěn yǒnggǎn, hěn yǒu zìxìn.

A: This young competitor knows no fear. When he faced the first-ranked competitor, he played with great courage and self-confidence.

Usage: Functions as predicate, or attributive of '精神', '劲儿', '劲头', or '勇气.' It can also be used singly.

Note: Humorous and complimentary in meaning.

156. 铁公鸡 (鐵公雞) tiě gōng jī

Translated character by character, 铁公鸡 means 'iron-rooster,' whereas the implied meaning of this proverb would be 'one who is stingy with money.' Its functional translation is 'miser,' or 'tightwad.'

Example 1:

A: 这次他捐了多少钱？

B: 一万块。

A: 他是亿万富翁，才捐了一万块，真是只**铁公鸡**。

A: Zhècì tā juānle duōshǎo qián?

B: Yí wàn kuài.

A: Tā shì yìwànfùwēng, cái juānle yí wàn kuài, zhēn shì zhī tiěgōngjī.

A: How much did he donate this time?

B: 10,000 RMB.

A: He's a multi-millionaire and he only donated 10,000 RMB? He really is a miser.

Example 2:

A: 他是**铁公鸡**，自己用过的旧东西包装一下就当礼物送给别人了。

A: Tā shì **tiěgōngjī**, zìjǐ yòngguò de jiù dōngxī bāozhuāng yíxià jiù dāng lǐwù sònggěi biérén le.

A: He's a tightwad. He wraps up things he's already used to serve as presents for others.

Usage: Functions as predicative.

Note: Slightly derogatory in meaning.

---

157. 无事不登三宝殿 (無事不登三寶殿)
wú shì bù dēng sān bǎo diàn

Translated character by character, 无事不登三宝殿 means 'no-issue-not-mount-three-treasure-temple,' whereas the implied meaning of this proverb would be 'one never visits unless they need something.'

Example 1:

A: （电话）老李，晚上有事吗？没事我过去跟你聊聊天儿。
B: 你是**无事不登三宝殿**，肯定有事找我。过来吧，我没事。

A: (diàn huà) Lǎo Lǐ, wǎnshang yǒu shì ma? Méi shì wǒ guòqù gēn nǐ liáoliáo tiānr.
B: Nǐ shì wú shì bù dēng sānbǎodiàn, kěndìng yǒu shì zhǎo wǒ. Guòlái ba, wǒ méi shì.

A: (On the phone) Old Li, are you up to anything tonight? If not, I'd like to come over and chat with you.
B: I only ever hear from you when you need help, so you definitely want something from me. Come on over. I'm free.

Example 2:

A: 大驾光临，欢迎欢迎。
B: 哪里哪里，我们是**无事不登三宝殿**，请您帮忙来了。

A: Dàjià guānglín, huānyíng huānyíng.
B: Nǎlǐ nǎlǐ, wǒmen shì wú shì bù dēng sānbǎodiàn, qǐng nín bāngmáng lái le.

A: We are honored by your presence. Welcome.
B: There's no need to stand on ceremony. We never visit unless we need something. We've come to ask you for help.

Usage: Functions as predicate or predicative.

Note: Neutral or humorous in meaning.

158. 马后炮 (馬後炮) mǎ hòu pào

Translated character by character, 马后炮 means '(of Chinese chess) horse-behind-cannon,' whereas the implied meaning of this proverb would be 'a belated action.' Its functional translation is 'to be wise after the fact.'

Example 1:

A: 我早就知道他们会分手，他们性格不合。

B: 你这不是**马后炮**嘛。以前你还说过他们俩挺般配的呢。

A: Wǒ zǎo jiù zhīdao tāmen huì fēnshǒu, tāmen xìnggé bùhé.

B: Nǐ zhè búshì mǎhòupào ma. Yǐqián nǐ hái shuōguo tāmen liǎ tǐng bānpèi de ne.

A: I knew long ago that they were going to break up. Their personalities didn't gel.

B: Aren't you being wise after the fact? You said before that they were a good match.

Example 2:

A: 你要是听了我的，买了这只股票，你就发了。

B: 你别给我**马后炮**了。我以前老听你的，吃的亏还少啊！

A: Nǐ yàoshi tīngle wǒde, mǎile zhè zhī gǔpiào, nǐ jiù fā le.

B: Nǐ bié gěi wǒ mǎhòupào le. Wǒ yǐqián lǎo tīng nǐde, chī de kuī hái shǎo a!

A: If you had listened to me and bought this stock, you would have been rich.

B: Don't be wise after the fact. I used to always listen to you and I lost a good deal of money.

Usage: Functions mainly as an object or predicate.

Note: Humorous and slightly derogatory in meaning. '马后炮' is a very formidable tactic in Chinese chess.

159. 掉链子 (掉鏈子) diào liànzi

Translated character by character, 掉链子 means 'slip off-(bike) chain,' whereas the implied meaning of this proverb would be 'to make a mistake at a crucial moment, resulting in the failure of a plan.' Its functional translation is 'to fumble the ball.'

Example 1:

A: 他是怎么搞的？怎么在法官面前结结巴巴？

B: 是啊，平时能说会道的，关键时候**掉链子**。

A: Tā shì zěnme gǎo de? Zěnme zài fǎguān miànqián jiējiebābā?

B: Shì a, píngshí néngshuō-huìdào de, guānjiàn shíhou diàoliànzi.

A: What's up with him? How could he stammer in front of the judge?
B: Yeah, normally he's eloquent, but at the critical moment he fumbled the ball.

Example 2:

A: 第一次约会紧张不紧张？
B: 说实话，挺紧张的。
A: 紧张一点儿没关系，只要不**掉链子**就行。

A: Dì-yī cì yuēhuì jǐnzhāng bù jǐnzhāng?
B: Shuō shíhuà, tǐng jǐnzhāng de.
A: Jǐnzhāng yìdiǎnr méiguānxì, zhǐyào bú diàoliànzi jiù xíng.

A: Are you nervous on your first date?
B: Honestly, I'm pretty nervous.
A: It doesn't matter if you're a little nervous, so long as you don't fumble the ball it's all good.

Usage: Functions as predicate.

Note: Neutral or humorous in meaning.

160. 纸老虎 (紙老虎) zhǐ lǎohǔ

Translated character by character, 纸老虎 means 'paper-tiger.' Its functional translation, popularized through Mao Zedong's usage of the phrase, is 'paper tiger.'

Example 1:

A: 毛泽东说过美国是**纸老虎**。

A: Máo Zédōng shuōguò Měiguó shì zhǐlǎohǔ.

A: Mao Zedong said the US is a paper tiger.

Example 2:

A: 他看起来那么厉害！
B: 别害怕，他就是只**纸老虎**，没有真本事。

A: Tā kàn qǐlái nàme lìhai!
B: Bié hàipà, tā jiù shì zhī zhǐlǎohǔ, méiyǒu zhēn běnshì.

A: He looks so imposing!
B: Don't be afraid, he's just a paper tiger. He doesn't have any real ability.

Usage: Functions as object or predicative.

Note: Slightly derogatory in meaning.

161. 狐狸精 (狐狸精) húli jīng

Translated character by character, 狐狸精 means 'fox-demon,' whereas the implied meaning of this proverb would be 'a shrewd and enticing woman.' Its functional translation is 'a vixen,' or 'a siren.'

Example 1:

A: 你这个**狐狸精**，勾引别人老公，要脸不要脸？

B: 骂人有什么用？有本事管住你自己的老公啊！

A: Nǐ zhègè húlijīng, gōuyǐn biérén lǎogōng, yào liǎn bú yào liǎn?

B: Màrén yǒu shénme yòng? Yǒu běnshi guǎn zhù nǐ zìjǐ de lǎogōng a!

A: You vixen, seducing other people's husbands. Have you no honor?

B: What use is berating people? You should have the ability to control your own husband!

Example 2:

A: 那个女人是个**狐狸精**，你不要被她迷上啊！

A: Nàgè nǚrén shì gè húlijīng, nǐ búyào bèi tā mí shàng a!

A: That woman is a siren. Don't let her seduce you!

Usage: Functions as predicative.

Note: Derogatory in meaning.

162. 丑话说在前头 (醜話説在前頭)
chǒu huà shuō zài qiántou

Translated character by character, 丑话说在前头 means 'ugly-words-speak-at-outset,' whereas the implied meaning of this proverb would be 'let's get the unpleasant part/unpleasantness out of the way,' or 'let's be candid here.'

Example 1:

A: 我说话算数。

B: 咱们把**丑话说在前头**。如果你说话不算数，我们只好法庭上见。

A: Wǒ shuōhuà suànshù.

B: Zánmen bǎ chǒu huà shuō zài qiántou. Rúguǒ nǐ shuōhuà bú suànshù, wǒmen zhǐhǎo fǎtíng shàng jiàn.

A: I stand by my word.

B: Let's get the unpleasantness out of the way. If your word doesn't hold, I'll see you in court.

Example 2:

A: 这件事意义至关重大，拜托你们加把劲儿。不过，**丑话说在前头**，如果谁让我丢脸，我就让谁丢饭碗。

A: Zhè jiàn shì yìyì zhìguān zhòngdà, bàituō nǐmen jiā bǎ jìnr. Búguò, chǒu huà shuō zài qiántou, rúguǒ shéi ràng wǒ diūliǎn, wǒ jiù ràng shéi diū fànwǎn.

A: The implications of this affair are huge. I'm asking you to work a little harder. But, let's be candid here, if anyone makes me lose face, I'll make them unemployed.

Usage: Functions as predicate.

Variant: 把丑话说在前头

Note: Neutral in meaning.

---

163.   半路杀出个程咬金 (半路殺出個程咬金)
bàn lù shā chū gè Chéng Yǎojīn

Translated character by character, 半路杀出个程咬金 means 'half-way-jump-out-a-Cheng Yaojin,' whereas the implied meaning of this proverb would be 'an unexpected opponent appears halfway.' Its functional translation is 'someone threw a wrench in the works.'

Example 1:

A: 会议开得怎么样？

B: 本来都商量好了，都觉得肯定没有问题了。没想到**半路杀出个程咬金**，王副市长极力反对，最后没成功。

A: Huìyì kāi de zěnmeyàng?

B: Běnlái dōu shāngliang hǎo le, dōu juéde méi wèntí le. Méixiǎngdào bànlù shā chū gè Chéng Yǎojīn, Wáng fùshìzhǎng jílì fǎnduì, zuìhòu méi chénggōng.

A: How was the meeting?

B: Everything had been hammered out, everyone thought there definitely wouldn't be any more issues. We wouldn't have guessed that Mayor Wangfu would throw a wrench in the works by unexpectedly doing his utmost to oppose the proposal. In the end, the proposal didn't succeed.

Example 2:

A: 这次法国网球公开赛，大家都以为四大天王中的一人会得冠军，结果**半路杀出个程咬金**，一个排名很低的选手击败了四大天王中的三个并最终夺冠。

A: Zhècì Fǎguó Wǎngqiú Gōngkāisài, dàjiā dōu yǐwéi sìdàtiānwáng zhōng de yì rén huì dé guànjūn, jiéguǒ bànlù shā chū gè Chéng Yǎojīn, yígè páimíng hěn dī de xuǎnshǒu jī bài le sìdàtiānwáng zhōng de sān gè bìng zuìzhōng duóguàn.

A: In this year's French Open, everyone thought that one of the 'Four Emperors' would take the championship. However, in the end, a low-ranked contestant threw a wrench in the works and beat three of the 'Four Emperors' to win the championship.

Usage: Functions as predicate.

Note: Humorous or neutral in meaning. Cheng Yaojin (589–665) was a general in the period between the Sui and Tang Dynasties. He often ambushed his enemies on roads and, as such, this proverb was born.

---

164. 麻雀虽小，五脏俱全 (麻雀雖小，五臟俱全)
má què suī xiǎo, wǔ zàng jù quán

Translated character by character, 麻雀虽小，五脏俱全 means 'sparrow-although-small, five-organs-all-complete,' whereas the implied meaning of this proverb would be 'even if something is small, it can still contain the essentials.'

Example 1:

A: 游轮虽然不太大，但是上面什么都有，客房、商店、饭馆、赌场、邮局、电子游戏厅、自动取款机等，**麻雀虽小，五脏俱全**。

A: Yóulún suīrán bú tài dà, dànshì shàngmiàn shénme dōu yǒu, kèfáng, shāngdiàn, fànguǎn, dǔchǎng, yóujú, diànzǐ yóuxìtīng, zìdòng qǔkuǎnjī děng, máquè suī xiǎo, wǔzàng jùquán.

A: Although the cruise ship wasn't so big, it had everything on board, including guest rooms, stores, restaurants, a casino, a post office, an arcade, an ATM, etc. Even though it isn't big, it has everything one needs.

Example 2:

A: 从一个小城市的治理也能看出这个国家的治理方式，因为**麻雀虽小，五脏俱全**。

A: Cóng yígè xiǎo chéngshì de zhìlǐ yě néng kànchū zhègè guójiā de zhìlǐ fāngshì, yīnwèi máquè suī xiǎo, wǔzàng jùquán.

A: From a small city's governance, you can see the way this country is governed, because even small things have all of the essential parts.

Usage: Used singly.

Note: Neutral in meaning.

165. 虎毒不食子 (虎毒不食子) hǔ dú bù shí zǐ

Translated character by character, 虎毒不食子 means 'tiger-vicious-not-eat-cub,' whereas the implied meaning of this proverb would be 'even a monster would not hurt its own children.'

Example 1:

A: 没想到他这么没有人性！

B: **虎毒不食子**，他竟然把亲生孩子给害死了！

A: Méi xiǎng dào tā zhème méiyǒu rénxìng!

B: Hǔ dú bù shí zǐ, tā jìngrán bǎ qīnshēng háizi gěi hàisǐ le!

A: I wouldn't have thought he was this inhuman.

B: Even a monster would not hurt its own children. He even killed his own child.

Example 2:

A: **虎毒不食子**，她怎么能对孩子下毒手！

A: Hǔ dú bù shí zǐ, tā zěnme néng duì háizi xià dúshǒu!

A: Even a monster would not hurt its own children. How could she beat the life out of her child?

Usage: Used singly.

Variant: 虎毒不吃子

Note: Neutral in meaning.

166. 小不忍则乱大谋 (小不忍則亂大謀) xiǎo bù rěn zé luàn dà móu

Translated character by character, 小不忍则乱大谋 means 'trivial-not-restrain-therefore-spoil-great-plan,' whereas the implied meaning of this proverb would be 'not being able to accept imperfection in a small issue will ruin larger plans.' Its functional translation is 'a little impatience will spoil great plans.'

Example 1:

A: 气死我了，他们这样做太过分了。

B: 别激动，**小不忍则乱大谋**。这个账我们会算的。

A: Qì sǐ wǒ le, tāmen zhèyàng zuò tài guòfèn le.

B: Bié jīdòng, xiǎo bù rěn zé luàn dà móu. Zhège zhàng wǒmen huì suàn de.

A: I'm so angry. They've gone too far doing this.

B: Don't jump the gun. A little impatience will spoil great plans. We will settle this score.

Example 2:

A: 我们行动吧？

B: 再等等，**小不忍则乱大谋**。

A: Wǒmen xíngdòng ba?

B: Zài děngděng, xiǎo bù rěn zé luàn dà móu.

A: Should we do it?

B: Wait a little longer. A little impatience will spoil great plans.

Usage: Used singly.

Note: Neutral in meaning.

167. 打狗还得看主人 (打狗還得看主人)
dǎ gǒu hái děi kàn zhǔ rén

Translated character by character, 打狗还得看主人 means 'beat-dog-still-must-see-master,' whereas the implied meaning of this proverb would be 'when one beats a dog, one must answer to its master.' Its functional translation can also be 'every action has consequences.'

Example 1:

A: 姓王的，你儿子把我儿子打成这样，**打狗还得看主人**，你以为我是好欺负的。我跟你没完。

A: Xìng Wáng de, nǐ érzǐ bǎ wǒ érzǐ dǎ chéng zhèyàng, dǎ gǒu hái děi kàn zhǔrén, nǐ yǐwéi wǒ shì hǎo qīfù de. Wǒ gēn nǐ méi wán.

A: Wang, your son beat my son up like this. Every action has consequences. You thought I could be bullied, but I'm not done with you.

Example 2:

A: 这小子喝醉了酒把我们的饭馆都砸了，我们还不动手？

B: 算了，**打狗还得看主人**，他爸是公安局长。我们就算吃个哑巴亏吧。

A: Zhè xiǎozi hē zuì le jiǔ bǎ wǒmen de fànguǎn dōu zá le, wǒmen hái bú dòngshǒu?

B: Suàn le, dǎ gǒu hái děi kàn zhǔrén, tā bà shì gōng'ān júzhǎng. Wǒmen jiù suàn chī gè yǎba kuī ba.

A: This kid got drunk and destroyed our restaurant and we're not going to take action?

B: Forget about it. When one beats a dog, one must answer to its master. His father is the police chief. Let's just bite our tongues.

Usage: Used singly.

Variants: 打狗还要看主人; 打狗看主人

Note: Neutral or humorous in meaning.

168.   万事俱备，只欠东风 (萬事俱備，只欠東風)
wàn shì jù bèi, zhǐ qiàn dōng fēng

Translated character by character, 万事俱备，只欠东风 means 'ten thousand-things-all-complete, only-lack-east-wind,' whereas the implied meaning of this proverb would be 'to be prepared but lack the crucial element.'

Example 1:

A: 你们准备得怎么样了？

B: **万事俱备**，只欠东风，就差您一句话了。只要您发话，我们马上动手。

A: Nǐmen zhǔnbèi de zěnmeyàng le?

B: Wànshì jùbèi, zhǐ qiàn dōngfēng, jiù chà nín yí jù huà le. Zhǐyào nín fāhuà, wǒmen mǎshàng dòngshǒu.

A: How are your preparations?

B: We're just waiting for the go-ahead from you. Just say the word and we'll get started immediately.

Example 2:

A: 公司什么时候能上市？

B: 现在**万事俱备**，只欠东风了。只要相关的政府机构批准就可以上市了。

A: Gōngsī shénme shíhòu néng shàngshì?

B: Xiànzài wànshì jùbèi, zhǐ qiàn dōngfēng le. Zhǐyào xiāngguān de zhèngfǔ jīgòu pīzhǔn jiù kěyǐ shàngshì le.

A: When can the company IPO?

B: We're just waiting for the all-clear now. Once the relevant government bodies approve it, we can IPO.

Usage: Functions as predicate.

Note: Neutral in meaning.

169. 不管黑猫白猫，会捉老鼠就是好猫 (不管黑貓白貓，會捉老鼠就是好貓)

bù guǎn hēi māo bái māo, huì zhuō lǎoshǔ jiù shì hǎo māo

Translated character by character, 不管黑猫白猫，会捉老鼠就是好猫 means 'no-matter-black-cat-white-cat, can-catch-mouse-then-is-good-cat,' whereas the implied meaning of this proverb would be 'so long as something functions properly, its form is irrelevant.' Its functional translation, popularized through Deng Xiaoping's use of this proverb, is 'it does not matter whether a cat is black or white so long as it catches mice.'

Example 1:

A: 这个办法是不是有些不太体面？

B: 管它呢，**不管黑猫白猫，会捉老鼠就是好猫**。再说，我们又没犯法。

A: Zhège bànfǎ shìbúshì yǒuxiē bú tài tǐmiàn?

B: Guǎn tā ne, bùguǎn hēi māo bái māo, huì zhuō lǎoshǔ jiùshì hǎo māo. Zàishuō, wǒmen yòu méi fànfǎ.

A: Is this solution a little too undignified?

B: Don't worry about it! It doesn't matter whether a cat is black or white so long as it catches mice. Moreover, we're not breaking the law.

Example 2:

A: 他是保守党的候选人，你还要选他吗？

B: **不管黑猫白猫，会捉老鼠就是好猫**。只要他能解决英国的经济问题，我就选他。

A: Tā shì bǎoshǒudǎng de hòu xuǎnrén, nǐ háiyào xuǎn tā ma?

B: Bùguǎn hēi māo bái māo, huì zhuō lǎoshǔ jiùshì hǎo māo. Zhǐyào tā néng jiějué Yīngguó de jīngjì wèntí, wǒ jiù xuǎn tā.

A: He's the Conservative Party candidate. Do you still want to vote for him?

B: It doesn't matter whether a cat is black or white so long as it catches mice. So long as he can solve Britain's economic problems, I'll vote for him.

Usage: Used singly.

Note: Humorous in meaning. This proverb is drawn from the Sichuan dialect. It won widespread popularity due to the Sichuan-born Chinese leader Deng Xiaoping's (1904–1997) high-profile invocation of the proverb in defense of economic liberalization.

170. 真金不怕火炼 (真金不怕火煉) zhēn jīn bú pà huǒ liàn

Translated character by character, 真金不怕火炼 means 'genuine-gold-not-fear-fire-temper,' whereas the implied meaning of this proverb would be 'a genuine talent fears not challenges or slander.' Its functional translation is 'true blue will never stain.'

Example 1:

A: 原来有人怀疑他的能力，后来把他调到另外一个工作岗位上，他照样干得很出色。现在没人怀疑他了吧？

B: 对呀，**真金不怕火炼**。他的确是个难得的人才。

A: Yuánlái yǒu rén huáiyí tā de nénglì, hòulái bǎ tā diào dào lìngwài yígè gōngzuò gǎngwèi shàng, tā zhàoyàng gàn de hěn chūsè. Xiànzài méi rén huáiyí tā le ba?

B: Duì ya, zhēn jīn bú pà huǒ liàn. Tā díquè shì gè nándé de réncái.

A: Before, there were people who doubted his ability. Afterwards, when he was transferred to another position, he did his job with the same distinction. Surely no one doubts him now, right?

B: That's right. True blue will never stain. He really is a rare talent.

Example 2:

A: 她的物理学理论发表后，不断受到挑战。但是，**真金不怕火炼**，没有人能推翻她的理论，她也因此获得诺贝尔奖。

A: Tā de wùlǐxué lǐlùn fābiǎo hòu, búduàn shòudào tiǎozhàn. Dànshì, zhēn jīn bú pà huǒ liàn, méiyǒu rén néng tuīfān tā de lǐlùn, tā yě yīncǐ huòdé Nuòbèi'ěr jiǎng.

A: After she announced her theory in physics, she was constantly challenged. But, true blue will never stain. As no one was able to overturn her theory, she won the Nobel Prize.

Usage: Used singly.

Note: Complimentary in meaning.

171. 狗改不了吃屎 (狗改不了吃屎) gǒu gǎi bù liǎo chī shǐ

Translated character by character, 狗改不了吃屎 means 'dog-change-not-able-eat-poop,' whereas the implied meaning of this proverb would be 'one can't kick a bad habit.' Its functional translation is 'the fox may grow grey, but never good.'

Example 1:

A: 她刚从戒毒所里出来，没两个月又因为吸毒被关进去了。

B: **狗改不了吃屎**，她再这样下去就没药可救了。

A: Tā gāng cóng jièdúsuǒ li chūlai, méi liǎng gè yuè yòu yīnwèi xīdú bèi guān jìnqù le.

B: Gǒu gǎi bùliǎo chī shǐ, tā zài zhèyàng xiàqù jiù méi yào kě jiù le.

A: She just got out of rehab, and less than two months later she was readmitted for doing drugs.

B: The fox may grow grey, but never good. There's no medicine that can save her.

Example 2:

A: 他因为赌博把房子和豪车都输了进去了，可是还去赌场。

B: **狗改不了吃屎**，让他不赌钱，除非太阳从西边出来。

A: Tā yīnwèi dǔbó bǎ fángzi hé háochē dōu shū jìnqù le, kěshì hái qù dǔchǎng.

B: Gǒu gǎi bùliǎo chī shǐ, ràng tā bù dǔqián, chúfēi tàiyang cóng xībian chūlai.

A: He gambled away his house and car, but he still goes to the casino.

B: The fox may grow grey, but never good. Him not gambling is like the sun rising from the west.

Usage: Used singly.

Note: Derogatory in meaning.

172. 杀手锏 (殺手鐧) shā shǒu jiǎn

Translated character by character, 杀手锏 means 'kill-hand-mace,' whereas the implied meaning of this proverb would be 'the best move that someone plays at a crucial moment.' Its functional translation is 'trump card,' or 'ace in the hole.'

Example 1:

A: 她违章停车，警察给了她罚单。她百般解释都没用，最后使出**杀手锏**。

B: 什么绝招？

A: 哭。

A: Tā wéizhāng tíngchē, jǐngchá gěile tā fádān. Tā bǎibān jiěshì dōu méiyòng, zuìhòu shǐ chū shāshǒujiǎn.

B: Shénme juézhāo?

A: Kū.

A: She parked illegally and the cops gave her a ticket. No matter which way she tried to explain it, it didn't help her. Finally, she played her trump card.

B: What was her trick?

A: She cried.

Example 2:

A: 在两大超市的竞争中，双方都使出了**杀手锏**——降价。

A: Zài liǎng dà chāoshì de jìngzhēng zhōng, shuāngfāng dōu shǐ chū le shāshǒujiǎn —jiàng jià.

A: In the competition between two large supermarkets, both played their ace in the hole – cutting prices.

Usage: Functions as object.

Variant: 撒手锏

Note: Neutral in meaning.

---

173. 饥不择食 (饑不擇食) jī bù zé shí

Translated character by character, 饥不择食 means 'hungry-not-choose-food,' whereas the implied meaning of this proverb would be 'one is not picky when in need.' Its functional translation is 'beggars can't be choosers.'

Example 1:

A: 经济萧条的时候任何一个工作机会都有数百人申请，人们已经**饥不择食**，根本不管工作性质，只要有活儿干就可以。

A: Jīngjì xiāotiáo de shíhòu rènhé yígè gōngzuò jīhuì dōu yǒu shù bǎi rén shēnqǐng, rénmen yǐjīng jī bù zé shí, gēnběn bùguǎn gōngzuò xìngzhì, zhǐyào yǒu huór gàn jiù kěyǐ.

A: In an economic depression, any job opportunity has hundreds of applicants. People are already beggars and not choosers, thoroughly indifferent about the nature of the job. So long as there's work to do, it's good enough.

Example 2:

A: 他们从认识到结婚只用了一个星期。

B: 都是大龄青年，自身条件又不够优秀，都**饥不择食**了。

A: Tāmen cóng rènshi dào jiéhūn zhǐ yòngle yígè xīngqī.

B: Dōu shì dàlíng qīngnián, zìshēn tiáojiàn yòu búgòu yōuxiù, dōu jī bù zé shí le.

A: It was only a week from the time they met until their marriage.

B: They're unmarried thirty-somethings and they're not sufficiently well-off. Beggars can't be choosers.

Usage: Functions as predicate or adverbial.

Note: Slightly derogatory in meaning.

174. 对事不对人 (對事不對人) duì shì bú duì rén

Translated character by character, 对事不对人 means 'toward-issue-not-toward-person,' whereas the implied meaning of this proverb would be 'it has no reflection on a particular person.' Its functional translation is 'it's nothing personal.'

Example 1:

A: 你不要想得太多，我的话是**对事不对人**。

A: Nǐ búyào xiǎng de tài duō, Wǒde huà shì duì shì bú duì rén.

A: Don't dwell on it too much. What I said was nothing personal.

Example 2:

A: 先生，可能我没说清楚，也可能我们之间的沟通有一些误解。能不能我先回去，请我的上司来跟您解释一下？

B: 不必了，我们办事**对事不对人**，谁来都一样。

A: Xiānsheng, kěnéng wǒ méi shuō qīngchu, yě kěnéng wǒmen zhījiān de gōutōng yǒuyìxiē wùjiě. Néngbunéng wǒ xiān huíqù, qǐng wǒde shàngsī lái gēn nín jiěshì yíxià?

B: Búbì le, wǒmen bànshì duì shì bú duì rén, shuí lái dōu yíyàng.

A: Sir, maybe I wasn't clear, or maybe we've had a little miscommunication. Can I go and ask my superior to come explain this to you?

B: That's not necessary. Our issue resolution is nothing personal. It doesn't matter who is involved.

Usage: Functions as predicate, predicative or attributive.

Note: Neutral in meaning.

175. 皮笑肉不笑 (皮笑肉不笑) pí xiào ròu bú xiào

Translated character by character, 皮笑肉不笑 means 'skin-smile-flesh-not-smile.' Its functional translation is 'fake smile.'

Example 1:

A: 他看起来挺和蔼的，整天笑。

B: 我看他挺虚伪的。别看他在笑，但是**皮笑肉不笑**，让人很不舒服。

A: Tā kàn qǐlái tǐng hé'ǎi de, zhěngtiān xiào.

B: Wǒ kàn tā tǐng xūwěi de. Bié kàn tā zài xiào, dànshì pí xiào ròu bú xiào, ràng rén hěn bù shūfu.

A: He looks pretty affable, smiling all the time.

B: He seems hypocritical to me. Don't be fooled by his smile, it's fake. It makes people very uncomfortable.

Example 2:

A: 他**皮笑肉不笑**地说："有空儿来坐坐，欢迎您再来。"

A: Tā **pí xiào ròu bú xiào** de shuō: "yǒu kòngr lái zuòzuò, huānyíng nín zài lái."

A: With a fake smile, he said, "Come back when you're free. You're welcome back again."

Usage: Functions as adverbial or predicate.

Note: Slightly derogatory in meaning.

---

176. 双刃剑 (雙刃劍) shuāng rèn jiàn

Translated character by character, 双刃剑 means 'double-edge-sword.' Its functional translation is 'double-edged sword.'

Example 1:

A: 咱们大量使用机器人来提高生产效率怎么样？

B: 这是一把**双刃剑**。机器人的确可以提高生产效率，但是我们人类是不是从此会渐渐失去智慧？

A: Zánmen dàliàng shǐyòng jīqìrén lái tígāo shēngchǎn xiàolǜ zěnmeyàng?

B: Zhè shì yì bǎ **shuāngrènjiàn**. Jīqìrén díquè kěyǐ tígāo shēngchǎn xiàolǜ, dànshì wǒmen rénlèi shìbúshì cóngcǐ huì jiànjiàn shīqù zhìhuì?

A: What about using a lot of robots to increase production efficiency?

B: That's a double-edged sword. Robots actually can increase production efficiency, but won't we humans start to slowly lose our intelligence?

Example 2:

A: 降低银行利率是把**双刃剑**。一方面可以刺激经济，另一方面也许会让通货膨胀抬头。

A: Jiàngdī yínháng lìlǜ shì bǎ **shuāngrènjiàn**. Yìfāngmiàn kěyǐ cìjī dāngqián xiāofèi, kěshì lìngyìfāngmiàn, yóuyú xiāofèi chāoqián, huì lā dī wèilái niánfèn de xiāofèi shuǐpíng.

A: Reducing bank interest rates is a double-edged sword. On the one hand, it can stimulate the economy, but, on the other hand, it might cause inflation to rear its head.

Usage: Functions as predicative.

Note: Neutral in meaning.

177. 热脸贴冷屁股 (熱臉貼冷屁股) rè liǎn tiē lěng pìgu

Translated character by character, 热脸贴冷屁股 means 'hot-face-snuggle-cold-butt,' whereas the implied meaning of this proverb would be 'to be completely ignored by someone.' Its functional translation is 'to not get the time of day from someone,' or 'to have someone not give you the time of day.'

Example 1:

A: 最近小马老是往牛局长办公室跑，可是每次待不了几分钟就出来。

B: 小马总是想打小报告，可是牛局长不吃这一套。小马**热脸贴了个冷屁股**。

A: Zuìjìn Xiǎo Mǎ lǎoshì wǎng Niú júzhǎng bàngōngshì pǎo, kěshì měicì dāi bùliǎo jǐ fēnzhōng jiù chūlái.

B: Xiǎo Mǎ zǒngshì xiǎng dǎ xiǎobàogào, kěshì Niú júzhǎng bù chī zhè yí tào. Xiǎo Mǎ rè liǎn tiēle gè lěng pìgu.

A: Recently, Little Ma has constantly been running to Chief Niu's office, but he always comes out after spending no more than a few minutes.

B: Little Ma always wants to tattle, but Chief Niu isn't having it. He doesn't give Little Ma the time of day.

Example 2:

A: 你怎么不像以前那样帮她了？

B: 她啊，以前我帮她，她还说感谢类的话；现在呢，不但不感谢，反倒觉得我在打搅她，我**热脸贴冷屁股**，何苦呢？

A: Nǐ zěnme bú xiàng yǐqián nàyàng bāng tā le?

B: Tā a, yǐqián wǒ bāng tā, tā hái shuō gǎnxiè lèi de huà; xiànzài ne, búdàn bù gǎnxiè, fǎndào juéde wǒ zài dǎjiǎo tā, wǒ rè liǎn tiē lěng pìgu, hékǔ ne?

A: Why aren't you helping her like before?

B: Her? When I helped her before, she would thank me. Now, she not only doesn't thank me, she rather thinks I'm disturbing her. She doesn't give me the time of day. Why bother?

Usage: Functions as predicate.

Note: Slightly derogatory in meaning.

178. 好了伤疤忘了疼 (好了傷疤忘了疼)
hǎo le shāngbā wàng le téng

Translated character by character, 好了伤疤忘了疼 means 'heal-ed-scar-forget-ed-pain,' whereas the implied meaning of this proverb would be 'to forget the pain once the wound is healed.' Its functional translation is 'once on shore, one prays no more.'

Example 1:

A: 他上次因为喝酒就犯心脏病住院了。这才出院多久啊就又开始喝上了。

B: **好了伤疤忘了疼**，看来上次伤得不重。

A: Tā shàngcì yīnwèi hējiǔ jiù fàn xīnzàngbìng zhùyuàn le. Zhè cái chūyuàn duōjiǔ a jiù yòu kāishǐ hēshang le.

B: Hǎole shāngbā wàngle téng, kànlái shàngcì shāng de bú zhòng.

A: Last time he was hospitalized with a heart attack because of his drinking. He's only been out of the hospital for a little while and he's started drinking again.

B: Once on shore, one prays no more. I can see he wasn't hurt badly enough last time.

Example 2:

A: 老百姓的钱又开始涌进股市了，他们忘了十年前的崩盘以及随后的熊市了。

B: **好了伤疤忘了疼**，人们的记性很差。

A: Lǎobǎixìng de qián yòu kāishǐ yǒngjìn gǔshì le, tāmen wàngle shí nián qián de bēngpán yǐjí suíhòu de xióngshì le.

B: Hǎole shāngbā wàngle téng, rénmen de jìxing hěn chà.

A: Ordinary people's money has started to flood into the stock market again. They've forgotten about the bubble bursting ten years ago and the resulting bear market.

B: Once on shore, one prays no more. People have very short memories.

Usage: Used singly or functions as predicate.

Note: Humorous or neutral in meaning.

179. 醋坛子 (醋罎子) cù tánzi

Translated character by character, 醋坛子 means 'vinegar-jar.' Its functional translation is 'jealous lover.'

Example 1:

A: 她是个**醋坛子**，只要丈夫跟别的女人说话，她就会凑上去，千方百计打断对话。

A: Tā shì gè cùtánzi, zhǐyào zhàngfu gēn biéde nǚrén shuōhuà, tā jiù huì còu shàngqù, qiānfāng-bǎijì dǎ duàn duìhuà.

A: She's a jealous lover. If she so much as sees her husband talking to other women, she goes up and does everything in her power to break up the conversation.

Example 2:

A: 他老婆是个有名的**醋坛子**，所以他的女同事没有一个人愿意去他家做客。

A: Tā lǎopo shì gè yǒumíng de cùtánzi, suǒyǐ tā de nǚ tóngshì méiyǒu yígè rén yuànyì qù tā jiā zuòkè.

A: His wife is known to be a jealous lover, so none of his female coworkers is willing to be a dinner guest at his home.

Usage: Functions mainly as predicative.

Variant: 醋罐子 (罐子 guànzi: canister)

Note: Slightly derogatory and humorous in meaning.

180. 君子之交淡如水 (君子之交淡如水)
jūnzǐ zhī jiāo dàn rú shuǐ

Translated character by character, 君子之交淡如水 means 'noble-man-'s-friendship-pure-like-water,' whereas the implied meaning of this proverb would be 'the friendship between gentlemen appears indifferent but is pure like water.'

Example 1:

A: 你跟我就不要客气了，咱们相识几十年了。
B: 虽说**君子之交淡如水**，但今天无论如何我要请你好好吃一顿。

A: Nǐ gēn wǒ jiù búyào kèqì le, zánmen xiāngshí jǐ shí nián le.
B: Suī shuō jūnzǐ zhī jiāo dàn rú shuǐ, dàn zhècì wúlùnrúhé wǒ yào qǐng nǐ hǎohāo chī yí dùn.

A: You don't need to be polite around me; we've known each other for decades.
B: Although they say the friendship between gentlemen appears indifferent, but is pure like water, today I would like to invite you to a big meal anyways.

Example 2:

A: 你最好的朋友是谁？
B: 老刘。
A: 是他啊？可是平常见你们来往不多。
B: 我们是**君子之交淡如水**，但是我们是真正理解对方的。

A: Nǐ zuìhǎo de péngyǒu shì shéi?

B: Lǎo Liú.

A: Shì tā a? Kěshì píngcháng jiàn nǐmen láiwǎng bù duō.

B: Wǒmen shì jūnzǐ zhī jiāo dàn rú shuǐ, dànshì wǒmen shì zhēnzhèng lǐjiě duìfāng de.

A: Who's your best friend?

B: Old Liu.

A: Him? But it seems you two don't usually interact.

B: For us, the friendship appears indifferent, but is pure like water. We really understand each other.

Usage: Functions as predicative or used singly.

Note: Neutral in meaning.

181. 三个和尚没水吃 (三個和尚沒水吃)
sān gè héshang méi shuǐ chī

Translated character by character, 三个和尚没水吃 means 'three-MW-monks-no-water-drink,' whereas the implied meaning of this proverb would be 'when many people are working together, they assume others will take responsibility for various tasks and, as a result, aren't efficient.' Its functional translation is 'everybody's business is nobody's business.'

Example 1:

A: 他们那个小组人员最多，可是贡献却不大。

B: 是啊，人多了就会出现**三个和尚没水吃**的问题。

A: Tāmen nàgè xiǎozǔ rényuán zuì duō, kěshì gòngxiàn què bú dà.

B: Shì a, rén duō le jiù huì chūxiàn sān gè héshang méi shuǐ chī de wèntí.

A: That group has the most employees, but they don't contribute much.

B: Yeah, when you've got a lot of people, the issue is that everybody's business is nobody's business.

Example 2:

A: 由于责任不明确，导致了人们之间相互推诿，**三个和尚反倒没水吃**。

A: Yóuyú zérèn bù míngquè, dǎozhì le rénmen zhījiān xiānghù tuīwěi, sān gè héshang fǎndǎo méi shuǐ chī.

A: Because the responsibilities were not clear, everyone was passing the buck. Everybody's business is nobody's business.

Usage: Functions as attributive or used singly.

Note: Slightly derogatory and humorous in meaning.

182. 赶鸭子上架 (趕鴨子上架) gǎn yāzi shàng jià

Translated character by character, 赶鸭子上架 means 'drive-duck-mount-trellis,' whereas the implied meaning of this proverb would be 'to force someone to do what they cannot.' Its functional translation is 'to force someone to put a square peg into a round hole.'

Example 1:

A: 请你今晚在宴会上给大家唱一个。

B: 我根本不会唱歌，现在你逼着我唱，这不是**赶鸭子上架**嘛？

A: Qǐng nǐ jīn wǎn zài yànhuì shàng gěi dàjiā chàng yígè.

B: Wǒ gēnběn búhuì chànggē, xiànzài nǐ bīzhe wǒ chàng, zhè búshì gǎn yāzi shàng jià ma?

A: Please sing everyone a song at tonight's banquet.

B: I really can't sing, and now you're forcing me to. Isn't that like forcing me to put a square peg into a round hole?

Example 2:

A: 她是出色的工程师，对行政一窍不通啊！让她当市长管理这么大一个城市，简直是**赶鸭子上架**。

A: Tā shì chūsè de gōngchéngshī, duì xíngzhèng yíqiào-bùtōng a! Ràng tā dāng shìzhǎng guǎnlǐ zhème dà yígè chéngshì, jiǎnzhí shì gǎn yāzi shàng jià.

A: She is an accomplished engineer, but she doesn't know the first thing about administration! Making her govern such a large city as mayor really is like forcing her to put a square peg into a round hole.

Usage: Functions as predicative or predicate.

Variant: 打鸭子上架 (in some Chinese dialects)

Note: Slightly derogatory and humorous in meaning.

183. 小白脸 (小白臉) xiǎo bái liǎn

Translated character by character, 小白脸 means 'little-white-face,' whereas the implied meaning of this proverb would be 'a pale-skinned young man with delicate features.' Its functional translation is 'pretty boy.'

Example 1:

A: 她养了一个**小白脸**。

A: Tā yǎngle yígè xiǎobáiliǎn.

A: She caught herself a pretty boy.

Example 2:

A: 那个富婆又结婚了。

B: 这次找了个**小白脸**。

A: Nàgè fùpó yòu jiéhūn le.

B: Zhècì zhǎole gè **xiǎobáiliǎn**.

A: That wealthy woman got married again.

B: This time she found a pretty boy.

Usage: Nominal element, functions mainly as object.

Note: Slightly derogatory in meaning.

184. 放长线，钓大鱼 (放長綫，釣大魚)
fàng cháng xiàn, diào dà yú

Translated character by character, 放长线，钓大鱼 means 'cast-long-line, catch-big-fish,' whereas the implied meaning of this proverb would be 'to approach something with an eye towards the long-term or a larger goal.' Its functional translation is 'to play the long game.'

Example 1:

A: 局长，我们怎么还不把那个毒贩抓起来？

B: 小马，我们是在**放长线钓大鱼**，目的是找到最大的老板，然后一网打尽。

A: Júzhǎng, wǒmen zěnme hái bù bǎ nàgè dúfàn zhuā qǐlai?

B: Xiǎo Mǎ, wǒmen shì fàng cháng xiàn, diào dàyú, mùdì shì zhǎodào zuìdà de lǎobǎn, ránhòu yìwǎng-dǎjìn.

A: Chief, why haven't we arrested that drug dealer yet?

B: Little Ma, we're playing the long game. Our goal is to find the kingpin and then roll them all up.

Example 2:

A: 有些公司开始把低端商品或硬件廉价卖给你，等着你脱离不了它的时候，它就会把高端商品或软件提价，赚取利润。这是一种**放长线钓大鱼**的策略。

A: Yǒuxiē gōngsī kāishǐ bǎ dīduān shāngpǐn huò yìngjiàn liánjià mài gěi nǐ, děngzhe nǐ tuólí bùliǎo tā de shíhou, tā jiù huì bǎ gāoduān shāngpǐn huò ruǎnjiàn tíjià, zhuànqǔ lìrùn. Zhè shì yìzhǒng fàng cháng xiàn, diào dàyú de cèluè.

A: There are some companies that sell you low-end products or hardware cheap up front, and once you can't live without it, they raise the price of high-end products or software to make a profit. That's a long-game type of strategy.

Usage: Functions mainly as predicate.

Note: Neutral in meaning.

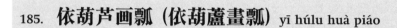

185. 依葫芦画瓢 (依葫蘆畫瓢) yī húlu huà piáo

Translated character by character, 依葫芦画瓢 means 'according to-gourd-draw-gourd dipper,' whereas the implied meaning of this proverb would be 'to copy mechanically.' Its functional translation is 'to follow suit.'

Example 1:

A: 这件事我做不了。

B: 没那么难，你就**依葫芦画瓢**，我怎么做你就怎么做。

A: Zhè jiàn shì wǒ zuò bùliǎo.

B: Méi nàme nán, nǐ jiù yī húlu huà piáo, wǒ zěnme zuò nǐ jiù zěnme zuò.

A: I can't do this.

B: It's not that hard. Just follow suit; do as I do.

Example 2:

A: 有人写了一本《丑陋的美国人》，很畅销，于是有人**依葫芦画瓢**，写了《丑陋的日本人》和《丑陋的中国人》等。

A: Yǒu rén xiěle yì běn Chǒulòu de Měiguórén, hěn chàngxiāo, yúshì yǒu rén yī húlu huà piáo, xiěle Chǒulòu de Rìběnrén hé Chǒulòu de Zhōngguórén děng.

A: Someone wrote a book called *Ugly Americans*, which sold very well, so someone else followed suit and wrote books called *Ugly Japanese*, *Ugly Chinese*, etc.

Usage: Functions as predicate.

Variant: 照葫芦画瓢

Note: Slightly derogatory or neutral in meaning.

186. 隔墙有耳 (隔牆有耳) gé qiáng yǒu ěr

Translated character by character, 隔墙有耳 means 'partition-wall-has-ears,' whereas the implied meaning of this proverb would be 'someone might be listening.' Its functional translation is 'walls have ears.'

Example 1:

A: 我们能不能这样办，……
B: 小点儿声，小心**隔墙有耳**。

A: Wǒmen néngbunéng zhèyàng bàn, ...
B: Xiǎo diǎn'r shēng, xiǎoxīn gé qiáng yǒu ěr.

A: Could we do this . . .
B: Quiet down; walls have ears.

Example 2:

A: 他们的对话非常重要，怕**隔墙有耳**，于是把旅馆电视的声音调得很大。

A: Tāmen de duìhuà fēicháng zhòngyào, pà gé qiáng yǒu ěr, yúshì bǎ lǚguǎn diànshì de shēngyīn tiáo de hěn dà.

A: Because their discussion was extremely important and they feared that the walls had ears, they turned the hotel television's volume up very loud.

Usage: Functions as object and usally used after '怕' or '小心.'

Note: Neutral in meaning.

187. 巧妇难为无米之炊 (巧婦難為無米之炊)
qiǎo fù nán wéi wú mǐ zhī chuī

Translated character by character, 巧妇难为无米之炊 means 'skillfull-housewife-hard-make-no-rice-food,' whereas the implied meaning of this proverb would be 'one cannot accomplish something without the necessary materials and conditions.' Its functional translation is 'you can't make bricks without straw.'

Example 1:

A: 总统整天在电视上讲要降低失业率，可是失业率就是下不去。
B: 这也难为总统了。**巧妇难为无米之炊**，经济这么疲软，就业率怎么上得去？

A: Zǒngtǒng zhěngtiān zài diànshì shàng jiǎng yào jiàngdī shīyèlǜ, kěshì shīyèlǜ jiùshì xià bú qù.
B: Zhè yě nánwéi zǒngtǒng le. Qiǎo fù nán wéi wú mǐ zhī chuī, jīngjì zhème píruǎn, jiùyèlǜ zěnme shàng de qù?

A: The president is always on TV talking about how we need to lower the unemployment rate, but it's not going down.
B: It's hard for the president. You can't make bricks without straw. With such a weak economy, how could employment rise?

Example 2:

A: 新市长怎么整天愁眉苦脸的，他不是很有能力吗？
B: 有能力是有能力，可是这个城市没有实力啊，还欠着一屁股外债呢。市长是**巧妇难为无米之炊**啊。

A: Xīn shìzhǎng zěnme zhěngtiān chóuméi-kǔliǎn de, tā búshì hěn yǒu nénglì ma?
B: Yǒu nénglì shì yǒu nénglì, kěshì zhègè chéngshì méiyǒu shílì a, hái qiànzhe yí pìgu wàizhài ne. Shìzhǎng shì qiǎo fù nán wéi wú mǐ zhī chuī a.

A: What's with the new mayor's long face? Isn't he very capable?
B: Capable is one thing, but this city doesn't have any power, and it still has a mountain of debt. He can't make bricks without straw.

Usage: Used singly.

Note: Neutral in meaning.

188. **不是吃素的 (不是吃素的)** bú shì chī sù de

Translated character by character, 不是吃素的 means 'not-a-vegetarian,' whereas the implied meaning of this proverb would be 'someone who is not a pushover.' Its functional translation is 'to be someone not to be trifled with.'

Example 1:

A: 你这样做他会同意吗？他可**不是吃素的**，把他惹急了，他可什么事都干得出来。

A: Nǐ zhèyàng zuò tā huì tóngyì ma? Tā kě búshì chīsùde, bǎ tā rě jí le, tā kě shénme shì dōu gàn de chūlái.

A: Will he agree with your doing this? He's not someone to be trifled with. If you provoke him, there's no saying what he'll do.

Example 2:

A: 看样子，他要跟我们斗个没完没了。
B: 让他来吧，咱们也**不是吃素的**，怕他什么。

A: Kànyàngzi, tā yào gēn wǒ men dòu gè méiwánméiliǎo.
B: Ràng tā lái ba, zánmen yě búshì chīsùde, pà tā shénme.

A: It looks like he wants to wage a perpetual war against us.
B: Let him. We're not to be trifled with. Why are you afraid of him?

Usage: Functions as predicative.

Note: Neutral in meaning.

189. 嫁鸡随鸡，嫁狗随狗 （嫁雞隨雞，嫁狗隨狗）
jià jī suí jī, jià gǒu suí gǒu

Translated character by character, 嫁鸡随鸡，嫁狗随狗 means 'married to-chicken-follow-chicken, married to-dog-follow-dog,' whereas the implied meaning of this proverb would be 'a woman follows her husband no matter how good or bad his lot.' Its functional translation is 'a woman should stand by her man.'

Example 1:

A: 在中国古代，女人的婚姻由父母做主，自己没有任何选择，**嫁鸡随鸡，嫁狗随狗**。

A: Zài Zhōngguó gǔdài, nǚrén de hūnyīn yóu fùmǔ zuòzhǔ, zìjǐ méiyǒu rènhé xuǎnzé, jià jī suí jī, jià gǒu suí gǒu.

A: In ancient China, a woman's marriage was determined by her parents and she had no choice in the matter. A woman needed to stand by her man.

Example 2:

A: 你想那么匆忙就嫁给一个老外，你了解他吗？不合适怎么办？
B: 咳，这就是命，**嫁鸡随鸡，嫁狗随狗**呗。

A: Nǐ xiǎng nàme cōngmáng jiù jià gěi yígè lǎowài, nǐ liǎojiě tā ma? Bù héshì zěnmebàn?
B: Hài, zhè jiùshì mìng, jià jī suí jī, jià gǒu suí gǒu bei.

A: Do you want to get married to a foreigner in such a hurry? Do you understand him? What will you do if he's not right for you?
B: Oh, that's fate. A woman should stand by her man.

Usage: Functions as predicate or used singly.

Note: Slightly derogatory in meaning.

190. 打开天窗说亮话 （打開天窗説亮話）
dǎ kāi tiān chuāng shuō liàng huà

Translated character by character, 打开天窗说亮话 means 'open-skylight-speak-bright-words,' whereas the implied meaning of this proverb would be 'to speak openly and directly.' Its functional translation is 'to lay one's cards on the table.'

Example 1:

A: 大哥，请坐，请坐。看您的脸色，谁把您给惹了？
B: 咱们**打开天窗说亮话**，你卖给我的假货到底能不能退？

A:　Dàgē, qǐngzuò, qǐngzuò. Kàn nín de liǎnsè, shéi bǎ nín gěi rě le?

B:　Zánmen dǎ kāi tiānchuāng shuō liàng huà, nǐ mài gěi wǒ de jiǎhuò dàodǐ néngbùnéng tuì?

A:　Brother, sit down, sit down. What an expression you have on your face; who got you worked up?

B:　Let's lay our cards on the table. Can the counterfeit goods you sold me really be returned?

Example 2:

A:　说话别转弯抹角的，有话直说。

B:　好，那我就**打开天窗说亮话**，我是为小王的事来的。

A:　Shuōhuà bié zhuǎnwān-mòjiǎo de, yǒu huà zhíshuō.

B:　Hǎo, nà wǒ jiù dǎ kāi tiānchuāng shuō liàng huà, wǒ shì wèi Xiǎo Wáng de shì lái de.

A:　Don't beat about the bush. If you have something to say, spit it out.

B:　Good, then I'll lay my cards on the table. I've come on Xiao Wang's behalf.

Usage: Functions as predicate.

Note: Neutral or humorous in meaning.

191. 人算不如天算 (人算不如天算) rén suàn bù rú tiān suàn

Translated character by character, 人算不如天算 means 'people-plan-not-better-heaven-plan,' whereas the implied meaning of this proverb would be 'no matter how much one plans something, one can't control everything.' Its functional translation is, 'the best laid plans of mice and men often go awry,' or 'man proposes, god disposes.'

Example 1:

A:　眼看她就成功了，可是支持她的一个重要人物出车祸死了，最后她仅仅以几票落选。

B:　可惜**人算不如天算**，看来她没这个命。

A:　Yǎnkàn tā jiù chénggōng le, kěshì zhīchí tā de yígè zhòngyào rénwù chū chēhuò sǐ le, zuìhòu tā jǐnjǐn yǐ jǐ piào luòxuǎn.

B:　Kěxī rén suàn bùrú tiān suàn, kànlái tā méi zhègè mìng.

A:　It looked like she was going to succeed, but an important figure who was supporting her died in a car crash and, in the end, she lost out by only a few votes.

B:　It's a shame. The best laid plans of mice and men often go awry. It looks like this isn't her destiny.

Example 2:

A: 我要坐的飞机晚起飞两个小时，我正生气呢，就在这时候，你猜，我碰到谁了？

B: 谁啊？

A: 我的偶像大卫·贝克汉姆！我赶快去跟他拍了张照片。

B: **人算不如天算**，要不然，你何年何月才能跟贝克汉姆拍一张照片啊？

A: Wǒ yào zuò de fēijī wǎn qǐfēi liǎng gè xiǎoshí, wǒ zhèng shēngqì ne, jiù zài zhè shíhòu, nǐ cāi, wǒ pèngdào shéi le?

B: Shéi a?

A: Wǒde ǒuxiàng Dàwèi Bèikèhànmǔ! Wǒ gǎnkuài qù gēn tā pāile zhāng zhàopiàn.

B: Rén suàn bùrú tiān suàn, yàobùrán, nǐ hénián-héyuè cáinéng gēn Bèikèhànmǔ pāi yì zhāng zhàopiàn a?

A: The flight I was going to take was delayed by two hours. I was angry, but guess who I ran into then?

B: Who?

A: My idol, David Beckham! I ran over to take a picture with him.

B: Man proposes, god disposes. Otherwise, when would you ever have been able to get a picture with David Beckham?

Usage: Used singly.

Note: Neutral in meaning.

192. 小动作 (小動作) xiǎo dòngzuò

Translated character by character, 小动作 means 'small-action,' whereas the implied meaning of this proverb would be 'a cheap shot,' or 'a cheap trick.'

Example 1:

A: 这是公平的竞争，可是他不时地在背后**搞小动作**，散布对手的流言。

A: Zhè shì gōngpíng de jìngzhēng, kěshì tā bùshí de zài bèihòu gǎo xiǎodòngzuò, sànbù duìshǒu de liúyán.

A: This is a fair competition, but he often pulls cheap tricks behind people's backs, spreading rumors about his opponents.

Example 2:

A: 我警告你，如果你敢在背后**搞小动作**，我就好好地收拾你。

A: Wǒ jǐnggào nǐ, rúguǒ nǐ gǎn zài bèihòu gǎo xiǎodòngzuò, wǒ jiù hǎohāo de shōushi nǐ.

A: I swear to god, if you dare pull a cheap trick behind my back, I'll end you.

Usage: Functions as object.

Variant: 搞小动作

Note: Slightly derogatory in meaning.

---

193. 远水解不了近渴 (遠水解不了近渴)
yuǎn shuǐ jiě bù liǎo jìn kě

Translated character by character, 远水解不了近渴 means 'distant-water-resolve-not-able-urgent-thirst,' whereas the implied meaning of this proverb would be 'aid that arrives too slowly is of no help at all.' Its functional translation is 'while the grass grows, the horse starves.'

Example 1:

A: 我们能不能请他帮忙？

B: 他倒是有能力帮我们，可是问题是，现在他人在外国，**远水解不了近渴**啊？

A: Wǒmen néngbùnéng qǐng tā bāngmáng?

B: Tā dàoshì yǒu nénglì bāng wǒmen, kěshì wèntí shì, xiànzài tā rén zài wàiguó, yuǎn shuǐ jiě bùliǎo jìn kě a?

A: Can we ask him to give us a hand?

B: He is capable of helping us, but the problem is that he's abroad at the moment. While the grass grows, the horse starves.

Example 2:

A: （灾区）现在最需要的是帐篷、毛毯、食物和饮用水。

B: 全国各地的救援物资正在往这里送。

A: **远水难解近渴**。我提议向中央请求使用战略储备。

A: (Zāiqū) Xiànzài zuì xūyào de shì zhàngpéng, máotǎn, shíwù hé yǐnyòngshuǐ.

B: Quánguó gèdì de jiùyuán wùzī zhèngzài wǎng zhèlǐ sòng.

A: Yuǎn shuǐ nán jiě jìn kě. Wǒ tíyì xiàng zhongyāng qǐngqiú shǐyòng zhànluè chǔbèi.

A: (In a disaster zone) What we need most now are tents, blankets, food, and drinking water.

B: Relief supplies are currently being shipped here from all parts of the country.

A: While the grass grows, the horse starves. I propose we petition the central government to use strategic reserves.

Usage: Functions mainly as predicate.

Variants: 远水难解近渴; 远水不解近渴

Note: Neutral in meaning.

194. 占着茅坑不拉屎 (佔著茅坑不拉屎)
zhàn zhe máokēng bù lāshǐ

Translated character by character, 占着茅坑不拉屎 means 'hog-ing-latrine pit-not-defecate,' whereas the implied meaning of this proverb would be, 'a man monopolizes a latrine but does not defecate.' Its functional translation is 'to be a dog in the manger.'

Example 1:

A: 总经理怎么还不退休啊？都六十了，什么出彩的事都没干出来过。

B: 他就是那种**占着茅坑不拉屎**的人，想让他退休，难着呢。

A: Zǒngjīnglǐ zěnme hái bú tuìxiū a? Dōu liùshí le, shénme chūcǎi de shì dōu méi gàn chūlái guo.

B: Tā jiùshì nà zhǒng zhànzhe máokēng bù lāshǐ de rén, xiǎng ràng tā tuìxiū, nánzhene.

A: How is it that the vice-general manager hasn't retired yet? He's already 60 and he's never done anything amazing.

B: He's just like a dog in the manger. Good luck getting him to retire.

Example 2:

A: 有些国会里的代表根本没提出过对老百姓有利的议案。

B: 对，这些人就是**占着茅坑不拉屎**。

A: Yǒuxiē Guóhuì lǐ de dàibiǎo gēnběn méi tíchū guo duì lǎobǎixìng yǒulì de yì'àn.

B: Duì, zhèxiē rén jiùshì zhànzhe máokēng bù lāshǐ.

A: Some congressional representatives simply haven't proposed legislation beneficial to the common people.

B: Yeah, these people are like dogs in the manger.

Usage: Functions as predicate or attributive.

Note: Derogatory in meaning. Latrines (茅坑) were used instead of toilets in ancient rural China. Although latrines are seldom seen today, one cannot replace 茅坑 (latrine) with 厕所 (toilet) in this proverb.

195. 碰一鼻子灰 (碰一鼻子灰) pèng yì bízi huī

Translated character by character, 碰一鼻子灰 means 'hit-one-nose-plaster dust,' whereas the implied meaning of this proverb would be 'to be stood up or ignored.' Its functional translation is 'to get the cold shoulder,' or 'to be left out in the cold.'

Example 1:

A: 他不是今天晚上请他的大学同学王市长吃饭吗？怎么还没走？

B: 已经回来了。他高高兴兴地去了，结果**碰了一鼻子灰**，连市长面都没见到。

A: Tā búshì jīntiān wǎnshang qǐng tā de dàxué tóngxué Wáng shìzhǎng chīfàn ma? Zěnme hái méi zǒu?

B: Yǐjīng huílái le. Tā gāogāoxìngxìng de qù le, jiéguǒ pèngle yì bízi hūi, lián shìzhǎng miàn dōu méi jiàndào.

A: Didn't he invite his college classmate, Mayor Wang, to dinner tonight? Why hasn't he left yet?

B: He's back already. He left very happy, but he got the cold shoulder. He didn't even see the mayor.

Example 2:

A: 那个小国的总统跑到某大国求助，结果**碰了一鼻子灰**。该大国的回答是"自己的事情自己解决"。

A: Nàgè xiǎo guó de zǒngtǒng pǎo dào mǒu dà guó qiúzhù, jiéguǒ pèngle yì bízi hūi. Gāi dà guó de huídá shì "zìjǐ de shìqíng zìjǐ jiějué".

A: The president of that small country went to a large country to ask for assistance, with the result being that he was left out in the cold. That large country's response was, "solve your own issues."

Usage: Functions as predicate.

Note: Neutral in meaning.

196. 死猪不怕开水烫 (死豬不怕開水燙)
sǐ zhū bú pà kāi shuǐ tàng

Translated character by character, 死猪不怕开水烫 means 'dead-pig-not-afraid-boiling-water-scald,' whereas the implied meaning of this proverb would be 'the situation is already so bad that to make it worse makes no real difference.'

Example 1:

A: 你怎么那么胆大，啥话都敢说？

B: 在这个单位我是没前途了，**死猪不怕开水烫**，大不了走人。

A: Nǐ zěnme nàme dǎndà, shá huà dōu gǎn shuō?

B: Zài zhège dānwèi wǒ shì méi qiántú le, sǐ zhū bú pà kāishuǐ tàng, dàbùliǎo zǒurén.

A: How are you so bold? Is there anything you don't dare say?

B: I simply don't have a future in this work unit anymore, so it doesn't affect me. At the worst, I'll just leave.

Example 2:

A: 他怎么抢了一家又一家银行？

B: 他是**死猪不怕开水烫**，抢一家就够在监狱待一辈子的。这家伙够疯狂的。

A: Tá zěnme qiǎngle yì jiā yòu yì jiā yínháng?

B: Tā shì sǐ zhū bú pà kāishuǐ tàng, qiǎng yì jiā jiù gòu zài jiānyù dāi yíbèizi de. Zhè jiāhuo gòu fēngkuáng de.

A: How does he rob bank after bank?

B: It makes no difference to him. Robbing one bank is enough to earn a life sentence. This guy is crazy.

Usage: Usually used singly.

Note: Slightly derogatory and humorous in meaning.

---

197. 换汤不换药 (換湯不換藥) huàn tāng bú huàn yào

Translated character by character, 换汤不换药 means 'change-water-not-change-medicine,' whereas the implied meaning of this proverb would be 'a change in form but not in content.' Its functional translation is 'putting old wine in new bottles.'

Example 1:

A: 政府又在精简机构呢。

B: **换汤不换药**，都精简好几次了，可是越简越多。

A: Zhèngfǔ yòu zài jīngjiǎn jīgòu ne.

B: Huàn tāng bú huàn yào, dōu jīngjiǎn hǎo jǐ cì le, kěshì yuè jiǎn yuè duō.

A: The government is downsizing again.

B: They're just putting old wine in new bottles. The government has been pared back time and again, but it gets bigger with every downsizing.

Example 2:

A: 马教授最近提出了一种新的理论。

B: 又是**换汤不换药**，跟三十年前的理论没一点区别。

A: Mǎ jiàoshòu zuìjìn tíchū le yìzhǒng xīnde lǐlùn.

B: Yòu shì huàn tāng bú huàn yào, gēn sānshí nián qián de lǐlùn méi yìdiǎnr qūbié.

A: Professor Ma put forward a new theory recently.

B: He's putting old wine in new bottles again; it's no different from the theory of 30 years ago.

Usage: Functions as predicate.

Note: Slightly derogatory in meaning. Chinese people used traditional Chinese medicine to diagnose and treat diseases in ancient times. Chinese medicine was the most popular means of medical intervention, and the medicine was generally made by steeping herbs in water. Comparatively speaking, the herbs were much more important than the water.

198. 救命稻草 (救命稻草) jiù mìng dào cǎo

Translated character by character, 救命稻草 means 'save-life-straw,' whereas the implied meaning of this proverb would be 'a potential remedy to a dire situation.' Its functional translation is 'a straw to clutch at.'

Example 1:

A: 股市低迷，取消印花税成了最后的**救命稻草**。

A: Gǔshì dīmí, qǔxiāo yìnhuāshuì chéngle zuìhòu de jiùmìng dàocǎo.

A: With the stock market depressed, repealing the stamp tax became a straw to clutch at.

Example 2:

A: 她失业一年半了，找了无数次工作都不成功。昨天有个公司给了她一份薪水很低的工作，她就像抓住了一根**救命稻草**，马上答应了下来。

A: Tā shīyè yì nián bàn le, zhǎole wúshù cì gōngzuò dōu bù chénggōng. Zuótiān yǒu gè gōngsī gěile tā yí fèn xīnshuǐ hěn dī de gōngzuò, tā jiù xiàng zhuāzhùle yì gēn jiùmìng dàocǎo, mǎshàng dāyìngle xiàlái.

A: She's been unemployed for a year and a half now, and hasn't been successful in her countless job searches. Yesterday, a company offered her a low-salary job and she, as though clutching at a straw, immediately committed.

Usage: Functions as object, usually after the verb '抓住.'

Note: Neutral in meaning.

199. 明枪易躲，暗箭难防 (明槍易躲，暗箭難防)
míng qiāng yì duǒ, àn jiàn nán fáng

Translated character by character, 明枪易躲，暗箭难防 means 'open-spear-easy-dodge, hidden-arrow-hard-guard,' whereas the implied meaning of this proverb would be 'open attacks are easy to plan against, but unexpected attacks are hard to prevent.' Its functional translation is 'better an open enemy than a false friend,' or 'an open foe may prove a curse; but a pretend friend is even worse.'

Example 1:

A: 最近他好像不再处处与你为敌了。

B: 希望如此。不过，**明枪易躲，暗箭难防**，我还得加点儿小心。

A: Zuìjìn tā hǎoxiàng búzài chùchù yǔ nǐ wéi dí le.

B: Xīwàng rúcǐ. Búguò, míng qiāng yì duǒ, àn jiàn nán fáng, wǒ hái děi jiā diǎnr xiǎoxīn.

A: Recently, he doesn't seem to be opposing you at every turn anymore.

B: I hope so. However, better an open enemy than a false friend. I should still be a little more careful.

Example 2:

A: 他极力提倡改革，因此触犯了保守派的利益。虽然他也很善于保护自己，但是毕竟**明枪易躲，暗箭难防**，保守派暗地里搜集到了一些对他不利的材料，最后用这些材料逼他辞职。

A: Tā jílì tíchàng gǎigé, yīncǐ chùfàn le bǎoshǒupài de lìyì. Suīrán tā yě hěn shànyú bǎohù zìjǐ, dànshì bìjìng míng qiāng yì duǒ, àn jiàn nán fáng, bǎoshǒupài àndìlǐ sōují dào le yìxiē duì tā búlì de cáiliào, zuìhòu yòng zhèxiē cáiliào bī tā cízhí.

A: He fervently advocates reform, so he went against the Conservative Party's interests. While he is very good at protecting himself, an open foe may prove a curse; but a pretend friend is even worse. The Conservative Party secretly found some materials that were damaging to him and, in the end, used them to force him to resign.

Usage: Used singly.

Note: Neutral in meaning.

200.　谋事在人，成事在天 (謀事在人，成事在天)
móu shì zài rén, chéng shì zài tiān

Translated character by character, 谋事在人，成事在天 means 'plan-event-on-person, accomplish-event-on-heaven,' whereas the implied meaning of this proverb would be 'the planning lies with man, the outcome with heaven.' Its functional translation is 'man proposes, god disposes,' or 'it's all in god's hands now.'

Example 1:

A: 我们有多大的胜算？

B: 别去想了，**谋事在人，成事在天**。

A: Wǒmen yǒu duō dà de shèngsuàn?

B: Bié qù xiǎng le, móu shì zài rén, chéng shì zài tiān.

A: What are our odds?

B: Don't worry about it. It's all in god's hands now.

Example 2:

A: 咳，这么优秀的人，居然没成功。

B: 是啊，**谋事在人，成事在天**，有时候你得信命。

A: Hài, zhème yōuxiù de rén, jūrán méi chénggōng.

B: Shì a, móu shì zài rén, chéng shì zài tiān, yǒushíhòu nǐ děi xìnmìng.

A: Oh, that impressive person surprisingly didn't succeed.

B: Yeah, man proposes, god disposes. Sometimes you need to accept fate.

Usage: Used singly.

Note: Neutral in meaning.

---

201. 三个女人一台戏 (三個女人一臺戲)
sān gè nǔ rén yì tái xì

Translated character by character, 三个女人一台戏 means 'three-women-a-MW-show,' whereas the implied meaning of this proverb would be 'there will be drama when many women are put together.' Its functional translation is 'three women make a market, four a fair.'

Example 1:

A: 把新来的小王安排到那个办公室吧。

B: 这恐怕不太合适吧？**三个女人一台戏**，现在四位小姐，还用干活儿吗？不得把办公室闹翻了天啊！

A: Bǎ xīn lái de Xiǎo Wáng ānpái dào nàgè bàngōngshì ba.

B: Zhè kǒngpà bú tài héshì ba? Sān gè nǔrén yì tái xì, xiànzài sì wèi xiǎojiě, hái yòng gàn huór ma? Bù děi bǎ bàngōngshì nào fān le tiān a!

A: Put the newly arrived Little Wang in that office.

B: I'm afraid that isn't so appropriate. Three women make a market, four a fair. With four ladies now, how can they do their work? They'll turn the office upside down!

Example 2:

A: 她们三个有矛盾。

B: 一定的，**三个女人一台戏**，以后有好戏看了。

A: Tāmen sān gè yǒu máodùn.

B: Yídìng de, sān gè nǔrén yì tái xì, yǐhòu yǒu hǎo xì kàn le.

A: There's an issue between the three of them.
B: That's for sure. Three women make a market, four a fair. This will be fun to watch.

Usage: Used singly.

Note: Derogatory in meaning.

---

202. 有鼻子有眼 (有鼻子有眼) yǒu bízi yǒu yǎn

Translated character by character, 有鼻子有眼 means 'have-nose-have-eyes,' whereas the implied meaning of this proverb would be 'to vividly describe something.' Its functional translation is '(to paint) a word picture.'

Example 1:

A: 他没去过法国，但是看过很多关于法国的书，所以说起法国的事也说得**有鼻子有眼**。

A: Tā méi qùguò Fǎguó, dànshì kànguò hěnduō guānyú Fǎguó de shū, suǒyǐ shuōqǐ fǎguó de shì yě shuō de yǒu bízi yǒu yǎn.

A: He's never been to France, but he's read a lot of books about France, so when he speaks about French things, he's still able to paint a word picture.

Example 2:

A: 他被警察带走了！
B: 真的吗？
A: 是真的，我听人说了，他就是中午吃饭的时候被带走的，饭馆里很多人都看见了。
B: 看他们说得**有鼻子有眼**的，好像真的，不过，都是谣言，因为刚才我看见他还在办公室。

A: Tā bèi jǐngchá dàizǒu le!
B: Zhēnde ma?
A: Shì zhēnde, wǒ tīng rén shuō le, tā jiùshì zhōngwǔ chīfàn de shíhòu bèi dàizǒu de, fànguǎn lǐ hěnduō rén dōu kànjiàn le.
B: Kàn tāmen shuō de yǒu bízi yǒu yǎn de, hǎoxiàng zhēnde, búguò, dōu shì yáoyán, yīnwèi gāngcái wǒ kànjiàn tā hái zài bàngōngshì.

A: He was taken away by the cops!
B: Really?
A: Really! I heard people talking. He was taken away when he was eating this afternoon. A lot of people in the restaurant saw.
B: Look, they painted a word picture and it seems true, but it's all hearsay, because I just now saw him still in his office.

Usage: Functions as complement. It is usually used after '说得.'

Note: Slightly derogatory in meaning.

203. 枪打出头鸟 （槍打出頭鳥） qiāng dǎ chū tóu niǎo

Translated character by character, 枪打出头鸟 means 'gun-shoot-stick-out-bird,' whereas the implied meaning of this proverb would be 'the hunter will shoot the bird that sticks its head out.'

Example 1:

A: 最近你低调一点儿，别太张扬了。

B: 怎么了？爸爸？

A: 现在媒体上反腐败的声势很大，**枪打出头鸟**，你别成第一个中枪的。

A: Zuìjìn nǐ dīdiào yìdiǎnr, bié tài zhāngyáng le.

B: Zěnme le? Bàba?

A: Xiànzài méitǐ shàng fǎn fǔbài de shēngshì hěn dà, qiāng dǎ chū tóu niǎo, nǐ bié chéng dì yī gè zhòngqiāng de.

A: You should be a little more low key these days. Don't be too overt.

B: What's wrong, dad?

A: The emphasis on anti-corruption in the media is very heavy now. The hunter will shoot the bird that sticks its head out. Don't be the first one to get caught.

Example 2:

A: 他的前途怎么样？

B: 这个年青人有能力，就是太喜欢出风头。**枪打出头鸟**，说不定哪天就倒霉了。

A: Tā de qiántú zěnmeyàng?

B: Zhège niánqīngrén yǒu nénglì, jiùshì tài xǐhuān chū fēngtou. Qiāng dǎ chū tóu niǎo, shuōbúdìng nǎ tiān jiù dǎoméi le.

A: How does his future look?

B: That young person is capable, but he's too fond of the limelight. The nail that sticks up gets hammered down. One can't say when his luck will run out.

Usage: Used singly.

Note: Slightly derogatory in meaning.

204. 碰钉子 (碰釘子) pèng dìngzi

Translated character by character, 碰钉子 means 'meet-nail,' whereas the implied meaning of this proverb would be 'to be met with rejection.' Its functional translation is 'to be rebuffed.'

Example 1:

A: 合作的事谈得怎么样？

B: 别提了，人家根本没什么兴趣。我**碰**了个**钉子**。

A: Hézuò de shì tán de zěnmeyàng?

B: Bié tí le, rénjia gēnběn méi shénme xìngqù. Wǒ pèngle gè dìngzi.

A: How're the cooperation negotiations going?

B: Don't bring that up. They really aren't interested at all. I've been rebuffed.

Example 2:

A: 这件事怎么这么顺利？

B: 其实也不是，开始的时候也**碰**了不少**钉子***。

A: Zhè jiàn shì zěnme zhème shùnlì?

B: Qíshí yě búshì, kāishǐ de shíhòu yě pèng le bùshǎo dìngzi.

A: How is this going so smoothly?

B: It actually isn't. At the outset we were rebuffed quite a few times.

Usage: Functions as predicate.

Note: Neutral in meaning.

205. 蹬鼻子上脸 (蹬鼻子上臉) dēng bízi shàng liǎn

Translated character by character, 蹬鼻子上脸 means 'climb-nose-mount-face.' Its implied meaning is 'to go too far.'

Example 1:

A: 姐夫敢打咱姐姐。

B: 上次就把姐姐气哭了，现在简直**蹬鼻子上脸**了。咱哥儿俩好好收拾收拾他，给他点儿颜色看看。

A: Jiěfu gǎn dǎ zán jiějie.

B: Shàng cì jiù bǎ jiějie qì kū le, xiànzài jiǎnzhí dēng bízi shàng liǎn le. Zánmen ger liǎ hǎohāo shōushi shōushi ta, gěi tā diǎnr yánsè kànkan.

A: How dare our brother-in-law beat our sister!

B: Last time he made our sister so angry she cried. Now he's truly gone too far. The two of us should go teach him a lesson and set him straight.

Example 2:

A: 小王又提出升职请求了。

B: 前段时间他闹涨工资，那次满足他了，这回**蹬鼻子上脸**了，看来他的胃口不小啊。

A: Xiǎo Wáng yòu tíchū shēngzhí qǐngqiú le.

B: Qián duàn shíjian tā nào zhǎng gōngzī, nà cì mǎnzú tā le, zhè huí dēng bízi shàng liǎn le, kànlai tā de wèikǒu bù xiǎo a.

A: Little Wang requested a promotion again.

B: He'd been agitating for a raise before and we obliged him. Now, he's gone too far. It seems he's just greedy.

Usage: Functions as predicate.

Note: Slightly derogatory and humorous in meaning.

---

206. 吃豆腐 (吃豆腐) chī dòufu

Translated character by character, 吃豆腐 means 'eat-tofu,' whereas the implied meaning of this proverb would be 'to eat tofu.' Its functional translation is 'to come on to' or 'to take advantage of a woman.'

Example 1:

A: 他这个人见到漂亮女人就拔不开步。

B: 总想**吃豆腐**。

A: Tā zhègè rén jiàndào piàoliang nǔrén jiù bá bù kāi bù.

B: Zǒng xiǎng chī dòufu.

A: When this guy spots a beautiful woman he can't just move on.

B: He always wants to make a move.

Example 2:

A: 大姐，今天没人请吃饭啊？

B: 那也轮不到你，想**吃**老娘的**豆腐**，你还嫩点儿。

A: Dàjiě, jīntiān méi rén qǐng chīfàn a?

B: Nà yě lún bú dào nǐ, xiǎng chī lǎoniáng de dòufu, nǐ hái nèng diǎnr.

A: Miss, has no one asked you out yet today?

B: It's not your turn yet. You're too young to be taking advantage of this old lady.

Usage: Functions as predicate. Some words, such as 'hers' (她的), 'mine' (我的), 'a beautiful woman's' (漂亮女人的), 'an old lady's' (老娘的), etc. can be inserted into this phrase without changing its idiomatic meaning.

Note: Humorous and slightly derogatory in meaning. 吃豆腐 comes from Southern dialects. As such, it is used more often in the South (including Taiwan).

---

207. 眉毛胡子一把抓 (眉毛鬍子一把抓)
méimao húzi yì bǎ zhuā

Translated character by character, 眉毛胡子一把抓 means 'eyebrow-beard-one-hand-grab,' whereas the implied meaning of this proverb would be 'to do everything at once.' Its functional translation is 'to tackle everything all at once,' or 'to deal with everything in one fell swoop.'

Example 1:

A: 我怎么老有干不完的事啊？

B: 每个人都有很多事，但事情的重要性不同，你不能**眉毛胡子一把抓**，要分清重点，做事讲先后。

A: Wǒ zěnme lǎo yǒu gàn bù wán de shì a?

B: Měigè rén dōu yǒu hěnduō shì, dàn shìqíng de zhòngyàoxìng bùtóng, nǐ bùnéng méimao húzi yì bǎ zhuā, yào fēnqīng zhòngdiǎn, zuòshì jiǎng xiānhòu.

A: Why do I always have things that I can't finish?

B: Everyone has a lot of issues, but those issues are of differing degrees of importance. You can't try to tackle everything all at once. You have to clearly identify your focus and prioritize things.

Example 2:

A: 他的报告内容丰富，有很多细节，但缺点是**眉毛胡子一把抓**，分不清主次。

A: Tā de bàogào nèiróng fēngfù, yǒu hěnduō xìjié, dàn quēdiǎn shì méimao húzi yì bǎ zhuā, fēn bù qīng zhǔcì.

A: His report had a lot of content and detail, but its weakness was that it tackled everything at once and wasn't organized.

Usage: Functions as predicate.

Note: Slightly derogatory and humorous in meaning.

208. 偷鸡不成反蚀把米 (偷雞不成反蝕把米)
tōu jī bù chéng fǎn shí bǎ mǐ

Translated character by character, 偷鸡不成反蚀把米 means 'steal-chicken-not-successful-instead-lose-handful-rice,' whereas the implied meaning of this proverb would be 'to seek to better oneself but end up losing what one already had.' Its functional translation is 'to go out for wool and come back shorn.'

Example 1:

A: 1997–98年的东南亚金融危机中，对冲基金在泰国、印尼等地大赚了一笔之后又想做空香港股市。没想到中国政府动用外汇储备，强力救市，结果对冲基金**偷鸡不成反蚀把米**，在香港吃了不小的亏。

A: 1997–98 nián de Dōngnányà jīnróng wēijī zhōng, duìchōng jījīn zài Tàiguó, Yìnní děng dì dà zhuàn le yì bǐ zhīhòu yòu xiǎng zuòkōng Xiānggǎng gǔshì. Méixiǎngdào Zhōngguó zhèngfǔ dòngyòng wàihuì chǔbèi, qiánglì jiùshì, jiéguǒ duìchōng jījīn tōu jī bù chéng fǎn shí bǎ mǐ, zài Xiānggǎng chī le bù xiǎo de kuī.

A: In the midst of the 1997–98 Southeast Asian financial crisis, after they made a killing in Thailand and Indonesia, hedge funds wanted to speculate in the Hong Kong stock market. They didn't expect China would employ its foreign currency reserves to wrestle the market back from the brink. In the end, the hedge funds went out for wool and came back shorn, having lost a great deal of money in Hong Kong.

Example 2:

A: 他们故意输球，就是为了在淘汰赛中避免遇到皇家马德里队。

B: 嘿嘿，他们做梦也没想到这个小组中的那支最弱的队居然战胜了另外一支强队。他们**偷鸡不成反蚀把米**，连小组赛都没有出线。

A: Tāmen gùyì shū qiú, jiùshì wèile zài táotàisài zhōng bìmiǎn yùdào Huángjiā Mǎdélǐ Duì.

B: Hēi hēi, tāmen zuòmèng yě méi xiǎngdào zhège xiǎozǔ zhōng de nà zhī zuì ruò de duì jūrán zhànshèngle lìngwài yì zhī qiáng duì. Tāmen tōu jī bù chéng fǎn shí bǎ mǐ, lián xiǎozǔsài dōu méiyǒu chūxiàn.

A: They threw the match so that they could face Real Madrid in the elimination rounds.

B: Haha, not even in their dreams would they imagine that the weakest team in the group stage would defeat another strong team. They went out for wool and came back shorn; they didn't even make it out of the group stage.

Usage: Functions as predicate.

Note: Slightly derogatory and humorous in meaning.

209. 众人拾柴火焰高 (眾人拾柴火焰高)
zhòng rén shí chái huǒ yàn gāo

Translated character by character, 众人拾柴火焰高 means 'many-people-collect-twig-fire-flame-high,' whereas the implied meaning of this proverb would be 'many people working together allows greater achievement.' Its functional translation is 'many hands make light work,' or 'little things add up.'

Example 1:

A: 我没好办法了。

B: 没关系，我们可以搞问卷调查，征求大家的意见，**众人拾柴火焰高**嘛。

A: Wǒ méi hǎo bànfǎ le.

B: Méiguānxì, wǒmen kěyǐ gǎo wènjuàn diàochá, zhēngqiú dàjiā de yìjiàn, zhòngrén shíchái huǒyàn gāo ma.

A: I don't have a good solution.

B: It's OK. We can conduct a questionnaire survey and solicit everyone's opinions. Many hands make light work.

Example 2:

A: 如果每人都捐助一块钱，但是人人都捐助的话，那么，**众人拾柴火焰高**，总量也是很大的。

A: Rúguǒ měi rén dōu juānzhù yī kuài qián, dànshì rénrén dōu juānzhù de huà, nàme, zhòngrén shíchái huǒyàn gāo, zǒngliàng yě shì hěn dà de.

A: If each person contributes a dollar, but everyone contributes, then little things will add up and the total will be very large.

Usage: Used singly.

Note: Complimentary in meaning.

210. 快刀斩乱麻 (快刀斬亂麻) kuài dāo zhǎn luàn má

Translated character by character, 快刀斩乱麻 means 'sharp-knife-chop-messy-knot,' whereas the implied meaning of this proverb would be 'to quickly solve a complicated problem by being decisive and taking resolute action.' Its functional translation is 'to cut the Gordian knot.'

Example 1:

A: 这事儿我再想想。

B: 还想什么啊？芝麻点儿事儿，本来很简单，让你越想越复杂。其实根本没那么复杂，你**快刀斩乱麻**，做完了就完了。

A:　Zhè shìr wǒ zài xiǎngxiǎng.

B:　Hái xiǎng shénme a? Zhīma diǎnr shìr, běnlái hěn jiǎndān, ràng nǐ yuè xiǎng yuè fùzá. Qíshí gēnběn méi nàme fùzá, nǐ kuài dāo zhǎn luàn má, zuò wánle jiù wán le.

A:　I'll think some more about this issue.

B:　What is there to think about? It's a trivial issue. It was very simple, but the more you thought the more complicated it got. But it's really not that complicated, you should cut the Gordian knot. When it's done, it's done.

Example 2:

A:　新政府**快刀斩乱麻**，只用了一年时间就解决了上届政府遗留下来的众多难题。办事效率真高。

A:　Xīn zhèngfǔ kuài dāo zhǎn luàn má, zhǐ yòngle yì nián shíjiān jiù jiějué le shàng jiè zhèngfǔ yíliú xiàlái de zhòngduō nántí. Bànshì xiàolǜ zhēn gāo.

A:　The new government cut the Gordian knot, solving the stubborn problems they inherited from the previous administration in only a year. Their problem solving efficacy is impressive.

Usage: Functions as predicate.

Note: Complimentary in meaning.

211.　吃软饭 (吃軟飯) chī ruǎn fàn

Translated character by character, 吃软饭 means 'eat-soft-rice.' Its functional translation is 'freeloader,' or 'to freeload.'

Example 1:

A:　他又帅又有魅力，事业又很成功。

B:　他啊，是个**吃软饭**的，全靠他老婆。没有他老婆，他顶多也就是个三线演员。

A:　Tā yòu shuài yòu yǒu mèilì, shìyè yòu hěn chénggōng.

B:　Tā a, shì gè chīruǎnfàn de, quán kào tā lǎopo. Méiyǒu tā lǎopo, tā dǐngduō yě jiùshì gè sān xiàn yǎnyuán.

A:　He's handsome, he's charming, and he's successful.

B:　Him? He's a freeloader. He relies on his wife for everything. If he didn't have his wife, he would be, at best, a C-list performer.

Example 2:

A:　老婆，再给我一次机会吧。

B:　你这个废物，就靠**吃软饭**活着，哪天像个男人来着。

A:　Lǎopo, zài gěi wǒ yí cì jīhuì ba.

B:　Nǐ zhège fèiwu, jiù kào chīruǎnfàn huózhe, nǎ tiān xiàng gè nánren láizhe.

A: Baby, give me another chance!

B: You're a good-for-nothing, freeloading to get by. When have you ever been a man?

Usage: Functions as predicate, or attributive.

Note: Used to be strongly derogatory, but has become slightly derogatory with time.

---

212.   一着不慎，满盘皆输（一招不慎，滿盤皆輸）
yì zhāo bú shèn, mǎn pán jiē shū

Translated character by character, 一着不慎，满盘皆输 means 'one-move-not-cautious, whole-board-all-lose.' Its functional translation is 'one false move may lose the game.'

Example 1:

A: 这是关系到两国外交关系的大事，务必格外谨慎，**一着不慎，满盘皆输**。

A: Zhè shì guānxì dào liǎng guó wàijiāo guānxì de dàshì, wùbì géwài jǐnshèn, yì zhāo bú shèn, mǎn pán jiē shū.

A: This is a big issue that will affect the diplomatic relationship between the two countries. We must be particularly careful. One false move may lose the game.

Example 2:

A: 两个人正在竞选市长，对各种利益集团的要求尽量满足，或者不明确表态，生怕**一着不慎，满盘皆输**。

A: Liǎng gè rén zhèngzài jìngxuǎn shìzhǎng, duì gèzhǒng lìyì jítuán de yāoqiú jìnliàng mǎnzú, huòzhě bù míngquè biǎotài, shēng pà yì zhāo bú shèn, mǎn pán jiē shū.

A: The two people currently running for mayor are trying their utmost to satisfy the demands of various interest groups, or to not express a clear stance, lest one false move lose the game.

Usage: Used singly.

Note: Neutral in meaning.

---

213.   听风就是雨（聽風就是雨） tīng fēng jiù shì yǔ

Translated character by character, 听风就是雨 means 'hear-wind-then-be-rain,' whereas the implied meaning of this proverb would be 'to jump to conclusions from insignificant evidence.'

Example 1:

A: 不好了，中东要打起来了。

B: 谁说的？你别**听风就是雨**。过去一艘航空母舰就一定会打仗吗？

A: Bù hǎo le, Zhōngdōng yào dǎ qǐlái le.

B: Shéi shuō de? Nǐ bié **tīng fēng jiùshì yǔ**. Guòqù yì sōu hángkōngmǔjiàn jiù yídìng huì dǎzhàng ma?

A: It's a mess. The Middle East is going to blow up.

B: Says who? Don't jump to conclusions from insignificant evidence. Do you think that war is coming whenever an aircraft carrier is sent over there?

Example 2:

A: 我们要有自信心，不能**听风就是雨**。

A: Wǒ men yào yǒu zìxìnxīn, bùnéng **tīng fēng jiùshì yǔ**.

A: We need to have self-confidence. We can't jump to conclusions from insignificant evidence.

Usage: Functions as predicate.

Note: Slightly derogatory in meaning.

214. 鸿门宴 (鴻門宴) Hóngmén yàn

Translated character by character, 鸿门宴 means 'Hongmen-banquet,' whereas the implied meaning of this proverb would be 'an event set up to provide the opportunity to attack an invitee.'

Example 1:

A: 听说他要请你吃饭。

B: 肯定是**鸿门宴**，我不想去。

A: Tīngshuō tā yào qǐng nǐ chīfàn.

B: Kěndìng shì **Hóngményàn**, wǒ bù xiǎng qù.

A: I heard he is going to ask you to dinner.

B: It's definitely an ambush. I don't want to go.

Example 2:

A: 我们摆下**鸿门宴**，看他们有没有胆量来。

A: Wǒmen bǎi xià **Hóngményàn**, kàn tāmen yǒu méi yǒu dǎnliàng lái.

A: Let's lay down an ambush and see if he has the guts to show up.

Usage: Functions as object.

Note: Neutral in meaning.

215. 吃哑巴亏 (吃啞巴虧) chī yǎba kuī

Translated character by character, 吃哑巴亏 means 'eat-mute-loss,' whereas the implied meaning of this proverb would be 'to silently accept a bad outcome.' Its functional translation is 'to bite one's tongue,' or 'to hold one's tongue.'

Example 1:

A: 初到美国的中国人，由于语言不通的关系，不少事情明知不合理，但是不能据理力争，只好**吃哑巴亏**。

A: Chū dào Měiguó de Zhōngguó rén, yóuyú yǔyán bù tōng de guānxì, bùshǎo shìqíng míngzhī bù hélǐ, dànshì bùnéng jùlǐ-lìzhēng, zhǐhǎo chī yǎba kuī.

A: Due to a language divide, Chinese people who have just arrived in America know perfectly well that many things are unjust, but can't elucidate their arguments, so they bite their tongues.

Example 2:

A: 有些女雇员受到男上司的性骚扰，不敢报警。一是怕证据不足，二是怕名声受到影响，所以**吃了不少哑巴亏**。

A: Yǒuxiē nǚ gùyuán shòudào nán shàngsī de xìngsāorǎo, bùgǎn bàojǐng. Yī shì pà zhèngjù bùzú, èr shì pà míngshēng shòudào yǐngxiǎng, suǒyǐ chīle bùshǎo yǎba kuī.

A: Some female employees suffer sexual harassment by male superiors and don't dare report it. First, they are afraid that there is insufficient evidence; second, they fear it will affect their reputation. So, they bite their tongues.

Usage: Functions as predicate.

Note: Slightly derogatory or neutral in meaning.

216. 眼中钉、肉中刺 (眼中釘、肉中刺)
yǎn zhōng dīng, ròu zhōng cì

Translated character by character, 眼中钉、肉中刺 means 'eye-inside-nail, flesh-inside-thorn,' whereas the implied meaning of this proverb would be 'an irritating impediment.' Its functional translation is 'a thorn in the side.'

Example 1:

A: 由于他屡屡在众人面前让领导难堪，领导决心拔掉这颗**眼中钉、肉中刺**，也就是把他解雇。

A: Yóuyú tā lǚlǚ zài zhòngrén miànqián ràng lǐngdǎo nánkān, lǐngdǎo juéxīn bádiào zhè kē yǎnzhōngdīng, ròuzhōngcì, yějiùshì bǎ tā jiěgù.

A: Because he embarrassed the leader in front of the public time and again, the leader was determined to remove this thorn from his side. That is to say: to fire him.

Example 2:

A: 朝鲜一直被一些国家视为**眼中钉**，他们总想借机颠覆朝鲜政权。

A: Cháoxiǎn yìzhí bèi yìxiē guójiā shìwéi yǎnzhōngdīng, ròuzhōngcì, tāmen zǒngshì xiǎng jièjī diānfù Cháoxiǎn zhèngquán.

A: North Korea has constantly been seen as a thorn in their side by a few countries, which are always looking for an opportunity to overthrow its regime.

Usage: Functions as objective.

Variant: 眼中钉、肉中刺

Note: Neutral in meaning.

---

217. 舍不得孩子套不住狼 (捨不得孩子套不住狼)
shě bù de háizi tào bú zhù láng

Translated character by character, 舍不得孩子套不住狼 means 'give up-not-able-child-catch-not-able-wolf,' whereas the implied meaning of this proverb would be 'one must take risks to reap rewards.' Its functional translation is 'you have to spend money to make money.'

Example 1:

A: 那个地方政府真是豁出去了，为了引进外资，答应外商无偿使用十五年土地。

B: **舍不得孩子套不住狼**，现在的狼胃口可大了。

A: Nàgè dìfāng zhèngfǔ zhēn shì huō chūqù le, wèile yǐnjìn wàizī, dāyìng wàishāng wúcháng shǐyòng shíwǔ nián tǔdì.

B: Shě bù de háizi tào bú zhù láng, xiànzài de láng wèikǒu kě dà le.

A: That municipal government really went all out. In order to attract foreign capital, they agreed to allow foreign businesses to use the land for free for fifteen years.

B: You have to spend money to make money. The appetites of foreign businessmen aren't easily satisfied nowadays.

Example 2:

A: 不行，我们这样亏大了。

B: 谁说不是呢？但是我们得把眼光放长远一点儿，**舍不得孩子套不住狼**。这次赔，下次赚。

A: Bùxíng, wǒmen zhèyàng kuī dà le.

B: Shéi shuō búshì ne? Dànshì wǒmen děi bǎ yǎnguāng fàng chángyuǎn yìdiǎnr, shě bù de háizi tào bú zhù láng. Zhècì péi, xiàcì zuàn.

A: That won't work. If we do that we'll lose a fortune.

B: Who said we wouldn't? But we need to set our sights a little further. You have to spend money to make money. This time we'll lose, next time we'll make a profit.

Usage: Used singly.

Variant: 舍不得孩子套不着狼

Note: Humorous in meaning.

---

218. 挂羊头、卖狗肉 (掛羊頭、賣狗肉)
guà yáng tóu, mài gǒu ròu

Translated character by character, 挂羊头、卖狗肉 means 'hang-goat-head, sell-dog-meat,' whereas the implied meaning of this proverb would be 'to sell dog meat while hanging a goat's head outside the shop/restaurant as advertisement.' Its functional translation is 'to cry wine and sell vinegar,' or 'to bait and switch.'

Example 1:

A: 咱们公司对面开了两家洗浴中心。

B: **挂羊头、卖狗肉**。鬼都知道那是色情服务场所。

A: Zánmen gōngsī duìmiàn kāile liǎng jiā xǐyù zhōngxin.

B: Guàyángtóu, màigǒuròu. Guǐ dōu zhīdao nà shì sèqíng fúwù chǎngsuǒ.

A: Two bathhouses opened across the way from our company.

B: That's crying wine and selling vinegar. Everyone knows those are 'massage parlours.'

Example 2:

A: 听说清华来的大教授要在我们学校开一门课，我想去注册。

B: 算了吧。前两年还有一个美国的教授开课呢，一个学期就见过一次面，剩下的都是助手教的。**挂羊头、卖狗肉**。

A: Tīngshuō Qīnghuá lái de dà jiàoshòu yào zài wǒmen xuéxiào kāi yì mén kè, wǒ xiǎng qù zhùcè.

B: Suàn le ba. Qián liǎng nián hái yǒu yígè Měiguó de jiàoshòu kāi kè ne, yígè xuéqī jiù jiànguò yí cì miàn, shèngxià de dōu shì zhùshǒu jiāo de. Guàyángtóu, màigǒuròu.

A: I hear that a famous professor from Tsinghua University is going to teach a class at our school. I want to go register.

B: Forget about it. Two years ago, there was an American professor teaching a course; I saw him only once that entire semester, the rest was taught by the TA. It's just a bait and switch.

Usage: Functions as predicate.

Note: Slightly derogatory in meaning.

219. 煮熟的鸭子飞了 (煮熟的鴨子飛了)
zhǔ shú de yāzi fēi le

Translated character by character, 煮熟的鸭子飞了 means 'boil-cooked-duck-fly-ed,' whereas the implied meaning of this proverb would be 'to lose something that is certain.' Its functional translation is 'to slip through one's fingers.'

Example 1:

A: 明天就决赛了，可是咱们的选手今天训练的时候受伤了。

B: 完了，**煮熟的鸭子飞了**，到手的金牌少了一块。

A: Míngtiān jiù juésài le, kěshì zánmen de xuǎnshǒu jīntiān xùnliàn de shíhou shòushāng le.

B: Wán le, zhǔ shú de yāzi fēi le, dàoshǒu de jīnpái shǎole yí kuài.

A: Tomorrow are the finals, but our contestant was injured during practice today.

B: That's it. It's slipped through our fingers. We'll get one fewer gold medal.

Example 2:

A: 对方已经同意了合同上的全部条款，明天就正式签约，不会再出现意外情况了吧？

B: 放心吧，**煮熟的鸭子飞不了**。

A: Duìfāng yǐjīng tóngyì le hétóng shàng de quánbù tiáokuǎn, míngtiān jiù zhèngshì qiānyuē, búhuì zài chūxiàn yìwài qíngkuàng le ba?

B: Fàngxīn ba, zhǔ shú de yāzi fēi bùliǎo.

A: They have already agreed to all of the conditions in the contract and are officially signing the document tomorrow. There won't be any more unexpected developments, right?

B: Relax! This won't slip through our fingers.

Usage: Used singly.

Note: Humorous in meaning.

220. **常在河边走，哪有不湿鞋 (常在河邊走，哪有不溼鞋)** cháng zài hé biān zǒu, nǎ yǒu bù shī xié

Translated character by character, 常在河边走，哪有不湿鞋 means 'often-on-river-side-walk, how-not-dampen-shoes,' whereas the implied meaning of this proverb would be 'you are marked by your surroundings.' Its functional translation is 'touch pitch, and you will be defiled.'

Example 1:

A: 听说咱们公司的现金出纳贪污了一万美元。

B: **常在河边走，哪有不湿鞋**的。大把大把的钞票每天从手里过，很难一点儿也不动心。

A: Tīngshuō zánmen gōngsī de xiànjīn chūnà tānwū le yíwàn měiyuán.

B: Cháng zài hé biān zǒu, nǎ yǒu bù shī xié de. Dà bǎ dà bǎ de chāopiào měitiān cóng shǒuli guò, hěn nán yìdiǎnr yě bú dòngxīn.

A: I heard our company's comptroller embezzled $10,000.

B: Touch pitch, and you will be defiled. Handling handfuls of bills every day, it's hard not to be tempted at least a little.

Example 2:

A: 她最初在酒吧只是唱歌，后来也陪客人喝酒了，有时候也陪客人出去过夜。

B: **常在河边走，哪能不湿鞋**？那种灯红酒绿的场合太腐蚀人了。

A: Tā zuìchū zài jiǔbā zhǐshì chànggē, hòulái yě péi kèren hējiǔ le, yǒushíhòu yě péi kèren chūqù guòyè.

B: Cháng zài hé biān zǒu, nǎ néng bù shī xié? Nàzhǒng dēnghóng-jiǔlǜ de chǎnghé tài fǔshí rén le.

A: At first, she only sang at the bar. Afterwards, she also started to drink with the clientele. Sometimes she also sleeps with them.

B: Touch pitch, and you shall be defiled. Those nightlife spots are too corrupting.

Usage: Used singly.

Variant: 常在河边走，哪能不湿鞋

Note: Humorous or neutral in meaning.

221. **三脚猫 (三腳貓)** sān jiǎo māo

Translated character by character, 三脚猫 means 'three-feet-cat,' whereas the implied meaning of this proverb would be 'to not have real skill.' Its functional translation is 'dilettantish,' or 'middling.'

Example 1:

A: 她开了一家影楼。

B: 以她那点儿**三脚猫**的照相技术，美女进去，丑八怪出来。

A: Tā kāile yì jiā yǐnglóu.

B: Yǐ tā nà diǎnr sānjiǎomāo de zhàoxiàng jìshù, měinǚ jìnqù, chǒubāguài chūlái.

A: He opened a photography studio.

B: With her dilettantish photography skills, beautiful women go in, and ugly monsters come out.

Example 2:

A: 他想在你面前显示显示他的能力。

B: 就他那点儿**三脚猫**的本事，还想在我面前耍，真是自不量力。

A: Tā xiǎng zài nǐ miànqián xiǎnshì xiǎnshì tā de nénglì.

B: Jiù tā nà diǎnr sānjiǎomāo de běnshì, hái xiǎng zài wǒ miànqián shuǎ, zhēn shì zìbúliànglì.

A: He wants to showcase his skills in front of you.

B: He wants to showcase his middling skills to me? He really overestimates himself.

Usage: Functions as predicative or attributive.

Note: Slightly derogatory in meaning.

---

222. 吃闭门羹 (吃閉門羹) chī bì mén gēng

Translated character by character, 吃闭门羹 means 'eat-shut-door-soup,' whereas the implied meaning of this proverb would be 'to be turned away at the door.' Its functional translation is 'to be left out in the cold,' or 'to get the cold shoulder.'

Example 1:

A: 我们一群人去了她家，结果**吃**了**闭门**羹。人家不在家。

A: Wǒmen yì qún rén qùle tā jiā, jiéguǒ chīle bìméngēng. Rénjia bú zài jiā.

A: The group of us went to her house and ended up being left out in the cold because she wasn't home.

Example 2:

A: 他是推销员，在**吃**了无数次**闭门**羹以后，练成了一开口就能吸引住别人的本领。

A: Tā shì tuīxiāoyuán, zài chīle wúshù cì bìméngēng yǐhòu, liàn chéng le yì kāi kǒu jiù néng xīyǐn zhù biérén de běnlǐng.

A: He's a salesman. After being cold-shouldered innumerable times, he developed the ability to captivate people quickly.

Usage: Functions as predicate.

Note: Neutral or humorous in meaning.

223. 三十年河东，三十年河西 (三十年河東，三十年河西) sānshí nián hé dōng, sānshí nián hé xī

Translated character by character, 三十年河东，三十年河西 means 'thirty-years-river-(flow) east, thirty-years-river-(flow) west,' whereas the implied meaning of this proverb would be 'things in life change often.' Its functional translation is 'change is the only constant,' or 'the wheel of fortune turns.'

Example 1:

A: 现在"毛泽东研究"又热了起来。

B: 真是三十年河东，三十年河西啊！

A: Xiànzài "Máo Zédōng Yánjiū" yòu rèle qǐlái.
B: Zhēn shì sānshí nián hé dōng, sānshí nián hé xī a!

A: The study of Mao Zedong has become hot again.
B: Change is the only constant, huh!

Example 2:

A: 史蒂夫·乔布斯创建了苹果公司，后来他被董事会解雇，再后来苹果陷入困境，公司又把乔布斯请了回来。

B: 三十年河东，三十年河西，乔布斯情何以堪啊？

A: Shǐdìfū Qiáobùsī chuàngjiàn le Píngguǒ gōngsī, hòulái tā bèi dǒngshìhuì jiěgù, zài hòulái Píngguǒ xiànrù kùnjìng, gōngsī yòu bǎ Qiáobùsī qǐngle huílái.
B: Sānshí nián hé dōng, sānshí nián hé xī, Qiáobùsī qínghéyǐkān a?

A: Steve Jobs founded Apple but later he was dismissed by the board. After that, when Apple fell on hard times, the company invited Jobs back again.
B: The wheel of fortune turns. For Jobs, love is too heavy, huh?

Usage: Functions as predicative or used singly.

Variant: 三十年河东河西

Note: Humorous in meaning.

224. 土包子 (土包子) tǔ bāozi

Translated character by character, 土包子 means 'rural-bun,' whereas the implied meaning of this proverb would be 'an extremely uncultured person from the countryside.' Its functional translation is 'a bumpkin,' or, when spoken of oneself, 'a boor.'

Example 1:

A: 这是什么东西啊？看起来味道不错。

B: **土包子**！什么都没见过。这是狗粮。

A: Zhè shì shénme dōngxī a? Kàn qǐlái wèidào búcuò.

B: Tǔ bāozi! Shénme dōu méi jiànguò. Zhè shì gǒuliáng.

A: What's this? It looks pretty tasty.

B: You bumpkin! You haven't seen anything. This is dog food.

Example 2:

A: 虽然他在中国的大城市住，但是到了上海以后就发现自己是个**土包子**。

A: Suīrán tā zài Zhōngguó de dàchéngshì zhù, dànshì dàole Shànghǎi yǐhòu jiù fāxiàn zìjǐ shì gè tǔbāozi.

A: While he lives in a big city in China, after he got to Shanghai, he realized he was a boor.

Usage: Nominal element, functions mainly as predicative or object.

Note: Derogatory in meaning.

225. 树大招风 (樹大招風) shù dà zhāo fēng

Translated character by character, 树大招风 means 'tree-big-catch-wind,' whereas the implied meaning of this proverb would be 'prominent people are at risk of being attacked.' Its functional translation is 'the winds howl around the highest peaks.'

Example 1:

A: 孩子，你怎么那么高调？不能低调一点儿吗？

B: 怎么了，爸爸？我的钱又不是偷来的、抢来的，我花自己的钱怎么不行？

A: 孩子，**树大招风**，你年轻轻的就有了几千万，别人会眼红的。

A: Háizi, nǐ zěnme nàme gāodiào? Bùnéng dīdiào yìdiǎnr ma?

B: Zénme le, bàba? Wǒde qián yòu búshì tōu lái de, qiǎng lái de, wǒ huā zìjǐ de qián zěnme bùxíng?

A: Háizi, shù dà zhāo fēng, nǐ niánqīngqing de jiù yǒule jǐ qiān wàn, biéren huì yǎnhóng de.

A: Son, why are you so flashy? Can't you be a little more low key?

B: What's wrong, Dad? My money isn't stolen. What's wrong about spending my own money?

A: Son, the winds howl around the highest peaks. You're already a multimillionaire at such a young age, people are apt to be jealous.

Example 2:

A: 这个艺人太张扬了，又是大摆生日宴，请666个名人参加；又是买私人城堡；还在全国招徒弟。

B: **树大招风**，估计税务局的人该盯上他了。

A: Zhègè yìrén tài zhāngyáng le, yòushì dà bǎi shēngriyàn, qǐng 666 gè míngrén cānjiā; yòushì mǎi sīrén chéngbǎo; hái zài quánguó zhāo túdi.

B: Shù dà zhao feng, gūji shuìwùjú de rén gāi dīng shang tā le.

A: That artist is too conspicuous. He threw a huge birthday party again, and invited 666 famous people to attend. He also bought his own castle. He's also scouring the world for an apprentice.

B: The winds howl around the highest peaks. The tax bureau might have paid attention to him.

Usage: Used singly.

Note: Neutral in meaning.

---

226. 酒逢知己千杯少 (酒逢知己千杯少)
jiǔ féng zhī jǐ qiān bēi shǎo

Translated character by character, 酒逢知己千杯少 means 'drinking-met-bosom-friend-thousand-toast-not enough.' Its functional translation is 'for a good friend, a thousand toasts are too few.'

Example 1:

A: 咱们再干一杯！

B: 不行，我已经喝了十几杯了。

A: 十几杯算什么！**酒逢知己千杯少**。我先干为敬！

A: Zánmen zài gān yì bēi!

B: Bùxíng, wǒ yǐjīng hēle shí jǐ bēi le.

A: Shí jǐ bēi suàn shénme? Jiǔ féng zhījǐ qiān bēi shǎo. Wǒ xiān gān wéi jìng.

A: Let's have another!

B: No, I've already had ten glasses.

A: What's ten glasses? For a good friend, a thousand toasts are too few. I'll show my respect by drinking first.

Example 2:

A: 今天难得大家这么高兴，**酒逢知己千杯少，**大家一定要尽兴！

A: Jīntiān nándé dàjiā zhème gāoxìng, jiǔ féng zhījǐ qiān bēi shǎo, dàjiā yídìng yào jìnxìng!

A: It's rare to see everyone as happy as today. For a good friend, a thousand toasts are too few. Everyone needs to let loose.

Usage: Used singly.

Note: Neutral in meaning.

227. 当一天和尚撞一天钟 (當一天和尚撞一天鐘)
dāng yì tiān héshang zhuàng yì tiān zhōng

Translated character by character, 当一天和尚撞一天钟 means 'be-one-day-monk-ring-one-day-bell,' whereas the implied meaning of this proverb would be 'to take a passive attitude towards one's work.' Its functional translation is 'to go through the motions.'

Example 1:

A: 反正我也不想在这家公司干了，混到年底拿到奖金就走人。

B: 你太缺乏职业精神了，**当一天和尚撞一天钟，**你得尽职尽责到最后一天。

A: Fǎnzhèng wǒ yě bù xiǎng zài zhè jiā gōngsī gàn le, hùn dào niándǐ ná dào jiǎngjīn jiù zǒurén.

B: Nǐ yě tài quēfá zhíyè jīngshen le, dāng yì tiān héshang zhuàng yì tiān zhōng, nǐ děi jìnzhí-jìnzé dào zuìhòu yì tiān.

A: I don't want to work at this company anymore. I'll coast until I get my bonus at the end of the year and then I'll leave.

B: You're so unprofessional, going through the motions. You need to stay diligent until your last day.

Example 2:

A: 他怎么每天都昏昏沉沉的，总是踩着点儿来，下班就走？

B: 他呀，啥时候努力过？总是**当一天和尚撞一天钟。**

A: Tā zěnme měi tiān dōu hūnhunchénchén de, zǒngshì cǎizhe diǎnr lái, xiàbān jiù zǒu.

B: Tā ya, shá shíhou nǔlì guò? Zǒngshì dāng yì tiān héshang zhuàng yì tiān zhōng.

A: How is he always so lethargic, arriving just in the nick of time and leaving as
      soon as work is over?

B: Him? When has he ever worked hard? He's always just going through the
      motions.

Usage: Functions as predicative, or used singly.

Variant: 做/作一天和尚撞一天钟

Note: Slightly derogatory and humorous in meaning.

228. 是骡子是马拉出来遛遛 (是騾子是馬拉出來遛遛)
shì luózi shì mǎ lā chūlai liùliu

Translated character by character, 是骡子是马拉出来溜溜 means 'is-mule-is-horse-
pull-out-to walk,' whereas the implied meaning of this proverb would be 'let's see
what you can do.' Its functional translation is 'actions speak louder than words,'
or 'it's time to see what someone is worth.'

Example 1:

A: 你有什么了不起？

B: 不服啊？**是骡子是马拉出来遛遛**。敢打一架吗？

A: Nǐ yǒu shénme liǎobùqǐ?

B: Bù fú a? Shì luózi shì mǎ lā chūlai liùliu. Gǎn dǎ yí jià ma?

A: What's so special about you?

B: You're not convinced? Actions speak louder than words. Do you dare go a
      round with me?

Example 2:

A: 世界杯足球赛就要举行了。

B: 这批球员平常养尊处优的，现在**是骡子是马**得**拉出来遛遛**了。

A: Shìjièbēi Zúqiúsài jiùyào jǔxíng le.

B: Zhè pī qiúyuán píngcháng yǎngzūn-chǔyōu de, xiànzài shì luózi shì mǎ děi lā
      chūlai liùliu le.

A: The FIFA World Cup is about to be held.

B: This group of soccer players normally lives in the lap of luxury, now it's time
      to see what they're worth.

Usage: Used singly.

Note: Slightly derogatory and humorous in meaning.

229. 一个鼻孔出气 (一個鼻孔出氣) yí gè bí kǒng chū qì

Translated character by character, 一个鼻孔出气 means 'one-nostril-out-breath,' whereas the implied meaning of this proverb would be 'to work together, often to dishonest ends.' Its functional translation is 'to be hand in glove.'

Example 1:

A: 她是这么说的。

B: 不要听她的。他们两个**一个鼻孔出气**。

A: Tā shì zhème shuō de.

B: Búyào tīng tā de. Tāmen liǎng gè yígè bíkǒng chūqì.

A: That's what she said.

B: Don't listen to her. The two of them are hand in glove.

Example 2:

A: 由于历史的关系，在国际舞台上，以色列和美国总是**一个鼻孔出气**。

A: Yóuyú lìshǐ de guānxi, zài guójì wǔtái shàng, Yǐsèliè hé Měiguó zǒngshì yígè bíkǒng chūqì.

A: Due to their history, on the international stage, Israel and the US are hand in glove.

Usage: Functions as predicate.

Note: Slightly derogatory in meaning.

230. 身在曹营心在汉 (身在曹營心在漢)
shēn zài Cáo yíng xīn zài Hàn

Translated character by character, 身在曹营心在汉 means 'body-in-Cao-camp-mind-in-Han,' whereas the implied meaning of this proverb would be 'to be physically present but have one's mind and allegiance elsewhere.' Its functional translation is 'to not have one's heart in something.'

Example 1:

A: 有的人工作之外还在网上开个小公司，因此上班的时候也是**身在曹营心在汉**，专心工作不了。

A: Yǒude rén gōngzuò zhīwài hái zài wǎngshàng kāi gè xiǎo gōngsī, yīncǐ shàngbān de shíhòu yě shì shēn zài Cáo yíng xīn zài Hàn, zhuānxīn gōngzuò bùliǎo.

A: Some people run a small business online outside of work. Because of this, their heart's not in it when they are in the office and they can't be focused on their work.

Example 2:

A: 你怎么又跟以前的女朋友联系？

B: 她最近有很多麻烦事。

A: 我有一件更大的麻烦事，那就是你。你跟我结婚了，可是**身在曹营心在汉**，心还在前任女友那里。

B: 不是，你误解我了。

A: Nǐ zěnme yòu gēn yǐqián de nǔpéngyǒu liánxì?

B: Tā zuìjìn yǒu hěnduō máfan shì.

A: Wǒ yǒu yí jiàn gèngdà de máfan shì, nà jiùshì nǐ. Nǐ gēn wǒ jiéhūn le, kěshì shēn zài Cáo yíng xīn zài Hàn, xīn hái zài qiánrèn nǔyǒu nàlǐ.

B: Búshì, nǐ wùjiě wǒ le.

A: Why did you get back in touch with your ex-girlfriend again?

B: She's been dealing with a lot of tough problems lately.

A: I have an even tougher problem. It's you. You married me but your heart's not in it. You're still in love with your ex-girlfriend.

B: No, you've misunderstood me.

Usage: Functions as predicative or predicate.

Note: Slightly derogatory in meaning. In the final years of the Eastern Han Dynasty, a very capable person, Xu Shu, was a counselor to the future emperor of the Shu Kingdom, Liu Bei. Knowing that Xu Shu was a dutiful son, Liu Bei's rival, Cao Cao, captured Xu Shu's mother in order to force him to help Cao Cao. Xu Shu was forced to abandon Liu Bei and go over to Cao Cao's camp, however, in his heart, he was still loyal to Liu Bei and he never contributed to Cao Cao's strategy.

231. 瘦死的骆驼比马大 (瘦死的駱駝比馬大)
shòu sǐ de luòtuo bǐ mǎ dà

Translated character by character, 瘦死的骆驼比马大 means 'skinny-die-camel-relative to-horse-bigger,' whereas the implied meaning of this proverb would be 'a starving camel is still bigger than a horse.'

Example 1:

A: 那次大地震以后，那个国家的经济就衰落了。

B: 我不这样认为，**瘦死的骆驼比马大**，它的经济基础很雄厚。

A: Nà cì dàdìzhèn yǐhòu, nàgè guójiā de jīngjì jiù shuāiluò le.

B: Wǒ bú zhèyàng rènwéi, shòu sǐ de luòtuo bǐ mǎ dà, tāde jīngjì jīchǔ hěn xiónghòu.

A: After that major earthquake, that country's economy collapsed.

B: I wouldn't agree; a starving camel is still bigger than a horse. The fundamentals of their economy are sound.

Example 2:

A:　上笔生意他赔惨了，可是他花钱还跟水儿似的。

B:　**瘦死的骆驼比马大**，人家拔根汗毛比咱们的腰都粗。

A:　Shàng bǐ shēngyì tā péi cǎn le, kěshì tā huāqián hái gēn shuǐr shìde.

B:　Shòu sǐ de luòtuo bǐ mǎ dà, rénjia bá gēn hànmáo bǐ zánmen de yāo dōu cū.

A:　He got clobbered on his last business deal, but he still spends money like it's water.

B:　A starving camel is still bigger than a horse. He's way wealthier than us.

Usage: Usually used singly.

Note: Humorous or neutral in meaning.

___

232. 树欲静而风不止 (樹欲靜而風不止)
shù yù jìng ér fēng bù zhǐ

Translated character by character, 树欲静而风不止 means 'tree-want-be still-but-wind-not-stop,' whereas the implied meaning of this proverb would be 'for a situation to take its own course regardless of someone's wishes.'

Example 1:

A:　哥哥，我们不要再跟他斗下去了，在这样下去会两败俱伤的。

B:　我也知道这个道理，可是**树欲静而风不止**啊？

A:　Gēge, wǒmen búyào zài gēn tā dòu xiàqù le, zài zhèyàng xiàqù huì liǎngbài-jùshāng de.

B:　Wǒ yě zhīdao zhègè dàoli, kěshì shù yù jìng ér fēng bù zhǐ a!

A:　Brother, we shouldn't keep fighting with him. If we continue like this, both sides will suffer.

B:　I know your reasoning, but this is out of our hands, right?

Example 2:

A:　只要存在着不同的意识形态，它们之间的斗争就会永远存在下去，即使一方想罢手也不行，因为**树欲静而风不止**。

A:　Zhǐyào cúnzàizhe bùtóng de yìshixíngtài, tāmen zhījiān de dòuzhēng jiùhuì yǒngyuǎn cúnzài xiàqu, jíshǐ yìfāng xiǎng bàshǒu yě bùxíng, yīnwèi shù yù jìng ér fēng bù zhǐ.

A:　So long as there exist different points of view, their conflict will continue forever. Even if one of them wants to give up, they can't, because it's taken on a life of its own.

Usage: Used singly and mainly in written form.

Note: Neutral in meaning.

233. 丑媳妇早晚也得见公婆 (醜媳婦早晚也得見公婆)
chǒu xífu zǎo wǎn yě děi jiàn gōng pó

Translated character by character, 丑媳妇早晚也得见公婆 means 'ugly-daughter-in-law-sooner or later-also-must-meet-parents-in-law,' whereas the implied meaning of this proverb would be 'one is unable to avoid an unpleasant experience forever.'

Example 1:

A: 书记，我第一次跟这么多大媒体的记者见面，心里有点儿虚。

B: 市长大人，这是你份内的事，再说**丑媳妇早晚也得见公婆**。别紧张，必要的时候我会帮你一下。

A: Shūjì, wǒ dì-yī cì gēn zhème duō dà méitǐ de jìzhě jiànmiàn, xīnlǐ yǒudiǎnr xū.

B: Shìzhǎng dàrén, zhè shì nǐ fènnèi de shì, zàishuō chǒu xífu zǎowǎn yě děi jiàn gōngpó. Bié jǐnzhāng, bìyào de shíhòu wǒ huì bāng nǐ yíxià.

A: Secretary, this will be the first time I've met with this many reporters from big media outlets; I'm a little bit nervous.

B: Mr. Mayor, these things are in your job description. Moreover, you can't avoid unpleasant experiences forever. Don't be nervous. When it's necessary, I'll help you.

Example 2:

A: 在钢琴大赛上，他明知自己弹得还不够完美，但是敢于抛开 “**丑媳妇怕见公婆**” 的心理，大胆地弹了起来。

A: Zài gāngqín dàsài shàng, tā míngzhī zìjǐ tán de hái búgòu wánměi, dànshì gǎnyú pāokāi "chǒu xífu pà jiàn gōngpó" de xīnlǐ, dàdǎn de tánle qǐlái.

A: At the big piano competition, he knew perfectly well that that he couldn't play well enough, but he dared to cast aside his mindset of wanting to avoid an unpleasant experience, and played bravely.

Usage: Used mainly singly.

Variant: 丑媳妇总要见公婆

Note: Neutral or humorous in meaning.

234. 胜者王侯败者贼 (勝者王侯敗者賊)
shèng zhě wáng hóu bài zhě zéi

Translated character by character, 胜者王侯败者贼 means 'winner-knight-loser-traitor,' whereas the implied meaning of this proverb would be 'victory absolves all sins and the defeated party is vilified.' Its functional translation, is 'history is written by the victors,' or 'winning isn't everything, it's the only thing.'

Example 1:

A: 媒体的焦点全部在胜选的总统候选人身上，而败选的总统候选人已
   经没人理了。可是几天前完全不是这个样子。

B: 这没什么。**胜者王侯败者贼**。败选的总统候选人已经成为历史了，
   没有人对历史感兴趣。

A: Méitǐ de jiāodiǎn quánbù zài shèngxuǎn de zǒngtǒng hòuxuǎnrén shēnshàng,
   ér bàixuǎn de zǒngtǒng hòuxuǎnrén yǐjīng méi rén lǐ le. Kěshì jǐ tiān qián
   wánquán búshì zhège yàngzi.

B: Zhè méi shénme. Shèng zhě wánghóu bài zhě zéi. Bàixuǎn de zǒngtǒng
   hòuxuǎnrén yǐjīng chéngwéi lìshǐ le, méiyǒu rén duì lìshǐ gǎn xìngqù.

A: All of the media's attention is focused on the winning presidential candidate
   and everyone has lost interest in the losing candidate already. But just a few
   days ago it was entirely different.

B: That's normal. History is written by the victors. The losing candidate is history
   already and no one's interested in history.

Example 2:

A: 这年头，大家都只认结果，没有人在意过程和手段，只要最后赢了
   就好。**胜者王侯败者贼**。

A: Zhè niántou, dàjiā dōu zhǐ rèn jiéguǒ, méiyǒu rén zàiyì guòchéng hé shǒuduàn,
   zhǐyào zuìhòu yíngle jiù hǎo. Shèng zhě wánghóu bài zhě zéi.

A: In years like this, everyone is only concerned with the result. Nobody cares
   about the process or methods, so long as they win in the end. Winning isn't
   everything, it's the only thing.

Usage: Used singly.

Note: Slightly derogatory or neutral in meaning.

---

235. 下三烂 (下三滥) xià sān làn

Translated character by character, 下三烂 means 'low-third-chaff,' whereas the implied
meaning of this proverb would be 'having less worth than the chaff left after three
siftings of processed grain.' Its functional translation is 'low-life,' or 'low-down.'

Example 1:

A: 他绑架了竞争对手的儿子来要挟对方。

B: 这么**下三烂**的手段他也想得出来！

A: Tā bǎngjià le jìngzhēng duìshǒu de érzi lái yāoxié duìfāng.

B: Zhème xiàsānlàn de shǒuduàn tā yě xiǎng de chūlái!

A: He kidnapped his opponent's son to coerce his opponent.

B: How did he think of such a low-down trick?

Example 2:

A: 以后别跟那些**下三烂**鬼混。

A: Yǐhòu bié gēn nàxiē xiàsānlàn guǐhùn.

A: In the future, don't hang around with those low-lifes.

Usage: Functions as attributive or object.

Note: Derogatory in meaning.

236. **上了贼船（上了贼船）** shàng le zéi chuán

Translated character by character, 上了贼船 means 'board-ed-pirate-ship,' whereas the implied meaning of this proverb would be 'to go past the point where one can turn back.' Its functional translation is 'to get in too deep,' or 'to cross the Rubicon.'

Example 1:

A: 你跟他走得那么近，小心**上了**他的**贼船**下不来啊。他的名声可不怎么样啊？

A: Nǐ gēn tā zǒu de nàme jìn, xiǎoxīn shàngle tā de zéichuán xià bùlái a. Tā de míngshēng kě bùzěnmeyàng a?

A: You've gotten so close with him. Be careful, once you get in too deep with him, there's no coming back. He's got a really bad reputation, huh?

Example 2:

A: 完了，我**上了贼船**了！

B: 怎么了？

A: 我把钱投入私募基金了，现在他们赔了，我想把本钱撤出来都不行。

A: Wán le, wǒ shàngle zéichuán le!

B: Zěnme le?

A: Wǒ bǎ qián tóurù sīmù jījīn le, xiànzài tāmen péi le, wǒ xiǎng bǎ běnqian chè chūlái dōu bùxíng.

A: That's it, there's no turning back now!

B: What's up?

A: I've put my money into a private equity fund. At this point, even if they make losses and I want to take my money out, I can't.

Usage: Functions as predicate.

Note: Derogatory and humorous in meaning.

237. 病急乱投医 (病急亂投醫) bìng jí luàn tóu yī

Translated character by character, 病急乱投医 means 'sick-severe-indiscriminate-seek-doctor,' whereas the implied meaning of this proverb would be 'when a situation is desperate, one will try anything.' Its functional translation is 'desperate times call for desperate measures,' or 'a drowning man will clutch at a straw.'

Example 1:

A: 求求你帮我一个忙，我的汽车又死火了。

B: 真是**病急乱投医**。我哪儿会修车啊？哪次不是给修车公司打电话？

A: Qiúqiú nǐ bāng wǒ yígè máng, wǒde qìchē yòu sǐhuǒ le.

B: Zhēnshì bìng jí luàn tóu yī. Wǒ nǎr huì xiūchē a? Nǎ cì búshì gěi xiūchē gōngsī dǎ diànhuà?

A: Please give me a hand. My car broke down again.

B: A drowning man really will clutch at a straw. How would I know how to fix a car? I always call a repair company to fix my car.

Example 2:

A: 那个国家的经济接近崩溃，**病急乱投医**，只好征收人头税。

A: Nàgè guójiā de jīngjì jiējìn bēngkuì, bìng jí luàn tóu yī, zhǐhǎo zhēngshōu réntóushuì.

A: Their country's economy is nearing collapse. Desperate times call for desperate measures; they've just imposed a poll tax!

Usage: Functions as predicative or predicate.

Note: Slightly derogatory in meaning.

238. 打如意算盘 (打如意算盤) dǎ rúyì suànpán

Translated character by character, 打如意算盘 means 'play-ideal-abacus,' whereas the implied meaning of this proverb would be 'to expect things to turn out as well as possible.' Its functional translation is 'to engage in wishful thinking.'

Example 1:

A: 希特勒的计划是德国从西边攻打苏联，日本从东边攻打，德、日在莫斯科会师。但是他的**如意算盘**落空了。

A: Xītèlè de jìhuà shì Déguó cóng xībiān gōngdǎ Sūlián, Rìběn cóng dōngbiān gōngdǎ, Dé, Rì zài Mòsīkē huìshī. Dànshì tā de rúyì suànpán luòkōng le.

A: Hitler's plan was to have Germany attack the Soviet Union from the West, and Japan attack from the East, with Germany and Japan meeting in Moscow. However, his wishful thinking didn't come to be.

Example 2:

A: 她嫁给那个老头就是为了分他的家产。

B: 我可以肯定地说，她的**如意算盘**打错了。据我所知，老头早就把遗嘱写好了，财产绝大多数分给了子女。

A: Tā jià gěi nàgè lǎotóu jiùshì wèile fēn tāde jiāchǎn.

B: Wǒ kěyǐ kěndìng de shuō, tā de rúyì suànpán dǎ cuò le. Jù wǒ suǒ zhī, lǎotóu zǎo jiù bǎ yízhǔ xiěhǎo le, cáichǎn juédàduōshù fēn gěi le zǐnǔ.

A: She married that geezer in order to share in his estate.

B: I can say with certainty, her wishful thinking is misinformed. As far as I know, the old man wrote his will long ago, and he bequeathed the lion's share of his assets to his children.

Usage: Functions mainly as predicate.

Note: Neutral in meaning.

---

239. 龙生龙，凤生凤 (龍生龍，鳳生鳳)
lóng shēng lóng, fèng shēng fèng

Translated character by character, 龙生龙，凤生凤 means 'dragon-give birth to-dragon, phoenix-give birth to-phoenix,' whereas the implied meaning of this proverb would be 'a child takes after its parents.' Its functional translation, is 'like father like son,' or 'like mother like daughter.'

Example 1:

A: 嘿，你看人家的儿子，北大毕业后直接进了外交部工作。

B: 可以理解，他老爸是北京市长，这叫**龙生龙，凤生凤**。

A: Hei, nǐ kàn rénjia de érzi, Běidà bìyè hòu zhíjiē jìnle wàijiāobù gōngzuò.

B: Kěyǐ lǐjiě, tā lǎobà shì Běijīng shìzhǎng, zhè jiào lóng shēng lóng, fèng shēng fèng.

A: Hey, look at his son. He went straight into a job at the Ministry of Foreign Affairs after graduating from Peking University.

B: That's understandable. His old man is the mayor of Beijing. That's what they call 'like father like son.'

Example 2:

A: 那个亿万富翁的儿子二十多岁就做几千万美元的生意。

B: 那是人家基因好，**龙生龙，凤生凤**。

A: Nàgè yìwàn fùwēng de érzi èrshí duō suì jiù zuò jǐ qiān wàn měiyuán de shēngyì.

B: Nà shì rénjia jīyīn hǎo, lóng shēng lóng, fèng shēng fèng.

A: That billionaire's son got a multimillion dollar contract in his twenties.
B: That's because he has good genes. Like father like son.

Usage: Used singly.

Note: Complimentary in meaning.

240. 不看僧面看佛面 (不看僧面看佛面)
bú kàn sēng miàn kàn fó miàn

Translated character by character, 不看僧面看佛面 means 'not-consider-monk-face-consider-Buddha-face,' whereas the implied meaning of this proverb would be 'to do something out of respect for a higher authority.' Its functional translation is 'for someone's sake.'

Example 1:

A: 我一定要处分他。
B: 老丁，还是算了吧。我们的老领导都出面说情了，**不看僧面看佛面**，这次就放过他吧。

A: Wǒ yídìng yào chǔfèn tā.
B: Lǎo Dīng, háishì suànle ba. Wǒmen de lǎo lǐngdǎo dōu chūmiàn shuōqíng le, bú kàn sēng miàn kàn fó miàn, zhècì jiù fàngguò tā ba.

A: I definitely want to punish him.
B: Old Ding, you should forget about it. Our ex-leader has already personally explained the situation. For our ex-leader's sake, let it go this time.

Example 2:

A: 钱市长，你家的公子在外面打着你的旗号可没少干好事啊！
B: 牛书记，我家教不严，应该好好反思。但是以前的事，请你**不看僧面看佛面**，给我点儿面子。

A: Qián shìzhǎng, nǐ jiā de gōngzi zài wàimiàn dǎzhe nǐde qíhào kě méi shǎo gàn hǎoshì a!
B: Niú shūjì, wǒ jiājiào bù yán, yīnggāi hǎohāo fǎnsī. Dànshì yǐqián de shì, qǐng nǐ bú kàn sēng miàn kàn fó miàn, gěi wǒ diǎnr miànzi.

A: Mayor Qian, your son has been using your good name to do many bad things.
B: Secretary Niu, I should reflect carefully on my lax parenting, but for what happened before, please forgive him for my sake and give me a little face.

Usage: Functions as predicate.

Note: Neutral in meaning.

241. 雷声大、雨点小 (雷聲大、雨點小)
léi shēng dà, yǔ diǎn xiǎo

Translated character by character, 雷声大、雨点小 means 'thunder-sound-loud, rain-drop-small,' whereas the implied meaning of this proverb would be 'someone doesn't make good on their promises or threats.' Its functional translation is 'all talk, no action.'

Example 1:

A: 他又信誓旦旦地说明年有什么宏伟的计划了。

B: 他总是**雷声大、雨点小**。他最近十年的计划没做成一两件。

A: Tā yòu xìnshì-dàndàn de shuō míngnián yǒu shénme hóngwěi de jìhuà le.

B: Tā zǒngshì léishēng dà, yǔdiǎn xiǎo. Tā zuìjìn shí nián de jìhuà méi zuòchéng yì liǎng jiàn.

A: He once again solemnly said that he had magnificent plans for next year.

B: He's always all talk and no action. He's barely accomplished one or two of his plans from the last ten years.

Example 2:

A: 国家三令五申要严厉打击领导干部任人唯亲的现象，但结果是**雷声大、雨点小**，腐败现象越来越严重了。

A: Guójiā sānlìng-wǔshēn yào yánlì dǎjī lǐngdǎo gànbù rènrén-wéiqīn de xiànxiàng, dàn jiéguǒ shì léishēng dà, yǔdiǎn xiǎo, fǔbài xiànxiàng yuèláiyuè yánzhòng le.

A: The nation has repeatedly warned that we must take strong measures against the phenomenon of our leaders and cadres engaging in nepotism, but it's all talk, no action. The corruption is getting worse and worse.

Usage: Functions as predicate.

Note: Slightly derogatory in meaning.

242. 脸红脖子粗 (臉紅脖子粗) liǎn hóng bózi cū

Translated character by character, 脸红脖子粗 means 'face-red-neck-flared,' whereas the implied meaning of this proverb would be 'to be extremely angry or agitated.' Its functional translation is 'to be red in the face,' or 'flushed with excitement or agitation.'

Example 1:

A: 因为一点小事，两个人争得**脸红脖子粗**。

A: Yīnwèi yìdiǎn xiǎoshì, liǎng gè rén zhēng de liǎn hóng bózi cū.

A: Because of a little trifle, two people fought until they were red in the face.

Example 2:

A: 他很尴尬，于是**脸红脖子粗**地嚷道，“关你什么事！

A: Tā hěn gāngà, yú shì liǎn hóng bózi cū de rǎng dào, "guān nǐ shénme shì!"

A: He was really embarrassed so, flushed with anger, he yelled, "It's none of your business!"

Usage: Functions as complement, adverbial or predicate.

Note: Neutral in meaning.

243. 一棍子打死 (一棍子打死) yí gùnzi dǎ sǐ

Translated character by character, 一棍子打死 means 'one-stick-beat-dead,' whereas the implied meaning of this proverb would be 'to completely discount something with some redeeming value due to a small flaw.' Its functional translation is 'to throw the baby out with the bathwater.'

Example 1:

A: 他这个人完全不能用。
B: 为什么？
A: 他喜欢喝酒，容易误事。
B: 他喜欢喝酒是喜欢喝酒，但是我们也不能**一棍子**把他**打死**。他的业务能力很强，这也是众所周知的。

A: Tā zhègè rén wánquán bùnéng yòng.
B: Wèishénme?
A: Tā xǐhuan hējiǔ, róngyì wùshì.
B: Tā xǐhuan hējiǔ shì xǐhuan hējiǔ, dànshì wǒmen yě bùnéng yí gùnzi bǎ tā dǎ sǐ. Tā de yèwù nénglì hěn qiáng, zhè yě shì zhòngsuǒ-zhōuzhī de.

A: You absolutely can't use that person.
B: Why?
A: He likes to drink; he's apt to hold things up.
B: So, he likes to drink, but we can't throw the baby out with the bathwater. His vocational competency is very strong; everyone knows that.

Example 2:

A: 这篇报告里的确有一、两处数据不准确，但是我们不能**一棍子打死**，报告还是有不少有价值的分析的。

A: Zhè piān bàogào lǐ díquè yǒu yī-liǎng chù shùjù bù zhǔnquè, dànshì wǒmen bùnéng yí gùnzi dǎ sǐ, bàogào háishì yǒu bùshǎo yǒu jiàzhí de fēnxī de.

A: This report definitely has one or two inaccurate statistics in it, but we can't throw the baby out with the bathwater. The report still has a good deal of valuable analysis.

Usage: Functions as predicate.

Note: Derogatory in meaning.

244.　拿鸡蛋碰石头 (拿雞蛋碰石頭) ná jīdàn pèng shítou

Translated character by character, 拿鸡蛋碰石头 means 'use-chicken-egg-hit-stone,' whereas the implied meaning of this proverb would be 'to court destruction.' Its functional translation is 'to pick a losing battle.'

Example 1:

A: 他要挑战世界拳击协会重量级冠军。
B: 虽然他这两年进步很大，但是要挑战拳王还是**拿鸡蛋碰石头**。

A: Tā yào tiǎozhàn Shìjiè Quánjī Xiéhuì zhòngliàngjí guànjūn.
B: Suīrán tā zhè liǎng nián jìnbù hěn dà, dànshì yào tiǎozhàn quánwáng háishì ná jīdàn pèng shítou.

A: He wants to challenge the World Boxing Association heavyweight champion.
B: Although he has made great strides in the last two years, if he challenges the champion, he'll be picking a losing battle.

Example 2:

A: 我要跟他打官司。
B: 忍了吧，怎么打也打不赢啊！他有权有势，你**拿着鸡蛋碰石头**，输定了。

A: Wǒ yào gēn tā dǎ guānsi.
B: Rěnle ba, zěnme dǎ yě dǎ bù yíng a! Tā yǒuquán-yǒushì, nǐ ná zhe jīdàn pèng shítou, shū dìng le.

A: I want to sue him.
B: Forget it, you'll never win. He's got power and influence. You're picking a losing battle. You'll lose for sure.

Usage: Functions as predicate.

Note: Neutral or slightly derogatory in meaning.

245. 没有不透风的墙 (沒有不透風的墙)
méiyǒu bú tòu fēng de qiáng

Translated character by character, 没有不透风的墙 means 'not-exist-impermeable-wall,' whereas the implied meaning of this proverb would be 'secrets will always come out.' Its functional translation is 'two may keep counsel, putting one away.'

Example 1:

A: 她怎么知道这件事了?

B: **没有不透风的墙**，你想那么多人都知道了，她怎么会不知道?

A: Tā zěnme zhīdao zhè jiàn shì le?

B: Méiyǒu bú tòu fēng de qiáng, nǐ xiǎng nàme duō rén dōu zhīdao le, tā zěnme huì bù zhīdao?

A: How does she know about that?

B: Two may keep counsel, putting one away. Just think, if that many people know already, how could she not know?

Example 2:

A: 两家公司的背后交易被媒体曝光了。

B: **没有不透风的墙**，当时有四、五个人知道内幕。

A: Liǎng jiā gōngsī de bèihòu jiāoyì bèi méitǐ bàoguāng le.

B: Méiyǒu bú tòu fēng de qiáng, dāngshí yǒu sì-wǔ gè rén zhīdao nèimù.

A: The media exposed the under-the-table dealings between the two companies.

B: Two may keep counsel, putting one away. At the time there were maybe five or six people who knew the inner workings.

Usage: Used singly.

Note: Neutral in meaning.

246. 人怕出名猪怕壮 (人怕出名豬怕壯)
rén pà chū míng zhū pà zhuàng

Translated character by character, 人怕出名猪怕壮 means 'person-fear-become-famous-pig-fear-fat,' whereas the implied meaning of this proverb would be 'famous people are liable to greater scrutiny and attack.' Its functional translation is 'fame can be a double-edged sword.'

Example 1:

A: 你怎么极少接受记者采访啊?

B: 你以为那全是好事啊? **人怕出名猪怕壮**，出了名以后，妒嫉、谣言什么的都来了。

A: Nǐ zěnme jí shǎo jiēshòu jìzhě cǎifǎng a?

B: Nǐ yǐwéi nà quán shì hǎoshì a? Rén pà chūmíng zhū pà zhuàng, chūle míng yǐhòu, dùjí, yáoyán shénme de dōu lái le.

A: Why do you so seldom accept interviews with reporters?

B: You think it's all good? Fame can be a double-edged sword. Once you're famous, the jealousy, rumors, and everything else start.

Example 2:

A: 他去年高调嫁女儿，两公里长的车队都是奔驰级别以上的。

B: 结果怎么样？现在因为偷税漏税进了监狱了吧？**人怕出名猪怕壮**，为人还是得低调点儿。

A: Tā qùnián gāodiào jià nǚ'ér, liǎng gōnglǐ cháng de chēduì dōu shì Bēnchí jíbié yǐshàng de.

B: Jiéguǒ zěnmeyàng? Xiànzài yīnwèi tōushuì lòushuì jìnle jiānyù le ba? Rén pà chūmíng zhū pà zhuàng, wéirén háishì děi dīdiào diǎnr.

A: He very publicly married off his daughter last year. The two-kilometer-long line of cars were all at least Mercedes-Benzes.

B: What happened? Has he now been jailed for evading taxes? Fame is a double-edged sword. People should be a little lower key.

Usage: Used singly.

Note: Slightly derogatory and humorous in meaning.

---

247. 山中无老虎，猴子称大王 (山中無老虎，猴子稱大王) shān zhōng wú lǎo hǔ, hóuzi chēng dà wáng

Translated character by character, 山中无老虎，猴子称大王 means 'mountain-on-no-tiger, monkey-claim-king,' whereas the implied meaning of this proverb would be 'when the top tier is not present, the second tier rules according to their whim.' Its functional translation is 'when the cat's away, the mice will play.'

Example 1:

A: 他居然赢了法国网球公开赛冠军。

B: 这次他太幸运了。世界前四名选手都因伤退出，**山中无老虎，猴子称大王**，他就得了冠军。

A: Tā jūrán yíngle Fǎguó Wǎngqiú Gōngkāisài guànjūn.

B: Zhècì tā tài xìngyùn le. Shìjiè qián sì míng xuǎnshǒu dōu yīn shāng tuìchū, shān zhōng wú lǎohǔ, hóuzi chēng dà wáng, tā jiù déle guànjūn.

A: He surprisingly won the French Open.

B: He was very lucky this time. The top four players in the world withdrew due to injuries. When the cat's away, the mice will play. That's how he won the championship.

Example 2:

A: 我出差才一个星期，公司怎么看起来乱七八糟的？

B: 我们都是按照李副主任的命令来做的。

A: 啊……！**山中无老虎，猴子称大王**，李副主任的胆子可真不小！

A: Wǒ chūchāi cái yígè xīngqī, gōngsī zěnme kànqǐlái luànqī-bāzāo de?

B: Wǒmen dōu shì ànzhào Lǐ fù zhǔrèn de mìnglìng lái zuò de.

A: À ......! Shān zhōng wú lǎohǔ, hóuzi chēng dà wáng, Lǐ fù zhǔrèn de dǎnzi kě zhēn bù xiǎo!

A: I've only been abroad on business for a week; how does the company seem to be such a mess?

B: We all did everything according to vice-director Li's orders.

A: Oh! When the cat's away the mice will play. Vice-director Li's really got guts!

Usage: Used singly.

Note: Slightly derogatory in meaning.

248. 杀鸡焉用宰牛刀 (殺雞焉用宰牛刀)
shā jī yān yòng zǎi niú dāo

Translated character by character, 杀鸡焉用宰牛刀 means 'kill-chicken-not-need-slaughter-cow-knife,' whereas the implied meaning of this proverb would be 'there's no need to go to town over a small issue.' Its functional translation is 'you don't need a sledgehammer to crack a nut.'

Example 1:

A: 这件事是不是需要我亲自去处理啊？

B: 老板，**杀鸡焉用宰牛刀**。您放心，一个星期之内一定给您摆平。

A: Zhè jiàn shì shìbúshì xūyào wǒ qīnzì qù chǔlǐ a?

B: Lǎobǎn, shā jī yān yòng zǎi niú dāo. Nín fàngxīn, yígè xīngqī zhīnèi yídìng gěi nín bǎipíng.

A: Is this an issue that I need to deal with personally?

B: Boss, you don't need a sledgehammer to crack a nut. Relax, I'll have it taken care of for you within a week.

Example 2:

A: 对手那么烂，怎么主教练派上了全部主力球员？这不是**杀鸡用牛刀**嘛。

A: Duìshǒu nàme làn, zěnme zhǔjiàoliàn pàishàngle quánbù zhǔlì zhènróng? Zhè búshì shā jī yòng niú dāo ma.

A: Our opponent is so bad, why did the head coach send his starting line? Isn't that using a sledgehammer to crack a nut?

Usage: Used singly.

Variants: 杀鸡用牛刀; 杀鸡焉用牛刀

Note: Humorous or neutral in meaning.

249. 大树底下好乘凉 (大樹底下好乘涼)
dà shù dǐxia hǎo chéngliáng

Translated character by character, 大树底下好乘凉 means 'big-tree-under-easy-get-shade,' whereas the implied meaning of this proverb would be 'benefits accrue to those close to influential people.' Its functional translation is 'follow closely behind heavy-laden wagons.'

Example 1:

A: 在中国，为什么那么多大学生毕业以后想到政府里去工作？

B: **大树底下好乘凉**，工资高、福利好、有实惠，还不用担心失业。

A: Zài Zhōngguó wèishénme nàme duō dàxuéshēng bìyè yǐhòu xiǎng dào zhèngfǔ lǐ qù gōngzuò?

B: Dà shù dǐxia hǎo chéngliáng, gōngzī gāo, fúlì hǎo, yǒu shíhui, hái búyòng dānxīn shīyè.

A: In China, why do so many college students want to work in government after they graduate?

B: Follow closely behind heavy-laden wagons. The salary is high, the benefits are good, there's material benefit, and you don't have to worry about losing your job.

Example 2:

A: 很多人想申请攻读那位诺贝尔化学奖得主的博士学位，目的无非是 **大树底下好乘凉**，将来发论文、评职称、申请项目容易一些。

A: Hěnduō rén xiǎng shēnqǐng gōngdú nà wèi Nuòbèi'ěr Huàxuéjiǎng dézhǔ de bóshì xuéwèi, mùdì wúfēi shì dà shù dǐxia hǎo chéngliáng, jiānglái fā lùnwén, píng zhíchēng, shēnqǐng xiàngmù róngyi yìxiē.

A: A lot of people want to apply to study for a doctorate with that Nobel Laureate in Chemistry. Their goal is simply to follow closely behind heavy-laden wagons. Afterwards, it will be easier to publish papers, get academic titles, and apply for grants.

Usage: Used singly.

Variant: 大树下面好乘凉

Note: Humorous or neutral in meaning.

250. 跑龙套 (跑龍套) pǎo lóng tào

Translated character by character, 跑龙套 means 'play-insignificant-role,' whereas the implied meaning of this proverb would be 'one who does various insignificant tasks for someone.' Its functional translation is 'to be a small player,' or 'act as a utility man.'

Example 1:

A: 你在这件事上起了很大的作用。

B: 哪儿啊！我就是个**跑龙套**的。

A: Nǐ zài zhè jiàn shì shàng qǐle hěndà de zuòyòng.

B: Nǎr a! Wǒ jiù shì gè pǎolóngtào de.

A: You had a big effect on this issue.

B: No, I didn't. I'm just a small player.

Example 2:

A: 他能帮多大的忙？

B: 我觉得帮不了多大的忙。他也就是个**跑龙套**的，说话不算数。

A: Tā néng bāng duōdà de máng?

B: Wǒ juéde bāng bùliǎo duōdà de máng. Tā yě jiùshì gè pǎolóngtào de, shuōhuà bú suànshù.

A: How much of a help can he be?

B: Not too much, I think. He's only a utility man; his word doesn't carry any weight.

Usage: Functions as predicate or used in the structure '是(一)个~的.'

Note: Neutral or humorous in meaning.

251. 七大姑，八大姨 (七大姑，八大姨) qī dà gū, bā dà yí

Translated character by character, 七大姑，八大姨 means 'seven-paternal aunts, eight-maternal aunts,' whereas the implied meaning of this proverb would be 'extremely distant relatives.'

Example 1:

A: 他当上市长以后，把**七大姑，八大姨**都安排进了市政府工作。

A: Tā dāngshàng shìzhǎng yǐhòu, bǎ qī dà gū, bā dà yí dōu ānpái jìnle shìzhèngfǔ gōngzuò.

A: After he became mayor, he arranged for all of his distant relatives to work in the municipal government.

Example 2:

A: 从我赚钱以后，**七大姑，八大姨**都找上门来了，说白了，都是借钱来了。这不，又冒出来一个二舅，我根本没见过。

A: Cóng wǒ zuànqián yǐhòu, qī dà gū, bā dà yí dōu zhǎoshàng mén lái le, shuō bái le, dōushì jièqián lái le. Zhè bú, yòu mào chūlái yígè èr jiù, wǒ gēnběn méi jiànguò.

A: After I made my money, all of my distant relatives came to my house. To be honest, they all came to borrow money. You see, even my mother's second oldest brother came out of the woodwork. I'd really never even met him.

Usage: Functions as object or subject.

Note: Slightly derogatory in meaning.

252.   一是一，二是二 (一是一，二是二) yī shì yī, èr shì èr

Translated character by character, 一是一, 二是二 means 'one-is-one, two-is-two,' whereas the implied meaning of this proverb would be 'to call things as they are,' or 'to do something how it should be done.' Its functional translation is 'to call a spade a spade.'

Example 1:

A: （父亲对孩子）你在那家公司里明明只实习了两个星期，但你的简历上为什么写一个月？

B: 这个……

A: 不能这样，做人得诚实，**一是一，二是二**。

A: (fùqīn duì háizi) Nǐ zài nà jiā gōngsī lǐ míngmíng zhǐ shíxí le liǎng gè xīngqī, dàn nǐde jiǎnlì shàng wèishénme xiě yígè yuè?

B: Zhè gè ......

A: Bùnéng zhèyàng, zuòrén děi chéngshi, yī shì yī, èr shì èr.

A: (Father to his child) You've only interned at that company for two weeks, so why did you write you worked there for a month on your resume?

B: Well . . .

A: You can't do that. Let's call a spade a spade. You have to be an honest person.

Example 2:

A: 市长光临我们小店我们感到非常荣幸，因此我们很高兴地把您选购的东西免费送给您。

B: 这样怎么能行？工作的时候我是市长，但是下班以后在超市购物，我就是普通消费者，咱们**一是一，二是二**。你的好意我心领了。

A: Shìzhǎng guānglín wǒmen xiǎo diàn wǒmen gǎndào fēicháng róngxìng, yīncǐ wǒmen hěn gāoxìng de bǎ nín xuǎngòu de dōngxi miǎnfèi sònggěi nín.

B: Zhèyàng zěnme néng xíng? Gōngzuò de shíhòu wǒ shì shìzhǎng, dànshì xiàbān yǐhòu zài chāoshì gòuwù, wǒ jiùshì pǔtōng xiāofèizhě, zánmen yī shì yī, èr shì èr. Nǐde hǎoyì wǒ xīnlǐng le.

A: We feel extremely honored to have the mayor visit our humble store, so we'll happily give you whatever you choose at no charge.

B: Don't do that. When I'm working I'm the mayor but, let's call a spade a spade. When I'm off work, buying things at the supermarket, I'm just a normal consumer. Your kindness is appreciated.

Usage: Functions as predicate.

Note: Neutral in meaning.

---

253. 多个朋友多条路 (多個朋友多條路)
duō gè péngyou duō tiáo lù

Translated character by character, 多个朋友多条路 means 'add-one-friend-create-one-path.' Its functional translation is 'the more friends you have, the more options you have in life.'

Example 1:

A: 老田，我有一个在电视台工作的朋友今天晚上过来，到时候你也来，咱们三个聊聊。

B: 算了吧，我跟他又不认识。

A: 一回生，二回熟嘛。再说，**多个朋友多条路**，认识一下有什么不好？

A: Lǎo Tián, wǒ yǒu yígè zài diànshìtái gōngzuò de péngyou jīntiān wǎnshang guòlai, dào shíhòu nǐ yě lái, zánmen sān gè liáoliao.

B: Suànle ba, wǒ gēn tā yòu bú rènshi.

A: Yì huí shēng, èr huí shú ma. Zàishuō, duō gè péngyou duō tiáo lù, rènshí yíxià yǒu shénme bùhǎo?

A: Old Tian, I have a friend who works at the TV station who's coming over tonight. You should come too. The three of us can talk.

B: Nah, I don't know him.

A: A stranger is just a friend you haven't met yet. That's to say, the more friends you have, the more options life offers. What do you stand to lose from meeting him quickly?

Example 2:

A: 做生意的人非常重视交际面，因为**多个朋友多条路**。

A: Zuò shēngyì de rén fēicháng zhòngshì jiāojìmiàn, yīnwèi duō gè péngyou duō tiáo lù.

A: People in business put extreme emphasis on networking, because the more friends you have, the more options life offers.

Usage: Used singly.

Note: Neutral in meaning.

---

254. 下台阶 (下臺階) xià tái jiē

Translated character by character, 下台阶 means 'go down-step,' whereas the implied meaning of this proverb would be 'to get out of an embarrassing predicament.' Its functional translation is 'to give someone an out.'

Example 1:

A: 她很会做人。
B: 是啊，即使别人错了，她也总是能让别人**下台阶**。

A: Tā hěn huì zuòrén.
B: Shì a, jíshǐ biérén cuò le, tā yě zǒngshì néng ràng biérén xiàtáijiē.

A: She's really good with people.
B: Yeah, even if other people are wrong, she's always able to give them an out.

Example 2:

A: 你说话太直了，即使你全对，你也得让对方**下**得了**台阶**啊。

A: Nǐ shuōhuà tài zhí le, jíshǐ nǐ quán duì, nǐ yě děi ràng duìfāng xiàdeliǎo táijiē a.

A: You speak too directly. Even if you're completely right, you have to allow the other person an out.

Usage: Functions as predicate.

Note: Neutral in meaning.

---

255. 打小算盘 (打小算盤) dǎ xiǎo suànpán

Translated character by character, 打小算盘 means 'use-small-abacus,' whereas the implied meaning of this proverb would be 'to act in one's own self-interest.'

Example 1:

A: 昨天说得好好的，今天大家都反对主任的提议。 可是该他发言的时候他却支支吾吾。

B: 他啊，在**打**自己的**小算盘**，怕惹了主任。

A: Zuótiān shuō de hǎohāo de, jīntiān dàjiā dōu fǎnduì zhǔrèn de tíyì. Kěshì gāi tā fāyán de shíhòu tā què zhīzhīwūwū.

B: Tā a, zài dǎ zìjǐ de xiǎosuànpán, pà rěle zhǔrèn.

A: It was talked out yesterday; everyone was going to oppose the chairman's proposal today. But when it was his turn to speak, he pussyfooted around it.

B: Him? He's acting out of self-interest. He's afraid to piss off the director.

Example 2:

A: 那个大城市的女人精得很，很会**打小算盘**，从来不肯吃一点儿亏。

A: Nàgè dà chéngshì de nǚrén jīng de hěn, hěn huì dǎ xiǎosuànpán, cónglái bùkěn chī yìdiǎnr kuī.

A: The women from that big city are extremely shrewd. They're very calculating, never willing to take a loss.

Usage: Functions as predicate.

Note: Slightly derogatory in meaning.

---

256.   坐山观虎斗 (坐山觀虎鬥) zuò shān guān hǔ dòu

Translated character by character, 坐山观虎斗 means 'sit-mountain-watch-tiger-fight,' whereas the implied meaning of this proverb would be 'to refrain from entering a dispute and instead wait until both sides are exhausted to take what one wants.' Its functional translation is 'to sit this one out and reap the spoils later.'

Example 1:

A: 我们的两个竞争对手现在正打官司呢。

B: 让他们打吧，我们**坐山观虎斗**。

A: Wǒmen de liǎng gè jìngzhēng duìshǒu xiànzài zhèng dǎ guānsī ne.

B: Ràng tāmen dǎ ba, wǒmen zuò shān guān hǔ dòu.

A: Our two competitors are currently in litigation.

B: Let them fight. We'll sit this one out and reap the spoils later.

Example 2:

A: 你说我们该帮哪一方呢？

B: 哪一方也不帮，我们**坐山观虎斗**。等双方两败俱伤了，我们就坐收渔利。

A: Nǐ shuō wǒmen gāi bāng nǎ yì fāng ne?

B: Nǎ yì fāng yě bù bāng, wǒmen zuò shān guān hǔ dòu. Děng shuāngfāng liǎngbài-jùshāng le, wǒmen jiù zuòshōu-yúlì.

A: Which side should we help?

B: Neither. We'll sit this one out. Once both sides have been hobbled, we'll reap the spoils.

Usage: Functions as predicate.

Note: Neutral in meaning.

257. 羊毛出在羊身上 (羊毛出在羊身上)
yáng máo chū zài yáng shēnshang

Translated character by character, 羊毛出在羊身上 means 'wool-come-from-sheep-body,' whereas the implied meaning of this proverb would be 'even if you receive something for free, you are paying for it in some way.' Its functional translation is 'there's no such thing as a free lunch.'

Example 1:

A: 喔，我们退休后的福利增加了百分之三。

B: 有什么高兴的？**羊毛出在羊身上**，没看见我们的退休年龄增长了两岁吗？

A: Wò, wǒmen tuìxiū hòu de fúlì zēngjiāle bǎi fēn zhī sān.

B: Yǒu shénme gāoxìng de? Yángmáo chū zài yáng shēnshang, méi kànjiàn wǒmen de tuìxiū niánlíng zēngzhǎngle liǎng suì ma?

A: Wow, our retirement benefits increased by 3 percent.

B: What's there to be happy about? There's no such thing as a free lunch. Didn't you see that our retirement age increased by two years?

Example 2:

A: 这个小区的房子真好，买一套房免费送一个车库！

B: **羊毛出在羊身上**，开发商不傻，肯定会在其他方面找回来。

A: Zhège xiǎoqū de fángzi zhēn hǎo, mǎi yí tào fáng miǎnfèi sòng yígè chēkù!

B: Yángmáo chū zài yáng shēnshang, kāifāshāng bù shǎ, kěndìng huì zài qítā fāngmiàn zhǎo huílai.

A: This community's houses are great. If you buy a house you get a garage for free!

B: There's no such thing as a free lunch. The developers aren't stupid. You can be sure they'll find another way to make that money back.

Usage: Used singly.

Note: Slightly derogatory and humorous in meaning.

258. 一口吃成个胖子 (一口吃成個胖子)
yì kǒu chī chéng gè pàngzi

Translated character by character, 一口吃成个胖子 means 'one-mouth-eat-into-a-fat-person,' whereas the implied meaning of this proverb would be 'to get what one wants instantly.' Its functional translation is 'to wave a magic wand and get what one wants.'

Example 1:

A: 我的进步怎么那么小呢?

B: 别想**一口吃成个胖子**，啥事慢慢儿来。

A: Wǒde jìnbù zěnme nàme xiǎo ne?

B: Bié xiǎng yì kǒu chī chéng gè pàngzi, shá shì mànmānr lái.

A: How have I improved so little?

B: Don't think you can wave a magic wand and be perfect. Some things take time.

Example 2:

A: 我们要一年一小步，三年一大步，十年一飞跃，超过所有的竞争对手。

B: ［对C小声说］又说胡话呢，**一口吃不成个胖子**。

A: Wǒmen yào yì nián yì xiǎo bù, sān nián yí dà bù, shí nián yì fēiyuè, chāoguò suǒyǒu de jìngzhēng duìshǒu.

B: [duì C xiǎoshēng shuō] Yòu húshuō ne, yì kǒu chī bù chéng gè pàngzi.

A: We need to take, in one year, a small step; in three years, one big step; in ten years, one flying leap; to surpass all of our competitors.

B: [whispering to C] He's spewing crap again. You can't just wave a magic wand.

Usage: Functions as predicate or used singly.

Note: Neutral in meaning. The negative form '一口吃不成胖子' is often seen too.

259. 屋漏偏逢连阴雨 (屋漏偏逢連陰雨)
wū lòu piān féng lián yīn yǔ

Translated character by character, 屋漏偏逢连阴雨 means 'room-leak-just-run-in-consecutive-rainy-days,' whereas the implied meaning of this proverb would be 'when bad things happen, many bad things happen concurrently.' Its functional translation is 'when it rains, it pours.'

Example 1:

A: 他最近可真可怜。上个月丢了工作，这个月老婆跟他离婚了，**屋漏偏逢连阴雨**，昨天他爸又死了。

A: Tā zuìjìn kě zhēn kělián. Shàng gè yuè diūle gōngzuò, zhègè yuè lǎopo gēn tā líhūn le, wū lòu piān féng lián yīn yǔ, zuótiān tā bà yòu sǐ le.

A: He's been really pitiful lately. He lost his job last month and his wife divorced him this month. When it rains, it pours. His father died yesterday as well.

Example 2:

A: 那家公司最近订单大减，资金周转出现问题，可是**屋漏偏逢连阴雨**，政府刚出台的政策严格限制贷款。

A: Nà jiā gōngsī zuìjìn dìngdān dà jiǎn, zījīn zhōuzhuǎn chūxiàn wèntí, kěshì wū lòu piān féng lián yīn yǔ, zhèngfǔ gāng chūtái de zhèngcè yángé xiànzhì dàikuǎn.

A: That company's backlog has recently shrunk drastically and it has run into issues with capital turnover, but when it rains, it pours; the policy that the government just unveiled seriously restricts loans.

Usage: Used singly.

Variant: 屋漏偏逢连夜雨

Note: Neutral in meaning.

---

260. 老油条 (老油條) lǎo yóu tiáo

Translated character by character, 老油条 means 'old-deep fried-dough stick,' whereas the implied meaning of this proverb would be 'one who has learned to be sly.' Its functional translation is 'a slippery one,' or 'wily old fox.'

Example 1:

A: 他说要为这次事故负全部责任。

B: 别听他的，他是官场上的**老油条**。不信你就看着，过不了几天他就会推出一个替罪羊。

A: Tā shuō yào wèi zhècì shìgù fù quánbù zérèn.

B: Bié tīng tā de, tā shì guānchǎng shàng de lǎoyóutiáo. Bú xìn nǐ jiù kàn zhe, guòbùliǎo jǐ tiān tā jiù huì tuī chū yígè tìzuìyáng.

A: He says he will take full responsibility for this accident.

B: Don't listen to him. He's the wily old fox of officialdom. If you don't believe me, just watch. In a few days, he's going to push out a scapegoat.

Example 2:

A: 跟他打交道要格外小心，他是个**老油条**，很难对付。

A: Gēn tā dǎjiāodào yào géwài xiǎoxīn, tā shì gè lǎoyóutiáo, hěn nán duìfu.

A: You should take care when interacting with him. He's a slippery one, hard to deal with.

Usage: Functions mainly as predicative.

Note: Slightly derogatory in meaning.

261. 捅马蜂窝 (捅馬蜂窩) tǒng mǎfēng wō

Translated character by character, 捅马蜂窝 means 'poke-hornet-nest,' whereas the implied meaning of this proverb would be 'to create a lot of trouble.' Its functional translation is 'to stir up a hornet's nest.'

Example 1:

A: 他在演讲的时候说有一些女性工作时不太专心，总想着孩子的事。这句话**捅**了**马蜂窝**。他的演讲当时就被抗议声和指责声打断。

A: Tā zài yǎnjiǎng de shíhòu shuō yǒu yìxiē nǚxìng gōngzuò shí bú tài zhuānxīn, zǒng xiǎngzhe háizi de shì. Zhè jù huà tǒngle mǎfēngwō. Tā de yǎnjiǎng dāngshí jiù bèi kàngyì shēng hé zhǐzé shēng dǎduàn.

A: While giving a speech, he said that there were a few women who weren't very focused on their work, always thinking about their children. These words stirred up a hornet's nest. At that time, his speech was broken up by the sound of protests and criticism.

Example 2:

A: 咱们公司员工的效率低。我想引进竞争机制，考核垫底的人被淘汰。

B: 你别去**捅**这个**马蜂窝**。咱们的员工被惯坏了，如果你想淘汰他们，我看啊，他们没被淘汰前，你先给淘汰了。

A: Zánmen gōngsī yuángōng de xiàolǜ dī. Wǒ xiǎng yǐnjìn jìngzhēng jīzhì, kǎohé diàndǐ de rén bèi táotài.

B: Nǐ bié qù tǒng zhègè mǎfēng wō. Zánmen de yuángōng bèi guànhuài le, rúguǒ nǐ xiǎng táotài tāmen, wǒ kàn a, tāmen méi bèi táotài qián, nǐ xiān gěi táotài le.

A: Our company's employees are inefficient. I want to recommend a system of competition, where the person with the worst evaluation is eliminated.

B: Don't stir up this hornet's nest. Our employees have been spoiled. If you want to eliminate them, my opinion is that you will be eliminated before they are gone.

Usage: Functions as predicate.

Note: Neutral in meaning.

262. 小意思 (小意思) xiǎo yìsi

Translated character by character, 小意思 means 'little-significance,' whereas the implied meaning of this proverb would be 'a small gift,' or 'something easy or unimportant.' Its functional translation is 'a token,' or 'not a big deal.'

Example 1:

A: 你能借给我一万块钱吗？我现在急需钱。
B: 一万块？**小意思**。现在就给你。

A: Nǐ néng jiè gěi wǒ yí wàn kuài qián ma? Wǒ xiànzài jíxū qián.
B: Yí wàn kuài? Xiǎoyìsi. Xiànzài jiù gěi nǐ.

A: Can you lend me 10,000 RMB? I urgently need money right now.
B: 10,000 RMB? No big deal. I'll give it to you right now.

Example 2:

A: （送给B很贵的酒。）
B: 你这是做什么？
A: 这是一点**小意思**，请您收下。

A: (sònggěi B hěn guì de jiǔ.)
B: Nǐ zhè shì zuò shénme?
A: Zhè shì yìdiǎn xiǎoyìsi, qǐng nín shōuxià.

A: (giving B expensive wine)
B: What are you doing?
A: This is just a small gift. Please accept it.

Usage: Functions as predicative or object.

Note: Neutral in meaning.

263. 倒打一耙 (倒打一耙) dào dǎ yì pá

Translated character by character, 倒打一耙 means 'reverse-hit-one-rake,' whereas the implied meaning of this proverb would be 'to make unsupported accusations of someone.' Its functional translation is 'to play the blame game.'

Example 1:

A: 听说你撞人了？

B: 哪儿啊？分明是他撞了我的车，他却**倒打一耙**，说我撞了他。

A: Tīngshuō nǐ zhuàng rén le?

B: Nǎr a? Fēnmíng shì tā zhuàngle wǒde chē, tā què dào dǎ yì pá, shuō wǒ zhuàngle tā.

A: I heard you hit someone?

B: What? Clearly it was him that hit my car. He's playing the blame game, saying I hit him.

Example 2:

A: S公司剽窃了A公司的专利，S公司不但不承认，反而**倒打一耙**，起诉A公司剽窃。

A: S gōngsī piāoqiè le A gōngsī de zhuānlì, S gōngsī búdàn bù chéngrèn, fǎn'ér dào dǎ yì pá, qǐsù A gōngsī piāoqiè.

A: Company S infringed on company A's patent, but not only is company S not admitting to it, they're playing the blame game, suing company A for infringement.

Usage: Functions as predicate.

Note: Slightly derogatory in meaning.

264. 陈芝麻、烂谷子 (陳芝蔴、爛穀子) chén zhīma, làn gǔzi

Translated character by character, 陈芝麻、烂谷子 means 'stale-sesame-seed, rotten-barley,' whereas the implied meaning of this proverb would be 'mundane, overhashed topics.' Its functional translation is 'idle chatter.'

Example 1:

A: 咱们上大学第一年，你跟我借⋯⋯

B: 有完没完？那点儿**陈芝麻、烂谷子**的事说多少回了？

A: Zánmen shàng dàxué dì-yī nián, nǐ gēn wǒ jiè......

B: Yǒu wán méi wán? Nà diǎnr chén zhīma làn gǔzi de shì shuō duōshao huí le?

A: In our freshman year of college, you borrowed my . . .

B: Shut up! How many times have you repeated that piece of idle chatter?

Example 2:

A: 那位大明星小时候姓黄，不是现在的姓。还有，她小时候是单眼皮。

B: 够了，别跟我提这种**陈芝麻、烂谷子**，我没兴趣。

A: Nà wèi dà míngxīng xiǎoshíhou xìng Huáng, búshì xiànzài de xìng. Háiyǒu, tā xiǎoshíhou shì dānyǎnpí.

B: Gòu le, bié gēn wǒ tí zhè zhǒng chén zhīma làn gǔzi, wǒ méi xìngqù.

A: When that movie star was younger, her surname was Huang, which isn't her current surname. Also, when she was younger, she had single-fold eyelids.

B: Enough! Don't bring up this sort of idle chatter with me. I'm not interested.

Usage: Functions as object.

Note: Slightly derogatory and humorous in meaning.

265. 一条龙 (一條龍) yì tiáo lóng

Translated character by character, 一条龙 means 'one-MW-dragon,' whereas the implied meaning of this proverb would be 'an integrated process.' Its functional translation is 'from soup to nuts.'

Example 1:

A: 这家留学服务公司为客户提供信息咨询、申请学校、办理签证、安排国外住宿等**一条龙**服务。

A: Zhèjiā liúxué fúwù gōngsī wèi kèhù tígōng xìnxī zīxún, shēnqǐng xuéxiào, bànlǐ qiānzhèng, ānpái guówài zhùsù děng yìtiáolóng fúwù.

A: This study abroad service company offers soup to nuts service for its clients, helping with consulting, applying to schools, obtaining a visa, arranging housing abroad, etc.

Example 2:

A: 沃尔玛不仅是大型连锁零售店，本身也生产，实现了生产、加工、销售、存储、运输**一条龙**的格局。

A: Wò'ěrmǎ bùjǐn shì dàxíng liánsuǒ língshòudiàn, běnshēn yě shēngchǎn, shíxiàn le shēngchǎn, jiāgōng, xiāoshòu, cúnchǔ, yùnshū yìtiáolóng de géjú.

A: Walmart is not just a large-scale retail chain, it also produces products, achieving a soup to nuts production, processing, sales, warehousing and shipping structure.

Usage: Functions as attributive.

Note: Neutral in meaning.

266. 四两拨千斤 (四兩撥千斤) sì liǎng bō qiān jīn

Translated character by character, 四两拨千斤 means 'four-taels-deflect-thousand-catty,' whereas the implied meaning of this proverb would be 'to solve a big issue with little effort.'

Example 1:

A: 他去调解两个人的矛盾，话虽不多，但是句句切中要害，起到**四两拨千斤**的效果。于是那两个人的矛盾很快化解了。

A: Tā qù tiáojiě liǎng gè rén de máodùn, huà suī bù duō, dànshì jù jù qièzhòng yàohài, qǐ dào sì liǎng bō qiān jīn de xiàoguǒ. Yúshì nà liǎng gè rén de máodùn hěnkuài huàjiě le.

A: He went to mediate two people's conflict. Not much was said, but every sentence hit the mark, creating an outsized effect. So, the conflict between those two people dissipated very quickly.

Example 2:

A: 两个人的辩论中，一方对另一方展开了猛烈地攻击，而另一方不慌不忙，用了一个笑话**四两拨千斤**，一下子就变被动为主动。

A: Liǎng gè rén de biànlùn zhōng, yī fāng duì lìng yī fāng zhǎnkāi le měngliè de gōngjī, ér lìng yī fāng bùhuāng-bùmáng, yòngle yígè xiàohua sì liǎng bō qiān jīn, yíxiàzi jiù biàn bèidòng wéi zhǔdòng.

A: In an argument between two people, one side launched a fierce attack against the other, but the other person, unflustered, used a joke to turn the tables. In a moment, he went from being on defense to being on offense.

Usage: Functions as attributive, predicate or predicative.

Note: Neutral in meaning.

267. 前怕狼，后怕虎 (前怕狼，後怕虎) qián pà láng, hòu pà hǔ

Translated character by character, 前怕狼，后怕虎 means 'ahead-fear-wolf-behind-fear-tiger,' whereas the implied meaning of this proverb would be 'to be overcome by fear and indecision.' Its functional translation is 'to be afraid to commit oneself.'

Example 1:

A: 他做不成大事，因为总是**前怕狼后怕虎**。

A: Tā zuò bù chéng dàshì, yīnwèi zǒngshì qián pà láng hòu pà hǔ.

A: He can't accomplish big things because he's always afraid to commit himself.

Example 2:

A: 改革就得付出代价，如果**前怕狼后怕虎**，那就永远不会发展。

A: Gǎigé jiù děi fùchū dàijià, rúguǒ qián pà láng hòu pà hǔ, nà jiù yǒngyuǎn búhuì fāzhǎn.

A: In order to reform, you must pay the price. If you're afraid to commit yourself, then you will never develop.

Usage: Functions as predicate.

Note: Slightly derogatory in meaning.

268.   吃水不忘挖井人 (吃水不忘挖井人)
chī shuǐ bú wàng wā jǐng rén

Translated character by character, 吃水不忘挖井人 means 'drink-water-don't-forget-dig-well-person.' Its functional translation is 'when drinking water, don't forget those who dug the well.'

Example 1:

A: 孩子，你也十几岁了，应该回爸爸的农村老家看一看。

B: 农村什么有意思的都没有，有什么看头？

A: 你怎么能这么说！你的父母和祖父母都从那里出生，都在那里长大。是那个地方养育了我们，没有那个地方就没有我们，也不会有现在的你。虽然现在我们生活好了，但是**吃水不忘挖井人**，你应该知道你现在的生活是怎么来的。

A: Háizi, nǐ yě shí jǐ suì le, yīnggāi huí bàba de nóngcūn lǎojiā kàn yí kàn.

B: Nóngcūn shénme yǒuyìsī de dōu méiyǒu, yǒu shénme kàntou?

A: Nǐ Zěnme néng zhème shuō! Nǐde fùmǔ hé zǔfùmǔ dōu cóng nàlǐ chūshēng, dōu zài nàlǐ zhǎngdà. Shì nàge dìfāng yǎngyù le wǒmen, méiyǒu nàge dìfāng jiù méiyǒu wǒmen, yě bú huì yǒu xiànzài de nǐ. Suīrán xiànzài wǒmen shēnghuó hǎo le, dànshì chī shuǐ bú wàng wā jǐng rén, nǐ yīnggāi zhīdào nǐ xiànzài de shēnghuó shì zěnme lái de.

A: Kiddo, now that you're a teenager, you should go see your father's rural, ancestral home.

B: There's nothing interesting in the country. What's there worth seeing?

A: How could you say that? Your father and grandparents were all born and raised there. It's that place that brought us up; without it we wouldn't be here and you wouldn't exist. Although we have a good life now, when drinking water, don't forget those who dug the well. You should know how your current lifestyle came to be.

Example 2:

A: 日本民间企业家促使中日关系正常化，**吃水不忘挖井人**，我们应该
感谢这些企业家们。

A: Rìběn mínjiān qǐyèjiā cùshǐ Zhōng-Rì guānxì zhèngchánghuà, chī shuǐ bú wàng
wā jǐng rén, wǒmen yīnggāi gǎnxiè zhèxiē qǐyèjiāmen.

A: Japanese civilian entrepreneurs pressed for the normalization of Sino-Japanese
relations. When drinking water, don't forget those who dug the well; we should
be grateful to those entrepreneurs.

Usage: Used singly.

Note: Neutral in meaning.

269. 有仇不报非君子 (有仇不報非君子)
yǒu chóu bú bào fēi jūnzǐ

Translated character by character, 有仇不报非君子 means 'have-feud-not-get revenge-
not-gentleman,' whereas the implied meaning of this proverb would be 'a good
man must avenge slights done unto him.' Its functional translation is 'a real man
must settle his scores.'

Example 1:

A: 今天他在大会上的发言明显是针对你的。
B: 是的，我会记住这笔帐的，**有仇不报非君子**，以后他的把柄不要落
到我手里。

A: Jīntiān tā zài dàhuì shàng de fāyán míngxiǎn shì zhēnduì nǐ de.
B: Shìde, wǒ huì jìzhù zhè bǐ zhàng de, yǒu chóu bú bào fēi jūnzǐ, yǐhòu tā de
bǎbǐng búyào luò dào wǒ shǒulǐ.

A: His address at the general assembly today was clearly directed at you.
B: Yeah, I'll remember this slight. A real man must settle his scores. He shouldn't
let me get my hooks into him in the future.

Example 2:

A: 他把你打了？
B: 这个王八蛋下手真狠，**有仇不报非君子**，以后我也找机会打他一顿。

A: Tā bǎ nǐ dǎ le?
B: Zhègè wángbādàn xiàshǒu zhēn hěn, yǒu chóu bú bào fēi jūnzǐ, yǐhòu wǒ yě
zhǎo jīhuì dǎ tā yí dùn.

A: Did he hit you?
B: That bastard has no mercy. But, a real man must settle his scores. I'll look for
an opportunity to beat him up in the future.

Usage: Used singly.

Note: Neutral in meaning.

---

270. 不倒翁 (不倒翁) bù dǎo wēng

Translated character by character, 不倒翁 means 'not-fall-man' whereas the implied meaning of this proverb would be 'someone who always lands on their feet no matter what the political environment.' Its functional translation is 'a tumbler.'

Example 1:

A: 他善于观察政治上的变化，每次都站在优胜者的一方，是政坛上的**不倒翁**。

A: Tā shànyú guānchá zhèngzhì shàng de biànhuà, měicì dōu zhàn zài yōushèngzhě de yì fāng, shì zhèngtán shàng de bùdǎowēng.

A: He's good at observing political change and always stands with the winning side. He's a political tumbler.

Example 2:

A: 他是个有名的**不倒翁**，做了十九年的美联储主席，不管哪个党派上台，对他都没有影响。

A: Tā shì gè yǒumíng de bùdǎowēng, zuòle shíjiǔ nián de Měiliánchǔ zhǔxí, bùguǎn nǎ gè dǎngpài shàngtái, duì tā dōu méiyǒu yǐngxiǎng.

A: He's a renowned tumbler. He's been chairman of the Federal Reserve for 19 years and no matter which party is in office, it doesn't affect him.

Usage: Functions as object.

Note: Slightly derogatory in meaning.

---

271. 干打雷，不下雨 (乾打雷，不下雨) gān dǎ léi, bú xià yǔ

Translated character by character, 干打雷，不下雨 means 'only-thunder-no-rain,' whereas the implied meaning of this proverb would be 'talking big, but not backing it up with action.' Its functional translation is 'to talk the talk but not walk the walk' or 'all bark and no bite.'

Example 1:

A: 高层总是说要改善我们的工作条件，但是一年了什么都没做啊！

B: 对啊，**干打雷，不下雨**。

A: Gāocéng zǒngshì shuō yào gǎishàn wǒmen de gōngzuò tiáojiàn, dànshì yì nián le shénme dōu méi zuò a!

B: Duì ā, gān dǎléi, bú xiàyǔ.

A: Management is always saying they're going to improve our working conditions, but it's been a year already and they haven't done a thing!

B: Yep, they're talking big but not backing it up with action.

Example 2:

A: 总说要反腐败，结果一个贪污犯也没抓起来。

B: **干打雷，不下雨**。

A: Zǒng shuō yào fǎn fǔbài, jiéguǒ yígè tānwūfàn yě méi zhuā qǐlái.

B: Gān dǎléi, bú xiàyǔ.

A: They're always saying they want to crack down on corruption, but they haven't even caught one corrupt person.

B: They are all bark and no bite.

Usage: Functions as predicate.

Note: Neutral or humorous in meaning.

---

272. 鸡飞狗跳 (雞飛狗跳) jī fēi gǒu tiào

Translated character by character, 鸡飞狗跳 means 'chicken-fly-dog-jump,' whereas the implied meaning of this proverb would be 'in an animated and disordered state.' Its functional translation is 'in a tizzy.'

Example 1:

A: 省里的干部要到一个小村子搞调查，村长觉得是一个在大干部面前表现的机会，赶紧让老百姓连夜打扫街道、栽花栽树，闹得全村**鸡飞狗跳**。

A: Shěng lǐ de gànbù yào dào yígè xiǎo cūnzi gǎo diàochá, cūnzhǎng juéde shì yígè zài dà gànbù miànqián biǎoxiàn de jīhuì, gǎnjǐn ràng lǎobǎixìng lián yè dǎsǎo jiēdào, zāi huā zāi shù, nào de quán cūn jī fēi gǒu tiào.

A: When province level cadres were going to survey a small town, the mayor thought it was an opportunity to shine in front of important cadres, so he quickly got the townsfolk to clean the streets and plant flowers and trees through the night, throwing the whole town into a tizzy.

Example 2:

A: 政府又在抓恐怖分子。

B: 什么恐怖分子？政府军倒像恐怖分子，把整个国家搞得**鸡飞狗跳**的。

A: Zhèngfǔ yòu zài zhuā kǒngbùfènzǐ.

B: Shénme kǒngbùfènzǐ? Zhèngfǔjūn dào xiàng kǒngbùfènzǐ, bǎ zhěng gè guójiā gǎo de jī fēi gǒu tiào de.

A: The government is catching terrorists again.

B: What terrorists? The army is really like the terrorists, throwing the whole country into a tizzy.

Usage: Functions as complement.

Variant: 鸡飞狗跳墙

Note: Derogatory in meaning.

273. 事后诸葛亮 (事後諸葛亮) shì hòu Zhūgé Liàng

Translated character by character, 事后诸葛亮 means 'event-after-Zhuge Liang,' whereas the implied meaning of this proverb would be 'to claim prescience after a result is known.' Its functional translation is 'hindsight is 20-20.'

Example 1:

A: 我说对了吧？别人都说她在这档选秀节目中过不了第一轮，我说她能得冠军。

B: 你别**事后诸葛亮**了。我可从来没听你说过她能得冠军。

A: Wǒ shuō duì le ba? Biérén dōu shuō tā zài zhè dàng xuǎnxiù jiémù zhōng guò bùliǎo dì-yī lún, wǒ shuō tā néng dé guànjūn.

B: Nǐ bié shì hòu Zhūgé Liàng le. Wǒ kě cónglái méi tīng nǐ shuōguò tā néng dé guànjūn.

A: Am I right? Everyone else said she wouldn't get past the first round of this talent search; I said she could be the winner.

B: Hindsight is 20-20. I never heard you say that she could win.

Example 2:

A: 比赛结束后，评论员大谈应该用哪个球员，应该使用什么战术。这不过是**事后诸葛亮**。

A: Bǐsài jiéshù hòu, pínglùnyuán dà tán yīnggāi yòng nǎ gè qiúyuán, yīnggāi shǐyòng shénme zhànshù. Zhè búguò shì shì hòu Zhūgé Liàng.

A: After the match ends, commentators talk big about which players should have been used, and which tactics should have been used. But hindsight is 20-20.

Usage: Functions as predicative or predicate.

Note: Slightly derogatory in meaning.

274.　落水狗 (落水狗) luò shuǐ gǒu

Translated character by character, 落水狗 means 'fall in-water-dog,' whereas the implied meaning of this proverb would be 'a bad person who has fallen out of favor.' Its functional translation is 'one who is down on their luck.'

Example 1:

A:　怎么这么多人批评他？

B:　你不知道，他以前有权的时候，对待别人非常粗暴；现在他成了**落水狗**，大家都想把以前的怨气出出来。

A:　Zěnme zhème duō rén pīpíng tā?

B:　Nǐ bù zhīdào, tā yǐqián yǒu quán de shíhòu, duìdài biérén fēicháng cūbào; xiànzài tā chéngle luòshuǐgǒu, dàjiā dōu xiǎng bǎ yǐqián de yuànqì chū chūlái.

A:　Why are so many people criticizing him?

B:　Don't you know? When he had power before, he treated others very rudely. Now that he's down on his luck, everyone wants to take out their anger on him.

Example 2:

A:　他看着挺可怜的。

B:　不能可怜他。我们要痛打**落水狗**。

A:　Tā kànzhe tǐng kělián de.

B:　Bùnéng kělián tā. Wǒmen yào tòng dǎ luòshuǐgǒu.

A:　He looks pretty pitiful.

B:　You can't pity him. We should hit a bad person even if he's down.

Usage: Nominal element, functions mainly as object.

Note: Slightly derogatory or neutral in meaning.

275.　板上钉钉 (板上釘釘) bǎn shàng dìng dīng

Translated character by character, 板上钉钉 means 'board-on-to nail-nail,' whereas the implied meaning of this proverb would be 'finalized,' or 'a guaranteed result.' Its functional translation is 'sure as shooting,' 'a shoo-in,' or 'a sure bet.'

Example 1:

A:　谁能当选下届市长？

B:　肯定是张副市长，这是**板上钉钉**的事。

A:　Shuí néng dāngxuǎn xià jiè shìzhǎng?

B:　Kěndìng shì Zhāng fùshìzhǎng, zhè shì bǎn shàng dìng dīng de shì.

A: Who could be elected to be the next mayor?
B: It will definitely be Vice-Mayor Zhang. That one's sure as shooting.

Example 2:

A: 说到奥运会男篮冠军，美国队是**板上钉钉**的。

A: Shuō dào Àoyùnhuì nánlán guànjūn, Měiguó duì shì **bǎn shàng dìng dīng** de.

A: As far as the Olympics men's basketball champion goes, Team USA is a shoo-in.

Usage: Functions as attributive or predicative.

Note: Neutral in meaning.

276. 一碗水端平 (一碗水端平) yì wǎn shuǐ duān píng

Translated character by character, 一碗水端平 means 'one-bowl-water-hold-even,' whereas the implied meaning of this proverb would be 'to treat equally without discrimination.' Its functional translation is 'to be impartial' or 'to take an impartial approach.'

Example 1:

A: 我们请他评评理去。
B: 谁不知道，你们俩是亲戚，他能**一碗水端平**吗？

A: Wǒmen qǐng tā píngping lǐ qù.
B: Shéi bù zhīdao, nǐmen liǎ shì qīnqi, tā néng yì wǎn shuǐ duān píng ma?

A: We asked him to referee for us.
B: Everyone knows you two are related. Can he be impartial?

Example 2:

A: 政府在收入分配政策上应该**一碗水端平**，不能叫弱势群体吃亏。

A: Zhèngfǔ zài shōurù fēnpèi zhèngcè shang yì wǎn shuǐ duān píng, bùnéng jiào ruòshì qúntǐ chīkuī.

A: The government should take an impartial approach to income distribution policy. It can't let the disadvantaged suffer.

Usage: Functions as predicate.

Note: Neutral in meaning.

277.　烫手的山芋 (燙手的山芋) tàng shǒu de shānyù

Translated character by character, 烫手的山芋 means 'scalding-hand-sweet potato,' whereas the implied meaning of this proverb would be 'something very annoying which no one wants to be saddled with.' Its functional translation is 'a hot potato.'

Example 1:

A: 恭喜你！现在你是国家队的主教练了。

B: 甭提了，你知道，这是个**烫手的山芋**，没人想干。我也不想干，可是上边非让我干不可。

A: Gōngxǐ nǐ! Xiànzài nǐ shì guójiāduì de zhǔjiàoliàn le.

B: Béng tí le, nǐ zhīdào, zhè shì gè tàngshǒu de shānyù, méi rén xiǎng gàn. Wǒ yě bù xiǎng gàn, kěshì shàngbiān fēi ràng wǒ gàn bùkě.

A: Congratulations! You're now the national team's head coach.

A: Don't mention it. You know, this job is like a hot potato; no one wants to have it. I also didn't want to do it, but the higher-ups wouldn't let me refuse.

Example 2:

A: 老城区改造是一块**烫手的山芋**，改好了，原有的居民感谢你；改不好，估计得让老百姓骂死。

A: Lǎochéngqū gǎizào shì yí kuài tàngshǒu de shānyù, gǎi hǎo le, yuányǒu de jūmín gǎnxiè nǐ; gǎi bù hǎo, gūjì děi ràng lǎobǎixìng mà sǐ.

A: Old city planning is a hot potato job. If you do a good job, the existing residents will thank you, but if you do a bad job, the public will probably scold you to death.

Usage: Functions mainly as predicative.

Note: Neutral or humorous in meaning.

278.　笑掉大牙 (笑掉大牙) xiào diào dà yá

Translated character by character, 笑掉大牙 means 'laugh-off-big-tooth,' whereas the implied meaning of this proverb would be 'to laugh one's head off.'

Example 1:

A: 你赶快回去换一身衣服吧？

B: 怎么了？不合适吗？

A: 岂止是不合适，简直是太不合适了！你穿这身衣服，会让人**笑掉大牙**的。

A: Nǐ gǎnkuài huíqù huàn yì shēn yīfú ba?

B: Zěnme le? Bù héshì ma?

A: Qǐzhǐ shì bù héshì, jiǎnzhí shì tài bù héshì le! Nǐ chuān zhè shēn yīfú, huì ràng rén xiào diào dà yá de.

A: Go back and change your outfit now!

B: What's wrong? Is it not appropriate?

A: It's not just inappropriate, it's honestly incredibly inappropriate. If you wear this outfit, people will laugh their heads off.

Example 2:

A: 庄子是谁？

B: 你真不知道？你还是学习中国哲学的，怎么连庄子都不知道？千万别跟别人说你不知道庄子，那会叫人**笑掉大牙**的。

A: Zhuāngzi shì shéi?

B: Nǐ zhēn bù zhīdào? Nǐ hái shì xuéxí Zhōngguó zhéxué de, zěnme lián Zhuāngzi dōu bù zhīdào? Qiānwàn bié gēn biérén shuō nǐ bù zhīdào Zhuāngzi, nà huì jiào rén xiào diào dà yá de.

A: Who is Zhuangzi?

B: Do you really not know? You studied Chinese philosophy; how do you not even know Zhuangzi? Don't, under any circumstances, tell people you don't know who Zhuangzi is. People would laugh their heads off.

Usage: Used in the structure '让/叫/令/被人~（的）.'

Note: Slightly derogatory or neutral in meaning.

279. 一回生，二回熟 （一回生，二回熟）
yī huí shēng, èr huí shú

Translated character by character, 一回生，二回熟 means 'first-time-strangers, second-time-intimates,' whereas the implied meaning of this proverb would be 'people become closer when they spend time together.' Its functional meaning is 'a stranger is just a friend you haven't met yet.'

Example 1:

A: 我来了一个高中同学，晚上过来热闹一下吧。

B: 我跟他不认识，还是你们自己热闹吧。

A: 没事儿，**一回生，二回熟**。再说我这个同学特别随和，很好相处。

A: Wǒ láile yígè gāozhōng tóngxué, wǎnshang guòlái rènào yíxià ba.

B: Wǒ gēn tā bú rènshí, háishì nǐmen zìjǐ rènào ba.

A: Méishìr, yī huí shēng, èr huí shú. Zàishuō wǒ zhègè tóngxué tèbié suíhé, hěn hǎo xiāngchǔ.

A: One of my high school classmates is coming to see me. Let's hang out tonight.

B: I don't know him. You two should just hang out yourselves.

A: Don't worry about it, a stranger is just a friend you haven't met yet. Moreover, this classmate of mine is extremely easy-going.

Example 2:

A: 对不起，刚才我很失礼，请您不要介意。

B: 哪里！以前我们不认识，才有这个误会；**一回生，二回熟**，下次就不会了。

A: Duìbùqǐ, gāngcái wǒ hěn shīlǐ, qǐng nín búyào jieyì.

B: Nǎ lǐ! Yǐqián wǒmen bú rènshí, cái yǒu zhège wùhuì; yī huí shēng, èr huí shú, xiàcì jiù bú huì le.

A: I'm sorry. I've been very rude. Please don't take offense.

B: Don't worry about it! We had this misunderstanding because we didn't know each other. A stranger is just a friend you haven't met yet. Next time we won't have this issue.

Usage: Used singly.

Note: Neutral in meaning.

---

280. 鱼与熊掌不可得兼 (魚與熊掌不可得兼)
yú yǔ xióng zhǎng bù kě dé jiān

Translated character by character, 鱼与熊掌不可得兼 means 'fish-and-bear-palm-not-able-get-both,' whereas the implied meaning of this proverb would be 'one cannot always have everything.' Its functional translation is 'one can't have everything in life.'

Example 1:

A: 从工作的角度，这是一个绝好的机会；但是从家庭的角度，我要付出太多。

B: 好好权衡一下吧，**鱼与熊掌不可得兼**，必须有取舍。

A: Cóng gōngzuò de jiǎodù, zhè shì yígè jué hǎo de jīhuì; dànshì cóng jiātíng de jiǎodù, wǒ yào fùchū tài duō.

B: Hǎohāo quánhéng yíxià ba, yú yǔ xióngzhǎng bùkě dé jiān, bìxū yǒu qǔshě.

A: From a work perspective, this is an outstanding opportunity but, from a family perspective, I'd have to give up too much.

B: Weigh up the pros and cons. You can't have everything in life. You have to give something up.

Example 2:

A: 我们得做出一个选择，是要利润还是要产品的知名度？**鱼和熊掌不可兼得**。

A: Wǒmen děi zuò chū yígè xuǎnzé, shì yào lìrùn háishì yào chǎnpǐn de zhīmíngdù? Yú hé xióngzhǎng bùkě jiān dé.

A: We have to make a choice. At this point, do we want profit, or product recognition? We can't have both.

Usage: Used singly.

Variant: 鱼与熊掌不可兼得

Note: Neutral or humorous in meaning.

---

281. 咸鱼翻身 (鹹魚翻身) xián yú fān shēn

Translated character by character, 咸鱼翻身 means 'salted-fish-turn over-body,' whereas the implied meaning of this proverb would be 'to revive something that is old or having difficulties.' Its functional translation is 'to give a new lease on life.'

Example 1:

A: 这个电影今年票房收入第一。
B: 是啊，男主角演电影三十年都没红过，这次凭这部电影**咸鱼翻身**了。

A: Zhègè diànyǐng jīnnián piàofáng shōurù dì-yī.
B: Shì a, nán zhǔjué yǎn diànyǐng sānshí nián dōu méi hóng guò, zhècì píng zhè bù diànyǐng xiányúfānshēn le.

A: This movie topped the box office this year.
B: Yeah, the movie's male lead hasn't been in a hot movie in 30 years, and was relying on this movie to give his career a new lease on life.

Example 2:

A: 他做实业越做越赔，后来炒股**咸鱼翻身**了。

A: Tā zuò shíyè yuè zuò yuè péi, hòulái chǎogǔ xiányúfānshēn le.

A: He was losing more and more in industry but, later, stock speculation gave him a new lease on life.

Usage: Functions as predicate.

Note: Slightly derogatory or neutral in meaning.

282.   一根绳上的蚂蚱 (一根繩上的螞蚱)
yì gēn shéng shàng de màzha

Translated character by character, 一根绳上的蚂蚱 means 'one-MW-string-on-locusts,' whereas the implied meaning of this proverb would be 'to have intertwined fates.' Its functional translation is 'to be in something together.'

Example 1:

A: 张局长怎么那么坚决地支持赵市长？

B: 你不知道，张局长是赵市长一手提拔起来的，他们是**一根绳上的蚂蚱**。如果赵市长下台，张局长也干不了了。

A: Zhāng júzhǎng zěnme nàme jiānjué de zhīchí Zhào shìzhǎng?

B: Nǐ bù zhīdao, Zhāng júzhǎng shì Zhào shìzhǎng yìshǒu tíbá qǐlái de, tāmen shì yì gēn shéng shàng de màzha. Rúguǒ Zhào shìzhǎng xiàtái, Zhāng júzhǎng yě gàn bùliǎo le.

A: Why is Minister Zhang supporting Mayor Zhao so steadfastly?

B: You don't know? Minister Zhang singlehandedly promoted Mayor Zhao. They are in this together. If Mayor Zhao is unseated, Minister Zhang will not be able to continue.

Example 2:

A: 大食品公司认为，只要食品药品管理局的官员收受了他们的巨额贿赂，从此他们就是**一根绳上的蚂蚱**。

A: Dà shípǐn gōngsī rènwéi, zhǐyào shípǐn yàopǐn guǎnlǐjú de guānyuán shōushòule tāmen de jù'é huìlù, cóngcǐ tāmen jiù shì yì gēn shéng shàng de màzha.

A: The big food company believes that if the FDA accepts their huge bribe, they will be in it together going forward.

Usage: Functions as object.

Variant: 一条绳上的蚂蚱

Note: Neutral or slightly derogatory in meaning.

283.   趟浑水 (趟渾水) tāng hún shuǐ

Translated character by character, 趟浑水 means 'wade-murky-water,' whereas the implied meaning of this proverb is 'to intentionally get involved in a messy situation.'

Example 1:

A: 我想去竞聘这个主任的位置。

B: 别去**趟**这个**浑水**，这里面的关系太复杂，太肮脏。你跟他们不是一路人。

A: Wǒ xiǎng qù jìngpìn zhègè zhǔrèn de wèizhì.

B: Bié qù tāng zhègè húnshuǐ, zhè lǐmiàn de guānxì tài fùzá, tài āngzāng. Nǐ gēn tāmen búshì yí lù rén.

A: I want to be a candidate for this post as director.

B: Don't get yourself into that mess. The situation is too complicated and too dirty. You're not that breed of person.

Example 2:

A: 你想不想解决那家公司的污染问题？

B: 我不想**趟浑水**。官司都打十年了，还墨墨迹迹的，我可不想管。

A: Nǐ xiǎng bù xiǎng jiějué nà jiā gōngsī de wūrǎn wèntí?

B: Wǒ bù xiǎng tānghúnshuǐ. Guānsi dōu dǎ shí nián le, hái mòmojīji de, wǒ kě bù xiǎng guǎn.

A: Do you want to deal with that company's pollution problem?

B: I don't want to get into that mess. The case has gone on for ten years already and it's still messy. I don't want any part of it.

Usage: Functions as predicate.

Note: Slightly derogatory in meaning.

---

284.   狗腿子 (狗腿子) gǒu tuǐ zi

Translated character by character, 狗腿子 means 'dog-leg,' whereas the implied meaning of this proverb would be 'a servile follower.' Its functional translation is 'henchman,' 'lackey,' or 'lapdog.'

Example 1:

A: 他跟领导走得很近。

B: 他就是领导的**狗腿子**，对领导溜须拍马，领导让他做什么他就做什么。

A: Tā gēn lǐngdǎo zǒu de hěn jìn.

B: Tā jiù shì lǐngdǎo de gǒutuǐzi, duì lǐngdǎo liūxū-pāimǎ, lǐngdǎo ràng tā zuò shénme tā jiù zuò shénme.

A: He's gotten very close to the boss.

B: He's the boss's lapdog. He fawns on the boss and does anything that the boss says.

Example 2:

A: 他手下有几个**狗腿子**，尤其是那个瘦子。

A: Tā shǒuxià yǒu jǐ gè gǒutuǐzi, yóuqí shì nàgè shòuzi.

A: He has a few lackeys at his command, especially the skinny one.

Usage: Functions as predicative or object.

Note: Derogatory in meaning.

285. 用在刀刃上（用在刀刃上）yòng zài dāo rèn shàng

Translated character by character, 用在刀刃上 means 'use-on-knife-edge,' whereas the implied meaning of this proverb would be 'to employ limited resources where they are most needed.'

Example 1:

A: 今年我的公司赚了一千万，我准备花一百万买辆跑车。

B: 你就知道乱花钱，钱得**用在刀刃上**，你能不能把那一百万用在改善生产设备上？

A: Jīn nián wǒde gōngsī zuànle yī qiān wàn, wǒ zhǔnbèi huā yì bǎi wàn mǎi liàng pǎochē.

B: Nǐ jiù zhīdào luàn huāqián, qián děi yòng zài dāorèn shàng, nǐ néngbùnéng bǎ nà yì bǎi wàn yòng zài gǎishàn shēngchǎn shèbèi shàng?

A: My company made 10 million RMB this year. I'm planning to spend a million to buy a sports car.

B: All you know how to do is waste money. You should use the money where it's needed. Can you use that million RMB on improving your production equipment?

Example 2:

A: 他可聪明了，游戏玩得好着呢。

B: 浪费了，好钢得**用在刀刃上**，学习那么差，游戏玩儿得好有什么用？

A: Tā kě cōngmíng le, yóuxì wán de hǎo zhe ne.

B: Làngfèi le, hǎo gāng děi yòng zài dāorèn shàng, xuéxí nàme chà, yóuxì wánr de hǎo yǒu shénme yòng?

A: He's very smart. He's really good at video games.

B: That's a waste. He should use his talents where they're most needed. What use is his being good at video games if his studies are in such a poor state?

Usage: Functions as predicate.

Variant: 好钢用在刀刃上

Note: Neutral in meaning.

286. 鸡飞蛋打 (雞飛蛋打) jī fēi dàn dǎ

Translated character by character, 鸡飞蛋打 means 'chicken-fled-egg-broken,' whereas the implied meaning of this proverb would be 'all is lost.' Its functional translation is 'to come up empty-handed.'

Example 1:

A: 他的女儿跟男朋友跑了。
B: 是啊，他本想跟男方多要些彩礼，谁知道要得太多了，结果不但没得到一分钱，女儿反倒跟人家跑了，**鸡飞蛋打**。

A: Tā de nǚ'ér gēn nánpéngyǒu pǎo le.
B: Shì a, tā běn xiǎng gēn nánfāng duō yào xiē cǎilǐ, shuízhīdào yào de tài duō le, jiéguǒ búdàn méi dédào yì fēn qián, nǚ'ér fǎndào gēn rénjia pǎo le, jī fēi dàn dǎ.

A: His daughter ran away with her boyfriend.
B: Yeah, he originally wanted to get a larger dowry from the man, but he was asking too much. In the end, he not only got no money, his daughter ran away with someone. He came up empty-handed.

Example 2:

A: 你不要太贪婪，差不多就行了，别最后弄得**鸡飞蛋打**。

A: Nǐ búyào tài tānlán, chàbuduō jiù xíng le, bié zuìhòu nòng de jī fēi dàn dǎ.

A: Don't be too greedy. Just leave well enough alone. Don't make it so that you come up empty-handed in the end.

Usage: Functions as predicate or complement.

Note: Neutral in meaning.

287. 胳膊扭不过大腿 (胳膊扭不過大腿) gēbo niǔ bú guò dàtuǐ

Translated character by character, 胳膊扭不过大腿 means 'arm-twist-not-able-thigh,' whereas the implied meaning of this proverb would be 'no amount of effort can make up for inherent weakness.' Its functional translation is 'the weak cannot contend with the strong.'

Example 1:

A: 这项规定太不合理了。不行，我要去上访。
B: 上诉也没有用，**胳膊扭不过大腿**，你告的可是一级政府啊！

A: Zhè xiàng guīdìng tài bù hélǐ le. Bùxíng, wǒ yào qù shàngfǎng.
B: Shàngsù yě méiyǒuyòng, gēbo niǔ bú guò dàtuǐ, nǐ gào de shì yì jí zhèngfǔ a!

A: This regulation is so unreasonable. This won't work; I'm going to appeal to a higher authority.

B: There's no use in going to court either. The weak cannot contend with the strong. You're going up against the government!

Example 2:

A: 老同学，不是我要说让你不高兴的话。你那家小书店还是关了吧，凭你的脑瓜，干什么不赚钱啊？

B: 不行，如果我的小店儿关了，周围的孩子、邻居看书就不方便了。

A: 你说得很对，可是**胳膊拧不过大腿**啊。网上购物兴起以后，全国的小书店都关了一半了。

A: Lǎotóngxué, búshì wǒ yào shuō ràng nǐ bù gāoxìng de huà. Nǐ nà jiā xiǎo shūdiàn háishi guānle ba, píng nǐde nǎoguā, gàn shénme bú zhuànqián a?

B: Bùxíng, rúguǒ wǒde xiǎodiànr guān le, zhōuwéi de háizi, línju kànshū jiù bù fāngbian le.

A: Nǐ shuō de hěn duì, kěshì gēbo nǐng bú guò dàtuǐ. Wǎngshàng gòuwù xīngqǐ yǐhòu, quánguó de xiǎo shūdiàn dōu guānle yíbàn le.

A: My friend, it's not that I want to say something that will make you unhappy, but you should close your little bookstore. Use your head; you can make money doing anything.

B: That won't work. If I close my small bookstore, it won't be convenient for the local children and residents to read books.

A: You're right, but the weak cannot contend with the strong. Since the rise of online shopping, half of the small bookstores in the country have closed.

Usage: Used singly.

Variant: 胳膊拧不过大腿 (拧 nǐng, to twist)

Note: Neutral or humorous in meaning.

288. 饱汉不知饿汉饥 (飽漢不知餓漢饑)
bǎo hàn bù zhī è hàn jī

Translated character by character, 饱汉不知饿汉饥 means 'full-man-not-know-hungry-man-starving,' whereas the implied meaning of this proverb would be 'one cannot understand someone's suffering without having experienced it.' Its functional translation is 'he jests at scars that never felt a wound,' or 'the wearer knows best where the shoe pinches.'

Example 1:

A: 过几天我再把钱打到你的账户上。

B: 你真是**饱汉子不知饿汉子饥**，我等你的钱都快等疯了。

A: Guò jǐ tiān wǒ zài bǎ qián dǎ dào nǐde zhànghù shàng.

B: Nǐ zhēn shì bǎo hànzi bù zhī è hànzi jī, wǒ děng nǐde qián dōu kuài děng fēng le.

A: In a few days, I'll wire more money into your account.

B: He jests at scars that never felt a wound. I'm about to go crazy waiting for the money.

Example 2:

A: 求他一点儿事，他却一拖再拖。

B: 他啊，**饱汉不知饿汉饥**，不理解我们的困难。

A: Qiú tā yìdiǎnr shì, tā què yìtuō-zàituō.

B: Tā a, bǎo hàn bù zhī è hàn jī, bù lǐjiě wǒmen de kùnnan.

A: I asked something of him and he just keeps pushing it back.

B: Him? The wearer knows best where the shoe pinches. He doesn't understand our troubles.

Usage: Functions as predicative.

Variant: 饱汉子不知饿汉子饥

Note: Derogatory and humorous in meaning.

---

289. 笑面虎 (笑面虎) xiào miàn hǔ

Translated character by character, 笑面虎 means 'smile-face-tiger,' whereas the implied meaning of this proverb would be 'one who hides their ferocity or malicious intent behind a façade of kindliness.' Its functional translation is 'a wolf in sheep's clothing.'

Example 1:

A: 他整天笑嘻嘻的，不过你要小心点儿，他是个**笑面虎**。

A: Tā zhěngtiān xiàoxīxī de, búguò nǐ yào xiǎoxīn diǎnr, tā shì gè xiàomiànhǔ.

A: He's always smiling, but you need to watch yourself. He's a wolf in sheep's clothing.

Example 2:

A: 律师个个都像**笑面虎**，表面上客客气气，收费的时候可是一点儿也不手软。

A: Lǜshī gègè dōu xiàng xiàomiànhǔ, biǎomiàn shàng kèkeqìqì, shōufèi de shíhòu kěshì yìdiǎnr yě bù shǒuruǎn.

A: Lawyers are all wolves in sheep's clothing. On the outside they're nice and polite, but when it comes time to collect the bills, they're coldhearted.

Usage: Functions as predicative or object.

Note: Slightly derogatory in meaning.

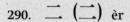

290. 二 (二) èr

Translated character by character, 二 means 'two,' whereas the implied meaning of this proverb would be 'clueless.'

Example 1:

A: 他太二了，连这话都不懂。

A: Tā tài èr le, lián zhè huà dōu bù dǒng.

A: He's so clueless. He doesn't even understand what this means.

Example 2:

A: 这个老外真二，把中国当成美国了。

A: Zhègè lǎowài zhēn èr, bǎ Zhōngguó dāngchéng Měiguó le.

A: This foreigner is really clueless. He thinks China is just like the US.

Usage: Functions as predicate.

Note: Slightly derogatory in meaning.

291. 给力 (給力) gěi lì

Translated character by character, 给力 means 'giving-power,' whereas the implied meaning of this proverb would be 'awesome,' or 'exciting.'

Example 1:

A: 这部电影真精彩，实在太**给力**了。

A: Zhè bù diànyǐng zhēn jīngcǎi, shízài tài gěilì le.

A: This movie is truly excellent. It's really so awesome.

Example 2:

A: 我给你拍照片呢。笑一笑，……再笑一笑，……不行，**给点儿力**好不好？

A: Wǒ gěi nǐ pāi zhàopiàn ne. Xiào yi xiào, ……zài xiào yi xiào, ……bùxíng, gěi diǎnr lì hǎobùhǎo?

A: I'll take your picture. Smile . . . ; smile again . . . ; that's no good. Look alive, OK?

Usage: Functions as predicate.

Note: Complimentary in meaning. Started to gain popularity in 2010. Sometimes referred to in English as 'gelivable.'

292. 母老虎 (母老虎) mǔ lǎohǔ

Translated character by character, 母老虎 means 'female-tiger,' whereas the implied meaning of this proverb would be 'a controlling or overbearing woman.' Its functional translation is 'shrew,' or 'battle-axe.'

Example 1:

A: 听说他老婆可厉害了。
B: 是个**母老虎**，把他管得跟个小猫似的。

A: Tīng shuō tā lǎopo kě lìhai le.
B: Shì gè mǔlǎohu, bǎ tā guǎn de gēn gè xiǎomāo shì de.

A: I hear his wife is really fierce.
B: She's a shrew. She's got him whipped.

Example 2:

A: 我的老板是只**母老虎**，非常凶。

A: Wǒde lǎobǎn shì zhī mǔlǎohu, fēicháng xiōng.

A: My boss is a battle-axe; very fierce.

Usage: Nominal element, functions as predicative or object.

Note: Slightly derogatory and humorous in meaning.

293. 五十步笑百步 (五十步笑百步) wǔshí bù xiào bǎi bù

Translated character by character, 五十步笑百步 means 'fifty-steps-laugh-one hundred-steps,' whereas the implied meaning of this proverb would be 'disparaging someone else for essentially the same thing you yourself have done.' Its functional translation is 'the pot calling the kettle black.'

Example 1:

A: 这个游戏有十关，你才过第二关，怎么这么慢？
B: 你别**五十步笑百步**，你不是还差五关呢吗？

A: Zhège yóuxì yǒu shí guān, nǐ cái guò dì-èr guān, zěnme zhème màn?
B: Nǐ bié wǔshí bù xiào bǎi bù, nǐ búshì hái chà wǔ guān ne ma?

A: This game has ten levels and you've only just beaten the second? How are you so slow?

B: The pot shouldn't call the kettle black. Don't you still have five levels left?

Example 2:

A: 你连比尔·克林顿都没听说过吗？你还算是美国人吗？

B: 你连老布什和小布什都不分呢，**五十步笑百步**。

A: Nǐ lián Bǐ'ěr Kèlíndùn dōu méi tīngshuō guò ma? Nǐ hái suàn shì Měiguórén ma?

B: Nǐ lián lǎo Bùshí hé xiǎo Bùshí dōu bù fēn ne, wǔshí bù xiào bǎi bù.

A: You haven't even heard of Bill Clinton? Are you really American?

B: You don't even know the difference between George H. W. Bush and George W. Bush. That's the pot calling the kettle black.

Usage: Functions as predicative or predicate.

Note: Slightly derogatory and humorous in meaning. 五十步笑百步 is an allusion from the Book of Mencius. A soldier who retreated fifty paces mocked one who retreated one hundred paces.

---

294. 门外汉 (門外漢) mén wài hàn

Translated character by character, 门外汉 means 'door-outside-man,' whereas the implied meaning of this proverb would be 'an inexperienced person.' Its functional translation is 'a layman.'

Example 1:

A: 对于艺术，我是个**门外汉**，所以最好不要乱发表看法。

A: Duìyú yìshù, wǒ shì gè ménwàihàn, suǒyǐ zuìhǎo búyào luàn fābiǎo kànfǎ.

A: With regards to art, I'm a layman, so I'd better not make comments lightly.

Example 2:

A: 经过不懈的努力，他从一个**门外汉**变成了内行。

A: Jīngguò búxiè de nǔlì, tā cóng yígè ménwàihàn biànchéng le nèiháng.

A: Through persistent effort, he went from being a layman to being an insider.

Usage: Nominal element, functions mainly as predicative or object.

Note: Neutral in meaning.

295. 前人栽树，后人乘凉 (前人栽樹，後人乘涼)
qián rén zāi shù, hòu rén chéng liáng

Translated character by character, 前人栽树，后人乘凉 means 'forefather-plant-tree, descendent-enjoy shade,' whereas the implied meaning of this proverb would be 'descendants benefit from the efforts of their forebears.' Its functional translation is 'walnuts and pears you plant for your heirs,' or 'for posterity's sake.'

Example 1:

A: 我们应该有一种奉献精神，**前人栽树，后人乘凉**，我们的子孙后代会感谢我们的付出的。

A: Wǒmen yīnggāi yǒu yìzhǒng fèngxiàn jīngshén, qián rén zāi shù, hòu rén chéng liáng, wǒmen de zǐsūn hòudài huì gǎnxiè wǒmen de fùchū de.

A: We should have a spirit of sacrifice. Walnuts and pears you plant for your heirs. Our descendants will be grateful for our efforts.

Example 2:

A: 这片荒漠何年何月才能改造成草原啊？值得吗？
B: 改造荒漠是**前人栽树，后人乘凉**。为了后世人，很值得。

A: Zhè piàn huāngmò hénián-héyuè cáinéng gǎizào chéng cǎoyuán a? Zhíde ma?
B: Gǎizào huāngmò shì qián rén zāi shù, hòu rén chéng liáng. Wèile hòushì rén, hěn zhíde.

A: Who knows when this piece of desert will finally be transformed into grassland? Is it worth it?
B: Transforming this desert is planting walnuts and pears for your heirs. For posterity, it's very much worth it.

Usage: Functions as predicative or used singly.

Note: Complimentary in meaning.

296. 烂泥扶不上墙 (爛泥扶不上墙) làn ní fú bú shàng qiáng

Translated character by character, 烂泥扶不上墙 means 'thin-mud-stick-not-upon-wall,' whereas the implied meaning of this proverb would be 'to help someone but have them fail to fulfill your expectations.' Its functional translation is 'to wash a pig is to waste both water and soap.'

Example 1:

A: 我们还应该再帮他一次。
B: 一次又一次，不知道已经多少次了，每次都是失败。他是**烂泥扶不上墙**的那种人。

A: Wǒmen hái yīnggāi zài bāng tā yí cì.

B: Yí cì yòu yí cì, bù zhīdào yǐjīng duōshǎo cì le, měicì dōu shì shībài. Tā shì làn ní fú bú shàng qiáng de nà zhǒng rén.

A: We should help him again.

B: It happens again and again. I don't know how many times we've helped him already, but he fails every time. To wash a pig is to waste both water and soap.

Example 2:

A: 这么多人帮他，他还是不能成功，真是**烂泥扶不上墙**。

A: Zhème duō rén bāng tā, tā hái shì bùnéng chénggōng, zhēn shì làn ní fú bú shàng qiáng.

A: So many people are helping him and he still can't succeed. To wash a pig is to waste both water and soap.

Usage: Functions as predicate or attributive.

Note: Derogatory and humorous in meaning.

297. 关公面前耍大刀 (關公面前耍大刀)
Guāngōng miàn qián shuǎ dà dāo

Translated character by character, 关公面前耍大刀 means 'in the face of-Lord Guan-play-broadsword,' whereas the implied meaning of this proverb would be 'to show off one's knowledge of some subject matter in front of a master.' Its functional translation is 'to teach one's grandmother how to suck eggs.'

Example 1:

A: 他写了一本应该怎么打网球的书，送了一本给费德勒。

B: 哇，他真好意思！这不是**关公面前耍大刀**么？

A: Tā xiěle yì běn yīnggāi zěnme dǎ wǎngqiú de shū, sòngle yì běn gěi Fèidélè.

B: Wà, tā zhēn hǎoyìsi! Zhè búshì Guāngōng miànqián shuǎ dà dāo me?

A: He wrote a book about how to play tennis and sent a copy to Roger Federer.

B: Wow, that's embarassing! Isn't that like teaching your grandmother how to suck eggs?

Example 2:

A: 你有什么看法，说出来听听？

B: 王教授，我可不敢。如果说了，那不是**关公面前耍大刀**嘛。

A: 学术上的事，不要那么谦虚，说来听听。

A: Nǐ yǒu shénme kànfǎ, shuō chūlái tīngtīng?
B: Wáng jiàoshòu, wǒ kě bùgǎn. Rúguǒ shuō le, nà búshì Guāngōng miànqián shuǎ dà dāo ma.
A: Xuéshù shàng de shì, búyào nàme qiānxū, shuō lái tīngtīng.

A: What do you think? Let's hear what you have to say.
B: Professor Wang, I don't dare. If I spoke, wouldn't that be like teaching your grandmother how to suck eggs?
A: Don't be so modest with regard to academic issues. Let's hear what you have to say.

Usage: Functions as predicative.

Note: Slightly derogatory in meaning.

---

298. 高不成，低不就 (高不成，低不就)
gāo bù chéng, dī bú jiù

Translated character by character, 高不成，低不就 means 'high-not able-achieve, low-not willing-accept,' whereas the implied meaning of this proverb would be 'to not be good enough to get what one wants, but unwilling to pursue something befitting one's talents.'

Example 1:

A: 他好像整天怀才不遇似的。
B: 哪儿啊，他是**高不成，低不就**。

A: Tā hǎoxiàng zhěngtiān huáicái-búyù shìde.
B: Nǎr a, tā shì gāobùchéng, dībújiù.

A: He seems to never be able to use his talents.
B: Not really. He's not good enough to do what he wants to do, but unwilling to do anything befitting his own talents.

Example 2:

A: 这个人有一定的才能，我想招聘他。
B: 再想想吧，他这个人**高不成，低不就**，干不成大事，抱怨倒不少。

A: Zhègè rén yǒu yídìng de cáinéng, wǒ xiǎng zhāopìn tā.
B: Zài xiǎngxiǎng ba, tā zhègè rén gāobùchéng, dībújiù, gàn bù chéng dàshì, bàoyuàn dào bùshǎo.

A: This person has some talent. I want to recruit him.
B: Think again. This guy is not good enough to do what he wants to do, but he's unwilling to do anything befitting his own talents. He can't get big things done and he complains a lot.

Usage: Functions as predicate.

Note: Slightly derogatory in meaning.

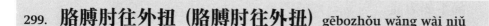

299. 胳膊肘往外扭 (胳膊肘往外扭) gēbozhǒu wǎng wài niǔ

Translated character by character, 胳膊肘往外扭 means 'arm-elbow-toward-outside-turn,' whereas the implied meaning of this proverb would be 'to side with outsiders instead of one's own people.'

Example 1:

A: 你也得为别人想想。

B: 你这话是怎么说的？你怎么不为我说话，**胳膊肘往外扭**啊？

A: Nǐ yě děi wèi biérén xiǎngxiǎng.

B: Nǐ zhè huà shì zěnme shuō de? Nǐ zěnme bú wèi wǒ shuōhuà, gēbozhǒu wǎng wài niǔ a?

A: You should also think about others.

B: How can you say that? Why didn't you take my side? You sided with outsiders instead of me.

Example 2:

A: X国其实对中国很好的。

B: 我看你像个汉奸，要不为什么**胳膊肘往外扭**？

A: X guó qíshí duì Zhōngguó hěnhǎo de.

B: Wǒ kàn nǐ xiàng gè hànjiān, yào bú wèishénme gēbozhǒu wǎng wài niǔ?

A: Country X is actually very good to China.

B: I think you sound like a traitor, otherwise why would you be supporting that country?

Usage: Functions as predicate.

Note: Neutral or humorous in meaning.

300. 长痛不如短痛 (長痛不如短痛)
cháng tòng bù rú duǎn tòng

Translated character by character, 长痛不如短痛 means 'long-agony-not-as good as-short-agony,' whereas the implied meaning of this proverb would be 'it is better to deal with painful things quickly.' Its functional translation is 'it's better to just rip the Band-Aid off now.'

Example 1:

A: 你看我跟我男朋友的关系，分分合合，好好坏坏，我们到底合适不合适？

B: 我看你们俩不合适。现在让你们分手，心里肯定会痛苦。但是，**长痛不如短痛**，与其一直痛苦下去，不如现在一刀两断。

A: Nǐ kàn wǒ gēn wǒ nánpéngyou de guānxì, fēnfenhéhé, hǎohǎohuàihuài, wǒmen dàodǐ héshì bú héshì?

B: Wǒ kàn nǐmen liǎ bù héshì. Xiànzài ràng nǐmen fēnshǒu, xīnlǐ kěndìng huì tòngkǔ. Dànshì, cháng tòng bùrú duǎn tòng, yǔqí yìzhí tòngkǔ xiàqù, bùrú xiànzài yìdāo-liǎngduàn.

A: Take a look at my relationship with my boyfriend. It's on and off, good and bad; are we right for each other or not?

B: I think you're not right for each other. If you break up now, it will definitely hurt, but it's better to just rip the Band-Aid off. It's better to make a clean break now than to continue being miserable.

Example 2:

A: 我在这家公司干得不如意，贡献多但是不受重视。想换家公司吧，但是现在总体就业形势不好。

B: **长痛不如短痛**。虽然现在就业形势不好，但是只要有机会就比你原来的公司强。

A: Wǒ zài zhè jiā gōngsī gàn de bù rúyì, gòngxiàn duō dànshì bú shòu zhòngshì. Xiǎng huàn jiā gōngsī ba, dànshì xiànzài zǒngtǐ jiùyè xíngshì bùhǎo.

B: Cháng tòng bùrú duǎn tòng. Suīrán xiànzài jiùyè xíngshì bùhǎo, dànshì zhǐyào yǒu jīhuì jiù bǐ nǐ yuánlái de gōngsī qiáng.

A: Working at this company hasn't turned out as I'd hoped. I've distinguished myself a lot, but I'm not valued. I want to move to another company, but the overall employment situation isn't good now.

B: It's better to just rip the Band-Aid off now. Although the employment situation isn't good now, if you get an opportunity, it'll be better than your old one.

Usage: Used singly.

Note: Neutral in meaning.

301. 酒香不怕巷子深 (酒香不怕巷子深)
jiǔ xiāng bú pà xiàngzi shēn

Translated character by character, 酒香不怕巷子深 means 'wine-fragrant-not-fear-alley-deep,' whereas the implied meaning of this proverb would be 'a good product needs no advertisement.' Its functional translation is 'good wine needs no bush.'

Example 1:

A: 张董，你们公司不怎么打广告，产品却卖得很火，有什么秘诀？

B: 什么也没有。我们只是注重质量，质量高了，**酒香不怕巷子深**，消费者自然也就喜欢了。其实我们不是不打广告，而是用消费者直接打广告。

A: Zhāng dǒng, nǐmen gōngsī bù zěnme dǎ guǎnggào, chǎnpǐn què mài de hěn huǒ, yǒu shénme mìjué?

B: Shénme yě méiyǒu. Wǒmen zhǐshì zhùzhòng zhìliàng, zhìliàng gāo le, jiǔ xiāng bú pà xiàngzi shēn, xiāofèizhě zìrán yě jiù xǐhuān le. Qíshí wǒmen búshì bù dǎ guǎnggào, érshì yòng xiāofèizhě zhíjiē dǎ guǎnggào.

A: Mr. Zhang, your company doesn't really advertise, but your products are flying off the shelves. What's your secret?

B: There is no secret. We just pay attention to quality. Good wine needs no bush. When the quality is good, consumers naturally like it. Really, it's not that we don't advertise; it's that we use consumers to advertise directly.

Example 2:

A: 可口可乐、麦当劳都做很多广告，看来**酒香也怕巷子深**。

A: Kěkǒu kělè, Màidāngláo dōu zuò hěn duō guǎnggào, kànlái jiǔ xiāng yě pà xiàngzi shēn.

A: Coca-Cola and McDonald's both advertise a lot. I see even good products need advertisement.

Usage: Used singly.

Variants: 酒好不怕巷子深; 好酒不怕巷子深

Note: Neutral in meaning.

---

302. 一条路走到黑 (一條路走到黑) yì tiáo lù zǒu dào hēi

Translated character by character, 一条路走到黑 means 'one-MW-road-walk-until-dark,' whereas the implied meaning of this proverb would be 'to persist in a quixotic endeavor until failure.' Its functional translation is 'to be as stubborn as a mule.'

Example 1:

A: 你去劝劝他，别再干下去了。这样肯定不行。

B: 我也劝过，但是不管用啊？他是**一条路走到黑**的人。

A: Nǐ qù quànquàn tā, bié zài gàn xiàqù le. Zhèyàng kěndìng bùxíng.

B: Wǒ yě quàn guò, dànshì bù guǎnyòng a? Tā shì yì tiáo lù zǒu dào hēi de rén.

A: Go have a talk with him; he can't keep doing that. It's just not OK.
B: I've spoken with him, but to what avail? He's stubborn as a mule.

Example 2:

A: 他怎么还做方便面生意啊？人们讲究饮食之后，这个行业一天比一天萎缩。

B: 他总是**一条路走到黑**，不会变通。

A: Tā zěnme hái zuò fāngbiànmiàn shēngyì a? Rénmen jiǎngjiū yǐnshí zhīhòu, zhège hángyè yì tiān bǐ yì tiān wěisuō.

B: Tā zǒngshì yì tiáo lù zǒu dào hēi, búhuì biàntōng.

A: How is he still in the instant noodle business? Since people became more discerning in their tastes, that industry has been shrinking constantly.
B: He's always been stubborn as a mule. He can't adapt.

Usage: Functions as predicate or attributive.

Variants: 一条路跑到黑；一条道走到黑；一条道跑到黑

Note: Slightly derogatory in meaning.

303. 不是鱼死，就是网破 (不是魚死，就是網破)
bú shì yú sǐ, jiù shì wǎng pò

Translated character by character, 不是鱼死，就是网破 means 'if-not-fish-die, then-is-net-break,' whereas the implied meaning of this proverb would be 'to be engaged in a fight to the end.' Its functional translation is 'it's either him or me.'

Example 1:

A: 你还想跟他争下去吗？

B: 我要跟他斗到底，**不是鱼死，就是网破**。

A: Nǐ hái xiǎng gēn tā zhēng xiàqù ma?
B: Wǒ yào gēn tā dòu dàodǐ, búshì yú sǐ, jiùshì wǎng pò.

A: You still want to keep fighting with him?
B: I want to fight him to the end. It's either him or me.

Example 2:

A: 事情已经发展到这一步了，**不是鱼死，就是网破**，妥协是不可能的了。

A: Shìqíng yǐjīng fā zhǎn dào zhè yí bù le, búshì yú sǐ, jiùshì wǎng pò, tuǒxié shì bù kěnéng de le.

A: Things have already come this far. It's either him or me. Compromise isn't a possibility anymore.

Usage: Functions as predicate.

Note: Neutral in meaning.

304. 冰山一角 (冰山一角) bīng shān yì jiǎo

Translated character by character, 冰山一角 means 'iceberg-one-corner,' whereas the implied meaning of this proverb would be 'the tip of the iceberg.'

Example 1:

A: 这起案件牵涉到很多重量级的人物。
B: 这只是**冰山一角**，真正的大人物还没出场呢。

A: Zhè qǐ ànjiàn qiānshè dào hěnduō zhòngliàngjí de rénwù.
B: Zhè zhǐshì bīngshān yì jiǎo, zhēnzhèng de dàrénwù hái méi chūchǎng ne.

A: This case has implicated a lot of heavyweights.
B: This is just the tip of the iceberg. The real big-hitters haven't come out yet.

Example 2:

A: 毒奶粉事件真可怕！
B: 这仅仅是食品行业**冰山**的**一角**，食用油、人工色素等问题还很多，并且更严重。

A: Dú nǎifěn shì jiàn zhēn kěpà!
B: Zhè jǐnjǐn shì shípǐn hángyè bīngshān de yì jiǎo, shíyòngyóu, réngōng sèsù děng wèntí hái hěnduō, bìngqiě gèng yánzhòng.

A: The tainted milk powder scandal was really frightening!
B: This is just the tip of the iceberg with the food industry. There are still a lot of issues, like those with cooking oil and artificial coloring, which are even more serious.

Usage: Functions mainly as predicative.

Note: Neutral in meaning.

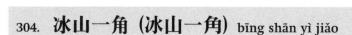

305. 身体是革命的本钱 (身體是革命的本錢) shēntǐ shì gémìng de běnqián

Translated character by character, 身体是革命的本钱 means 'body-is-revolution-'s-capital,' whereas the implied meaning of this proverb would be 'good health is a prerequisite for work.'

Example 1:

A: 小高，你得注意身体啊，工作别太辛苦了。

B: 谢谢您的关心，我的身体很棒。

A: **身体是革命的本钱**。工作可以慢慢干，但累坏了身体可就不容易恢复了。

A: Xiǎo Gāo, nǐ děi zhùyì shēntǐ a, gōngzuò bié tài xīnkǔ le.

B: Xièxiè nín de guānxīn, wǒde shēntǐ hěn bàng.

A: Shēntǐ shì gémìng de běnqian. Gōngzuò kěyǐ mànmān gàn, dàn lèihuàile shēntǐ kě jiù bù róngyì huīfù le.

A: Little Gao, you have to be careful of your health. Don't work too hard.

B: Thank you for your concern. I'm very healthy.

A: Good health is a prerequisite for work. Work can be done slowly, but if you tire yourself out, it's not easy to recover.

Example 2:

A: 你少喝点儿酒吧，**身体是革命的本钱**。

A: Nǐ shǎo hē diǎnr jiǔ ba, shēntǐ shì gémìng de běnqian.

A: Drink a little less. Good health is a prerequisite for work.

Usage: Used singly.

Note: Neutral or humorous in meaning.

---

306. 说风凉话 (説風涼話) shuō fēng liáng huà

Translated character by character, 说风凉话 means 'speak-sarcastic-remark,' whereas the implied meaning of this proverb would be 'to make sarcastic comments.' Its functional translation is 'to crack wise.'

Example 1:

A: 就那点活儿，干了一个星期了，还没干完呢。

B: 你要是想帮，就过来帮个忙；要是不想帮，也别在这儿**说风凉话**。

A: Jiù nà diǎn huór, gànle yígè xīngqī le, hái méi gàn wán ne.

B: Nǐ yàoshì xiǎng bāng, jiù guòlái bāng gè máng; yàoshì bù xiǎng bāng, yě bié zài zhèr shuō fēngliánghuà.

A: You've been working on that little task for a week and you still haven't finished?

B: If you want to help then come over and help. If you don't want to help, don't just stand here cracking wise.

Example 2:

A: 她做事很有主见。

B: 对，那么多人**说风凉话**，可是她一点也不在乎。

A: Tā zuòshì hěn yǒu zhǔjiàn.

B: Duì, nàme duō rén shuō fēngliánghuà, kěshì tā yìdiǎn yě bú zàihu.

A: She has her own way of doing things.

B: Yeah, so many people crack, wise but she doesn't care at all.

Usage: Functions as predicate.

Note: Slightly derogatory in meaning.

---

307. 紧箍咒 （緊箍咒） jǐn gū zhòu

Translated character by character, 紧箍咒 means 'tighten-headband-incantation,' whereas the implied meaning of this proverb would be 'a method by which one controls another person.' Its functional translation is 'to tug on the yoke,' or 'a yoke on the shoulders.'

Example 1:

A: 他老是提我上大学的时候吸大麻被警察抓住那件事。

B: 又念**紧箍咒**了吧，肯定是你最近让他不满意了。

A: Tā lǎoshì tí wǒ shàng dàxué de shíhòu xī dàmá bèi jǐngchá zhuāzhù nà jiàn shì.

B: Yòu niàn jǐngūzhòu le ba, kěndìng shì nǐ zuìjìn ràng tā bù mǎnyì le.

A: He always reminds me of how I was arrested by the police for smoking marijuana when we were in college.

B: He's tugging on the yoke again. You obviously have upset him recently.

Example 2:

A: 百分之八的经济增长率就像戴在各级政府领导头上的一道**紧箍咒**。

A: Bǎi fēn zhī bā de jīngjì zēngzhǎnglǜ jiù xiàng dài zài gè jí zhèngfǔ lǐngdǎo tóu shàng de yí dào jǐngūzhòu.

A: An 8 percent economic growth rate is like a yoke on the shoulders of government leaders at all levels.

Usage: Functions mainly as object.

Note: Neutral or humorous in meaning.

308. 唱双簧 (唱雙簧) chàng shuāng huáng

Translated character by character, 唱双簧 means 'play-double-reed,' whereas the implied meaning of this proverb would be 'to scheme with someone.' Its functional translation is 'a carefully choreographed dance.'

Example 1:

A: 这两个人真会演戏。

B: 怎么讲？

A: 那个女的在电视上哭诉遇到家庭暴力，另一个男的接受采访时说男女平等，坚决反对家庭暴力。其实谁都知道他们在**唱双簧**，女的是有夫之妇，男的是有妇之夫，但是两个人早就有不正当男女关系了。

A: Zhè liǎng gè rén zhēn huì yǎnxì.

B: Zěnme jiǎng?

A: Nàgè nǚde zài diànshì shàng kūsù yùdào jiātíng bàolì, lìngyígè nánde jiēshòu cǎifǎng shí shuō nánnǚ píngděng, jiānjué fǎnduì jiātíng bàolì. Qíshí shéi dou zhīdào tāmen zài chàngshuānghuáng, nǚde shì yǒufūzhīfù, nánde shì yǒufùzhīfū, dànshì liǎng gè rén zǎo jiù yǒu bú zhèngdāng nánnǚ guānxì le.

A: Those two really can act.

B: What do you mean?

A: On TV, that woman said through her tears that she suffered domestic abuse, and when another man was being interviewed, he said men and women are equal and that he is firmly opposed to domestic violence. But everyone knew they were taking part in a carefully choreographed dance. The woman was married and the man was married, but the two of them had been having inappropriate relations for a long time.

Example 2:

A: 美、日元首的新闻发布会就像**唱双簧**，表面上好像有些分歧意见，本质上是一个立场。

A: Měi, Rì yuánshǒu de xīnwén fābùhuì jiù xiàng chàngshuānghuáng, biǎomiànshàng hǎoxiàng yǒu xiē fēnqí yìjiàn, běnzhìshàng shì yígè lìchǎng.

A: The press conference held by the US and Japanese heads of state was like a carefully choreographed dance. On the face of it, it seemed as though there were some divergent opinions, but, in essence, they have the same position.

Usage: Functions as predicate.

Note: Slightly derogatory in meaning.

309. 开空白支票 (開空白支票) kāi kòng bái zhī piào

Translated character by character, 开空白支票 means 'write-blank-check,' whereas the implied meaning of this proverb would be 'to make a promise one cannot keep.' Its functional translation is 'to write a check one can't cash.'

Example 1:

A: 他对员工许诺说如果公司今年盈利，年底会多发一个月的工资作为奖金。谁知道他**开**出的是一张**空白支票**，盈利是盈利了，可是奖金根本没有。

A: Tā duì yuángōng xǔnuò shuō rúguǒ gōngsī jīnnián yínglì, niándǐ huì duō fā yígè yuè de gōngzī zuòwéi jiǎngjīn. Shuízhīdào tā kāi chū de shì yì zhāng kòngbái zhīpiào, yínglì shì yínglì le, kěshì jiǎngjīn gēnběn méiyǒu.

A: He promised his employees that if the company made a profit this year, he would give an extra month's pay to each employee as a bonus. Who knew he was writing a check he couldn't cash? While the company made a profit, there was no bonus.

Example 2:

A: 我保证三个月之内把本钱及利息全部还给你。
B: 你也不用给我**开空白支票**了，咱们白纸黑字写下来好不好？

A: Wǒ bǎozhèng sān gè yuè zhīnèi bǎ běnqián jí lìxī quánbù hái gěi nǐ.
B: Nǐ yě búyòng gěi wǒ kāi kòngbái zhīpiào le, zánmen báizhǐ-hēizì xiě xiàlái hǎo bù hǎo?

A: I promise I will repay all of the capital with interest to you within three months.
B: Don't write me a check you can't cash. Let's put it in writing, OK?

Usage: Functions as predicate.

Variant: 开空头支票

Note: Neutral in meaning.

310. 保护伞 (保護傘) bǎo hù sǎn

Translated character by character, 保护伞 means 'protective-umbrella,' whereas the implied meaning of this proverb would be 'something providing legal or political cover for someone.'

Example 1:

A: 现在有的警察充当黑社会的**保护伞**。

A: Xiànzài yǒude jǐngchá chōngdāng hēishèhuì de bǎohùsǎn.

A: Now, some cops run interference for the underworld.

Example 2:

A: 有的公司明目张胆地制假售假，就是因为有政府官员为他们当**保护伞**。

A: Yǒude gōngsī míngmù-zhāngdǎn de zhìjiǎ shòujiǎ, jiùshì yīnwèi yǒu zhèngfǔ guānyuán wèi tāmen dāng bǎohùsǎn.

A: Some companies openly produce and sell counterfeit goods because they have government officials running interference for them.

Usage: Functions mainly as object.

Note: Neutral in meaning.

311. 一个萝卜一个坑（一個蘿蔔一個坑）
yí gè luóbo yí gè kēng

Translated character by character, 一个萝卜一个坑 means 'one-MW-turnip-one-MW-hole,' whereas the implied meaning of this proverb would be 'each has his own task and there's nobody to spare.'

Example 1:

A: 经理，我想请两天假去参加我表弟的婚礼。
B: 小李，你知道，咱们公司缺人手，**一个萝卜一个坑**，你休假，只好我去做你的工作了。

A: Jīnglǐ, wǒ xiǎng qǐng liǎng tiān jià qù cānjiā wǒ biǎodì de hūnlǐ.
B: Xiǎo Lǐ, nǐ zhīdao, zánmen gōngsī quē rénshǒu, yígè luóbo yígè kēng, nǐ xiūjià, zhǐhǎo wǒ qù zuò nǐde gōngzuò le.

A: Manager, I'd like to take two days' leave to attend my cousin's wedding.
B: Little Li, you know, our company is short-handed; each person has their own task and there's nobody to spare. If you take time off, I'll have to do your work myself.

Example 2:

A: 这次考核，他怎么那么紧张？
B: 你想，他的工作那么好，并且只有几个位置，**一个萝卜一个坑**，你走了，有的是人想占那个位置。

A: Zhècì kǎohé, tā zěnme nàme jǐnzhāng?
B: Nǐ xiǎng, tāde gōngzuò nàme hǎo, bìngqiě zhǐyǒu jǐ gè wèizhì, yígè luóbo yígè kēng, nǐ zǒu le, yǒudeshì rén xiǎng zhàn nàge wèizhì.

A: Why is he so nervous about this evaluation?

B: Think about it. He's got such a good job and there are only a few positions. Every position is filled. If you leave, there will be plenty of people who want to take that position.

Usage: Mostly used singly.

Note: Neutral in meaning. Since the 1990s, Beijing's charter middle schools have been harder than ever to get into. As these schools choose from academically qualified students with an electronic lottery, students must not only be very intelligent, but also very lucky to get in. Parents who were concerned with their children's education soon realized that they could improve their children's chances of being accepted if they enrolled them in afterschool tutoring classes offered by these charter schools. Therefore, parents scrambled to enroll their children in these classes. Parents call these kinds of classes '坑班' or '占坑班.'

---

312. 狗咬狗 (狗咬狗) gǒu yǎo gǒu

Translated character by character 狗咬狗 means 'dog-bite-dog,' whereas the implied meaning of this proverb is 'a fight between two bad people.' Its functional translation is 'dogfight.'

Example 1:

A: 他们两个人吵起来了。

B: 他们是**狗咬狗**，没一个好东西。

A: Tāmen liǎng gè rén chǎo qǐlái le.

B: Tāmen shì gǒuyǎogǒu, méi yígè hǎodōngxi.

A: The two of them started fighting.

B: It's a dogfight. Neither of them is a good person.

Example 2:

A: 他们两派互相攻击得厉害。

B: 让他们**狗咬狗**去吧，最好都咬死。

A: Tāmen liǎng pài hùxiāng gōngjī de lìhai.

B: Ràng tāmen gǒuyǎogǒu qù ba, zuìhǎo dōu yǎo sǐ.

A: Their two camps are attacking each other fiercely.

B: Let them have a dogfight. Let's hope they kill each other.

Usage: Functions as predicate.

Note: Derogatory and humorous in meaning.

313. 唱高调 (唱高調) chàng gāo diào

Translated character by character, 唱高调 means 'sing-high-pitch,' whereas the implied meaning of this proverb would be 'to say something that sounds good but not act in such a way as to back it up.' Its functional translation is 'to posture.'

Example 1:

A: 她说她管理的那家非赢利组织的利润都捐给贫困人口了。

B: 净**唱高调**。我看钱都让她挥霍了，剩下的几毛钱可能捐出去了。

A: Tā shuō tā guǎnlǐ de nà jiā fēiyínglì zǔzhī de lìrùn dōu juān gěi pínkùn rénkǒu le.

B: Jìng chànggāodiào. Wǒ kàn qián dōu ràng tā huīhuò le, shèngxià de jǐ máo qián kěnéng juān chūqù le.

A: She said the non-profit organization she runs donates all of its profits to the underprivileged.

B: She's just posturing. I think she blows all of the money and maybe donates the few cents that are left over.

Example 2:

A: 他说要把公司员工的利益放在第一位。

B: **唱高调**呢。他的做法却是把他自己的分红放在第一位。

A: Tā shuō yào bǎ gōngsī yuángōng de lìyì fàng zài dì-yī wèi.

B: Chànggāodiào ne. Tā de zuòfǎ què shì bǎ tā zìjǐ de fēnhóng fàng zài dì-yī wèi.

A: He said he was going to put the interests of the company's employees first.

B: He's posturing. What he really does is put his own dividends first.

Usage: Functions as predicate.

Note: Slightly derogatory in meaning.

314. 打水漂 (打水漂) dǎ shuǐ piāo

Translated character by character, 打水漂 means 'play-water-skipping stones,' whereas the implied meaning of this proverb would be 'to make ducks and drakes of.'

Example 1:

A: 你那笔投资赚了多少钱？

B: 甭提了，都**打水漂**了。

A: Nǐ nà bǐ tóuzī zuànle duōshǎo qián?

B: Béng tí le, dōu dǎshuǐpiāo le.

A: How much did he make from that investment?
B: Don't mention it. He made ducks and drakes of it.

Example 2:

A: 现在股市低迷，正是买股票的大好时机。你从银行借钱也得买。
B: 我从银行借的钱如果**打**了**水漂**，那我怎么还啊？

A: Xiànzài gǔshì dīmí, zhèng shì mǎi gǔpiào de dà hǎo shíjī. Nǐ cóng yínháng jièqián yě děi mǎi.
B: Wǒ cóng yínháng jiè de qián rúguǒ dǎ le shuǐpiāo, nà wǒ zěnme huán a?

A: The stock market is depressed. Now is a very good opportunity to buy stocks. Even if you have to borrow from the bank, you need to buy.
B: If I make ducks and drakes of the money I borrow from the bank, how will I pay it back?

Usage: Functions as predicate.

Note: Neutral or humorous in meaning.

315. 开小差 (開小差) kāi xiǎo chāi

Translated character by character, 开小差 means 'grant-secret-leave,' whereas the implied meaning of this proverb would be 'to be distracted or unfocused.' Its functional translation is 'to let one's mind wander,' or 'to zone out.'

Example 1:

A: 司机开车的时候脑子不能**开小差**，否则太危险。
B: 外科医生做手术的时候更不能，如果**开小差**，那受伤的可不是自己，而是病人。

A: Sījī kāichē de shíhòu nǎozi bùnéng kāixiǎochāi, fǒuzé tài wēixiǎn.
B: Wàikē yīshēng zuò shǒushù de shíhòu gèng bùnéng, rúguǒ kāixiǎochāi, nà shòushāng de kě búshì zìjǐ, érshì bìngrén.

A: When driving, a driver can't zone out, otherwise it's too dangerous.
B: Even more so when a surgeon is performing surgery. If they zone out, it won't be them that gets hurt, but their patient.

Example 2:

A: 你们单位领导讲话有意思吗？
B: 一点儿意思都没有。他讲话的时候下边的人都**开小差**，玩儿手机游戏的，递小纸条的，闭目养神的，干什么的都有，就是没有听讲话的。

A: Nǐmen dānwèi lǐngdǎo jiǎnghuà yǒu yìsi ma?

B: Yìdiǎnr yìsi dōu méiyǒu. Tā jiǎnghuà de shíhòu xiàbiān de rén dōu kāixiǎochāi, wánr shǒujī yóuxì de, dì xiǎo zhǐtiáo de, bìmù-yǎngshén de, gàn shénme de dōu yǒu, jiùshì méiyǒu tīng jiǎnghuà de.

A: Is your work unit's boss an interesting speaker?

B: Not at all. When he speaks, the audience zones out, playing cell phone games, passing notes, and resting their eyes. People do all kinds of things, except listen.

Usage: Functions as predicate.

Note: Slightly derogatory in meaning.

---

316. 两面派 (兩面派) liǎng miàn pài

Translated character by character, 两面派 means 'double-face-person/style,' whereas the implied meaning of this proverb would be 'double-dealer,' or 'double dealing.'

Example 1:

A: 对他要小心一点儿。

B: 为什么？

A: 他是个典型的**两面派**，说话不可靠。

A: Duì tā yào xiǎoxīn yìdiǎnr.

B: Wèishénme?

A: Tā shì gè diǎnxíng de liǎngmiànpài, shuōhuà bù kěkào.

A: You need to be a little careful with him.

B: Why?

A: He's a typical double-dealer. You can't trust what he says.

Example 2:

A: 在这个问题上，外交部耍**两面派**手法，一方面对国内的民众说支持某国的学生运动；另一方面又偷偷地与该国的军政府保持密切联系。

A: Zài zhège wèntí shàng, wàijiāobù shuǎ liǎngmiànpài shǒufǎ, yīfāngmiàn duì guónèi de mínzhòng shuō zhīchí mǒu guó de xuéshēng yùndòng; lìngyīfāngmiàn yòu tōutōu de yǔ gāi guó de jūnzhèngfǔ bǎochí mìqiè liánxì.

A: In this case, the Foreign Ministry employed double dealing methods. On the one hand, they said to their citizens that they supported some country's student movement; on the other hand, they secretly maintained their close ties with that country's military junta.

Usage: Functions as attributive, predicative or object.

Note: Derogatory in meaning.

317. 一盘散沙 (一盤散沙) yì pán sǎn shā

Translated character by character, 一盘散沙 means 'a-plate-loose-sands,' whereas the implied meaning of this proverb would be 'to be in a state of disunity.'

Example 1:

A: 他们人很多。

B: 不用担心，人虽然多，但是是**一盘散沙**。

A: Tāmen rén hěnduō.

B: Búyòng dānxīn, rén suīrán duō, dànshì shì yì pán sǎnshā.

A: There are a lot of them.

B: Don't worry. While there are a lot of them, they're in a state of disunity.

Example 2:

A: 有人认为一个中国人很可能是一条龙，可是一群中国人却是**一盘散沙**。

A: Yǒurén rènwéi yígè Zhōngguórén hěn kěnéng shì yì tiáo lóng, kěshì yì qún Zhōngguórén què shì yì pán sǎnshā.

A: Some people think one Chinese person can be a dragon, but a group of Chinese actually has no cohesion.

Usage: Functions mainly as predicative.

Note: Slightly derogatory in meaning.

318. 和稀泥 (和稀泥) huò xī ní

Translated character by character, 和稀泥 means 'mix-thin-mud,' whereas the implied meaning of this proverb would be 'to mediate a dispute without determining fault.' Its functional translation is 'to paper over something.'

Example 1:

A: 两个人吵了起来，有人赶快上来**和稀泥**，说："哟，下班时间都过了，你们两个人是为了公事吵。我看你们先各自回家，明天上班以后再吵好不好？"

A: Liǎng gè rén chǎole qǐlái, yǒu rén gǎnkuài shànglái huòxīní, shuō: "yò, xiàbān shíjiān dōu guò le, nǐmen liǎng gè rén shì wèile gōngshì chǎo. Wǒ kàn nǐmen xiān gèzì huíjiā, míngtiān shàngbān yǐhòu zài chǎo hǎobuhǎo?"

A: When two people started fighting, someone quickly stepped forward to paper over the issue, saying, "Hey, the work day's over, you two are fighting over work issues. I think you two should both go home, and when work starts tomorrow, you can continue fighting, OK?"

Example 2:

A: 双方争执不下，他就在中间**和稀泥**，反正不明确表态到底站在哪一方。

A: Shuāngfāng zhēngzhí búxià, tā jiù zài zhōngjiān huòxīní, fǎnzhèng bù míngquè biǎotài dàodǐ zhàn zài nǎ yì fāng.

A: Two sides were in the middle of an argument, so he papered over the issue between them. However, he didn't clearly express which side he stood with.

Usage: Functions as predicate.

Note: Slightly derogatory in meaning.

---

319. 敲竹杠 (敲竹杠) qiāo zhú gàng

Translated character by character, 敲竹杠 means 'knock-bamboo-pole,' whereas the implied meaning of this proverb would be 'to extract money from someone,' or 'to charge an exorbitantly high price.' Its functional translation is 'to fleece,' or 'highway robbery.'

Example 1:

A: 刚才市政府来了两个人，说是请咱们公司为什么什么活动赞助一下。
B: 又是来**敲竹杠**的。不过，怎么也得表示一下，要不然会麻烦不断。

A: Gāngcái shìzhèngfǔ láile liǎng gè rén, shuō shì qǐng zánmen gōngsī wèi shénme shénme huódòng zànzhù yíxià.
B: Yòu shì lái qiāozhúgàng de. Búguò, zěnme yě děi biǎoshì yíxià, yàobùrán huì máfan búduàn.

A: Two people from the municipal government just came by. They said they were asking our company to sponsor some event.
B: They came to fleece us again. Anyways, we have to make a show of it, otherwise we'll have endless trouble.

Example 2:

A: 昨天我被当地老百姓**敲**了一次**竹杠**。
B: 怎么回事？
A: 他们那里修路，大路不通。他们跟我要了二百块钱，才把我从小路带过去。

A: Zuótiān wǒ bèi dāngdì lǎobǎixìng qiāole yí cì zhúgàng.
B: Zěnme huí shì?
A: Tāmen nàlǐ xiūlù, dàlù bù tōng. Tāmen gēn wǒ yàole èrbǎi kuài qián, cái bǎ wǒ cóng xiǎolù dài guòqù.

A: I got fleeced by the locals there yesterday.

B: What happened?

A: They're fixing the road there, and the main road is closed. They asked me for 200 RMB to take me through the back roads.

Usage: Functions as predicate.

Note: Derogatory in meaning. There are many stories regarding the etymology of '敲竹杠.' One such etymology is as follows: In the mountainous region of Sichuan, when wealthy people went into the mountains to burn incense, they sat on a palanquin made of bamboo which was carried by palanquin bearers. When they got halfway up the mountain, the palanquin bearers would fleece their passengers for more money, refusing to carry on without a raise. The passengers had no option but to pay up.

320. 扯后腿 (扯後腿) chě hòu tuǐ

Translated character by character, 扯后腿 means 'pull-back-leg,' whereas the implied meaning of this proverb would be 'to hold someone back.'

Example 1:

A: 他办事怎么这么不爽快？

B: 不是他不爽快，而是他老婆总**扯后腿**。

A: Tā bànshì zěnme zhème bù shuǎngkuài?

B: Búshì tā bù shuǎngkuài, érshì tā lǎopo zǒng chěhòutuǐ.

A: Why is he so indecisive?

B: It's not that he's indecisive, but rather that his wife is always holding him back.

Example 2:

A: 看来他要大刀阔斧地改革了。

B: 没那么容易，他想改革，可是**扯后腿**的多着呢。

A: Kànlái tā yào dàdāo-kuòfǔ de gǎigé le.

B: Méi nàme róngyì, tā xiǎng gǎigé, kěshì chěhòutuǐ de duō zhe ne.

A: I think he wants to boldly and resolutely institute reforms.

B: It's not that easy. He wants to reform, but there are many people holding him back.

Usage: Functions as predicate.

Note: Slightly derogatory in meaning.

321. 穿小鞋 (穿小鞋) chuān xiǎo xié

Translated character by character, 穿小鞋 means 'wear-small-shoes,' whereas the implied meaning of this proverb would be 'to create trouble for someone.' Its functional translation is 'to stack the deck against someone.'

Example 1:

A: 我受不了了。

B: 怎么了？

A: 他老是给我**穿小鞋**，存心给我制造麻烦。

A: Wǒ shòu bùliǎo le.

B: Zěnme le?

A: Tā lǎoshì gěi wǒ chuānxiǎoxié, cúnxīn gěi wǒ zhìzào máfan.

A: I can't take it anymore!

B: What's wrong?

A: He's always stacking the deck against me, deliberately making trouble for me.

Example 2:

A: 他为人怎么样？

B: 不太公正，谁惹了他他就给谁**穿小鞋**。

A: Tā wéirén zěnmeyàng?

B: Bú tài gōngzhèng, shéi rěle tā tā jiù gěi shéi chuānxiǎoxié.

A: What kind of person is he?

B: Not very fair. If anyone annoys him, he'll stack the deck against them.

Usage: Functions as predicate.

Note: Slightly derogatory in meaning.

322. 给他一点颜色看看 (給他一點顏色看看)
gěi tā yì diǎn yánsè kàn kàn

Translated character by character, 给他一点颜色看看 means 'give-him-a-bit-color-see-see,' whereas the implied meaning of this proverb would be 'to punish someone for what they've done.' Its functional translation is 'to take someone down a peg,' or 'to fix someone's wagon.'

Example 1:

A: 他也太狂了！

B: 我们**给他一点颜色看看**，让他以后老实点儿。

A: Tā yě tài kuáng le!

B: Wǒmen gěi tā yìdiǎn yánsè kànkan, ràng tā yǐhòu lǎoshi diǎnr.

A: He's just too arrogant!

B: Let's take him down a peg and make him a little more obedient in the future.

Example 2:

A: 我们做什么，他总是反对。

B: 他存心跟我们过意不去，那我们就**给他一点颜色看看**。

A: Wǒmen zuò shénme, tā zǒngshì fǎnduì.

B: Tā cúnxīn gēn wǒmen guòyìbúqù, nà wǒmen jiù gěi tā yìdiǎn yánsè kànkan.

A: Whatever we do, he always opposes us.

B: He's deliberately causing trouble for us, so let's fix his wagon.

Usage: Functions as predicate.

Note: Neutral or humorous in meaning.

---

323. 天高皇帝远 (天高皇帝遠) tiān gāo huángdì yuǎn

Translated character by character, 天高皇帝远 means 'heaven-high-emperor-far away,' whereas the implied meaning of this proverb would be 'when one is far away from authority, the powers that be will not intervene.'

Example 1:

A: 有些地方领导怎么那么大胆，连违法的事都敢做？

B: 中国太大了，**天高皇帝远**，中央政府对偏远地区的地方政府控制不够。

A: Yǒuxiē dìfāng lǐngdǎo zěnme nàme dàdǎn, lián wéifǎ de shì dōu gǎn zuò?

B: Zhōngguó tài dà le, tiān gāo huángdì yuǎn, zhōngyāng zhèngfǔ duì piānyuǎn dìqū de dìfāng zhèngfǔ kòngzhì búgòu.

A: How are some regional leaders so bold? They even dare to do illegal things.

B: China's too big; when one is far away from authority, the powers that be will not intervene. The central government doesn't exercise enough control over the governments of far-flung areas.

Example 2:

A: 你们部门的人工作效率不高啊！

B: 我们这块儿**山高皇帝远**，公司不重视，干好干坏一个样。

A: Nǐmen bùmén de rén gōngzuò xiàolǜ bù gāo a!

B: Wǒmen zhè kuàir shān gāo huángdì yuǎn, gōngsī bú zhòngshì, gàn hǎo gàn huài yígè yàng.

A: The efficiency of your division's workers is low!

B: Because they are far away, the management doesn't bother us; the company doesn't pay attention. Whether we do a good job or a bad job, it's all the same.

Usage: Functions as predicate.

Variant: 山高皇帝远

Note: Neutral in meaning.

324. 拣软柿子捏 (揀軟柿子捏) jiǎn ruǎn shìzi niē

Translated character by character, 拣软柿子捏 means 'pick-soft-persimmon-to pinch,' whereas the implied meaning of this proverb would be 'to run after a train with a full mouth.' Its functional translation is 'to pick on an easy target.'

Example 1:

A: 这次裁员，就我们小组被裁的人多。

B: 倒霉啊！咱们小组的头儿废物，上头也是专**拣软柿子捏**啊！

A: Zhècì cáiyuán, jiù wǒmen xiǎozǔ bèi cái de rén duō.

B: Dǎoméi a! Zánmen xiǎozǔ de tóur fèiwu, shàngtou yě shì zhuān jiǎn ruǎnshìzi niē a!

A: There were more layoffs in our group in this round of cuts.

B: What a mess! Our group leader is useless. The guys upstairs are just picking on an easy target.

Example 2:

A: 大家都迟到了，领导为什么只批评我？

B: 谁叫你那么老实来着，领导总是**拣软柿子捏**。

A: Dàjiā dōu chídào le, lǐngdǎo wèishénme zhǐ pīpíng wǒ?

B: Shéi jiào nǐ nàme lǎoshí láizhe, lǐngdǎo zǒngshì jiǎn ruǎnshìzi niē.

A: Everyone was late, why did the leader only chastise me?

B: Who made you so naïve? The boss always picks on easy targets.

Usage: Functions as predicate.

Variant: 挑软柿子捏(挑 tiāo, to pick)

Note: Neutral in meaning. 软柿子 alone is a colloquial expression, meaning 'coward, pushover (person).'

325. 打马虎眼 (打馬虎眼) dǎ mǎhu yǎn

Translated character by character, 打马虎眼 means 'act-careless-eye,' whereas the implied meaning of this proverb would be 'to pretend not to know what someone is talking about,' or 'to seek to deceive someone.' Its functional translation is 'to play dumb,' or 'to demur.'

Example 1:

A: 这项任务能不能按时完成？

B: 大家正在努力做。

A: 你别给我**打马虎眼**。我问你能不能完成，只要回答"能"或者"不能"就行了。

A: Zhè xiàng rènwù néngbùnéng ànshí wánchéng?

B: Dàjiā zhèng zài nǔlì zuò.

A: Nǐ bié gěi wǒ dǎ mǎhuyǎn. Wǒ wèn nǐ néngbùnéng wánchéng, zhǐyào huídá "néng" huòzhě "bùnéng" jiù xíng le.

A: Can this task be completed on time?

B: Everyone is working hard on it now.

A: Don't play dumb. I asked you if it could be completed; you only need to answer with a "yes" or a "no."

Example 2:

A: 别人跟她聊工作，她聊得很细。但是当被人问她收入的时候，她**打了个马虎眼**，说"还可以"。

A: Biérén gēn tā liáo gōngzuò, tā liáo de hěn xì. Dànshì dāng biérén wèn tā shōurù de shíhòu, tā dǎle gè mǎhǔyǎn, shuō "hái kěyǐ".

A: When other people talk shop with her, she gets into the details, but when she's asked what her income is, she demurs, saying, "It's OK."

Usage: Functions as predicate.

Note: Slightly derogatory in meaning.

326. 千里马 (千里馬) qiān lǐ mǎ

Translated character by character, 千里马 means 'thousand-mile-horse,' whereas the implied meaning of this proverb would be 'a person (particularly a young person) of great talent.' Its functional translation is 'wunderkind,' or 'prodigy.'

Example 1:

A: 这个年轻人怎么样？

B: 我认为是匹**千里马**，前途无限。

A: Zhège niánqīngrén zěnmeyàng?

B: Wǒ rènwéi shì pǐ qiānlǐmǎ, qiántú wúxiàn.

A: What's that young person like?

B: I think he's a prodigy. His potential is limitless.

Example 2:

A: 领导的一部分职责就是在下属中发现**千里马**，然后好好培养。

A: Lǐngdǎo de yíbùfēn zhízé jiùshì zài xiàshǔ zhōng fāxiàn qiānlǐmǎ, ránhòu hǎohao péiyǎng.

A: Part of a leader's responsibility is to uncover prodigies among his subordinates and train them well.

Usage: Nominal element, functions as predicative or object.

Note: Complimentary in meaning.

---

327. 打擦边球 (打擦邊球) dǎ cā biān qiú

Translated character by character, 打擦边球 means 'hit-brush-edge-ball,' whereas the implied meaning of this proverb would be 'to push the limits of rules or laws.' Its functional translation is 'to push the envelope.'

Example 1:

A: 有的公司利用国家有关法律、法规不严谨的空子，专门**打**法律的**擦边球**。

A: Yǒude gōngsī lìyòng guójiā yǒuguān fǎlǜ, fǎguī bù yánjǐn de kòngzi, zhuānmén dǎ fǎlǜ de cābiānqiú.

A: Some companies use the loopholes in the relevant laws and regulations of a country, intentionally pushing the legal envelope.

Example 2:

A: 他对别人说上级领导应该充分发掘下级的潜力，否则就称不上是一个令人信服的上级。

B: 他是在**打擦边球**，是批评我专权。

A: Tā duì biérén shuō shàngjí lǐngdǎo yīnggāi chōngfèn fājué xiàjí de qiánlì, fǒuzé jiù chēng búshàng shì yígè lìng rén xìnfú de shàngjí.

B: Tā shì zài dǎ cābiānqiú, shì pīpíng wǒ zhuānquán.

A: He tells other people that high-level leaders should fully develop the potential of their inferiors, otherwise they cannot be called an inspiring leader.

B: He's pushing the envelope, criticizing my monopoly on power.

Usage: Functions as predicate.

Note: Slightly derogatory in meaning.

---

328.   摸着石头过河 (摸著石頭過河) mō zhe shítou guò hé

Translated character by character, 摸着石头过河 means 'touch-ing-stones-cross-river,' whereas the implied meaning of this proverb would be 'to learn something by trial and error.' As this proverb was made famous by Deng Xiaoping, it is generally delivered according to its character by character translation, 'to cross the river by touching stones.'

Example 1:

A: 邓小平说中国的改革开放得**摸着石头过河**，因为以前没有现成的经验。

A: Dèng Xiǎopíng shuō Zhōngguó de Gǎigé Kāifàng děi mōzhe shítou guò hé, yīnwèi yǐqián méiyǒu xiànchéng de jīngyàn.

A: Deng Xiaoping said China's Reform and Opening needed to cross the river by touching stones, because the country had no relevant experience.

Example 2:

A: 你对这个计划有信心吗？

B: 说实话，我心里也没底，咱们就**摸着石头过河**，走一步看一步吧。

A: Nǐ duì zhègè jìhuà yǒu xìnxīn ma?

B: Shuō shíhuà, wǒ xīnli yě méidǐ, zánmen jiù mōzhe shítou guò hé, zǒu yí bù kàn yí bù ba.

A: Are you confident in this plan?

B: To be honest, I'm not sure. Let's just cross the river by touching stones and play it by ear.

Usage: Functions as predicate.

Variant: 摸石头过河

Note: Neutral in meaning.

329. 半路出家 (半路出家) bàn lù chū jiā

Translated character by character, 半路出家 means 'middle-road-become-monk,' whereas the implied meaning of this proverb would be 'to move into a field one is not familiar with.' Its functional translation is 'mid-life career change.'

Example 1:

A: 她的画真棒，一定从小就有名师指点。

B: 不是，她四十多岁才学画，是**半路出家**。

A: Tā de huà zhēn bàng, yídìng cóngxiǎo jiù yǒu míngshī zhǐdiǎn.

B: Búshì, tā sìshí duō suì cái xué huà, shì bànlù chūjiā.

A: Her paintings are really great. She must have been tutored by a master from a young age.

B: No, she only learned how to paint in her 40s. It was a mid-life career change.

Example 2:

A: 他原来是学物理的，后来**半路出家**，搞起了法律。

A: Tā yuánlái shì xué wùlǐ de, hòulái bànlù chūjiā, gǎoqǐle fǎlǜ.

A: He used to be a physics student, then he made a mid-life career change and took up law.

Usage: Functions mainly as predicative or predicate.

Note: Neutral or humorous in meaning.

330. 老狐狸 (老狐狸) lǎo húli

Translated character by character, 老狐狸 means 'old-fox,' whereas the implied meaning of this proverb would be 'sly old fox.'

Example 1:

A: 我觉得他挺和蔼的。

B: 别上他的当，他是只**老狐狸**。

A: Wǒ juéde tā tǐng hé'ǎi de.

B: Bié shàng tā de dàng, tā shì zhī lǎohúli.

A: I think he's very affable.

B: Don't be taken in by him. He's a sly old fox.

Example 2:

A: 他是生意场上的**老狐狸**，骗人无数。

A: Tā shì shēngyìchǎng shàng de **lǎohúli**, piànrén wúshù.

A: He's the sly old fox of the business world, having cheated countless people.

Usage: Nominal element, functions as predicative.

Note: Slightly derogatory in meaning.

331. 一窝蜂 (一窩蜂) yì wō fēng

Translated character by character, 一窝蜂 means 'a-hive of-bees,' whereas the implied meaning of this proverb would be 'swarm.'

Example 1:

A: 最近人们好像都疯了！
B: **一窝蜂**似的去整容，好像谁的鼻子矮一点儿就是丑八怪了。

A: Zuìjìn rénmen hǎoxiàng dōu fēng le!
B: Yìwōfēng shìde qù zhěngróng, hǎoxiàng shéi de bízi ǎi yìdiǎnr jiù shì chǒubāguài le.

A: It seems like everyone's gone crazy recently!
B: They're going to get their makeup done in swarms. It seems like people believe that anyone whose nose looks small is a monster.

Example 2:

A: 看到这种商品大卖，不少商家**一窝蜂**地生产起了这种商品。

A: Kàn dào zhèzhǒng shāngpǐn dà mài, bùshǎo shāngjiā yìwōfēng de shēngchǎn qǐle zhèzhǒng shāngpǐn.

A: When they saw that this sort of merchandise was selling well, many store owners swarmed to produce it.

Usage: Functions as adverbial.

Note: Slightly derogatory in meaning.

332. 开夜车 (開夜車) kāi yè chē

Translated character by character, 开夜车 means 'drive-night-car,' whereas the implied meaning of this proverb would be 'to work or study late into the night, sometimes for days in a row.' Its functional translation is 'to burn the midnight oil.'

Example 1:

A: 报告明天就要交了，现在我还没写完呢。

B: 我也没写完呢，今天得**开夜车**了。

A: Bàogào míngtiān jiùyào jiāo le, xiànzài wǒ hái méi xiěwán ne.

B: Wǒ yě méi xiěwán ne, jīntiān děi kāiyèchē le.

A: I have to turn in my report tomorrow and I still haven't finished it.

B: I also haven't finished it. I'll have to burn the midnight oil tonight.

Example 2:

A: 很多大学生平常学习不太努力，都是等到考试前几天**开夜车**。

A: Hěnduō dàxuéshēng píngcháng xuéxí bú tài nǔlì, dōu shì děngdào kǎoshì qián jǐ tiān kāiyèchē.

A: A lot of college students ordinarily don't study very diligently, waiting until the days before a test to burn the midnight oil.

Usage: Functions as predicate.

Note: Neutral in meaning.

---

333. 手心手背都是肉 (手心手背都是肉)
shǒu xīn shǒu bèi dōu shì ròu

Translated character by character, 手心手背都是肉 means 'hand-palm-hand-back-all-are-flesh,' whereas the implied meaning of this proverb would be 'to be unable to choose between two choices.' Its functional translation is 'a tough call.'

Example 1:

A: 你的两个孩子打架打得那么厉害，你怎么不惩罚一下理亏的那个？

B: 我舍不得啊！**手心手背都是肉**，让我惩罚哪个我都不忍心。

A: Nǐde liǎng gè háizi dǎjià dǎ de nàme lìhai, nǐ zěnme bù chéngfá yíxià lǐkuī de nàgè?

B: Wǒ shěbùdé a! Shǒuxīn shǒubèi dōu shì ròu, ràng wǒ chéngfá nǎ gè wǒ dōu bù rěnxīn.

A: Your two children are fighting so intensely, why don't you punish whichever one is in the wrong?

B: I couldn't stand it! It's a tough call; I couldn't bear to punish either.

Example 2:

A: 国家也很为难，不管是城市居民，还是农民，**手心手背都是肉**，国家都不忍心使他们受到伤害。

A: Guójiā yě hěn wéinán, bùguǎn shì chéngshì jūmín, háishì nóngmín, shǒuxīn shǒubèi dōu shì ròu, guójiā dōu bù rěnxīn shǐ tāmen shòudào shānghài.

A: It's also difficult for the country. Whether it's the city-dwellers or the rural population, it's a tough call. The country can't bear to subject any of them to harm.

Usage: Used singly.

Note: Neutral in meaning.

334. 缩头乌龟 (縮頭烏龜) suō tóu wūguī

Translated character by character, 缩头乌龟 means 'withdraw-head-tortoise,' whereas the implied meaning of this proverb would be 'a cowardly or easily frightened person.' Its functional translation is 'a chicken,' or 'a scaredy cat.'

Example 1:

A: 他在故意挑衅你，你不要上他的当。
B: 不行，如果我当**缩头乌龟**，以后怎么见别人？

A: Tā zài gùyì tiǎoxìn nǐ, nǐ búyào shàng tā de dàng.
B: Bùxíng, rúguǒ wǒ dāng suō tóu wūguī, yǐhòu zěnme jiàn biérén?

A: He's intentionally provoking you. Don't fall for it.
B: No. If I'm a chicken, how could I face people?

Example 2:

A: 别看他平时好像牛哄哄的，可是在外国人面前就像个**缩头乌龟**，连个屁都不敢放。

A: Bié kàn tā píngshí hǎoxiàng niúhōnghōng de, kěshì zài wàiguórén miànqián jiù xiàng gè suō tóu wūguī, lián gè pì dōu bùgǎn fàng.

A: Although he normally seems cocky, he's a chicken in the company of foreigners. He doesn't dare make a peep.

Usage: Functions mainly as object of verbs like '成了,' '当,' or '做.'

Note: Derogatory in meaning.

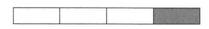

335. 走过场 (走過場) zǒu guò chǎng

Translated character by character, 走过场 means 'go-interlude,' whereas the implied meaning of this proverb would be 'to act as though one is doing something, but not work hard.' Its functional translation is 'to go through the motions,' or 'to do something as a formality.'

Example 1:

A: 下个星期上级来检查，我们得好好准备准备。

B: 不用紧张，这都是**走过场**，关键是要招待好。

A: Xià gè xīngqī shàngjí lái jiǎnchá, wǒmen děi hǎohāo zhǔnbèi zhǔnbèi.

B: Búyòng jǐnzhāng, zhè dōushì zǒuzǒu guòchang, guānjiàn shì yào zhāodài hǎo.

A: Next week the higher-ups are coming to do an inspection. We need to prepare well.

B: Don't worry, this is just a formality. What's crucial is that we receive them well.

Example 2:

A: 国会里自由党和保守党对政府预算赤字已经辩论好几天了，如果明天还达不成协议，政府就要关门了，真让人紧张。

B: 放松，放松，肯定会达成协议的。其实协议早就达成了，现在不过是**走过场**，好让选民觉得他们在代表选民说话。

A: Guóhuì lǐ Zìyóudǎng hé Bǎoshǒudǎng duì zhèngfǔ yùsuàn chìzì yǐjīng biànlùn hǎo jǐ tiān le, rúguǒ míngtiān hái dá bù chéng xiéyì, zhèngfǔ jiù yào guānmén le, zhēn ràng rén jǐnzhāng.

B: Fàngsōng, fàngsōng, kěndìng huì dáchéng xiéyì de. Qíshí xiéyì zǎojiù dáchéng le, xiànzài búguò shì zǒu guòchang, hǎo ràng xuǎnmín juéde tāmen zài dàibiǎo xuǎnmín shuōhuà.

A: The liberal and conservative parties have already been debating the government budget deficit in Congress for a number of days. If they still haven't reached an agreement by tomorrow, the government will close. It's nerve-racking.

B: Relax, relax. They'll definitely come to an agreement. In fact, they came to an agreement long ago; now they're just going through the motions to make voters believe they are representing constituent interests.

Usage: Functions mainly as predicate.

Note: Neutral in meaning.

---

336. 做文章 (做文章) zuò wénzhāng

Translated character by character, 做文章 means 'write-composition,' whereas the implied meaning of this proverb would be 'to make a big deal of something.' Its functional translation is 'to seize on,' or 'to make an issue of something.'

Example 1:

A: 请您对我们面包店的发展提出宝贵的意见。

B: 你们的长处是声誉好，所以可以在形象上大**作文章**；至于面包的品种，可以逐渐多样化。

A: Qǐng nín duì wǒmen miànbāodiàn de fāzhǎn tíchū bǎoguì de yìjiàn.

B: Nǐmen de chángchù shì shēngyù hǎo, suǒyǐ kěyǐ zài xíngxiàng shàng dà zuò wénzhāng; zhìyú miànbāo de pǐnzhǒng, kěyǐ zhújiàn duōyànghuà.

A: Please give us your valuable insights on our bakery's development.

B: Your strong point is that you have a good reputation, so you can really seize on that image. As for your assortment of breads, you can slowly diversify.

Example 2:

A: 他在搜集你上大学时的言论，好像想在这方面攻击你。

B: 嗯，想在这方面**做文章**，用心真是险恶啊。

A: Tā zài sōují nǐ shàng dàxué shí de yánlùn, hǎoxiàng xiǎng zài zhè fāngmiàn gōngjī nǐ.

B: Èn, xiǎng zài zhè fāngmiàn zuòwénzhāng, yòngxīn zhēn shì xiǎn'è a.

A: He's gathering your speeches from when you were in college. It seems like he wants to attack you on that.

B: Yeah. If he's looking to make an issue of this, his intentions really are sinister.

Usage: Functions as predicate.

Variant: 作文章

Note: Slightly derogatory or neutral in meaning.

337. 吃大锅饭 (吃大鍋飯) chī dà guō fàn

Translated character by character, 吃大锅饭 means 'eat-big-pot-meal,' whereas the implied meaning of this proverb would be 'to be compensated without regard to performance.'

Example 1:

A: 你们公司怎么样？

B: 不怎么样。干好干坏都一样，**吃大锅饭**。

A: Nǐmen gōngsī zěnmeyàng?

B: Bù zěnmeyàng. Gàn hǎo gàn huài dōu yíyàng, chī dàguōfàn.

A: What's your company like?

B: Not so good. Whether you do a good job or a bad job, it's all the same. The compensation is not performance-based.

Example 2:

A: 你们饭馆得到的小费怎么分？

B: **吃大锅饭**，平均分配。

A: Nǐmen fànguǎn dédào de xiǎofèi zěnme fēn?

B: Chī dàguōfàn, píngjūn fēnpèi.

A: How do you divide up the tips the restaurant gets?

B: It's not performance-based; we divide them up equally.

Usage: Functions as predicate.

Note: Slightly derogatory in meaning.

338.   戴高帽 (戴高帽) dài gāo mào

Translated character by character, 戴高帽 means 'put on-high-hat,' whereas the implied meaning of this proverb would be 'to overstate someone's skills or standing.' Its functional translation is 'to oversell someone.'

Example 1:

A: 老婆，你的厨艺天下第一。

B: 你又给我**戴高帽**呢，在咱们家第一我就满足了。

A: Lǎopó, nǐde chúyì tiānxià dì-yī.

B: Nǐ yòu gěi wǒ dàigāomào ne, zài zánmen jiā dì-yī wǒ jiù mǎnzú le.

A: Honey, you're the best chef on earth.

B: You're overselling me again. I'm happy just to be the best in our home.

Example 2:

A: 现在的领导见了面，都是互相**戴高帽**，吹嘘了别人，也吹嘘了自己。

A: Xiànzài de lǐngdǎo jiànle miàn, dōu shì hùxiāng dàigāomào, chuīxū le biérén, yě chuīxū le zìjǐ.

A: When today's leaders meet, it's all patting each other on the back. They boast about themselves while boasting about others.

Usage: Functions as predicate.

Note: Slightly derogatory in meaning.

339. 秋后算账 (秋後算賬) qiū hòu suàn zhàng

Translated character by character, 秋后算账 means 'fall-after-calculate-bill,' whereas the implied meaning of this proverb would be 'to settle one's accounts at an opportune moment.' Its functional translation is 'revenge is a dish best served cold.'

Example 1:

A: 我跟老板的矛盾解决了，他没有生气。
B: 现在没生气，但是得小心他**秋后算账**。

A: Wǒ gēn lǎobǎn de máodùn jiějué le, tā méiyǒu shēngqì.
B: Xiànzài méi shēngqì, dànshì děi xiǎoxīn tā qiū hòu suànzhàng.

A: I've resolved my conflict with my boss and he didn't get angry.
B: He hasn't yet, but be careful. Revenge is a dish best served cold.

Example 2:

A: B国常常用所谓的人权问题指责C国。C国的策略是，在B国申请成为联合国常任理事国问题上坚决反对，**秋后算账**。

A: B guó chángcháng yòng suǒwèi de rénquán wèntí zhǐzé C guó. C guó de cèlüè shì, zài B guó shēnqǐng chéngwéi Liánhéguó Chángrèn Lǐshìguó wèntí shàng jiānjué fǎnduì, qiū hòu suànzhàng.

A: Country B often uses so-called human rights issues to criticize country C. Country C's strategy is to firmly oppose country B when they apply to become a standing member of the UN Security Council. Revenge is a dish best served cold.

Usage: Functions as predicate.

Note: Slightly derogatory or neutral in meaning.

340. 僧多粥少 (僧多粥少) sēng duō zhōu shǎo

Translated character by character, 僧多粥少 means 'monk-many-porridge-little,' whereas the implied meaning of this proverb would be 'a situation in which there is not enough of a desired commodity to go around.' Its functional translation is 'too many boats chasing too few fish.'

Example 1:

A: 文秘市场**僧多粥少**，因此很多中文系文秘专业毕业的学生毕业就等于失业。

A: Wénmì shìchǎng sēng duō zhōu shǎo, yīncǐ hěnduō zhōngwénxì wénmì zhuānyè bìyè de xuéshēng bìyè jiù děngyú shīyè.

A: In the secretary market, there are too many boats chasing too few fish. So, a lot of Chinese Department graduates with secretary majors are unemployed after graduation.

Example 2:

A: 老刘，想想办法，把我的外甥女安排进你们单位。

B: 老王，不是我不想帮啊，而是我们单位**僧多粥少**。实话告诉你，下周就要裁三十人啊。

A: Lǎo Liú, xiǎngxiǎng bànfǎ, bǎ wǒde wàishēngnǔ ānpái jìn nǐmen dānwèi.
B: Lǎo Wáng, búshì wǒ bù xiǎng bāng a, érshì wǒmen dānwèi sēng duō zhōu shǎo. Shíhuà gàosù nǐ, xià zhōu jiù yào cái sānshí rén a.

A: Old Liu, think of a way to use my niece in your work unit.
B: Old Wang, it's not that I don't want to help you, but in our work unit, there are too many boats chasing too few fish. To tell you the truth, we're going to have to lay off 30 people next week.

Usage: Functions as predicate or attributive.

Note: Neutral or humorous in meaning.

341. 坐冷板凳 (坐冷板凳) zuò lěng bǎndèng

Translated character by character, 坐冷板凳 means 'sit-cold-bench,' whereas the implied meaning of this proverb would be 'to be ignored in an unimportant position.' Its functional translation is 'to be sidelined.'

Example 1:

A: 搞基础研究的人必须能够**坐得了冷板凳**。

A: Gǎo jīchǔ yánjiū de rén bìxū nénggòu zuò de liǎo lěngbǎndèng.

A: Those who do basic research need to be able to deal with sitting on the sidelines.

Example 2:

A: 他**坐**了十年**冷板凳**，终于写出了一本震惊世界的书。

A: Tā zuòle shí nián lěngbǎndèng, zhōngyú xiěchūle yì běn zhènjīng shìjiè de shū.

A: He was sidelined for ten years, but he finally wrote a book that shocked the world.

Usage: Functions as predicate.

Note: Neutral in meaning.

342. 不当家不知柴米贵 (不當家不知柴米貴)
bù dāng jiā bù zhī chái mǐ guì

Translated character by character, 不当家不知柴米贵 means 'not-run-household-not-know-firewood-rice-expensive,' whereas the implied meaning of this proverb would be 'if one is not in someone else's situation, one cannot understand that person's trouble.'

Example 1:

A: 他儿子又跟他要钱买辆新车。

B: 这个儿子太不争气了。**不当家不知柴米贵**，他老爸挣钱容易吗？

A: Tā érzǐ yòu gēn tā yào qián mǎi liàng xīn chē.

B: Zhègè érzǐ tài bù zhēngqì le. Bù dāngjiā bù zhī chái mǐ guì, tā lǎobà zhèngqián róngyì ma?

A: His son's asking him for money again to buy a new car.

B: That kid is such a disappointment. He doesn't understand his father's trouble. Money doesn't grow on trees.

Example 2:

A: 老板，我们的福利不能再增加一点儿吗？

B: 增加？我还想减少呢！你真是**不当家不知柴米贵**，现在公司用钱的地方太多了。

A: Lǎobǎn, wǒmen de fúlì bùnéng zài zēngjiā yìdiǎnr ma?

B: Zēngjiā? Wǒ hái xiǎng jiǎnshǎo ne! Nǐ zhēn shì bù dāngjiā bù zhī chái mǐ guì, xiànzài gōngsī yòngqián de dìfāng tài duō le.

A: Boss, can't you increase our benefits a little bit?

B: Increase them? I actually want to decrease them! You don't understand my trouble. There are many things the company is going to spend a lot of money on now.

Usage: Functions as predicate or predicative.

Note: Slightly derogatory and humorous in meaning.

343. 红眼病 (紅眼病) hóng yǎn bìng

Translated character by character, 红眼病 means 'red-eye-illness,' whereas the implied meaning of this proverb would be 'jealousy.' Its functional translation is 'the green-eyed monster.'

Example 1:

A: 你得了奖，别人看起来好像很不高兴。

B: 他们得了**红眼病**。

A: Nǐ déle jiǎng, biérén kàn qǐlái hǎoxiàng hěn bù gāoxìng.

B: Tāmen déle hóngyǎnbìng.

A: When you got the award, the others looked like they were very unhappy.

B: They got a touch of the green-eyed monster.

Example 2:

A: 改革开放初期，有一小部分人先富了起来，结果不少人得了**红眼病**，抱怨政府为什么那些人先富了而他们却没富。

A: Gǎigé kāifàng chūqī, yǒu yì xiǎo bùfèn rén xiān fùle qǐlái, jiéguǒ bùshǎo rén déle hóngyǎnbìng, bàoyuàn zhèngfǔ wèishénme nàxiē rén xiān fùle ér tāmen què méi fù.

A: In the beginning of the Reform and Opening, there was a small portion of the population that became wealthy first, causing a lot of people to be bitten by the green-eyed monster and complain to the government about why those people got rich first and they still hadn't.

Usage: Functions as object.

Note: Slightly derogatory and humorous in meaning.

---

344. 葫芦里卖的是什么药 (葫蘆裏賣的是什麼藥)
húlu lǐ mài de shì shénme yào

Translated character by character, 葫芦里卖的是什么药 means 'gourd-inside-sell-is-what-medicine,' whereas the implied meaning of this proverb would be 'to not be able to see what someone has planned.' Its functional translation is 'to have something up one's sleeve.'

Example 1:

A: 她说她有一个好主意。你知道那是什么吗？

B: 不知道，不知道她**葫芦里卖的是什么药**。

A: Tā shuō tā yǒu yígè hǎo zhúyì. Nǐ zhīdào nà shì shénme ma?

B: Bù zhīdào, bù zhīdào tā húlu lǐ mài de shì shénme yào.

A: She says she has a good idea. Do you know what it is?

B: No. I don't know what she has up her sleeve.

Example 2:

A: 他明天要跟你单独谈？

B: 对，但是我不知道他**葫芦里卖的是什么药**。

A: Tā míngtiān yào gēn nǐ dāndú tán?

B: Duì, dànshì wǒ bù zhī dào tā húlu lǐ mài de shì shénme yào.

A: He wants to talk with you alone tomorrow?

B: Yeah, but I don't know what he's got up his sleeve.

Usage: Functions mainly as object of '不知道.'

Note: Neutral or humorous in meaning.

345. 三句话不离本行 (三句話不離本行)
sān jù huà bù lí běn háng

Translated character by character, 三句话不离本行 means 'three-MW-sentences-not-away-own-profession,' whereas the implied meaning of this proverb would be 'to hardly be able to talk about anything other than one's work.'

Example 1:

A: 今天咱们只聊中学时候的事儿，不许聊工作上的事。……听说，那家公司的股票……

B: 你啊，**三句话不离本行**，不说股票你就受不了。

A: Jīntiān zánmen zhǐ liáo zhōngxué shíhòu de shìr, bùxǔ liáo gōngzuò shàng de shì. ……tīng shuō, nà jiā gōngsī de gǔpiào ……

B: Nǐ a, sān jù huà bù lí běnháng, bù shuō gǔpiào nǐ jiù shòu bùliǎo.

A: Today, we're only going to talk about stuff from middle school; we're not allowed to talk about work things . . . I heard that company's stock . . .

B: You're a shop talk junkie. You can't stand not talking about stocks.

Example 2:

A: 她是电视台记者，跟人说话的时候，**三句话不离本行**，总是问别人"最近有什么新鲜事吗？"

A: Tā shì diànshìtái jìzhě, gēn rén shuōhuà de shíhòu, sān jù huà bù lí běnháng, zǒngshì wèn biérén "zuìjìn yǒu shénme xīnxiān shì ma?"

A: She's a TV reporter. When she's talking with people, she can hardly talk about anything other than her work. She's always asking others, "Has anything interesting happened recently?"

Usage: Functions as predicate or used singly.

Note: Slightly derogatory or neutral in meaning.

346. 糖衣炮弹 (糖衣炮彈) táng yī pào dàn

Translated character by character, 糖衣炮弹 means 'sugar-coated-cannon-shell,' whereas the implied meaning of this proverb would be 'an advance that one has convinced another person to gladly accept through clever camouflage.' Its functional translation is 'a Trojan Horse.'

Example 1:

A: 王局长最近好像对奢侈品和美女很感兴趣。

B: 这是**糖衣炮弹**啊！作为政府官员，必须警惕这些东西。

A: Wáng júzhǎng zuìjìn hǎoxiàng duì shēchǐpǐn hé měinǚ hěn gǎn xìngqù.

B: Zhè shì tángyī pàodàn a! Zuòwéi zhèngfǔ guānyuán, bìxū jǐngtì zhèxiē dōngxī.

A: Director Wang seems to have become interested in luxury goods and beautiful women recently.

B: It's a Trojan Horse! As a government official, you need to be on the alert about these things.

Example 2:

A: 不少大学生被西方国家的民主与自由这两颗**糖衣炮弹**击中。

A: Bùshǎo dàxuéshēng bèi xīfāng guójiā de mínzhǔ yǔ zìyóu zhè liǎng kē tángyī pàodàn jīzhòng.

A: Many college students have taken in the Trojan Horses of western countries, democracy and freedom.

Usage: Nominal element, functions as predicative or object.

Note: Slightly derogatory and humorous in meaning.

347. 树倒猢狲散 (樹倒猢猻散) shù dǎo húsūn sàn

Translated character by character, 树倒猢狲散 means 'tree-fallen-monkey-scatter,' whereas the implied meaning of this proverb would be 'when an influential person falls from power, those beneath him tend to flee.' Its functional translation is 'rats leaving a sinking ship.'

Example 1:

A: 那个王牌节目主持人的栏目没被电视台续约，结果那个主持人手下的人纷纷自谋出路。

B: **树倒猢狲散**，以前的大树靠不住了。

A: Nàgè wángpái jiémù zhǔchírén de lánmù méi bèi diànshìtái xùyuē, jiéguǒ nàgè zhǔchírén shǒuxià de rén fēnfēn zìmóu-chūlù.

B: Shù dǎo húsūn sàn, yǐián de dàshù kào búzhù le.

A: That ace TV host's program wasn't picked up for another season by the station, so his subordinates found a way out.

B: Rats leaving a sinking ship. What was once a great ship is now unstable.

Example 2:

A: 首相被逼下台，原来的内阁大臣们纷纷与他划清界线。

B: 咳，**树倒猢狲散**，人啊，有时候挺无情的。

A: Shǒuxiàng bèi bī xiàtái, yuánlái de nèigé dàchénmen fēnfēn yǔ tā huà qīng jièxiàn.

B: Hài, shù dǎo húsūn sàn, rén a, yǒushíhou tǐng wúqíng de.

A: The prime minister was forced to step down. His former cabinet ministers severed ties with him.

B: Oh, rats leaving a sinking ship. People are quite ruthless sometimes.

Usage: Used singly.

Note: Slightly derogatory in meaning.

348. 硬骨头 (硬骨頭) yìng gǔtou

Translated character by character, 硬骨头 means 'hard-bone,' whereas the implied meaning of this proverb would be 'a difficult issue,' or 'a person who doesn't fold under pressure.' Its functional translation is 'a tough nut to crack,' or 'one tough cookie.'

Example 1:

A: 这项研发任务最重，派谁去负责呢？

B: 这是一块**硬骨头**，非得能力出众、责任心又强的人去才行。

A: Zhè xiàng yánfā rènwù zuìzhòng, pài shéi qù fùzé ne?

B: Zhè shì yí kuài yìnggǔtou, fēiděi nénglì chūzhòng, zérènxīn yòu qiáng de rén qù cái ràng rén fàngxīn.

A: The responsibilities associated with this R&D program are the greatest. Who do you want to make responsible for it?

B: This is a tough nut to crack. This position needs to be filled by a very capable and very responsible person.

Example 2:

A: 犯罪集团用金钱、美女，甚至恐吓都没能诱惑或吓唬住他。

B: 他真是**硬骨头**。

A: Fànzuì jítuán yòng jīnqián, měinǚ, shènzhì kǒnghè dōu méi néng yòuhuò huò xiàhu zhù tā.

B: Tā zhēn shì yìnggǔtou.

A: The crime syndicate hasn't been able to entice or frighten him with money,
    beautiful women, or even threats.

B: He really is one tough cookie.

Usage: Functions as object or attributive.

Note: Complimentary in meaning when used to describe a person.

---

349. 二虎相争，必有一伤（二虎相爭，必有一傷）
èr hǔ xiāng zhēng, bì yǒu yì shāng

Translated character by character, 二虎相争，必有一伤 means 'two-tiger-each other-fight, must-get-one-hurt,' whereas the implied meaning of this proverb would be 'when two powerful people clash, at least one is bound to get hurt.' Its functional translation is 'when two tigers clash, one is sure to get hurt.'

Example 1:

A: 他们两个争得很厉害。

B: 最好别让他们争下去了，**二虎相争，必有一伤**啊！

A: Tāmen liǎng gè zhēng de hěn lìhai.

B: Zuìhǎo bié ràng tāmen zhēng xiàqù le, èr hǔ xiāng zhēng, bì yǒu yì shāng a!

A: They're both fighting really fiercely.

B: You shouldn't let them continue fighting. When two tigers fight, one is sure
    to get hurt.

Example 2:

A: 美国副总统和国务卿都要竞选下届总统。

B: **二虎相争，必有一伤**，即使赢了的一方也会遍体鳞伤。

A: Měiguó fùzǒngtǒng hé guówùqīng dōu yào jìngxuǎn xiàjiè zǒngtǒng.

B: Èr hǔ xiāng zhēng, bì yǒu yì shang, jíshǐ yíngle de yìfāng yě huì biàntǐ línshāng.

A: Both the vice-president and the secretary of state for the US want to run for
    president next cycle.

B: When two tigers fight, one is sure to get hurt. Even the winner will get beaten
    black and blue.

Usage: Used singly.

Note: Neutral in meaning.

350. 拆东墙，补西墙 (拆東墙，補西墙)
chāi dōng qiáng, bǔ xī qiáng

Translated character by character, 拆东墙，补西墙 means 'tear down-east-wall, mend-west wall,' whereas the implied meaning of this proverb would be 'to take things from one place in order to resupply another.' Its functional translation is 'to rob Peter to pay Paul.'

Example 1:

A: 他跟我借一万块钱。
B: 他早就跟我借过八千块钱，现在他就是在**拆东墙，补西墙**。

A: Tā gēn wǒ jiè yí wàn kuài qián.
B: Tā zǎo jiù gēn wǒ jièguò bā qiān kuài qián, xiànzài tā jiùshì zài chāidōngqiáng, bǔxīqiáng.

A: He borrowed 10,000 RMB from me.
B: He borrowed 8,000 RMB from me a long time ago. Now, he's just robbing Peter to pay Paul.

Example 2:

A: 政府财政赤字太大了，也没有理由加税了，于是**拆东墙，补西墙**，把社会养老金提前用了。

A: Zhèngfǔ cáizhèng chìzì tài dà le, yě méiyǒu lǐyóu jiāshuì le, yúshì chāidōngqiáng, bǔxīqiáng, bǎ shèhuì yǎnglǎojīn tíqián yòng le.

A: The government's budget deficit is too large, and they have no reason to increase taxes, so they're robbing Peter to pay Paul, using social security's trust fund.

Usage: Functions as predicate.

Note: Slightly derogatory and humorous in meaning.

351. 大鱼吃小鱼 (大魚吃小魚) dà yú chī xiǎo yú

Translated character by character, 大鱼吃小鱼 means 'big-fish-eat-little-fish,' whereas the implied meaning of this proverb would be 'the strong outcompete the weak.' Its functional translation is 'the law of the jungle.'

Example 1:

A: 生意真难做啊！弄不好就会被对手吃掉。
B: 是啊，商业领域就是**大鱼吃小鱼**，没有什么同情心可言。

A: Shēngyì zhēn nán zuò a! Nòng bùhǎo jiù huì bèi duìshǒu chīdiào.
B: Shì a, shāngyè lǐngyù jiùshì dà yú chī xiǎo yú, méiyǒu shénme tóngqíngxīn kě yán.

A: Business is really tough! If you mess up, you'll be swallowed up by your competitors.

B: Yeah, in the field of business, the law of the jungle applies. There's no compassion to speak of.

Example 2:

A: 洗发水行业原有数十家企业，后来竞争极其激烈，结果是**大鱼吃小鱼**，最后只剩下四、五家了。

A: Xǐfàshuǐ hángyè yuán yǒu shù shí jiā qǐyè, hòulái jìngzhēng jíqí jīliè, jiéguǒ shì dà yú chī xiǎo yú, zuìhòu zhǐ shèngxià sì-wǔ jiā le.

A: The shampoo industry used to have tens of companies, but as a result of extremely intense competition, the law of the jungle applied. In the end, only four or five companies were left.

Usage: Functions as predicative or attributive, or used singly.

Note: Neutral or humorous in meaning.

352. 狐狸尾巴露出来了 (狐狸尾巴露出來了)
húli wěiba lòu chūlái le

Translated character by character, 狐狸尾巴露出来了 means 'fox-tail-show-out,' whereas the implied meaning of this proverb would be 'a bad person has accidentally made their true nature known.' Its functional translation is 'to show one's true colors,' or 'the jig is up.'

Example 1:

A: 他是一个外国志愿者，怎么也跑到市中心广场上与当地市民一起抗议去了？

B: 没那么简单，他肯定是个间谍，现在**狐狸尾巴露出来了**。

A: Tā shì yígè wàiguó zhìyuànzhě, zěnme yě pǎo dào shìzhōngxīn guǎngchǎng shàng yǔ dāngdì shìmín yìqǐ kàngyì qù le?

B: Méi nàme jiǎndān, tā kěndìng shì gè jiàndié, xiànzài húli wěiba lòu chūlái le.

A: He is a foreign volunteer, why did he go into the square in the city center to protest with local city residents?

B: It's not that simple; he's definitely a spy. Now the jig is up.

Example 2:

A: 她平常好像对您很尊敬，可是在这么重要的问题上怎么敢强烈地反对您？

B: 她是只小狐狸，平常掩盖得很深，现在**露出了狐狸尾巴**。

A: Tā píngcháng hǎoxiàng duì nín hěn zūnjìng, kěshì zài zhème zhòngyào de wèntí shàng zěnme gǎn qiángliè de fǎnduì nín?

B: Tā shì zhī xiǎo húli, píngcháng yǎngài de hěn shēn, xiànzài lòu chūle húli wěiba.

A: She usually seems to respect you a lot; how could she dare to strongly oppose you on such an important issue?

B: She's a slippery one. She usually buries her inclinations deep, but now she's shown her true colors.

Usage: Functions as predicate.

Note: Slightly derogatory and humorous in meaning.

---

353. 开绿灯 (開綠燈) kāi lǜ dēng

Translated character by character, 开绿灯 means 'turn on-green-light,' whereas the implied meaning of this proverb would be 'to signal one's approval of something,' or 'to expedite.' Its functional translation is 'to give the green light,' or 'to give the go-ahead.'

Example 1:

A: 这些药是怎么流入市场的？

B: 按说这些劣质药品根本不可能通过检验的，但是制药公司花费巨资行贿，所以审批部门、检验部门处处**开绿灯**，最后药品就进入市场了。

A: Zhèxiē yào shì zěnme liúrù shìchǎng de?

B: Ànshuō zhèxiē lièzhì yàopǐn gēnběn bù kěnéng tōngguò jiǎnyàn de, dànshì zhǐyào gōngsī huāfèi jùzī xínghuì, suǒyǐ shěnpī bùmén, jiǎnyàn bùmén chùchù kāilǜdēng, zuìhòu yàopǐn jiù jìnrù shìchǎng le.

A: How did these drugs get onto the market?

B: They say these substandard drugs really couldn't have passed inspection, but the drug company spent an enormous amount of money on bribes, so the examination and approval agency and the inspection agency both gave the go-ahead and, in the end, the drug got onto the market.

Example 2:

A: 当地政府为了吸引外资高科技企业，在企业投产前的许多环节都大**开绿灯**，以便企业尽快入驻。

A: Dāngdì zhèngfǔ wèile xīyǐn wàizī gāokējì qǐyè, zài qǐyè tóuchǎn qián de xǔduō huánjié dōu dà kāi lǜdēng, yǐbiàn qǐyè jìnkuài rùzhù.

A: In order to attract foreign high-tech companies, the local government expedited many of the pre-production steps in order to facilitate the companies' earliest tenancy.

Usage: Functions as predicate.

Note: Neutral in meaning.

354. 歪瓜裂枣 (歪瓜裂棗) wāi guā liè zǎo

Translated character by character, 歪瓜裂枣 means 'asymmetrical-melon-split-date,' whereas the implied meaning of this proverb would be 'an ugly person.' Its functional translation is 'a troll.'

Example 1:

A: 你要把他介绍给王小姐？

B: 是啊？

A: 他长得**歪瓜裂枣**的，怎么配得上王小姐？

A: Nǐ yào bǎ tā jièshào gěi Wáng xiǎojiě?
B: Shì a?
A: Tā zhǎng de wāi guā liè zǎo de, zěnme pèi de shàng Wáng xiǎojiě?

A: You want to introduce him to Miss Wang?
B: Yeah, why?
A: He looks like a troll. How will he match up to Miss Wang?

Example 2:

A: 你们办公室的男人怎么那么丑？

B: 你们办公室的帅吗？个个都是**歪瓜裂枣**。

A: Nǐmen bàngōngshì de nánrén zěnme nàme chǒu?
B: Nǐmen bàngōngshì de shuài ma? Gègè dōu shì wāi guā liè zǎo.

A: How are all the men in your office so ugly?
B: Are the ones in your office handsome? All of yours are trolls.

Usage: Functions mainly as object.

Note: Derogatory in meaning.

355. 小辫子 (小辮子) xiǎo biànzi

Translated character by character, 小辫子 means 'short-pigtail,' whereas the implied meaning of this proverb would be 'one's weak point.' Its functional translation is 'short hairs,' or 'chink in one's armor.'

Example 1:

A: 他对你怎么那么客气？

B: 他有**小辫子**在我手里。

A: Tā duì nǐ zěnme nàme kèqì?

B: Tā yǒu xiǎobiànzi zài wǒ shǒulǐ.

A: Why is he so polite to you?

B: I've got him by the short hairs.

Example 2:

A: 他被对手抓住了**小辫子**，最后不得不认输。

A: Tā bèi duìshǒu zhuāzhù le xiǎobiànzi, zuìhòu bùdebù rènshū.

A: His opponent got him by the short hairs. In the end, he had no choice but to admit defeat.

Usage: Functions as object.

Note: Neutral or humorous in meaning.

356. 一头雾水 （一頭霧水） yì tóu wù shuǐ

Translated character by character, 一头雾水 means 'full-head-mist,' whereas the implied meaning of this proverb would be 'in a befuddled or confused state.' Its functional translation is 'at a loss.'

Example 1:

A: 她的报告的主要观点是什么？

B: 不知道。她的思维太跳跃，听得我一**头雾水**。

A: Tā de bàogào de zhǔyào guāndiǎn shì shénme?

B: Bù zhīdào. Tā de sīwéi tài tiàoyuè, tīng de wǒ yì tóu wùshuǐ.

A: What was the main conclusion of her report?

B: I don't know. Her thought process was too jumpy; I was at a loss to understand it.

Example 2:

A: 电影怎么样？

B: 人物关系太复杂，我看得一**头雾水**，到最后也没看明白谁是男主角。

A: Diànyǐng zěnmeyàng?

B: Rénwù guānxì tài fùzá, wǒ kàn de yì tóu wùshuǐ, dào zuìhòu yě méi kàn míngbai shéi shì nán zhǔjué.

A: How was the movie?
B: The interpersonal relationships were too complicated. At the end I was still at a loss as to who the main male character was.

Usage: Functions as complement and usually used in the structure '看/听/搞 + 得 + (Subject) + ~.'

Note: Neutral or humorous in meaning.

357.　隔行如隔山 (隔行如隔山) gé háng rú gé shān

Translated character by character, 隔行如隔山 means 'different-profession-like-dividing-mountain,' whereas the implied meaning of this proverb would be 'one is uninformed about trades other than one's own.' Its functional translation is 'different professions are different worlds.'

Example 1:

A: 你试一下，很简单。
B: 没那么容易吧？ **隔行如隔山**，我以前根本没接触过。

A: Nǐ shì yíxià, hěn jiǎndān.
B: Méi nàme róngyì ba? Gé háng rú gé shān, wǒ yǐqián gēnběn méi jiēchù guò.

A: Give it a try. It's simple.
B: Can it be that easy? Different professions are different worlds. I haven't had any experience with it.

Example 2:

A: 在今天的报告中，那位大教授说了不合适的话，因为虽然他在自己的领域是大牛，但是**隔行如隔山**，在这个领域他几乎一无所知。

A: Zài jīntiān de bàogào zhōng, nà wèi dà jiàoshòu shuōle bú héshì de huà, yīnwèi suīrán tā zài zìjǐ de lǐngyù shì dàniú, dànshì gé háng rú gé shān, zài zhègè lǐngyù tā jīhū yìwúsuǒzhī.

A: In today's speech, that prominent professor made some misinformed comments because, even though he's a big shot in his field, different professions are different worlds. He knows almost nothing about this field.

Usage: Used singly.

Note: Neutral in meaning.

358. 一亩三分地 (一畝三分地) yì mǔ sān fēn dì

Translated character by character, 一亩三分地 means 'one-point-three-*mu* (666.66 m²)-land,' whereas the implied meaning of this proverb would be 'an area in which one's word goes.' Its functional translation is 'personal fief.'

Example 1:

A: 请您多关照。

B: 小意思，这块地方是我的**一亩三分地**，什么事我都能摆平。

A: Qǐng nín duō guānzhào.

B: Xiǎoyìsi, zhè kuài dìfāng shì wǒde yì mǔ sān fēn dì, shénme shì wǒ dōu néng bǎipíng.

A: Please take care of me.

B: It's nothing. This area is my personal fief; I can smooth anything over here.

Example 2:

A: 校长，会不会有人反对？

B: 有用吗？这是我的**一亩三分地**，只有我说了算。

A: Xiàozhǎng, huìbúhuì yǒu rén fǎnduì?

B: Yǒuyòng ma? Zhè shì wǒde yì mǔ sān fēn dì, zhǐyǒu wǒ shuōle suàn.

A: Principal, will people resist?

B: What's the use? This is my personal fief; only what I say goes.

Usage: Functions as object.

Note: Neutral in meaning.

359. 成也萧何，败也萧何 (成也蕭何，敗也蕭何) chéng yě Xiāo Hé, bài yě Xiāo Hé

Translated character by character, 成也萧何，败也萧何 means 'succeed-also-(because) Xiao He, defeat-also-(because) Xiao He,' whereas the implied meaning of this proverb would be 'one's successes and failures are both due to the same person.'

Example 1:

A: 这家公司的兴起是因为他，衰败也是因为他。

B: 真是**成也萧何，败也萧何**。这就是命啊！

A: Zhè jiā gōngsī de xìngqǐ shì yīnwèi tā, shuāibài yěshì yīnwèi tā.

B: Zhēn shì chéng yě Xiāo Hé, bài yě Xiāo Hé. Zhè jiùshì mìng a!

A: This company's rise was due to him, and its fall was also due to him.

B: Both their successes and failures really were due to him. This is fate!

Example 2:

A: 这个大牌球星虽然篮球技术很高，但是太独断。球队赢球靠他，输球也往往是因为他，可谓**成也萧何，败也萧何**。

A: Zhègè dàpái qiúxīng suīrán lánqiú jìshù hěn gāo, dànshì tài dúduàn. Qiúduì yíng qiú kào tā, shū qiú yě wǎngwǎng shì yīnwèi tā, kěwèi chéng yě Xiāo Hé, bài yě Xiāo Hé.

A: While that superstar is very talented at basketball, he's not a team player. The team relies on him to win, but when they lose, it's often because of him. You could say their successes and failures are all due to him.

Usage: Functions as predicative.

Note: Neutral in meaning.

360. 大水冲了龙王庙 (大水冲了龍王廟)
dà shuǐ chōng le lóng wáng miào

Translated character by character, 大水冲了龙王庙 means 'flood-overflow-ed-Dragon-King's-temple,' whereas the implied meaning of this proverb would be 'to accidentally wrong an ally,' or 'conflicts arise between people on one's own side.' Its functional translation is 'friendly fire.'

Example 1:

A: 告诉你一件新鲜事儿。我有个邻居，是法官，今天因为他家的宠物与另一个邻居发生了冲突，结果这个法官被告上了法庭。

B: 哟，这不是**大水冲了龙王庙**嘛。

A: Gàosù nǐ yí jiàn xīnxiān shìr. Wǒ yǒu gè línjū, shì fǎguān, jīntiān yīnwèi tā jiā de chǒngwù yǔ lìngyígè línjū fāshēng le chōngtu, jiéguǒ zhègè fǎguān bèi gào shàngle fǎtíng.

B: Yò, zhè búshì dà shuǐ chōngle lóngwáng miào ma.

A: Let me tell you something interesting. I have a neighbor who is a judge. Today, he got into an altercation with another neighbor because of his pet, resulting in his being sued.

B: Oh, aren't things like that not supposed to happen?

Example 2:

A: （与B争吵……）其实，我是反对堕胎的。

B: 是嘛，既然这样，我们还吵什么啊，**大水冲了龙王庙**了。

A: (yǔ B zhēngchǎo ……) Qíshí, wǒ shì fǎnduì duòtāi de.

B: Shì ma, jìrán zhèyàng, wǒmen hái chǎo shénme a, dà shuǐ chōngle lóngwáng miào le.

A: (arguing with B) In reality, I'm opposed to abortion.

B: Really? If that's the case, what're we fighting about? This is friendly fire.

Usage: Functions as predicative or used singly.

Note: Neutral or humorous in meaning.

---

361. 乱弹琴 (亂彈琴) luàn tán qín

Translated character by character, 乱弹琴 means 'blindly-play-zither,' whereas the implied meaning of this proverb would be 'to speak or act without sound reasons.'

Example 1:

A: 您不在这几天，他把您的规定改了很多。

B: 简直是**乱弹琴**！马上把他叫来。

A: Nín bú zài zhè jǐ tiān, tā bǎ nín de guīdìng gǎile hěnduō.

B: Jiǎnzhí shì luàntánqín! Mǎshàng bǎ tā jiào lái.

A: In the days that you weren't here, he changed your rules a lot.

B: He really acts without thinking. Tell him to see me immediately!

Example 2:

A: 他说社会的发展一定是前进两步、后退一步。

B: **乱弹琴**！看来他连最基本的历史都不了解。

A: Tā shuō shèhuì de fāzhǎn yídìng shì qiánjìn liǎng bù, hòutuì yí bù.

B: Luàntánqín! Kànlái tā lián zuì jīběn de lìshǐ dōu bù liǎojiě.

A: He says social development is definitely two steps forward, one step back.

B: He doesn't think before speaking! I can see he doesn't even understand the most basic things about history.

Usage: Functions as predicate or used singly.

Note: Slightly derogatory and humorous in meaning.

---

362. 挤牙膏 (擠牙膏) jǐ yá gāo

Translated character by character, 挤牙膏 means 'squeeze-toothpaste,' whereas the implied meaning of this proverb would be 'to speak slowly and haltingly,' or 'to advance with difficulty.' Its functional translation is 'to draw something out,' or 'to be like pulling teeth.'

Example 1:

A: 是这么回事。我……我……，这么说吧，……
B: 你别**挤牙膏**了，有话就快说。

A: Shì zhème huí shì. Wǒ......wǒ......, zhème shuō ba, ...
B: Nǐ bié jǐyágāo le, yǒu huà jiù kuài shuō.

A: It's like this. I . . . I . . . Let's say . . .
B: Spit it out! If you have something to say, say it fast.

Example 2:

A: 这部电视连续剧的进展也太慢了，跟**挤牙膏**似的。
B: 怪不得一拍就是八十集呢。

A: Zhè bù diànshì liánxùjù de jìnzhǎn yě tàimàn le, gēn jǐyágāo shìde.
B: Guàibude yì pāi jiùshì bāshí jí ne.

A: This TV series develops too slowly. It's like pulling teeth.
B: No wonder they shoot 80 episodes at a time.

Usage: Functions as predicate.

Note: Slightly derogatory and humorous in meaning.

363. 墙倒众人推 (墙倒衆人推) qiáng dǎo zhòng rén tuī

Translated character by character, 墙倒众人推 means 'wall-fallen-crowd-push,' whereas the implied meaning of this proverb would be 'when a wall is about to collapse, everyone gives it a push.' Its functional translation is 'everyone kicks a man who is down.'

Example 1:

A: 看今天的报纸，怎么全是批评他的？
B: 很简单，他的性丑闻被曝光，政治生命结束，**墙倒众人推**，媒体也开始一致批评他了。

A: Kàn jīntiān de bàozhǐ, zěnme quán shì pīpíng tā de?
B: Hěn jiǎndān, tāde xìngchǒuwén bèi bàoguāng, zhèngzhì shēngmìng jiéshù, qiáng dǎo zhòngrén tuī, méitǐ yě kāishǐ yízhì pīpíng tā le.

A: Look at today's paper. How is it all criticizing him?
B: It's simple. His sex scandal has been brought to light; his political career is over. Everyone hits a man who is down and now the media has started to criticize him as one.

Example 2:

A: 兄弟，还能撑得住吧？

B: 大哥，你真够朋友。在我落难的时候别人都**墙倒众人推**，就你一个人跟平常一样照顾小弟。

A: Xiōngdi, hái néng chēng de zhù ba?

B: Dàgē, nǐ zhēn gòupéngyou. Zài wǒ luònàn de shíhou biérén dōu qiáng dǎo zhòngrén tuī, jiù nǐ yígè rén gēn píngcháng yíyàng zhàogù xiǎodì.

A: Brother, can you still stand it?

B: Big brother, you're so good to me. When I fell on hard times, everyone else kicked me while I was down; only you cared for your little brother as usual.

Usage: Used singly or functions as predicate.

Note: Slightly derogatory in meaning.

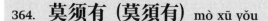

364. 莫须有 （莫须有） mò xū yǒu

Translated character by character, 莫须有 means 'maybe-exist,' whereas the implied meaning of this proverb would be 'groundless,' or 'trumped-up.'

Example 1:

A: 有的公司以**莫须有**的理由解聘员工。

B: 这还算好的，更糟糕的是，美国大使馆会以**莫须有**的理由拒绝签证申请。

A: Yǒude gōngsī yǐ mòxūyǒu de lǐyóu jiěpìn yuángōng.

B: Zhè hái suàn hǎo de, gèng zāogāo de shì, Měiguó dàshǐguǎn huì yǐ mòxūyǒu de lǐyóu jùjué qiānzhèng shēnqǐng.

A: Some companies dismiss employees on trumped-up grounds.

B: That's not so bad. What's worse is that the American embassy will reject visa applications without grounds.

Example 2:

A: 他在监狱中关了五年，出狱后的第一件事就是对媒体说对他的指控都是**莫须有**。

A: Tā zài jiānyù zhōng guānle wǔ nián, chūyù hòu de dì-yī jiàn shì jiùshì duì méitǐ shuō duì tā de zhǐkòng dōu shì mòxūyǒu.

A: He was held in prison for five years. After he got out, the first thing he did was say the charges against him were groundless.

Usage: Functions as attributive or predicative.

Note: Derogatory in meaning. This phrase alludes to an answer that the infamous Chancellor Qin Hui of the Song Dynasty gave on the question of whether General Yue Fei had betrayed his country. There are several different interpretations of the meaning of 莫须有, but the translation here is the most popular one.

365.   拿鸡毛当令箭 (拿雞毛當令箭) ná jī máo dāng lìng jiàn

Translated character by character, 拿鸡毛当令箭 means 'use-chicken-feather-as-(authoritative) arrow,' whereas the implied meaning of this proverb would be 'to use a made-up directive to order people around.'

Example 1:

A: 这是主任的话，你们爱听不听。

B: 你别**拿鸡毛当令箭**。主任有话可以自己说嘛，干嘛要让你转达？

A: Zhè shì zhǔrèn de huà, nǐmen ài tīng bù tīng.

B: Nǐ bié ná jīmáo dāng lìngjiàn. Zhǔrèn yǒu huà kěyǐ zìjǐ shuō ma, gàn ma yào ràng nǐ zhuǎndá?

A: This is what the director says, but decide for yourself whether or not you want to listen.

B: Don't make things up in order to order people around. If the director has something to say, he can say it himself. What's he doing making you relay?

Example 2:

A: 她说话这么牛？

B: 没办法，她是领导的红人，整天**拿着鸡毛当令箭**，别人都对她客气三分。

A: Tā shuōhuà zhème niú?

B: Méi bànfǎ, tā shì lǐngdǎo de hóngrén, zhěngtiān názhe jīmáo dāng lìngjiàn, biérén dōu duì tā kèqì sān fēn.

A: Why does she speak so arrogantly?

B: There's nothing we can do about it. She is the boss's favorite, always making things up to boss people around. Everyone is quite polite to her.

Usage: Functions as predicate.

Note: Slightly derogatory in meaning.

366. 捅破窗户纸 (捅破窗戶紙) tǒng pò chuānghu zhǐ

Translated character by character, 捅破窗户纸 means 'poke-broken-window-paper,' whereas the implied meaning of this proverb would be 'to reveal the truth and speak openly about a secret.' Its functional translation is 'to affirm an open secret,' or 'to address the elephant in the room.'

Example 1:

A: 大家都觉得他是同性恋，可是没有人公开说过。今天他自己**捅破**了这层**窗户纸**，主动告诉别人他就是同性恋。

A: Dà jiā dōu juéde tā shì tóngxìngliàn, kěshì méiyǒu rén gōngkāi shuō guò. Jīntiān tā zìjǐ tǒng pò le zhè céng chuānghu zhǐ, zhǔdòng gàosù biérén tā jiùshì tóngxìngliàn.

A: Everyone thought he was gay, but no one had stated it openly. Today, he addressed the elephant in the room and took it upon himself to tell everyone he was gay.

Example 2:

A: 你说，这种事怎么好意思让女人先开口？
B: 都这年代了，还考虑什么谁先谁后的？把这层**窗户纸捅破**了就行了。

A: Nǐ shuō, zhèzhǒng shì zěnme hǎoyìsi ràng nǚrén xian kāikǒu?
B: Dōu zhè niándài le, hái kǎolǜ shénme shéi xiān shéi hòu de? Bǎ zhè céng chuānghu zhǐ tǒng pò le jiù xíng le.

A: Hey, how could you allow a woman to bring an issue like this up first?
B: In this day and age, you still worry about something like who brings something up? You just need to deal with the elephant in the room.

Usage: Functions as predicate.

Note: Neutral in meaning.

367. 三字经 (三字經) sān zì jīng

Translated character by character, 三字经 means 'three-character-scripture.' Its implied meaning is 'curse.'

Example 1:

A: 这是谁xxx干的？
B: 不许带**三字经**。

A: Zhè shì shéi xxx gàn de?
B: Bùxǔ dài sānzìjīng.

A: Who the #&%@ did this?
B: You can't say curse words!

Example 2:

A: 他十分生气，说着说着**三字经**就出来了。

A: Tā shífēn shēngqì, shuōzhe shuōzhe sānzìjīng jiù chūlái le.

A: He's extremely angry. As he was speaking, curses came out.

Usage: Nominal element, functions as object or subject.

Note: Neutral or humorous in meaning.

---

368. 苍蝇不叮无缝的蛋 (蒼蠅不叮無縫的蛋)
cāngying bù dīng wú fèng de dàn

Translated character by character, 苍蝇不叮无缝的蛋 means 'fly-not-suck-without-cracked-egg,' whereas the implied meaning of this proverb would be 'if you don't have any faults, bad people won't gravitate to you.' Its functional translation is 'to bring bad things upon oneself as a result of one's bad character.'

Example 1:

A: 那么多花花公子老是缠着她。
B: **苍蝇不叮无缝的蛋**，如果她严辞拒绝，不会有那么多人的。

A: Nàme duō huāhuāgōngzi lǎoshì chánzhe tā.
B: Cāngying bù dīng wú fèng de dàn, rúguǒ tā yáncí jùjué, búhuì yǒu nàme duō rén de.

A: So many playboys are pursuing her.
B: She's bringing it upon herself. If she rejected them forcefully there wouldn't be so many.

Example 2:

A: 在电视上他哭哭啼啼地说他刚当干部的时候是多么清廉，后来不断有人给他送礼，他拒绝不了才受贿的。
B: **苍蝇不叮无缝的蛋**，如果他内心真的很清廉，什么时候都不会收受贿赂。

A: Zài diànshì shang tā kūkutíti de shuō tā gāng dāng gànbù de shíhou shì duōme qīnglián, hòulái búduàn yǒu rén gěi tā sònglǐ, tā jùjué bùliǎo cái shòuhuì de.
B: Cāngying bù dīng wú fèng de dàn, rúguǒ tā nèixīn zhēnde hěn qīnglián, shénme shíhou dōu búhuì shòuhuì.

A: On television, he said, sobbing, how honest he was when he first became a cadre and that later, people were constantly giving him gifts. Only when he couldn't refuse them did he start taking bribes.

B: He brought it upon himself. If he was truly honest at heart, he would never have taken bribes.

Usage: Used singly.

Note: Derogatory in meaning.

369. 大跌眼镜 (大跌眼鏡) dà diē yǎn jìng

Translated character by character, 大跌眼镜 means 'truly-drop-glasses,' whereas the implied meaning of this proverb would be 'to be surprising.' Its functional translation is 'to have one's jaw drop,' or 'to be slack-jawed.'

Example 1:

A: 在这起贿赂案中，让人**大跌眼镜**的是，他不但没有受到惩罚，反而升了官。

A: Zài zhè qǐ huìlù'àn zhōng, ràng rén dà diē yǎnjìng de shì, tā búdàn méiyǒu shòudào chéngfá, fǎn'ér shēngle guān.

A: What was really jaw-dropping about this bribery case was that he not only wasn't punished, but instead was promoted in the government.

Example 2:

A: 在七八个总统候选人中，开始人气最低的人最终当选总统，这让众多媒体和时事评论员**大跌眼镜**。

A: Zài qī-bā gè zǒngtǒng hòuxuǎnrén zhōng, kāishǐ rénqì zuì dī de rén zuìzhōng dāngxuǎn zǒngtǒng, zhè ràng zhòngduō méitǐ hé shíshì pínglùnyuán dà diē yǎnjìng.

A: Out of seven or eight presidential candidates, the one who was least popular at the beginning won in the end. This left a lot of commentators and members of the media slack-jawed.

Usage: Functions as predicate, usually after '让/令人.'

Variant: 跌破眼镜

Note: Neutral in meaning.

370.   说一千，道一万 (説一千，道一萬)
shuō yì qiān, dào yí wàn

Translated character by character, 说一千，道一万 means 'say-one thousand, say-ten thousand,' whereas the implied meaning of this proverb would be 'no matter what you say.' Its functional translation is 'there are no two ways about it.'

Example 1:

A: 这件事真的很难办，不是我不使劲。

B: 算了，**说一千道一万**，你还是没办了，你以前是怎么保证来着？

A: Zhè jiàn shì zhēnde hěn nán bàn, búshì wǒ bù shǐjìn.

B: Suànle, shuō yì qiān dào yí wàn, nǐ háishì méi bàn liǎo, nǐ yǐqián shì zěnme bǎozhèng láizhe?

A: This issue is really hard to handle. It's not that I'm not putting in the effort.

B: Forget it, there are no two ways about it; you still haven't dealt with it. How did you promise me before?

Example 2:

A: 发展经济，保护环境，**说一千道一万**，都要以人为本。如果人民没能满意，这些都是空话。

A: Fāzhǎn jīngjì, bǎohù huánjìng, shuō yì qiān dào yí wàn, dōu yào yǐ rén wéi běn. Rúguǒ rénmín méi néng mǎnyì, zhèxiē dōu shì kōnghuà.

A: There are no two ways about it, developing the economy and protecting the environment both have to be based on people. If people aren't able to be satisfied, this is all empty talk.

Usage: Functions as parenthetical between subject and object, or used at the beginning of a sentence.

Note: Neutral in meaning.

371.   绊脚石 (絆腳石) bàn jiǎo shí

Translated character by character, 绊脚石 means 'stumbling-foot-stone,' whereas the implied meaning of this proverb would be 'stumbling block.'

Example 1:

A: 我们的计划非常好，就是他是一块**绊脚石**，怎么办？

B: 能绕过去就绕过去，实在绕不过去就赶走他。

A: Wǒmen de jìhuà fēicháng hǎo, jiùshì tā shì yí kuài bànjiǎoshí, zěnme bàn?

B: Néng rào guòqù jiù rào guòqù, shízài rào bú guòqù jiù gǎnzǒu tā.

A:　Our plan is really good. He's the only stumbling block. What should we do?

B:　If we can go around him, we'll go around him. If we really can't go around, we'll drive him away.

Example 2:

A:　老同志从领导岗位上退下来以后就不要再干涉年轻人的工作了，不能成为他们前进路上的**绊脚石**。

A:　Lǎo tóngzhì cóng lǐngdǎo gǎngwèi shàng tuì xiàlái yǐhòu jiù búyào zài gānshè niánqīngrén de gōngzuò le, bùnéng chéngwéi tāmen qiánjìn lùshàng de bànjiǎoshí.

A:　After old comrades retire from their positions as leaders, they shouldn't continue to interfere in the work of younger people. They can't become a stumbling block on the younger people's work paths.

Usage: Functions as object or predicative.

Note: Neutral in meaning.

---

372. 过五关、斩六将 (過五關、斬六將)
guò wǔ guān , zhǎn liù jiàng

Translated character by character, 过五关、斩六将 means 'to pass-five-pass, decapitate-six-general,' whereas the implied meaning of this proverb is 'to overcome great challenges and have the glory to show for it.'

Example 1:

A:　我上高中的时候是学校的足球队长，是全校男生崇拜的对象，也是众多女生追求的目标。

B:　行了吧，谁年青的时候没有**过五关、斩六将**的经历。

A:　Wǒ shàng gāozhōng de shíhòu shì xuéxiào de zúqiú duìzhǎng, shì quánxiào nánshēng chóngbài de duìxiàng, yěshì zhòngduō nǚshēng zhuīqiú de mùbiāo.

B:　Xíng le ba, shéi niánqīng de shíhòu méi yǒu guò wǔ guān zhǎn liù jiàng de jīnglì.

A:　When I was in high school, I was the captain of the soccer team, I was worshipped by every guy at the school, and I was pursued by many girls.

B:　That's enough. Who doesn't have achievements to be proud of from their youth?

Example 2:

A:　他以坚实的业务能力、良好的沟通技巧和出色的宏观视野，**过五关、斩六将**，征服了所有的招聘者，得到了一个非常重要的职位。

A: Tā yǐ jiānshí de yèwù nénglì, liánghǎo de gōutōng jìqiǎo hé chūsè de hóngguān shìyě, guò wǔ guān, zhǎn liù jiàng, zhēngfú le suǒyǒu de zhāopìnzhě, dédào le yígè fēicháng zhòngyào de zhíwèi.

A: Relying on his solid vocational skills, his very good communication skills and his outstanding holistic understanding of situations, he overcame great challenges, won over all of the interviewers, and got an extremely important post.

Usage: Functions as predicate.

Note: Complimentary in meaning.

373. 求爷爷、告奶奶 (求爺爺、告奶奶) qiú yéye, gào nǎinai

Translated character by character, 求爷爷、告奶奶 means 'beg-grandpa-call-grandma.' Its implied meaning is 'to go around begging for help.'

Example 1:

A: 你的银行贷款的担保人是谁？
B: 别提这事儿了！谁也不愿意当。**我求爷爷、告奶奶**，到处找人，最后还是一位大学同学当的保人。

A: Nǐde yínháng dàikuǎn de dānbǎorén shì shéi?
B: Bié tí zhè shìr le! Shéi yě bú yuànyì dāng. Wǒ qiú yéye gào nǎinai, dàochù zhǎo rén, zuìhòu háishì yí wèi dàxué tóngxué dāng de bǎorén.

A: Who is the guarantor for your bank loan?
B: I don't want to talk about it! No one was willing to be my guarantor. I went around begging for help, looking everywhere, and in the end it was a college classmate who became my guarantor.

Example 2:

A: 咳，这个专业的毕业生真可怜，拿了博士学位以后还得**求爷爷、告奶奶**到处找用人单位，最后很多人都去当中学老师了。

A: Hài, zhègè zhuānyè de bìyèshēng zhēn kělián, nále bóshì xuéwèi yǐhòu hái děi qiú yéye gào nǎinai de dàochù zhǎo yòngrén dānwèi, zuìhòu hěnduō rén dōu qù dāng zhōngxué lǎoshī le.

A: Oh, grad students in this field are really pitiful. After they get their PhDs, they still have to go around begging for help, looking for work units that are hiring. In the end, many go become middle school teachers.

Usage: Functions as predicate.

Note: Neutral in meaning.

374. 羡慕嫉妒恨 (羡慕嫉妒恨) xiànmù jídù hèn

Translated character by character, 羡慕嫉妒恨 means 'jealous-envious-hate,' whereas the implied meaning of this proverb would be 'to be very jealous.' Its functional translation is 'to be green with envy.'

Example 1:

A: 我的州的个人所得税率还不到百分之十。

B: 什么？不到百分之十？你真让我**羡慕嫉妒恨**。

A: Wǒde zhōu de gèrén suǒdéshuìlǜ hái bú dào bǎi fēn zhī shí.

B: Shénme? Bú dào bǎi fēn zhī shí? Nǐ zhēn ràng wǒ xiànmù jídù hèn.

A: My state income tax rate is even less than 10 percent.

B: What? Less than 10 percent? You're really making me green with envy.

Example 2:

A: 我一周工作二十个小时就可以了。

B: 你的工作是什么？这真是让人**羡慕嫉妒恨**的工作。

A: Wǒ yī zhōu gōngzuò èrshí gè xiǎoshí jiù kěyǐ le.

B: Nǐde gōngzuò shì shénme? Zhè zhēnshì ràng rén xiànmù jídù hèn de gōngzuò.

A: I only need to work twenty hours a week.

B: What do you do? That really is a job that could make someone green with envy.

Usage: Functions as predicate or attributive.

Note: Humorous in meaning.

375. 打掉门牙往肚里咽 (打掉門牙往肚里咽)
dǎ diào mén yá wǎng dù lǐ yàn

Translated character by character, 打掉门牙往肚里咽 means 'knock-out-front-teeth-into-stomach-swallow,' whereas the implied meaning of this proverb would be 'to refrain from addressing or speaking the truth about an insult one has endured.' Its functional translation is 'to bite one's tongue.'

Example 1:

A: 他本想借助别人的力量发展自己，没想到不但没能发展自己，反倒被别人侵占了他自己不少利益。他得罪不起人家，只好**打掉门牙往肚里咽**。

A: Tā běnxiǎng jièzhù biérén de lìliàng fāzhǎn zìjǐ, méixiǎngdào búdàn méi néng fāzhǎn zìjǐ, fǎndǎo bèi biérén qīnzhàn le tā zìjǐ bùshǎo lìyì. Tā dézuì bùqǐ rénjia, zhǐhǎo dǎ diào ményá wǎng dù lǐ yàn.

A: He originally wanted to use other people's strength to advance himself. He never thought that he would not be able to advance himself, but rather that other people would expropriate his benefits. He didn't have the power to resist the others, so he bit his tongue.

Example 2:

A: 他辞去了国内待遇优厚的工作，不顾一切地到了国外，以为国外就是天堂。但是他在国外混得并不如意，远远不如国内成功，有时候甚至得去饭馆刷盘子。国内的人问起他国外怎么样时，他**打掉门牙往肚里咽**，说"挺好的"。

A: Tā cíqù le guónèi dàiyù yōuhòu de gōngzuò, búgù yíqiè de dàole guówài, yǐwéi guówài jiùshì tiāntáng. Dànshì tā zài guówài hùn de bìng bù rúyì, yuǎnyuǎn bùrú guónèi chénggōng, yǒushíhòu shènzhì děi qù fànguǎn shuā pánzi. Guónèi de rén wèn qǐ tā guówài zěnmeyàng shí, tā dǎ diào ményá wǎng dù lǐ yàn, shuō "tǐng hǎo de."

A: He gave up a cushy domestic job, recklessly going abroad, believing that other countries were heaven. But things didn't pan out for him as he had expected abroad, with much less success than he had at home. Sometimes, he even had to wash dishes at restaurants. When people from home asked him how abroad was, he bit his tongue, saying, "Quite good."

Usage: Functions as predicate.

Variants: 打掉门牙(or 牙齿)和血吞 (和 huò, with)

Note: Neutral in meaning.

---

376. 唱对台戏 (唱對臺戲) chàng duì tái xì

Translated character by character, 唱对台戏 means 'sing-opposing-stage-drama,' whereas the implied meaning of this proverb would be 'to do what an opponent is doing with the intention of foiling their plans or distracting attention.' Its functional translation is 'to steal someone's thunder,' or 'to take the wind out of someone's sails.'

Example 1:

A: 老板，我们举办产品发布会的消息刚发布，我们的对手也发布消息说在同一天召开产品发布会。

B: 他们总是跟我们**唱对台戏**。

A: Lǎobǎn, wǒmen jǔbàn chǎnpǐn fābùhuì de xiāoxī gāng fābù, wǒmen de duìshǒu yě fābù xiāoxī shuō zài tóng yì tiān zhàokāi chǎnpǐn fābùhuì.

B: Tāmen zǒngshì gēn wǒmen chàng duìtáixì.

A: Boss, the news that we're hosting a product launch was just released. Our competitor also announced that they will be holding a product launch on the same day.

B: They're always trying to steal our thunder.

Example 2:

A: 那个国家专门跟美国**唱对台戏**，美国支持什么，那个国家就反对什么。

A: Nàgè guójiā zhuānmén gēn Měiguó **chàng duìtáixì**, Měiguó zhīchí shénme, nàgè guójiā jiù fǎnduì shénme.

A: That country is specifically trying to take the wind out of the sails of the US. Anything that the US supports, that country opposes.

Usage: Functions as predicate. It is usually used after '跟/和 somebody.'

Note: Slightly derogatory or neutral in meaning.

377.   分一杯羹 (分一杯羹) fēn yì bēi gēng

Translated character by character, 分一杯羹 means 'share-a-cup-bouillon,' whereas the implied meaning of this proverb would be 'to receive one's portion of a windfall.' Its functional translation is 'to take one's share of the loot.'

Example 1:

A: 他怎么突然变得这么积极？

B: 不是快见成果了吗？他也想**分一杯羹**。

A: Tā zěnme tūrán biàn de zhème jījí?

B: Búshì kuài jiàn chéngguǒ le ma? Tā yě xiǎng **fēn yì bēi gēng**.

A: Why has he suddenly become so proactive?

B: Isn't the result about to be known? He wants to take his share of the loot.

Example 2:

A: 中国政府放开某类商品市场，于是外国公司蜂拥而入，都希望**分**得**一杯羹**。

A: Zhōngguó zhèngfǔ fàng kāi mǒu lèi shāngpǐn shìchǎng, yúshì wàiguó gōngsī fēngyōng'érrù, dōu xīwàng **fēn dé yì bēi gēng**.

A: China's government opened some commodity markets. As a result, foreign companies flooded in, all of them wanting to take their share of the loot.

Usage: Functions as predicate or object of 希望, 想 etc.

Note: Slightly derogatory or neutral in meaning.

378. 变色龙 (變色龍) biàn sè lóng

Translated character by character, 变色龙 means 'change-color-lizard,' whereas the implied meaning of this proverb would be 'chameleon.'

Example 1:

A: 领导好像都挺喜欢他的。

B: 他是**变色龙**，只要领导变，他就变。

A: Lǐngdǎo hǎoxiàng dōu tǐng xǐhuān tā de.

B: Tā shì biànsèlóng, zhǐyào lǐngdǎo biàn, tā jiù biàn.

A: The boss seems to like him a lot.

B: He's a chameleon. When the boss changes his mind, so does he.

Example 2:

A: 在政治上他是**变色龙**，民众需要什么他就许诺什么。

A: Zài zhèngzhì shàng tā shì biànsèlóng, mínzhòng xūyào shénme tā jiù xǔnuò shénme.

A: He's a political chameleon. Whatever the people need, he promises it to them.

Usage: Nominal element, functions as predicative.

Note: Slightly derogatory in meaning.

379. 独木不成林 (獨木不成林) dú mù bù chéng lín

Translated character by character, 独树不成林 means 'single-tree-not-become-forest,' whereas the implied meaning of this proverb would be 'one person alone cannot accomplish much.' Its functional translation is 'a single tree does not a forest make.'

Example 1:

A: 你能不能自己干？

B: 我倒是想过，不过，**独木不成林**。在现在的单位，毕竟有几个关系不错的能照应一下。

A: Nǐ néngbùnéng zìjǐ gàn?

B: Wǒ dàoshì xiǎngguò, búguò, dú mù bù chéng lín. Zài xiànzài de dānwèi, bìjìng yǒu jǐ gè guānxì búcuò de néng zhàoyìng yíxià.

A: Can you do it yourself?

B: Although I did think about it, a single tree does not a forest make. After all, I'm pretty friendly with a number of people in my current work unit who can lend me a hand.

Example 2:

A: 他的想法怎么样？

B: 好是好，可是支持的人少，**独木不成林**，很难成功。

A: Tā de xiǎngfǎ zěnmeyàng?

B: Hǎo shì hǎo, kěshì zhīchí de rén shǎo, dú mù bù chéng lín, hěn nán chénggōng.

A: How is his idea?

B: It's good, but there aren't many people supporting it. A single tree does not a forest make. It'll be hard to succeed.

Usage: Used singly.

Note: Neutral in meaning.

---

380. 既生瑜，何生亮？ （既生瑜，何生亮？）
jì shēng Yú, hé shēng Liàng?

Translated character by character, 既生瑜，何生亮? means 'since-born-Zhou Yu, why-born-Zhuge Liang,' whereas the implied meaning of this proverb would be 'if god made someone so excellent, why did he make someone even better?'

Example 1:

A: 真可惜，希拉里·克林顿如果不是与奥巴马竞争，一定会成为一位出色的总统。

B: **既生瑜，何生亮**啊！

A: Zhēn kěxī, Xīlālǐ Kèlíndùn rúguǒ búshì yǔ Àobāmǎ jìngzhēng, yídìng huì chéngwéi yí wèi chūsè de zǒngtǒng.

B: Jì shēng Yú, hé shēng Liàng a!

A: It's a shame. If Hillary Clinton hadn't been competing with Obama, she definitely would have become a distinguished president.

B: If god made someone so excellent, why did he make someone even better?

Example 2:

A: 你们两个是天生的冤家，竞争了几十年，而他的运气常常比你好一点儿。

B: **既生瑜，何生亮**？老天对我如此不公。

A: Nǐmen liǎng gè shì tiānshēng de yuānjia, jìngzhēng le jǐ shí nián, ér tā de yùnqì chángcháng bǐ nǐ hǎo yìdiǎnr.

B: Jì shēng Yú, hé shēng Liàng? Lǎotiān duì wǒ rúcǐ bùgōng.

A: You two are born enemies. You've been competing for decades and his luck has often been a little better than yours.

B: If god made me so excellent, why did he make him even better? God is so unfair to me.

Usage: Used singly.

Note: Neutral in meaning.

---

381. 撂挑子 (撂挑子) liào tiāozi

Translated character by character, 撂挑子 means 'drop-shoulder pole,' whereas the implied meaning of this proverb would be 'to quit one's job,' or 'to shirk one's responsibilities.'

Example 1:

A: 我宁可失业，也不干这份苦差事了。

B: 你想**撂挑子**啦？别那么着急做决定。

A: Wǒ nìngkě shīyè, yě bú gàn zhè fèn kǔ chāishì le.

B: Nǐ xiǎng liàotiāozǐ la? Bié nàme zháojí zuò juédìng.

A: I'd rather be unemployed than do this drudgery.

B: You want to quit your job? Don't be in such a hurry to make a decision.

Example 2:

A: 这个老太太体弱多病，多亏小保姆精心照顾，要不然早就不行了。老太太知道这份工作非常辛苦，一般人没有耐心做，所以她对小保姆格外好，生怕小保姆**撂挑子**不干了。

A: Zhège lǎotàitai tǐruò-duōbìng, duōkuī xiǎo bǎomǔ jīngxīn zhàogù, yàobùrán zǎo jiù bùxíng le. Lǎotàitai zhīdào zhè fèn gōngzuò fēicháng xīnkǔ, yìbān rén méiyǒu nàixīn zuò, suǒyǐ tā duì xiǎo bǎomǔ géwài hǎo, shēng pà xiǎo bǎomǔ liàotiāozi bú gàn le.

A: This old lady is frail and sick. Without the painstaking care of her caretaker, she would have died long ago. The old lady knows this job is extremely taxing and the average person doesn't have the patience for it, so she is especially nice to her caretaker, lest she quit her job.

Usage: Functions as predicate.

Note: Slightly derogatory and humorous in meaning.

---

382. 敲门砖 (敲門磚) qiāo mén zhuān

Translated character by character, 敲门砖 means 'knock-door-brick,' whereas the implied meaning of this proverb would be 'something that one needs or uses as a tool to gain fortune and fame.' Its functional translation is 'a step on the path to,' or 'prerequisite for.'

Example 1:

A: 你儿子无论如何也得上一所藤校。

B: 为什么一定要上藤校？

A: 藤校是他毕业以后找工作的**敲门砖**。

A: Nǐ érzǐ wúlùnrúhé yě děi shàng yì suǒ Téngxiào.
B: Wèishénme yídìng yào shàng Téngxiào?
A: Téngxiào shì tā bìyè yǐhòu zhǎo gōngzuò de qiāoménzhuān.

A: In any case, your son needs to attend an Ivy League school.
B: Why does he need to go to an Ivy?
A: An Ivy is a step on the path to his finding a job after he graduates.

Example 2:

A: 那个俱乐部的成员好像都很有钱。

B: 一亿美元财产和会说法语是那家俱乐部的**敲门砖**。

A: Nàgè jùlèbù de chéngyuán hǎoxiàng dōu hěn yǒu qián.
B: Yī yì měiyuán cáichǎn hé huì shuō Fǎyǔ shì nà jiā jùlèbù de qiāoménzhuān.

A: It seems all of the members in that club are rich.
B: Having $100 million and speaking French are the prerequisites for entry into that club.

Usage: Functions as predicative or predicate.

Note: Neutral or humorous in meaning.

383. 试金石 (試金石) shì jīn shí

Translated character by character, 试金石 means 'test-gold-stone,' whereas the implied meaning of this proverb would be 'a standard or criterion by which something is judged.' Its functional translation is 'touchstone.'

Example 1:

A: 他们两个人结婚三个月就离婚了。

B: 时间是婚姻的**试金石**，看来他们真的不合适。

A: Tāmen liǎng gè rén jiéhūn sān gè yuè jiù líhūn le.
B: Shíjiān shì hūnyīn de shìjīnshí, kànlái tāmen zhēnde bù héshì.

A: The two of them were only married for three months when they divorced.
B: Time is the touchstone by which marriage is tested. I guess they really aren't suitable for each other.

Example 2:

A: 市场是企业产品的**试金石**。

A: Shìchǎng shì qǐyè chǎnpǐn de shìjīnshí.

A: The market is the touchstone by which products are assessed.

Usage: Functions as predicative.

Note: Neutral in meaning.

384. 火烧眉毛 (火燒眉毛) huǒ shāo méi máo

Translated character by character, 火烧眉毛 means 'fire-burn-eyebrow,' whereas the implied meaning of this proverb would be 'to be in an urgent situation.' Its functional translation is 'the chips are down,' or 'pressing.'

Example 1:

A: 好，这样吧，我先考虑考虑，明天回复你。
B: 还考虑什么啊！都**火烧眉毛**了，赶快行动吧！

A: Hǎo, zhèyàng ba, wǒ xiān kǎolǜ kǎolǜ, míngtiān huífù nǐ.
B: Hái kǎolǜ shénme a! Dōu huǒ shāo méimáo le, gǎnkuài xíngdòng ba!

A: OK. Why don't we do this? I'll think about it and get back to you tomorrow.
B: What's left to consider? The chips are down, you need to act soon!

Example 2:

A: 王总，您真沉得住气，**火烧眉毛**的事一大堆，您还能安心地钓鱼啊？
B: 你不知道，其实我正在想办法。

A: Wáng zǒng, nín zhēn chéndezhù qì, huǒ shāo méimáo de shì yí dà duī, nín hái néng ānxīn de diàoyú a?
B: Nǐ bù zhī dào, qí shí wǒ zhèng zài xiǎng bànfǎ.

A: Mr. Wang, you really can handle pressure. There are loads of pressing issues and you can still fish calmly?
B: You don't know it, but I'm thinking of solutions right now.

Usage: Functions as predicate or attributive.

Variant: 火烧眉毛到眼前

Note: Neutral or humorous in meaning.

385. 空手套白狼 (空手套白狼) kōng shǒu tào bái láng

Translated character by character, 空手套白狼 means 'empty-hands-catch-white-wolf,' whereas the implied meaning of this proverb would be 'to gain something without risking anything of one's own.'

Example 1:

A: 她一点儿都不想付出啊？

B: 光想着**空手套白狼**了。天下哪儿有那么多好事？

A: Tā yìdiǎnr dōu bù xiǎng fùchū a?

B: Guāng xiǎngzhe kōngshǒu tào báiláng le. Tiānxià nǎr yǒu nàme duō hǎoshì?

A: She doesn't want to put up anything?

B: She only wants to gain something without risking anything of her own. Where on earth are there so many good opportunities?

Example 2:

A: 有人认为咨询公司没有什么实物资产，做生意就是**空手套白狼**。

A: Yǒurén rènwéi zīxún gōngsī méiyǒu shénme shíwù zīchǎn, zuò shēngyì jiùshì kōngshǒu tào báiláng.

A: Some people think consulting companies don't have any real assets and their business is gaining something without risking anything of their own.

Usage: Functions mainly as predicate.

Note: Slightly derogatory or neutral in meaning.

386. 一瓶子不满，半瓶子晃荡 (一瓶子不滿，半瓶子晃蕩) yì píngzi bù mǎn, bàn píngzi huàngdang

Translated character by character, 一瓶子不满，半瓶子晃荡 means 'one-bottle-not-full, half-bottle-slosh,' whereas the implied meaning of this proverb would be 'those who know don't speak, those who speak don't know.' Its functional translation is 'empty barrels make the most noise.'

Example 1:

A: 他刚学了几句法语，就在大家面前炫耀。

B: **一瓶子不满，半瓶子晃荡**，其实只懂三五句。

A: Tā gāng xuéle jǐ jù Fǎyǔ, jiù zài dàjiā miànqián xuànyào.

B: Yì píngzi bù mǎn, bàn píngzi huàngdang, qíshí zhǐ dǒng sān-wǔ jù.

A: He's only learned a little French and he's showing off in front of everyone.
B: Empty barrels make the most noise. He really only knows a few phrases.

Example 2:

A: 她总是觉得自己高人一头，比别人有见识。
B: **一瓶子不满，半瓶子晃荡**，这样的人肤浅得很。

A: Tā zǒngshi juéde zìjǐ gāorén-yìtóu, bǐ biéren yǒu jiànshi.
B: Yī píngzi bù mǎn, bàn píngzi huàngdang, zhèyàng de rén fūqiǎn de hěn.

A: She always thinks she's head and shoulders above the rest, that she's more experienced than others.
B: Empty barrels make the most noise. Those kinds of people are very shallow.

Usage: Used singly.

Variants: 一瓶(子)不满半瓶晃; 一瓶不响, 半瓶晃荡

Note: Slightly derogatory and humorous in meaning.

---

387. 脱了裤子放屁 (脱了褲子放屁) tuō le kùzi fàng pì

Translated character by character, 脱了裤子放屁 means 'take off-ed-pants-fart,' whereas the implied meaning of this proverb would be 'to be excessive and unnecessary.' Its functional translation is 'as useless as tits on a bull.'

Example 1:

A: 我要买辆中档的日本车，但是还差三千美元呢。你能不能借给我两、三千块？
B: 买日本车干什么？德国车多好。
A: 你这不是**脱了裤子放屁**嘛？日本车我还买不起呢，更不用说德国车了。

A: Wǒ yào mǎi liàng zhōngdàng de Rìběn chē, dànshì hái chà sānqiān měiyuán ne. Nǐ néngbùnéng jiègěi wǒ liǎng, sān qiān kuài?
B: Mǎi Rìběn chē gàn shénme? Déguó chē duō hǎo.
A: Nǐ zhè búshì tuōle kùzi fàngpì ma? Rìběn chē wǒ hái mǎi bù qǐ ne, gèng búyòng shuō Déguó chē le.

A: I want to buy a mid-range Japanese car, but I'm still three thousand dollars short. Can you lend me two or three thousand bucks?
B: What're you doing buying a Japanese car? German cars are great.
A: That comment is as useless as tits on a bull. I can't even afford a Japanese car, to say nothing of a German car.

Example 2:

A: 快春节了，报纸上又说了，"领导干部在节日期间不能收受红包或礼物"。

B: 简直是**脱了裤子放屁**！分明是在提醒老百姓应该给领导送礼。

A: Kuài chūnjié le, bàozhǐ shàng yòu shuō le, "lǐngdǎo gànbù zài jiérì qījiān bùnéng shōushòu hóngbāo huò lǐwù".

B: Jiǎnzhí shì tuōle kùzi fàngpì! Fēnmíng shì zài tíxǐng lǎobǎixìng yīnggāi gěi lǐngdǎo sònglǐ.

A: It's almost Lunar New Year. In the newspaper it said, "Leaders and cadres cannot accept holiday money or gifts during the holidays."

B: That's as useless as tits on a bull! Clearly they're just reminding people that they should give gifts to officials.

Usage: Functions as predicative.

Note: Derogatory in meaning.

---

388.   借东风 (借東風) jiè dōng fēng

Translated character by character, 借东风 means 'borrow-east-wind,' whereas the implied meaning of this proverb would be 'to turn a trend or situation to one's advantage,' or 'to learn from someone else's experience.' Its functional translation is 'to ride the wave.'

Example 1:

A: 这是千载难逢的好机会，我们要**借**政策的**东风**，把我们的事业推上一个台阶。

A: Zhè shì qiānzǎi-nánféng de hǎo jīhuì, wǒmen yào jiè zhèngcè de dōngfēng, bǎ wǒmen de shìyè tuī shàng yígè táijiē.

A: This is a once in a lifetime opportunity. We need to ride the wave of this policy and take our careers to the next level.

Example 2:

A: 今年全国的失业率平均百分之八，我们省的是百分之十，但是邻省的只有百分之五。

B: 我们得到邻省**借东风**，好好看看人家是怎么搞的。

A: Jīnnián quánguó de shīyèlǜ píngjūn bǎi fēn zhī bā, wǒmen shěng de shì bǎifēnzhī shí, dànshì lín shěng de zhǐyǒu bǎifēnzhī wǔ.

B: Wǒmen děi dào lín shěng jièdōngfēng, hǎohāo kànkàn rénjia shì zěnme gǎo de.

A: The national unemployment rate is 8 percent and our state's unemployment
    rate is 10 percent, but the neighboring state's is only 4 percent.
B: We need to go there to learn from their experience and see how they do it.

Usage: Functions as predicate.

Note: Neutral in meaning.

389. 白开水 (白開水) bái kāi shuǐ

Translated character by character, 白开水 means 'plain-boiled-water,' whereas the
implied meaning of this proverb would be 'very boring.' Its functional translation
is 'vanilla.'

Example 1:

A: 你的老板怎么样？
B: 只知道工作，别的都不感兴趣，跟一杯**白开水**似的。

A: Nǐde lǎobǎn zěnmeyàng?
B: Zhǐ zhīdào gōngzuò, biéde dōu bù gǎn xìngqù, gēn yì bēi báikāishuǐ shìde.

A: What is your boss like?
B: All he knows is work; he's not interested in anything else. He's very vanilla.

Example 2:

A: 生活太无聊了。
B: 是啊，就像**白开水**。不行，我才三十岁，得找些刺激的事做。

A: Shēnghuó tài wúliáo le.
B: Shì a, jiù xiàng báikāishuǐ. Bùxíng, wǒ cái sānshí suì, děi zhǎo xiē cìjī de shì zuò.

A: Life is so boring.
B: Yeah, it's very vanilla. I need to do something about that. I'm only 30, I need
    to find some exciting things to do.

Usage: Functions as predicative.

Note: Slightly derogatory in meaning.

390. 鲤鱼跳龙门 (鯉魚跳龍門) lǐ yú tiào lóng mén

Translated character by character, 鲤鱼跳龙门 means 'carp-jump-dragon-gate,'
whereas the implied meaning of this proverb would be 'to advance to a point at
which one's success is guaranteed.' Its functional translation is 'to get one's big
break.'

Example 1:

A: 他用了二十年心血，终于进入了这个委员会。

B: **鲤鱼跳龙门**了，以后可以大有作为了。

A: Tā yòngle èrshí nián xīnxuè, zhōngyú jìnrùle zhègè wěiyuánhuì.

B: Lǐyú tiào Lóngmén le, yǐhòu kěyǐ dàyǒuzuòwéi le.

A: With twenty years of blood and toil, he finally got onto this committee.

B: He's gotten his big break. Now he can do great things.

Example 2:

A: 如果一位不知名的作家的小说能被《纽约时报》推荐，那就像**鲤鱼跃**过了**龙门**，作家的名气一下子就大了。

A: Rúguǒ yí wèi bù zhīmíng de zuòjiā de xiǎoshuō néng bèi "Niǔyuē Shíbào" tuījiàn, nà jiù xiàng lǐyú yuè guò le Lóngmén, zuòjiā de míngqì yíxiàzi jiù dà le.

A: If an unknown author's novel is recommended by the *New York Times*, it's a big break. The author will immediately become famous.

Usage: Functions as predicate.

Variant: 鲤鱼跃龙门

Note: Neutral or humorous in meaning. Legend has it that if a carp can jump over a gate called 'Dragon Gate' in a stretch of the Yellow River located in Shanxi Province, it will become a dragon.

---

391. 强龙压不住地头蛇 (強龍壓不住地頭蛇)
qiáng lóng yā bú zhù dìtóushé

Translated character by character, 强龙压不住地头蛇 means 'powerful-dragon-suppress-not-able-local-snake,' whereas the implied meaning of this proverb would be 'even a powerful outsider cannot crush a local bully.' Its functional translation is 'you can't beat someone on their home turf.'

Example 1:

A: 那么大牌的歌星到一个小县城去开演唱会，结果演砸了。听说是让几个小混混搞的。

B: **强龙压不住地头蛇**，对这些地头蛇，谁也没办法。

A: Nàme dàpái de gēxīng dào yígè xiǎo xiànchéng qù kāi yǎnchànghuì, jiéguǒ yǎn zá le. Tīngshuō shì ràng jǐ gè xiǎohùnhun gǎo de.

B: Qiáng lóng yā bú zhù dìtóushé, duì zhèxiē dìtóushé, shéi yě méi bànfa.

A: That huge pop star went to a small county seat to give a concert and it was a failure. I heard it was the doing of a few punks.

B: You can't beat someone on their home turf. No one can handle them.

Example 2:

A: 总统侯选人竞选的时候到了某地都要事先打听当地的头面人物有谁。

B: 是啊，**强龙不压地头蛇**，在地方办事还需要他们。

A: Zǒngtǒng hòuxuǎnrén jìngxuǎn de shíhou dàole mǒu dì dōu yào shìxiān dǎting dāngdì de tóumiàn rénwù shì shéi.

B: Shì a, qiáng lóng yā bú zhù dìtóushé, zài dàngdì bànshì hái xūyào tāmen.

A: When running for president, upon arriving in a particular location, the candidate must first inquire as to who the most important people are.

B: Yeah, you can't beat someone on their home turf. In order to do things in their area, you need them.

Usage: Used singly.

Variants: 强龙斗不过地头蛇; 强龙难压地头蛇

Note: Neutral in meaning.

392. 这山望着那山高 (這山望著那山高)
zhè shān wàng zhe nà shān gāo

Translated character by character, 这山望着那山高 means 'this-mountain-look-ing-that-mountain-tall,' whereas the implied meaning of this proverb would be 'the other mountain always looks higher.' Its functional translation is 'the grass is always greener on the other side.'

Example 1:

A: 有的人总想换工作。

B: **这山望着那山高**，总会有更好的工作，永远换不完。

A: Yǒude rén zǒng xiǎng huàn gōngzuò.

B: Zhè shān wàngzhe nà shān gāo, zòng huì yǒu gèng hǎo de gōngzuò, yǒngyuǎn huàn bù wán.

A: Some people are always itching to change jobs.

B: The grass is always greener on the other side. There will always be a better job. They will never stop moving.

Example 2:

A: 他从中国到了美国，现在又想去欧洲。

B: 是啊，**这山望着那山高**，不过，欧洲的确比美国好。

A: Tā cóng Zhōngguó dàole Měiguó, xiànzài yòu xiǎngqù Ōuzhōu.

B: Shì a, zhè shān wàngzhe nà shān gāo, búguò, Ōuzhōu díquè bǐ Měiguó hǎo.

A: He came to the US from China; now he wants to go to Europe.

B: Yes, the grass is always greener on the other side, but Europe actually is better than the US.

Usage: Used singly.

Note: Slightly derogatory in meaning.

393. 光脚的不怕穿鞋的 (光腳的不怕穿鞋的)
guāng jiǎo de bú pà chuān xié de

Translated character by character, 光脚的不怕穿鞋的 means 'bare-foot-*de* (people)-not-fear-wear-shoes-*de* (people),' whereas the implied meaning of this proverb would be 'those with nothing do not fear those with power.' Its functional translation is 'he who is down need fear no fall.'

Example 1:

A: 你一个普通老百姓，敢抗拒政府拆迁的命令，不怕有人收拾你吗？

B: **光脚的不怕穿鞋的**，他们还能把我怎么样？大不了坐几年监狱。

A: Nǐ yígè pǔtōng lǎobǎixìng, gǎn kàngjù zhèngfǔ chāiqiān de mìnglìng, bú pà yǒurén shōushi nǐ ma?

B: Guāngjiǎo de bú pà chuānxié de, tāmen hái néng bǎ wǒ zěnmeyàng? Dàbùliǎo zuò jǐ nián jiānyù.

A: You're an average person, how do you dare resist the government's demolition order? Aren't you worried someone is going to rough you up?

B: He who is down need fear no fall. What else can they do to me? Nothing worse than a few years in jail.

Example 2:

A: 这场球赛有啥看头？中国男足的实力与巴西队是天上地下啊！

B: 别这么说，**光脚的不怕穿鞋的**，中国男足如果像爷们儿一样去踢，不一定输得太难看。

A: Zhè cháng qiúsài yǒu shá kàntou? Zhōngguó nánzú de shílì yǔ Bāxīduì shì tiānshang-dìxia a!

B: Bié zhème shuō, guāngjiǎo de bú pà chuānxié de, Zhōngguó nánzú rúguǒ xiàng yémenr yíyàng qù tī, bùyídìng shū de tài nánkàn.

A: What's worth watching about this match? China's men's soccer team is nowhere near as strong as Brazil's.

B: Don't say that. He who is down need fear no fall. If our team plays like men, we won't necessarily lose that badly.

Usage: Used singly.

Note: Humorous in meaning.

394. 不成功，便成仁 (不成功，便成仁)
bù chénggōng, biàn chéng rén

Translated character by character, 不成功，便成仁 means 'not-became-successful, then-die for-justice,' whereas the implied meaning of this proverb would be 'I'll stake something on it,' or 'to win or die trying.'

Example 1:

A: 老板，把这件事交给我办吧？

B: 这件事难度不小，而且一旦失败，影响很大。

A: 您放心，我**不成功，便成仁**。如果失败，我主动辞职。

A: Lǎobǎn, bǎ zhèjiàn shì jiāogěi wǒ bàn ba?

B: Zhèjiàn shì nándù bùxiǎo, érqiě yídàn shībài, yǐngxiǎng hěn dà.

A: Nín fàngxīn, wǒ bù chénggōng, biàn chéng rén. Rúguǒ shībài, wǒ zhǔdòng cízhí.

A: Boss, you're giving me that issue to deal with, right?

B: This is a difficult issue. If you happen to fail, the repercussions will be very large.

A: Relax, I'll stake my career on it. If I fail, I'll proffer my resignation.

Example 2:

A: 我看他孤注一掷了，把希望都寄托在女性选民身上了。

B: 是啊，这次**不成功就**得**成仁**了，因为他把大部分男性选民都惹了。

A: Wǒ kàn tā gūzhù-yízhì le, bǎ xīwàng dōu jìtuō zài nǚxìng xuǎnmín shēnshàng le.

B: Shì a, zhècì bù chénggōng jiù děi chéng rén le, yīnwèi tā bǎ dàbùfen nánxìng xuǎnmín dōu rě le.

A: I think he's putting all of his eggs in one basket, putting all of his hopes on female voters.

B: Yeah. This time, he'll win or die trying, because he offended a lot of male voters.

Usage: Functions as predicate.

Variant: 不成功, 则成仁

Note: Neutral in meaning.

395. 滚刀肉 (滚刀肉) *gǔn dāo ròu*

Translated character by character, 滚刀肉 means 'rolling-knife-meat,' whereas the implied meaning of this proverb would be 'a person who is annoying and difficult to deal with.' Its functional translation is 'a real piece of work.'

Example 1:

A: 无论她说什么你都别跟她吵。
B: 为什么？
A: 她是个**滚刀肉**。

A: Wúlùn tā shuō shénme nǐ dōu bié gēn tā chǎo.
B: Wèishénme?
A: Tā shì gè gǔndāoròu.

A: No matter what she says, don't argue with her.
B: Why?
A: She's a real piece of work.

Example 2:

A: 他从小就是个**滚刀肉**，没有人敢惹他。

A: Tā cóngxiǎo jiù shì gè gǔndāoròu, méiyǒu rén gǎn rě tā.

A: Ever since he was young, he's been a real piece of work. No one dares rile him up.

Usage: Nominal element, functions as predicative.

Note: Slightly derogatory and humorous in meaning.

396. 久病成良医 (久病成良醫) *jiǔ bìng chéng liáng yī*

Translated character by character, 久病成良医 means 'prolonged-illness-make-good-doctor,' whereas the implied meaning of this proverb would be 'prolonged illness makes the patient a good doctor.'

Example 1:

A: 你真厉害，连汽车都会修！
B: 哪儿啊！我那辆老爷车整天坏，去修车铺都修不起，只好自己鼓捣，现在**久病成良医**了。

A: Nǐ zhēn lìhai, lián qìchē dōu huì xiū!
B: Nǎr a! Wǒ nà liàng lǎoyechē zhěngtiān huài, qù xiūchēpù dōu xiū bùqǐ, zhǐhǎo zìjǐ gǔdao, xiànzài jiǔ bìng chéng liángyī le.

A: You're awesome. You can even fix cars!

B: It's nothing! That old car of mine is always broken, and I can't afford to have it fixed at the shop, so I tinker with it myself. Now, prolonged illness has made the patient a good doctor.

Example 2:

A: 这种水果伤胃，不能跟糖一起吃。

B: 你怎么知道这么多养生知识？

A: 我从小体弱多病，**久病成良医**，算是半个医生吧。

A: Zhèzhǒng shuǐguǒ shāng wèi, bùnéng gēn táng yìqǐ chī.

B: Nǐ zěnme zhīdào zhème duō yǎngshēng zhīshi?

A: Wǒ cóngxiǎo tǐruò-duōbìng, jiǔ bìng chéng liángyī, suànshì bàngè yīshēng ba.

A: This kind of fruit can harm your stomach. You can't eat it with sugar.

B: How do you know so much about staying healthy?

A: I've had a fragile constitution since I was little. Prolonged illness makes a good doctor. I guess I'm practically a doctor now.

Usage: Functions as predicate or used singly.

Note: Neutral or humorous in meaning.

---

397. 枕边风 (枕邊風) zhěn biān fēng

Translated character by character, 枕边风 means 'pillow-side-wind,' whereas the implied meaning of this proverb would be 'the conversation that a couple has in bed before going to sleep.' Its functional translation would be 'pillow talk.'

Example 1:

A: 他昨天还说要那样做来着，今天怎么就变了？

B: 肯定是他老婆吹**枕边风**了。

A: Tā zuótiān hái shuō yào nàyàng zuò láizhe, jīntiān zěnme jiù biàn le?

B: Kěndìng shì tā lǎopo chuī zhěnbiānfēng le.

A: He said yesterday that he wanted to do it that way. How has he changed his mind today?

B: It's definitely his wife's pillow talk.

Example 2:

A: 我们怎么才能改变他的决定呢？

B: 你这样吧，先试着找他老婆谈谈。如果他老婆愿意帮忙，吹吹**枕边风**，他可能就会改变决定了。

A: Wǒmen zěnme cáinéng gǎibiàn tā de juédìng ne?

B: Nǐ zhèyàng ba, xiān shìzhe zhǎo tā lǎopo tántán. Rúguǒ tā lǎopo yuànyì bāngmáng, chuīchuī zhěnbiānfēng, tā kěnéng jiù huì gǎibiàn juédìng le.

A: How can we change his decision?

B: This is what you need to do: first, try to find his wife and talk to her. If his wife is willing to help and work it into her pillow talk, he might just change his decision.

Usage: Functions mainly as object of '吹.'

Note: Slightly derogatory and humorous in meaning.

---

398. 一锤子买卖 (一錘子買賣) yì chuízi mǎimai

Translated character by character, 一锤子买卖 means 'a-hammer-business,' whereas the implied meaning of this proverb would be 'a one-time deal.' Its functional translation is 'to skin the sheep.'

Example 1:

A: 他们公司产品的服务靠得住吗？

B: 根本靠不住。他们公司干的都是**一锤子买卖**，赚钱以后就跑了。

A: Tāmen gōngsī chǎnpǐn de fúwù kào de zhù ma?

B: Gēnběn kào bú zhù. Tāmen gōngsī gàn de dōu shì yì chuízi mǎimai, zuàn qián yǐhòu jiù pǎo le.

A: Is their company's customer service reliable?

B: It really isn't. Their company is of the 'skin the sheep' mindset. Once they've gotten their money, they disappear.

Example 2:

A: 我们给合作方的利润太高了。

B: 是很高，但是我们的目的是长期合作，所以不搞**一锤子买卖**。

A: Wǒmen gěi hézuòfāng de lìrùn tài gāo le.

B: Shì hěn gāo, dànshì wǒmen de mùdì shì chángqī hézuò, suǒyǐ bù gǎo yì chuízi mǎimai.

A: We give too much profit to our collaborators.

B: It is a lot, but our goal is long-term cooperation, so we don't skin the sheep.

Usage: Functions as object of verbs like '是,' '搞,' or '做.'

Note: Neutral or humorous in meaning.

399. 横挑鼻子竖挑眼 (橫挑鼻子豎挑眼)
héng tiāo bízi shù tiāo yǎn

Translated character by character, 横挑鼻子竖挑眼 means 'this way-criticize-nose-that way-criticize-eyes,' whereas the implied meaning of this proverb would be 'to pick out small flaws.' Its functional translation is 'to do one's utmost to find problems where there are none.'

Example 1:

A: 他跟我过不去，总是**横挑鼻子竖挑眼**。

A: Tā gēn wǒ guòbúqù, zǒngshì héng tiāo bízi shù tiāo yǎn.

A: He's out to get me. He's always finding problems where there are none.

Example 2:

A: 你们俩关系好像有点儿紧张。

B: 说白了吧，他忌妒我，所以就借着手里的权力对我的工作**横挑鼻子竖挑眼**。

A: Nǐmen liǎ guānxì hǎoxiàng yǒudiǎnr jǐnzhāng.

B: Shuōbáile ba, tā jìdù wǒ, suǒyǐ jiù jièzhe shǒulǐ de quánlì duì wǒde gōngzuò héng tiāo bízi shù tiāo yǎn.

A: It seems that the relationship between you two is a little tense.

B: To speak candidly, he's jealous of me, so he uses the power he has in his hands to find problems in my work where there are none.

Usage: Functions as predicate.

Note: Slightly derogatory in meaning.

400. 唱空城计 (唱空城計) chàng kōng chéng jì

Translated character by character, 唱空城计 means 'play-empty-city-stratagem,' whereas the implied meaning of this proverb would be 'to act confident and bold in order to conceal weakness,' or 'to not be at home.' Its functional translation is 'to bluff,' or 'to not be at home.'

Example 1:

A: 找到他没有？

B: 这小子跟我**唱空城计**，连家都不回。

A: Zhǎo dào tā méi yǒu?

B: Zhè xiǎozi gēn wǒ chàng kōngchéngjì, lián jiā dōu bù huí.

A: Did you find him?
B: That kid's avoiding me. He doesn't even go home.

Example 2:

A: 他说他要买瑞士银行的股票。

B: **唱空城计**呢吧？是不是想卖啊？

A: Tā shuō tā yào mǎi Ruìshì Yínháng de gǔpiào.
B: Chàng kōngchéngjì ne ba? Shìbúshì xiǎng mài a?

A: He said he wants to buy UBS stock.
B: He's bluffing, right? Doesn't he want to sell?

Usage: Functions as predicate.

Note: Neutral or humorous in meaning.

401. 一刀切 (一刀切) yì dāo qiē

Translated character by character, 一刀切 means 'one-knife-cut,' whereas the implied meaning of this proverb would be 'to make hard and fast rules.' Its functional translation is 'cookie-cutter,' or 'use cookie-cutter methods.'

Example 1:

A: 在处理问题的时候不能搞一**刀切**，要具体事情具体分析。

A: Zài chǔlǐ wèntí de shíhou bùnéng gǎo yìdāoqiē, yào jùtǐ shìqing jùtǐ fēnxi.

A: When fixing problems, you can't use cookie-cutter methods. You need to tailor your response.

Example 2:

A: 在小学课本的编写上，要充分考虑到各地的文化差异，防止一**刀切**，全国只有一套课本。

A: Zài xiǎoxué kèběn de biānxiě shang, yào chōngfèn kǎolǜ dào gèdì de wénhuà chāyì, fángzhǐ yìdāoqiē, quánguó zhǐyǒu yí tào kèběn.

A: In writing an elementary school textbook, one needs to fully consider the cultural differences of different regions in order to prevent the whole country from having just one, cookie-cutter textbook.

Usage: Functions mainly as predicate, usually after '搞' or '防止.'

Note: Neutral in meaning.

402. 旧瓶装新酒 (舊瓶裝新酒) jiù píng zhuāng xīn jiǔ

Translated character by character, 旧瓶装新酒 means 'old-bottle-hold-new-wine,' whereas the implied meaning of this proverb would be 'new content in an old form.'

Example 1:

A: 社会上的很多流行语实际上套用的是以前的固定语的格式，**旧瓶装新酒**，只是内容新而已。

A: Shèhuì shàng de hěnduō liúxíngyǔ shíjìshang tàoyòng de shì yǐqián de gùdìngyǔ de géshì, jiù píng zhuāng xīn jiǔ, zhǐshì nèiróng xīn éryǐ.

A: A lot of society's popular sayings actually borrow the constructions of existing expressions. It's new content in an old form. The only thing that's new is the content.

Example 2:

A. 这是一个当代梁祝的故事，导演极力想**旧瓶装新酒**，给这个故事新的内涵。

A: Zhè shì yígè dāngdài Liángzhù de gùshi, dǎoyǎn jílì xiǎng jiù píng zhuāng xīn jiǔ, gěi zhègè gùshì xīn de nèihán.

A: This is a modern day Romeo and Juliet story. The director badly wants to put new content into an old form and give the story a new connotation.

Usage: Functions as predicate or used singly.

Note: Neutral in meaning.

403. 两面三刀 (兩面三刀) liǎng miàn sān dāo

Translated character by character, 两面三刀 means 'two-faces-three-blades,' whereas the implied meaning of this proverb would be 'deceitful and insincere.' Its functional translation is 'two-faced,' or 'double-dealing.'

Example 1:

A: 他是我的朋友，会帮我的。

B: 他也是你的对手的朋友，也会帮他的。这个人**两面三刀**的，不可靠。

A: Tā shì wǒde péngyǒu, huì bāng wǒde.

B: Tā yě shì nǐde duìshǒu de péngyǒu, yě huì bāng tā de. Zhègè rén liǎngmiàn-sāndāo de, bù kěkào.

A: He's my friend. He'll help me.

B: He's also your competitor's friend and will help him. He's a double-dealer. He can't be relied upon.

Example 2:

A: 她是一个**两面**三刀的女人，对她要留一个心眼儿。

A: Tā shì yígè liǎngmiàn-sāndāo de nǚrén, duì tā yào liú yígè xīnyǎnr.

A: She's a two-faced woman. You have to keep an eye on her.

Usage: Functions as attributive or predicate.

Note: Derogatory in meaning.

404. 一把钥匙开一把锁 (一把鑰匙開一把鎖)
yì bǎ yàoshi kāi yì bǎ suǒ

Translated character by character, 一把钥匙开一把锁 means 'one-MW-key-open-one-MW-lock,' whereas the implied meaning of this proverb would be 'there is a discrete answer to every problem.' Its functional translation is 'there is a key for every lock.'

Example 1:

A: 她怎么那么不开心？你去劝劝她。

B: 你把她惹得那么不高兴，**一把钥匙开一把锁**，还是你自己去劝吧？

A: Tā zěnme nàme bù kāixīn? nǐ qù quànquàn tā.

B: Nǐ bǎ tā rě de nàme bù gāoxìng, yì bǎ yàoshi kāi yì bǎ suǒ, háishì nǐ zìjǐ qù quàn ba?

A: How is she so unhappy? You should go comfort her.

B: You're the one who made her so unhappy. There is a key for every lock; maybe you should go comfort her yourself.

Example 2:

A: 每个国家都有自己的难处，没有一种解决办法能够包打天下。**一把钥匙开一把锁**，适合这个国家的办法在别的国家就很可能行不通。

A: Měi gè guójiā dōu yǒu zìjǐ de nánchù, méiyǒu yìzhǒng jiějué bànfǎ nénggòu bāodǎ-tiānxià. Yì bǎ yàoshi kāi yì bǎ suǒ, shìhé zhègè guójiā de bànfǎ zài biéde guójiā jiù hěn kěnéng xíng bù tōng.

A: Every country has its own difficulties and there is no all-encompassing solution. There is a key for every lock and a fitting solution for this country might very well not work in another country

Usage: Used singly.

Note: Neutral in meaning.

405. 打一巴掌，给个甜枣 (打一巴掌，給個甜棗)
dǎ yì bāzhang, gěi gè tián zǎo

Translated character by character, 打一巴掌，给个甜枣 means 'give-one-slap, give-a-sweet-date,' whereas the implied meaning of this proverb would be 'to severely punish someone and give them something good afterwards to keep their spirits up.' Its functional translation is 'to throw someone a bone,' or 'to use the carrot and stick approach.'

Example 1:

A: 在这次换届中，他没能如愿从副系主任升为系主任，真够委屈的。

B: 也不尽然，上头**打一巴掌，给个甜枣**，虽说没让他升为系主任，但是职称从副教授升为正教授了。

A: Zài zhècì huànjiè zhōng, tā méi néng rúyuàn cóng fù xìzhǔrèn shēng wéi xìzhǔrèn, zhēn gòu wěiqū de.

B: Yě bú jìnrán, shàngtou dǎ yì bāzhang, gěi gè tián zǎo, suīshuō méi ràng tā shēngwéi xìzhǔrèn, dànshì zhíchēng cóng fùjiàoshòu shēngwéi zhèngjiàoshòu le.

A: In this transition, he wasn't promoted from associate department chair to department chair as he'd hoped. It's so wrong.

B: Not necessarily. His superior threw him a bone. While they didn't allow him to become a department chair, his title was elevated from associate professor to full professor.

Example 2:

A: 一个男生手捧一束鲜花去请一个女生吃饭，可是女生断然拒绝。为了使男生免于过分尴尬，女生**打一巴掌**后**给个甜枣**，说以后有好电影可以考虑一起去看。

A: Yígè nánshēng shǒupěng yí shù xiānhuā qù qǐng yígè nǚshēng chīfàn, kěshì nǚshēng duànrán jùjué. Wèile shǐ nánshēng miǎnyú guòfèn gāngà, nǚshēng dǎ yì bāzhang hòu gěi gè tián zǎo, shuō yǐhòu yǒu hǎo diànyǐng kěyǐ kǎolǜ yìqǐ qù kàn.

A: A man asked a woman out with a bunch of flowers in his hand, but the woman flatly refused him. In order to avoid making the man feel too awkward, the woman threw him a bone, saying that if there were a good movie later, she would consider seeing it with him.

Usage: Functions as predicate.

Note: Slightly derogatory and humorous in meaning.

406. 先君子后小人 (先君子後小人) xiān jūnzǐ hòu xiǎorén

Translated character by character, 先君子后小人 means 'first-gentleman-after-mean-person,' whereas the implied meaning of this proverb would be 'to prefer peaceful negotiation but resort to force if reason cannot be found.' Its functional translation is 'let's not let this get ugly.'

Example 1:

A: 就这样定了，咱们**先君子后小人**，如果违约，虽然咱们是好朋友，也得法庭上见了。

B: 你放心吧。我对不起谁也不能对不起你啊！

A: Jiù zhèyàng dìng le, zánmen xiān jūnzǐ hòu xiǎorén, rúguǒ wéiyuē, suīrán zánmen shì hǎo péngyǒu, yě děi fǎtíng shàng jiàn le.

B: Nǐ fàngxīn ba. wǒ duìbùqǐ shuí yě bùnéng duìbùqǐ nǐ a!

A: Let's settle it this way. Let's not let this get ugly. If you break the contract, even though we are good friends, I'll have to see you in court.

B: Relax, I could wrong others but I would never wrong you!

Example 2:

A: 他为人圆滑，在自己的利益上寸步不让，凡事都**先君子后小人**，滴水不漏。

A: Tā wéirén yuánhuá, zài zìjǐ de lìyì shàng cùn bù bú ràng, fánshì dōu xiān jūnzǐ hòu xiǎorén, dī shuǐ bú lòu.

A: He's shrewd. He refuses to budge an inch when it comes to his interests and he always makes the terms watertight before he strikes a deal.

Usage: Functions as predicate.

Note: Neutral in meaning.

407. 尺有所短，寸有所长 (尺有所短，寸有所長)
chǐ yǒu suǒ duǎn, cùn yǒu suǒ cháng

Translated character by character, 尺有所短，寸有所长 means 'foot-have-its-shortness, inch-have-its-length,' whereas the implied meaning of this proverb would be 'no one is perfect, but no one is worthless either.'

Example 1:

A: 没想到，这次是以前完全不起眼的他解决了这个大难题。

B: 是啊，**尺有所短，寸有所长**，以后我们还真得好好挖掘一下每个人的长处。

A: Méi xiǎng dào, zhècì shì yǐqián wánquán bùqǐyǎn de tā jiějué le zhègè dà
      nántí.
B: Shì a, chǐ yǒu suǒ duǎn, cùn yǒu suǒ cháng, yǐhòu wǒmen hái zhēn děi hǎohāo
      wājué yíxià měi gè rén de chángchù.

A: I wouldn't have thought that that previously utterly undistinguished guy would
      solve this big problem.
B: Yeah, no one is perfect, but no one is worthless either. We should really
      thoroughly uncover every person's merits.

Example 2:

A: 他是一个乡巴佬，能有什么本事？
B: 话不能这么说，**尺有所短，寸有所长**，单说他的勤奋精神，就是我
      们在座的都比不了的。

A: Tā shì yígè xiāngbalǎo, néng yǒu shénme běnshì?
B: Huà bùnéng zhème shuō, chǐ yǒu suǒ duǎn, cùn yǒu suǒ cháng, dān shuō tā
      de qínfèn jīngshén, jiùshì wǒmen zàizuò de dōu bǐ bùliǎo de.

A: He's a bumpkin. What could he be good at?
B: You can't say that. No one is perfect, but no one is worthless either. Just in
      terms of his work ethic, no one here can compete with him.

Usage: Used singly.

Variant: 寸有所长

Note: Neutral or slightly complimentary in meaning.

---

408. 出来混的，总要还的 (出来混的，總要還的)
chūlái hùn de, zǒng yào huán de

Translated character by character, 出来混的，总要还的 means 'leave-home-make a
living, some day-will-pay for-it,' whereas the implied meaning of this proverb would
be 'every bad deed will eventually have its consequences.' Its functional translation
is 'chickens come home to roost.'

Example 1:

A: 他都要退休了，还是因为受贿被判刑了。
B: **出来混的，总要还的。**

A: Tā dōu yào tuìxiū le, háishì yīnwèi shòuhuì bèi pànxíng le.
B: Chūlái hùn de, zǒng yào huán de.

A: He was going to retire, but he was still convicted for accepting bribes.
B: Chickens will always come home to roost.

Example 2:

A: 他年轻的时候对别人太苛刻，现在年纪大了，结果连一个朋友都没有。

B: **出来混，迟早要还的**。

A: Tā niánqīng de shíhòu duì biérén tài kēkè, xiànzài niánjì dà le, jiéguǒ lián yígè péngyǒu dōu méiyǒu.

B: Chūlai hùn, chízǎo yào huán de.

A: When he was young, he was too hard on others. Now that he's old, he doesn't have even one friend.

B: Chickens come home to roost.

Usage: Used singly.

Variant: 出来混，总要还的

Note: Humorous in meaning. This proverb comes from a line in a 2003 movie: "出来混，迟早要还的." It has become popular in the last few years.

---

409. 画虎不成反类犬 (畫虎不成反類犬)
huà hǔ bù chéng fǎn lèi quǎn

Translated character by character, 画虎不成反类犬 means 'draw-tiger-not-successful-instead-resemble-dog,' whereas the implied meaning of this proverb would be 'to try to imitate something and fail miserably.' Its functional translation is '(to try to emulate something beyond one's ability and) fall flat on one's face.'

Example 1:

A: 他觉得什么都是西方的好，于是拼命模仿，但是缺乏真正理解，结果**画虎不成反类犬**。

A: Tā juéde shénme dōu shì xīfāng de hǎo, yúshì pīnmìng mófǎng, dànshì quēfá zhēnzhèng lǐjiě, jiéguǒ huà hǔ bù chéng fǎn lèi quǎn.

A: He thinks all Western things are better, so he kills himself emulating them even though he lacks real understanding. The result is that his imitation is poor and he falls flat on his face.

Example 2:

A: 我认为绘画艺术中的野兽派色彩强烈，表现力强。我准备学习这种风格。

B: 好好想想，这种风格并不适合中国的环境，别最后出现**画虎不成反类犬**的情况。

A: Wǒ rènwéi huìhuà yìshù zhōng de Yěshòupài sècǎi qiángliè, biǎoxiànlì qiáng.
    Wǒ zhǔnbèi xuéxí zhè zhǒng fēnggé.

B: Hǎohāo xiǎngxiang, zhè zhǒng fēnggé bìng bú shìhé Zhōngguó de huánjìng,
    bié zuìhòu chūxiàn huà hǔ bù chéng fǎn lèi quǎn de qíngkuàng.

A: I think the colors in the Fauvist style of painting are bold. It's very impressive.
    I plan on studying this style.

B: Make sure to look before you leap. This style doesn't fit with the appetites of
    Chinese people. Don't try to imitate it and end up falling flat on your face.

Usage: Functions as predicate or attributive.

Variant: 画虎不成反类狗

Note: Slightly derogatory or neutral in meaning.

410. 大意失荆州 (大意失荊州) dà yì shī Jīngzhōu

Translated character by character, 大意失荆州 means 'careless-lose-Jingzhou,'
whereas the implied meaning of this proverb would be 'to suffer a serious setback
as the result of a careless mistake.'

Example 1:

A: 奥运会上，美国男子篮球队轻视对手，结果**大意失荆州**，输给了欧
    洲的一支球队。

A: Àoyùnhuì shàng, Měiguó nánzǐ lánqiúduì qīngshì duìshǒu, jiéguǒ dàyi shī
    Jīngzhōu, shū gěi le Ōuzhōu de yì zhī qiúduì.

A: In the Olympics, the US men's basketball team underestimated their opponents
    and, as a result, suffered a loss, losing to a European team.

Example 2:

A: 现任总统在谋求连任时与一位名不见经传的对手展开竞选，他以为
    自己会轻松连任，因此竞选活动并不积极。没想到**大意失荆州**，最
    后没能连任。

A: Xiàn rèn zǒngtǒng zài móuqiú liánrèn shí yǔ yí wèi míng bú jiàn jīngzhuàn
    de duìshǒu zhǎnkāi jìngxuǎn, tā yǐwéi zìjǐ huì qīngsōng liánrèn, yīncǐ jìngxuǎn
    huódòng bìngbù jījí. Méi xiǎng dào dàyi shī Jīngzhōu, zuìhòu méi néng liánrèn.

A: While seeking a second term, the incumbent president wasn't proactive about
    holding campaign events, because he mistakenly believed that he would win
    reelection easily against an unknown candidate. He hadn't imagined that he
    would suffer a loss and, in the end, be unable to serve another term.

Usage: Functions as predicate.

Note: Neutral in meaning. Jingzhou (located in modern Hubei province) was a city of strategic importance during the Three Kingdoms Period. The emperor of the Shu Kingdom, Liu Bei sent his most reliable and capable general, Guan Yu to protect the city. But, in the end, Guan Yu lost Jingzhou due to a careless mistake, causing the Shu Kingdom to go on the defensive for the rest of the Three Kingdoms period.

411. 卸磨杀驴 (卸磨殺驢) xiè mò shā lǘ

Translated character by character, 卸磨杀驴 means 'unload-mill-kill-donkey,' whereas the implied meaning of this proverb would be 'to get rid of someone as soon as they've done their job.' Its functional translation is 'to kick someone to the curb when they've outlived their usefulness.'

Example 1:

A: 老朱，别生那么大气了，小心身体。

B: 我能不生气吗？我为公司工作了四十年，最后被打发到那个偏远的小地方，他们是**卸磨杀驴**。

A: Lǎo Zhū, bié shēng nàme dà qì le, xiǎoxīn shēntǐ.

B: Wǒ néng bù shēngqì ma? Wǒ wèi gōngsī gōngzuò le sìshí nián, zuìhòu bèi dǎfa dào nàgè piānyuǎn de xiǎo dìfāng, tāmen shì xiè mò shā lǘ.

A: Old Zhu, don't get so angry. You need to consider your health.

B: How could I not be angry? I worked for that company for forty years and, in the end, they sent me to that small, remote area. They kicked me to the curb when I'd outlived my usefulness.

Example 2:

A: 他为自己的党派与反对派拼命争斗，可是赢了之后，该党却**卸磨杀驴**，把所有的过错都让他一个人承担了。

A: Tā wèi zìjǐ de dǎngpài yǔ fǎnduìpài pīnmìng zhēngdòu, kěshì yíngle zhīhòu, gāi dǎng què xiè mò shā lǘ, bǎ suǒyǒu de guòcuò dōu ràng tā yígè rén chéngdān le.

A: He fought tooth and nail for his party against the opposition party but, after they won, his party kicked him to the curb, loading him down with all of their mistakes.

Usage: Functions as predicate.

Note: Derogatory in meaning.

412. 躺着都中枪 (躺著都中槍) tǎng zhe dōu zhòng qiāng

Translated character by character, 躺着都中枪 means 'lie-ing-however-got-shot,' whereas the implied meaning of this proverb would be 'to be dragged into something one tried, unsuccessfully, to avoid.' Its functional translation is 'to get caught in the crossfire.'

Example 1:

A: 这件事怎么把你也给卷进去了？

B: 人要是倒霉了，**躺着都中枪**。就是因为他们俩都姓王，而我也姓王，所以就给卷进去了。

A: Zhè jiàn shì zěnme bǎ nǐ yě gěi juǎn jìnqù le?

B: Rén yàoshì dǎoméi le, tǎngzhe dōu zhòng qiāng. Jiùshì yīnwèi tāmen liǎ dōu xìng Wáng, ér wǒ yě xìng Wáng, suǒyǐ jiù gěi juǎn jìnqù le.

A: How did you get sucked into this mess?

B: If you're unlucky, you get caught in the crossfire. I got dragged into it because they both have the last name Wang and so do I.

Example 2:

A: 现在的独生子女啊，没有任何独立生活能力，全靠父母，尤其是大城市的。

B: （对C）你是独生子女吗？

C: **我躺着也中枪**。我不但是独生子女，而且是上海的独生子女。

A: Xiànzài de dúshēng zǐnǚ a, méiyǒu rènhé dúlì shēnghuó nénglì, quán kào fùmǔ, yóuqí shì dà chéngshì de.

B: (duì C) nǐ shì dúshēng zǐnǚ ma?

C: Wǒ tǎngzhe yě zhòng qiāng. Wǒ búdàn shì dúshēng zǐnǚ, érqiě shì Shànghǎi de dúshēng zǐnǚ.

A: Only children today . . . they're completely incapable of fending for themselves; they rely completely on their parents, especially those children that live in big cities.

B: (To C) Are you an only child?

C: I guess I've gotten caught in the crossfire here. I'm not only an only child, I'm an only child from Shanghai.

Usage: Functions as predicate.

Variant: 躺枪

Note: Neutral or humorous in meaning.

413. 脚正不怕鞋歪 (腳正不怕鞋歪) jiǎo zhèng bú pà xié wāi

Translated character by character, 脚正不怕鞋歪 means 'foot-straight-not-feat-shoe-crooked,' whereas the implied meaning of this proverb would be 'a righteous person is not influenced by rumors.' Its functional translation is 'an honest man fears no gossip.'

Example 1:

A: 最近很多人在背后说你利用职权招聘了你的小姨子进了咱们公司。

B: 老王，随他们说去吧。他们只看到她是我的小姨子，怎么不想想我的小姨子是北大十佳大学生呢？我**脚正不怕鞋歪**，别人爱怎么说就怎么说吧。

A: Zuìjìn hěnduō rén zài bèihòu shuō nǐ lìyòng zhíquán zhāopìn le nǐde xiǎoyízǐ jìnle zánmen gōngsī.

B: Lǎo Wáng, suí tāmen shuō qù ba. Tāmen zhǐ kàndào tā shì wǒde xiǎoyízǐ, zěnme bù xiǎngxiǎng wǒde xiǎoyízǐ shì Běidà shí jiā dàxuéshēng ne? Wǒ jiǎo zhèng bú pà xié wāi, biérén ài zěnme shuō jiù zěnme shuō ba.

A: Recently, a lot of people have been saying, behind your back, that you used your authority to hire your sister-in-law into our office.

B: Old Wang, let them say what they want. They only see that she is my sister-in-law; why don't they consider that she was top ten in her class at Peking University? An honest man fears no gossip. Let them say what they want.

Example 2:

A: 我们领导同志要时时刻刻把人民的利益挂在心头，至于社会上的流言蜚语，根本不用在乎。**脚正不怕鞋歪**，人民的眼睛是雪亮的，是会对我们有一个公正的评价的。

A: Wǒmen lǐngdǎo tóngzhì yào shíshí kèkè bǎ rénmín de lìyì guà zài xīntóu, zhìyú shèhuì shàng de liúyán-fēiyǔ, gēnběn búyòng zàihū. Jiǎo zhèng bú pà xié wāi, rénmín de yǎnjīng shì xuěliàng de, shì huì duì wǒmen yǒu yígè gōngzhèng de píngjià de.

A: As leaders, we should have the best interests of the people at heart at all times. As for society's rumors, they can simply be ignored. An honest man fears no gossip. The people are perceptive; they will have a fair opinion of us.

Usage: Used singly.

Note: Complimentary in meaning.

414. **有奶就是娘**（有奶就是娘）yǒu nǎi jiù shì niáng

Translated character by character, 有奶就是娘 means 'have-milk-just-is-mother,' whereas the implied meaning of this proverb would be 'whoever suckles me is my mother.' Its functional translation is 'to sell one's allegience to the highest bidder.'

Example 1:

A: 新领导刚上台，他就不停地拍马屁。

B: 这个人**有奶就是娘**。你再看看他怎么对待刚下台的领导就行了，见了面连招呼都不打。

A: Xīn lǐngdǎo gāng shàngtái, tā jiù bùtíng de pāimǎpì.
B: Zhège rén yǒu nǎi jiù shì niáng. Nǐ kànkan tā zěnme duìdài gāng xiàtái de lǐngdǎo jiù xíng le, jiànle miàn lián zhāohu dōu bù dǎ.

A: The new leader has just taken office and he's already incessantly kissing up to him.
B: This guy sells his allegiance to the highest bidder. Just look at how he treats our former leader. He doesn't even acknowledge him when he sees him.

Example 2:

A: 昨天说得好好的，今天签合同。怎么突然变卦了？

B: 另一家公司的报价比我们高出一万块钱，他们就不讲信誉了。他们啊，**有奶就是娘**。

A: Zuótiān shuō de hǎohāo de, jīntiān qiān hétóng. Zěnme tūrán jiù biànguà le?
B: Lìng yì jiā gōngsī de bàojià bǐ wǒmen gāo chū yíwàn kuàiqian, tāmen jiù bù jiǎng xìnyù le. Tāmen a, yǒu nǎi jiù shì niáng.

A: Yesterday we talked it out and today we signed a contract. How did it suddenly fall through?
B: Another company's offer was 10,000 RMB more than ours. They don't take reputation into account; they sell their allegiance to the highest bidder.

Usage: Functions as predicate.

Variant: 有奶便是娘

Note: Derogatory in meaning.

415. **肉烂在锅里**（肉爛在鍋裏）ròu làn zài guō lǐ

Translated character by character, 肉烂在锅里 means 'meat-melt-inside-pot,' whereas the implied meaning of this proverb would be 'one's interests have been affected, but the benefits have not accrued to someone else.' Its functional translation is 'it's all in the family.'

Example 1:

A:　今天打麻将赢了多少？

B:　不知道，玩儿以前没数，玩儿以后也没数。

A:　你真是，赌博不在乎输赢！

B:　那也不是，因为都是亲戚，输赢没关系，反正**肉烂在锅里**。

A:　Jīntiān dǎ májiàng yíngle duōshǎo?

B:　Bù zhīdào, wánr yǐqián méi shǔ, wánr yǐhòu yě méi shǔ.

A:　Nǐ zhēnshi, dǔbó bú zàihū shūyíng!

B:　Nà yě búshì, yīnwèi dōu shì qīnqi, shūyíng méi guānxi, fǎnzhèng ròu làn zài guōli.

A:　How much did you win playing Mah-jong today?

B:　I don't know. I didn't count before or after.

A:　Look at you, not caring whether you win or lose when you gamble.

B:　It's not like that. Because we're relatives, winning or losing doesn't matter. After all, it's all in the family.

Example 2:

A:　贪污腐败阻碍经济发展。

B:　这话也对也不对。贪污腐败当然不对；不过，只要不把钱转移到国外，最终**肉**还是**烂在锅里**，钱还是国家的。

A:　Tānwū fǔbài zǔ'ài jīngjì fāzhǎn.

B:　Zhè huà yě duì yě bú duì. Tānwū fǔbài dāngrán búduì; búguò, zhǐyào bù bǎ qián zhuǎnyí dào guówài, zuìzhōng ròu hái shì làn zài guōli, qián háishì guójiā de.

A:　Graft impedes economic development.

B:　That's partially correct. Graft definitely isn't right, but so long as the money isn't transferred abroad, in the end, it's all in the family. The money is still in the country.

Usage: Usually used after '反正.'

Note: Neutral or humorous in meaning.

416.　说你胖你就喘（說你胖你就喘）
shuō nǐ pàng nǐ jiù chuǎn

Translated character by character, 说你胖你就喘 means 'say-you-fat-you-just-pant,' whereas the implied meaning of this proverb would be 'to believe a flattering comment said in jest reflects one's true nature.' Its functional translation is 'flattery, like perfume, should be smelled, not swallowed.'

Example 1:

A: 你这个娱乐记者一定采访过很多大明星吧？

B: 当然啦，像成龙啊，周润发啊经常请我喝茶。

A: **说你胖你就喘**上了，你一个狗仔队，人家见到你不骂你就算你幸运了。

A: Nǐ zhège yúlè jìzhě yídìng cǎifǎngguò hěnduō dà míngxīng ba?

B: Dāngrán la, xiàng Chénglóng a, Zhōu Rùnfā a jīngcháng qǐng wǒ hēchá.

A: Shuō nǐ pàng nǐ jiù chuǎn shàng le, nǐ yígè gǒuzǎiduì, rénjia jiàn dào nǐ bú mà nǐ jiù suàn nǐ xìngyùn le.

A: As an entertainment reporter, you must have interviewed a lot of movie stars, right?

B: Of course! Like, Jackie Chan and Chow Yun-fat often invite me for tea.

A: Flattery, like perfume, should be smelled, not swallowed. You paparazzi, you should consider yourself lucky if they see you and don't berate you.

Example 2:

A: 你们的产品最近好像很畅销。

B: 是啊。我们已经占领了本省市场，下一步是全国市场，再下一步是全球市场。我们准备三年内超过英国对手，五年内超过美国对手。

A: 好家伙，**说你胖你就喘**。什么时候超过火星上的对手啊？

A: Nǐmen de chǎnpǐn zuìjìn hǎoxiàng hěn chàngxiāo.

B: Shì a. Wǒmen yǐjīng zhànlǐngle běn shěng shìchǎng, xiàyíbù shì quánguó shìchǎng, zài xiàyíbù shì quánqiú shìchǎng. Wǒmen zhǔnbèi sān nián nèi chāoguò Yīngguó duìshǒu, wǔ nián nèi chāoguò Měiguó duìshǒu.

A: Hǎo jiāhuo, shuō nǐ pàng nǐ jiù chuǎn. Shénme shíhòu chāoguò Huǒxīng shàng de duìshǒu a?

A: It seems like your products have been selling well recently.

B: Yeah. We've already captured the market in this province; next we'll capture the national market, then the world market. We are prepared to overtake our English rivals in three years, and our American rivals within five years.

A: Wow. Flattery, like perfume, should be smelled, not swallowed, buddy. When are you going to overtake your competitors on Mars?

Usage: Used singly.

Note: Slightly derogatory and humorous in meaning.

417. 擦屁股 (擦屁股) cā pìgu

Translated character by character, 擦屁股 means 'wipe-butt' whereas the implied meaning of this proverb would be 'to resolve the problems someone has caused.' Its functional translation is 'to clean up someone's mess.'

Example 1:

A: 叔叔，我又有点儿麻烦事。

B: 你小子，总是在外面惹是生非，每次都让我替你**擦屁股**。

A: Shūshu, wǒ yòu yǒu diǎnr máfan shì.

B: Nǐ xiǎozi, zǒngshì zài wàimiàn rěshì-shēngfēi, měi cì dōu ràng wǒ tì nǐ cā pìgu.

A: Uncle, I've gotten in trouble again.

B: You, boy, are always out stirring up trouble, and I always have to clean up your mess for you.

Example 2:

A: 邮政局福利高，可是员工效率低，连年亏损，但是政府总是给他们**擦屁股**，不断地补贴他们。

A: Yóuzhèngjú fúlì gāo, kěshì yuángōng xiàolǜ dī, lián nián kuīsǔn, dànshì zhèngfǔ zǒngshì gěi tāmen cā pìgu, búduàn de bǔtiē tāmen.

A: The benefits in the postal service are good, but the efficiency of their employees is low and they've lost money many years in a row. But the government always cleans up their mess, continually subsidizing them.

Usage: Functions as predicate.

Note: Derogatory and humorous in meaning.

418. 皇帝女儿不愁嫁 (皇帝女兒不愁嫁)
huáng dì nǔ ér bù chóu jià

Translated character by character, 皇帝女儿不愁嫁 means 'emperor-daughter-not-worry-marriage,' whereas the implied meaning of this proverb would be 'to be in an advantageous situation and rely on that for success.' Its functional translation is 'sitting pretty.'

Example 1:

A: 以前，清华、北大的毕业生可以说是**皇帝女儿不愁嫁**，但是现在不同了。

A: Yǐqián, Qīnghuá, Běidà de bìyèshēng kěyǐ shuō shì huáng dì nǔ ér bù chóu jià, dànshì xiànzài bùtóng le.

A: Before, you could say that Tsinghua and Peking University students were sitting pretty, but things are different now.

Example 2:

A: 这种产品怎么二十年来技术上都没有提高，还是那么不好用？

B: 它们受到政府的保护，处于垄断地位，产品呢，自然是**皇帝女儿不愁嫁**，好坏都卖得出去。

A: Zhè zhǒng chǎnpǐn zěnme èrshí nián lái jìshù shàng dōu méiyǒu tígāo, háishì nàme bù hǎoyòng?

B: Tāmen shòudào zhèngfǔ de bǎohù, chǔyú lǒngduàn dìwèi, chǎnpǐn ne, zìrán shì huáng dì nǚ ér bù chóu jià, hǎohuài dōu mài de chūqù.

A: How is this product still so inconvenient? How has it not improved technologically in the last twenty years?

B: They're protected by the government and have monopolistic standing. As for the product, naturally it's sitting pretty; it'll sell whether it's good or bad.

Usage: Functions as predicative or attributive.

Note: Neutral or humorous in meaning.

419. 一朝天子一朝臣（一朝天子一朝臣）
yì cháo tiānzǐ yì cháo chén

Translated character by character, 一朝天子一朝臣 means 'one-reign-emperor-one-reign-feudal officials,' whereas the implied meaning of this proverb would be 'new leaders appoint new counsellors.'

Example 1:

A: 有什么事需要王市长办就赶快去找他。

B: 急什么？

A: 听说王市长明年要调到其他城市去了，**一朝天子一朝臣**，王市长现在手下的大部分人都得换，这样王市长以后再说话也就不好使了。

A: Yǒu shénme shì xūyào Wáng shìzhǎng bàn jiù gǎnkuài qù zhǎo tā.

B: Jí shénme?

A: Tīngshuō Wáng shìzhǎng míngnián yào diào dào qítā chéngshì qù le, yì cháo tiānzǐ yì cháo chén, Wáng shìzhǎng xiànzài shǒuxià de dàbùfēn rén dōu děi huàn, zhèyàng Wáng shìzhǎng yǐhòu zài shuōhuà yě jiù bù hǎoshǐ le.

A: If you have anything you need Mayor Wang to do, you should see him soon.

B: What's the hurry?

A: I hear that Mayor Wang is going to be transferred to another city next year. New leaders appoint new counsellors. Most of the people currently under Mayor Wang must be replaced, so Mayor Wang won't have much influence afterwards.

Example 2:

A: 英国不搞领导终身制，**一朝天子一朝臣**，执政党若下台，基本上所有的高级官员都要下台。

A: Yīngguó bù gǎo lǐngdǎo zhōngshēnzhì, yì cháo tiānzǐ yì cháo chén, zhízhèngdǎng ruò xiàtái, jīběnshang suǒyǒu de gāojí guānyuán dōu yào xiàtái.

A: As Britain doesn't have lifelong tenure, and a new leader appoints new counsellors, if the ruling party is unseated, basically all of the high-level officials must step down.

Usage: Used singly.

Note: Neutral or slightly derogatory in meaning.

---

420. 活人让尿憋死 (活人讓尿憋死) huó rén ràng niào biē sǐ

Translated character by character, 活人让尿憋死 means 'live-person-let-urine-hold in-die,' whereas the implied meaning of this proverb would be 'to not be adaptable.'

Example 1:

A: 你怎么走回来了？为什么不打车？

B: 我的钱不够。

A: 你真笨，你不会先打车回来，然后从家里取钱给司机，**活人**还**让尿憋死**啊？

A: Nǐ zěnme zǒu huílai le? Wèishénme bù dǎchē?

B: Wǒde qián búgòu.

A: Nǐ zhēn bèn, nǐ búhuì xiān dǎchē huílai, ránhòu cóng jiāli qǔ qián gěi sījī, huórén hái ràng niào biē sǐ a?

A: Why did you walk back? Why didn't you take a cab?

B: I didn't have enough money.

A: You're an idiot. Couldn't you take a cab home and get cash from your house to pay the driver? Why don't you use your head?

Example 2:

A: 咱们这个城市失业率上升、犯罪率上升，生活质量越来越差，怎么办呢？

B: 那就搬走呗，**活人**总不能**让尿给憋死**。

A: Zánmen zhègè chéngshì shīyèlǜ shàngshēng, fànzuìlǜ shàngshēng, shēnghuó zhìliàng yuèláiyuè chà, zěnmebàn?

B: Nà jiù bānzǒu bei, huórén zǒngbùnéng ràng niào gěi biē sǐ.

A: The unemployment rate in our city is rising, the crime rate is rising, and the quality of life is getting worse and worse. What should we do?

B: Just leave. You can't be as stubborn as a mule.

Usage: Used singly.

Variants: (活)人不能让尿(给)憋死

Note: Slightly derogatory and humorous in meaning.

---

421. 走马灯 (走馬燈) zǒu mǎ dēng

Translated character by character, 走马灯 means 'rotate-horse-lantern,' whereas the implied meaning of this proverb would be 'an incessant turnover of personnel.' Its functional translation is 'a revolving door,' or 'musical chairs.'

Example 1:

A: 日本和意大利有一段时间政局不稳定，首相或总理**走马灯**似的换。

A: Rìběn hé Yìdàlì yǒu yí duàn shíjiān zhèngjú bù wěndìng, shǒuxiàng huò zǒnglǐ zǒumǎdēng shìde huàn.

A: Japan and Italy had periods of political instability, changing prime ministers or premiers like musical chairs.

Example 2:

A: 这个老板脾气古怪，很难相处，秘书**走马灯**似的换。

A: Zhège lǎobǎn píqì gǔguài, hěn nán xiāngchǔ, mìshū zǒumǎdēng shìde huàn.

A: That boss has a bizarre temperament and is tough to get along with. Secretaries have come and gone like musical chairs.

Usage: Functions as adverbial.

Note: Neutral in meaning.

---

422. 花无百日红 (花無百日紅) huā wú bǎi rì hóng

Translated character by character, 花无百日红 means 'flower-no-hundred-day-red,' whereas the implied meaning of this proverb would be 'an ideal state cannot last long.' Its functional translation is 'nothing good lasts forever.'

Example 1:

A: 我们曾经的性感女神也老了。

B: 是啊，**花无百日红**。

A: Wǒmen céngjīng de xìnggǎn nǔshén yě lǎo le.

B: Shì a, huā wú bǎi rì hóng.

A: Our old sex symbol has also aged.

B: Yeah, nothing good lasts forever.

Example 2:

A: 你为什么想离开咱们单位？

B: 咱们单位的确不错，工作稳定，各方面的待遇也很好；但是就是给人一种缺乏激情的感觉。趁现在还年轻，我想到外边去闯一闯。**花无百日红**，也许再过十年，我就不会想换工作了。

A: Nǐ wèishénme xiǎng líkāi zánmen dānwèi?

B: Zánmen dānwèi díquè búcuò, gōngzuò wěndìng, gè fāngmiàn de dàiyù yě hěnhǎo; dànshì jiùshì gěi rén yìzhǒng quēfá jīqíng de gǎnjué. Chèn xiànzài hái niánqīng, wǒ xiǎng dào wàibiān qù chuǎngyìchuǎng. Huā wú bǎi rì hóng, yěxǔ zài guò shí nián, wǒ jiù búhuì xiǎng huàn gōngzuò le.

A: Why do you want to leave our work unit?

B: Our work unit is really pretty good; the work is stable, and in many regards we're treated very well, but it makes me feel deprived of excitement here. I want to see the world outside while I'm still young. Nothing good lasts forever; maybe in another ten years I won't want to change jobs anymore.

Usage: Used singly.

Note: Neutral in meaning.

---

423. 东风压倒西风 (東風壓倒西風) dōng fēng yā dǎo xī fēng

Translated character by character, 东风压倒西风 means 'east-wind-prevail-over-west-wind,' whereas the implied meaning of this proverb would be 'the forces of good far outpower the forces of evil.' Its functional translation is 'the good guys win.'

Example 1:

A: 日本自民党选举哪派赢了？

B: 我没关注，因为结果不是**东风压倒西风**，就是西风压倒东风，但是，哪派上台都差不多。

A: Rìběn Zìmíndǎng xuǎnjǔ nǎ pài yíng le?

B: Wǒ méi guānzhù, yīnwèi jiéguǒ búshì dōngfēng yādǎo xīfēng, jiùshì xīfēng yādǎo dōngfēng, dànshì, nǎ pài shàngtái dōu chàbuduō.

A: Which faction won in Japan's Liberal Democratic Party's election?

B: I haven't been following it, because if one group doesn't win, the other will. But it makes no difference which is in power.

Example 2:

A: 这届冬奥会上，**东风压倒**了**西风**，亚洲国家赢得了更多金牌。

A: Zhè jiè Dōng'àohuì shàng, dōngfēng yādǎo le xīfēng, Yàzhōu guójiā yíngdé le gèng duō jīnpái.

A: At this Winter Olympics, our side won. Asian countries won more gold medals.

Usage: Functions as predicate or predicative.

Note: Neutral in meaning.

---

424.   岁月是把杀猪刀 (歲月是把殺豬刀)
　　　 suìyuè shì bǎ shā zhū dāo

Translated character by character, 岁月是把杀猪刀 means 'age-is-MW-slaughter-pig-knife,' whereas the implied meaning of this proverb would be 'time isn't kind to anyone.'

Example 1:

A: 哇，几年不见，他竟然这么老了！
B: **岁月是把杀猪刀**啊！

A: Wà, jǐ nián bú jiàn, tā jìngrán zhème lǎo le!
B: Suìyuè shì bǎ shā zhū dāo a!

A: Wow, I hadn't seen him for a few years, I'm surprised he looks so old!
B: Time isn't kind to anyone.

Example 2:

A: 咳，前几年还是玉女呢，怎么几年以后就成了大妈了呢？
B: **岁月是把杀猪刀**。

A: Hài, qián jǐ nián háishì yùnǚ ne, zěnme jǐ nián yǐhòu jiù chéngle dàmā le ne?
B: Suìyuè shì bǎ shā zhū dāo.

A: Oh, she was still young and beautiful a few years ago. How has she now turned into an old lady?
B: Time isn't kind to anyone.

Usage: Used singly.

Note: Neutral or humorous in meaning.

425. 丁是丁，卯是卯 (丁是丁，卯是卯)
dīng shì dīng, mǎo shì mǎo

Translated character by character, 丁是丁，卯是卯 means 'nail-is-nail, rivet-is-rivet,' whereas the implied meaning of this proverb would be 'to be meticulous.'

Example 1:

A: 他做起工作来**丁是丁，卯是卯**，让人很放心。

A: Tā zuò qǐ gōngzuò lái dīng shì dīng, mǎo shì mǎo, ràng rén hěn fàngxīn.

A: He's a very meticulous worker. It makes people feel confident.

Example 2:

A: 严市长是个**丁是丁，卯是卯**的人，公私分明。

A: Yán shìzhǎng shì gè dīng shì dīng, mǎo shì mǎo de rén, gōngsī fēnmíng.

A: Mayor Yan is very meticulous. He keeps his work separate from his personal life.

Usage: Functions as predicate or attributive.

Note: Complimentary in meaning.

426. 多年的媳妇熬成婆 (多年的媳婦熬成婆)
duō nián de xífu áo chéng pó

Translated character by character, 多年媳妇熬成婆 means 'many-year-'s-daughter-in-law-(finally)-turned-into-mother-in-law,' whereas the implied meaning of this proverb would be 'to reap rewards one has patiently endured hardship to merit.' Its functional translation is 'to have paid one's dues and get what one deserves.'

Example 1:

A: 他在副市长的位置上干了十年，现在终于提上了正市长。
B: 不容易啊！**多年的媳妇熬成**了**婆**。

A: Tā zài fù shìzhǎng de wèizhì shàng gànle shí nián, xiànzài zhōngyú tí shàng le zhèng shìzhǎng.
B: Bù róngyì a! Duō nián de xífu áo chéng le pó.

A: He's been vice-mayor for ten years and has finally been promoted to mayor.
B: That doesn't come easily! He's paid his dues, now he's getting what he deserves.

Example 2:

A: 他在这家公司说话终于算数了。
B: 是啊，**多年的媳妇熬成婆**了。

A: Tā zài zhè jiā gōngsī shuōhuà zhōngyú suànshù le.

B: Shì a, duō nián de xífu áo chéng pó le.

A: His word finally carries weight at this company.

B: Yeah. He's paid his dues, now he's getting what he deserves.

Usage: Used singly.

Note: Neutral or humorous in meaning.

427. 强将手下无弱兵 (強將手下無弱兵)
qiáng jiàng shǒu xià wú ruò bīng

Translated character by character, 强将手下无弱兵 means 'able-general-under-no-weak-soldier,' whereas the implied meaning of this proverb would be 'a good leader has no weak subordinates.' Its functional translation, is 'there are no poor soldiers under an able general.'

Example 1:

A: 这个团队怎么这么能干？

B: 主要是因为有一个特别能干的头儿，**强将手下无弱兵**。

A: Zhège tuánduì zěnme zhème nénggàn?

B: Zhǔyào shì yīnwèi yǒu yígè tèbié nénggàn de tóur, qiáng jiàng shǒuxià wú ruò bīng.

A: How is this team so capable?

B: It's mainly because of the extremely capable leader. There are no poor soldiers under an able general.

Example 2:

A: 那位诺贝尔化学奖得主的学生们个个都很出色。

B: 那当然，**强将手下无弱兵**嘛。

A: Nà wèi Nuòbèi'ěr huàxuéjiǎng dézhǔ de xuéshēngmen gègè dōu hěn chūsè.

B: Nà dāngrán, qiáng jiàng shǒuxià wú ruò bīng ma.

A: That Nobel laureate's students are all very distinguished.

B: Of course. There are no poor soldiers under an able general.

Usage: Used singly.

Note: Complimentary in meaning.

428. 头痛医头，脚痛医脚 (頭痛醫頭，腳痛醫腳)
tóu tòng yī tóu, jiǎo tòng yī jiǎo

Translated character by character, 头痛医头，脚痛医脚 means 'head-ache-treat-head, foot-ache-treat-foot,' whereas the implied meaning of this proverb would be 'to treat symptoms as they occur without addressing the underlying issue.' Its functional translation is 'to slap a Band-Aid on something.'

Example 1:

A: 那么多农民在街头当小贩，乱糟糟的，太破坏我们城市的形象了。应该把他们都赶回农村去。

B: 这种办法不是**头痛医头，脚痛医脚**吗？归根结底是农村的生活差，所以农民才跑到城市里来。

A: Nàme duō nóngmín zài jiētóu dāng xiǎofàn, luànzāozāo de, tài pòhuài wǒmen chéngshì de xíngxiàng le. Yīnggāi bǎ tāmen dōu gǎn huí nóngcūn qù.

B: Zhèzhǒng bànfǎ búshì tóu tòng yī tóu, jiǎo tòng yī jiǎo ma? Guīgēn-jiédǐ shì nóngcūn de shēnghuó chà, suǒyǐ nóngmín cái pǎodào chéngshì lǐ lái.

A: There are so many farmers turned peddlers on the streets. It's a mess, and it's so damaging to the image of our city. They should shoo them all back to the countryside.

B: Isn't that just slapping a Band-Aid on the problem? The root of it is that country life is bad, so the farmers come flooding into the cities.

Example 2:

A: 分析事情的时候要能联系地看，抓住事情的本质，然后对症下药，不能**头痛医头，脚痛医脚**。

A: Fēnxī shìqíng de shíhòu yào néng liánxì de kàn, zhuāzhù shìqíng de běnzhì, ránhòu duìzhèng-xiàyào, bùnéng tóu tòng yī tóu, jiǎo tòng yī jiǎo.

A: When you analyze a situation, you need to be able to see things holistically; grasp the essence of the situation. You can't just slap a Band-Aid on it.

Usage: Functions as predicative, attributive or predicate.

Note: Slightly derogatory in meaning.

429. 拉不出屎来怨茅房 (拉不出屎來怨茅房)
lā bù chū shǐ lái yuàn máofáng

Translated character by character, 拉不出屎来怨茅房 means 'pull-not-out-poop-blame-outhouse,' whereas the implied meaning of this proverb would be 'to blame someone or something else for one's own inability to perform.' Its functional translation is 'to pass the buck,' or, in the negative form, 'a good carpenter doesn't blame his tools.'

Example 1:

A: 都怪你不好。

B: 你这个人怎么回事？**拉不出屎来怨茅房**啊？明明是你自己的事，怎么怪到我头上来了？

A: Dōu guài nǐ bùhǎo.

B: Nǐ zhège rén zěnmehuíshì? Lā bù chū shǐ lái yuàn máofáng a? Míngming shì nǐ zìjǐ de cuò, zěnme guài dào wǒ tóushang lái le?

A: It's all your fault.

B: What's wrong with you, passing the buck on to me? This is clearly your problem. How are you blaming me?

Example 2:

A: 总统把竞选连任失败的责任归到美联储主席头上来了。

B: 瞎扯，那纯粹是**拉不出屎来怨茅房**。他自己的经济政策不成功怨不得别人。

A: Zǒngtǒng bǎ jìngxuǎn liánrèn shībài de zérèn guī dào Měiliánchǔ zhǔxí tóushang lái le.

B: Xiāchě, nà chúncuì shì lā bù chū shǐ lái yuàn máofáng. Tā zìjǐ de jīngjì zhèngcè bù chénggōng yuàn bu de biérén.

A: The president placed the blame for his reelection loss on the shoulders of the Federal Reserve chairman.

B: That's nonsense! That's only him passing the buck. His economic policies were not successful. He shouldn't blame others.

Usage: Usually used singly.

Note: Derogatory in meaning.

---

430. 东方不亮西方亮 (東方不亮西方亮)
dōng fāng bú liàng xī fāng liàng

Translated character by character, '东方不亮西方亮' means 'eastern-world-not-lit-western-world-lit,' whereas the implied meaning of this proverb is 'while something isn't workable in one place, it might be workable somewhere else.'

Example 1:

A: 新能源这个行业有前途吗？

B: 别担心，不行咱们就转行。**东方不亮西方亮**，哪个行业能赚钱，我们就干哪个行业。

A: Xīnnéngyuán zhège hángyè yǒu qiántú ma?

B: Bié dānxīn, bùxíng zánmen jiù zhuǎnháng. Dōngfāng bú liàng xīfāng liàng, nǎge hángyè néng zuànqián, wǒmen jiù gàn nǎge hángyè.

A: Is there a future in the renewable energy industry?

B: Don't worry, if not we'll change professions. We might find success elsewhere. We'll work in whatever profession we can make money in.

Example 2:

A: 大企业的产品和服务往往多元化，企业希望**东方不亮西方亮**，因此在竞争中立于不败之地。

A: Dà qǐyè de chǎnpǐn hé fúwù wǎngwǎng duōyuánhuà, qǐyè xīwàng dōngfāng bú liàng xīfāng liàng, yīncǐ zài jìngzhēng zhōng lì yú bú bài zhī dì.

A: The products and services of large corporations are often diversified in the hope that if something doesn't succeed, something else will. So, in competition, they can't lose.

Usage: Used singly.

Variant: 东边不亮西边亮

Note: Neutral in meaning.

431. 老牛拉破车 (老牛拉破車) lǎo niú lā pò chē

Translated character by character, 老牛拉破车 means 'old-cow-pull-broken-cart,' whereas the implied meaning of this proverb would be 'to move slowly and haltingly.' Its functional translation is 'to trundle along.'

Example 1:

A: 你怎么才到？怎么开的车？

B: 怎么才到？就那辆破车，五十迈都跑不了，**老牛拉破车**，能到就谢天谢地了。

A: Nǐ zěnme cái dào? Zěnme kāi de chē?

B: Zěnme cái dào? Jiù nà liàng pò chē, wǔshí mài dōu pǎobuliǎo, lǎo niú lā pò chē, néng dào jiù xiètiān-xièdì le.

A: How did you only just get here? How were you driving?

B: How did I only just get here? I was trundling along in that old car, which can't even make 50 miles an hour. I thank god I even got here.

Example 2:

A: 那家企业员工众多，但是生产效率低，管理混乱，给人一种**老牛拉破车**的感觉，倒闭只是时间早晚的问题了。

A: Nà jiā qǐyè yuángōng zhòngduō, dànshì shēngchǎn xiàolǜ dī, guǎnlǐ hùnluàn, gěi rén yìzhǒng lǎo niú lā pò chē de gǎnjué, dǎobì zhǐshì shíjiān zǎowǎn de wèntí le.

A: That company has a huge number of employees, its production efficiency is low and its management is chaotic. It feels like it's just trundling along. It's just a matter of time until it goes bankrupt.

Usage: Functions mainly as attributive or adverbial.

Note: Slightly derogatory in meaning.

432. 放卫星 (放衛星) fàng wèi xīng

Translated character by character, 放卫星 means 'launch-satellite,' whereas the implied meaning of this proverb would be 'to talk the talk,' or 'to talk big.'

Example 1:

A: 厂长说要在三年内把产量翻一番。
B: 他在**放卫星**。有点儿常识的人都知道这不可能。

A: Chǎngzhǎng shuō yào zài sān nián nèi bǎ chǎnliàng fān yī fān.
B: Tā zài fàng wèixīng. Yǒu diǎnr chángshi de rén dōu zhīdào zhè bù kěnéng.

A: The plant manager said he wanted to double production within three years.
B: He's talking big. Anyone with common sense knows that's not possible.

Example 2:

A: 我们能3:0赢你们。
B: 你们就会**放卫星**，谁赢谁输还不一定呢。

A: Wǒmen néng 3.0 yíng nǐmen.
B: Nǐmen jiù huì fàng wèixīng, shéi yíng shéi shū hái bùyídìng ne.

A: We'll beat you 3-0.
B: So, you can talk the talk, but the jury's still out on who's going to win.

Usage: Functions as predicate.

Note: Slightly derogatory in meaning.

433. 鸡同鸭讲 (雞同鴨講) jī tóng yā jiǎng

Translated character by character, 鸡同鸭讲 means 'chicken-to-duck-speak,' whereas the implied meaning of this proverb would be 'to be speaking to the wrong audience.' Its functional translation is 'whistling in the wind.'

Example 1:

A: 他跟一个文盲介绍毕加索的油画。

B: 那不是**鸡同鸭讲**嘛，对方怎么能听得懂？

A: Tā gēn yígè wénmáng jièshào Bìjiāsuǒ de yóuhuà.

B: Nà búshì jī tóng yā jiǎng ma, duìfāng zěnme néng tīng de dǒng?

A: He was explaining Picasso's paintings to an uncultured person.

B: He's whistling in the wind. How could the other guy understand?

Example 2:

A: 有些老年人很认真地对他们的孙子、孙女讲他们的人生观和价值观，希望孙辈们接受。

B: 可怜他们的一片苦心，不过，这完全是**鸡同鸭讲**。

A: Yǒuxiē lǎoniánrén hěn rènzhēn de duì tāmen de sūnzǐ, sūnnǚ jiǎng tāmen de rénshēngguān hé jiàzhíguān, xīwàng sūnbèi men jiēshòu.

B: Kělián tāmen de yí piàn kǔxīn, búguò, zhè wánquán shì jī tóng yā jiǎng.

A: Some old people solemnly impart their values and outlook on life to their grandchildren in the hopes that they will take them to heart.

B: I empathize with their effort, but they're absolutely whistling in the wind.

Usage: Functions mainly as predicative.

Note: Derogatory and humorous in meaning.

---

434. 一锅端 (一鍋端) yì guō duān

Translated character by character, 一锅端 means 'whole-pot-removed,' whereas the implied meaning of this proverb would be 'to be wiped out all at once.'

Example 1:

A: 咱们这里的社会治安以后几年会好很多。

B: 是啊，最大的黑社会组织被**一锅端**了。

A: Zánmen zhèlǐ de shèhuì zhì'ān yǐhòu jǐ nián huì hǎo hěnduō.

B: Shì a, zuì dà de hēishèhuì zǔzhī bèi yìguōduān le.

A: Public order will be much better here in the next few years.

B: Yeah, the biggest crime syndicate was wiped out.

Example 2:

A: 多少人被免职了？

B: 上自市长，下至办公室秘书，**一锅端**了。

A: Duōshao rén bèi miǎnzhí le?

B: Shàng zì shìzhǎng, xiàzhì bàngōngshì mìshū, yìguōduān le.

A: How many people were let go?

B: From the mayor to the office secretaries, they were all wiped out.

Usage: Functions as predicate.

Variants: 一窝端; 连锅端; 连窝端 (窝 wō: nest, den)

Note: Neutral in meaning.

435. 老皇历 (老皇曆) lǎo huángli

Translated character by character, 老皇历 means 'old-emperor-calendar.' Its functional translation is 'anachronistic,' or 'an anachronistic practice.'

Example 1:

A: 子女结婚得征得父母的同意。

B: 这都是**老皇历**了，现在时兴父母再婚得征得子女同意。

A: Zǐnǚ jiéhūn děi zhēngdé fùmǔ de tóngyì.

B: Zhè dōu shì lǎohuángli le, xiànzài shíxīng fùmǔ zàihūn děi zhēngdé zǐnǚ tóngyì.

A: Children need to ask their parents' approval to get married.

B: That's an anachronistic practice. Now, the trend is for parents to have to ask their children's approval to get remarried.

Example 2:

A: 男60岁、女55岁退休成了**老皇历**，现在都是65岁。

A: Nán 60 suì, nǚ 55 suì tuìxiū chéngle lǎohuángli, xiànzài dōu shì 65 suì.

A: Men retiring at 60 and women at 55 is an anachronistic practice. Now, it's 65 for both.

Usage: Functions as object or predicative.

Note: Slightly derogatory and humorous in meaning.

436. 家花没有野花香 (家花沒有野花香)
jiā huā méi yǒu yě huā xiāng

Translated character by character, 家花没有野花香 means 'home-flower-not-as-wild-flower-fragrant,' whereas the implied meaning of this proverb would be 'other women seem better than your significant other.' Its functional translation is 'the grass is always greener (on the other side of the fence).'

Example 1:

A: 他老婆长得挺漂亮的，他怎么还在外面乱搞？

B: **家花没有野花香**，男人都喜新厌旧。

A: Tā lǎopo zhǎng de tǐng piàoliang de, tā zěnme hái zài wàimiàn luàn gǎo?

B: Jiā huā méi yǒu yě huā xiāng, nánrén dōu xǐxīn-yànjiù.

A: His wife is quite pretty, why is he out philandering?

B: The grass is always greener. Men have a short attention span.

Example 2:

A: 王子也搞婚外恋啊？

B: **家花没有野花香**。

A: Wángzǐ yě gǎo hūnwàiliàn a?

B: Jiā huā méi yǒu yě huā xiāng.

A: Does the prince also have extramarital affairs?

B: The grass is always greener.

Usage: Used singly.

Note: Neutral in meaning.

---

437. 又想当婊子又想立牌坊 (又想當婊子又想立牌坊)
yòu xiǎng dāng biǎozi yòu xiǎng lì páifang

Translated character by character, 又想当婊子又想立牌坊 means 'not only-want-be-whore-also-want-erect-arch,' whereas the implied meaning of this proverb would be 'to want to be able to do immoral things while maintaining a good name.'

Example 1:

A: 那个国家侵占了周围的小国，还大言不惭地说为了被侵占国家人民的利益着想。

B: 那个国家**又想当婊子又想立牌坊**，纯粹是流氓政府。

A: Nàgè guójiā qīnzhànle zhōuwéi de xiǎo guó, hái dàyán-bùcán de shuō wèile bèi qīnzhàn guójiā rénmín de lìyì zhuóxiǎng.

B: Nàgè guójiā yòu xiǎng dāng biǎozi yòu xiǎng lì páifang, chúncuì shì liúmáng zhèngfǔ.

A: That country invaded the small neighboring country, shamelessly boasting that they were doing it for the good of the people of the invaded country.

B: That country wants to do bad things while maintaining a good name. It's simply a rogue state.

Example 2:

A: 他设下圈套陷害竞争对手，把人家送进监狱，还假惺惺地说很同情老朋友，对结果很遗憾。

B: 这个王八蛋**又想当婊子又想立牌坊**，将来不得好死。

A: Tā shè xià quāntào xiànhài jìngzhēng duìshǒu, bǎ rénjia sòng jìn jiānyù, hái jiǎxīngxing de shuō hěn tóngqíng lǎopéngyou, duì jiéguǒ hěn yíhàn.

B: Zhègè wángbādàn yòu xiǎng dāng biǎozi yòu xiǎng lì páifang, jiānglái bù dé hǎo sǐ.

A: He framed his competitor and had him sent to jail, hypocritically saying he sympathized with his old friend and that he was very sorry about the result.

B: That bastard wants to do bad things and keep a good name. I hope he dies a violent death.

Usage: Functions as predicate.

Variant: 又想当婊子又想立贞节牌坊 (贞节 zhēnjié, chastity)

Note: Derogatory in meaning.

---

438. 遮羞布 (遮羞布) zhē xiū bù

Translated character by character, 遮羞布 means 'cover up-shame (private parts)-cloth,' whereas the implied meaning of this proverb would be 'something with which one covers up an embarrassing fact or problem.' Its functional translation is 'a fig leaf.'

Example 1:

A: 他赤裸裸地排挤、打击与他意见不同的人，提拔只会吹捧他的人，还美其名曰"选拔人才"。

B: "选拔人才"只是一块**遮羞布**。

A: Tā chìluǒluo de páijǐ, dǎjī yǔ tā yìjiàn bùtóng de rén, tíbá zhǐ huì chuīpěng tā de rén, hái měiqímíngyuē "xuǎnbá réncái".

B: "Xuǎnbá réncái" zhǐ shì yí kuài zhēxiūbù.

A: He unabashedly attacked and pushed out those people whose opinions were different than his and promoted those who would only flatter him. He even put lipstick on it and called it "personnel selection."

B: "Personnel selection" is just a fig leaf.

Example 2:

A: 如果把我逼急了，我就把内幕都抖出来。

B: 最好别撕下这块**遮羞布**，那对谁都不好。

A: Rúguǒ bǎ wǒ bī jí le, wǒ jiù bǎ nèimù dōu dǒu chūlái.

B: Zuìhǎo bié sī xià zhè kuài zhēxiūbù, nà duì shéi dōu bùhǎo.

A: If you push me, I'll reveal all of your secrets.

B: You'd better not remove that fig leaf. That would be bad for everyone involved.

Usage: Functions as object.

Note: Neutral in meaning.

439. 耍花枪 (耍花槍) shuǎ huā qiāng

Translated character by character, 耍花枪 means 'flourish-spear,' whereas the implied meaning of this proverb would be 'to be dishonest,' or 'to cheat.' Its functional translation is 'to toy with someone.'

Example 1:

A: 我不是故意的，是一时糊涂。

B: 你少给我**耍花枪**，这么大的事能糊涂吗？

A: Wǒ búshì gùyì de, shì yìshí hútu.

B: Nǐ shǎo gěi wǒ shuǎhuāqiāng, zhème dà de shì néng hútu ma?

A: I didn't do it on purpose. I was confused at the time.

B: Don't toy with me. How could you be confused about such an important issue?

Example 2:

A: 你不要以为他是认真的，其实他在跟你**耍花枪**呢。

A: Nǐ búyào yǐwéi tā shì rènzhēn de, qíshí tā zài gēn nǐ shuǎhuāqiāng ne.

A: Don't make the mistake of thinking he's serious when he's really toying with you.

Usage: Functions as predicate.

Note: Slightly derogatory in meaning.

440. 又要马儿跑，又要马儿不吃草 (又要馬兒跑，又要馬兒不吃草) yòu yào mǎ ér pǎo, yòu yào mǎ ér bù chī cǎo

Translated character by character, 又要马儿好，又要马儿不吃草 means 'on one hand-require-horse-run, on other hand-require-horse-not-eat-grass,' whereas the implied meaning of this proverb would be 'to want to have something both ways.' Its functional translation is 'to have one's cake and eat it too.'

Example 1:

A: 小牛，周末加班把这个活儿干完。

B: 老板，你怎么也得表示一下，总不能**又要马儿跑，又要马儿不吃草**吧？

A: Xiǎo Niú, zhōumò jiābān bǎ zhègè huór gàn wán.

B: Lǎobǎn, nǐ zěnme yě děi biǎoshì yíxià, zǒng bùnéng **yòu yào mǎ ér pǎo, yòu yào mǎ ér bù chī cǎo** ba?

A: Little Niu, work overtime this weekend and get this project finished.

B: Boss, you need to give an incentive. You can't have your cake and eat it too.

Example 2:

A: 奖惩得分明，对努力工作的人就应该奖励，不能**又要马儿跑，又要马儿不吃草**。

A: Jiǎngchéng děi fēnmíng, duì nǔlì gōngzuò de rén jiù yīnggāi jiǎnglì, bùnéng **yòu yào mǎ ér pǎo, yòu yào mǎ ér bù chī cǎo**.

A: You have to be clear about rewards and punishments. You should encourage and reward those who work diligently. You can't have your cake and eat it too.

Usage: Functions as predicate.

Note: Slightly derogatory and humorous in meaning.

---

441. 牛不喝水强按头 (牛不喝水強按頭)
niú bù hē shuǐ qiáng àn tóu

Translated character by character, 牛不喝水强按头 means 'cow-not-drink-water-force-push down-head,' whereas the implied meaning of this proverb would be 'to force someone to do something.' Its functional translation is 'to impose one's will on someone.'

Example 1:

A: 这件事就由他吧，你就别再强迫他了。

B: 不行，他小小年纪懂什么？就得听我的。

A: **牛不喝水强按头**，你强迫他接受，但他会心服口服吗？

A: Zhè jiàn shì jiù yóu tā ba, nǐ jiù bié zài qiángpò tā le.

B: Bùxíng, tā xiǎoxiǎo niánjì dǒng shénme? Jiù děi tīng wǒ de.

A: Niú bù hēshuǐ qiáng àn tóu, nǐ qiángpò tā jiēshòu, dàn tā huì xīnfú-kǒufú ma?

A: This is his issue to deal with. Stop trying to force him.

B: No, what does he understand at this young age? He must obey me.

A: You can impose your will on him and he will accept it, but will he take it to heart?

Example 2:

A: 他不接受我们的意见怎么办？

B: 不接受？那我们只好**牛不喝水强按头**了。

A: Tā bù jiēshòu wǒmen de yìjiàn zěnme bàn?
B: Bù jiēshòu? Nà wǒmen zhǐhǎo niú bù hēshuǐ qiáng àn tóu le.

A: What will we do if he doesn't accept our advice?
B: If he doesn't accept? Then we'll just have to impose our will on him.

Usage: Mainly used singly.

Note: Neutral in meaning.

---

442. 摆乌龙（擺烏龍）bǎi wū lóng

Translated character by character, 摆乌龙 means 'waggle-black-dragon,' whereas the implied meaning of this proverb would be 'to say something that later turns out to be false.' Its functional translation is 'to put one's foot in it.'

Example 1:

A: 这回CNN**摆乌龙**了。

B: 怎么回事？

A: 为了吸引读者和观众，在最高法院对这起案件宣判之前半个小时，CNN就抢先播报了。可是判决的结果正好与CNN播报的相反。

A: Zhè huí CNN bǎiwūlóng le.
B: Zěnme huí shì?
A: Wèile xīyǐn dúzhě hé guānzhòng, zài zuìgāo fǎyuàn duì zhè qǐ ànjiàn xuānpàn zhīqián bàn gè xiǎoshí, CNN jiù qiǎngxiān bōbào le. Kěshì pànjué de jiéguǒ zhènghǎo yǔ CNN bōbào de xiāngfǎn.

A: CNN put their foot in it this time.
B: What happened?
A: In order to attract readers and viewers, CNN was the first to report the Supreme Court's ruling in this case, a half an hour before it was announced. But, in the end, the ruling was the opposite of what CNN had reported.

Example 2:

A: 这位"打假"英雄出大丑了。

B: 打错了吗？

A: 没打错，而是自己被打了。他以前总是揭露别人的论文造假，可是这次大**摆乌龙**，他读博士期间发表的一篇论文被人揭露造假，连他的博士导师都承认那篇文章有问题。

A: Zhè wèi "dǎ jiǎ" yīngxióng chū dà chǒu le.

B: Dǎ cuò le ma?

A: Méi dǎ cuò, érshì zìjǐ bèi dǎ le. Tā yǐqián zǒngshì jiēlù biérén de lùnwén zàojiǎ, kěshì zhècì dà bǎi wūlóng, tā dú bóshì qījiān fābiǎo de yì piān lùnwén bèi rén jiēlù zàojiǎ, lián tā de bóshì dǎoshī dōu chéngrèn nà piān wénzhāng yǒu wèntí.

A: This anti-fakery crusader really screwed up.

B: Did he wrongly accuse someone?

A: No, he was caught himself. Before, he would always reveal other people's plagiarism, but, this time, he really put his foot in it. One of the papers he published when he was a doctoral student was revealed to be plagiarized. Even his PhD advisor admitted that that paper was plagiarized.

Usage: Functions as predicate.

Variant: 自摆乌龙

Note: Neutral or humorous in meaning.

---

443. 各打五十大板 (各打五十大板) gè dǎ wǔshí dà bǎn

Translated character by character, 各打五十大板 means 'each-strike-fifty-hard-switch,' whereas the implied meaning of this proverb would be 'to punish both parties equally without considering guilt.'

Example 1:

A: 在足球比赛中，两个球员粗野地动起手来了，主裁和边裁都没有看清楚事件的起因，所以**各打五十大板**，两个球员都被罚下。

A: Zài zúqiú bǐsài zhōng, liǎng gè qiúyuán cūyě de dòng qǐ shǒu lái le, zhǔcái hé biāncái dōu méiyǒu kàn qīngchu shìjiàn de qǐyīn, suǒyǐ gè dǎ wǔshí dàbǎn, liǎng gè qiúyuán dōu bèi fáxià.

A: In a soccer match, two players got into a vicious fistfight. Neither the main referee or the linesman saw clearly what caused the incident, so they penalized both players without regard for guilt.

Example 2:

A: 你们俩的矛盾在公司中造成了极不好的影响，因此公司决定把你们两个分别调到不同的部门。

B: 怎么？**各打五十大板**啊？那么谁该负主要的责任呢？

A: Nǐmen liǎ de máodùn zài gōngsī zhōng zàochéngle jí bùhǎo de yǐngxiǎng, yīncǐ gōngsī juédìng bǎ nǐmen liǎng gè fēnbié diào dào bùtóng de bùmén.

B: Zénme? Gè dǎ wǔshí dàbǎn a? Nàme shéi gāi fù zhǔyào de zérèn ne?

A: The conflict between the two of you had a very negative impact on the company, so the company has decided to transfer you separately to different divisions.

B: What? You're punishing us both equally? Then who should shoulder the brunt of the blame?

Usage: Functions as predicate.

Note: Neutral or humorous in meaning.

444.　一个将军一个令 (一個將軍一個令)
　　yí gè jiāngjūn yí gè lìng

Translated character by character, 一个将军一个令 means 'one-MW-general-one-MW-order,' whereas the implied meaning of this proverb would be 'each leader has his own policies.' Its functional translation is 'new lords, new laws,' or 'too many chiefs and not enough Indians.'

Example 1:

A: 新领导上台了，以前的政策还会延续吗？

B: 我看不会，**一个将军一个令**，谁都想施行自己的政策。

A: Xīn lǐngdǎo shàngtái le, yǐqián de zhèngcè hái huì yánxù ma?

B: Wǒ kàn búhuì, yígè jiāngjūn yígè lìng, shéi dōu xiǎng shīxíng zìjǐ de zhèngcè.

A: Will the old policies be continued once the new leader takes office?

B: I don't think so. New lords, new laws. Everyone wants to institute their own policies.

Example 2:

A: 你们单位人不多，但是管理怎么那么混乱？

B: 干活儿的不多，但是指挥的人多，**一个将军一个令**，能不乱吗？

A: Nǐmen dānwèi rén bùduō, dànshì guǎnlǐ zěnme nàme hùnluàn?

B: Gànhuór de bùduō, dànshì zhǐhuī de rén duō, yígè jiāngjūn yígè lìng, néng bú luàn ma?

A: There aren't many people in your work unit. How is the management so chaotic?

B: There aren't many workers, but there are a lot of people giving commands. There are too many chiefs and not enough Indians. How can it not be a mess?

Usage: Used singly.

Note: Slightly derogatory or neutral in meaning.

445. 抱大腿 (抱大腿) bào dà tuǐ

Translated character by character, 抱大腿 means 'embrace-big-thigh,' whereas the implied meaning of this proverb would be 'to cozy up to someone powerful.'

Example 1:

A: 她不是有个帅哥男朋友吗？怎么又跟这个富商谈恋爱了？

B: **抱大腿**呗。你想，如果能跟这个富商结婚，那就一辈子吃喝不愁了。

A: Tā búshì yǒu gè shuàigē nánpéngyǒu ma? Zěnme yòu gēn zhègè fùshāng tán liàn'ài le?

B: Bàodàtuǐ bei. Nǐ xiǎng, rúguǒ néng gēn zhègè fùshāng jiéhūn, nà jiù yíbèizi chīhēbùchóu le.

A: Doesn't she have a handsome boyfriend? Why has she taken up with that rich businessman?

B: She's cozying up to someone powerful. Think about it, if she can marry this rich businessman, she'll never have to worry about money again.

Example 2:

A: 新领导刚上台，他就不停地拍马屁。

B: 他这个人就是善于**抱粗腿**。

A: Xīn lǐngdǎo gāng shàngtái, tā jiù bù tíng de pāimǎpì.

B: Tā zhègè rén jiùshì shànyú bàocūtuǐ.

A: The new leader has just taken office and he is constantly sucking up.

B: That guy is just good at cozying up to powerful people.

Usage: Functions as predicate.

Variant: 抱粗腿

Note: Slightly derogatory in meaning.

446. 砸了锅 (砸了鍋) zá le guō

Translated character by character, 砸了锅 means 'break-ed-pot,' whereas the implied meaning of this proverb would be 'to screw something up.' Its functional translation is 'to drop the ball.'

Example 1:

A: 怎么这么不开心？

B: 有一个电话面试，结果太紧张，**砸了锅**。对方当时就说我不适合他们公司。

A: Zěnme zhème bù kāixīn?

B: Yǒu yígè diànhuà miànshì, jiéguǒ tài jǐnzhāng, záleguō. Duìfāng dāngshí jiù shuō wǒ bú shìhé tāmen gōngsī.

A: Why are you so unhappy?

B: I had a phone interview and because I was so nervous, I dropped the ball. The interviewer said to me, on the spot, that I wasn't right for their company.

Example 2:

A: 这次演出一定要成功。

B: 我保证一定成功。

A: 如果你演**砸锅了**，我就砸你的饭碗。

A: zhècì yǎnchū yídìng yào chénggōng.

B: Wǒ bǎozhèng yídìng chénggōng.

A: Rúguǒ nǐ yǎn záguō le, wǒ jiù zá nǐde fànwǎn.

A: Your act needs to work this time.

B: I promise it will.

A: If you drop the ball, I'll fire you.

Usage: Functions as predicate.

Note: Neutral in meaning.

447. 会哭的孩子有奶吃 (會哭的孩子有奶吃)
huì kū de háizi yǒu nǎi chī

Translated character by character, 会哭的孩子有奶吃 means 'good at-crying-baby-have-breast milk-to eat,' whereas the implied meaning of this proverb would be, 'if a baby is good at pretending to cry, he will be rewarded with his mother's breast milk.' Its functional translation is, 'those who complain the loudest get the most attention,' or 'the squeaky wheel gets the grease.'

Example 1:

A: 你看这些人，整天上街游行。结果怎么样？国会很重视。

B: **会哭的孩子有奶吃**。咱们亚洲人就是吃亏。

A: Nǐ kàn zhèxiē rén, zhěngtiān shàngjiē yóuxíng. Jiéguǒ zěnmeyàng? Guóhuì hěn zhòngshì.

B: Huì kū de háizi yǒu nǎi chī. Zánmen Yàzhōurén jiùshì chīkuī.

A: Look at these people, always protesting in the street. And what happens? Congress pays attention.

B: The squeaky wheel gets the grease; we Asians just lose out.

Example 2:

A: 他又去找老板抱怨别人了。

B: **会哭的孩子有奶吃**。你不说话，老板就不重视你。

A: Tā yòu qù zhǎo lǎobǎn bàoyuàn biérén le.

B: Huì kū de háizi yǒu nǎi chī. Nǐ bù shuōhuà, lǎobǎn jiù bú zhòngshì nǐ.

A: He went to the boss again to complain about other people.

B: Those who complain the loudest get the most attention. If you don't speak out, the boss won't pay attention to you.

Usage: Used singly.

Note: Slightly derogatory in meaning. The '奶' in this proverb should be translated as '母乳' (breast milk), not '牛奶' (cow's milk).

---

448. 二一添作五 (二一添作五) èr yī tiān zuò wǔ

Translated character by character, 二一添作五 means 'two-to divide-one-add-five,' whereas the implied meaning of this proverb would be 'to split equally.' Its functional translation is 'to split something down the middle,' or 'go fifty-fifty.'

Example 1:

A: 赚钱之后咱俩四六开，你拿大头，我拿小头。

B: 你这么客气干嘛。别说了，**二一添作五**，你一半我一半。

A: Zuànqián zhīhòu zán liǎ sì-liù kāi, nǐ ná dàtóu, wǒ ná xiǎotóu.

B: Nǐ zhème kèqì gàn ma. Bié shuō le, èr yī tiān zuò wǔ, nǐ yíbàn wǒ yíbàn.

A: After we get the money, we'll split it 40–60; you take the big share, I'll take the small one.

B: What're you being so polite for? Don't argue, we'll split it down the middle; half for you, half for me.

Example 2:

A: 在这个项目的投入上，中外双方二一**添作五**，中方出场地，外方出资金。

A: Zài zhègè xiàngmù de tóurù shàng, zhōngwài shuāngfāng èr yī tiān zuò wǔ, zhōngfāng chū chǎngdì, wàifāng chū zījīn.

A: In terms of the investment in this project, the Chinese and foreigners are splitting it down the middle. The Chinese are providing the land, the foreigners the capital.

Usage: Functions as predicate.

Note: Neutral in meaning. 二一添作五 is a rule to be followed when using an abacus.

449.   风一阵，雨一阵 (風一陣，雨一陣)
fēng yí zhèn, yǔ yí zhèn

Translated character by character, 风一阵，雨一阵 means 'wind-a-while, rain-a-while,' whereas the implied meaning of this proverb would be 'to change back and forth quickly and unpredictably.' Its functional translation is 'to flit from one thing to another.'

Example 1:

A: 她怎么今天想干这，明天想干那？

B: 她总是**风一阵，雨一阵**的，做事很不成熟。

A: Tā zěnme jīntiān xiǎng gàn zhè, míngtiān xiǎng gàn nà?

B: Tā zǒngshì fēng yí zhèn yǔ yí zhèn de, zuòshì hěn bù chéngshú.

A: How does she want to do this today and something else tomorrow?

B: She's always flitting from one thing to another. She conducts herself in a very immature way.

Example 2:

A: 下个月我要去参加选秀节目。

B: 你别整天**风一阵，雨一阵**的，安安心心把工作干好是大事。

A: Xià gè yuè wǒ yào qù cānjiā xuǎnxiù jiémù.

B: Nǐ bié zhěng tiān fēng yí zhèn yǔ yí zhèn de, ānanxīnxīn bǎ gōngzuò gànhǎo shì dàshì.

A: I want to go participate in a talent search contest next month.

B: Don't flit from one thing to another all the time. Keeping your mind on getting your work done is the main issue.

Usage: Functions as predicate.

Note: Slightly derogatory in meaning.

450.   剃头挑子一头热 (剃頭挑子一頭熱) tì tóu tiāozi yī tóu rè

Translated character by character, 剃头挑子一头热 means 'shave-head-carrying pole-one-end-hot,' whereas the implied meaning of this proverb would be 'one person wants something but the other has no interest.' Its functional translation is 'A is not buying what B is selling,' or 'not having any of it.'

Example 1:

A: 他跟我们大学的校花谈恋爱了？

B: 校花？笑话吧？肯定是**剃头挑子一头热**。校花早就有亿万富翁的儿子追求了。

A: Tā gēn wǒmen dàxué de xiàohuā tánliàn'ài le?

B: Xiàohuā? Xiàohuà ba? Kěndìng shì tìtóu tiāozi yī tóu rè. Xiàohuā zǎo jiù yǒu yìwàn fùwēng de érzǐ zhuīqiú le.

A: Is he seeing the most beautiful girl at our university?

B: The most beautiful girl in the school? You're kidding, right? She's definitely not buying what he's selling. She's been getting courted by billionaires' sons for a long time now.

Example 2:

A: 听说那两家公司正在研究合并的可能性。

B: 有一家都快破产了还想合并？**剃头挑子一头热**，另一方愿意收购就不错了。

A: Tīngshuō nà liǎng jiā gōngsī zhèngzài yánjiū hébìng de kěnéngxìng.

B: Yǒu yì jiā dōu kuài pòchǎn le hái xiǎng hébìng? Tìtóu tiāozi yī tóu rè, lìng yì fāng yuànyì shōugòu jiù búcuò le.

A: I heard those two companies are currently researching the possibility of a merger.

B: One of them is nearly bankrupt and they still want to merge? The other company's not buying what they're selling. If the other company is even willing to acquire them it should be considered a good result.

Usage: Functions as predicative or used singly.

Note: Slightly derogatory and humorous in meaning. In ancient China, street barbers carried a pole over their shoulder. On one end of the pole was a coal brazier, which was hot; on the other end of the pole was a stool and their tools, which were cold.

---

451. 远来的和尚会念经 (遠來的和尚會念經)
yuǎn lái de héshang huì niàn jīng

Translated character by character, 远来的和尚会念经 means 'distant-come-monk-good at-chant-scripture,' whereas the implied meaning of this proverb would be 'all that is foreign must be better.'

Example 1:

A: 他在剑桥大学也就是个普通的教授，这次来咱们大学报告，校长亲自到飞机场去接，面子够大的。

B: **远来的和尚会念经**，人家是英国剑桥大学的。

A: Tā zài Jiànqiáo Dàxué yě jiùshì gè pǔtōng de jiàoshòu, zhècì lái zánmen dàxué bàogào, xiàozhǎng qīnzì dào fēijīchǎng qù jiē, miànzi gòu dà de.

B: Yuǎn lái de héshang huì niànjīng, rénjia shì Yīngguó Jiànqiáo Dàxué de.

A: He was only an ordinary professor at Cambridge, but when he came to present at our university, the president himself went to the airport to pick him up. What an honor.

B: All that is foreign must be better. He's a professor at Cambridge (University).

Example 2:

A: 这个老外的观点真的很新颖。

B: 是啊，**外来的和尚会念经**，老外的理论就是新。

A: Zhègè lǎowài de guāndiǎn zhēnde hěn xīnyǐng.

B: Shì a, wài lái de héshang huì niànjīng, lǎowài de lǐlùn jiùshì xīn.

A: This foreigner's opinion is very original.

B: Yes. All that is foreign must be better; foreigners' theories are truly new.

Usage: Used singly.

Variant: 外来的和尚会念经

Note: Neutral in meaning.

---

452. 揪辫子 (揪辮子) jiū biànzi

Translated character by character, 揪辫子 means 'seize-pigtail,' whereas the implied meaning of this proverb would be 'to seize on someone's shortcomings,' or 'to get one's hooks into someone.'

Example 1:

A: 你千万别把任何把柄留给她。

B: 怎么讲？

A: 她会**揪**住你的**辫子**不放。

A: Nǐ qiānwàn bié bǎ rènhé bǎbǐng liúgěi tā.

B: Zěnme jiǎng?

A: Tā huì jiū zhù nǐde biānzi bú fàng.

A: You absolutely must not give her any leverage.

B: Why do you say that?

A: She'll get her hooks into you and never let go.

Example 2:

A: 民主党和共和党在这个问题上争论不休，互相**揪小辫**。

A: Mínzhǔdǎng hé Gònghédǎng zài zhègè wèntí shàng zhēnglùn bù xiū, hùxiāng jiū xiǎobiàn.

A: The Democrats and Republicans quarreled endlessly about this issue, seizing on each other's shortcomings.

Usage: Functions as predicate.

Variant: 揪小辫

Note: Slightly derogatory in meaning.

---

453. 小姐的身子丫鬟的命 (小姐的身子丫鬟的命)
xiǎo jiě de shēnzi yāhuán de mìng

Translated character by character, 小姐的身子丫鬟的命 means 'princess-'s-body-maiden-'s-fate,' whereas the implied meaning of this proverb would be 'a good lady with bad fortune.'

Example 1:

A: 你怎么那么瞧不起她？

B: 她也太把自己当回事儿了。不就是一个服务员吗？有什么了不起的？**小姐的身子丫鬟的命**。

A: Nǐ zěnme nàme qiáobùqǐ tā?

B: Tā yě tài bǎ zìjǐ dāng huí shìr le. Bú jiùshì yígè fúwùyuán ma? Yǒu shénme liǎobùqǐ de? Xiǎojie de shēnzi yāhuán de mìng.

A: Why do you look down on her so much?

B: She thinks too highly of herself. Isn't she just a waitress? What's so special about her? No matter what she thinks of herself, she is still poor.

Example 2:

A: 她的命怎么那么不好？婆婆和丈夫都虐待她？

B: 可惜了，这么好的一个姑娘，**小姐的身子丫鬟的命**。

A: Tā de mìng zěnme nàme bù hǎo? Pópo hé zhàngfu dōu nuèdài tā?

B: Kěxī le, zhème hǎo de yígè gūniang, xiǎojie de shēnzi yāhuán de mìng.

A: How does she have such bad luck, with her mother-in-law and husband both abusing her?

B: It's a shame that such a good girl has such bad fortune.

Usage: Functions as predicate or used singly.

Variant: 小姐的身子丫环的命

Note: Slightly derogatory and humorous in meaning.

454. 只见树木，不见森林 (只見樹木，不見森林)
zhǐ jiàn shùmù, bú jiàn sēnlín

Translated character by character, 只见树木，不见森林 means 'only-seen-trees-not-seen-forest,' whereas the implied meaning of this proverb would be 'to only see parts of the whole and be unable to comprehend the larger issue.' Its functional translation is 'to not see the forest for the trees.'

Example 1:

A: 那个国家有很多问题，比方说民主的问题，平等的问题和创新的问题，所以那个国家是没有前途的。

B: 话不能这样说。我们得全面地、历史地看问题，否则就会**只见树木，不见森林**。那个国家最近二十年来在你提到的那些方面都取得了明显的进步。

A: Nàgè guójiā yǒu hěnduō wèntí, bǐfāngshuō mínzhǔ de wèntí, píngděng de wèntí hé chuàngxīn de wèntí, suǒyǐ nàgè guójiā shì méiyǒu qiántú de.

B: Huà bùnéng zhèyàng shuō. Wǒmen děi quánmiàn de, lìshǐ de kàn wèntí, fǒuzé jiù huì zhǐ jiàn shùmù, bú jiàn sēnlín. Nàgè guójiā zuìjìn èrshí nián lái zài nǐ tídào de nàxiē fāngmiàn dōu qǔdé le míngxiǎn de jìnbù.

A: That country has no future because it has many issues, with democracy, equality, and innovation to name a few.

B: You can't say that. We have to look at the issues comprehensively, and with an eye to the past, otherwise we won't see the forest for the trees. In the last twenty years, that country has achieved clear progress in the few areas you mentioned.

Example 2:

A: 下结论不能太武断，要全面分析问题，不能**只见树木，不见森林**。

A: Xià jiélùn bùnéng tài wǔduàn, yào quánmiàn fēnxī wèntí, bùnéng zhǐ jiàn shùmù, bú jiàn sēnlín.

A: You can't make conclusions subjectively. You need to analyze the issue comprehensively. Don't fail to see the forest for the trees.

Usage: Functions as predicate or attributive.

Variant: 见树不见林

Note: Slightly derogatory or neutral in meaning.

455. 屁股决定脑袋 (屁股决定脑袋) pìgu juédìng nǎodai

Translated character by character, 屁股决定脑袋 means 'butt-determine-head,' whereas the implied meaning of this proverb would be 'one's position determines one's views and behavior.'

Example 1:

A: 他在学生时代思想很激进的，现在说话怎么都是官腔？

B: 不难理解，**屁股决定脑袋**。现在他是副市长。

A: Tā zài xuéshēng shídài sīxiǎng hěn jījìn de, xiànzài shuōhuà zěnme dōu shì guānqiāng?

B: Bù nán lǐjiě, pìgu juédìng nǎodai. Xiànzài tā shì fù shìzhǎng.

A: When he was a student, his thinking was very radical. How does he now speak like an official?

B: It's not hard to understand. His thought process is determined by his position. He's a vice-mayor now.

Example 2:

A: 咱们从小一起长大，可是现在他的想法跟我们很不同。

B: 那就对了，他是当官的，我们是老百姓，**屁股决定脑袋**。

A: Zánmen cóngxiǎo yìqǐ zhǎngdà, kěshì xiànzài tā de xiǎngfǎ gēn wǒmen hěn bùtóng.

B: Nà jiù duì le, tā shì dāngguān de, wǒmen shì lǎobǎixìng, pìgu juédìng nǎodai.

A: We all grew up together, but now his views are very different from ours.

B: That's right. He's an official, we're common people; one's position determines one's views.

Usage: Used singly.

Note: Slightly derogatory and humorous in meaning.

456. 兔子尾巴长不了 (兔子尾巴長不了)
tùzi wěiba cháng bù liǎo

Translated character by character, 兔子尾巴长不了 means 'rabbit-tail-unable-longer,' whereas the implied meaning of this proverb would be 'something (often bad people or institutions) cannot last.' Its functional translation is 'something's days are numbered.'

Example 1:

A: 这届政府十分腐败，只会加税，其他什么都不会干。

B: 看着吧，**兔子尾巴长不了**，过不了两年就会下台。

A: Zhè jiè zhèngfǔ shífēn fǔbài, zhǐ huì jiāshuì, qítā shénme dōu búhuì gàn.

B: Kànzhe ba, tùzi wěiba cháng bùliǎo, guò bùliǎo liǎng nián jiù huì xiàtái.

A: This administration is extremely corrupt. All they do is raise taxes; they can't do anything else.

B: Look, their days are numbered. They'll be out of office in less than two years.

Example 2:

A: 最近股市好像很牛。

B: 都是假象，**兔子尾巴长不了**，熊市马上就到了。

A: Zuìjìn gǔshì hǎoxiàng hěn niú.

B: Dōu shì jiǎxiàng, tùzi wěiba cháng bùliǎo, xióngshì mǎshàng jiù dào le.

A: The stock market seems to be really bullish lately.

B: It's all an illusion. The bull market's days are numbered; the bear market is right around the corner.

Usage: Used singly.

Note: Slightly derogatory in meaning.

457. 骑马找马 (騎馬找馬) qí mǎ zhǎo mǎ

Translated character by character, 骑马找马 means 'ride-horse-find-horse,' whereas the implied meaning of this proverb would be 'to look for another job while keeping one's current position.'

Example 1:

A: 这个工作不太理想，我不太想去。

B: 你现在一份工作都没有，就不要挑三拣四了。先有一份工作，然后 **骑马找马**，再找下一份好工作。

A: Zhègè gōngzuò bú tài lǐxiǎng, wǒ bú tài xiǎng qù.

B: Nǐ xiànzài yī fèn gōngzuò dōu méiyǒu, jiù búyào tiāosān-jiǎnsì le. Xiān yǒu yí fèn gōngzuò, ránhòu qí mǎ zhǎo mǎ, zài zhǎo xià yí fèn hǎo gōngzuò.

A: This job isn't ideal. I don't really want to go.

B: You don't even have a job right now. Don't be picky. First get a job, and then you can look for another job while keeping that position.

Example 2:

A: 我想辞职。

B: 找到下家没有？

A: 还没有。

B: 那我建议你还是暂时不要辞职，**骑马找马**，现在找一份工作多不容易！

A: Wǒ xiǎng cízhí.

B: Zhǎodào xiàjiā méiyǒu?

A: Hái méiyǒu.

B: Nà wǒ jiànyì nǐ háishì zànshí búyào cízhí, qí mǎ zhǎo mǎ, xiànzài zhǎo yí fèn gōngzuò duō bù róngyì!

A: I want to resign.

B: Have you found your next employer yet?

A: Not yet.

B: Then I would suggest you temporarily remain at your job and look for another job while keeping that position. It's very difficult to find a job now.

Usage: Functions as predicate.

Variant: 骑驴找马

Note: Neutral or humorous in meaning.

---

458. 敲锣边儿 (敲鑼邊兒) qiāo luó biānr

Translated character by character, 敲锣边儿 means 'beat-gong-edge,' whereas the implied meaning of this proverb would be 'to meddle with the intent of causing or intensifying an altercation.' Its functional translation is 'to stir the pot.'

Example 1:

A: 其实我们两个人之间的矛盾没有那么大。

B: 我也这样觉得。这次我们闹得这么不愉快都是因为他**敲锣边儿**。

A: Qíshí wǒmen liǎng gè rén zhījiān de máodùn méiyǒu nàme dà.

B: Wǒ yě zhèyàng juéde. Zhècì wǒmen nào de zhème bù yúkuài dōu shì yīnwèi tā qiāoluóbiānr.

A: Really, the issue between the two of us isn't that serious.

B: I don't think so either. The reason we fought so bitterly this time was because he was stirring the pot.

Example 2:

A: 对她的话你要多个心眼儿。

B: 怎么了？

A: 她特别喜欢**敲锣边儿**，就希望别人打起来，她好从中得到好处。

A: Duì tā de huà nǐ yào duō gè xīnyǎnr.

B: Zěnme le?

A: Tā tèbié xǐhuān qiāoluóbiānr, jiù xīwàng biérén dǎ qǐlái, tā hǎo cóngzhōng dédào hǎochù.

A: You need to be wary of what she says.
B: What's wrong?
A: She really likes to stir the pot. She hopes that when others start fighting, she can benefit from it.

Usage: Functions as predicate.

Note: Slightly derogatory in meaning.

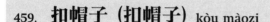

459. 扣帽子 (扣帽子) kòu màozi

Translated character by character, 扣帽子 means 'place-hat (on someone),' whereas the implied meaning of this proverb would be 'to give someone an unfitting and unflattering label.' Its functional translation is 'to paint someone as something,' or 'to call someone names.'

Example 1:

A: 这家伙真坏。
B: 怎么了？
A: 他在所有的同事面前给我**扣**了一个"破坏团结"的大**帽子**。

A: Zhè jiāhuo zhēn huài.
B: Zěnme le?
A: Tā zài suǒyǒu de tóngshì miànqián gěi wǒ kòule yígè "pòhuài tuánjié" de dà màozi.

A: That guy is really bad.
B: What's wrong?
A: He painted me as someone who is a "destroyer of unity" in front of all of our colleagues.

Example 2:

A: 今天的辩论基本上算是实事求是，没有人给对方**扣帽子**。

A: Jīntiān de biànlùn jīběnshàng suàn shì shíshì-qiúshì, méiyǒu rén gěi duìfāng kòumàozi.

A: Today's debate was mainly based on fact. There was no undeserved name-calling.

Usage: Functions as predicate.

Note: Slightly derogatory in meaning.

460. 拔出萝卜带出泥 (拔出蘿蔔帶出泥)
bá chū luóbo dài chū ní

Translated character by character, 拔出萝卜带出泥 means 'pull-out-turnip-bring-up-mud,' whereas the implied meaning of this proverb would be 'one thing brings about another.'

Example 1:

A: 省长的秘书出事了。

B: 看着吧，**拔出萝卜带出泥**，过不了多久这个省长也得出事。

A: Shěngzhǎng de mìshū chūshì le.

B: Kànzhe ba, bá chū luóbo dài chū ní, guò bùliǎo duōjiǔ zhègè shěngzhǎng yě děi chūshì.

A: The governor's secretary is in trouble.

B: You just watch, one thing will bring about another. It won't be too long until that governor is also in trouble.

Example 2:

A: 经济腐败案一般都会涉及到一群人，抓住一个，**拔出萝卜带出泥**，很快就能发现其他人。

A: Jīngjì fǔbài àn yìbān dōu huì shèjí dào yì qún rén, zhuāzhù yígè, bá chū luóbo dài chū ní, hěnkuài jiù néng fāxiàn qítā rén.

A: Economic corruption cases generally implicate a group of people. When one person is caught, one thing leads to another and others are quickly found out.

Usage: Used singly.

Note: Slightly derogatory in meaning.

461. 满嘴跑火车 (滿嘴跑火車) mǎn zuǐ pǎo huǒchē

Translated character by character, 满嘴跑火车 means 'full-mouth-run-train,' whereas the implied meaning of this proverb would be 'to run after a train with a full mouth.' Its functional translation is 'to blow smoke,' or 'to be full of it.'

Example 1:

A: 他好像很有理想。

B: 别听他的，这家伙整天**满嘴跑火车**，没一句话是真的。

A: Tā hǎoxiàng hěn yǒu lǐxiǎng.

B: Bié tīng tāde, zhè jiāhuo zhěngtiān mǎn zuǐ pǎo huǒchē, méi yí jù huà shì zhēnde.

A: He seems to be very idealistic.

B: Don't listen to him. This guy is always blowing smoke; not a word of what he says is true.

Example 2:

A: 你又喝多了，**满嘴跑火车**。

B: 谁喝多了！你才喝多了呢。我呀，再喝三瓶二锅头也醉不了。

A: Nǐ yòu hē duō le, mǎn zuǐ pǎo huǒchē.

B: Shéi hē duō le! Nǐ cái hē duō le ne. Wǒ ya, zài hē sān píng èrguōtóu yě zuì bùliǎo.

A: You're drunk again. You're full of it.

B: I'm drunk? You're the one that's drunk. As for me, I could drink another three bottles of *Erguotou* (a liquor popular in Beijing) and not get drunk.

Usage: Functions as predicate.

Note: Humorous and slightly derogatory in meaning.

462. 温水煮青蛙 (溫水煮青蛙) wēn shuǐ zhǔ qīngwā

Translated character by character, 温水煮青蛙 means 'tepid-water-boil-frog,' whereas the implied meaning of this proverb would be 'to attempt to defeat someone without their knowing of a plot against them.' Its functional translation is 'to boil the frog slowly.'

Example 1:

A: 行动不能太快，否则对手会发现我们的意图。

B: 对，我们来个**温水煮青蛙**，等对手发现威胁的时候已经晚了。

A: Xíngdòng bùnéng tài kuài, fǒuzé duìshǒu huì fāxiàn wǒmen de yìtú.

B: Duì, wǒmen lái gè wēnshuǐ zhǔ qīngwā, děng duìshǒu fāxiàn wēixié de shíhou yǐjīng wǎn le.

A: You can't move too fast, or else our opponent will realize our intentions.

B: Right, we'll boil the frog slowly. By the time they uncover the threat, it'll already be over.

Example 2:

A: 要慢慢买入目标公司的股票，不要让他们觉察到危险。

B: 好，我们**温水煮青蛙**，先让他们暂时舒服几个月。

A: Yào mànmàn mǎi rù mùbiāo gōngsī de gǔpiào, búyào ràng tāmen chájué dào wēixiǎn.

B: Hǎo, wǒmen wēnshuǐ zhǔ qīngwā, xiān ràng tāmen zànshí shūfu jǐ gè yuè.

A: We need to slowly increase our holdings in the target company. We can't let them see the danger.

B: OK. We'll boil the frog slowly; allow them their false sense of security for a few months.

Usage: Functions as predicate.

Note: Neutral in meaning.

---

463. 万金油 (萬金油) wàn jīn yóu

Translated character by character, 万金油 means 'ten thousand-gold-oil,' whereas the implied meaning of this proverb would be 'someone who can do many things,' or 'a remedy for many ills.' Its functional translation is 'jack of all trades,' or 'panacea.'

Example 1:

A: 我们要招 个公关部经理。

B: 她是**万金油**，让她干正合适。

A: Wǒmen yào zhāo yígè gōngguānbù jīnglǐ.

B: Tā shì wànjīnyóu, ràng tā gàn zhèng héshì.

A: We need to hire a manager for our PR department.

B: She's a jack-of-all-trades. She'd be just right for it.

Example 2:

A: 很多人批评政府对经济的调控太多，有很多负面作用，说要让市场发挥真正的主导作用。但是市场不是**万金油**，并不能解决所有问题。

A: Hěnduō rén pīpíng zhèngfǔ duì jīngjì de tiáokòng tài duō, yǒu hěnduō fùmiàn zuòyòng, shuō yào ràng shìchǎng fāhuī zhēnzhèng de zhǔdǎo zuòyòng. Dànshì shìchǎng búshì wànjīnyóu, bìng bùnéng jiějué suǒyǒu wèntí.

A: A lot of people criticize the government for interfering excessively in the economy, as there are a lot of negative externalities and they want to allow the market to exert its guiding influence. But the market isn't a panacea; it can't solve all problems.

Usage: Functions as predicative.

Note: Neutral in meaning.

464. 树挪死，人挪活 (樹挪死，人挪活)
shù nuó sǐ, rén nuó huó

Translated character by character, 树挪死，人挪活 means 'tree-transplant-die, person-move-live,' whereas the implied meaning of this proverb would be 'sometimes change is good for people.' Its functional translation is 'people, unlike trees, thrive on change.'

Example 1:

A: 咱们这儿发展越来越差，怎么办呢？
B: **树挪死，人挪活**。到南方去碰碰运气吧。

A: Zánmen zhèr fāzhǎn yuèláiyuè chà, zěnmebàn ne?
B: Shù nuó sǐ, rén nuó huó. Dào nánfāng qù pèngpèng yùnqì ba.

A: Things are getting worse and worse for us here. What should we do?
B: People, unlike trees, thrive on change. You should go to the South and try your hand there.

Example 2:

A: 你在这家公司工作了十年了，一点儿没发展，要不你换家公司吧？
B: 我都工作十年了，也有一定的基础了，离开了怪可惜的。
A: **树挪死，人挪活**。凭你的本事，在别的地方肯定成功。

A: Nǐ zài zhè jiā gōngsī gōngzuòle shí nián le, yìdiǎnr méi fāzhǎn, yàobù nǐ huàn jiā gōngsī ba?
B: Wǒ dōu gōngzuò shí nián le, yě yǒu yídìng de jīchǔ le, líkāi le guài kěxī de.
A: Shù nuó sǐ, rén nuó huó. Píng nǐde běnshì, zài biéde dìfāng kěndìng chénggōng.

A: You've worked at this company for ten years now, and you haven't advanced at all. Why don't you move to another company?
B: I've worked here for ten years now and I have a certain foundation. It would be a real shame if I left.
A: People, unlike trees, thrive on change. With your skills, you will definitely succeed somewhere else.

Usage: Used singly.

Note: Neutral in meaning.

465. 按下葫芦起了瓢 (按下葫蘆起了瓢) àn xià húlu qǐ le piáo

Translated character by character, 按下葫芦起了瓢 means 'press-down-gourd-rise-ed-gourd dipper,' whereas the implied meaning of this proverb would be 'if it's not one thing it's another.' Its functional translation is 'to be like Whac-A-Mole.'

Example 1:

A: 最近他倒霉事不断，公司财务状况不佳，这两天公司的情况刚稍好一点儿，他儿子又因为伤人进了监狱。

B: 是啊，**按下葫芦起了瓢**，最麻烦的是他老婆要跟他离婚。

A: Zuìjìn tā dǎoméi shì búduàn, gōngsī cáiwù zhuàngkuàng bùjiā, zhè liǎng tiān gōngsī de qíngkuàng gāng shāo hǎo yìdiǎnr, tā érzi yòu yīnwèi shāng rén jìnle jiānyù.

B: Shì a, àn xià húlu qǐle piáo, zuì máfan de shì tā lǎopo yào gēn tā líhūn.

A: Recently, he's been deluged by unlucky events. The company's financial situation wasn't good and when, in the last two days, the situation improved a little bit, his son was sent to jail for injuring someone.

A: Yeah. It's like Whac-A-Mole. The worst part is that his wife wants to divorce him.

Example 2:

A: 美国最近挺乱的。

B: 共和党和民主党争吵了快一年才在预算案上达成妥协，**按下葫芦起了瓢**，最近股市又大起大落。

A: Méiguó zuìjìn tǐng luàn de.

B: Gònghédǎng hé Mínzhǔdǎng chǎole kuài yì nián cái zài yùsuàn'àn shang dáchéng tuǒxié, àn xià húlu qǐle piáo, zuìjìn gǔshì yòu dàqǐ-dàluò.

A: Recently, America has been a mess.

B: After almost a year of fighting, the Republicans and Democrats have finally come to a compromise on the budget. But, it's like Whac-A-Mole. Recently, the stock market has been fluctuating wildly.

Usage: Used singly.

Variants: 按下葫芦浮起瓢; 按下葫芦起瓢; 按倒葫芦浮起瓢

Note: Neutral or humorous in meaning.

466. 到什么山唱什么歌 (到什麼山唱什麼歌)
dào shénme shān chàng shénme gē

Translated character by character, 到什么山唱什么歌 means 'arrive-what-mountain-sing-what-song,' whereas the implied meaning of this proverb would be 'to change one's tune when talking to different people.'

Example 1:

A: 她怎么到哪里都吃香？

B: 她嘴很甜，**到什么山唱什么歌**。

A: Tā zěnme dào nǎlǐ dōu chīxiāng?
B: Tā zuǐ hěn tián, dào shénme shān chàng shénme gē.

A: How is she popular everywhere?
B: She's a sweet talker. She changes her tune when talking to different people.

Example 2:

A: 那个推销员的业绩很好。

B: 他见什么人说什么话，**到什么山唱什么歌**。

A: Nàgè tuīxiāoyuán de yèjì hěn hǎo.
B: Tā jiàn shénme rén shuō shénme huà, dào shénme shān chàng shénme gē.

A: That salesman is very accomplished.
B: He changes his tune when talking to different people.

Usage: Functions as predicate.

Note: Neutral in meaning.

---

467. 拔根汗毛比腰粗 (拔根汗毛比腰粗)
bá gēn hàn máo bǐ yāo cū

Translated character by character, 拔根汗毛比腰粗 means 'pull-MW-body-hair-relative to-waist-thick,' whereas the implied meaning of this proverb would be 'to be significantly richer or more powerful than others.'

Example 1:

A: 我就是要跟他比。

B: 比什么啊！人家**拔根汗毛比**咱的**腰都粗**。

A: Wǒ jiùshì yào gēn tā bǐ.
B: Bǐ shénme a! Rénjia bá gēn hànmáo bǐ zán de yāo dōu cū.

A: I want to compete with him.
B: What're you thinking? We're nothing compared to him.

Example 2:

A: 小李，去年你借我的两千块钱还没还我呢。

B: 哟，你还记着哪。你**拔根汗毛比**我的**腰还粗**，这点儿小钱还要啊？

A: Xiǎo Lǐ, qùnián nǐ jiè wǒ de liǎngqiān kuài qián hái méi huán wǒ ne.
B: Yò, nǐ hái jìzhe na. Nǐ bá gēn hànmáo bǐ wǒde yāo hái cū, zhè diǎnr xiǎoqián hái yào a?

A: Little Li, you still haven't repaid the two thousand dollars you borrowed from me last year.
B: Oh, you still remember. You're much richer than me; you still want such a small sum of money?

Usage: Functions as predicate.

Note: Derogatory and humorous in meaning.

468. 阎王好见，小鬼难搪 (閻王好見，小鬼難搪)
Yánwáng hǎo jiàn, xiǎo guǐ nán táng

Translated character by character, 阎王好见，小鬼难搪 means 'devil-easy-meet, lesser-demon-hard-evade,' whereas the implied meaning of this proverb would be 'important people are very welcoming, but their handlers are less so.' Its functional translation is 'getting past the gatekeeper is the hard part.'

Example 1:

A: 我要写检举信给省长反映咱们县的腐败案。

B: 如果省长看了大概会起作用，但是**阎王好见，小鬼难搪**，估计这封信根本到不了省长手里，在秘书那里就被扣下了。

A: Wǒ yào xiě jiǎnjǔxìn gěi shěng lingdào fǎnyìng zánmen xiàn de fǔbài àn.

B: Rúguǒ shěngzhǎng kànle dàgài huì qǐ zuòyòng, dànshì Yánwáng hǎo jiàn, xiǎoguǐ nán táng, gūjì zhè fēng xìn gēnběn dàobùliǎo shěngzhǎng shǒulǐ, zài mìshū nàlǐ jiù bèi kòuxià le.

A: I want to write a letter of accusation reflecting the corruption case in our county to the provincial governor.

B: If the provincial governor receives it, it will probably have an effect, but getting past the gatekeeper is the hard part. That letter might not even reach the governor; it'll be culled by the secretary.

Example 2:

A: 我想见我们局长，可是每次秘书都说局长开会去了。

B: 很明显，你没有打点好秘书，**阎王好见，小鬼难搪**，下次先把秘书打点好了，也就能见到领导了。

A: Wǒ xiǎng jiàn wǒmen júzhǎng, kěshì měi cì mìshū dōu shuō júzhǎng kāihuì qù le.

B: Hěn míngxiǎn, nǐ méiyǒu dǎdiǎn hǎo mìshū, Yánwáng hǎo jiàn, xiǎoguǐ nán táng, xià cì xiān bǎ mìshū dǎdiǎn hǎo le, yě jiù néng jiàndào lǐngdǎo le.

A: I want to see our director, but his secretary always tells me he's in a meeting.

B: It's obvious that you haven't buttered up the secretary well enough. Getting past the gatekeeper is the hardest part. Next time, once you've first made nice with the secretary, you'll be able to see the boss.

Usage: Used singly.

Variants: 阎王好见, 小鬼难缠; 阎王好见, 小鬼难当 (缠 chán, tangle)

Note: Slightly derogatory and humorous in meaning.

469. 不见兔子不撒鹰 (不見兔子不撒鷹)
bú jiàn tùzi bù sā yīng

Translated character by character, 不见兔子不撒鹰 means 'not-see-hare-not-release-eagle,' whereas the implied meaning of this proverb would be 'to refrain from acting until something is certain.' Its functional translation is 'to not commit oneself until success is certain.'

Example 1:

A: 为什么骗子在中国北方屡屡得手，而在南方却很难得手呢？
B: 北方人实在，别人说的话都信；南方人精明，**不见兔子不撒鹰**。

A: Wèishénme piànzi zài Zhōngguó běifāng lǚlǚ déshǒu, ér zài nánfāng què hěn nán déshǒu ne?
B: Běifāng rén shízai, biérén shuō de huà dōu xìn; nánfāng rén jīngmíng, bú jiàn tùzi bù sā yīng.

A: Why do cheats succeed time and again in northern China but find it hard to succeed in the south?
B: Northerners are naïve; they believe everything other people tell them. Southerners are shrewd; they won't commit themselves until success is certain.

Example 2:

A: 找他借钱吧。
B: 估计很难，他这个人**不见兔子不撒鹰**，手紧得很。

A: Zhǎo tā jièqián ba.
B: Gūjì hěn nán, tā zhègè rén bú jiàn tùzi bù sā yīng, shǒu jǐn de hěn.

A: Go borrow money from him.
B: It'll probably be very difficult. That guy is very careful with his money. He won't commit himself unless he is certain of success.

Usage: Functions as predicate.

Note: Neutral in meaning.

470. 当面锣，对面鼓 (當面鑼，對面鼓)
dāng miàn luó, duì miàn gǔ

Translated character by character, 当面锣，对面鼓 means 'facing-gong-opposing-drum,' whereas the implied meaning of this proverb would be 'to argue about or discuss something face-to-face.' Its functional translation is 'to hash things out in the open.'

Example 1:

A: 在背后散布谣言算什么本事？有本事就站出来**当面锣，对面鼓**地辩论一次！

A: Zài bèihòu sànbù yáoyán suàn shénme běnshì? Yǒu běnshì jiù zhàn chūlái dāng miàn luó duì miàn gǔ de biànlùn yí cì!

A: What kind of integrity is spreading rumors behind people's backs? Someone with character would stand up and hash things out in the open!

Example 2:

A: 这样吧，我把你们两个都约出来。大家**当面锣，对面鼓**，把话说明白。

A: Zhèyàng ba, wǒ bǎ nǐmen liǎng gè dōu yuē chūlái. Dàjiā dāng miàn luó duì miàn gǔ, bǎ huà shuō míngbai.

A: Here's what we'll do, I'll put you two together. Everyone will hash things out in the open and make themselves understood.

Usage: Functions as adverbial or predicate.

Note: Neutral in meaning.

471. 眼大肚子小 (眼大肚子小) yǎn dà dùzi xiǎo

Translated character by character, 眼大肚子小 means 'eyes-big-stomach-small,' whereas the implied meaning of this proverb would be 'to want to tackle more than one is able.' Its functional translation is 'to have eyes bigger than one's stomach.'

Example 1:

A: 再多吃点儿！
B: 这桌子菜这么好吃，我想吃光它们，可是**眼大肚子小**，再也吃不下了。

A: Zài duō chī diǎnr!
B: Zhè zhuōzi cài zhème hǎochī, wǒ xiǎng chī guāng tāmen, kěshì yǎn dà dùzi xiǎo, zài yě chī bú xià le.

A: Eat some more!
B: The food on this table is so good, I want to eat it all, but my eyes are bigger than my stomach. I can't get anything else down.

Example 2:

A: 他是个书迷，看见书就想买，可惜**眼大肚子小**，买了很多，看得不多。

A: Tā shì gè shūmí, kàn jiàn shū jiù xiǎng mǎi, kěxī yǎn dà dùzi xiǎo, mǎile hěn duō, kàn de bù duō.

A: He's a bookworm. If he sees a book, he wants to buy it. It's a shame his eyes are bigger than his stomach. He's bought a lot of books but read few.

Usage: Functions as predicate.

Note: Slightly derogatory and humorous in meaning.

472. 浅水养不了大鱼 (淺水養不了大魚)
qiǎn shuǐ yǎng bù liǎo dà yú

Translated character by character, 浅水养不了大鱼 means 'shallow-water-raise-not-able-big-fish,' whereas the implied meaning of this proverb would be 'ambitious or talented people need room to grow.' Its functional translation is 'a big fish needs a big pond.'

Example 1:

A: 听说他也交了辞职报告走了。
B: 是啊，咱们是小公司，他是大能人，**浅水养不了大鱼**，离开是早晚的事。

A: Tīngshuō tā yě jiāole cízhí bàogào zǒu le.
B: Shì a, zánmen shì xiǎo gōngsī, tā shì dà néngrén, qiǎnshuǐ yǎng bùliǎo dàyú, líkāi shì zǎowǎn de shì.

A: I heard he also proffered his resignation and left.
B: Yeah. We're a small company and he's a wunderkind. A big fish needs a big pond; he was going to leave sooner or later.

Example 2:

A: 经理，他的求职简历看起来太好了。
B: 这不是挺好吗？
A: 我担心**浅水养不了大鱼**，他只是拿咱们公司做个跳板。

A: Jīnglǐ, tā de qiúzhí jiǎnlì kàn qǐlái tài hǎo le.
B: Zhè búshì tǐng hǎo ma?
A: Wǒ dānxīn qiǎnshuǐ yǎng bùliǎo dàyú, tā zhǐshì ná zánmen gōngsī zuò gè tiàobǎn.

A: Manager, his CV looks too good.
B: Isn't that a good thing?
A: I'm worried that a big fish needs a big pond and he's just using our company as a springboard.

Usage: Functions as predicate or object.

Variant: 浅水养不住大鱼

Note: Neutral or humorous in meaning.

---

473. **吃别人嚼过的馍不香** (吃别人嚼過的饃不香)
chī bié rén jiáo guò de mó bù xiāng

Translated character by character, 吃别人嚼过的馍不香 means 'eat-other-person-chew-ed-naan-not-tasty,' whereas the implied meaning of this proverb would be 'getting to something second is not enjoyable.' Its functional translation is 'if you're not first, you're last.'

Example 1:

A: 艺术家们最不愿意**吃别人嚼过的馍**，他们总是追求独树一帜。

A: Yìshùjiāmen zuì bú yuànyì chī biérén jiáoguò de mó, tāmen zǒngshì zhuīqiú dúshù-yízhì.

A: Artists are completely unwilling to do what others have done before. They're always seeking to blaze a new trail.

Example 2:

A: 我有一个新想法，……。
B: 你已经说了已经有别人这样做了，那你还是想点儿别的吧。**吃别人嚼过的馍不香**。

A: Wǒ yǒu yígè xīn xiǎngfǎ, ...
B: Nǐ yǐjīng shuōle yǐjīng yǒu biérén zhèyàng zuò le, nà nǐ háishì xiǎng diǎnr biéde ba. Chī biérén jiáoguò de mó bù xiāng.

A: I've got a new idea, . . .
B: You already said that someone else did that already, so you should think of something else. If you're not first, you're last.

Usage: Functions as predicate or used singly.

Note: Slightly derogatory and humorous in meaning.

---

474. **起大早，赶晚集** (起大早，趕晚集) qǐ dà zǎo, gǎn wǎn jí

Translated character by character, 起大早，赶晚集 means 'get up-(in) early morning-arrive at-market-late,' whereas the implied meaning of this proverb would be 'to be first to start but the last to finish.' Its functional translation, is 'first off the blocks, but last over the line.'

Example 1:

A: 日本那家电子公司在显示技术上够倒霉的。

B: 怎么讲？

A: **起了个大早，赶了个晚集**。他们是最先提出改善显示技术的，并且投入了很多研究经费，可是最后被美国和韩国的公司领先了。

A: Rìběn nà jiā diànzǐ gōngsī zài xiǎnshì jìshù shàng gòu dǎoméi de.

B: Zěnme jiǎng?

A: Qǐle gè dà zǎo, gǎnle gè wǎn jí. Tāmen shì zuìxiān tíchū gǎishàn xiǎnshì jìshù de, bìngqiě tóurù le hěnduō yánjiū jīngfèi, kěshì zuìhòu bèi Měiguó hé Hánguó de gōngsī lǐngxiān le.

A: That Japanese electronics company was very unlucky with display technologies.

B: Why do you say that?

A: They were first off the blocks but last over the line. They were the first to suggest improving display technology, and they invested a lot in R&D, but, in the end, they were surpassed by American and Korean companies.

Example 2:

A: 有人认为中国在同性恋问题上是**起大早，赶晚集**，因为在古代人们对同性恋的态度比较宽容，而到了现代则越来越不包容。

A: Yǒurén rènwéi Zhōngguó zài tóngxìngliàn wèntí shàng shì qǐ dà zǎo gǎn wǎn jí, yīnwèi zài gǔdài rénmen duì tóngxìngliàn de tàidù bǐjiào kuānróng, ér dàole xiàndài zé yuèláiyuè bù bāoróng.

A: Some people believe that, in terms of gay rights, China was first off the blocks but last over the line, because their attitude towards homosexuals during ancient times was relatively tolerant, but in modern times has become more and more intolerant.

Usage: Functions as predicate.

Note: Neutral or humorous in meaning.

475. 打不着狐狸惹身骚 (打不着狐狸惹身骚)
dǎ bù zháo húli rě shēn sāo

Translated character by character, 打不着狐狸惹身骚 means 'get-not-able-fox-catch-body-odor,' whereas the implied meaning of this proverb would be 'to not only not succeed in achieving one's objective, but also cause oneself trouble.' Its functional translation is 'to wake a sleeping giant.'

Example 1:

A: （公安局长）这个人臭名昭著并且很难对付，如果没有绝对把握不能
草率行动，免得**打不着狐狸惹身骚**。

A: (gōng'ān júzhǎng) Zhègè rén chòumíng-zhāozhù bìngqiě hěn nán duìfù, rúguǒ
méiyǒu juéduì bǎwò bùnéng cǎoshuài xíngdòng, miǎnde dǎ bù zháo húli rě
shēn sāo.

A: (Police chief) This person is notorious and hard to handle so, in order to avoid
waking a sleeping giant, if we do not have absolute certainty, we cannot act
rashly.

Example 2:

A: 我想联合一些人把他赶下台。
B: 小心啊！他可是只老狐狸，弄不好你们**打不着狐狸还惹一身骚**。

A: Wǒ xiǎng liánhé yìxiē rén bǎ tā gǎn xià tái.
B: Xiǎoxīn a! Tā kě shì zhī lǎohúli, nòng bù hǎo nǐmen dǎ bù zháo húli hái rě yì
shēn sāo.

A: I want to get a few people together to unseat him.
B: Be careful! He's a wily old fox. If you screw up, you'll be waking a sleeping
giant.

Usage: Functions as predicate.

Note: Slightly derogatory or neutral in meaning.

---

476. 多面手 (多面手) duō miàn shǒu

Translated character by character, 多面手 means 'multi-facet-hand(person),' whereas
the implied meaning of this proverb would be 'someone with a diverse set of skills
and knowledge.' Its functional translation is 'a renaissance man/woman,' or 'a
polymath.'

Example 1:

A: 他是个难得的人才。
B: 对，业务又精通，又会搞人际关系，是个**多面手**。

A: Tā shì gè nándé de réncái.
B: Duì, yèwù yòu jīngtōng, yòu huì gǎo rénjì guānxì, shì gè duōmiànshǒu.

A: He's a rare talent.
B: Yeah. He's proficient at his work and he has good interpersonal skills. He's a
renaissance man.

Example 2:

A: 她既能唱，又能跳，还会弹乐器，也会作曲，是一位**多面手**。

A: Tā jì néng chàng, yòu néng tiào, hái huì tán yuèqì, yě huì zuòqǔ, shì yí wèi **duōmiànshǒu**.

A: She can dance, she can sing, she can play instruments, and she can compose. She's a renaissance woman.

Usage: Functions as object.

Note: Complimentary in meaning.

477. 鸟枪换炮 (鳥槍換炮) niǎo qiāng huàn pào

Translated character by character, 鸟枪换炮 means 'bird-gun-change-cannon,' whereas the implied meaning of this proverb would be 'to see one's situation improve dramatically.' Its functional translation is 'to be moving on up.'

Example 1:

A: 哟，一年不见，开上大奔了，**鸟枪换炮**了啊！

A: Yò, yì nián bú jiàn, kāi shàng dà Bēn le, niǎo qiāng huàn pào le a!

A: Oh, I haven't seen you in a year and you're driving a Mercedes-Benz now. You're moving on up!

Example 2:

A: 以前该公司的设备一直比较落后，现在**鸟枪换炮**了，采用的都是世界上最先进的设备。

A: Yǐ qián gāi gōngsī de shèbèi yìzhí bǐjiào luòhòu, xiànzài niǎo qiāng huàn pào le, cǎiyòng de dōu shì shìjiè shàng zuì xiānjìn de shèbèi.

A: Before, this company's equipment was always pretty outdated, but now they're moving on up. Everything they're using is the world's most advanced equipment.

Usage: Functions as predicate.

Note: Humorous in meaning.

478. 矬子里拔将军 (矬子裏拔將軍) cuózi lǐ bá jiāngjūn

Translated character by character, 矬子里拔将军 means 'dwarf-amongst-choose-general,' whereas the implied meaning of this proverb would be 'to pick the best out of a bad group.' Its functional translation is 'the best house in a bad neighborhood,' or 'in the land of the blind, the one-eyed man is king.'

Example 1:

A:　他就是你们那里最优秀的了？

B:　也不是。我们那里最优秀的几个都病了，现在只能**矬子里拔将军**，所以选上了他。

A:　Tā jiùshì nǐmen nàlǐ zuì yōuxiù de le?

B:　Yě búshì. Wǒmen nàlǐ zuì yōuxiù de jǐ gè dōu bìng le, xiànzài zhǐnéng cuózi lǐ bá jiāngjūn, suǒyǐ xuǎnshàngle tā.

A:　He's the best you've got?

B:　Not really, our best few are all sick. For now, he's the best house in a bad neighborhood, so we chose him.

Example 2:

A:　他什么能力都没有，怎么被选上州长了？

B:　咳，这届州长候选人不是有这样的问题就是有那样的问题。他虽然没有能力，但是问题少，所以**矬子里拔将军**，就把他选上了。

A:　Tā shénme nénglì dōu méiyǒu, zěnme bèi xuǎnshàng zhōuzhǎng le?

B:　Hài, zhè jiè zhōuzhǎng hòuxuǎnrén búshì yǒu zhèyàng de wèntí jiùshì yǒu nàyàng de wèntí. Tā suīrán méiyǒu nénglì, dànshì wèntí shǎo, suǒyǐ cuózi lǐ bá jiāngjūn, jiù bǎ tā xuǎnshàng le.

A:　He's completely incapable; how was he elected governor?

B:　Oh, in this governor's race, if a candidate didn't have one issue, he had another. While this guy is incapable, he had few issues, so we picked the best house in a bad neighborhood.

Usage: Functions mainly as predicate

Variant: 矮子里拔将军 (used more frequently in written form)

Note: Slightly derogatory and humorous in meaning.

---

479. 给个棒槌就当针 (給個棒槌就當針)
gěi gè bàngchui jiù dāng zhēn

Translated character by character, 给个棒槌就当针 means 'given-a-club-just-use as-needle,' whereas the implied meaning of this proverb would be 'to take something too literally or seriously.'

Example 1:

A:　他可真够幼稚的，没听出来别人是跟他客套，**给个棒槌就当针**了。

A:　Tā kě zhēn gòu yòuzhì de, méi tīng chūlái biérén shì gēn tā kètào, gěi gè bàngchui jiù dāngzhēn le.

A: He really is incredibly naïve. He can't tell that other people are just standing on ceremony. He's so naïve.

Example 2:

A: 你怎么那么傻，别人**给**你**个棒槌你就当针**了。他们是逗你玩儿呢。

A: Nǐ zěnme nàme shǎ, biérén gěi nǐ gè bàngchui nǐ jiù dāngzhēn le. Tāmen shì dòu nǐ wánr ne.

A: How can you be so stupid? You take what they say to you seriously; they're having a laugh at your expense.

Usage: Functions as predicate.

Note: Slightly derogatory and humorous in meaning. 真 is homophone of 针. 当真 means 'to take at face value; to take seriously.'

---

480.   捧臭脚 (捧臭脚) pěng chòu jiǎo

Translated character by character, 捧臭脚 means 'uphold-stinky-foot,' whereas the implied meaning of this proverb would be 'to shamelessly flatter.' Its functional translation is 'to lick someone's boots.'

Example 1:

A: 领导说了应该这么办，我们就得这么办。
B: 你就会**捧臭脚**。领导让你死，你去死吗？

A: Lǐngdǎo shuōle yīnggāi zhème bàn, wǒmen jiù děi zhème bàn.
B: Nǐ jiù huì pěngchòujiǎo. Lǐngdǎo ràng nǐ sǐ, nǐ qù sǐ ma?

A: The boss said we should do it this way, so we have to do it this way.
B: You just lick his boots. If he told you to kill yourself, would you?

Example 2:

A: 他就是一个**捧臭脚**的，就会拍马屁。

A: Tā jiùshì yígè pěngchòujiǎo de, jiù huì pāimǎpì.

A: He's a bootlicker. He's only good at sucking up to people.

Usage: Functions as predicate.

Note: Derogatory in meaning.

481. 咬人的狗不露齿 (咬人的狗不露齒)
yǎo rén de gǒu bú lòu chǐ

Translated character by character, 咬人的狗不露齿 means 'bite-person-dog-not-show-teeth,' whereas the implied meaning of this proverb would be 'things that seem harmless are always the most dangerous.' Its functional translation is 'beware of a silent dog and still water.'

Example 1:

A: 他看起来挺面善的，做起事来不至于这么狠吧？

B: 你太幼稚了。**咬人的狗不露齿**，让你防不胜防啊？

A: Tā kàn qǐlái tǐng miànshàn de, zuò qǐ shì lái bú zhìyú zhème hěn ba?

B: Nǐ tài yòuzhì le. Yǎo rén de gǒu bú lòu chǐ, ràng nǐ fángbúshèngfáng a?

A: He looks pretty kind-faced. He can't be that vicious, right?

B: You're so naïve, that's to catch you off balance. Beware of a silent dog and still water.

Example 2:

A: 你要小心。他在背后没少说你坏话。

B: 不至于吧？他人挺好的。

A: **咬人的狗不露齿**，看着老实，咬起人来才凶呢。

A: Nǐ yào xiǎoxīn. Tā zài bèihòu méi shǎo shuō nǐ huàihuà.

B: Bú zhìyú ba? Tā rén tǐng hǎo de.

A: Yǎo rén de gǒu bú lòu chǐ, kànzhe lǎoshi, yǎo qǐ rén lái cái xiōng ne.

A: You need to watch out. He's been saying a lot of bad things about you behind your back.

B: Can that be? He's a good person.

A: Beware of a silent dog and still water. He looks honest, but when he attacks people, he's fierce.

Usage: Used singly.

Note: Derogatory in meaning.

482. 炒冷饭 (炒冷飯) chǎo lěng fàn

Translated character by character, 炒冷饭 means 'stir-cold-rice,' whereas the implied meaning of this proverb would be 'to hype something old without adding anything new.' Its functional translation is 'to rehash.'

Example 1:

A: 今天的报告人又讲鲁迅的小说。

B: 又在**炒冷饭**，已经讲了一百多年了。

A: Jīntiān de bàogàorén yòu jiǎng Lǔxùn de xiǎoshuō.

B: Yòu zài chǎolěngfàn, yǐjīng jiǎngle yì bǎi duō nián le.

A: Today's presenter talked about Lu Xun's novels again.

B: Still rehashing it. It's already been talked about for over a hundred years.

Example 2:

A: 媒体又在评选最伟大的足球运动员。

B: 这是**炒冷饭**，几乎每隔十年八年就炒一次。

A: Méitǐ yòu zài píngxuǎn zuì wěidà de zúqiú yùndòngyuán.

B: Zhè shì chǎolěngfàn, jīhū měi gé shí nián bā nián jiù chǎo yí cì.

A: The media is polling to select the greatest soccer player again.

B: That's rehashing. They remake the story practically every eight or ten years.

Usage: Functions as predicate or predicative.

Note: Slightly derogatory and humorous in meaning.

---

483. 一只羊是赶，一群羊也是放 (一隻羊是趕， 一群羊也是放) yì zhī yáng shì gǎn, yì qún yáng yě shì fàng

Translated character by character, 一只羊是赶，一群羊也是放 means 'one-MW-sheep-is-drive, one-flock-sheep-also-is-herd,' whereas the implied meaning of this proverb would be 'one more is not a burden.' Its functional translation is 'what's one more?'

Example 1:

A: 他们家已经有三个孩子了，现在老婆又大肚子了，还要生啊？

B: 那有什么，**一只羊是赶，一群羊也是放**。

A: Tāmen jiā yǐjīng yǒu sān gè háizi le, xiànzài lǎopo yòu dàdùzi le, háiyào shēng a?

B: Nà yǒu shénme, yì zhī yáng shì gǎn, yì qún yáng yě shì fàng.

A: They already have three kids, but the wife is pregnant again. Are they having another?

B: That's not a big deal. What's one more?

Example 2:

A: 老牛，上头决定这项工作也由你负责。

B: 领导这么信任我，把工作都给我干了。对我来说无所谓，**一只羊是赶，一群羊也是放**，只要领导不挑剔质量就行了。

A: Lǎo Niú, shàngtou juédìng zhè xiàng gōngzuò yě yóu nǐ fùzé.

B: Lǐngdǎo zhème xìnrèn wǒ, bǎ gōngzuò dōu gěi wǒ gàn le. Duì wǒ láishuō wúsuǒwèi, yì zhī yáng shì gǎn, yì qún yáng yě shì fàng, zhǐyào lǐngdǎo bù tiāoti zhìliàng jiù xíng le.

A: Old Niu, the boss has decided that you'll be responsible for this task.

B: The boss really trusts me, giving me all of the work. I don't care, what's one more? As long as he's not picky about quality, it's fine.

Usage: Used singly.

Note: Neutral in meaning.

---

484. **虱子多了不咬，账多了不愁 (蝨子多了不咬，賬多了不愁)** shīzi duō le bù yǎo, zhàng duō le bù chóu

Translated character by character, 虱子多了不咬, 账多了不愁 means 'lice-many-not-bite, debts-many-not-worry,' whereas the implied meaning of this proverb would be 'when one is up to one's ears in debt, one stops worrying.' Its functional translation is 'worry is interest paid on trouble before it is due.'

Example 1:

A: 你欠那么多债，不担心债主去告你啊？

B: 我啊？**虱子多了不咬，账多了不愁**。他们把我送进监狱，更一分钱都得不到了，所以现在他们对我客气着呢。

A: Nǐ qiàn nàme duō zhài, bù dānxīn zhàizhǔ qù gào nǐ a?

B: Wǒ a? Shīzi duōle bù yǎo, zhàng duō le bù chóu. Tāmen bǎ wǒ sòngjìn jiānyù, gèng yī fēn qián dōu dé búdào le, suǒyǐ xiànzài tāmen duì wǒ kèqì zhe ne.

A: You're so deep in debt, aren't you worried the creditor will sue you?

B: Me? If I owe you a pound, I have a problem; if I owe you a million, the problem is yours. If they send me to jail, they won't get even a penny, so now they're being polite to me.

Example 2:

A: 还有三天就大考了，你怎么还那么轻松？

B: 我以前欠得太多了，现在**虱子多了不咬，账多了不愁**，反正也考不好了。

A: Hái yǒu sān tiān jiù dàkǎo le, nǐ zěnme hái nàme qīngsōng?

B: Wǒ yǐqián qiàn de tài duō le, xiànzài shīzi duōle bù yǎo, zhàng duōle bù chóu, fǎnzhèng yě kǎo bù hǎo le.

A: The big test is in just three days; how are you still so calm?

B: I've already fallen too far behind. At this point, worry is just interest paid on trouble before it's due. In any case, I won't do well.

Usage: Functions as predicate or used singly.

Note: Slightly derogatory and humorous in meaning.

---

485. 攒鸡毛，凑掸子 (攢雞毛，湊撢子) zǎn jī máo, còu dǎnzi

Translated character by character, 攒鸡毛，凑掸子 means 'accumulate-chicken-feather-make up-duster,' whereas the implied meaning of this proverb would be 'quantity does not make up for inferior quality.'

Example 1:

A: 咱们的竞争对手联合了二十家小公司，要跟咱们对抗。

B: 别说二十家，就是二百家也不是咱们的对手啊。他们就是**攒鸡毛，凑掸子**。

A: Zánmen de jìngzhēng duìshǒu liánhé le èrshí jiā xiǎo gōngsī, yào gēn zánmen duìkàng.

B: Bié shuō èrshí jiā, jiùshì èr bǎi jiā yě búshì zánmen de duìshǒu a. Tāmen jiùshì zǎn jīmáo, còu dǎnzi.

A: Our competitor combined twenty small companies and wants to compete with us.

B: It doesn't matter if it's 20 or 200 companies, they're not our competitor. They're just trying to use quantity to make up for quality.

Example 2:

A: 房子首付凑齐了吗？

B: 终于齐了。

A: 找了好多人吧？

B: 可不是，东借西借，**攒鸡毛，凑掸子**，终于凑齐了。

A: Fángzi shǒufù còu qí le ma?

B: Zhōngyú qí le.

A: Zhǎole hǎo duō rén ba?

B: Kěbúshì, dōng jiè xī jiè, zǎn jīmáo, còu dǎnzi, zhōngyú còu qí le.

A: Have you pieced together the down payment yet?

B: Yes, finally.

A: Did you ask a lot of people?

B: Yeah, I borrowed from everyone. Piece by piece, I finally got the down payment together.

Usage: Functions as predicate.

Note: Slightly derogatory in meaning.

486. 骑脖子拉屎 (騎脖子拉屎) qí bózi lāshǐ

Translated character by character, 骑脖子拉屎 means 'sit-neck-poop,' whereas the implied meaning of this proverb would be 'to treat someone like garbage.'

Example 1:

A: 这些房地产商，强行征了人家的住宅，还找人把人家打得吐血，太残忍了。

B: 这不是**骑脖子拉屎**吗？让人家怎么活啊？

A: Zhèxiē fángdìchǎnshāng, qiángxíng zhēngle rénjia de zhùzhái, hái zhǎo rén bǎ rénjia dǎ de tùxiě, tài cánrěn le.

B: Zhè búshì qí bózi lāshǐ ma? Ràng rénjia zěnme huó a?

A: That real estate developer forcefully took someone's home and asked some people to severely beat him. It's so cruel.

B: Isn't he treating others like garbage? How can he live like that?

Example 2:

A: 他在我眼前调戏我老婆。

B: 简直**骑着你脖子拉屎**，你怎么办了？

A: Tā zài wǒ yǎnqián tiáoxì wǒ lǎopo.

B: Jiǎnzhí qízhe nǐ bózi lāshǐ, nǐ zěnme bàn le?

A: He flirted with my wife right in front of me.

B: He really treated you like garbage. What did you do about it?

Usage: Functions as predicate or predicative.

Variant: 骑着脖子拉屎

Note: Derogatory in meaning.

487. 指着和尚骂秃子 (指著和尚罵秃子)
zhǐ zhe héshang mà tūzi

Translated character by character, 指着和尚骂秃子 means 'point-ing-monk-curse-bald-person,' whereas the implied meaning of this proverb would be 'to say something to someone that doesn't appear to be about them, but is, in fact, a thinly veiled criticism.'

Example 1:

A: 那个女人有过很多男朋友，可是他在她面前总是提到"妓女"。

B: 喔，这不是**指着和尚骂秃子**嘛。

A: Nàgè nǚrén yǒu guò hěnduō nánpéngyou, kěshì tā zài tā miànqián zǒngshì tídào "jìnǚ".

B: Wò, zhè búshì zhǐzhe héshang mà tūzi ma.

A: That woman has had a lot of boyfriends, but he was always mentioning "prostitutes" in front of her.

B: Oh, isn't he just criticizing her to her face?

Example 2:

A: 你什么意思？

B: 你自己心里清楚。

A: 有种就说出来，别**指着和尚骂秃子**。

A: Nǐ shénme yìsi?

B: Nǐ zìjǐ xīnli qīngchu.

A: Yǒu zhǒng jiù shuō chūlái, bié zhǐ zhe héshang mà tūzi.

A: What do you mean?

B: You know what I mean.

A: If you have the guts, just spit it out. Don't beat around the bush.

Usage: Functions as predicate or predicative.

Note: Derogatory and humorous in meaning.

488. 蚂蚱也是肉 (螞蚱也是肉) màzha yě shì ròu

Translated character by character, 蚂蚱也是肉 means 'locust-also-is-meat,' whereas the implied meaning of this proverb would be 'a buck is a buck.'

Example 1:

A: 利润这么低的生意你也做？

B: **蚂蚱也是肉**！这年头生意不好做啊。

A: Lìrùn zhème dī de shēngyì nǐ yě zuò?
B: Màzha yě shì ròu! Zhè nián tóu shēngyì bù hǎo zuò a.

A: You even engage in such low-profit business?
B: A buck is a buck! In this sort of an environment, business is hard.

Example 2:

A: 银行在那个服务项目上增收了一毛钱。
B: 一毛钱虽然少，但是**蚂蚱腿也是肉**，多了就显出来了。

A: Yínháng zài nàgè fúwù xiàngmù shàng zēngshōu le yì máo qián.
B: Yì máo qián suīrán shǎo, dànshì màzha tuǐ yě shì ròu, duōle jiù xiǎn chūlái le.

A: The bank raised fees by ten cents on that service.
B: While ten cents is not much, a buck is a buck. It adds up.

Usage: Used singly.

Variants: 蚂蚱腿也是肉; 蚂蚱虽小也是肉

Note: Neutral or humorous in meaning.

---

489. 背着抱着一般沉 (背著抱著一般沉)
bēi zhe bào zhe yìbān chén

Translated character by character, 背着抱着一般沉 means 'carry on back-ing-carry in arms-ing-equal-heavy,' whereas the implied meaning of this proverb would be 'it's more or less the same.' Its functional translation is 'six of one, half a dozen of the other.'

Example 1:

A: 我是买精装房，还是买毛坯房然后自己再装修？
B: **背着抱着一般沉**，看你急不急住了。

A: Wǒ shì mǎi jīngzhuāngfáng, háishi mǎi máopīfáng ránhòu zìjǐ zài zhuāngxiū?
B: Bēizhe bàozhe yìbān chén, kàn nǐ jí bù jí zhù le.

A: Should I buy a finished house, or should I buy a semi-finished house and then renovate it myself?
B: It's six of one, half a dozen of the other. It depends on whether you're anxious to move in or not.

Example 2:

A: 我的个人所得税，是先少交些然后再补，还是先多交些然后再退税呢？
B: **背着抱着一般沉**，先多交省心。

A: Wǒde gèrénsuǒdéshuì, shì xiān shǎo jiāo xiē ránhòu zài bǔ, háishi xiān duō jiāo xiē ránhòu zài tuìshuì ne?

B: Bēizhe bàozhe yìbān chén, xiān duō jiāo shěngxīn.

A: For my income taxes, should I underpay first and then supplement, or should I overpay and then get a refund?

B: It's six of one, half a dozen of the other. Overpaying first saves you the worry.

Usage: Used singly.

Note: Neutral in meaning.

490. 一言堂 (一言堂) yì yán táng

Translated character by character, 一言堂 means 'one-speaking-hall,' whereas the implied meaning of this proverb would be 'an area where one person's word goes.'

Example 1:

A: 他叫别人发言的时候，别人怎么不说话？

B: 开始的时候有人说，后来发现说不说都是一个样。表面上他很民主，但实际上搞**一言堂**，听不进去别人的建议。

A: Tā jiào biérén fāyán de shíhòu, biérén zěnme bù shuōhuà?

B: Kāishǐ de shíhòu yǒu rén shuō, hòulái fāxiàn shuō bù shuō dōu shì yígèyàng. Biǎomiàn shàng tā hěn mínzhǔ, dàn shíjìshàng gǎo yìyántáng, tīng bú jìnqù biérén de jiànyì.

A: When he calls on people to speak, why don't people talk?

B: People spoke at first, but they later realized that it makes no difference whether they speak or not. On the surface, he seems very democratic, but in reality, he rules the roost. He doesn't take people's suggestions into account.

Example 2:

A: 在那个公司的会议上基本上没人讲话，整个会议差不多成了首席执行官的**一言堂**。

A: Zài nàgè gōngsī de huìyì shàng jīběnshàng méi rén jiǎnghuà, zhěnggè huìyì chàbùduō chéngle shǒuxízhíxíngguān de yìyántáng.

A: At that company's meeting, practically no one spoke. The whole meeting pretty much turned into the CEO show.

Usage: Functions as object, often after verb '搞.'

Note: Slightly derogatory in meaning.

491.   乱拳打死老师傅 (亂拳打死老師傅)
luàn quán dǎ sǐ lǎo shīfu

Translated character by character, 乱拳打死老师傅 means 'chaos-fist-beat-to death-old-master,' whereas the implied meaning of this proverb would be 'an inexperienced person defeats a master by throwing out the rules or traditions.'

Example 1:

A: 英格兰队赢了意大利队？

B: 真的？怎么可能？意大利队踢得那么好。

A: 按理说赢不了，但是今天的比赛英格兰队的战术很奇怪，根本不讲究章法，一阵乱攻，**乱拳打死老师傅**。

A: Yīnggélán duì yíngle Yìdàlì duì?

B: Zhēnde? Zěnme kěnéng? Yìdàlì duì tī de nàme hǎo.

A: Àn lǐ shuō yíng bùliǎo, dànshì jīntiān de bǐsài Yīnggélán duì de zhànshù hěn qíguài, gēnběn bù jiǎngjiū zhāngfǎ, yí zhèn luàn gōng, luàn quán dǎ sǐ lǎo shīfu.

A: England's team beat Italy's?

B: Really? How's that possible? Italy's team is so good.

A: Logically speaking, it isn't possible, but England's tactics today were very odd. They really weren't concerned with organization and attacked haphazardly. They beat the Italians by throwing out the rules.

Example 2:

A: 这个年轻人与一个资深政客竞选，大家都以为两个人不是一个级别的，没想到年轻人的竞选行动完全不讲规则，最后**乱拳打死老师傅**，竟然赢了。

A: Zhège niánqīngrén yǔ yígè zīshēn zhèngkè jìngxuǎn, dàjiā dōu yǐwéi liǎng gè rén búshì yígè jíbié de, méi xiǎng dào niánqīngrén de jìngxuǎn xíngdòng wánquán bù jiǎng guīzé, zuìhòu luàn quán dǎ sǐ lǎo shīfu, jìngrán yíng le.

A: When this young person was running against a powerful politician, everyone thought they weren't on the same level. No one thought that the young person's campaign events would completely flout tradition and that, in the end, he would surprisingly win by throwing out the rules.

Usage: Functions as predicate.

Note: Neutral or humorous in meaning.

492. 端起碗来吃肉，放下筷子骂娘 (端起碗來吃肉，放下筷子罵娘) duān qǐ wǎn chī ròu, fàng xià kuàizi mà niáng

Translated character by character, 端起碗来吃肉，放下筷子骂娘 means 'hold-up-bowl-eat-meat, put-down-chopsticks-scold-mother,' whereas the implied meaning of this proverb would be 'to be ungrateful for that which is provided to them and want more.' Its functional translation is 'to drink the ocean and then call it salty.'

Example 1:

A: 他又在发牢骚，说工作太辛苦。

B: 让他闭嘴。**端起碗吃肉，放下筷子骂娘**。工资那么高，还想不干活，简直做梦。

A: Tā yòu zài fā láosao, shuō gōngzuò tài xīnkǔ.

B: Ràng tā bìzuǐ. Duān qǐ wǎn chī ròu, fàngxià kuàizi mà niáng. Gōngzī nàme gāo, hái xiǎng bú gànhuó, jiǎnzhí zuòmèng.

A: He's grumbling again, saying his job is too arduous.

B: Make him shut up. He drinks the ocean and then calls it salty. His salary is huge and he still doesn't want to work; he's really dreaming.

Example 2:

A: 政治家们也不容易，千方百计地想为老百姓多做些好事，可是老百姓现在很难满足，总是批评政府。

B: 是啊。**端起碗吃肉，放下筷子骂娘**。是不是老百姓的要求太高了？

A: Zhèngzhìjiāmen yě bù róngyi, qiānfāng-bǎijì de xiǎng wèi lǎobǎixìng duō zuò xiē hǎoshì, kěshì lǎobǎixìng xiànzài hěn nán mǎnzú, zǒngshì pīpíng zhèngfǔ.

B: Shì a. Duān qǐ wǎn chī ròu, fàngxià kuàizi mà niáng. Shìbúshì lǎobǎixìng de yāoqiú tài gāo le?

A: Politicians also have it bad. They do everything in their power to try to do more good for the people, but the people are very hard to satisfy, always criticizing the government.

B: Yes, they drink the ocean and then call it salty. Aren't the people's demands too extravagant?

Usage: Used singly.

Variants: 端起碗吃肉，放下筷子骂娘; 拿起筷子吃肉，放下筷子骂娘

Note: Derogatory and humorous in meaning.

493. 出头的椽子先烂 (出頭的椽子先爛)
chū tóu de chuánzi xiān làn

Translated character by character, 出头的椽子先烂 means 'stick-out-rafter-first-rot,' whereas the implied meaning of this proverb would be 'those who stand out are subject to attack.' Its functional translation is 'the nail that sticks out gets hammered down.'

Example 1:

A: 医院的新规定大家都觉得不合理，怎么没人提意见？

B: 没看出来吗？这次医院不惜代价推行新规定，如果有人反对，肯定没有好下场。**出头的椽子先烂**，你还是别带这个头儿吧。

A: Yīyuàn de xīn guīdìng dàjiā dōu juéde bù hélǐ, zěnme méi rén tí yìjian?

B: Méi kàn chūlai ma? Zhècì yīyuàn bùxī dàijià tuīxíng xīn guīdìng, rúguǒ yǒu rén fǎnduì, kěndìng méiyǒu hǎo xiàchang. Chūtóu de chuánzi xiān làn, nǐ háishi bié dài zhègè tóur ba.

A: Everyone thinks that the hospital's new rule is unreasonable; so why hasn't anyone spoken up?

B: Haven't you noticed? This time around, the hospital has spared no expense in implementing the new rule. If anyone objects, it won't end well. The nail that sticks up gets hammered down. You best not lead on this one.

Example 2:

A: 部分领导干部在改革的步子上太小，总是跟在别人的后面，担心**出头的椽子先烂**。

A: Bùfen lǐngdǎo gànbù zài gǎigé de bùzi shang tài xiǎo, zǒngshì gēn zài biéren de hòumian, dānxīn chūtóu de chuánzi xiān làn.

A: Some party cadres are moving too slowly toward reform, always following behind the others. They're afraid that they will be punished for taking the lead.

Usage: Usually used singly.

Note: Neutral or humorous in meaning.

494. 一马勺坏一锅 (一馬勺壞一鍋) yì mǎsháo huài yì guō

Translated character by character, 一马勺坏一锅 means 'one-ladle-spoil-one-pot,' whereas the implied meaning of this proverb would be 'one bad thing can spoil the lot.' Its functional translation is 'one bad apple spoils the barrel.'

Example 1:

A: 其实绝大多数神父都是好的，就有那么一两个变童的，结果神职人员的形象大受影响。

B: **一马勺坏一锅。**

A: Qíshí juédàduōshù shénfù dōu shì hǎo de, jiù yǒu nàme yì-liǎng gè luántóng de, jiéguǒ shénzhí rényuán de xíngxiàng dà shòu yǐngxiǎng.

B: Yì mǎsháo huài yì guō.

A: In reality, the vast majority of priests are good. Only a couple are pedophiles, but this seriously affected the image of the clergy.

B: One bad apple spoils the barrel.

Example 2:

A: 这批产品中被抽查出来有一件不合格，影响了整批产品的价格。

B: 是啊，**一马勺坏一锅。**

A: Zhè pī chǎnpǐn zhōng bèi chōuchá chūlái yǒu yí jiàn bù hégé, yǐngxiǎngle zhěng pī chǎnpǐn de jiàgé.

B: Shì a, yì mǎsháo huài yì guō.

A: An inspection revealed that there was one substandard item in this batch of product, and it affected the price of the whole batch.

B: Yes, one bad apple spoils the barrel.

Usage: Used singly.

Note: Slightly derogatory in meaning.

---

495. 终日打雁，让雁啄了眼 (終日打雁，讓雁啄了眼)
zhōng rì dǎ yàn, ràng yàn zhuó le yǎn

Translated character by character, 终日打雁，让雁啄了眼 means 'all-day-hunt-eagle, by-eagle-pecked-eye,' whereas the implied meaning of this proverb would be 'to be unexpectedly bested by one's quarry.' Its functional translation is 'the hunter has become the hunted.'

Example 1:

A: 今天我现眼了。

B: 怎么回事儿？

A: 我干代理怎么说也有二十年了，什么样的客户没见过？谁能骗得了我？可是今天我却被一个大学生模样的人骗了，**终日打雁，让雁啄了眼**。

A: Jīntiān wǒ xiànyǎn le.

B: Zěnme huí shìr?

A: Wǒ gàn dàilǐ zěnme shuō yě yǒu èrshí nián le, shénmeyàng de kèhù méi jiànguò? Shéi néng piàndeliǎo wǒ? Kěshì jīntiān wǒ què bèi yígè dàxuéshēng múyàng de rén piàn le, zhōng rì dǎ yàn, ràng yàn zhuóle yǎn.

A: I made a fool of myself today.

B: What happened?

A: I've been an agent for at least twenty years now, and I've seen every kind of client. Who could cheat me? But, today I was duped by someone who looked like a college student. The hunter has become the hunted.

Example 2:

A: 那个主持人总喜欢开别人的玩笑，可是今天被别人开了玩笑，**终日打雁，却被雁啄了眼**。

A: Nàgè zhǔchírén zǒng xǐhuan kāi biérén de wánxiào, kěshì jīntiān bèi biérén kāile wánxiào, zhōng rì dǎ yàn, què bèi yàn zhuóle yǎn.

A: That show host always enjoys making fun of other people, but today he got made fun of by someone. The hunter became the hunted.

Usage: Functions as predicate or used singly.

Variants: 终日打雁，叫雁啄了眼; 终日打雁，被雁啄了眼

Note: Slightly derogatory or neutral in meaning.

---

496. 老鸹嫌猪黑 (老鴰嫌豬黑) lǎogua xián zhū hēi

Translated character by character, 老鸹嫌猪黑 means 'crow-mock-pig-darker,' whereas the implied meaning of this proverb would be 'to criticize someone about something that would also apply to oneself.' Its functional translation is 'it's the pot calling the kettle black.'

Example 1:

A: 她自己的英语那么差，还说别人的不好。

B: 是啊，**老鸹嫌猪黑**。

A: Tā zìjǐ de yīngyǔ nàme chà, hái shuō biérén de bùhǎo.

B: Shì a, lǎogua xián zhū hēi.

A: Her English is so poor, yet she says that other person's English is no good.

B: Yeah, it's the pot calling the kettle black.

Example 2:

A: 他总是嘲笑那些不太聪明的人。

B: 他有什么资格？他自己的智商超不过八十，**老鸹嫌猪黑**。

A: Tā zǒngshì cháoxiào nàxiē bú tài cōngmíng de rén.

B: Tā yǒu shénme zīgé? Tā zìjǐ de zhìshāng chāo bú guò bāshí, lǎogua xián zhū hēi.

A: He's always laughing at those people who aren't so bright.

B: What right does he have? His IQ can't be any higher than 80. It's the pot calling the kettle black.

Usage: Used singly.

Note: Derogatory and humorous in meaning.

497. 别人牵驴你拔橛 (別人牽驢你拔橛)
bié rén qiān lú nǐ bá jué

Translated character by character, 别人牵驴你拔橛 means 'other-person-lead-donkey-you-pull-stake,' whereas the implied meaning of this proverb would be 'to shoulder the blame and not get what one wants.' Its functional translation is 'to get caught holding the bag.'

Example 1:

A: 听说那个省的人正在抢购盐呢。

B: 是啊，价格已经炒上去十倍了，政府已经很关注了。

A: 那我们也赶快贩一批盐过去吧？

B: 诶，**别人牵驴你拔橛**。你没听见刚才我说政府已经盯上了吗？你一去不是正好被政府抓到吗？

A: Tīngshuō nàgè shěng de rén zhèngzài qiǎnggòu yán ne.

B: Shì a, jiàgé yǐjīng chǎo shàngqù shí bèi le, zhèngfǔ yǐjīng hěn guānzhù le.

A: Nà wǒmen yě gǎnkuài fàn yì pī yán guòqù ba?

B: Èi, biérén qiān lú nǐ bá jué. Nǐ méi tīngjiàn gāngcái wǒ shuō zhèngfǔ yǐjīng dīng shàng le ma? Nǐ yí qù búshì zhènghǎo bèi zhèngfǔ zhuā dào ma?

A: I hear people in that province are making a run on salt.

B: Yeah. The price has already been jacked up ten times; the government is already monitoring it closely.

A: Then let's quickly move a shipment of salt there to sell.

B: Huh? And get caught holding the bag? Didn't you just hear me say that the government is already onto it? Wouldn't you get caught by the government once you got there?

Example 2:

A: （医生甲）你看，报纸上又在骂咱们呢，说咱们收费过高了。

B: （医生乙）咱们这一行真倒霉，钱都让别人赚走了大头儿，**别人牵**走**了驴，咱**们成了**拔橛**的了。

A: (yīsheng jiǎ) Nǐ kàn, bàozhǐ shàng yòu zài mà zánmen ne, shuō zánmen shōufèi
guò gāo le.

B: (yīsheng yǐ) Zánmen zhè yì háng zhēn dǎoméi, qián dōu ràng biérén zuàn
zǒule dàtóur, biérén qiān zǒu le lú, zánmen chéngle bá jué de le.

A: (Doctor A) Look, they're slandering us in the newspaper again, saying our fees
are too high.

B: (Doctor B) Our industry is such a mess. The vast majority of the money has all
been taken by other people and we've been left holding the bag.

Usage: Used singly.

Variants: 别人(or 人家)牵驴(or 牛)你拔橛(or 桩)

Note: Derogatory and humorous in meaning.

---

498. 仔卖爷田不心疼 (仔賣爺田不心疼)
zǎi mài yé tián bù xīn téng

Translated character by character, 仔卖爷田不心疼 means 'child-sell-grandfather-
field-not-heart-painful,' whereas the implied meaning of this proverb would be 'to
sell one's inheritance with no regret.' Its functional translation is 'to sell one's
birthright for a mess of pottage.'

Example 1:

A: 因为不喜欢做餐饮，他把他爸爸传给他的、经营了几十年的一家在
当地很受欢迎的比萨饼店转手卖给别人了。

B: 咳，**仔卖爷田不心疼**，他爸要是活着不得气死啊！

A: Yīnwèi bù xǐhuan zuò cānyǐn, tā bǎ tā bàba chuán gěi tā de, jīngyíngle jǐshí
nián de yì jiā zài dāngdì hěn shòu huānyíng de bǐsàbǐng diàn zhuǎnshǒu mài
gěi biérén le.

B: Hài, zǎi mài yé tián bù xīn téng, tā bà yàoshi huózhe bùděi qì sǐ a!

A: Because he doesn't like to run a restaurant, he sold the pizza parlor that his
father ran for decades and passed down to him, to another person.

B: He sold his birthright for a mess of pottage. If his father were still alive, he
would be furious.

Example 2:

A: 这么大的国有企业，以不到市场价格的三分之一卖给私人企业了。

B: 这帮领导啊，**仔卖爷田不心疼**，反正亏的不是他们自己。他们从中
反倒捞了一把。

A: Zhème dà de guóyǒu qǐyè, yǐ búdào shìchǎng jiàgé de sān fēn zhī yī mài gěi
sīrén qǐyè le.

B: Zhè bāng lǐngdǎo a, zǎi mài yé tián bù xīn téng, fǎnzhèng kuī de búshì tāmen
zìjǐ. Tāmen cóngzhōng fǎndào lāole yì bǎ.

A: That large state owned enterprise was sold to a private company for less than one third of its market value.

B: These leaders will sell their birthrights for a mess of pottage. After all, they got something out of it.

Usage: Used singly or functions as predicate.

Variants: 仔(or 崽)卖爷田不心疼(or 痛)

Note: Slightly derogatory and humorous in meaning.

---

499. **萝卜快了不洗泥 (蘿蔔快了不洗泥)**
luóbo kuài le bù xǐ ní

Translated character by character, 萝卜快了不洗泥 means 'radish-(sell) fast-not-wash-mud,' whereas the implied meaning of this proverb would be 'haste creates an inferior product.' Its functional translation, is 'the hasty bitch brings forth blind puppies.'

Example 1:

A: 这家公司的产品的质量怎么越来越差了，反倒不如前几年的好？

B: 自从他们的产品一炮走红之后，销量有了保证。**萝卜快了不洗泥**，质量差了点儿，但是销量还不错。

A: Zhè jiā gōngsī de chǎnpǐn de zhìliàng zěnme yuèláiyuè chà le, fǎndào bùrú qián jǐ nián de hǎo?

B: Zìcóng tāmen de chǎnpǐn yípàozǒuhóng zhīhòu, xiāoliàng yǒule bǎozhèng. Luóbo kuàile bù xǐ ní, zhìliàng chàle diǎnr, dànshì xiāoliàng hái búcuò.

A: How does the quality of this company's product keep getting worse and worse? On the contrary, it's not even as good as last year.

B: Ever since their product became a hit overnight, their sales volume was guaranteed. The hasty bitch brings forth blind puppies. While the quality has suffered a little, their sales numbers are still good.

Example 2:

A: 这位小说家自从获得诺贝尔文学奖以后，每年都出版好几本小说。当然，**萝卜快了不洗泥**，质量也越来越差。

A: Zhè wèi xiǎoshuōjiā zìcóng huòdé Nuòbèi'ěr wénxuéjiǎng yǐhòu, měinián dōu chūbǎn hǎo jǐ běn xiǎoshuō. Dāngrán, luóbo kuàile bù xǐ ní, zhìliàng yě yuèláiyuè chà.

A: Ever since that novelist won the Nobel Prize, she's been publishing many books each year. Of course, the hasty bitch brings forth blind puppies. The quality of her novels is deteriorating.

Usage: Used singly.

Note: Neutral in meaning.

Translated character by character, 接地气 means 'connect with-earth-vapor,' whereas the implied meaning of this proverb would be 'connected with ordinary people or circumstances.' Its functional translation is 'grounded,' or 'down to earth.'

Example 1:

A: 你好像很不舒服，是不是？

B: 没有哇。我怎么了？

A: 那你说话的时候怎么总是耸肩，我还以为你病了呢。

B: 哪儿啊！我就是留学几年，习惯西方的 body language 了。

A: 对了，你又耸肩，说话又夹洋文，在中国这儿不**接地气**啊。

A: Nǐ hǎoxiàng hěn bù shūfu, shìbúshì?

B: Méiyǒu wa. Wǒ zěnme le?

A: Nà nǐ shuōhuà de shíhòu zěnme zǒngshì sǒngjiān, wǒ hái yǐwéi nǐ bìngle ne?

B: Nǎr a! Wǒ jiùshì liúxué jǐ nián, xíguàn le xīfāng de body language le.

A: Duìle, nǐ yòu sǒngjiān, shuōhuà yòu jiā yángwén, zài Zhōngguó zhèr bù jiēdìqì a.

A: You seem very uncomfortable. Are you?

B: No. What's wrong?

A: Then why do you keep shrugging when you speak? I thought you were sick.

B: Not at all! It's just because I've gotten used to Western body language after studying abroad for several years.

B: Right. You not only shrug, you also use words from other languages when you speak Chinese. In China, that's not down-to-earth.

Example 2:

A: 冯导演的电影之所以很受观众欢迎就是因为他的电影**接地气**。

A: Féng dǎoyǎn de diànyǐng zhīsuǒyǐ hěn shòu guānzhòng huānyíng jiùshì yīnwèi tā de diànyǐng jiēdìqì.

A: The reason that Director Feng's films are very popular is that they are grounded.

Usage: Functions as predicate.

Note: Complimentary in meaning.

Appendix one: Pinyin index of 500 common Chinese proverbs and colloquial expressions

References are to entry numbers.

A

àn xià húlu qǐ le piáo 按下葫芦起了瓢 (465)

B

bā jiǔ bù lí shí 八九不离十 (122)

bā zì hái méi yì piě 八字还没一撇 (119)

bá chū luóbo dài chū ní 拔出萝卜带出泥 (460)

bá gēn hàn máo bǐ yāo cū 拔根汗毛比腰粗 (467)

bái kāi shuǐ 白开水 (389)

bǎi wū lóng 摆乌龙 (442)

bān qǐ shítou zá zìjǐ de jiǎo 搬起石头砸自己的脚 (71)

bǎn shàng dìng dīng 板上钉钉 (275)

bàn lù chū jiā 半路出家 (329)

bàn lù shā chū gè Chéng Yǎojīn 半路杀出个程咬金 (163)

bàn jiǎo shí 绊脚石 (371)

bǎo hàn bù zhī è hàn jī 饱汉不知饿汉饥 (288)

bǎo hù sǎn 保护伞 (310)

bào dà tuǐ 抱大腿 (445)

bào fó jiǎo 抱佛脚 (91)

bēi hēi guō 背黑锅 (127)

bēi zhe bào zhe yìbān chén 背着抱着一般沉 (489)

biàn sè lóng 变色龙 (378)

bié rén qiān lǘ nǐ bá juè 别人牵驴你拔橛 (497)

bīng dòng sān chǐ, fēi yí rì zhī hán 冰冻三尺，非一日之寒 (130)

bīng shān yì jiǎo 冰山一角 (304)

bìng jí luàn tóu yī 病急乱投医 (237)

bù chénggōng, biàn chéng rén 不成功，便成仁 (394)

bù dāng jiā bù zhī chái mǐ guì 不当家不知柴米贵 (342)

bù dǎo wēng 不倒翁 (270)

bú dào Huáng Hé xīn bù sǐ 不到黄河心不死 (134)

bù fēn qīng hóng zào bái 不分青红皂白 (54)

bù guǎn hēi māo bái māo, huì zhuō lǎoshǔ jiù shì hǎo māo 不管黑猫白猫，会捉老鼠就是好猫 (169)

bùguǎn sān qī èrshíyī 不管三七二十一 (23)

bú jiàn guāncai bú luò lèi 不见棺材不落泪 (94)

bú jiàn tùzi bù sā yīng 不见兔子不撒鹰 (469)

bú kàn sēng miàn kàn fó miàn 不看僧面看佛面 (240)

bú pà yí wàn, jiù pà wànyī 不怕一万，就怕万一 (21)

bú rù hǔ xuè, yān dé hǔ zǐ 不入虎穴，焉得虎子 (116)

bú shì chī sù de 不是吃素的 (188)

bú shì shěng yóu de dēng 不是省油的灯 (125)

bú shì yú sǐ, jiù shì wǎng pò 不是鱼死，就是网破 (303)

C

cā pìgu 擦屁股 (417)

cāngying bù dīng wú fèng de dàn 苍蝇不叮无缝的蛋 (368)

chāi dōng qiáng, bǔ xī qiáng 拆东墙，补西墙 (350)

cháng tòng bù rú duǎn tòng 长痛不如短痛 (300)

cháng zài hé biān zǒu, nǎ yǒu bù shī xié 常在河边走，哪有不湿鞋 (220)

chàng duì tái xì 唱对台戏 (376)

chàng gāo diào 唱高调 (313)

chàng kōng chéng jì 唱空城计 (400)

chàng shuāng huáng 唱双簧 (308)

chǎo lěng fàn 炒冷饭 (482)

chǎo yóu yú 炒鱿鱼 (66)

chē dào shān qián bì yǒu lù 车到山前必有路 (82)

chě hòu tuǐ 扯后腿 (320)

chén zhīma, làn gǔzi 陈芝麻、烂谷子 (264)

chéng shì bù zú, bài shì yǒu yú 成事不足，败事有余 (38)

chéng yě Xiāo Hé, bài yě Xiāo Hé 成也萧何，败也萧何 (359)

chī bì mén gēng 吃闭门羹 (222)

chī bié rén jiáo guò de mó bù xiāng 吃别人嚼过的馍不香 (473)

chī bú dào pútao jiù shuō pútao suān 吃不到葡萄就说葡萄酸 (43)

chī bù liǎo dōu zhe zǒu 吃不了兜着走 (84)

chī dà guō fàn 吃大锅饭 (337)

chī dòufu 吃豆腐 (206)

chī ruǎn fàn 吃软饭 (211)

chī shuǐ bú wàng wā jǐng rén 吃水不忘挖井人 (268)

chī xiāng de, hē là de 吃香的，喝辣的 (77)

chī yǎba kuī 吃哑巴亏 (215)

chī yí qiàn, zhǎng yí zhì 吃一堑，长一智 (7)

chī zhe wǎn lǐ de, kàn zhe guō lǐ de 吃着碗里的，看着锅里的 (24)

chǐ yǒu suǒ duǎn, cùn yǒu suǒ cháng 尺有所短，寸有所长 (407)

chǒu huà shuō zài qiántou 丑话说在前头 (162)

chǒu xífu zǎo wǎn yě děi jiàn gōng pó 丑媳妇早晚也得见公婆 (233)

chūlai hùn de, zǒng yào huán de 出来混的，总要还的 (408)

chū qì tǒng 出气筒 (121)

chū tóu de chuánzi xiān làn 出头的椽子先烂 (493)

chū shēng niú dú bú pà hǔ 初生牛犊不怕虎 (155)

chuān xiǎo xié 穿小鞋 (321)

chuī niú pí 吹牛皮 (98)

cǐ dì wú yín sānbǎi liǎng 此地无银三百两 (42)

cù tánzi 醋坛子 (179)

cuózi lǐ bá jiāngjūn 矬子里拔将军 (478)

D

dǎ bù zháo húli rě shēn sāo 打不着狐狸惹身骚 (475)

dǎ cā biān qiú 打擦边球 (327)

dǎ diào mén yá wǎng dù lǐ yàn 打掉门牙往肚里咽 (375)

dǎ gǒu hái děi kàn zhǔ rén 打狗还得看主人 (167)

dǎ jiàngyóu 打酱油 (20)

dǎ kāi tiān chuāng shuō liàng huà 打开天窗说亮话 (190)

dǎ mǎhu yǎn 打马虎眼 (325)

dǎ rúyì suànpán 打如意算盘 (238)

dǎ shuǐ piāo 打水漂 (314)

dǎ tuì táng gǔ 打退堂鼓 (146)

dǎ xiǎo suànpán 打小算盘 (255)

dǎ yì bāzhang, gěi gè tián zǎo 打一巴掌，给个甜枣 (405)

dǎ zhǒng liǎn chōng pàngzi 打肿脸充胖子 (85)

dà diē yǎn jìng 大跌眼镜 (369)

dà shù dǐxia hǎo chéngliáng 大树底下好乘凉 (249)

dà shuǐ chōng le lóng wáng miào 大水冲了龙王庙 (360)

dà yì shī Jīngzhōu 大意失荆州 (410)

dà yú chī xiǎo yú 大鱼吃小鱼 (351)

dài gāo mào 戴高帽 (338)

dāng ěr páng fēng 当耳旁风 (87)

dāng miàn luó, duì miàn gǔ 当面锣，对面鼓 (470)

dāng yì tiān héshang zhuàng yì tiān zhōng 当一天和尚撞一天钟 (227)

daozi zuǐ, dòufu xīn 刀子嘴，豆腐心 (63)

dào dǎ yì pá 倒打一耙 (263)

dào shénme shān chàng shénme gē 到什么山唱什么歌 (466)

dé piányi mài guāi 得便宜卖乖 (124)

dēng bízi shàng liǎn 蹬鼻子上脸 (205)

diào liànzi 掉链子 (159)

dīng shì dīng, mǎo shì mǎo 丁是丁，卯是卯 (425)

dōng fāng bú liàng xī fāng liàng 东方不亮西方亮 (430)

dōng fēng yā dǎo xī fēng 东风压倒西风 (423)

dú mù bù chéng lín 独木不成林 (379)

duān qǐ wǎn chī ròu, fàng xià kuàizi mà niáng 端起碗来吃肉，放下筷子骂娘 (492)

duì hào rù zuò 对号入座 (141)

duì shì bú duì rén 对事不对人 (174)

duō gè péngyou duō tiáo lù 多个朋友
多条路 (253)

duō miàn shǒu 多面手 (476)

duō nián de xífu áo chéng pó 多年的媳妇
熬成婆 (426)

duǒ de guò chū-yī, duǒ bù guò shíwǔ
躲得过初一，躲不过十五 (76)

E

èr 二 (290)

èr bǎi wǔ 二百五 (6)

èr hǔ xiāng zhēng, bì yǒu yì shāng
二虎相争，必有一伤 (349)

èr yī tiān zuò wǔ 二一添作五 (448)

F

fàng gēzi 放鸽子 (113)

fàng wèi xīng 放卫星 (432)

fàng cháng xiàn, diào dà yú 放长线，
钓大鱼 (184)

féi shuǐ bù liú wài rén tián 肥水不流外人田
(52)

fēn yì bēi gēng 分一杯羹 (377)

fēng mǎ niú bù xiāng jí 风马牛不相及 (148)

fēng yí zhèn, yǔ yí zhèn 风一阵，雨一阵
(449)

G

gǎn yāzi shàng jià 赶鸭子上架 (182)

gān dǎ léi, bú xià yǔ 干打雷，不下雨 (271)

gāo bù chéng, dī bú jiù 高不成，低不就
(298)

gēbo niǔ bú guò dàtuǐ 胳膊扭不过大腿
(287)

gēbozhǒu wǎng wài niǔ 胳膊肘往外扭 (299)

gé háng rú gé shān 隔行如隔山 (357)

gé qiáng yǒu ěr 隔墙有耳 (186)

gè dǎ wǔshí dà bǎn 各打五十大板 (443)

gěi gè bàngchui jiù dāng zhēn 给个棒槌
就当针 (479)

gěi lì 给力 (291)

gěi tā yì diǎn yánsè kàn kàn 给他一点颜色
看看 (322)

gōng shuō gōng yǒu lǐ, pó shuō pó yǒu lǐ
公说公有理，婆说婆有理 (144)

gǒu gǎi bù liǎo chī shǐ 狗改不了吃屎 (171)

gǒu jí le tiào qiáng 狗急了跳墙 (135)

gǒu tuǐ zi 狗腿子 (284)

gǒu yǎn kàn rén dī 狗眼看人低 (136)

gǒu yǎo gǒu 狗咬狗 (312)

gǒu zuǐ lǐ tǔ bù chū xiàng yá 狗嘴里吐不出
象牙 (59)

guà yáng tóu, mài gǒu ròu 挂羊头、卖狗肉
(218)

Guāngōng miàn qián shuǎ dà dāo
关公面前耍大刀 (297)

guāng jiǎo de bú pà chuān xié de 光脚的
不怕穿鞋的 (393)

gǔn dāo ròu 滚刀肉 (395)

guò hé chāi qiáo 过河拆桥 (105)

guò le zhè ge cūn, jiù méi zhè ge diàn
过了这个村，就没这个店 (90)

guò wǔ guān, zhǎn liù jiàng 过五关、
斩六将 (372)

H

hǎo hàn bù chī yǎn qián kuī 好汉不吃
眼前亏 (50)

hǎo le shāngbā wàng le téng 好了伤疤
忘了疼 (178)

hǎo mǎ bù chī huí tóu cǎo 好马不吃回头草
(1)

hǎo xì zài hòutou 好戏在后头 (97)

hèn tiě bù chéng gāng 恨铁不成钢 (88)

héng tiāo bízi shù tiāo yǎn 横挑鼻子竖挑眼
(399)

hóng yǎn bìng 红眼病 (343)

Hóngmén yàn 鸿门宴 (214)

hóu nián mǎ yuè 猴年马月 (31)

húli jīng 狐狸精 (161)

húli wěiba lòu chūlái le 狐狸尾巴露出来了
(352)

húlu lǐ mài de shì shénme yào 葫芦里卖的
是什么药 (344)

hǔ dú bù shí zǐ 虎毒不食子 (165)

huā wú bǎi rì hóng 花无百日红 (422)

huà hǔ bù chéng fǎn lèi quǎn 画虎不成
反类犬 (409)

huàn tāng bú huàn yào 换汤不换药 (197)

huáng dì nǚ ér bù chóu jià 皇帝女儿不愁嫁
(418)

huángshang bù jí tàijian jí 皇上不急太监急
(39)

huì kū de háizi yǒu nǎi chī 会哭的孩子有
奶吃 (447)

huó rén ràng niào biē sǐ 活人让尿憋死
(420)

huǒ shāo méi máo 火烧眉毛 (384)
huò xī ní 和稀泥 (318)

J

jī bù zé shí 饥不择食 (173)
jīdàn lǐ tiāo gútou 鸡蛋里挑骨头 (83)
jī fēi dàn dǎ 鸡飞蛋打 (286)
jī fēi gǒu tiào 鸡飞狗跳 (272)
jī máo suàn pí 鸡毛蒜皮 (28)
jī tóng yā jiǎng 鸡同鸭讲 (433)
jǐ suǒ bú yù, wù shī yú rén 己所不欲，
    勿施于人 (15)
jǐ yá gāo 挤牙膏 (362)
jì shēng Yú, hé shēng Liàng? 既生瑜，
    何生亮？ (380)
jiā cháng biàn fàn 家常便饭 (45)
jiā chǒu bù kě wài yang 家丑不可外扬 (126)
jiā huā méi yǒu yě huā xiāng 家花没有
    野花香 (436)
jiā jiā yǒu běn nán niàn de jīng 家家有本
    难念的经 (100)
jià jī suí jī, jià gǒu suí gǒu 嫁鸡随鸡，
    嫁狗随狗 (189)
jiǎn ruǎn shìzi niē 拣软柿子捏 (324)
jiāng shì lǎo de là 姜是老的辣 (33)
jiǎo cǎi liǎng zhī chuán 脚踩两只船 (41)
jiǎo zhèng bú pà xié wāi 脚正不怕鞋歪 (413)
jiē dì qì 接地气 (500)
jiě líng hái xū jì líng rén 解铃还须系铃人
    (51)
jiè dōng fēng 借东风 (388)
jǐn gū zhòu 紧箍咒 (307)
jìn shuǐ lóu tái xiān dé yuè 近水楼台先得月
    (103)
jìn zhū zhě chì, jìn mò zhě hēi 近朱者赤，
    近墨者黑 (9)
jǐng shuǐ bú fàn hé shuǐ 井水不犯河水
    (111)
jìng jiǔ bù chī chī fá jiǔ 敬酒不吃吃罚酒
    (75)
jiū biànzi 揪辫子 (452)
jiǔ niú èr hǔ zhī lì 九牛二虎之力 (74)
jiǔ bìng chéng liáng yī 久病成良医 (396)
jiǔ féng zhī jǐ qiān bēi shǎo 酒逢知己
    千杯少 (226)
jiǔ xiāng bú pà xiàngzi shēn 酒香不怕
    巷子深 (301)
jiù píng zhuāng xīn jiǔ 旧瓶装新酒 (402)
jiù mìng dào cǎo 救命稻草 (198)
jūnzǐ zhī jiāo dàn rú shuǐ 君子之交淡如水 (180)

K

kāi kòng bái zhī piào 开空白支票 (309)
kāi lǜ dēng 开绿灯 (353)
kāi xiǎo chāi 开小差 (315)
kāi yè chē 开夜车 (332)
kōng shǒu tào bái láng 空手套白狼 (385)
kòu màozi 扣帽子 (459)
kuài dāo zhǎn luàn má 快刀斩乱麻 (210)

L

lā bù chū shǐ lái yuàn máofáng 拉不出屎来
    怨茅房 (429)
làiháma xiǎng chī tiān'é ròu 癞蛤蟆想吃
    天鹅肉 (46)
làn ní fú bú shàng qiáng 烂泥扶不上墙 (296)
lǎo diào yá 老掉牙 (70)
lǎogua xián zhū hēi 老鸹嫌猪黑 (496)
lǎo húli 老狐狸 (330)
lǎo huángli 老皇历 (435)
lǎo niú lā pò chē 老牛拉破车 (431)
lǎo yóu tiáo 老油条 (260)
léi shēng dà, yǔ diǎn xiǎo 雷声大、雨点小
    (241)
lǐ yú tiào lóng mén 鲤鱼跳龙门 (390)
liǎn hóng bózi cū 脸红脖子粗 (242)
liǎng miàn pài 两面派 (316)
liǎng miàn sān dāo 两面三刀 (403)
liào tiāozi 撂挑子 (381)
línzi dà le, shénme niǎo dōu yǒu
    林子大了，什么鸟都有 (27)
liú dé qīng shān zài, bú pà méi chái shāo
    留得青山在，不怕没柴烧 (34)
lóng shēng lóng, fèng shēng fèng 龙生龙，
    凤生凤 (239)
lòu mǎ jiǎo 露马脚 (143)
luàn tán qín 乱弹琴 (361)
luàn quán dǎ sǐ lǎo shīfu 乱拳打死老师傅 (491)
luóbo báicài, gè yǒu suǒ ài 萝卜白菜，
    各有所爱 (58)
luóbo kuài le bù xǐ ní 萝卜快了不洗泥 (499)
luò shuǐ gǒu 落水狗 (274)
lǜ màozi 绿帽子 (109)

M

má què suī xiǎo, wǔ zàng jù quán 麻雀
    虽小，五脏俱全 (164)
mǎ hòu pào 马后炮 (158)
màzha yě shì ròu 蚂蚱也是肉 (488)

mài guānzi 卖关子 (72)

mǎn zuǐ pǎo huǒchē 满嘴跑火车 (461)

méiyǒu bú tòu fēng de qiáng 没有不透风的
墙 (245)

méimao húzi yì bǎ zhuā 眉毛胡子一把抓
(207)

mén wài hàn 门外汉 (294)

míng qiāng yì duǒ, àn jiàn nán fang 明枪
易躲，暗箭难防 (199)

mō zhe shítou guò hé 摸着石头过河 (328)

mó dāo bú wù kǎn chái gōng 磨刀不误
砍柴工 (147)

mò xū yǒu 莫须有 (364)

móu shì zài rén, chéng shì zài tiān
谋事在人，成事在天 (200)

mǔ lǎohǔ 母老虎 (292)

N

ná de qǐ, fàng de xià 拿得起，放得下 (35)

ná jīdàn pèng shítou 拿鸡蛋碰石头 (244)

ná jī máo dāng lìng jiàn 拿鸡毛当令箭 (365)

nǎ hú bù kāi tí nǎ hú 哪壶不开提哪壶 (65)

nǐ zǒu nǐ de yáng guān dào, wǒ guò wǒ de
dú mù qiáo 你走你的阳关道，我过我的
独木桥 (89)

niǎo qiāng huàn pào 鸟枪换炮 (477)

niú bù hē shuǐ qiáng àn tóu 牛不喝水
强按头 (441)

niú tóu bú duì mǎ zuǐ 牛头不对马嘴 (80)

P

pāi mǎ pì 拍马屁 (18)

pǎo le héshang pǎo bù liǎo miào 跑了和尚
跑不了庙 (108)

pǎo lóng tào 跑龙套 (250)

péi le fūren yòu zhé bīng 赔了夫人又折兵
(117)

pěng chòu jiǎo 捧臭脚 (480)

pèng dìngzi 碰钉子 (204)

pèng yì bízi huī 碰一鼻子灰 (195)

pí xiào ròu bú xiào 皮笑肉不笑 (175)

pìgu juédìng nǎodai 屁股决定脑袋 (455)

pō lěng shuǐ 泼冷水 (152)

pò guànzi pò shuāi 破罐子破摔 (56)

Q

qī dà gū, bā dà yí 七大姑，八大姨 (251)

qí bózi lāshǐ 骑脖子拉屎 (486)

qí mǎ zhǎo mǎ 骑马找马 (457)

qǐ dà zǎo, gǎn wǎn jí 起大早，赶晚集 (474)

qiān lǐ mǎ 千里马 (326)

qián pà láng, hòu pà hǔ 前怕狼，后怕虎
(267)

qián rén zāi shù, hòu rén chéng liáng
前人栽树，后人乘凉 (295)

qiǎn shuǐ yǎng bù liǎo dà yú 浅水养不了
大鱼 (472)

qiāng dǎ chū tóu niǎo 枪打出头鸟 (203)

qiáng jiàng shǒu xià wú ruò bīng 强将手下
无弱兵 (427)

qiáng lóng yā bú zhù dìtóushé 强龙压不住
地头蛇 (391)

qiáng niǔ de guā bù tián 强扭的瓜不甜 (69)

qiáng dǎo zhòng rén tuī 墙倒众人推 (363)

qiáng tóu cǎo 墙头草 (101)

qiāo luó biānr 敲锣边儿 (458)

qiāo mén zhuān 敲门砖 (382)

qiāo zhú gang 敲竹杠 (319)

qiǎo fù nán wéi wú mǐ zhī chuī 巧妇难为
无米之炊 (187)

qíngrén yǎn lǐ chū Xīshī 情人眼里出西施
(19)

qiū hòu suàn zhàng 秋后算账 (339)

qiú yéye, gào nǎinai 求爷爷，告奶奶 (373)

R

rè liǎn tiē lěng pìgu 热脸贴冷屁股 (177)

rén bù kě mào xiàng, hǎi shuǐ bù kě dǒu
liáng 人不可貌相，海水不可斗量 (26)

rén pà chū míng zhū pà zhuàng 人怕出名
猪怕壮 (246)

rén suàn bù rú tiān suàn 人算不如天算
(191)

rén wǎng gāo chù zǒu, shuǐ wǎng dī chù
liú 人往高处走，水往低处流 (67)

ròu làn zài guō lǐ 肉烂在锅里 (415)

S

sān gè chòu pí jiàng, dǐng gè Zhūgé Liàng
三个臭皮匠，顶个诸葛亮 (40)

sān gè héshang méi shuǐ chī 三个和尚
没水吃 (181)

sān gè nǚ rén yì tái xì 三个女人一台戏
(201)

sān jiǎo māo 三脚猫 (221)

sān jù huà bù lí běn hang 三句话不离本行
(345)

sānshíliù jì zǒu wéi shàng 三十六计走为上 (86)

sānshí nián hé dōng, sānshí nián hé xī 三十年河东，三十年河西 (223)

sān tiān dǎ yú, liǎng tiān shài wǎng 三天打鱼，两天晒网 (60)

sān xià wǔ chú èr 三下五除二 (151)

sān cháng liǎng duǎn 三长两短 (95)

sān zì jīng 三字经 (367)

sēng duō zhōu shǎo 僧多粥少 (340)

shā jī gěi hóu kàn 杀鸡给猴看 (153)

shā jī yān yòng zǎi niú dāo 杀鸡焉用宰牛刀 (248)

shā shǒu jiǎn 杀手锏 (172)

shān zhōng wú lǎo hǔ, hóuzi chēng dà wáng 山中无老虎，猴子称大王 (247)

shàng dāo shān, xià huǒ hǎi 上刀山，下火海 (145)

shàng le zéi chuán 上了贼船 (236)

shàng liáng bú zhèng xià liáng wāi 上梁不正下梁歪 (115)

shě bù de háizi tào bú zhù láng 舍不得孩子套不住狼 (217)

shēntǐ shì gémìng de běnqián 身体是革命的本钱 (305)

shēn zài Cáo yíng xīn zài Hàn 身在曹营心在汉 (230)

shēng mǐ zuò chéng shú fàn 生米做成熟饭 (154)

shèng zhě wáng hóu bài zhě zéi 胜者王侯败者贼 (234)

shīzi duō le bù yǎo, zhàng duō le bù chóu 虱子多了不咬，账多了不愁 (484)

shí wàn bā qiān lǐ 十万八千里 (142)

shí shí wù zhě wéi jùn jié 识时务者为俊杰 (110)

shì hòu Zhūgé Liàng 事后诸葛亮 (273)

shì jīn shí 试金石 (383)

shì luózi shì mǎ lā chūlai liùliu 是骡子是马拉出来遛遛 (228)

shǒu xīn shǒu bèi dōu shì ròu 手心手背都是肉 (333)

shòu sǐ de luòtuo bǐ mǎ dà 瘦死的骆驼比马大 (231)

shù dà zhāo fēng 树大招风 (225)

shù dǎo húsūn sàn 树倒猢狲散 (347)

shù nuó sǐ, rén nuó huó 树挪死，人挪活 (464)

shù yù jìng ér fēng bù zhǐ 树欲静而风不止 (232)

shuǎ huā qiāng 耍花枪 (439)

shuāng rèn jiàn 双刃剑 (176)

shuō Cáo Cāo, Cáo Cāo dào 说曹操，曹操到 (4)

shuō de bǐ chàng de hǎo tīng 说得比唱得好听 (68)

shuō fēng liáng huà 说风凉话 (306)

shuō nǐ pàng nǐ jiù chuǎn 说你胖你就喘 (416)

shuō yì qiān, dào yí wàn 说一千，道一万 (370)

sǐ mǎ dāng huó mǎ yī 死马当活马医 (139)

sǐ zhū bú pà kāi shuǐ tang 死猪不怕开水烫 (196)

sì liǎng bō qiān jīn 四两拨千斤 (266)

suìyuè shì bǎ shā zhū dāo 岁月是把杀猪刀 (424)

suō tóu wūguī 缩头乌龟 (334)

T

tàiyáng cóng xī biān chūlai 太阳从西边出来 (3)

tāng hún shuǐ 趟浑水 (283)

táng yī pào dàn 糖衣炮弹 (346)

tǎng zhe dōu zhòng qiāng 躺着都中枪 (412)

tàng shǒu de shānyù 烫手的山芋 (277)

tì tóu tiāozi yī tóu rè 剃头挑子一头热 (450)

tì zuì yang 替罪羊 (102)

tiān gāo huángdì yuǎn 天高皇帝远 (323)

tiānshang diào xiànbǐng 天上掉馅饼 (14)

tiān wú jué rén zhī lù 天无绝人之路 (47)

tiānxià méiyǒu bú sàn de yánxí 天下没有不散的筵席 (13)

tiānxià wūyā yìbān hēi 天下乌鸦一般黑 (133)

tiào jìn Huáng Hé xǐ bù qīng 跳进黄河洗不清 (17)

tiě fàn wǎn 铁饭碗 (129)

tiě gōng jī 铁公鸡 (156)

tīng fēng jiù shì yǔ 听风就是雨 (213)

tǒng mǎ fēng wō 捅马蜂窝 (261)

tǒng pò chuānghu zhǐ 捅破窗户纸 (366)

tōu jī bù chéng fǎn shí bǎ mǐ 偷鸡不成反蚀把米 (208)

tōu jī mō gǒu 偷鸡摸狗 (138)

tóu tòng yī tóu, jiǎo tòng yī jiǎo 头痛医头，脚痛医脚 (428)

tǔ bāozi 土包子 (224)

tùzi bù chī wō biān cǎo 兔子不吃窝边草 (128)

tùzi wěiba cháng bù liǎo 兔子尾巴长不了 (456)

tuō le kùzi fàng pì 脱了裤子放屁 (387)

W

wāi guā liè zǎo 歪瓜裂枣 (354)

wàn jīn yóu 万金油 (463)

wàn shì jù bèi, zhǐ qiàn dōng fēng
万事俱备，只欠东风 (168)

wáng pó mài guā, zì mài zì kuā 王婆卖瓜，
自卖自夸 (11)

wēn shuǐ zhǔ qīngwā 温水煮青蛙 (462)

wūyā zuǐ 乌鸦嘴 (5)

wū lòu piān féng lián yīn yǔ 屋漏偏逢
连阴雨 (259)

wú fēng bù qǐ làng 无风不起浪 (123)

wú shì bù dēng sān bǎo diàn 无事不登
三宝殿 (157)

wǔshí bù xiào bǎi bù 五十步笑百步 (293)

wù yǐ xī wéi guì 物以稀为贵 (10)

X

xiā māo pèng shàng sǐ hàozi 瞎猫碰上
死耗子 (49)

xià mǎ wēi 下马威 (132)

xià sān làn 下三烂 (235)

xià tái jiē 下台阶 (254)

xiān jūnzǐ hòu xiǎorén 先君子后小人
(406)

xiān huā chā zài niú fèn shàng 鲜花插在
牛粪上 (29)

xián yú fān shēn 咸鱼翻身 (281)

xiànmù jídù hèn 羡慕嫉妒恨 (374)

xiǎo bái liǎn 小白脸 (183)

xiǎo biànzi 小辫子 (355)

xiǎo bù rěn zé luàn dà móu 小不忍则乱
大谋 (166)

xiǎo cài yì dié 小菜一碟 (2)

xiǎo dòngzuò 小动作 (192)

xiǎo ér kē 小儿科 (78)

xiǎo jiě de shēnzi yāhuán de mìng
小姐的身子丫鬟的命 (453)

xiǎo wū jiàn dà wū 小巫见大巫 (104)

xiǎo yìsi 小意思 (262)

xiào diào dà yá 笑掉大牙 (278)

xiào miàn hǔ 笑面虎 (289)

xiè mò shā lǘ 卸磨杀驴 (411)

xīn jí chī bù liǎo rè dòufu 心急吃不了
热豆腐 (44)

xīn yǒu yú ér lì bù zú 心有余而力不足
(53)

xīn guān shàng rèn sān bǎ huǒ 新官上任
三把火 (140)

Y

Yánwáng hǎo jiàn, xiǎo guǐ nán tang
阎王好见，小鬼难搪 (468)

yǎn bú jiàn wéi jìng 眼不见为净 (32)

yǎn dà dùzi xiǎo 眼大肚子小 (471)

yǎn lǐ róu bù de shāzi 眼里揉不得沙子
(150)

yǎn zhōng dīng, ròu zhōng cì 眼中钉、
肉中刺 (216)

yáng máo chū zài yáng shēnshang
羊毛出在羊身上 (257)

yǎo rén de gǒu bú lòu chǐ 咬人的狗不露齿
(481)

yì bǎ yàoshi kāi yì bǎ suǒ 一把钥匙开一把锁
(404)

yī bú zuò, èr bù xiū 一不做，二不休 (106)

yí bù yí gè jiǎoyìn 一步一个脚印 (114)

yì zhāo bèi shé yǎo, shí nián pà jǐng shéng
一朝被蛇咬，十年怕井绳 (61)

yì cháo tiānzǐ yì cháo chén 一朝天子一朝臣
(419)

yì chuízi mǎimai 一锤子买卖 (398)

yì dāo qiē 一刀切 (401)

yī fēn qián yī fēn huò 一分钱一分货 (73)

yí gè bāzhang pāi bù xiǎng 一个巴掌拍不响
(79)

yí gè bí kǒng chū qì 一个鼻孔出气 (229)

yí gè jiāngjūn yí gè ling 一个将军一个令
(444)

yí gè luóbo yí gè kēng 一个萝卜一个坑
(311)

yì gēn shéng shàng de màzha 一根绳上的
蚂蚱 (282)

yí gùnzi dǎ sǐ 一棍子打死 (243)

yì guō duān 一锅端 (434)

yī huí shēng, èr huí shú 一回生，二回熟
(279)

yī kē shù shàng diào sǐ 一棵树上吊死
(112)

yì kǒu chī chéng gè pàngzi 一口吃成个胖子
(258)

yì mǎsháo huài yì guō 一马勺坏一锅 (494)

yì mǔ sān fēn dì 一亩三分地 (358)

yì pán sǎn shā 一盘散沙 (317)

yì píngzi bù mǎn, bàn píngzi huàngdang
一瓶子不满，半瓶子晃荡 (386)

yī shān bù róng èr hǔ 一山不容二虎 (149)

yì shī zú chéng qiān gǔ hèn 一失足成
千古恨 (64)

yī shì yī, èr shì èr 一是一，二是二 (252)

yì tiáo long 一条龙 (265)

yì tiáo lù zǒu dào hēi 一路走到黑 (302)

yì tóu wù shuǐ 一头雾水 (356)

yì wǎn shuǐ duān píng 一碗水端平 (276)

yì wō fēng 一窝蜂 (331)

yì yán tang 一言堂 (490)

yì zhāo bú shèn, mǎn pán jiē shū 一着不慎，满盘皆输 (212)

yì zhī yáng shì gǎn, yì qún yáng yě shì fang 一只羊是赶，一群羊也是放 (483)

yī húlu huà piáo 依葫芦画瓢 (185)

yǐ qí rén zhī dào huán zhì qí rén zhī shēn 以其人之道还治其人之身 (36)

yǐ xiǎorén zhī xīn, duó jūnzǐ zhī fù 以小人之心，度君子之腹 (81)

yǐ yá huán yá, yǐ yǎn huán yǎn 以牙还牙，以眼还眼 (107)

yīngxióng nán guò měirén guān 英雄难过美人关 (62)

yìng gǔtou 硬骨头 (348)

yòng zài dāo rèn shàng 用在刀刃上 (285)

yǒu bízi yǒu yǎn 有鼻子有眼 (202)

yǒu chóu bú bào fēi jūnzǐ 有仇不报非君子 (269)

yǒu nǎi jiù shì niáng 有奶就是娘 (414)

yǒu qí fù bì yǒu qí zǐ 有其父必有其子 (93)

yǒu qián néng shǐ guǐ tuī mò 有钱能使鬼推磨 (92)

yǒu xīn zāi huā huā bù zhǎng, wú xīn chā liǔ liǔ chéng yīn 有心栽花花不长，无心插柳柳成荫 (118)

yǒu yǎn bù shí Tài Shān 有眼不识泰山 (120)

yòu xiǎng dāng biǎozi yòu xiǎng lì páifang 又想当婊子又想立牌坊 (437)

yòu yào mǎ ér pǎo, yòu yào mǎ ér bù chī cǎo 又要马儿跑，又要马儿不吃草 (440)

yú yǔ xióng zhǎng bù kě dé jiān 鱼与熊掌不可得兼 (280)

yù sù zé bù dá 欲速则不达 (99)

yuǎn lái de héshang huì niàn jīng 远来的和尚会念经 (451)

yuǎn qīn bù rú jìn lín 远亲不如近邻 (131)

yuǎn shuǐ jiě bù liǎo jìn kě 远水解不了近渴 (193)

Z

zá le guō 砸了锅 (446)

zǎi mài yé tián bù xīn téng 仔卖爷田不心疼 (498)

zǎn jī máo, còu dǎnzi 攒鸡毛，凑掸子 (485)

zhàn zhe máokēng bù lāshǐ 占着茅坑不拉屎 (194)

zhàn zhe shuōhuà bù yāo téng 站着说话不腰疼 (12)

zhē xiū bù 遮羞布 (438)

zhè shān wàng zhe nà shān gāo 这山望着那山高 (392)

zhēn jīn bú pà huǒ liàn 真金不怕火炼 (170)

zhěn biān fēng 枕边风 (397)

zhēng yǎn xiā 睁眼瞎 (16)

zhēng yì zhī yǎn, bì yì zhī yǎn 睁一只眼，闭一只眼 (55)

zhēng zhe yǎnjing shuō xiā huà 睁着眼睛说瞎话 (8)

zhǐ jiàn shùmù, bú jiàn sēnlín 只见树木，不见森林 (454)

zhǐ xǔ zhōu guān fàng huǒ, bù xǔ bǎixìng diǎn dēng 只许州官放火，不许百姓点灯 (137)

zhǐ bāo bú zhù huǒ 纸包不住火 (96)

zhǐ lǎohǔ 纸老虎 (160)

zhǐ zhe héshang mà tūzi 指着和尚骂秃子 (487)

zhōng rì dǎ yàn, ràng yàn zhuó le yǎn 终日打雁，让雁啄了眼 (495)

zhòng guā dé guā, zhòng dòu dé dòu 种瓜得瓜，种豆得豆 (57)

zhòng rén shí chái huǒ yàn gāo 众人拾柴火焰高 (209)

zhǔ shú de yāzi fēi le 煮熟的鸭子飞了 (219)

zǒu guò chǎng 走过场 (335)

zǒu hòu mén 走后门 (48)

zǒu mǎ dēng 走马灯 (421)

zǒu táo huā yùn 走桃花运 (37)

zǒu zhe qiáo 走着瞧 (22)

zuān niú jiǎo jiān 钻牛角尖 (25)

zuì wēng zhī yì bú zài jiǔ 醉翁之意不在酒 (30)

zuò lěng bǎndèng 坐冷板凳 (341)

zuò shān guān hǔ dòu 坐山观虎斗 (256)

zuò wénzhāng 做文章 (336)

Appendix two: stroke index of 500 common Chinese proverbs and colloquial expressions

References are to entry numbers.

One stroke

一刀切 (401)
一口吃成个胖子 (258)
一山不容二虎 (149)
一个巴掌拍不响 (79)
一个将军一个令 (444)
一个萝卜一个坑 (311)
一个鼻孔出气 (229)
一马勺坏一锅 (494)
一不做，二不休 (106)
一分钱一分货 (73)
一只羊是赶，一群羊也是放 (483)
一失足成千古恨 (64)
一头雾水 (356)
一回生，二回熟 (279)
一把钥匙开一把锁 (404)
一步一个脚印 (114)
一条龙 (265)
一条路走到黑 (302)
一言堂 (490)
一亩三分地 (358)
一是一，二是二 (252)
一根绳上的蚂蚱 (282)
一瓶子不满，半瓶子晃荡 (386)
一盘散沙 (317)
一着不慎，满盘皆输 (212)
一朝天子一朝臣 (419)
一朝被蛇咬，十年怕井绳 (61)
一棵树上吊死 (112)
一棍子打死 (243)
一锅端 (434)
一窝蜂 (331)
一碗水端平 (276)
一锤子买卖 (398)

Two strokes

二 (290)
二一添作五 (448)
二百五 (6)
二虎相争，必有一伤 (349)
丁是丁，卯是卯 (425)
十万八千里 (142)
七大姑，八大姨 (251)
人不可貌相，海水不可斗量 (26)
人往高处走，水往低处流 (67)
人怕出名猪怕壮 (246)
人算不如天算 (191)
八九不离十 (122)
八字还没一撇 (119)
九牛二虎之力 (74)
刀子嘴，豆腐心 (63)
又要马儿跑，又要马儿不吃草 (440)
又想当婊子又想立牌坊 (437)

Three strokes

三十六计走为上 (86)
三十年河东，三十年河西 (223)
三下五除二 (151)
三个女人一台戏 (201)
三个和尚没水吃 (181)
三个臭皮匠，顶个诸葛亮 (40)
三天打鱼，两天晒网 (60)
三长两短 (95)
三句话不离本行 (345)
三字经 (367)
三脚猫 (221)
干打雷，不下雨 (271)
土包子 (224)

下三烂 (235)
下马威 (132)
下台阶 (254)
大水冲了龙王庙 (360)
大鱼吃小鱼 (351)
大树底下好乘凉 (249)
大跌眼镜 (369)
大意失荆州 (410)
万事俱备，只欠东风 (168)
万金油 (463)
上了贼船 (236)
上刀山，下火海 (145)
上梁不正下梁歪 (115)
小儿科 (78)
小不忍则乱大谋 (166)
小白脸 (183)
小动作 (192)
小巫见大巫 (104)
小姐的身子丫鬟的命 (453)
小菜一碟 (2)
小意思 (262)
小辫子 (355)
山中无老虎，猴子称大王 (247)
千里马 (326)
久病成良医 (396)
门外汉 (294)
己所不欲，勿施于人 (15)
马后炮 (158)

Four strokes

王婆卖瓜，自卖自夸 (11)
井水不犯河水 (111)
开小差 (315)
开夜车 (332)
开空白支票 (309)
开绿灯 (353)
天下乌鸦一般黑 (133)
天下没有不散的筵席 (13)
天上掉馅饼 (14)
天无绝人之路 (47)
天高皇帝远 (323)
无风不起浪 (123)
无事不登三宝殿 (157)
五十步笑百步 (293)
不入虎穴，焉得虎子 (116)
不见兔子不撒鹰 (469)
不见棺材不落泪 (94)
不分青红皂白 (54)
不成功，便成仁 (394)
不当家不知柴米贵 (342)

不到黄河心不死 (134)
不怕一万，就怕万一 (21)
不是吃素的 (188)
不是鱼死，就是网破 (303)
不是省油的灯 (125)
不看僧面看佛面 (240)
不倒翁 (270)
不管三七二十一 (23)
不管黑猫白猫，会捉老鼠就是好猫 (169)
太阳从西边出来 (3)
车到山前必有路 (82)
手心手背都是肉 (333)
牛不喝水强按头 (441)
牛头不对马嘴 (80)
长痛不如短痛 (300)
分一杯羹 (377)
公说公有理，婆说婆有理 (144)
风一阵，雨一阵 (449)
风马牛不相及 (148)
乌鸦嘴 (5)
火烧眉毛 (384)
心有余而力不足 (53)
心急吃不了热豆腐 (44)
尺有所短，寸有所长 (407)
丑话说在前头 (162)
丑媳妇早晚也得见公婆 (233)
以小人之心，度君子之腹 (81)
以牙还牙，以眼还眼 (107)
以其人之道还治其人之身 (36)
双刃剑 (176)

Five strokes

打一巴掌，给个甜枣 (405)
打小算盘 (255)
打马虎眼 (325)
打开天窗说亮话 (190)
打不着狐狸惹身骚 (475)
打水漂 (314)
打如意算盘 (238)
打肿脸充胖子 (85)
打狗还得看主人 (167)
打退堂鼓 (146)
打掉门牙往肚里咽 (375)
打酱油 (20)
打擦边球 (327)
巧妇难为无米之炊 (187)
龙生龙，凤生凤 (239)
东风压倒西风 (423)
东方不亮西方亮 (430)
占着茅坑不拉屎 (194)

旧瓶装新酒 (402)
只见树木，不见森林 (454)
只许州官放火，不许百姓点灯 (137)
四两拨千斤 (266)
生米做成熟饭 (154)
白开水 (389)
仔卖爷田不心疼 (498)
用在刀刃上 (285)
鸟枪换炮 (477)
饥不择食 (173)
半路出家 (329)
半路杀出个程咬金 (163)
头痛医头，脚痛医脚 (428)
出气筒 (121)
出头的椽子先烂 (493)
出来混的，总要还的 (408)
皮笑肉不笑 (175)
对号入座 (141)
对事不对人 (174)
母老虎 (292)

Six strokes

扣帽子 (459)
老牛拉破车 (431)
老狐狸 (330)
老油条 (260)
老皇历 (435)
老掉牙 (70)
老鸹嫌猪黑 (496)
过了这个村，就没这个店 (90)
过五关、斩六将 (372)
过河拆桥 (105)
有仇不报非君子 (269)
有心栽花花不长，无心插柳柳成荫 (118)
有奶就是娘 (414)
有其父必有其子 (93)
有钱能使鬼推磨 (92)
有眼不识泰山 (120)
有鼻子有眼 (202)
死马当活马医 (139)
死猪不怕开水烫 (196)
成也萧何，败也萧何 (359)
成事不足，败事有余 (38)
此地无银三百两 (42)
光脚的不怕穿鞋的 (393)
当一天和尚撞一天钟 (227)
当耳旁风 (87)
当面锣，对面鼓 (470)
吃一堑，长一智 (7)
吃大锅饭 (337)

吃不了兜着走 (84)
吃不到葡萄就说葡萄酸 (43)
吃水不忘挖井人 (268)
吃闭门羹 (222)
吃豆腐 (206)
吃别人嚼过的馍不香 (473)
吃软饭 (211)
吃哑巴亏 (215)
吃香的，喝辣的 (77)
吃着碗里的，看着锅里的 (24)
岁月是把杀猪刀 (424)
肉烂在锅里 (415)
先君子后小人 (406)
会哭的孩子有奶吃 (447)
杀手锏 (172)
杀鸡给猴看 (153)
杀鸡焉用宰牛刀 (248)
众人拾柴火焰高 (209)
各打五十大板 (443)
多个朋友多条路 (253)
多年的媳妇熬成婆 (426)
多面手 (476)
冰山一角 (304)
冰冻三尺，非一日之寒 (130)
羊毛出在羊身上 (257)
关公面前耍大刀 (297)
好了伤疤忘了疼 (178)
好马不吃回头草 (1)
好汉不吃眼前亏 (50)
好戏在后头 (97)
红眼病 (343)

Seven strokes

远水解不了近渴 (193)
远来的和尚会念经 (451)
远亲不如近邻 (131)
扯后腿 (320)
走马灯 (421)
走过场 (335)
走后门 (48)
走桃花运 (37)
走着瞧 (22)
花无百日红 (422)
苍蝇不叮无缝的蛋 (368)
求爷爷、告奶奶 (373)
两面三刀 (403)
两面派 (316)
听风就是雨 (213)
吹牛皮 (98)
别人牵驴你拔橛 (497)

乱拳打死老师傅 (491)
乱弹琴 (361)
你走你的阳关道，我过我的独木桥 (89)
身在曹营心在汉 (230)
身体是革命的本钱 (305)
近水楼台先得月 (103)
近朱者赤，近墨者黑 (9)
坐山观虎斗 (256)
坐冷板凳 (341)
这山望着那山高 (392)
没有不透风的墙 (245)
快刀斩乱麻 (210)
初生牛犊不怕虎 (155)
识时务者为俊杰 (110)
君子之交淡如水 (180)
屁股决定脑袋 (455)
陈芝麻、烂谷子 (264)
鸡飞狗跳 (272)
鸡飞蛋打 (286)
鸡毛蒜皮 (28)
鸡同鸭讲 (433)
鸡蛋里挑骨头 (83)
纸包不住火 (96)
纸老虎 (160)

Eight strokes

拔出萝卜带出泥 (460)
拔根汗毛比腰粗 (467)
拣软柿子捏 (324)
拍马屁 (18)
拆东墙，补西墙 (350)
抱大腿 (445)
抱佛脚 (91)
拉不出屎来怨茅房 (429)
英雄难过美人关 (62)
林子大了，什么鸟都有 (27)
板上钉钉 (275)
枪打出头鸟 (203)
枕边风 (397)
画虎不成反类犬 (409)
事后诸葛亮 (273)
卖关子 (72)
到什么山唱什么歌 (466)
虎毒不食子 (165)
明枪易躲，暗箭难防 (199)
物以稀为贵 (10)
和稀泥 (318)
依葫芦画瓢 (185)
舍不得孩子套不住狼 (217)
肥水不流外人田 (52)

鱼与熊掌不可得兼 (280)
兔子不吃窝边草 (128)
兔子尾巴长不了 (456)
狐狸尾巴露出来了 (352)
狐狸精 (161)
狗改不了吃屎 (171)
狗咬狗 (312)
狗急了跳墙 (135)
狗眼看人低 (136)
狗腿子 (284)
狗嘴里吐不出象牙 (59)
饱汉不知饿汉饥 (288)
变色龙 (378)
放卫星 (432)
放长线，钓大鱼 (184)
放鸽子 (113)
炒冷饭 (482)
炒鱿鱼 (66)
浅水养不了大鱼 (472)
泼冷水 (152)
空手套白狼 (385)
试金石 (383)
虱子多了不咬，账多了不愁 (484)
终日打雁，让雁啄了眼 (495)
绊脚石 (371)

Nine strokes

挂羊头、卖狗肉 (218)
指着和尚骂秃子 (487)
挤牙膏 (362)
按下葫芦起了瓢 (465)
树大招风 (225)
树挪死，人挪活 (464)
树倒猢狲散 (347)
树欲静而风不止 (232)
咸鱼翻身 (281)
歪瓜裂枣 (354)
耍花枪 (439)
背着抱着一般沉 (489)
背黑锅 (127)
是骡子是马拉出来遛遛 (228)
蚂蚱也是肉 (488)
咬人的狗不露齿 (481)
哪壶不开提哪壶 (65)
卸磨杀驴 (411)
种瓜得瓜，种豆得豆 (57)
秋后算账 (339)
保护伞 (310)
皇上不急太监急 (39)
皇帝女儿不愁嫁 (418)

胜者王侯败者贼 (234)
独木不成林 (379)
姜是老的辣 (33)
前人栽树，后人乘凉 (295)
前怕狼，后怕虎 (267)
烂泥扶不上墙 (296)
剃头挑子一头热 (450)
活人让尿憋死 (420)
恨铁不成钢 (88)
穿小鞋 (321)
说一千，道一万 (370)
说风凉话 (306)
说你胖你就喘 (416)
说曹操，曹操到 (4)
说得比唱得好听 (68)
既生瑜，何生亮？ (380)
屋漏偏逢连阴雨 (259)
眉毛胡子一把抓 (207)
给力 (291)
给个棒槌就当针 (479)
给他一点颜色看看 (322)

Ten strokes

赶鸭子上架 (182)
起大早，赶晚集 (474)
换汤不换药 (197)
热脸贴冷屁股 (177)
捅马蜂窝 (261)
捅破窗户纸 (366)
莫须有 (364)
真金不怕火炼 (170)
砸了锅 (446)
破罐子破摔 (56)
紧箍咒 (307)
钻牛角尖 (25)
铁公鸡 (156)
铁饭碗 (129)
笑面虎 (289)
笑掉大牙 (278)
借东风 (388)
倒打一耙 (263)
拿鸡毛当令箭 (365)
拿鸡蛋碰石头 (244)
拿得起，放得下 (35)
胳膊扭不过大腿 (287)
胳膊肘往外扭 (299)
留得青山在，不怕没柴烧 (34)
高不成，低不就 (298)
病急乱投医 (237)
站着说话不腰疼 (12)

酒香不怕巷子深 (301)
酒逢知己千杯少 (226)
烫手的山芋 (277)
家丑不可外扬 (126)
家花没有野花香 (436)
家家有本难念的经 (100)
家常便饭 (45)

Eleven strokes

捧臭脚 (480)
掉链子 (159)
接地气 (500)
萝卜白菜，各有所爱 (58)
萝卜快了不洗泥 (499)
救命稻草 (198)
常在河边走，哪有不湿鞋 (220)
睁一只眼，闭一只眼 (55)
睁眼瞎 (16)
睁着眼睛说瞎话 (8)
眼大肚子小 (471)
眼不见为净 (32)
眼中钉、肉中刺 (216)
眼里揉不得沙子 (150)
唱双簧 (308)
唱对台戏 (376)
唱空城计 (400)
唱高调 (313)
做文章 (336)
偷鸡不成反蚀把米 (208)
偷鸡摸狗 (138)
得便宜卖乖 (124)
欲速则不达 (99)
脚正不怕鞋歪 (413)
脚踩两只船 (41)
脸红脖子粗 (242)
脱了裤子放屁 (387)
麻雀虽小，五脏俱全 (164)
阎王好见，小鬼难搪 (468)
鸿门宴 (214)
情人眼里出西施 (19)
谋事在人，成事在天 (200)
骑马找马 (457)
骑脖子拉屎 (486)
绿帽子 (109)

Twelve strokes

替罪羊 (102)
揪辫子 (452)
煮熟的鸭子飞了 (219)

葫芦里卖的是什么药 (344)
敬酒不吃吃罚酒 (75)
落水狗 (274)
硬骨头 (348)
跑了和尚跑不了庙 (108)
跑龙套 (250)
赔了夫人又折兵 (117)
矬子里拔将军 (478)
猴年马月 (31)
羡慕嫉妒恨 (374)
温水煮青蛙 (462)
强龙压不住地头蛇 (391)
强扭的瓜不甜 (69)
强将手下无弱兵 (427)
隔行如隔山 (357)
隔墙有耳 (186)

Thirteen strokes

摸着石头过河 (328)
摆乌龙 (442)
搬起石头砸自己的脚 (71)
碰一鼻子灰 (195)
碰钉子 (204)
雷声大、雨点小 (241)
跳进黄河洗不清 (17)
躲得过初一，躲不过十五 (76)
解铃还须系铃人 (51)
新官上任三把火 (140)
满嘴跑火车 (461)
滚刀肉 (395)
嫁鸡随鸡，嫁狗随狗 (189)

Fourteen strokes

墙头草 (101)
墙倒众人推 (363)
撂挑子 (381)
僧多粥少 (340)
鲜花插在牛粪上 (29)

敲门砖 (382)
敲竹杠 (319)
敲锣边儿 (458)
遮羞布 (438)
瘦死的骆驼比马大 (231)
端起碗来吃肉，放下筷子骂娘 (492)
缩头乌龟 (334)

Fifteen strokes

趟浑水 (283)
横挑鼻子竖挑眼 (399)
醋坛子 (179)
醉翁之意不在酒 (30)
瞎猫碰上死耗子 (49)
躺着都中枪 (412)
鲤鱼跳龙门 (390)

Sixteen strokes

磨刀不误砍柴工 (147)
糖衣炮弹 (346)

Seventeen strokes

戴高帽 (338)
擦屁股 (417)

Eighteen strokes

癞蛤蟆想吃天鹅肉 (46)

Nineteen strokes

攒鸡毛，凑掸子 (485)
蹬鼻子上脸 (205)

Twenty-one strokes

露马脚 (143)

Appendix three: Chinese word index of 500 common Chinese proverbs and colloquial expressions

References are to entry numbers.

矮：矬子里拔将军 (478)
爱：萝卜白菜，各有所爱 (58)
爱情：脚踩两只船 (41)
按下：牛不喝水强按头 (441)；按下葫芦
　　起了瓢 (465)
按照：依葫芦画瓢 (185)
暗地：明枪易躲，暗箭难防 (199)
熬：多年的媳妇熬成婆 (426)
熬夜：开夜车 (332)

八：八九不离十 (122)；八字还没一撇 (119)
巴掌：一个巴掌拍不响 (79)；打一巴掌，
　　给个甜枣 (405)
拔：拔出萝卜带出泥 (460)；拔根汗毛比腰粗
　　(467)；矬子里拔将军 (478)；别人牵驴
　　你拔橛 (497)
拔除：眼中钉、肉中刺 (216)
把柄：小辫子 (355)；揪辫子 (452)
罢工：撂挑子 (381)
霸道：只许州官放火，不许百姓点灯 (137)
白菜：萝卜白菜，各有所爱 (58)
白开水：白开水 (389)
白脸：小白脸 (183)
百日：花无百日红 (422)
百姓：只许州官放火，不许百姓点灯 (137)；
　　接地气 (500)
摆乌龙：摆乌龙 (442)
败者：胜者王侯败者贼 (234)
搬：搬起石头砸自己的脚 (71)
板凳：坐冷板凳 (341)
板子：各打五十大板 (443)；板上钉钉 (275)
半：一瓶子不满，半瓶子晃荡 (386)
半路：半路出家 (329)；半路杀出个程咬金
　　(163)

绊：绊脚石 (371)
绊脚石：绊脚石 (371)
帮凶：狗腿子 (284)
帮助：多个朋友多条路 (253)；远亲不如近邻
　　(131)；借东风 (388)
榜样：上梁不正下梁歪 (115)；杀鸡给猴看
　　(153)
棒槌：给个棒槌就当针 (479)
包：纸包不住火 (96)
包庇：纸包不住火 (96)
包子：土包子 (224)
保护：大树底下好乘凉 (249)；保护伞 (310)
保护伞：保护伞 (310)
报恩：过河拆桥 (105)
报复：以牙还牙，以眼还眼 (107)；有仇不报
　　非君子 (269)
报应：出来混的，总要还的 (408)
抱：抱大腿 (445)；抱佛脚 (91)；背着抱着
　　一般沉 (489)
抱大腿：抱大腿 (445)
抱佛脚：抱佛脚 (91)
抱怨：会哭的孩子有奶吃 (447)
暴露：此地无银三百两 (42)；露马脚 (143)
杯：酒逢知己千杯少 (226)
背：背着抱着一般沉 (489)；背黑锅 (127)
背黑锅：背黑锅 (127)
背后：小动作 (192)
被：一朝被蛇咬，十年怕井绳 (61)；
　　终日打雁，让雁啄了眼 (495)
被逼：狗急了跳墙 (135)
本行：三句话不离本行 (345)
本钱：留得青山在，不怕没柴烧 (34)；身体
　　是革命的本钱 (305)
本人：对事不对人 (174)

本事：是骡子是马拉出来遛遛 (228)
本质：狐狸尾巴露出来了 (352)；背着抱着
　　一般沉 (489)；是骡子是马拉出来遛遛
　　(228)；睁眼瞎 (16)
笨蛋：二百五 (6)
鼻孔：一个鼻孔出气 (229)
鼻子：一个鼻孔出气 (229)；有鼻子有眼
　　(202)；碰一鼻子灰 (195)；横挑鼻子竖挑眼
　　(399)；蹬鼻子上脸 (205)
比：拔根汗毛比腰粗 (467)；说得比唱得好听
　　(68)；瘦死的骆驼比马大 (231)
必：二虎相争，必有一伤 (349)
必定：车到山前必有路 (82)；有其父必有
　　其子 (93)
必输：拿鸡蛋碰石头 (244)
闭：睁一只眼，闭一只眼 (55)
闭门：吃闭门羹 (222)
庇护：保护伞 (310)
边：敲锣边儿 (458)
变成：一口吃成个胖子 (258)
变化：人算不如天算 (191)；三十年河东，
　　三十年河西 (223)
变老：岁月是把杀猪刀 (424)
变色龙：变色龙 (378)
变通：一棵树上吊死 (112)；东方不亮西方亮
　　(430)；活人让尿憋死 (420)
便：不成功，便成仁 (394)
便饭：家常便饭 (45)
辫子：小辫子 (355)；揪辫子 (452)
表达：挤牙膏 (362)
表面：冰山一角 (304)
表象：纸老虎 (160)
婊子：又想当婊子又想立牌坊 (437)
憋死：活人让尿憋死 (420)
别人：己所不欲，勿施于人 (15)；吃别人
　　嚼过的馍不香 (473)；别人牵驴你拔橛 (497)
冰：冰冻三尺，非一日之寒 (130)
冰冻：冰冻三尺，非一日之寒 (130)
冰山：冰山一角 (304)
兵：赔了夫人又折兵 (117)；强将手下无弱兵
　　(427)
病：久病成良医 (396)；红眼病 (343)；病急
　　乱投医 (237)
拨动：四两拨千斤 (266)
脖子：脸红脖子粗 (242)；骑脖子拉屎 (486)
补：拆东墙，补西墙 (350)
补偿：打一巴掌，给个甜枣 (405)
不：一个巴掌拍不响 (79)；八九不离十
　　(122)；又要马儿跑，又要马儿不吃草
　　(440)；三句话不离本行 (345)；干打雷，
　　不下雨 (271)；不入虎穴，焉得虎子 (116)；

不见兔子不撒鹰 (469)；不见棺材不落泪
　　(94)；不分青红皂白 (54)；不成功，便成仁
　　(394)；不当家不知柴米贵 (342)；不到黄河
　　心不死 (134)；不怕一万，就怕万一 (21)；
　　不看僧面看佛面 (240)；牛不喝水强按头
　　(441)；牛头不对马嘴 (80)；风马牛不相及
　　(148)；心急吃不了热豆腐 (44)；打不着
　　狐狸惹身骚 (475)；占着茅坑不拉屎 (194)；
　　只见树木，不见森林 (454)；只许州官放火，
　　不许百姓点灯 (137)；仔卖爷田不心疼
　　(498)；饥不择食 (173)；对事不对人 (174)；
　　有仇不报非君子 (269)；有心栽花花不长，
　　无心插柳柳成荫 (118)；有眼不识泰山
　　(120)；死猪不怕开水烫 (196)；光脚的不怕
　　穿鞋的 (393)；吃不到葡萄就说葡萄酸
　　(43)；吃水不忘挖井人 (268)；吃别人嚼过
　　的馍不香 (473)；好马不吃回头草 (1)；
　　好汉不吃眼前亏 (50)；远亲不如近邻 (131)；
　　苍蝇不叮无缝的蛋 (368)；没有不透风的墙
　　(245)；初生牛犊不怕虎 (155)；纸包不住火
　　(96)；虎毒不食子 (165)；舍不得孩子套
　　不住狼 (217)；肥水不流外人田 (52)；兔子
　　不吃窝边草 (128)；饱汉不知饿汉饥 (288)；
　　虱子多了不咬，账多了不愁 (484)；树欲静
　　而风不止 (232)；咬人的狗不露齿 (481)；
　　皇上不急太监急 (39)；皇帝女儿不愁嫁
　　(418)；独木不成林 (379)；烂泥扶不上墙
　　(296)；恨铁不成钢 (88)；换汤不换药
　　(197)；真金不怕火炼 (170)；胳膊扭不过
　　大腿 (287)；留得青山在，不怕没柴烧 (34)；
　　高不成，低不就 (298)；站着说话不腰疼
　　(12)；酒香不怕巷子深 (301)；家丑不可外
　　扬 (126)；萝卜快了不洗泥 (499)；常在
　　河边走，哪有不湿鞋 (220)；眼不见为净
　　(32)；眼里揉不得沙子 (150)；偷鸡不成反
　　蚀把米 (208)；欲速则不达 (99)；脚正不怕
　　鞋歪 (413)；敬酒不吃吃罚酒 (75)；跑了
　　和尚跑不了庙 (108)；强龙压不住地头蛇
　　(391)；强扭的瓜不甜 (69)；醉翁之意不
　　在酒 (30)；磨刀不误砍柴工 (147)
不成：画虎不成反类犬 (409)；偷鸡不成反
　　蚀把米 (208)
不倒翁：不倒翁 (270)
不定：风一阵，雨一阵 (449)
不断：按下葫芦起了瓢 (465)
不感激：端起碗来吃肉，放下筷子骂娘 (492)
不公正：各打五十大板 (443)
不关心：打酱油 (20)
不管：不分青红皂白 (54)；不管三七二十一
　　(23)；不管黑猫白猫，会捉老鼠就是好猫
　　(169)

不见：眼不见为净 (32)

不开：哪壶不开提哪壶 (65)

不可：人不可貌相，海水不可斗量 (26)；
鱼与熊掌不可得兼 (280)；家丑不可外扬
(126)

不可能：太阳从西边出来 (3)

不了：吃不了兜着走 (84)；兔子尾巴长不了
(456)；狗改不了吃屎 (171)；浅水养不了
大鱼 (472)；跑了和尚跑不了庙 (108)；
躲得过初一，躲不过十五 (76)

不灵活：钻牛角尖 (25)

不怕：不怕一万，就怕万一 (21)；初生牛犊
不怕虎 (155)；真金不怕火炼 (170)；留得
青山在，不怕没柴烧 (34)；酒香不怕
巷子深 (301)；脚正不怕鞋歪 (413)

不如：远亲不如近邻 (131)；家花没有野花香
(436)

不是：不是吃素的 (188)；不是鱼死，就是
网破 (303)；不是省油的灯 (125)

不嫌弃：蚂蚱也是肉 (488)

不相干：你走你的阳关道，我过我的独木桥
(89)

不相关：打酱油 (20)

不要：一不做，二不休 (106)；己所不欲，
勿施于人 (15)

不再：过了这个村，就没这个店 (90)

不在：醉翁之意不在酒 (30)

不在意：当耳旁风 (87)

不正当：走后门 (48)

不知：饱汉不知饿汉饥 (288)

不自量力：拿鸡蛋碰石头 (244)

不自责：拉不出屎来怨茅房 (429)

不自知：癞蛤蟆想吃天鹅肉 (46)

不足：心有余而力不足 (53)；成事不足，
败事有余 (38)

布：遮羞布 (438)

步：一步一个脚印 (114)；五十步笑百步
(293)

擦：擦屁股 (417)

擦边：打擦边球 (327)

擦屁股：擦屁股 (417)

猜不透：葫芦里卖的是什么药 (344)

财力：拔根汗毛比腰粗 (467)

踩：脚踩两只船 (41)

残忍：虎毒不食子 (165)

惨重：赔了夫人又折兵 (117)

苍蝇：苍蝇不叮无缝的蛋 (368)

操心：皇上不急太监急 (39)

曹操：身在曹营心在汉 (230)；说曹操，
曹操到 (4)

草：好马不吃回头草 (1)；兔子不吃窝边草
(128)；墙头草 (101)

测量：人不可貌相，海水不可斗量 (26)

测验：试金石 (383)

插：鲜花插在牛粪上 (29)

插柳：有心栽花花不长，无心插柳柳成荫
(118)

差不多：八九不离十 (122)

差距：八字还没一撇 (119)；小巫见大巫
(104)

拆：拆东墙，补西墙 (350)

拆解：拆东墙，补西墙 (350)

拆桥：过河拆桥 (105)

柴：留得青山在，不怕没柴烧 (34)；
磨刀不误砍柴工 (147)

柴火：众人拾柴火焰高 (209)

柴米：不当家不知柴米贵 (342)

掺和：趟浑水 (283)

谄媚：捧臭脚 (480)

长：尺有所短，寸有所长 (407)；兔子尾巴
长不了 (456)

长…短…：长痛不如短痛 (300)；三长两短
(95)

长线：放长线，钓大鱼 (184)

常常：常在河边走，哪有不湿鞋 (220)

常年：终日打雁，让雁啄了眼 (495)

畅销：萝卜快了不洗泥 (499)

唱：说得比唱得好听 (68)；唱双簧 (308)；
唱对台戏 (376)；唱空城计 (400)；唱高调
(313)

唱高调：唱高调 (313)

唱歌：到什么山唱什么歌 (466)

唱双簧：唱双簧 (308)

唱戏：唱对台戏 (376)

朝：一朝天子一朝臣 (419)

朝代：一朝天子一朝臣 (419)

嘲笑：笑掉大牙 (278)

炒：炒冷饭 (482)；炒鱿鱼 (66)

炒饭：炒冷饭 (482)

炒冷饭：炒冷饭 (482)

炒鱿鱼：炒鱿鱼 (66)

车：车到山前必有路 (82)；老牛拉破车 (431)

扯：扯后腿 (320)

扯后腿：扯后腿 (320)

臣：一朝天子一朝臣 (419)

沉：背着抱着一般沉 (489)

陈旧：老掉牙 (70)；陈芝麻、烂谷子 (264)；
炒冷饭 (482)

成…败…：成也萧何，败也萧何 (359)；
成事不足，败事有余 (38)；胜者王侯败者
贼 (234)

成功：不成功，便成仁 (394)；成也萧何，败也萧何 (359)；成事不足，败事有余 (38)；高不成，低不就 (298)；谋事在人，成事在天 (200)

成仁：不成功，便成仁 (394)

乘凉：大树底下好乘凉 (249)；前人栽树，后人乘凉 (295)

程咬金：半路杀出个程咬金 (163)

惩罚：打一巴掌，给个甜枣 (405)；各打五十大板 (443)

吃：一口吃成个胖子 (258)；大鱼吃小鱼 (351)；心急吃不了热豆腐 (44)；吃一堑，长一智 (7)；吃大锅饭 (337)；吃不了兜着走 (84)；吃不到葡萄就说葡萄酸 (43)；吃水不忘挖井人 (268)；吃闭门羹 (222)；吃豆腐 (206)；吃别人嚼过的馍不香 (473)；吃软饭 (211)；吃哑巴亏 (215)；吃香的，喝辣的 (77)；吃着碗里的，看着锅里的 (24)；会哭的孩子有奶吃 (447)；好马不吃回头草 (1)；好汉不吃眼前亏 (50)；虎毒不食子 (165)；兔子不吃窝边草 (128)；狗改不了吃屎 (171)；敬酒不吃吃罚酒 (75)；端起碗来吃肉，放下筷子骂娘 (492)；癞蛤蟆想吃天鹅肉 (46)

吃…喝…：吃香的，喝辣的 (77)

吃草：又要马儿跑，又要马儿不吃草 (440)

吃豆腐：吃豆腐 (206)

吃饭：吃大锅饭 (337)；吃软饭 (211)

吃亏：偷鸡不成反蚀把米 (208)；吃哑巴亏 (215)；好汉不吃眼前亏 (50)

吃肉：端起碗来吃肉，放下筷子骂娘 (492)

吃软饭：吃软饭 (211)

吃屎：狗改不了吃屎 (171)

吃水：三个和尚没水吃 (181)；吃水不忘挖井人 (268)

吃素：不是吃素的 (188)

尺…寸…：尺有所短，寸有所长 (407)

齿：咬人的狗不露齿 (481)

赤：近朱者赤，近墨者黑 (9)

冲：大水冲了龙王庙 (360)

仇：有仇不报非君子 (269)

愁：虱子多了不咬，账多了不愁 (484)

丑：丑话说在前头 (162)；丑媳妇早晚也得见公婆 (233)

丑陋：歪瓜裂枣 (354)

丑事：家丑不可外扬 (126)

臭：捧臭脚 (480)

出丑：摆乌龙 (442)

出家：半路出家 (329)

出来：出来混的，总要还的 (408)

出名：人怕出名猪怕壮 (246)

出气：一个鼻孔出气 (229)；出气筒 (121)

出气筒：出气筒 (121)

出生：既生瑜，何生亮？ (380)

出头：出头的椽子先烂 (493)；枪打出头鸟 (203)

出自：羊毛出在羊身上 (257)

初生：初生牛犊不怕虎 (155)

初始：下马威 (132)

初一…十五…：躲得过初一，躲不过十五 (76)

除掉：一锅端 (434)

处理：烫手的山芋 (277)；擦屁股 (417)

穿：穿小鞋 (321)

穿小鞋：穿小鞋 (321)

穿鞋：光脚的不怕穿鞋的 (393)

船：上了贼船 (236)；脚踩两只船 (41)

椽子：出头的椽子先烂 (493)

喘：说你胖你就喘 (416)

窗户：捅破窗户纸 (366)

窗户纸：捅破窗户纸 (366)

闯荡：出来混的，总要还的 (408)

吹牛：放卫星 (432)；吹牛皮 (98)

吹牛皮：吹牛皮 (98)

吹捧：戴高帽 (338)

吹嘘：吹牛皮 (98)

锤子：一锤子买卖 (398)

刺：眼中钉、肉中刺 (216)

凑：攒鸡毛，凑掸子 (485)

粗：拔根汗毛比腰粗 (467)；脸红脖子粗 (242)

醋：醋坛子 (179)

醋坛子：醋坛子 (179)

村子：过了这个村，就没这个店 (90)

存心：哪壶不开提哪壶 (65)

忖度：以小人之心，度君子之腹 (81)

矬子：矬子里拔将军 (478)

达：欲速则不达 (99)

打：一棍子打死 (243)；打一巴掌，给个甜枣 (405)；打小算盘 (255)；打马虎眼 (325)；打不着狐狸惹身骚 (475)；打水漂 (314)；打如意算盘 (238)；打狗还得看主人 (167)；打退堂鼓 (146)；打酱油 (20)；打擦边球 (327)；各打五十大板 (443)；枪打出头鸟 (203)；终日打雁，让雁啄了眼 (495)；倒打一耙 (263)

打掉：打掉门牙往肚里咽 (375)

打击：出头的椽子先烂 (493)；泼冷水 (152)；枪打出头鸟 (203)

打酱油：打酱油 (20)

打劫：一锤子买卖 (398)；敲竹杠 (319)

打开：打开天窗说亮话 (190)
打雷：干打雷，不下雨 (271)
打乱：小不忍则乱大谋 (166)
打破：鸡飞蛋打 (286)
打扰：无事不登三宝殿 (157)
打水漂：打水漂 (314)
打死：一棍子打死 (243)；乱拳打死老师傅 (491)
打鱼：三天打鱼，两天晒网 (60)
打肿：打肿脸充胖子 (85)
大：林子大了，什么鸟都有 (27)；树大招风 (225)；起大早，赶晚集 (474)；眼大肚子小 (471)；雷声大、雨点小 (241)；瘦死的骆驼比马大 (231)
大…小…：眼大肚子小 (471)
大本营：跑了和尚跑不了庙 (108)
大臣：一朝天子一朝臣 (419)
大大地：大跌眼镜 (369)
大刀：关公面前耍大刀 (297)
大水：大水冲了龙王庙 (360)
大头：放长线，钓大鱼 (184)
大腿：抱大腿 (445)；胳膊扭不过大腿 (287)
大王：山中无老虎，猴子称大王 (247)
大牙：笑掉大牙 (278)
大意：大意失荆州 (410)
大鱼：放长线，钓大鱼 (184)；浅水养不了大鱼 (472)
代价：舍不得孩子套不住狼 (217)
代替：替罪羊 (102)
带：拔出萝卜带出泥 (460)
带头：出头的椽子先烂 (493)
戴：戴高帽 (338)
戴高帽：戴高帽 (338)
单方：一个巴掌拍不响 (79)；剃头挑子一头热 (450)
单相思：剃头挑子一头热 (450)
单向：热脸贴冷屁股 (177)
耽误：磨刀不误砍柴工 (147)
胆小：缩头乌龟 (334)
掸子：攒鸡毛，凑掸子 (485)
淡：君子之交淡如水 (180)
弹琴：乱弹琴 (361)
蛋：苍蝇不叮无缝的蛋 (368)；鸡飞蛋打 (286)
当：当一天和尚撞一天钟 (227)；当耳旁风 (87)；拿鸡毛当令箭 (365)
当家：不当家不知柴米贵 (342)
当面：当面锣，对面鼓 (470)
当事者：解铃还须系铃人 (51)
当真：给个棒槌就当针 (479)
当作：死马当活马医 (139)

刀：一刀切 (401)；岁月是把杀猪刀 (424)；杀鸡焉用宰牛刀 (248)；关公面前耍大刀 (297)；两面三刀 (403)；快刀斩乱麻 (210)；磨刀不误砍柴工 (147)
刀刃：用在刀刃上 (285)
刀山：上刀山，下火海 (145)
刀子：一刀切 (401)；刀子嘴，豆腐心 (63)
捣乱：和稀泥 (318)
倒：树倒猢狲散 (347)；倒打一耙 (263)；墙倒众人推 (363)
倒霉：屋漏偏逢连阴雨 (259)；躺着都中枪 (412)
倒向：墙头草 (101)
到：说曹操，曹操到 (4)
到手：煮熟的鸭子飞了 (219)
道：以其人之道还治其人之身 (36)
道理：公说公有理，婆说婆有理 (144)
道路：天无绝人之路 (47)
稻草：救命稻草 (198)
得：打狗还得看主人 (167)；得便宜卖乖 (124)
得尺进尺：蹬鼻子上脸 (205)
得到：近水楼台先得月 (103)；鱼与熊掌不可得兼 (280)；种瓜得瓜，种豆得豆 (57)
灯：只许州官放火，不许百姓点灯 (137)；走马灯 (421)
蹬：蹬鼻子上脸 (205)
低：狗眼看人低 (136)；高不成，低不就 (298)
低处：人往高处走，水往低处流 (67)
敌意：当面锣，对面鼓 (470)
底下：大树底下好乘凉 (249)
地：一亩三分地 (358)；接地气 (500)
地方：此地无银三百两 (42)
地方势力：强龙压不住地头蛇 (391)
地盘：一亩三分地 (358)
地气：接地气 (500)
地头蛇：强龙压不住地头蛇 (391)
地位：多年的媳妇熬成婆 (426)；屁股决定脑袋 (455)
地域：近水楼台先得月 (103)
点灯：只许州官放火，不许百姓点灯 (137)
店铺：过了这个村，就没这个店 (90)
吊死：一棵树上吊死 (112)
钓鱼：放长线，钓大鱼 (184)
掉：天上掉馅饼 (14)；掉链子 (159)
掉链子：掉链子 (159)
掉牙：老掉牙 (70)
跌落：大跌眼镜 (369)
丁：丁是丁，卯是卯 (425)
叮：苍蝇不叮无缝的蛋 (368)

顶：三个臭皮匠，顶个诸葛亮 (40)
钉：板上钉钉 (275)；眼中钉、肉中刺 (216)；
　　丁是丁，卯是卯 (425)
钉子：板上钉钉 (275)；碰钉子 (204)
丢失：大意失荆州 (410)
东…西…：东风压倒西风 (423)；东方不亮
　　西方亮 (430)；拆东墙，补西墙 (350)
东方：东方不亮西方亮 (430)
东风：万事俱备，只欠东风 (168)；东风压倒
　　西风 (423)；借东风 (388)
动作：小动作 (192)
兜：吃不了兜着走 (84)
斗：人不可貌相，海水不可斗量 (26)；坐山
　　观虎斗 (256)
豆：种瓜得瓜，种豆得豆 (57)
豆腐：刀子嘴，豆腐心 (63)；心急吃不了
　　热豆腐 (44)；吃豆腐 (206)
毒：虎毒不食子 (165)
独：独木不成林 (379)
独断：一言堂 (490)
独木桥：你走你的阳关道，我过我的独木桥
　　(89)
肚子：打掉门牙往肚里咽 (375)；眼大肚子小
　　(471)
妒嫉：人怕出名猪怕壮 (246)；醋坛子 (179)
端掉：一锅端 (434)
端平：一碗水端平 (276)
端起：端起碗来吃肉，放下筷子骂娘 (492)
短：尺有所短，寸有所长 (407)
对：对事不对人 (174)
对待：以牙还牙，以眼还眼 (107)；以其人
　　之道还治其人之身 (36)
对付：阎王好见，小鬼难搪 (468)
对面：当面锣，对面鼓 (470)
对台戏：唱对台戏 (376)
对外：家丑不可外扬 (126)
对应：牛头不对马嘴 (80)；对号入座 (141)
多：多个朋友多条路 (253)；多年的媳妇熬成
　　婆 (426)；多面手 (476)；虱子多了不咬，
　　账多了不愁 (484)；僧多粥少 (340)
多面手：多面手 (476)；万金油 (463)
…多…少：僧多粥少 (340)
多余：脱了裤子放屁 (387)
躲：躲得过初一，躲不过十五 (76)
躲避：明枪易躲，暗箭难防 (199)；躲得过
　　初一，躲不过十五 (76)；跑了和尚跑不了
　　庙 (108)

恶人：狗咬狗 (312)
恶习：狗改不了吃屎 (171)
恶语：狗嘴里吐不出象牙 (59)

饿：饱汉不知饿汉饥 (288)
儿子：有其父必有其子 (93)
耳：隔墙有耳 (186)
耳朵：当耳旁风 (87)
二：一回生，二回熟 (279)；一是一，
　　二是二 (252)；二 (290)；二虎相争，
　　必有一伤 (349)；九牛二虎之力 (74)
二百五：二百五 (6)

发愁：皇帝女儿不愁嫁 (418)；家家有本难念
　　的经 (100)
发展：兔子尾巴长不了 (456)
乏味：老掉牙 (70)
罚酒：敬酒不吃吃罚酒 (75)
翻身：咸鱼翻身 (281)
烦恼：眼不见为净 (32)
反倒：画虎不成反类犬 (409)；倒打一耙
　　(263)；偷鸡不成反蚀把米 (208)
饭：巧妇难为无米之炊 (187)；生米做成熟饭
　　(154)；吃软饭 (211)；炒冷饭 (482)；
　　家常便饭 (45)
饭碗：铁饭碗 (129)
方便：远亲不如近邻 (131)
方面：多面手 (476)
方式：以其人之道还治其人之身 (36)
防备：温水煮青蛙 (462)
妨碍：绊脚石 (371)
房梁：上梁不正下梁歪 (115)
放：一只羊是赶，一群羊也是放 (483)；
　　放卫星 (432)；放长线，钓大鱼 (184)；
　　放鸽子 (113)；拿得起，放得下 (35)
放鸽子：放鸽子 (113)
放火：只许州官放火，不许百姓点灯 (137)
放屁：脱了裤子放屁 (387)
放卫星：放卫星 (432)
放下：拿得起，放得下 (35)；端起碗来吃
　　肉，放下筷子骂娘 (492)；撂挑子 (381)
放羊：一只羊是赶，一群羊也是放 (483)
飞：鸡飞狗跳 (272)；鸡飞蛋打 (286)；
　　煮熟的鸭子飞了 (219)
飞黄腾达：鲤鱼跳龙门 (390)
非：有仇不报非君子 (269)；冰冻三尺，
　　非一日之寒 (130)
肥水：肥水不流外人田 (52)
费力：九牛二虎之力 (74)
分：一亩三分地 (358)
分不清：眉毛胡子一把抓 (207)
分配：吃大锅饭 (337)；僧多粥少 (340)
分散：一盘散沙 (317)
分手：天下没有不散的筵席 (13)
分享：分一杯羹 (377)

粪：鲜花插在牛粪上 (29)
风：风马牛不相及 (148)；东风压倒西风 (423)；当耳旁风 (87)；听风就是雨 (213)；枕边风 (397)；树大招风 (225)；树欲静而风不止 (232)；借东风 (388)
风…雨…：风一阵，雨一阵 (449)；听风就是雨 (213)
风浪：无风不起浪 (123)
风凉话：说风凉话 (306)；站着说话不腰疼 (12)
风头：枪打出头鸟 (203)
蜂：一窝蜂 (331)
蜂拥：一窝蜂 (331)
逢：屋漏偏逢连阴雨 (259)；酒逢知己千杯少 (226)
缝隙：苍蝇不叮无缝的蛋 (368)
凤：龙生龙，凤生凤 (239)
佛：不看僧面看佛面 (240)；抱佛脚 (91)
夫人：赔了夫人又折兵 (117)
敷衍：当一天和尚撞一天钟 (227)
扶：烂泥扶不上墙 (296)
扶助：烂泥扶不上墙 (296)
腐烂：出头的椽子先烂 (493)；陈芝麻、烂谷子 (264)
腐蚀：糖衣炮弹 (346)
父…子…：有其父必有其子 (93)
父亲：有其父必有其子 (93)
付出：又要马儿跑，又要马儿不吃草 (440)；空手套白狼 (385)；站着说话不腰疼 (12)
复活：咸鱼翻身 (281)
复兴：咸鱼翻身 (281)
富余：心有余而力不足 (53)
腹：以小人之心，度君子之腹 (81)

改：狗改不了吃屎 (171)
改变：一条路走到黑 (302)；树挪死，人挪活 (464)
尴尬：哪壶不开提哪壶 (65)
赶：一只羊是赶，一群羊也是放 (483)；赶鸭子上架 (182)
赶集：起大早，赶晚集 (474)
感恩：吃水不忘挖井人 (268)
感染：近朱者赤，近墨者黑 (9)
干涉：你走你的阳关道，我过我的独木桥 (89)
钢：恨铁不成钢 (88)
杠：敲竹杠 (319)
高：众人抬柴火焰高 (209)；这山望着那山高 (392)；戴高帽 (338)
高…低…：高不成，低不就 (298)
高潮：好戏在后头 (97)

高处：人往高处走，水往低处流 (67)
高调：唱高调 (313)
搞砸：砸了锅 (446)
告：求爷爷、告奶奶 (373)
胳膊：胳膊扭不过大腿 (287)；胳膊肘往外扭 (299)
胳膊肘：胳膊肘往外扭 (299)
鸽子：放鸽子 (113)
歌：到什么山唱什么歌 (466)
革命：身体是革命的本钱 (305)
隔：隔行如隔山 (357)；隔墙有耳 (186)
隔行：隔行如隔山 (357)
个人：对事不对人 (174)
各：各打五十大板 (443)
各自：公说公有理，婆说婆有理 (144)
给：打一巴掌，给个甜枣 (405)；给个棒槌就当针 (479)
给力：给力 (291)
根据：对号入座 (141)
根植：接地气 (500)
羹：分一杯羹 (377)；吃闭门羹 (222)
更替：一朝天子一朝臣 (419)；走马灯 (421)
工夫：磨刀不误砍柴工 (147)
公…婆…：公说公有理，婆说婆有理 (144)
公鸡：铁公鸡 (156)
公开：当面锣，对面鼓 (470)
公婆：丑媳妇早晚也得见公婆 (233)
公正：一碗水端平 (276)
攻击：倒打一耙 (263)
勾当：偷鸡摸狗 (138)
沟通：鸡同鸭讲 (433)
狗：打狗还得看主人 (167)；鸡飞狗跳 (272)；狗改不了吃屎 (171)；狗咬狗 (312)；狗急了跳墙 (135)；狗眼看人低 (136)；狗腿子 (284)；狗嘴里吐不出象牙 (59)；挂羊头、卖狗肉 (218)；咬人的狗不露齿 (481)；偷鸡摸狗 (138)；落水狗 (274)；嫁鸡随鸡，嫁狗随狗 (189)
狗：画虎不成反类犬 (409)
狗肉：挂羊头、卖狗肉 (218)
狗腿子：狗腿子 (284)
狗咬狗：狗咬狗 (312)
姑：七大姑，八大姨 (251)
姑且：死马当活马医 (139)
谷子：陈芝麻、烂谷子 (264)
骨头：鸡蛋里挑骨头 (83)；硬骨头 (348)
鼓：打退堂鼓 (146)；当面锣，对面鼓 (470)
故意：唱对台戏 (376)
顾及：不看僧面看佛面 (240)
顾忌：死猪不怕开水烫 (196)；光脚的不怕穿鞋的 (393)

瓜：王婆卖瓜，自卖自夸 (11)；歪瓜裂枣 (354)；种瓜得瓜，种豆得豆 (57)；强扭的瓜不甜 (69)

瓜…豆…：种瓜得瓜，种豆得豆 (57)

瓜…枣…：歪瓜裂枣 (354)

挂：挂羊头、卖狗肉 (218)

关公：关公面前耍大刀 (297)

关键：成也萧何，败也萧何 (359)

关键时刻：掉链子 (159)

关联：拔出萝卜带出泥 (460)

关系：走后门 (48)

关系到：一着不慎，满盘皆输 (212)

关注：会哭的孩子有奶吃 (447)

关子：卖关子 (72)

观：坐山观虎斗 (256)

官：新官上任三把火 (140)

官员：只许州官放火，不许百姓点灯 (137)

棺材：不见棺材不落泪 (94)

罐子：破罐子破摔 (56)

光：干打雷，不下雨 (271)

光脚：光脚的不怕穿鞋的 (393)

光说不做：说得比唱得好听 (68)

鬼：有钱能使鬼推磨 (92)；阎王好见，小鬼难搪 (468)

贵：不当家不知柴米贵 (342)

贵重：物以稀为贵 (10)

滚刀肉：滚刀肉 (395)

棍子：一棍子打死 (243)

锅：一马勺坏一锅 (494)；一锅端 (434)；吃大锅饭 (337)；吃着碗里的，看着锅里的 (24)；肉烂在锅里 (415)；背黑锅 (127)；砸了锅 (446)

锅…碗…：吃着碗里的，看着锅里的 (24)

果断：快刀斩乱麻 (210)

过：过了这个村，就没这个店 (90)；你走你的阳关道，我过我的独木桥 (89)

过场：走过场 (335)

过关：过五关、斩六将 (372)；英雄难过美人关 (62)

过河：过河拆桥 (105)；摸着石头过河 (328)

过时：老皇历 (435)；陈芝麻、烂谷子 (264)

过头：虱子多了不咬，账多了不愁 (484)

蛤蟆：癞蛤蟆想吃天鹅肉 (46)

还：以牙还牙，以眼还眼 (107)；出来混的，总要还的 (408)

孩子：会哭的孩子有奶吃 (447)；舍不得孩子套不住狼 (217)

海水：人不可貌相，海水不可斗量 (26)

寒冷：冰冻三尺，非一日之寒 (130)

汉朝：身在曹营心在汉 (230)

汉子：饱汉不知饿汉饥 (288)

汗毛：拔根汗毛比腰粗 (467)

行：隔行如隔山 (357)

行动：干打雷，不下雨 (271)；雷声大、雨点小 (241)

好：不管黑猫白猫，会捉老鼠就是好猫 (169)；好了伤疤忘了疼 (178)；好戏在后头 (97)

好处：肉烂在锅里 (415)；羊毛出在羊身上 (257)；鱼与熊掌不可得兼 (280)

好汉：好汉不吃眼前亏 (50)

好景：花无百日红 (422)

好马：好马不吃回头草 (1)

好色：家花没有野花香 (436)

好听：说得比唱得好听 (68)

号码：对号入座 (141)

耗子：瞎猫碰上死耗子 (49)

喝：吃香的，喝辣的 (77)

喝酒：敬酒不吃吃罚酒 (75)

喝水：牛不喝水强按头 (441)

何必：既生瑜，何生亮？ (380)

和尚：三个和尚没水吃 (181)；当一天和尚撞一天钟 (227)；远来的和尚会念经 (451)；指着和尚骂秃子 (487)；跑了和尚跑不了庙 (108)；僧多粥少 (340)

和稀泥：和稀泥 (318)

河：过河拆桥 (105)；常在河边走，哪有不湿鞋 (220)；摸着石头过河 (328)；跳进黄河洗不清 (17)

河边：常在河边走，哪有不湿鞋 (220)

河水：井水不犯河水 (111)

黑：一条路走到黑 (302)；天下乌鸦一般黑 (133)；老鸹嫌猪黑 (496)；近朱者赤，近墨者黑 (9)

黑锅：背黑锅 (127)

很久：久病成良医 (396)

恨：一失足成千古恨 (64)；恨铁不成钢 (88)；羡慕嫉妒恨 (374)

恒心：三天打鱼，两天晒网 (60)

横…竖…：横挑鼻子竖挑眼 (399)

衡量：试金石 (383)

红：红眼病 (343)；花无百日红 (422)；脸红脖子粗 (242)

红眼病：红眼病 (343)

鸿门：鸿门宴 (214)

鸿门宴：鸿门宴 (214)

哄抢：一窝蜂 (331)

猴：杀鸡给猴看 (153)；猴年马月 (31)

猴子：树倒猢狲散 (347)；山中无老虎，猴子称大王 (247)

后：先君子后小人 (406)；前怕狼，后怕虎 (267)

后备：骑马找马 (457)
后代：仔卖爷田不心疼 (498)
后果：打不着狐狸惹身骚 (475)；吃不了
　　兜着走 (84)
后悔：好马不吃回头草 (1)
后门：走后门 (48)
后人：前人栽树，后人乘凉 (295)
后头：好戏在后头 (97)
后腿：扯后腿 (320)
后遗症：一朝被蛇咬，十年怕井绳 (61)
厚望：恨铁不成钢 (88)
忽略：坐冷板凳 (341)
狐狸：打不着狐狸惹身骚 (475)；
　　老狐狸 (330)；狐狸尾巴露出来了 (352)；
　　狐狸精 (161)
狐狸精：狐狸精 (161)
胡乱：眉毛胡子一把抓 (207)
胡说：乱弹琴 (361)；满嘴跑火车 (461)
胡子：眉毛胡子一把抓 (207)
壶：哪壶不开提哪壶 (65)
葫芦：依葫芦画瓢 (185)；按下葫芦起了瓢
　　(465)；葫芦里卖的是什么药 (344)
猢狲：树倒猢狲散 (347)
虎：一山不容二虎 (149)；九牛二虎之力
　　(74)；不入虎穴，焉得虎子 (116)；坐山观
　　虎斗 (256)；初生牛犊不怕虎 (155)；画虎
　　不成反类犬 (409)；虎毒不食子 (165)；
　　前怕狼，后怕虎 (267)；笑面虎 (289)
虎穴：不入虎穴，焉得虎子 (116)
花：有心栽花花不长，无心插柳柳成荫
　　(118)；花无百日红 (422)；家花没有野花香
　　(436)；鲜花插在牛粪上 (29)
花枪：耍花枪 (439)
画：画虎不成反类犬 (409)；依葫芦画瓢
　　(185)
话：三句话不离本行 (345)；丑话说在前头
　　(162)；打开天窗说亮话 (190)
坏：一马勺坏一锅 (494)
坏人：天下乌鸦一般黑 (133)
坏事：成事不足，败事有余 (38)
缓慢：老牛拉破车 (431)；挤牙膏 (362)
换：鸟枪换炮 (477)；换汤不换药 (197)
换位：饱汉不知饿汉饥 (288)
皇帝：一朝天子一朝臣 (419)；天高皇帝远
　　(323)；皇帝女儿不愁嫁 (418)
皇历：老皇历 (435)
皇上：皇上不急太监急 (39)
黄河：不到黄河心不死 (134)；跳进黄河洗不
　　清 (17)；三十年河东，三十年河西 (223)
晃：一瓶子不满，半瓶子晃荡 (386)
晃荡：一瓶子不满，半瓶子晃荡 (386)

幌子：挂羊头、卖狗肉 (218)
灰：碰一鼻子灰 (195)
回：一回生，二回熟 (279)
回头：好马不吃回头草 (1)
回头客：一锤子买卖 (398)
会：会哭的孩子有奶吃 (447)；远来的和尚会
　　念经 (451)
浑水：趟浑水 (283)
混：出来混的，总要还的 (408)
混乱：鸡飞狗跳 (272)
活：死马当活马医 (139)；树挪死，人挪活
　　(464)
活该：搬起石头砸自己的脚 (71)
活马：死马当活马医 (139)
活人：活人让尿憋死 (420)
火：火烧眉毛 (384)；只许州官放火，不许
　　百姓点灯 (137)；众人拾柴火焰高 (209)；
　　纸包不住火 (96)；真金不怕火炼 (170)；
　　新官上任三把火 (140)
火车：满嘴跑火车 (461)
火海：上刀山，下火海 (145)
火焰：众人拾柴火焰高 (209)
货：一分钱一分货 (73)
获得：不入虎穴，焉得虎子 (116)

饥…饱…：饱汉不知饿汉饥 (288)
饥饿：饥不择食 (173)；饱汉不知饿汉饥
　　(288)
机会：过了这个村，就没这个店 (90)
鸡：杀鸡给猴看 (153)；杀鸡焉用宰牛刀
　　(248)；鸡飞蛋打 (286)；鸡毛蒜皮 (28)；
　　鸡同鸭讲 (433)；鸡蛋里挑骨头 (83)；
　　铁公鸡 (156)；拿鸡毛当令箭 (365)；
　　拿鸡蛋碰石头 (244)；偷鸡不成反蚀把米
　　(208)；偷鸡摸狗 (138)；嫁鸡随鸡，
　　嫁狗随狗 (189)；攒鸡毛，凑掸子 (485)
鸡…狗…：鸡飞狗跳 (272)；偷鸡摸狗 (138)；
　　嫁鸡随鸡，嫁狗随狗 (189)
鸡…鸭…：鸡同鸭讲 (433)
鸡蛋：苍蝇不叮无缝的蛋 (368)；鸡蛋里挑
　　骨头 (83)；拿鸡蛋碰石头 (244)
鸡毛：鸡毛蒜皮 (28)；拿鸡毛当令箭 (365)；
　　攒鸡毛，凑掸子 (485)
积累：姜是老的辣 (33)
积习：狗改不了吃屎 (171)
基础：身体是革命的本钱 (305)；磨刀不误
　　砍柴工 (147)
急：狗急了跳墙 (135)；皇上不急太监急
　　(39)；病急乱投医 (237)
棘手：烫手的山芋 (277)
集体：众人拾柴火焰高 (209)

嫉妒：羡慕嫉妒恨 (374)
嫉妒：吃不到葡萄就说葡萄酸 (43)；红眼病
　(343)；既生瑜，何生亮？(380)
挤：挤牙膏 (362)
挤牙膏：挤牙膏 (362)
计划：人算不如天算 (191)；小不忍则乱大谋
　(166)
技巧：四两拨千斤 (266)
忌惮：打狗还得看主人 (167)
既然：既生瑜，何生亮？(380)
家：家丑不可外扬 (126)；家花没有野花香
　(436)；家家有本难念的经 (100)
家产：仔卖爷田心不疼 (498)
家常：家常便饭 (45)
家丑：家丑不可外扬 (126)
家底：赔了夫人又折兵 (117)
假借：拿鸡毛当令箭 (365)
假象：笑面虎 (289)
假装：睁一只眼，闭一只眼 (55)；唱双簧
　(308)；得便宜卖乖 (124)
价格：物以稀为贵 (10)
嫁：嫁鸡随鸡，嫁狗随狗 (189)
嫁人：皇帝女儿不愁嫁 (418)
奸猾：不倒翁 (270)；老狐狸 (330)
坚决：不管三七二十一 (23)
坚强：硬骨头 (348)
艰难：硬骨头 (348)
兼得：鱼与熊掌不可得兼 (280)
拣：拣软柿子捏 (324)
见：丑媳妇早晚也得见公婆 (233)；
　阎王好见，小鬼难搪 (468)
见不得人：偷鸡摸狗 (138)
剑：双刃剑 (176)
铜：杀手锏 (172)
箭：明枪易躲，暗箭难防 (199)
将：强将手下无弱兵 (427)
将就：矬子里拔将军 (478)；高不成，低不就
　(298)
将军：一个将军一个令 (444)；过五关、
　斩六将 (372)；矬子里拔将军 (478)
姜：姜是老的辣 (33)
讲：鸡同鸭讲 (433)
酱油：打酱油 (20)
交往：君子之交淡如水 (180)；一回生，
　二回熟 (279)
嚼：吃别人嚼过的馍不香 (473)
角：冰山一角 (304)
狡诈：两面三刀 (403)
脚：一步一个脚印 (114)；三脚猫 (221)；
　头痛医头，脚痛医脚 (428)；抱佛脚 (91)；
　绊脚石 (371)；捧臭脚 (480)；脚正不怕

鞋歪 (413)；脚踩两只船 (41)；搬起石头
　砸自己的脚 (71)
脚印：一步一个脚印 (114)
搅和：和稀泥 (318)
搅坏：一马勺坏一锅 (494)
教训：一朝被蛇咬，十年怕井绳 (61)；
　吃一堑，长一智 (7)；好了伤疤忘了疼
　(178)；给他一点颜色看看 (322)
皆：一着不慎，满盘皆输 (212)
接：接地气 (500)
节省：不是省油的灯 (125)
结果：生米做成熟饭 (154)；有心栽花
　花不长，无心插柳柳成荫 (118)
解：解铃还须系铃人 (51)
解雇：炒鱿鱼 (66)
解决：远水解不了近渴 (193)；一把钥匙开
　一把锁 (404)
届时：秋后算账 (339)
界限：打擦边球 (327)
借：借东风 (388)
借东风：借东风 (388)
借题发挥：做文章 (336)
斤…两…：四两拨千斤 (266)
金：试金石 (383)；真金不怕火炼 (170)
紧箍咒：紧箍咒 (307)
紧急：火烧眉毛 (384)；病急乱投医 (237)
谨慎：一着不慎，满盘皆输 (212)
尽头：一条路走到黑 (302)
进展：好戏在后头 (97)
近：远水解不了近渴 (193)；远亲不如近邻
　(131)；近水楼台先得月 (103)；近朱者赤，
　近墨者黑 (9)
经书：远来的和尚会念经 (451)
经验：姜是老的辣 (33)
荆州：大意失荆州 (410)
精：狐狸精 (161)
精神：开小差 (315)
井绳：一朝被蛇咬，十年怕井绳 (61)
井水：井水不犯河水 (111)
警告：杀鸡给猴看 (153)；给他一点颜色看看
　(322)
警示：给他一点颜色看看 (322)
竞争：大鱼吃小鱼 (351)；二虎相争，
　必有一伤 (349)
敬酒：敬酒不吃吃罚酒 (75)
静：树欲静而风不止 (232)
究竟：说一千，道一万 (370)
揪：揪辫子 (452)
揪辫子：揪辫子 (452)
九：八九不离十 (122)；九牛二虎之力
　(74)

酒：酒香不怕巷子深 (301)；敬酒不吃吃罚酒 (75)；醉翁之意不在酒 (30)；酒逢知己千杯少 (226)

酒瓶：旧瓶装新酒 (402)

旧题材：炒冷饭 (482)

救命：救命稻草 (198)

就：不成功，便成仁 (394)

就是：不是鱼死，就是网破 (303)；有奶就是娘 (414)；听风就是雨 (213)

拒绝：吃闭门羹 (222)；碰钉子 (204)

俱备：万事俱备，只欠东风 (168)

俱全：麻雀虽小，五脏俱全 (164)

距离：十万八千里 (142)

卷进：躺着都中枪 (412)

决定：屁股决定脑袋 (455)；谋事在人，成事在天 (200)

决心：长痛不如短痛 (300)

绝技：杀手锏 (172)

绝境：狗急了跳墙 (135)

绝望：天无绝人之路 (47)；狗急了跳墙 (135)

橛子：别人牵驴你拔橛 (497)

军营：身在曹营心在汉 (230)

君子：以小人之心，度君子之腹 (81)；有仇不报非君子 (269)；先君子后小人 (406)；君子之交淡如水 (180)

俊杰：识时务者为俊杰 (110)

开：一把钥匙开一把锁 (404)；开空白支票 (309)；开绿灯 (353)

开车：开夜车 (332)

开绿灯：开绿灯 (353)

开水：白开水 (389)；死猪不怕开水烫 (196)

开小差：开小差 (315)

开夜车：开夜车 (332)

砍柴：磨刀不误砍柴工 (147)

看：打狗还得看主人 (167)；吃着碗里的，看着锅里的 (24)；杀鸡给猴看 (153)；狗眼看人低 (136)

看见：不见兔子不撒鹰 (469)；不见棺材不落泪 (94)；只见树木，不见森林 (454)

看清：识时务者为俊杰 (110)；睁眼瞎 (16)

考虑：病急乱投医 (237)

考验：真金不怕火炼 (170)

靠山：树倒猢狲散 (347)

科班：半路出家 (329)

科室：小儿科 (78)

可能：莫须有 (364)

可笑：笑掉大牙 (278)

渴：远水解不了近渴 (193)

客观：对事不对人 (174)

肯定：板上钉钉 (275)

坑：一个萝卜一个坑 (311)

空白：开空白支票 (309)

空城计：唱空城计 (400)

空手：空手套白狼 (385)

空谈：唱高调 (313)

控制：天高皇帝远 (323)

口：一口吃成个胖子 (258)

口渴：远水解不了近渴 (193)

扣：扣帽子 (459)

扣帽子：扣帽子 (459)

哭：会哭的孩子有奶吃 (447)

裤子：脱了裤子放屁 (387)

夸耀：王婆卖瓜，自卖自夸 (11)

快：快刀斩乱麻 (210)；萝卜快了不洗泥 (499)

筷子：端起碗来吃肉，放下筷子骂娘 (492)

亏：偷鸡不成反蚀把米 (208)

亏：好汉不吃眼前亏 (50)

捆绑：一根绳上的蚂蚱 (282)

困境：饥不择食 (173)

困难：不当家不知柴米贵 (342)

拉：老牛拉破车 (431)

拉出来：是骡子是马拉出来遛遛 (228)

拉屎：占着茅坑不拉屎 (194)；拉不出屎来怨茅房 (429)；骑脖子拉屎 (486)

辣：姜是老的辣 (33)

来不及：远水解不了近渴 (193)

来得及：磨刀不误砍柴工 (147)

癞蛤蟆：癞蛤蟆想吃天鹅肉 (46)

烂：肉烂在锅里 (415)

烂泥：烂泥扶不上墙 (296)

狼：舍不得孩子套不住狼 (217)；空手套白狼 (385)；前怕狼，后怕虎 (267)

浪费：打水漂 (314)；杀鸡焉用宰牛刀 (248)

老：老牛拉破车 (431)；老狐狸 (330)；老油条 (260)；老皇历 (435)；老掉牙 (70)；乱拳打死老师傅 (491)；姜是老的辣 (33)

老底：瘦死的骆驼比马大 (231)

老掉牙：老掉牙 (70)

老鸹：老鸹嫌猪黑 (496)

老狐狸：老狐狸 (330)

老虎：山中无老虎，猴子称大王 (247)；母老虎 (292)；纸老虎 (160)；一山不容二虎 (149)

老皇历：老皇历 (435)

老牛：老牛拉破车 (431)

老鼠：不管黑猫白猫，会捉老鼠就是好猫 (169)

老鹰：不见兔子不撒鹰 (469)

老油条：老油条 (260)

雷：雷声大、雨点小 (241)
雷声：雷声大、雨点小 (241)
类似：画虎不成反类犬 (409)
累积：冰冻三尺，非一日之寒 (130)；
　攒鸡毛，凑掸子 (485)
累赘：扯后腿 (320)
冷：坐冷板凳 (341)
冷…热…：热脸贴冷屁股 (177)
冷饭：炒冷饭 (482)
冷水：泼冷水 (152)
冷遇：热脸贴冷屁股 (177)；碰一鼻子灰
　(195)
离：八九不离十 (122)
离开：三句话不离本行 (345)
里：十万八千里 (142)
鲤鱼：鲤鱼跳龙门 (390)
力：九牛二虎之力 (74)；心有余而力不足
　(53)
力气：九牛二虎之力 (74)
厉害：母老虎 (292)
立场：两面派 (316)
立功：卸磨杀驴 (411)
利落：快刀斩乱麻 (210)
利益：打小算盘 (255)；有奶就是娘 (414)；
　有钱能使鬼推磨 (92)；肥水不流外人田
　(52)
利益相关：兔子不吃窝边草 (128)
利用：过河拆桥 (105)；借东风 (388)
连累：打不着狐狸惹身骚 (475)
连锁：一条龙 (265)
连夜雨：屋漏偏逢连阴雨 (259)
连阴雨：屋漏偏逢连阴雨 (259)
联系：对号入座 (141)
脸：小白脸 (183)；打肿脸充胖子 (85)；
　热脸贴冷屁股 (177)；脸红脖子粗 (242)；
　蹬鼻子上脸 (205)
脸红：脸红脖子粗 (242)
炼：真金不怕火炼 (170)
链子：掉链子 (159)
梁：上梁不正下梁歪 (115)
两：二虎相争，必有一伤 (349)；三天打鱼，
　两天晒网 (60)；两面派 (316)；脚踩两只船
　(41)
两空：鸡飞蛋打 (286)
两面：两面派 (316)
两面派：两面派 (316)
两难：高不成，低不就 (298)
亮：东方不亮西方亮 (430)
撂：撂挑子 (381)
撂挑子：撂挑子 (381)
裂开：歪瓜裂枣 (354)

邻近：兔子不吃窝边草 (128)
邻居：远亲不如近邻 (131)
林：独木不成林 (379)
临时：抱佛脚 (91)
灵活：一棵树上吊死 (112)；好汉不吃眼前亏
　(50)
灵巧：巧妇难为无米之炊 (187)
灵验：说曹操，曹操到 (4)
铃铛：解铃还须系铃人 (51)
领导：强将手下无弱兵 (427)
领域：隔行如隔山 (357)
令：一个将军一个令 (444)
令箭：拿鸡毛当令箭 (365)
刘邦：鸿门宴 (214)
留不住：浅水养不了大鱼 (472)
留下：留得青山在，不怕没柴烧 (34)
流：人往高处走，水往低处流 (67)
流动：人往高处走，水往低处流 (67)
流入：肥水不流外人田 (52)
流失：肉烂在锅里 (415)
柳：有心栽花花不长，无心插柳柳成荫 (118)
遛：是骡子是马拉出来遛遛 (228)
龙：一条龙 (265)；龙生龙，凤生凤 (239)；
　变色龙 (378)；强龙压不住地头蛇 (391)
龙…凤…：龙生龙，凤生凤 (239)
龙门：鲤鱼跳龙门 (390)
龙套：跑龙套 (250)
龙王：大水冲了龙王庙 (360)
娄子：捅马蜂窝 (261)
楼台：近水楼台先得月 (103)
漏雨：屋漏偏逢连阴雨 (259)
路：一条路走到黑 (302)；车到山前必有路
　(82)；多个朋友多条路 (253)
露：露马脚 (143)
露齿：咬人的狗不露齿 (481)
露出来：狐狸尾巴露出来了 (352)
露马脚：露马脚 (143)
露馅：露马脚 (143)
乱：乱拳打死老师傅 (491)；乱弹琴 (361)；
　快刀斩乱麻 (210)；病急乱投医 (237)
乱弹琴：乱弹琴 (361)
乱来：乱弹琴 (361)
萝卜：一个萝卜一个坑 (311)；拔出萝卜
　带出泥 (460)；萝卜白菜，各有所爱 (58)；
　萝卜快了不洗泥 (499)
锣：当面锣，对面鼓 (470)；敲锣边儿 (458)
锣边：敲锣边儿 (458)
骡子：是骡子是马拉出来遛遛 (228)
骆驼：瘦死的骆驼比马大 (231)
落：落水狗 (274)
落空：吃闭门羹 (222)

落泪：不见棺材不落泪 (94)
落水：落水狗 (274)
落水狗：落水狗 (274)
驴：别人牵驴你拔橛 (497)；卸磨杀驴 (411)；
　猴年马月 (31)
绿：绿帽子 (109)
绿灯：开绿灯 (353)
绿帽子：绿帽子 (109)

麻：快刀斩乱麻 (210)
麻烦：不是省油的灯 (125)；穿小鞋 (321)；
　捅马蜂窝 (261)；眼中钉、肉中刺 (216)
麻利：三下五除二 (151)
麻雀：麻雀虽小，五脏俱全 (164)
马：又要马儿跑，又要马儿不吃草 (440)；
　下马威 (132)；千里马 (326)；马后炮
　(158)；风马牛不相及 (148)；死马当活马医
　(139)；拍马屁 (18)；是骡子是马拉出来
　遛遛 (228)；骑马找马 (457)；猴年马月
　(31)；瘦死的骆驼比马大 (231)
马蜂：捅马蜂窝 (261)
马蜂窝：捅马蜂窝 (261)
马后炮：马后炮 (158)
马虎：打马虎眼 (325)
马脚：露马脚 (143)
马屁：拍马屁 (18)
马勺：一马勺坏一锅 (494)
马嘴：牛头不对马嘴 (80)
蚂蚱：一根绳上的蚂蚱 (282)；蚂蚱也是肉
　(488)
骂：三字经 (367)；指着和尚骂秃子 (487)；
　端起碗来吃肉，放下筷子骂娘 (492)
骂娘：端起碗来吃肉，放下筷子骂娘 (492)
埋怨：拉不出屎来怨茅房 (429)
买卖：一锤子买卖 (398)
卖：王婆卖瓜，自卖自夸 (11)；仔卖爷田不
　心疼 (498)；卖关子 (72)；挂羊头、卖狗肉
　(218)；葫芦里卖的是什么药 (344)
卖乖：得便宜卖乖 (124)
卖关子：卖关子 (72)
卖药：葫芦里卖的是什么药 (344)
满：一瓶子不满，半瓶子晃荡 (386)；
　满嘴跑火车 (461)
猫：三脚猫 (221)；不管黑猫白猫，会捉老鼠
　就是好猫 (169)；瞎猫碰上死耗子 (49)
矛盾：三个女人一台戏 (201)
茅房：拉不出屎来怨茅房 (429)
茅坑：占着茅坑不拉屎 (194)
卯：丁是丁，卯是卯 (425)
铆：丁是丁，卯是卯 (425)
冒充：打肿脸充胖子 (85)

冒犯：大水冲了龙王庙 (360)
冒险：不入虎穴，焉得虎子 (116)；舍不得
　孩子套不住狼 (217)
帽：戴高帽 (338)
帽子：扣帽子 (459)；绿帽子 (109)
貌：人不可貌相，海水不可斗量 (26)
没：过了这个村，就没这个店 (90)
没出息：下三烂 (235)
没完：走着瞧 (22)
没有：天下没有不散的筵席 (13)；没有不
　透风的墙 (245)；留得青山在，不怕没柴烧
　(34)；家花没有野花香 (436)
眉毛：火烧眉毛 (384)；眉毛胡子一把抓
　(207)
美女：鲜花插在牛粪上 (29)
美人：英雄难过美人关 (62)
媚外：胳膊肘往外扭 (299)
门：门外汉 (294)；敲门砖 (382)
门外汉：门外汉 (294)
门牙：打掉门牙往肚里咽 (375)
蒙混：眼里揉不得沙子 (150)
迷惑：一头雾水 (356)
米：巧妇难为无米之炊 (187)；生米做成熟饭
　(154)；偷鸡不成反蚀把米 (208)
秘密：没有不透风的墙 (245)
蜜蜂：一窝蜂 (331)
勉强：强扭的瓜不甜 (69)
面：两面三刀 (403)；两面派 (316)；笑面虎
　(289)
面前：关公面前耍大刀 (297)
面子：不看僧面看佛面 (240)；下台阶 (254)；
　打狗还得看主人 (167)
庙：大水冲了龙王庙 (360)；跑了和尚跑
　不了庙 (108)
名声：跳进黄河洗不清 (17)
名声：人怕出名猪怕壮 (246)
明…暗…：明枪易躲，暗箭难防 (199)
明确：一是一，二是二 (252)
命：小姐的身子丫鬟的命 (453)
命令：一个将军一个令 (444)；拿鸡毛当令箭
　(365)
命运：既生瑜，何生亮？ (380)；嫁鸡随鸡，
　嫁狗随狗 (189)
摸：偷鸡摸狗 (138)；摸着石头过河 (328)
摸索：摸着石头过河 (328)
馍：吃别人嚼过的馍不香 (473)
模仿：依葫芦画瓢 (185)
磨：卸磨杀驴 (411)；磨刀不误砍柴工 (147)
磨刀：磨刀不误砍柴工 (147)
陌生：一回生，二回熟 (279)
莫：一不做，二不休 (106)

莫须有：莫须有 (364)
墨：近朱者赤，近墨者黑 (9)
谋：谋事在人，成事在天 (200)
谋划：小不忍则乱大谋 (166)
母：母老虎 (292)
母老虎：母老虎 (292)
亩：一亩三分地 (358)
木：独木不成林 (379)
目标：树大招风 (225)
目的：醉翁之意不在酒 (30)

拿：拿鸡毛当令箭 (365)；拿鸡蛋碰石头
　　(244)；拿得起，放得下 (35)
拿起：拿得起，放得下 (35)
哪：哪壶不开提哪壶 (65)
哪有：常在河边走，哪有不湿鞋 (220)
奶：有奶就是娘 (414)；会哭的孩子有奶吃
　　(447)
奶奶：求爷爷、告奶奶 (373)
耐心：放长线，钓大鱼 (184)
男人：吃软饭 (211)
难：巧妇难为无米之炊 (187)；英雄难过
　　美人关 (62)；明枪易躲，暗箭难防 (199)；
　　家家有本难念的经 (100)；阎王好见，
　　小鬼难搪 (468)
难缠：滚刀肉 (395)
难免：常在河边走，哪有不湿鞋 (220)
难事：家家有本难念的经 (100)
脑袋：屁股决定脑袋 (455)
内耗：二虎相争，必有一伤 (349)
内容：旧瓶装新酒 (402)
能：有钱能使鬼推磨 (92)
能干：拿得起，放得下 (35)
能力：高不成，低不就 (298)；眼大肚子小
　　(471)
能手：多面手 (476)
能说：说得比唱得好听 (68)
泥：拔出萝卜带出泥 (460)；和稀泥 (318)；
　　萝卜快了不洗泥 (499)
你…我…：你走你的阳关道，我过我的
　　独木桥 (89)
年：三十年河东，三十年河西 (223)；
　　多年的媳妇熬成婆 (426)
…年…月：猴年马月 (31)
念叨：说曹操，曹操到 (4)
念经：远来的和尚会念经 (451)；家家有本
　　难念的经 (100)
娘：有奶就是娘 (414)；端起碗来吃肉，
　　放下筷子骂娘 (492)
鸟：林子大了，什么鸟都有 (27)；
　　枪打出头鸟 (203)

鸟枪：鸟枪换炮 (477)
尿：活人让尿憋死 (420)
捏：拣软柿子捏 (324)
牛：九牛二虎之力 (74)；牛不喝水强按头
　　(441)；风马牛不相及 (148)；杀鸡焉用
　　宰牛刀 (248)
牛犊：初生牛犊不怕虎 (155)
牛粪：鲜花插在牛粪上 (29)
牛角尖：钻牛角尖 (25)
牛皮：吹牛皮 (98)
牛头：牛头不对马嘴 (80)
扭：胳膊扭不过大腿 (287)；胳膊肘往外扭
　　(299)；强扭的瓜不甜 (69)
挪：树挪死，人挪活 (464)
懦弱：拣软柿子捏 (324)
女儿：皇帝女儿不愁嫁 (418)
女人：母老虎 (292)；吃豆腐 (206)；
　　吃软饭 (211)；狐狸精 (161)；三个女人
　　一台戏 (201)

耙：倒打一耙 (263)
怕：一朝被蛇咬，十年怕井绳 (61)；人怕
　　出名猪怕壮 (246)；死猪不怕开水烫 (196)；
　　光脚的不怕穿鞋的 (393)；初生牛犊不怕虎
　　(155)；前怕狼，后怕虎 (267)；留得
　　青山在，不怕没柴烧 (34)
拍：一个巴掌拍不响 (79)；拍马屁 (18)
拍马屁：拍马屁 (18)
牌坊：又想当婊子又想立牌坊 (437)
派：两面派 (316)
攀附：抱大腿 (445)
盘：一盘散沙 (317)；一着不慎，满盘皆输
　　(212)
判断：人不可貌相，海水不可斗量 (26)；
　　以小人之心，度君子之腹 (81)
旁边：当耳旁风 (87)；枕边风 (397)
旁观：坐山观虎斗 (256)；说风凉话 (306)
胖：说你胖你就喘 (416)
胖子：一口吃成个胖子 (258)；打肿脸充胖子
　　(85)
抛弃：卸磨杀驴 (411)
跑：又要马儿跑，又要马儿不吃草 (440)；
　　跑了和尚跑不了庙 (108)；跑龙套 (250)；
　　满嘴跑火车 (461)
跑龙套：跑龙套 (250)
炮：马后炮 (158)；鸟枪换炮 (477)
炮弹：糖衣炮弹 (346)
赔：赔了夫人又折兵 (117)
配角：跑龙套 (250)
朋友：多个朋友多条路 (253)；君子之交
　　淡如水 (180)

捧：捧臭脚 (480)
捧臭脚：捧臭脚 (480)
碰：拿鸡蛋碰石头 (244)；碰一鼻子灰 (195)；
　碰钉子 (204)
碰钉子：碰钉子 (204)
碰上：瞎猫碰上死耗子 (49)
皮…肉…：皮笑肉不笑 (175)
皮匠：三个臭皮匠，顶个诸葛亮 (40)
屁：脱了裤子放屁 (387)
屁股：屁股决定脑袋 (455)；热脸贴冷屁股
　(177)；擦屁股 (417)
偏偏：屋漏偏逢连阴雨 (259)
便宜：得便宜卖乖 (124)
片面：只见树木，不见森林 (454)；
　头痛医头，脚痛医脚 (428)
瓢：依葫芦画瓢 (185)；按下葫芦起了瓢
　(465)
撇：八字还没一撇 (119)
拼凑：攒鸡毛，凑掸子 (485)
平常：家常便饭 (45)
平淡：白开水 (389)
平凡：三个臭皮匠，顶个诸葛亮 (40)
平分：二一添作五 (448)
平均：吃大锅饭 (337)
瓶：旧瓶装新酒 (402)
瓶子：一瓶子不满，半瓶子晃荡 (386)
泼：泼冷水 (152)
泼冷水：泼冷水 (152)
泼皮：滚刀肉 (395)
婆：多年的媳妇熬成婆 (426)
破：不是鱼死，就是网破 (303)；老牛拉破车
　(431)；破罐子破摔 (56)
破车：老牛拉破车 (431)
破坏：一马勺坏一锅 (494)
葡萄：吃不到葡萄就说葡萄酸 (43)
普通：家常便饭 (45)

七…八…：七大姑，八大姨 (251)
期望：高不成，低不就 (298)
欺负：不是吃素的 (188)；拣软柿子捏 (324)；
　骑脖子拉屎 (486)
欺辱：骑脖子拉屎 (486)
奇怪：林子大了，什么鸟都有 (27)
骑：骑马找马 (457)；骑脖子拉屎 (486)
骑马：骑马找马 (457)
起：按下葫芦起了瓢 (465)
起因：解铃还须系铃人 (51)
起早：起大早，赶晚集 (474)
气筒：出气筒 (121)
恰当：用在刀刃上 (285)
恰好：一个萝卜一个坑 (311)

千：酒逢知己千杯少 (226)
千…万…：说一千，道一万 (370)
千方百计：横挑鼻子竖挑眼 (399)
千古：一失足成千古恨 (64)
千斤：四两拨千斤 (266)
千里马：千里马 (326)
牵：别人牵驴你拔橛 (497)
谦虚：一瓶子不满，半瓶子晃荡 (386)
前…后…：前人栽树，后人乘凉 (295)；
　前怕狼，后怕虎 (267)
前人：前人栽树，后人乘凉 (295)
前提：敲门砖 (382)
前头：丑话说在前头 (162)
前途：兔子尾巴长不了 (456)
钱：一分钱一分货 (73)；有钱能使鬼推磨 (92)
浅：浅水养不了大鱼 (472)
欠：万事俱备，只欠东风 (168)
堑：吃一堑，长一智 (7)
枪：枪打出头鸟 (203)；明枪易躲，暗箭难防
　(199)；躺着都中枪 (412)
枪…炮…：鸟枪换炮 (477)
强：强龙压不住地头蛇 (391)；强扭的瓜不甜
　(69)；强将手下无弱兵 (427)
强…弱…：强将手下无弱兵 (427)
强龙：强龙压不住地头蛇 (391)
强迫：赶鸭子上架 (182)；牛不喝水强按头
　(441)
强弱：胳膊扭不过大腿 (287)
强硬：敬酒不吃吃罚酒 (75)
墙：没有不透风的墙 (245)；拆东墙，补西墙
　(350)；狗急了跳墙 (135)；烂泥扶不上墙
　(296)；隔墙有耳 (186)；墙头草 (101)；
　墙倒众人推 (363)
墙头：墙头草 (101)
墙头草：墙头草 (101)
敲：敲门砖 (382)；敲竹杠 (319)；敲锣边儿
　(458)
敲锣边：敲锣边儿 (458)
敲门砖：敲门砖 (382)
敲竹杠：敲竹杠 (319)
桥：过河拆桥 (105)；你走你的阳关道，
　我过我的独木桥 (89)
瞧：走着瞧 (22)
巧合：瞎猫碰上死耗子 (49)
切：一刀切 (401)
侵犯：井水不犯河水 (111)
亲戚：远亲不如近邻 (131)；七大姑，八大姨
　(251)
青山：留得青山在，不怕没柴烧 (34)
青蛙：温水煮青蛙 (462)
轻率：听风就是雨 (213)

轻视：坐冷板凳 (341)
清：跳进黄河洗不清 (17)
清白：跳进黄河洗不清 (17)
清净：眼不见为净 (32)
情人：情人眼里出西施 (19)
秋：秋后算账 (339)
秋后：秋后算账 (339)
求：求爷爷、告奶奶 (373)
求救：抱佛脚 (91)
球：打擦边球 (327)
驱动：有钱能使鬼推磨 (92)
屈辱：打掉门牙往肚里咽 (375)
取舍：鱼与熊掌不可得兼 (280)
取笑：五十步笑百步 (293)
圈套：鸿门宴 (214)
权势：大树底下好乘凉 (249)；拔根汗毛比
　腰粗 (467)；抱大腿 (445)
权威：一个将军一个令 (444)
全部：一锅端 (434)
全局：一着不慎，满盘皆输 (212)；
　只见树木，不见森林 (454)
拳头：乱拳打死老师傅 (491)
犬：画虎不成反类犬 (409)
缺点：苍蝇不叮无缝的蛋 (368)

让：终日打雁，让雁啄了眼 (495)
让步：先君子后小人 (406)
惹：打不着狐狸惹身骚 (475)
热：心急吃不了热豆腐 (44)；剃头挑子
　一头热 (450)；热脸贴冷屁股 (177)
热闹：三个女人一台戏 (201)
热情：泼冷水 (152)
人：人不可貌相，海水不可斗量 (26)；人往
　高处走，水往低处流 (67)；人怕出名猪怕
　壮 (246)；人算不如天算 (191)；天无绝人
　之路 (47)；以其人之道还治其人之身
　(36)；对事不对人 (174)；吃水不忘挖井人
　(268)；狗眼看人低 (136)；树挪死，人挪活
　(464)；咬人的狗不露齿 (481)；谋事在人，
　成事在天 (200)；解铃还须系铃人 (51)；
　墙倒众人推 (363)
人…事…：对事不对人 (174)
人…天…：人算不如天算 (191)
人才：人往高处走，水往低处流 (67)；
　千里马 (326)；门外汉 (294)；浅水养不了
　大鱼 (472)
人为：穿小鞋 (321)
仁：不成功，便成仁 (394)
忍耐：小不忍则乱大谋 (166)
刃：双刃剑 (176)
认为：物以稀为贵 (10)

认真：说你胖你就喘 (416)；给个棒槌就当针
　(479)
任何：不分青红皂白 (54)；不管三七二十一
　(23)
日出：太阳从西边出来 (3)
容：一山不容二虎 (149)
容纳：一山不容二虎 (149)
容颜：岁月是把杀猪刀 (424)
容易：大树底下好乘凉 (249)；小儿科 (78)；
　小菜一碟 (2)；小意思 (262)；阎王好见，
　小鬼难搪 (468)；明枪易躲，暗箭难防 (199)
揉：眼里揉不得沙子 (150)
肉：手心手背都是肉 (333)；肉烂在锅里
　(415)；挂羊头、卖狗肉 (218)；蚂蚱也是肉
　(488)；眼中钉、肉中刺 (216)；滚刀肉
　(395)；端起碗来吃肉，放下筷子骂娘
　(492)；癞蛤蟆想吃天鹅肉 (46)
如：君子之交淡如水 (180)；隔行如隔山 (357)
如意：打如意算盘 (238)
入座：对号入座 (141)
软：吃软饭 (211)；拣软柿子捏 (324)
弱：强将手下无弱兵 (427)

撒：不见兔子不撒鹰 (469)
三：三个女人一台戏 (201)；三个和尚没水吃
　(181)；三个臭皮匠，顶个诸葛亮 (40)；
　三天打鱼，两天晒网 (60)；三句话不离
　本行 (345)；三脚猫 (221)；下三烂 (235)；
　新官上任三把火 (140)
三…两…：三天打鱼，两天晒网 (60)；
　三长两短 (95)；两面三刀 (403)
三把火：新官上任三把火 (140)
三百：此地无银三百两 (42)
三尺：冰冻三尺，非一日之寒 (130)
三脚猫：三脚猫 (221)
三十：三十年河东，三十年河西 (223)
三十六计：三十六计走为上 (86)
三字经：三字经 (367)
伞：保护伞 (310)
散：天下没有不散的筵席 (13)
散开：树倒猢狲散 (347)
散沙：一盘散沙 (317)
骚气：打不着狐狸惹身骚 (475)
森林：只见树木，不见森林 (454)
僧：不看僧面看佛面 (240)；僧多粥少 (340)
杀：半路杀出个程咬金 (163)；岁月是把杀
　猪刀 (424)；杀鸡给猴看 (153)；杀鸡焉用
　宰牛刀 (248)；卸磨杀驴 (411)
杀手锏：杀手锏 (172)
沙子：一盘散沙 (317)；眼里揉不得沙子
　(150)

傻：二 (290)

晒网：三天打鱼，两天晒网 (60)

山：一山不容二虎 (149)；山中无老虎，
　　猴子称大王 (247)；车到山前必有路 (82)；
　　坐山观虎斗 (256)；这山望着那山高 (392)；
　　到什么山唱什么歌 (466)；留得青山在，
　　不怕没柴烧 (34)；隔行如隔山 (357)

山芋：烫手的山芋 (277)

善变：变色龙 (378)

善于：会哭的孩子有奶吃 (447)

伤：二虎相争，必有一伤 (349)

伤疤：好了伤疤忘了疼 (178)

伤害：双刃剑 (176)

伤心：不见棺材不落泪 (94)

上：蹬鼻子上脸 (205)

上…下…：上梁不正下梁歪 (115)

上策：三十六计走为上 (86)

上船：上了贼船 (236)

上吊：一棵树上吊死 (112)

上架：赶鸭子上架 (182)

上任：新官上任三把火 (140)

烧：火烧眉毛 (384)；留得青山在，不怕没
　　柴烧 (34)

少：酒逢知己千杯少 (226)；僧多粥少 (340)

蛇：一朝被蛇咬，十年怕井绳 (61)；强龙
　　压不住地头蛇 (391)

舍得：舍不得孩子套不住狼 (217)

社会：出来混的，总要还的 (408)

身…心…：身在曹营心在汉 (230)

身份：多年的媳妇熬成婆 (426)

身体：身在曹营心在汉 (230)；身体是革命的
　　本钱 (305)

身子：小姐的身子丫鬟的命 (453)

深：酒香不怕巷子深 (301)

什么：林子大了，什么鸟都有 (27)；
　　到什么山唱什么歌 (466)

慎：一着不慎，满盘皆输 (212)

升级：鸟枪换炮 (477)

生：一回生，二回熟 (279)；龙生龙，凤生凤
　　(239)

生…熟…：生米做成熟饭 (154)

生动：有鼻子有眼 (202)

生疏：一回生，二回熟 (279)

生育：龙生龙，凤生凤 (239)

生长：有心栽花花不长，无心插柳柳成荫
　　(118)

声势：雷声大、雨点小 (241)

声誉：酒香不怕巷子深 (301)

绳：一根绳上的蚂蚱 (282)

绳子：一根绳上的蚂蚱 (282)

胜…败…：胜者王侯败者贼 (234)

胜者：胜者王侯败者贼 (234)

失败：成也萧何，败也萧何 (359)；
　　成事不足，败事有余 (38)

失去：过了这个村，就没这个店 (90)

失势：落水狗 (274)；墙倒众人推 (363)

失手：终日打雁，让雁啄了眼 (495)

失业：铁饭碗 (129)

失真：画虎不成反类犬 (409)

失足：一失足成千古恨 (64)

师傅：乱拳打死老师傅 (491)

虱子：虱子多了不咬，账多了不愁 (484)

施加：己所不欲，勿施于人 (15)

湿：常在河边走，哪有不湿鞋 (220)

十：八九不离十 (122)

十年：一朝被蛇咬，十年怕井绳 (61)

十万八千：十万八千里 (142)

石：绊脚石 (371)

石头：试金石 (383)；拿鸡蛋碰石头 (244)；
　　摸着石头过河 (328)；搬起石头砸自己的脚
　　(71)

时务：识时务者为俊杰 (110)

识别：有眼不识泰山 (120)

实力：胳膊扭不过大腿 (287)

实用：不管黑猫白猫，会捉老鼠就是好猫
　　(169)

实质：换汤不换药 (197)

拾柴：众人拾柴火焰高 (209)

食物：饥不择食 (173)

蚀：偷鸡不成反蚀把米 (208)

屎：占着茅坑不拉屎 (194)；拉不出屎来怨
　　茅房 (429)；狗改不了吃屎 (171)；骑脖子
　　拉屎 (486)

势力：一亩三分地 (358)；东风压倒西风
　　(423)；独木不成林 (379)

势利：狗眼看人低 (136)；变色龙 (378)；
　　墙头草 (101)；墙倒众人推 (363)

事：万事俱备，只欠东风 (168)

事端：无风不起浪 (123)

事故：按下葫芦起了瓢 (465)

事关：成也萧何，败也萧何 (359)

事后：马后炮 (158)

事情：无事不登三宝殿 (157)；对事不对人
　　(174)；成事不足，败事有余 (38)；事后
　　诸葛亮 (273)；谋事在人，成事在天 (200)

试：试金石 (383)

试金石：试金石 (383)

试探：敲门砖 (382)

柿子：拣软柿子捏 (324)

收获：空手套白狼 (385)；种瓜得瓜，
　　种豆得豆 (57)

收拾：擦屁股 (417)

手：手心手背都是肉 (333)；烫手的山芋 (277)

手背：手心手背都是肉 (333)

手下：强将手下无弱兵 (427)

手心：手心手背都是肉 (333)

受罚：替罪羊 (102)

受过：背黑锅 (127)

受伤：二虎相争，必有一伤 (349)

瘦：瘦死的骆驼比马大 (231)

疏忽：一着不慎，满盘皆输 (212)

输：一着不慎，满盘皆输 (212)

熟：一回生，二回熟 (279)；煮熟的鸭子飞了 (219)

熟识：一回生，二回熟 (279)

树：一棵树上吊死 (112)；大树底下好乘凉 (249)；树大招风 (225)；树挪死，人挪活 (464)；树倒猢狲散 (347)；树欲静而风不止 (232)；前人栽树，后人乘凉 (295)

树林：林子大了，什么鸟都有 (27)；独木不成林 (379)

树木：只见树木，不见森林 (454)

树荫：有心栽花花不长，无心插柳柳成荫 (118)

耍：关公面前耍大刀 (297)；耍花枪 (439)

耍花枪：耍花枪 (439)

摔：破罐子破摔 (56)

双：双刃剑 (176)；唱双簧 (308)

双方：一个巴掌拍不响 (79)

双簧：唱双簧 (308)

双刃剑：双刃剑 (176)

爽约：放鸽子 (113)

水：一碗水端平 (276)；人往高处走，水往低处流 (67)；大水冲了龙王庙 (360)；井水不犯河水 (111)；白开水 (389)；死猪不怕开水烫 (196)；远水解不了近渴 (193)；近水楼台先得月 (103)；君子之交淡如水 (180)；浅水养不了大鱼 (472)；泼冷水 (152)；落水狗 (274)；温水煮青蛙 (462)；趟浑水 (283)

水漂：打水漂 (314)

说：丑话说在前头 (162)；打开天窗说亮话 (190)；吃不到葡萄就说葡萄酸 (43)；说你胖你就喘 (416)；说曹操，曹操到 (4)；说得比唱得好听 (68)；睁着眼睛说瞎话 (8)

说…道…：说一千，道一万 (370)

说话：乌鸦嘴 (5)；说风凉话 (306)；站着说话不腰疼 (12)

说谎：睁着眼睛说瞎话 (8)

私情：绿帽子 (109)

思想：屁股决定脑袋 (455)

死：一棵树上吊死 (112)；一棍子打死 (243)；不是鱼死，就是网破 (303)；死马当活马医 (139)；死猪不怕开水烫 (196)；树挪死，人挪活 (464)；瘦死的骆驼比马大 (231)；瞎猫碰上死耗子 (49)

死马：死马当活马医 (139)

死心：不到黄河心不死 (134)

四两：四两拨千斤 (266)

松手：不见兔子不撒鹰 (469)

怂恿：敲锣边儿 (458)

诉苦：吃哑巴亏 (215)

速：欲速则不达 (99)

酸：吃不到葡萄就说葡萄酸 (43)

蒜：鸡毛蒜皮 (28)

蒜皮：鸡毛蒜皮 (28)

算：人算不如天算 (191)

算盘：打小算盘 (255)；打如意算盘 (238)

算账：秋后算账 (339)

虽：麻雀虽小，五脏俱全 (164)

随：嫁鸡随鸡，嫁狗随狗 (189)

岁月：岁月是把杀猪刀 (424)

缩：缩头乌龟 (334)

缩头：缩头乌龟 (334)

琐碎：鸡毛蒜皮 (28)

锁：一把钥匙开一把锁 (404)

踏实：一步一个脚印 (114)

台阶：下台阶 (254)

太监：皇上不急太监急 (39)

太阳：太阳从西边出来 (3)

泰山：有眼不识泰山 (120)

贪婪：吃着碗里的，看着锅里的 (24)；蹬鼻子上脸 (205)

贪心：这山望着那山高 (392)

坛子：醋坛子 (179)

探索：摸着石头过河 (328)

汤药：换汤不换药 (197)

堂：一言堂 (490)

搪塞：打马虎眼 (325)

糖：糖衣炮弹 (346)

糖衣炮弹：糖衣炮弹 (346)

躺：躺着都中枪 (412)

躺枪：躺着都中枪 (412)

烫：死猪不怕开水烫 (196)；烫手的山芋 (277)

烫手：烫手的山芋 (277)

趟：趟浑水 (283)

趟浑水：趟浑水 (283)

逃避：丑媳妇早晚也得见公婆 (233)

逃跑：三十六计走为上 (86)

桃花：走桃花运 (37)

讨好：两面派 (316)
套：舍不得孩子套不住狼 (217)；空手套白狼 (385)
疼：仔卖爷田不心疼 (498)；好了伤疤忘了疼 (178)；站着说话不腰疼 (12)
提：哪壶不开提哪壶 (65)
体谅：饱汉不知饿汉饥 (288)
剃头：剃头挑子一头热 (450)
替：替罪羊 (102)
替代：出气筒 (121)
替人：背黑锅 (127)
替罪羊：替罪羊 (102)
天：人算不如天算 (191)；三天打鱼，两天晒网 (60)；天无绝人之路 (47)；天高皇帝远 (323)；当一天和尚撞一天钟 (227)；谋事在人，成事在天 (200)
天窗：打开天窗说亮话 (190)
天鹅：癞蛤蟆想吃天鹅肉 (46)
天鹅肉：癞蛤蟆想吃天鹅肉 (46)
天亮：东方不亮西方亮 (430)
天上：天上掉馅饼 (14)
天下：天下乌鸦一般黑 (133)；天下没有不散的筵席 (13)
天子：一朝天子一朝臣 (419)
田：仔卖爷田不心疼 (498)；肥水不流外人田 (52)
甜：打一巴掌，给个甜枣 (405)；强扭的瓜不甜 (69)
填补：拆东墙，补西墙 (350)
挑：鸡蛋里挑骨头 (83)；横挑鼻子竖挑眼 (399)
挑刺：鸡蛋里挑骨头 (83)
挑剔：眼里揉不得沙子 (150)；横挑鼻子竖挑眼 (399)
挑战：唱对台戏 (376)
挑子：剃头挑子一头热 (450)；撂挑子 (381)
条件：巧妇难为无米之炊 (187)
调停：和稀泥 (318)
跳：鸡飞狗跳 (272)；跳进黄河洗不清 (17)；鲤鱼跳龙门 (390)
跳进：跳进黄河洗不清 (17)
跳墙：狗急了跳墙 (135)
贴：热脸贴冷屁股 (177)
铁：恨铁不成钢 (88)；铁公鸡 (156)；铁饭碗 (129)
铁公鸡：铁公鸡 (156)
听：听风就是雨 (213)
听天由命：嫁鸡随鸡，嫁狗随狗 (189)
停止：树欲静而风不止 (232)；一不做，二不休 (106)
挺不住：掉链子 (159)

通奸：绿帽子 (109)
捅：捅马蜂窝 (261)；捅破窗户纸 (366)
捅破：捅破窗户纸 (366)
痛：长痛不如短痛 (300)；头痛医头，脚痛医脚 (428)
痛苦：长痛不如短痛 (300)
偷：偷鸡不成反蚀把米 (208)；偷鸡摸狗 (138)
偷摸：偷鸡摸狗 (138)
偷听：隔墙有耳 (186)
头：一头雾水 (356)；牛不喝水强按头 (441)；挂羊头、卖狗肉 (218)；缩头乌龟 (334)
头…脚…：头痛医头，脚痛医脚 (428)
头痛：头痛医头，脚痛医脚 (428)
投机：酒逢知己千杯少 (226)
投入：种瓜得瓜，种豆得豆 (57)
投医：病急乱投医 (237)
透风：没有不透风的墙 (245)
秃子：指着和尚骂秃子 (487)
土：土包子 (224)
土包子：土包子 (224)
土气：土包子 (224)
吐：狗嘴里吐不出象牙 (59)
兔子：不见兔子不撒鹰 (469)；兔子不吃窝边草 (128)；兔子尾巴长不了 (456)
团结：一盘散沙 (317)
推：墙倒众人推 (363)
推磨：有钱能使鬼推磨 (92)
推诿：三个和尚没水吃 (181)
腿：扯后腿 (320)；狗腿子 (284)；胳膊扭不过大腿 (287)
退出：打退堂鼓 (146)
退堂：打退堂鼓 (146)
脱：脱了裤子放屁 (387)

挖井：吃水不忘挖井人 (268)
歪：上梁不正下梁歪 (115)；歪瓜裂枣 (354)；脚正不怕鞋歪 (413)
外：门外汉 (294)
外表：人不可貌相，海水不可斗量 (26)
外界：树欲静而风不止 (232)
外来：远来的和尚会念经 (451)
外流：肥水不流外人田 (52)
外人：肥水不流外人田 (52)
外扬：家丑不可外扬 (126)
外因：树欲静而风不止 (232)
完备：麻雀虽小，五脏俱全 (164)
完成：八字还没一撇 (119)
晚：起大早，赶晚集 (474)
碗：一碗水端平 (276)；吃着碗里的，看着锅里的 (24)；铁饭碗 (129)；端起碗来吃肉，放下筷子骂娘 (492)

万：万事俱备，只欠东风 (168)
万金油：万金油 (463)
万一：不怕一万，就怕万一 (21)
王侯：胜者王侯败者贼 (234)
王婆：王婆卖瓜，自卖自夸 (11)
网：不是鱼死，就是网破 (303)
往外：胳膊肘往外扭 (299)
忘：好了伤疤忘了疼 (178)
忘记：吃水不忘挖井人 (268)
望：这山望着那山高 (392)
危急：病急乱投医 (237)
危险：上刀山，下火海 (145)
威严：下马威 (132)
微薄：独木不成林 (379)
为难：赶鸭子上架 (182)
伪装：咬人的狗不露齿 (481)
尾巴：兔子尾巴长不了 (456)；狐狸尾巴
　　露出来了 (352)
猥琐男：鲜花插在牛粪上 (29)
卫星：放卫星 (432)
位置：一个萝卜一个坑 (311)；占着茅坑不
　　拉屎 (194)
畏缩：前怕狼，后怕虎 (267)
胃口：卖关子 (72)
温水：温水煮青蛙 (462)
文章：做文章 (336)
翁：不倒翁 (270)；醉翁之意不在酒 (30)
窝：一窝蜂 (331)；兔子不吃窝边草 (128)；
　　捅马蜂窝 (261)
窝案：拔出萝卜带出泥 (460)
窝边草：兔子不吃窝边草 (128)
乌龟：缩头乌龟 (334)
乌龙：摆乌龙 (442)
乌鸦：天下乌鸦一般黑 (133)；乌鸦嘴 (5)；
　　老鸹嫌猪黑 (496)
乌鸦嘴：乌鸦嘴 (5)
污蔑：脚正不怕鞋歪 (413)
污染：常在河边走，哪有不湿鞋 (220)
巫师：小巫见大巫 (104)
诬陷：扣帽子 (459)
屋子：屋漏偏逢连阴雨 (259)
无：天无绝人之路 (47)；无风不起浪 (123)；
　　无事不登三宝殿 (157)；有心栽花花不长，
　　无心插柳柳成荫 (118)；此地无银三百两
　　(42)；花无百日红 (422)；苍蝇不叮无缝的
　　蛋 (368)；强将手下无弱兵 (427)
无常：三十年河东，三十年河西 (223)
无耻：睁着眼睛说瞎话 (8)
无价值：鸡毛蒜皮 (28)
无赖：滚刀肉 (395)
无趣：白开水 (389)

无望：死马当活马医 (139)
无心：有心栽花花不长，无心插柳柳成荫
　　(118)
无意：有心栽花花不长，无心插柳柳成荫
　　(118)
五十：五十步笑百步 (293)；各打五十大板
　　(443)
五脏：麻雀虽小，五脏俱全 (164)
勿：己所不欲，勿施于人 (15)
物：物以稀为贵 (10)
物极必反：虱多了不咬，账多了不愁 (484)
误会：大水冲了龙王庙 (360)
雾水：一头雾水 (356)

西边：太阳从西边出来 (3)
西方：东方不亮西方亮 (430)
西风：东风压倒西风 (423)
西施：情人眼里出西施 (19)
吸收：远来的和尚会念经 (451)
希望：己所不欲，勿施于人 (15)；天无绝人
　　之路 (47)；车到山前必有路 (82)
稀泥：和稀泥 (318)
稀少：物以稀为贵 (10)
媳妇：丑媳妇早晚也得见公婆 (233)；多年的
　　媳妇熬成婆 (426)
洗：萝卜快了不洗泥 (499)；跳进黄河洗不清
　　(17)
喜好：萝卜白菜，各有所爱 (58)
喜新厌旧：家花没有野花香 (436)
戏：三个女人一台戏 (201)；好戏在后头
　　(97)；唱对台戏 (376)
戏耍：放鸽子 (113)
系：解铃还须系铃人 (51)
瞎：睁眼瞎 (16)；瞎猫碰上死耗子 (49)
瞎话：睁着眼睛说瞎话 (8)
瞎猫：瞎猫碰上死耗子 (49)
狭隘：钻牛角尖 (25)
下贱：又想当婊子又想立牌坊 (437)；
　　下三烂 (235)
下降：萝卜快了不洗泥 (499)
下马威：下马威 (132)
下三烂：下三烂 (235)
下台阶：下台阶 (254)
下一步：骑马找马 (457)
下一代：龙生龙，凤生凤 (239)
下雨：干打雷，不下雨 (271)
吓唬：唱空城计 (400)
先：出头的椽子先烂 (493)；先君子后小人
　　(406)；近水楼台先得月 (103)
先…后…：先君子后小人 (406)
先发：起大早，赶晚集 (474)

先决条件：敲门砖 (382)

先验：事后诸葛亮 (273)

鲜花：鲜花插在牛粪上 (29)

咸鱼：咸鱼翻身 (281)

嫌：老鸹嫌猪黑 (496)

显眼：树大招风 (225)

限制：巧妇难为无米之炊 (187)

线：放长线，钓大鱼 (184)

馅饼：天上掉馅饼 (14)

羡慕：羡慕嫉妒恨 (374)；人怕出名猪怕壮 (246)

相爱：情人眼里出西施 (19)

相差：十万八千里 (142)

相处：一山不容二虎 (149)

相当于：三个臭皮匠，顶个诸葛亮 (40)

相关：风马牛不相及 (148)

相貌：人不可貌相，海水不可斗量 (26)

相同：手心手背都是肉 (333)；背着抱着一般沉 (489)

香：吃别人嚼过的馍不香 (473)；吃香的，喝辣的 (77)；酒香不怕巷子深 (301)；家花没有野花香 (436)

响：一个巴掌拍不响 (79)

想：癞蛤蟆想吃天鹅肉 (46)

想得开：拿得起，放得下 (35)

项羽：鸿门宴 (214)

巷子：酒香不怕巷子深 (301)

象牙：狗嘴里吐不出象牙 (59)

萧何：成也萧何，败也萧何 (359)

小：小白脸 (183)；小动作 (192)；小辫子 (355)；眼大肚子小 (471)；麻雀虽小，五脏俱全 (164)；雷声大、雨点小 (241)

小…大…：小不忍则乱大谋 (166)；小巫见大巫 (104)

小白脸：小白脸 (183)

小菜：小菜一碟 (2)

小动作：小动作 (192)

小儿：小儿科 (78)

小儿科：小儿科 (78)

小鬼：阎王好见，小鬼难搪 (468)

小姐：小姐的身子丫鬟的命 (453)

小气：铁公鸡 (156)

小巧：麻雀虽小，五脏俱全 (164)

小人：以小人之心，度君子之腹 (81)；先君子后小人 (406)

小鞋：穿小鞋 (321)

小意思：小菜一碟 (2)；小意思 (262)

笑：皮笑肉不笑 (175)；笑面虎 (289)；笑掉大牙 (278)

笑掉：笑掉大牙 (278)

笑面虎：笑面虎 (289)

鞋：光脚的不怕穿鞋的 (393)；穿小鞋 (321)；常在河边走，哪有不湿鞋 (220)

泄漏：没有不透风的墙 (245)

卸：卸磨杀驴 (411)

谢：脚正不怕鞋歪 (413)

心：刀子嘴，豆腐心 (63)；不到黄河心不死 (134)；心有余而力不足 (53)；心急吃不了热豆腐 (44)；以小人之心，度君子之腹 (81)；仔卖爷田不心疼 (498)

心病：眼中钉、肉中刺 (216)

心急：心急吃不了热豆腐 (44)；一口吃成个胖子 (258)；欲速则不达 (99)

心软：刀子嘴，豆腐心 (63)

心思：身在曹营心在汉 (230)

新：新官上任三把火 (140)

新…旧…：旧瓶装新酒 (402)

新官：新官上任三把火 (140)

新颖：吃别人嚼过的馍不香 (473)

新政：新官上任三把火 (140)

形式：旧瓶装新酒 (402)；走过场 (335)

形势：识时务者为俊杰 (110)

凶恶：咬人的狗不露齿 (481)

熊掌：鱼与熊掌不可得兼 (280)

休：一不做，二不休 (106)

须：解铃还须系铃人 (51)

虚假：皮笑肉不笑 (175)

虚实：指着和尚骂秃子 (487)

虚伪：打肿脸充胖子 (85)；笑面虎 (289)

许诺：开空白支票 (309)

宣扬：家丑不可外扬 (126)

悬念：葫芦里卖的是什么药 (344)

选拔：矮子里拔将军 (478)

选择：饥不择食 (173)

炫耀：关公面前耍大刀 (297)

丫环：小姐的身子丫鬟的命 (453)

丫鬟：小姐的身子丫鬟的命 (453)

压倒：东风压倒西风 (423)

压制：强龙压不住地头蛇 (391)

鸭：鸡同鸭讲 (433)

鸭子：赶鸭子上架 (182)；煮熟的鸭子飞了 (219)

牙：以牙还牙，以眼还眼 (107)；打掉门牙往肚里咽 (375)；老掉牙 (70)；笑掉大牙 (278)

牙膏：挤牙膏 (362)

哑巴：吃哑巴亏 (215)

咽：打掉门牙往肚里咽 (375)

焉：不入虎穴，焉得虎子 (116)；杀鸡焉用宰牛刀 (248)

严谨：丁是丁，卯是卯 (425)
严肃：丁是丁，卯是卯 (425)
言：一言堂 (490)
阎王：阎王好见，小鬼难搪 (468)
筵席：天下没有不散的筵席 (13)
颜色：给他一点颜色看看 (322)
掩藏：纸包不住火 (96)
掩盖：此地无银三百两 (42)；家丑不可外扬 (126)
掩饰：耍花枪 (439)
眼：以牙还牙，以眼还眼 (107)；打马虎眼 (325)；狗眼看人低 (136)；终日打雁，让雁啄了眼 (495)；睁一只眼，闭一只眼 (55)；睁眼瞎 (16)；眼大肚子小 (471)；眼不见为净 (32)；眼中钉、肉中刺 (216)；眼里揉不得沙子 (150)；情人眼里出西施 (19)；横挑鼻子竖挑眼 (399)
眼睛：有眼不识泰山 (120)；有鼻子有眼 (202)；红眼病 (343)；睁着眼睛说瞎话 (8)
眼镜：大跌眼镜 (369)
眼泪：不见棺材不落泪 (94)
眼里：情人眼里出西施 (19)
眼前：火烧眉毛 (384)；好汉不吃眼前亏 (50)；眼不见为净 (32)
演戏：唱双簧 (308)
艳遇：走桃花运 (37)
宴：鸿门宴 (214)
宴席：天下没有不散的筵席 (13)
雁：终日打雁，让雁啄了眼 (495)
央求：求爷爷、告奶奶 (373)
羊：一只羊是赶，一群羊也是放 (483)；羊毛出在羊身上 (257)；挂羊头、卖狗肉 (218)；替罪羊 (102)
羊毛：羊毛出在羊身上 (257)
羊头：挂羊头、卖狗肉 (218)
阳关道：你走你的阳关道，我过我的独木桥 (89)
养：浅水养不了大鱼 (472)
妖媚：狐狸精 (161)
要挟：敲竹杠 (319)
腰：拔根汗毛比腰粗 (467)；站着说话不腰疼 (12)
腰疼：站着说话不腰疼 (12)
遥远：十万八千里 (142)；猴年马月 (31)；天高皇帝远 (323)
咬：一朝被蛇咬，十年怕井绳 (61)；狗咬狗 (312)；虱子多了不咬，账多了不愁 (484)；咬人的狗不露齿 (481)
咬人：咬人的狗不露齿 (481)
药：换汤不换药 (197)；葫芦里卖的是什么药 (344)

钥匙：一把钥匙开一把锁 (404)
爷：仔卖爷田不心疼 (498)
爷爷：求爷爷、告奶奶 (373)
野花：家花没有野花香 (436)
夜：开夜车 (332)
一：一回生，二回熟 (279)；一是一，二是二 (252)
一…二…：一山不容二虎 (149)；一不做，二不休 (106)；一回生，二回熟 (279)；一是一，二是二 (252)
一把：眉毛胡子一把抓 (207)
一百：五十步笑百步 (293)
一般：天下乌鸦一般黑 (133)；背着抱着一般沉 (489)
一旦：一朝被蛇咬，十年怕井绳 (61)
一定：二虎相争，必有一伤 (349)
一分：一分钱一分货 (73)
一概：一棍子打死 (243)
一律：一刀切 (401)
一千：说一千，道一万 (370)
一群：一只羊是赶，一群羊也是放 (483)
一条龙：一条龙 (265)
一头：剃头挑子一头热 (450)
一万：不怕一万，就怕万一 (21)；说一千，道一万 (370)
一窝端：一锅端 (434)
一窝蜂：一窝蜂 (331)
一言堂：一言堂 (490)
一样：天下乌鸦一般黑 (133)
医生：久病成良医 (396)；病急乱投医 (237)
医治：头痛医头，脚痛医脚 (428)；死马当活马医 (139)
依附：吃软饭 (211)
依照：依葫芦画瓢 (185)
姨：七大姑，八大姨 (251)
遗传：有其父必有其子 (93)
遗憾：一失足成千古恨 (64)
以：以小人之心，度君子之腹 (81)；以牙还牙，以眼还眼 (107)；以其人之道还治其人之身 (36)
以…为…：物以稀为贵 (10)
以后：事后诸葛亮 (273)
以偏概全：一棍子打死 (243)
义务：当一天和尚撞一天钟 (227)
异想天开：癞蛤蟆想吃天鹅肉 (46)
意外：三长两短 (95)；大跌眼镜 (369)；不怕一万，就怕万一 (21)；半路杀出个程咬金 (163)
银子：此地无银三百两 (42)
隐藏：狐狸尾巴露出来了 (352)
英雄：英雄难过美人关 (62)

英勇：过五关、斩六将 (372)
应对：阎王好见，小鬼难搪 (468)
硬：硬骨头 (348)
硬骨头：硬骨头 (348)
勇敢：上刀山，下火海 (145)
用：用在刀刃上 (285)
优劣：尺有所短，寸有所长 (407)
优势：近水楼台先得月 (103)
优秀：久病成良医 (396)
优越：吃香的，喝辣的 (77)
油灯：不是省油的灯 (125)
油滑：老油条 (260)；耍花枪 (439)
油条：老油条 (260)
鱿鱼：炒鱿鱼 (66)
有：有仇不报非君子 (269)；有奶就是娘
　(414)；有其父必有其子 (93)；有钱能使
　鬼推磨 (92)；有眼不识泰山 (120)；有鼻子
　有眼 (202)；林子大了，什么鸟都有 (27)
有理：公说公有理，婆说婆有理 (144)
有钱：有钱能使鬼推磨 (92)
有市场：皇帝女儿不愁嫁 (418)
有恃无恐：皇帝女儿不愁嫁 (418)
有心：有心栽花花不长，无心插柳柳成荫
　(118)
有余：成事不足，败事有余 (38)
又…又…：又要马儿跑，又要马儿不吃草
　(440)；又想当婊子又想立牌坊 (437)
诱惑：狐狸精 (161)
鱼：大鱼吃小鱼 (351)；不是鱼死，就是网破
　(303)；鱼与熊掌不可得兼 (280)；放长线，
　钓大鱼 (184)；浅水养不了大鱼 (472)；
　鲤鱼跳龙门 (390)
鱼…水…：浅水养不了大鱼 (472)
渔利：坐山观虎斗 (256)
愚蠢：二 (290)；二百五 (6)；活人让尿憋死
　(420)
愚钝：有眼不识泰山 (120)
雨：听风就是雨 (213)；屋漏偏逢连阴雨
　(259)；雷声大、雨点小 (241)
雨点：雷声大、雨点小 (241)
预测：乌鸦嘴 (5)；事后诸葛亮 (273)
欲：树欲静而风不止 (232)；欲速则不达 (99)
欲望：眼大肚子小 (471)
遇到：屋漏偏逢连阴雨 (259)
冤枉：别人牵驴你拔橛 (497)
原则：到什么山唱什么歌 (466)
远：远来的和尚会念经 (451)
远…近…：远水解不了近渴 (193)；
　远亲不如近邻 (131)
远亲：七大姑，八大姨 (251)
怨：拉不出屎来怨茅房 (429)

月亮：近水楼台先得月 (103)
允许：只许州官放火，不许百姓点灯 (137)

砸：砸了锅 (446)；搬起石头砸自己的脚 (71)
砸锅：砸了锅 (446)
栽倒：吃一堑，长一智 (7)
栽花：有心栽花花不长，无心插柳柳成荫
　(118)
栽树：前人栽树，后人乘凉 (295)
仔：仔卖爷田不心疼 (498)
宰：杀鸡焉用宰牛刀 (248)
再起：留得青山在，不怕没柴烧 (34)
在于：谋事在人，成事在天 (200)
攒：攒鸡毛，凑掸子 (485)
早…晚…：起大早，赶晚集 (474)
早晚：丑媳妇早晚也得见公婆 (233)
枣：打一巴掌，给个甜枣 (405)；歪瓜裂枣
　(354)
造福：前人栽树，后人乘凉 (295)
则：欲速则不达 (99)
责备：倒打一耙 (263)
责任：三个和尚没水吃 (181)；不当家不知
　柴米贵 (342)
贼：上了贼船 (236)；胜者王侯败者贼 (234)
怎么：不入虎穴，焉得虎子 (116)
增长：吃一堑，长一智 (7)
扎实：一步一个脚印 (114)；三脚猫 (221)
债务：拆东墙，补西墙 (350)
斩：过五关、斩六将 (372)；快刀斩乱麻
　(210)
占便宜：吃豆腐 (206)；偷鸡不成反蚀把米
　(208)；得便宜卖乖 (124)
占据：占着茅坑不拉屎 (194)
站：站着说话不腰疼 (12)
张扬：枪打出头鸟 (203)
章法：乱拳打死老师傅 (491)
账：虱子多了不咬，账多了不愁 (484)；
　秋后算账 (339)
招风：树大招风 (225)
招架：阎王好见，小鬼难搪 (468)
朝：一朝被蛇咬，十年怕井绳 (61)
找：骑马找马 (457)
找碴：鸡蛋里挑骨头 (83)
找麻烦：做文章 (336)
照顾：开绿灯 (353)
遮：遮羞布 (438)
遮羞：遮羞布 (438)
遮羞布：遮羞布 (438)
折兵：赔了夫人又折兵 (117)
这：过了这个村，就没这个店 (90)
这…那…：这山望着那山高 (392)

着数：一着不慎，满盘皆输 (212)
贞洁：又想当婊子又想立牌坊 (437)
针：给个棒槌就当针 (479)
针对：对事不对人 (174)
珍惜：仔卖爷田不心疼 (498)
真金：真金不怕火炼 (170)
真相：露马脚 (143)
真正：君子之交淡如水 (180)
枕边风：枕边风 (397)
枕头：枕边风 (397)
争：二虎相争，必有一伤 (349)
争吵：脸红脖子粗 (242)
睁：睁一只眼，闭一只眼 (55)；睁眼瞎 (16)；
    睁着眼睛说瞎话 (8)
睁眼瞎：睁眼瞎 (16)
正：上梁不正下梁歪 (115)；脚正不怕鞋歪
    (413)
正直：脚正不怕鞋歪 (413)
支票：开空白支票 (309)
只：万事俱备，只欠东风 (168)；只见树木，
    不见森林 (454)；只许州官放火，不许百姓
    点灯 (137)
芝麻：陈芝麻、烂谷子 (264)
知道：不当家不知柴米贵 (342)
知己：酒逢知己千杯少 (226)
直接：打开天窗说亮话 (190)
直说：捅破窗户纸 (366)
纸：纸包不住火 (96)；纸老虎 (160)；
    捅破窗户纸 (366)
纸老虎：纸老虎 (160)
指：指着和尚骂秃子 (487)
制服：紧箍咒 (307)
质变：鲤鱼跳龙门 (390)
质量：一分钱一分货 (73)；萝卜快了不洗泥
    (499)
治：以其人之道还治其人之身 (36)
智慧：吃一堑，长一智 (7)
中枪：躺着都中枪 (412)
中伤：明枪易躲，暗箭难防 (199)
忠于：身在曹营心在汉 (230)；脚踩两只船
    (41)
终究：跑了和尚跑不了庙 (108)；躲得过
    初一，躲不过十五 (76)
终日：终日打雁，让雁啄了眼 (495)
钟：当一天和尚撞一天钟 (227)
种：种瓜得瓜，种豆得豆 (57)
众人：众人拾柴火焰高 (209)；墙倒众人推
    (363)
州官：只许州官放火，不许百姓点灯 (137)
周瑜：既生瑜，何生亮？ (380)
粥：僧多粥少 (340)

咒：紧箍咒 (307)
朱：近朱者赤，近墨者黑 (9)
诸葛亮：三个臭皮匠，顶个诸葛亮 (40)；
    事后诸葛亮 (273)；既生瑜，何生亮？
    (380)；唱空城计 (400)
猪：人怕出名猪怕壮 (246)；老鸹嫌猪黑
    (496)；死猪不怕开水烫 (196)；岁月是把
    杀猪刀 (424)
竹杠：敲竹杠 (319)
主次：眉毛胡子一把抓 (207)
主妇：巧妇难为无米之炊 (187)
主人：打狗还得看主人 (167)
煮：煮熟的鸭子飞了 (219)；温水煮青蛙
    (462)
注定：谋事在人，成事在天 (200)；
    嫁鸡随鸡，嫁狗随狗 (189)
抓：眉毛胡子一把抓 (207)
抓住：揪辫子 (452)
专业：半路出家 (329)
砖：敲门砖 (382)
装：旧瓶装新酒 (102)
壮：人怕出名猪怕壮 (246)
撞钟：当一天和尚撞一天钟 (227)
捉：不管黑猫白猫，会捉老鼠就是好猫 (169)
捉弄：既生瑜，何生亮？ (380)
捉住：空手套白狼 (385)
啄：终日打雁，让雁啄了眼 (495)
子：虎毒不食子 (165)
自暴自弃：破罐子破摔 (56)
自不量力：关公面前耍大刀 (297)
自残：二虎相争，必有一伤 (349)；
    狗咬狗 (312)
自己：双刃剑 (176)；己所不欲，勿施于人
    (15)；王婆卖瓜，自卖自夸 (11)；
    搬起石头砸自己的脚 (71)
自救：树倒猢狲散 (347)
自身：以其人之道还治其人之身 (36)；
    羊毛出在羊身上 (257)
自私：打小算盘 (255)
自相矛盾：摆乌龙 (442)
自知：老鸹嫌猪黑 (496)
自作自受：搬起石头砸自己的脚 (71)
总要：出来混的，总要还的 (408)
总账：秋后算账 (339)
走：一条路走到黑 (302)；人往高处走，
    水往低处流 (67)；三十六计走为上 (86)；
    吃不了兜着走 (84)；走后门 (48)；走着瞧
    (22)；你走你的阳关道，我过我的独木桥
    (89)；常在河边走，哪有不湿鞋 (220)
走过场：走过场 (335)
走后门：走后门 (48)

走马灯：走马灯 (421)
走思：开小差 (315)
走运：走桃花运 (37)
走着瞧：走着瞧 (22)
阻碍：绊脚石 (371)
祖辈：仔卖爷田不心疼 (498)
钻：钻牛角尖 (25)
嘴：刀子嘴，豆腐心 (63)；乌鸦嘴 (5)；
　满嘴跑火车 (461)
嘴里：狗嘴里吐不出象牙 (59)
嘴硬：刀子嘴，豆腐心 (63)

罪：替罪羊 (102)
醉：醉翁之意不在酒 (30)
醉翁：醉翁之意不在酒 (30)
醉翁之意：醉翁之意不在酒 (30)
作为：占着茅坑不拉屎 (194)
坐：坐山观虎斗 (256)；坐冷板凳 (341)
座位：对号入座 (141)
做：一不做，二不休 (106)；做文章 (336)
做成：生米做成熟饭 (154)
做梦：天上掉馅饼 (14)
做文章：做文章 (336)